The Tragedy of Martina Castro

THE SECRET HISTORY OF SANTA CRUZ COUNTY SERIES
Edited by Derek R. Whaley

This series brings to light long out-of-print books, dusty manuscripts, and other lost material documenting the history of the county from pre-colonial times to the present.

The History of Rancho Soquel Augmentation
The Tragedy of Martina Castro by Ronald G. Powell
The Reign of the Lumber Barons by Ronald G. Powell
The Shadow of Loma Prieta by Ronald G. Powell

Ronald G. Powell

The Tragedy of Martina Castro

Part One of the History of
Rancho Soquel Augmentation

Edited by Derek R. Whaley
With a foreword by Stanley D. Stevens

First published in 2020 by
ZAYANTE PUBLISHING
Santa Cruz, California, USA

www.zayantepublishing.com

© 2021 Zayante Publishing

Third revision, October 2022

Designed by Derek R. Whaley
Cover and layout: Derek R. Whaley

The moral right of the authors has been asserted.

Material from this book courtesy the Ronald G. Powell Collection, Special Collections, McHenry Library, University of California, Santa Cruz.

Front: Portrait of Martina Castro, from the Santa Cruz Museum of Art & History

Back: Map of Part of Rancho Soquel Augmentation Survey, November 1881, from the UCSC Library Map Collection; Portrait of Thomas Fallon, from a lithograph, and Portrait of Carmel Fallon, from the History San José Photographic Collection

All rights reserved. Without limiting the rights under copyright reserved above, no part of this publication may be reproduced, stored or introduced into a retrieval system, or transmitted, in any form or by any means (electronic, mechanical, photocopying, recording or otherwise), without the prior written permission of the copyright owner.

ISBN 978-1-953609-38-0 (printed book)
ISBN 978-1-953609-39-7 (ebook)

In memory of
Ronald Gabriel Powell
1931 – 2010

Contents

A Remembrance by Stanley D. Stevens ix
Introduction by Derek R. Whaley xiii

The Tragedy of Martina Castro
- Chapter 1: At the Edge of the Empire 3
- Chapter 2: Echoes from the East 73
- Chapter 3: In Defense of My Own 123
- Chapter 4: Soquel in the Balance 223
- Chapter 5: Enter the King 291
- Chapter 6: Road to Partition 351
- Chapter 7: Divided and Conquered 465
- Epilogue: In the Matter of the Estate of Martina Castro, Deceased 535

Notes 557
Bibliography 577
Index 583

A Remembrance
by Stanley D. Stevens

Ron was born on February 26, 1931 in Oakland, California. He graduated from Fremont High School in Oakland in 1950 and then went to Cogswell Polytechnic Institute in San Francisco and received an electrical engineering degree in 1953. Soon afterwards, he went to work at Beckman (later Berkeley Instruments), where he remained until 1956. Following this, he worked at Lockheed's Missile Systems Division from 1956 to 1971 and then Raytheon and GTE Sylvania through the 1970s. In the 1980s and 1990s, during semi-retirement and while working on the research of which this book is one product, he worked with his brother Dick at the Bicycle Outfitter in Los Altos.

Generally speaking, Ron lived a reclusive lifestyle. He explained to me once that for most of his adult life he suffered from an ailment, best described as sensitivity to atmospheric pressure. Similar to the effect of migraine headaches, these episodes made it so he could not function. Consultation with doctors did not help—they apparently thought he imagined the symptoms. In retrospect, I am amazed that he accomplished all that he did. Ron died on September 11, 2010 at Santa Clara Kaiser Hospital.

Stanley D. Stevens

He is survived by his son, John, his daughters, Susan Rogers and Ronell Elwin, and his brother, Dick.

Ron was an amateur photographer and enjoyed hiking throughout northern California parks and historical sites. The Online Archive of California (OAC) includes a Collection Guide to the Ronald G. Powell Photographs at the University of California, Santa Cruz, Special Collections and Archives (see http://oac2-prd.cdlib.org/findaid/ark:/13030/kt9779s2tn/dsc/#dsc-1.3.9). An examination of that Collection Guide reveals the range of dates when he took these photos:

Alameda & Santa Clara Counties, 1981–1984
Marin & Sonoma Counties, 1981–1985
Santa Cruz County, 1982–1984
Monterey & San Benito Counties, 1983
Mendocino & Humboldt Counties, 1983–1985
San Mateo County, 1985

It is not surprising that he would explore areas close to his San Mateo County and Santa Clara County residences. After the 1989 Loma Prieta Earthquake, which had its epicenter within the Soquel Augmentation Rancho northeast of Aptos, he returned to focus on the history of that area.

My association with Ron began sometime before 1998, when he frequented the Map Room at the McHenry Library at UC Santa Cruz. I don't have an exact date when I realized that his interest was solely on the history of Santa Cruz County, particularly the Mexican ranchos of Martina Castro: Rancho Soquel and Rancho Soquel Augmentation. His research focused on logging railroads and land ownership. It overlapped with my own interest in land ownership because it involved the many thousands of acres acquired by Frederick Augustus Hihn, the focus of my research.

During the years that Ron was conducting his research, we talked about the sources available; in particular, the records that I had collected about F. A. Hihn. He sought my advice on how to assemble this history. I suggested that if I were to undertake a project of that scope, I would find all the facts available, starting with the original land grant system of early California, and lay out those facts in chronological order. That would, of course, begin

A Remembrance

with the Castro Family. One would want to know how Martina Castro had acquired the Soquel Rancho and, subsequently, the augmentation to that land grant. Along the way, I hoped he would find the "story of F. A. Hihn" and I would be able to add that story to my knowledge of how Hihn had acquired thousands of acres within those ranchos. That story would provide the details of Hihn's development of the towns of Aptos, Capitola, and Soquel. The railroad history that touched this area, especially within the Soquel Augmentation Rancho, was of great interest to the general public. Early in my career, I was not knowledgeable about the subject and questions addressed to me as Map Librarian went unanswered. I had hopes that Ron would provide the answers, and I was not disappointed.

I supported Ron by making a deal with him: he would share his discoveries about Hihn and provide me copies of related articles (generated from newspapers on microfilm), and I would cover the cost of photocopies that he needed on the two ranchos. This association led to his documentation of "The Frederick Augustus Hihn Story," as related in Ron's fifty-two volumes now held in the Hihn-Younger Archive at the McHenry Library. The collection is the only comprehensive study of Rancho Soquel and the Soquel Augmentation Rancho. The volumes include many original maps of the ranchos and original documents about historic sites, land ownership, roads, and railroad lines.

Documents in my files at home express Ron's attitude about sharing his research. The first is a Letter of Gift dated March 7, 1998. In this letter, he specifies that: "the materials included in this gift shall be identified as the Ronald Powell Collection and when used and/or copied for research purposes, reference to this source will be included as an acknowledgment." Another document dated June 15, 2005 states Ron's condition for the use of his research: "All my books and photos are designed for public use and may be copied and reproduced in any medium with the stipulation that acknowledgment is given to the source: The Ronald G. Powell Collection." Other publications that he produced—for example, The Castros of Soquel, a 395-page history of that family—make no assertion of copyright and include a simple line that the work was compiled "by Ronald Powell."

After my August 11, 2000 visit with Ron at his Los Altos residence, I wrote a thank you letter for his taking the time to give me a grand tour of

Stanley D. Stevens

his collection. I wrote that "the Ron Powell Collection is undoubtedly the best-organized research collection that I have seen during my thirty years as a librarian. It is a researcher's dream to come upon such a user-friendly collection."

None of his research, in whatever form, was submitted for copyright protection. He wanted to share his work without restriction but thought he should be credited for the more than thirty years of devotion and expense that he invested in his research. Anyone who uses, reproduces, or quotes from Ron's published works salutes him by acknowledging his authorship.

For thirty years, Ron compiled his history of the Soquel Augmentation Rancho and the Soquel Rancho. I classify his work as monumental. I defer to others to evaluate his interpretations, his accuracy, and his impact.

Stanley D. Stevens
Librarian Emeritus
Founder, The Hihn-Younger Archive
McHenry Library, UC Santa Cruz
March 25, 2020

Introduction
by Derek R. Whaley

Like many Santa Cruzans, I had heard vague whispers of a woman named Martina Castro for many years before I ever encountered Ronald G. Powell's manuscript. I recalled that she was one of the Mexican land grantees who owned Rancho Soquel and its accompanying Augmentation, which I knew from my research encompassed parts of Capitola, Soquel, Aptos, and basically everything north of those places to the summit of the Santa Cruz Mountains. I also knew that her family was very well connected and owned several other land grants in Santa Cruz County, from Rancho San Andrés near Watsonville to Rancho Refugio up the North Coast. What I did not know was her tragic tale of how a Californio, born and raised, received massive tracts of land—nearly ten percent of modern Santa Cruz County—and then lost it through betrayal, subterfuge, and failed schemes, ending her life virtually destitute as a boarder in her own daughter's granny flat. It was an amazing story that deserved a proper telling.

    I had no intention of publishing this book when I first encountered it. In May 2019, I was deep into researching and writing my next *Santa Cruz Trains* book when Stanley Stevens unintentionally introduced me to a massive unpublished collection of documents gathered, organized, and curated by Powell. The subjects of my research at that moment were the lumber companies that operated along the Loma Prieta Branch of the Southern Pacific Railroad, which once meandered seven miles into The Forest of Nisene Marks State Park. Stevens sent me part five of seven of Powell's magnum opus, and I was immediately intent on seeing the other six volumes.

As Stevens notes in his Remembrance, Powell gifted his writings and research material to the McHenry Library at the University of California, Santa Cruz prior to his death in 2010. For many years, a digital version of the collection was available to the public via a dedicated Hihn-Younger Archive webpage, but that was taken down during a website revamp in the mid-2010s. Thus, it was fortunate that Stevens inadvertently made me aware of Powell's work and was able to provide me the source files. The collection encompasses fifty-one PDF files, including the seven volumes that make up Powell's monolithic *Santa Cruz County under California as the 31st State plus The Frederick Augustus Hihn Story*. The pages before you are an adaptation of the first three volumes of that manuscript, which focus primarily on the life and times of Martina Castro. Since Powell did not formally name his tome, I adopted the title *The Tragedy of Martina Castro* for the first part, since it seemed to fit its themes and focus. The remaining four volumes comprise the second book in my adaptation, *The Reign of the Lumber Barons*, which documents the history of the Augmentation from the mid-1860s—when logging first began in earnest—to the present. Running as an undercurrent throughout both books is the story of Frederick A. Hihn, a German immigrant who became the wealthiest and most influential person in Santa Cruz County and was deeply involved in both the fate of Martina Castro's lands and their commercial exploitation.

The Augmentation—*aumento* in Spanish—was the second of two grants made to Castro by the Mexican government in the 1830s and 1840s. Its name derives from the fact that it increased—augmented—the land of Rancho Soquel, which was the first grant. Rancho Soquel was in reality quite small, although on par with other coastal land grants in Santa Cruz County. Its boundaries ranged from today's Capitola on the east bank of Soquel Creek to about a half a mile north of Soquel Drive. From there,

Introduction

the boundary ran due east until reaching Borregas Gulch, where it turned down the gulch until returning to the Monterey Bay at New Brighton State Beach. As in most ranchos, cattle breeding was its main activity and leather its primary product, although in later years Rancho Soquel was developed into real estate subdivisions and a vacation resort known as Camp Capitola.

Encroachment onto her land by neighboring Rancho Aptos prompted Castro to petition the government for additional land, which was granted to her in the form of an augmentation to her original grant. Although this was not strictly speaking a formal land grant like Rancho Soquel had been, the United States government later confirmed it as such under the name Rancho Shoquel or Shoquel Augmentation. The Augmentation was poorly defined initially but its eventual boundaries followed Soquel Creek to its headwaters in the west and then along the ridgeline to the summit of Loma Prieta in the east, thereby encompassing much of the Summit area and making a small part of it fall within Santa Clara County. From Loma Prieta, it continued due south, taking in most of the Aptos and Valencia Creek watersheds, until reaching the boundary of Rancho Aptos about a mile north of California State Route 1. Unlike Rancho Soquel, the Augmentation was composed almost entirely of old growth redwood forest, which is why it drew such interest from local logging concerns beginning in the 1860s and why most of it has since become two state parks: The Forest of Nisene Marks and the Soquel Demonstration Forest.

Powell's fascination with Castro and her two ranchos grew out of an interest in the logging and railroading history of the area, evidence of which Powell photographed and scrutinized intensely in writing his manuscript. Although not well known outside of a small circle of historians, Powell was most studious and thorough in his research. He made dozens of trips to the California State Archives in Sacramento, the Bancroft Library in Berkeley, the Santa Cruz County Recorder's Department, the Santa Cruz Public Library, and the McHenry Library at UC Santa Cruz. He sought the help of translators, local historians, county clerks, librarians, professional researchers, and even psychiatric ward staff. And many of the secondary sources that he called upon were not traditional history books written in the past fifty years but rather texts from the nineteenth century, written by people who had personally known their subjects and documented events that were still unfolding around them. The result was the most authoritative history of Castro and her properties that has ever existed. Unfortunately, Powell only ever published an abridged edition of his work, *The Castros of Soquel* in 1994, and the bulk of his findings languished in storage for nearly two decades.

The book before you is not what we would typically consider to be a traditional history book. As a trained historian of the Middle Ages, I know a chronicle when I see one, and Powell most certainly followed in the footsteps of his medieval predecessors. At their most basic level, chronicles are chronologically organized records of history derived from primary- and secondary-source material, often with very little obvious historical interpretation or analysis. However, chronicles have a lot of editorial oversight, meaning that the people who compiled them chose which materials to include and which to leave out in order to better tell their stories. Using this definition, Powell's method of writing history fits perfectly. His goal throughout his work is to explain in precise detail how Martina Castro came into possession of Rancho Soquel and the Augmentation, and then how she lost it all. There are occasional tangents, as with all chronicles, and some material does not initially seem connected, but all of it serves a purpose in the story. More pointedly, Powell omitted or reworked any sources that directly contradicted his conclusions in order to better serve his goals. The chronicle style is thus unconsciously manipulative in that it causes the reader to make conclusions based on often incomplete or heavily biased data, a tactic Powell occasionally employs to his advantage. Readers of this book must, therefore, remember that they are not reading an impartial history—Powell chose every passage for a reason.

All of that being said, Powell never edited his manuscript nor prepared it in any way for publication. As a result, it had several issues that I, as both a historian and an editor, felt needed to be addressed before it could be published. These included making corrections and updates for readability and reliability. Broadly speaking, I have rewritten the majority of the text to be more consistent in style and to reduce Powell's tendency to duplicate information. Powell was never one for suspense and so revealed the end of Castro's story far earlier than was necessary, so I have also restructured those moments to avoid spoiling the ending. More importantly, I have eliminated two sources that contained many errors and did not advance the story in any meaningful way. The first of these is *A California Cavalier: The Journal of Captain Thomas Fallon* by Thomas McEnery. This book purports itself to be a lost journal written by Fallon but is, in fact, a chronology of Fallon's life intermixed with stories and anecdotes that are fantasies of the author or drawn from the lives of other contemporaries, who admired Fallon such that, as mayor of San José, he commissioned a statue to the man. The second source is Estelle Latta's *Controversial Mark Hopkins: The Great Swindle of American History*, which attempts to decouple the histories of two men named Mark Hopkins who lived in Sacramento in the early 1850s. In attempting to detangle the two men, though, Latta actually made the issue incredibly more complicated by incorrectly attributing facts about each man's life. Several historians have since roundly debunked her conclusions and I felt it reckless to include them here.

Powell borrowed several other important styles from the chronicle format that I have retained in this book. He includes titles for individual passages to divide the book into thematic sections, which he organizes chronologically whenever possible. This adherence to chronology often breaks storylines apart, which is also a relic of the chronicle format and helps motivate the reader to continue reading. Powell does not include chapters in his manuscript but rather splits the book into periods of California occupation—California under Mexican rule, for example—but these divisions cease following California statehood in 1850 and I did not retain them. Instead, I have divided the book into seven chapters with thematic titles and an epilogue and have added dates to the top corners of each page to help guide the reader. Other lesser changes I have made include standardizing the endnotes for consistency, cleaning up Powell's extensive selection of maps and figures, most of which he created himself, and removing currency conversions, since several inflation calculators can now be found online. One final touch I added was Joaquín Castro's cattle brand to the cover and ends of most chapters. While it is unknown what Martina Castro's personal brand looked like, clues provided by her siblings' brands suggest that it likely resembled that of her father's.

This work was a massive undertaking for Powell and editing it and its sequels has been an unexpected journey for me. Whereas Powell spent years researching and gathering the information into a succinct and well-organized tale, I have spent much of the last year cleaning up the manuscript to make it presentable to a wider audience. I must thank Dr. Kara Kennedy for proofreading the entire book, Kanda Whaley for providing stylistic advice, Dr. Lindsay Breach for verifying the legitimacy and viability of all of the legal jargon, and Andria Burdette for providing the index.

This book deserves recognition as a foundational text in the history of Santa Cruz County. The story of Martina Castro is a vital record of life in colonial California, when settlements were centered around missions, small towns, and private ranches, and the primary markers of success were the number of native converts and tanned hides. It was in this environment that Castro emerged as one of the great baronesses of the New World—an aristocrat with no palace, no court, and no vassals, ruling a rugged domain at the furthest edge of a world-spanning empire.

Derek R. Whaley
May 25, 2020

The Tragedy of
Martina Castro

Chapter 1

~

At the Edge of the Empire

Pope Alexander VI declares the partition of the world between Spain and Portugal

Shortly after Columbus returned to the Spanish court and reported his discovery of the New World, conflict arose between the two most powerful maritime countries of that time—Portugal and Spain—concerning possession of the newly-discovered territories. To settle the dispute between the two crowns, Pope Alexander VI issued the papal bull *Inter caetera* on May 4, 1493. The decree established a line of demarcation between the two crowns 100 leagues west of the Azores—roughly the 38.5° West longitudinal line today.

Because the makeup of the New World was unknown, the line did not produce a sensible geographic division. It cut through the easternmost portion of South America (today Brazil). All of the land west of this line became the personal property of Queen Isabella I of Castile and her heirs, and it consisted of most of South America and all of North America. The bull was amended in 1494 by the Treaty of Tordesillas, which changed some geographic boundaries in South America, but the treaty did not affect what would become California. Within a few decades, Spain established Tenochtitlan (México City), the former capital of the Aztec Empire, as the capital of the Viceroyalty of New Spain (North America).[1]

Juan Cabrillo explores along the California Coast

Juan Rodríguez Cabrillo, a Portuguese navigator serving under the flag of Castile, left the port of Navidad in México at the end of June 1542. He arrived in San Diego Bay, the first European explorer to reach Alta California by land or sea. After departing the bay, he explored the coast of California by ship as far north as the Russian River (in today's Sonoma County). The primary goal of his expedition was to find the Strait of Anián, a mythical waterway that connected the west and east coasts of North America via a northwest passage.[2]

Juan Cabrillo anchors in La Bahía de los Piños

On his return journey, Juan Cabrillo anchored in what he called La Bahía de los Piños" (Pine Trees Bay) on November 16, 1542. Several historians believe that this location was on the northern side of Monterey Bay. He did not come ashore because the surf was too heavy. It would be another sixty years before a description of the Santa Cruz coastline would be entered into an explorer's log. A week after his discovery of La Bahía de los Piños, Cabrillo was injured on Santa Catalina Island and later died from his wound.[3]

Sebastián Vizcaíno anchors in Monterey Bay

In the sixteenth and early seventeenth centuries, Imperial Spain was developing and conquering new lands on the basis of their ability to produce mineral wealth. They believed that the Pacific Ocean was a "Spanish Lake," situated between New Spain and Peru and the Philippines, and to a great extent, up to the mid-eighteenth century, it was. But English explorers invaded that lake as early as 1579, and over the next 200 years, the English,

French, and even the Dutch were sending ships to the Pacific Coast of Asia while the Russians were establishing outposts in Alaska and even exploring the Pacific coastline as far south as California.

Although California was thought to have little value, Spain gave Sebastián Vizcaíno three ships with instructions to explore and chart the California coast in order to find a suitable port to serve the trade routes of New Spain in the Pacific Ocean. He was promised command of a Manila galleon as reward if a port was found. On December 15, 1602, as he headed home, his ships entered Monterey Bay, which Vizcaíno named in honor of Gaspar de Zúñiga Avecedo y Fonseca, Viceroy of New Spain and Count of Monterrey, under whose authority he was commissioned. It was some sixty years after Cabrillo had supposedly also entered the bay and only seven years after Sebastián Rodríguez Cermeño had sailed there. Cermeño was a Portuguese merchant and adventurer on a mission similar to that undertaken by Vizcaíno, but he had lost his galleon at Drakes Bay—which he had renamed San Francisco—and Spanish authorities discounted his discoveries.

In his logs, Vizcaíno described Monterey Bay as "the best port that could be desired, for besides being sheltered from all winds, it has many pines for masts and yards, and live oak and white oaks, and water in great quantity, all near the shore." He recommended Monterey Bay as a safe haven for the Manila galleons returning from the East. During his explorations of the area, he named Punta de los Piños to the south of the bay, and Punta Año Nuevo to the north, as well as the Río del Carmelo (Carmel River), flowing into the ocean just to the south of today's town of Monterey. Vazcaíno, like all earlier explorers, missed San Francisco Bay mostly due to the fog.

During his two week-stay anchored in Monterey Bay, he and his crew made a number of trips ashore and met the local Native Americans. Vizcaíno wrote of them as follows:

> *The land is well populated with Indians without number, many of whom came on different occasions to our camp. They seemed to be gentle and peaceful people; they say with signs that there are many villages inland. The sustenance which these Indians eat most of daily, besides fish and shellfish, is*

> *acorns and another fruit larger than a chestnut; this is what we could understand of them.*
>
> *There are Indians, although they are distrustful of dealing with us. That is to say that the aforesaid Indians came in peace, and from appearances are good people; they brought us shellfish and made great efforts to bring us to their town, which they made signs was inland.*

Father Antonio de la Ascensión, who accompanied Vizcaíno, stated: "The port is all surrounded with rancherias of affable, good natives and well-disposed, who like to give what they have; here they brought us skins of bears and lions and deer. They use the bow and arrow and have their form of government. They were very pleased that we should have settled in their country. They go naked at this port."

When Vizcaíno's ships finally set sail for home, they were but a few days from the end of their journey. By this time, half of his men were either dead or dying and his enthusiasm to leave the Monterey Bay must have carried a note of urgency to his superiors. But this urgency might have lost some of its legendary luster had they known that Vizcaíno was not the first to discover the bay, as discussed earlier. It will also be remembered that Vizcaíno had a personal interest in the success of this mission. His journey of exploration was a failure until his three ships entered Monterey Bay. Although the bay is an arc—hardly "sheltered from all winds"—Vizcaíno reported to Spanish authorities what they hoped to hear.

The viceroy of New Spain was delighted to have the harbor bear his name and, in return, he awarded Vizcaíno with the promised captainship of a galleon. But shortly afterward, a new viceroy was appointed, one more skeptical of Vizcaíno, and he revoked the captaincy. Among the men to suffer the most from the explorer's fraudulent claims of a magnificent port at Monterey Bay was Martinez Palacios, Vizcaíno's mapmaker. He was convicted of forgery and hanged for his role in the misrepresentation. Despite the preceding events, rumors of the fabled port of Monterey persisted.[4]

The Society of Jesus begins establishing missions in Baja California

In 1534, the Roman Catholic priest Ignatius Loyola founded a religious order which he named the Society of Jesus, commonly known as the Jesuits. Beginning in 1697, the order established several missions among the Native American people of Baja (Lower) California.[5]

José de Gálvez is appointed Visitor-General of New Spain

In 1765, José de Gálvez was appointed *visitador generál* (inspector general) of New Spain by King Charles III. Gálvez was a forceful, intelligent, ambitious, and competent man who was known to possess several idiosyncrasies that at times caused many to consider him a bit crazy.

Gálvez helped reorganize the government in New Spain in an effort to increase its financial revenue and stop its declining regional power. But his plan to encourage settlement in Alta (Upper) California was a personal project. He believed that by consolidating the northwest region into one governmental unit that included both Californias, Spain's international image would improve, as would his own prospects for career advancement.

Listening to rumors concerning increased British and Russian interest along the northern coastline of Alta California, Gálvez convinced the Spanish government that it was time to locate and settle the fabled harbor at Monterey Bay. This began a military and religious thrust northward, while Gálvez also hinted that settlement in Alta California would provide new sources of revenue. As it happened, the primary result of his project was the establishment of a chain of missions that would ultimately prove to be a financial drain on Spain until the Mexican government took over the area around 1822.[6]

The Jesuits are expelled from Baja California

In 1767, José de Gálvez was tasked with expelling the Jesuits from New Spain. Fearing the power, militancy, and independence of the order in Baja

California, King Charles III demanded they be removed from positions of authority. But when Gálvez went to carry out the order, he discovered that the missions were decaying and nearly deserted. He turned them over to the military under Gaspar de Portolá who, in turn, gave the properties to the Franciscan Order, led by Father Junípero Serra, in 1768.

Portolá was born in 1723 in Os de Balageur, Spain. He entered the military at the age of eleven, later fighting for the Spanish crown in Portugal and Italy with distinction. He was sent to the New World specifically to expel the Jesuits and establish a reliable bulwark in the Californias against Russian and English encroachment. Serra, meanwhile, had been born on the island of Majorca off the coast of Spain. He became a priest in 1737 and taught philosophy on Majorca, where he met his later companions, Francisco Palóu and Juan Crespí. In 1749, all three friars travelled to New Spain and took up positions at the College of San Fernando de México in México City, where Serra served as a missionary and inquisitor. It was in this capacity that he was recruited to join Portolá on his mission to eject the Jesuits from Baja California.[7]

The Portolá Expedition enters Alta California

With the transference of the Jesuit possessions to the Franciscans complete, José de Gálvez was able to proceed with his plan to explore and settle Alta California. He first set up a supply base at San Blas on the west coast of México and sailed from there to Baja California. Once there, he finished his plans for the expedition to Monterey Bay. Originally, the expedition was to include several divisions: two parties travelling by land and three ships following along the coastline. Unfortunately for Gálvez, the original approach was blocked by revolts in Sonora that were sparked by the expulsion of the Jesuits. These rebellions delayed the first push into Alta California.

Finally, in the winter of 1768, all of the necessary elements for the trip to Monterey Bay were assembled. On January 9, 1769, everyone set out, with parties travelling by both land and sea. Gálvez addressed them with words of encouragement, readying them for the dangers they would meet. The military leader appointed to lead the expedition was Gaspar de Portolá, while Father Serra headed the Franciscan missionary contingent.

San Carlos, the first of Portolá's three ships, left for San Diego Bay on January 11, 1769 to establish a waystation and wait for the two land parties. The second ship, *San Antonio*, left a month later, on February 15. In the meantime, the two land expeditions left for San Diego with Serra traveling in the second party, which was under the leadership of Portolá.

The two arrived in San Diego on July 1. On the way north, some of the Native Americans who had accompanied them from México died and several of the soldiers deserted. The *San Carlos* and *San Antonio* were waiting at anchor as the party reached the port. Two weeks later, the expedition began the long trek north in search of the lost port of Monterey, although Serra remained behind to establish the first mission in Alta California, San Diego de Alcalá, construction on which began on July 16. As the oldest church in the state, Mission San Diego is often referred to as the "Mother of the Alta California Missions" by historians. Father Crespí accompanied Portolá north as the replacement for Serra.

The party reached the Monterey Bay on October 4 but continued north, not recognizing the bay due to its shallow depth and lack of shelter. As they marched on, surveyors in the party reasoned that their calculations were in error and that the bay must be further north. Ten days later, the group reached Soquel Creek. After crossing the creek, Crespí wrote in his journal: "We stopped on the bank of a small stream, which was about four *varas* [11 feet] of deep running water. It has on its bank a good growth of cottonwoods and alders." He named the stream El Rosario del Beato Serafin de Asculi (The Rosary of the Blessed Seraphim of Ascoli). St. Seraphin of Montegranaro was a sixteenth century Capuchin monk who was canonized by Pope Clement XIII in 1767, only two years before the Portolá expedition. His feast day is celebrated on October 12, two days before Father Crespí encountered Soquel Creek. The lead cartographer of the party, Miguel Costansó, also mentioned the creek in his diary, noting it as a "ditch in which, to descend and ascend its sides, we had to open a path."

On the last day of October, a weary party set up camp at a place where they could see the great ocean and, to the north, Point Reyes and the rocky islets of the Farallons. After the camp was established, Portolá sent one of his men, José Francisco Ortega, to explore. Some of the soldiers who remained in camp resolved to forage. Near evening, they reported that they had viewed a vast arm of the sea which stretched far inland. Wondering if this could be the lost port of Monterey, they all headed out the next day, quickly finding themselves looking down onto not the bay they had set out to find but San Francisco and San Pablo Bays.

After an absence of eight months, Portolá returned to San Diego in March 1770, leaving behind most of the surviving members of his party incapacitated by illness. While he had been away, Serra had accomplished little toward construction of the mission at San Diego. The party leader reported to the authorities of his failure to find the lost port of Monterey, but the success of finding San Francisco Bay, which was received with little enthusiasm at first. Desiring to take *San Carlos* and return to New Spain with the surviving members of his party, Portolá was convinced by Serra that his failure to find Monterey was due to mistakes made by Cabrillo while mapping the coast. Serra compared Cabrillo's maps to the ones Vizcaíno made during his 1602 voyage. Portolá, this time with Serra beside him, set out again for the north and arrived at Point Pinos overlooking the Monterey Bay on May 24. A week later, on June 3, Serra held the first mass on the shores of Monterey Bay, after which he established Alta California's second mission, San Carlos Borromeo de Monterey, at the site of the future presidio.[8]

Mission San Carlos Borromeo de Monterey is moved

Because the intended site for Mission San Carlos Borromeo de Monterey was too close to a planned presidio at Monterey, the mission site was moved in 1771 to its present location in Carmel and renamed San Carlos Borromeo de Carmelo.[9]

Control of Baja California missions given to Dominican Order

In 1772, after failing to rehabilitate the former Jesuit missions, the Franciscans lost their authority over Baja California and it was transferred to the Dominican Order, which eventually succeeded in establishing a mission chain throughout the peninsula. Meanwhile, the Franciscans shifted their focus to Alta California.

Spanish Crown begins giving land grants to worthy recipients

Beginning in 1773, the military commandant of California, who served as the territorial governor, was given authority by the Spanish Crown via the Viceroy of New Spain to grant land to deserving individuals. This was considered an important aspect of the settlement plan for Alta California, which included the establishment of missions, presidios, and pueblos (towns). The principal recipients of grants during this period were officers and soldiers upon their retirement from service. A grant to an individual was made only to the person and could not be deeded or willed to another. When the grantee died, the land reverted back to the Crown. Spanish grants and claims were respected by the Mexican government when it assumed control around 1821. Many grantees took the precaution to have their grant renewed by the Mexican government.[10]

The Santa Clara Valley is explored and Mission Santa Cruz is established

In 1774, an exploratory party led by Governor Fernando Javier Rivera y Moncada and accompanied by Father Palóu left Mission Carmel and headed into the Santa Clara Valley to explore it up to the southern end of San Francisco Bay. After their explorations were completed, the party returned to Mission Carmel by following the western side of the Santa Cruz Mountains (along the route established by the Portolá party) until the San Lorenzo River was reached. Before crossing the river, they established the future site of Mission Santa Cruz.[11]

Juan Bautista de Anza leads two expeditions into Alta California

Between January 8, 1774 and March 10, 1776, Captain Juan Bautista de Anza, standing "forth in the double capacity of both explorer and colony leader," led two expeditions into Alta California.[12]

The first expedition began by land, departing from Tubac (south of modern-day Tucson, Arizona) on January 8, 1774. Anza's primary goal was to reach Mission San Gabriel Arcángel (Los Angeles). In his party were two Franciscan friars, thirty-one other men, 140 horses, and sixty-five heads of cattle. The party reached San Gabriel on April 10, 1774. Here the cattle, horses, and twenty-three men remained while Anza with the six remaining men and two friars continued their journey toward Monterey. The party reached Monterey on April 20, at which point Anza immediately turned back to return to San Gabriel alone.

Anza reached San Gabriel again on May 1, 1774 and then left for Tubac, arriving there around May 26. After a short rest, he continued to México City, arriving in July, where he recounted the results of his remarkable journey to his superiors.

This first expedition by land into Alta California made a definite contribution to western pathfinding. His journey to and from Monterey from Tubac covered over 1,500 miles. To then go on to the viceroy in México City involved a horseback journey of an additional 1,250 miles. For his success, and to encourage him to pursue a second expedition, Anza was promoted to the ranch of lieutenant-colonel in October 1774.

The next month, Anza, on behalf of the viceroy, wrote and signed a decree on November 24, 1774 that stated his intention to lead a second expedition into Alta California. Immediately after signing the decree, he rushed to San Felipé y Santiago de Sinaloa (modern-day Sinaloa de Leyva in México) to raise the necessary force and supplies for the trip northward. The purpose of the expedition was to bring settlers with their families to Monterey, where a presidio had been under construction since 1770. The plan was that, after the families reached the vicinity of the presidio and were settled, Monterey would be established as the official capital of Alta California.

Anza successfully gathered a group of thirty soldiers with their families plus a number of additional families by late 1775. The party left from San Felipe for San Miguel de Horcasitas in Sonora, further to the north. By the time Horcasitas was reached, the party consisted of 177 people. At Tubac, an additional sixty-three people joined the group, including the family of Joaquín Isidro Castro, a soldier stationed at Tubac.

It was planned that, at each waypoint, a number of soldiers would leave and be replaced with new, fresh troops from the local garrison. San

Gabriel provided the first such troops. By the time the party finally arrived in Monterey on March 10, 1776, 250 people and 800 heads of livestock had been brought to Monterey to support the presidio, mission, and settlement.

While his achievements as an explorer were what he became best known for, Anza's role as a colony leader was just as remarkable. Herbert Eugene Bolton writes: "With slender equipment he organized and conducted a large company of men, women, and children some sixteen hundred miles, from the Sinaloa mainland to Monterey. When it left its last rendezvous at Tubac, his colony comprised of two hundred and forty persons. On the first day out from the post a woman paid the extreme price of motherhood. But this was the only death during the whole journey, and to offset the loss three infants were born on the way and all reached their destination safe and sound. This is a remarkable record, never excelled—perhaps never equaled—in all the history of the great pioneer trek of peoples to the Pacific Coast before, during, or after the Gold Rush. Anza's brilliant success can not be attributed to the ease of the journey, for it was made amid varying conditions of drought, cold, snow, and rain. The march of sixteen hundred miles from Culiacán to Monterey, in which only one human being was lost, was so difficult that it cost the lives of nearly a hundred head of stock which died of hardship on the way."

Three months after reaching Monterey, on June 17, about seventy-five men, including soldiers, headed north under the command of Lieutenant José Joaquín Moraga to establish the presidio and a site for Mission San Francisco de Asís. On their return journey, the men also established the site for Mission Santa Clara de Asís in the Santa Clara Valley.[13]

El Pueblo de San José de Guadalupe is established and José Joaquín Castro becomes one of its first residents

As part of the Spanish program to civilize and Christianize the local Native Americans, three pueblos with formal charters were initially founded. While the purpose of the California missions was to be settled by *gente de razon* (people of reason), the Spanish brought colonists to California for the expressed purpose of having a politically reliable population under civil, not church, control. They were also intended to accelerate population growth since the missions were unable to accomplish this. The first such settlement was El Pueblo de San José de Guadalupe, founded by José Moraga on November 29, 1777 in the Santa Clara Valley. It evolved into the modern-day city of San José.

One of the first residents of San José was Joaquín Isidro Castro, who had travelled to Monterey on Anza's second expedition into Alta California. The Castro family, according to Spanish historian Julio de Atienza, was one of five families in Old Castile that descended from the first kings. As Spanish influence spread throughout the world, the family was at the forefront. Joaquín Castro was born in 1732 in Sinaloa. Prior to the expedition, Castro served as a scout in Tubac, where he and seven other soldiers were recruited to join Anza's party to Monterey in 1776. He and his wife set out with seven children, but an eighth was born during the trip and a ninth was later born in California. During their journey, their oldest daughter, Ana Josefa, was courted by José Antonio María Soberanes. When they reached Monterey, she was married to Soberanes on May 29, 1776 by Father Serra. Soberanes had served as a scout and guide in three expeditions into Alta California: with Portolá in 1769, with Pedro Fagas in 1772, and with Anza in 1776.

The Castro family did not initially settle in Monterey but continued on to the presidio at San Francisco, where they lived for a year. But they were sent in 1776 to help establish Mission Santa Clara and the family settled in the adjacent Pueblo de San José the next year. By the late 1780s, Castro became co-owner of Rancho Buena Vista, a royal grant near Monterey alongside Soberanes. Rancho Buena Vista was one of six land grants listed in the Monterey District in January 1795.

Castro's wife, María Martina Botiller, was born in 1733 in France. Leon Rowland states that: "Legend is that she was a French woman of noble blood, exiled to Spain, where she married Joaquin Castro, with whom she went to Sinaloa and with whom she later came to California." The couple had nine known children, including:

1. *Ignacio Clemente.* Born in 1756, he was around twenty when he came to Alta California with his parents. He was a soldier in Monterey from 1790 to 1793 and *alcalde* (mayor)

of the Pueblo of San José in 1799, 1804, and 1809-1810. He drowned in the Arroyo de la Alameda on March 4, 1817.

2. *Ana Josefa.* Born in 1758, she was eighteen when she entered Alta California. After marrying José María Soberanes in 1776, she lived at Mission Carmel. The couple moved to the newly founded Mission Nuestra Señora Dolores de la Soledad in 1791, where Soberanes was stationed. As previously discussed, he became a co-grantee, along with Joaquín Castro, of Rancho Buena Vista.

   Soberanes died in 1803 and was buried on September 22 in the cemetery of Mission Carmel. Afterwards, Ana returned to Monterey with four of her children and, on May 12, 1816, in the chapel of the Presidio of Monterey, married José Miguel Eduardo Uribe y López. She died six years later on July 30, 1822. Out of Ana's two marriages, two of Alta California's most prominent families descended: the Soberanes and Bernals.

3. *María Encarnación.* Born in 1764, she was approximately twelve when she arrived in California. She married José Joaquín de Avila on January 7, 1782, and later moved to México City with her husband in around 1800.

4. *María del Carmen Martina.* Born in 1766, she was around ten when she entered California and she married Ventura Amézquita in Santa Clara in around 1814.

5. *José Mariano.* Born in 1765, José was about nine when he traveled on the second Anza expedition. He married María Josefa Romero on February 19, 1791 at Mission Santa Barbara. He was grantee of Rancho de las Ánimas in Santa Clara County in 1802. This is said to have been the only vice-regal land grant in California. He died in 1828 at the age of 37.

6. *José Joaquín.* Born in 1770, he was six years old when he came to California. He was the father of, among several others, María Martina Castro, who is the primary focus of this book. He and Martina will be discussed in further detail below.

7. *Francisco María.* Born in 1774, he was only two when the Anza expedition set off from Tubac. Some sources state he was born in 1773, and these also disagree on whether he was born in Spain or Sinaloa, where his siblings were born. He married María Gabriela Berryessa on February 16, 1795 at Mission Santa Clara. He died at San Pablo on November 5, 1831.

8. *Carlos Antonio.* Possibly born in Fuerte, Sonora (New Spain) in 1774, Carlos is more often noted as having been born on the second Anza expedition before it reached Mission San Gabriel in late 1775. The date of his death is equally uncertain, with several sources listing him dying as early as 1845, but others stating mid-1848.

9. *María Isabel.* Born in Alta California and baptized on November 19, 1777, Isabel died young in San Francisco on July 3, 1779.

Joaquín Castro died on December 31, 1801 and was buried in the cemetery of Mission Carmel. After his death, Soberanes gained full ownership of Rancho Buena Vista until his own death in 1803. Meanwhile, María Martina died in the Pueblo de Branciforte in 1813 and was buried in the Mission Santa Cruz cemetery.[14]

El Pueblo de Nuestra Señora la Reina de los Ángeles sobre el Río Porciúncula is established

The second Spanish settlement, El Pueblo de Nuestra Señora la Reina de los Ángeles sobre el Río Porciúncula (Town of Our Lady, Queen of the Angels, on the River Porciuncula), was established in September 1781. It eventually developed into the city of Los Angeles.

Father Junípero Serra dies

Father Junípero Serra died on August 28, 1784. Shortly afterwards, Father Fermín Lasuén was elected by the Franciscans of New Spain to serve as the new head of the missions in Alta California.[15]

Father Lasuén blesses site of Mission Santa Cruz and establishes the Franciscan Trail

In mid-1791, Father Lasuén decided that the time had arrived to found Alta California's twelfth mission near the site of the planned Branciforte pueblo. He wanted to bless the exact spot that had been established earlier by Father Palóu in 1774 and then establish the best route between the mission and Mission Santa Clara to the north.

The party led by Lasuén left Mission Carmel and headed inland and then north along a partially established road (which today follows, for the most part, State Route 82) until they were opposite today's town of Woodside. Here, the party crossed the Santa Cruz Mountains. When they reached the ocean, the party turned south toward the San Lorenzo River, where the site of the twelfth mission had been selected.

After Lasuén planted a cross at the site of the future mission and blessed the ground on August 29, 1791, the party headed north through the Santa Cruz Mountains (roughly down modern-day State Route 17, Scotts Valley Drive, and Glenwood Drive). Near where Mountain Charley Road begins today, they continued up along the top of the narrow ridge between Mountain Charley Gulch to the west and Bean Creek to the east. When the party reached a point about a mile below the crest of the Santa Cruz Mountains, they stopped along the side of a small body of water soon to be called "Laguna del Sargento."

After leaving the lagoon behind, they reached the crest of the Santa Cruz Mountains. Much of the route that the party followed to Los Gatos

Creek is speculative. They probably crossed the future State Route 17 where Mountain Charley Road meets Summit Road. From here, they continued down Mountain Charley Road along the east side of State Route 17 until reaching Old Santa Cruz Highway, from where they continued to the creek and followed it to Mission Santa Clara.[16]

Baptism of local Native Americans begins at Mission Santa Cruz

After Lasuén's party left the site of Mission Santa Cruz, a military detachment from the presidio in San Francisco set up camp in the area to supervise the erection of the mission's buildings. Soon after construction was underway, the troops began gathering the Native Americans from the surrounding area to be baptized. Prior to the erection of the mission, local Costanoan tribal people were brought to Missions Carmel, San Francisco, and Santa Clara for conversion and resettlement, which meant there were few Native Americans left along the coast for Mission Santa Cruz. Nonetheless, the first baptisms at Santa Cruz occurred on September 24, 1791. Because the local Native Americans were either too hard to manage or were too few in number to perform the tasks assigned to them by the friars, neophytes (converted Native Americans) were brought from Mission Santa Clara. The mission site was chosen on Christmas Day 1791.

The first buildings of the new mission were temporary affairs made of poles and crudely split redwood planks, cut in the forests of the Santa Cruz Mountains to the north. By the end of the year, eighty-seven local Native Americans had been baptized at the mission site. Meanwhile, their lands were slowly converted for stock raising by the Franciscans in order to achieve self-sufficiency for the mission. They raised cattle, sheep, and goats, but largely ignored the redwood trees in the interior, which were too difficult to cut for use.[17]

José Joaquín Castro marries María Antonia Amador y Noriega

On December 23, 1791, José Joaquín, the sixth child and third son of Joaquín

Isidro Castro and María Martina Botiller, married María Antonia Amador y Noriega, the daughter of his sergeant, Pedro Antonio Amador. Castro had enlisted in the Spanish army while his family lived in San Francisco and was still stationed there at the time of his marriage. While they lived in San Francisco, Joaquín and Antonia produced their first two children:

1. *José Ignacio*, baptized on March 1, 1793 and buried on January 10, 1811 at the Mission San Juan Bautista cemetery.

2. *María Antonia Dionisia*, baptized on April 10, 1795. She married Juan José Feliz in 1849 at Mission Santa Clara de Asís.

Shortly after their second child was born, Joaquín was transferred to the Presidio of Monterey, where the family remained until he retired after ten years of service in 1798. They had no more children while they lived in Monterey.[18]

Construction of Mission Santa Cruz begins

On February 27, 1793, construction of the first permanent buildings for the church and mission at Santa Cruz began on the floodplain along the west bank of the San Lorenzo River. However, after the first rainy season and subsequent flooding of the San Lorenzo River, the Spanish soldiers and Franciscan friars decided that the sites of both the church and the mission were too close to the river. To solve the problem, they moved the mission and church to higher ground and began constructing new buildings composed entirely of adobe and redwood. These structures, complete with five-foot-thick adobe walls and tile roofs supported by redwood beams, were dedicated on May 10, 1794. Despite the improved location and use of stronger building materials, the mission and its associated structures would continue to suffer from winter storms throughout their relatively short existence.[19]

Franciscan Trail improved

After Father Lasuén established the rugged Franciscan Trail between

Mission Santa Cruz and Mission Santa Clara, it served as the main route between the two locations. In 1795, Governor Diego de Borica ordered that the road be improved. Pedro Amador, Joaquín Castro's father-in-law, was assigned the task.

The governor wanted the road improved for two main reasons: first, to shorten the travel time between the two missions, and, second, to support the first wave of settlers who would shortly be arriving in the newly authorized Pueblo de Branciforte. Nonetheless, the trail was less a road and more of a game trail, difficult and dangerous to navigate even in the best circumstances. John Young explains that "steep, rough, and in the summer a wondrous place for dust, the trail in winter was a dangerous place for pack trains and men alike." And then there was always the danger from grizzly bears and mountain lions. The Franciscan Trail, with its many short-cuts and rerouting over short distances, would serve as the main route between San José and Branciforte for more than fifty years.[20]

The population at Mission Santa Cruz reaches 523

By 1796, the population at Mission Santa Cruz reached 523 people, the highest it would ever achieve. As such, it supported the lowest population of all twenty-one missions in Alta California.[21]

Branciforte pueblo established

On March 3, 1796, Pedro de Alberni and Alberto de Córdoba of the Royal Corps of Engineers were commissioned to find a site for a third pueblo and decided upon the west bank of the San Lorenzo River across from Mission Santa Cruz. As soon as the area was surveyed and a map prepared, Governor Borica authorized construction of the pueblo to begin. When the governor approved the location of the town, he broke a colonial law that forbade the founding of any pueblo within a league (two and a half miles) of a mission. Mission Santa Cruz was located less than a mile away across the river. However, this rule was conveniently overlooked by secular authorities. Instead, the friars were directed to support the new town in flagrant violation of both custom and legality. In early 1797, the

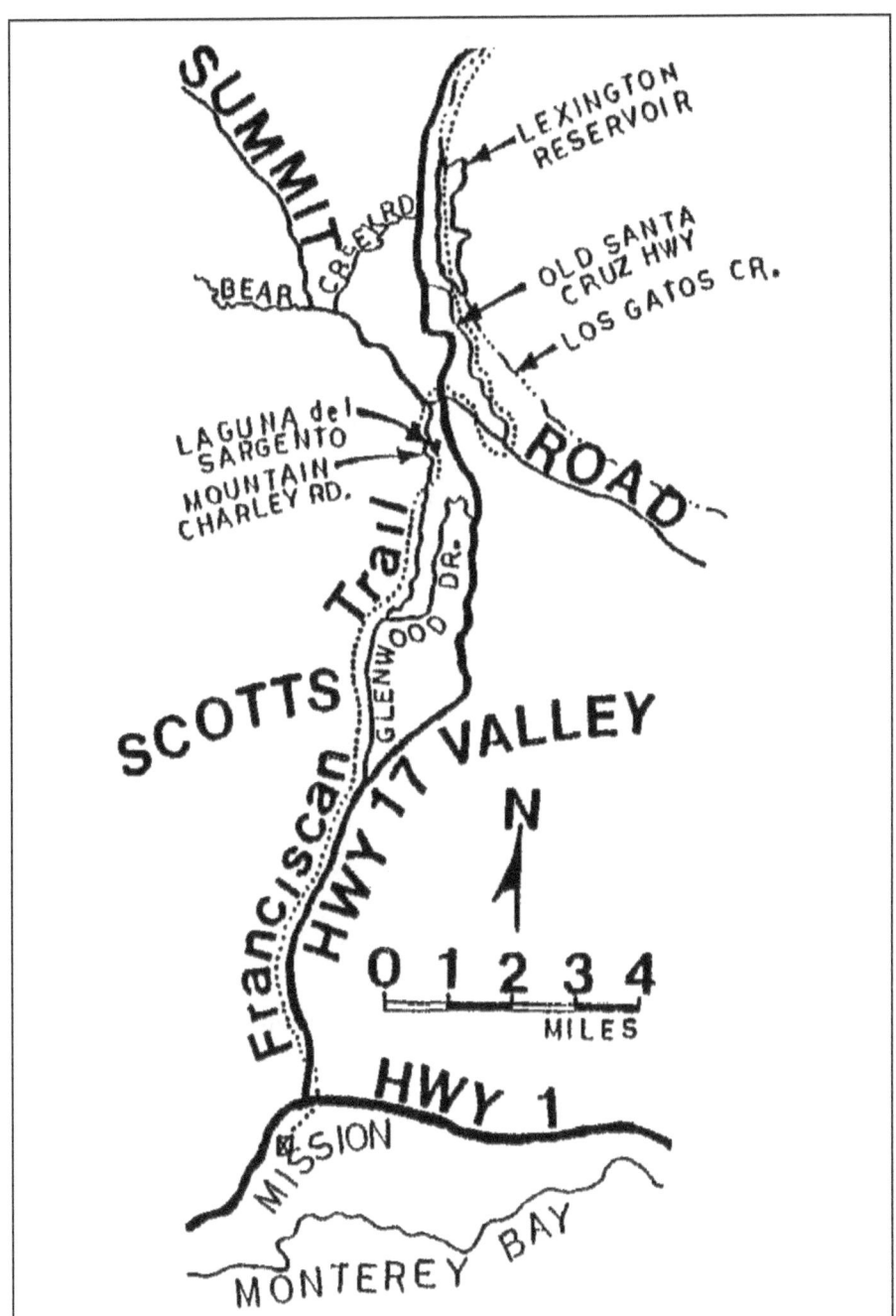

Figure 1.1 Route of the Franciscan Trail between Mission Santa Cruz and Los Gatos Creek

pueblo was given the name Branciforte, named in honor of the Viceroy Miguel de la Grúa Talamanca, Marqués de Branciforte. It remained the smallest chartered pueblo in Alta California.

The first colonists came to Monterey on the schooner *Concepción* and arrived in Branciforte on May 12. Gabriel Moraga, son of José Moraga and later made famous for his own expeditions into the Central Valley, was transferred from the Pueblo de San José and given authority over the new settlement as its *comisionado* (military administrator).

Historians over the years have taken delight in the fact that the first eight male inhabitants were criminals. But what type of criminals were they? They were not killers or thieves but natives of Old México who had run afoul of its rigorous political laws. They were given the choice of going before a judge and possibly serving time in jail for political disobedience or moving to Alta California as settlers. As inducement, they were promised transportation, 430 pesos distributed over five years, an adobe home with tile roof, and livestock, farm tools, a plow, and a musket to be paid in installments.

The first residents were not picked randomly—by the governor's request they included a carpenter, tailor, miner, merchant, engraver, two farmers, and one unclassified person. According to Leon Rowland, three—or perhaps four—brought wives and two of the couples had children.

When they reached Branciforte, their promised houses were not waiting, so they were forced to put up huts of split redwood and tule thatching. The subsidies came in cash or supplies, convincing at least six of the original eight men to remain in the pueblo.[22]

First *invalidos* arrive at Branciforte

In 1798, six *invalidos* (from which the non-pejorative term "invalided out" derives) arrived at Branciforte from the Presidio of Monterey. Five of them played a part in the future history of Santa Cruz County, three in a major role, two in a minor. Each was promised a pension in exchange for agreeing to return to arms in the event of a military emergency, a very real likelihood in Alta California, where Native American revolts led to the abandonment of some of the missions as late as 1824. As was usual for a time when the resources of the Spanish Empire were stretched thin and under threat by

At the Edge of the Empire 1798

foreign powers, the individuals in the farthest outposts were exploited without receiving their promised compensation.

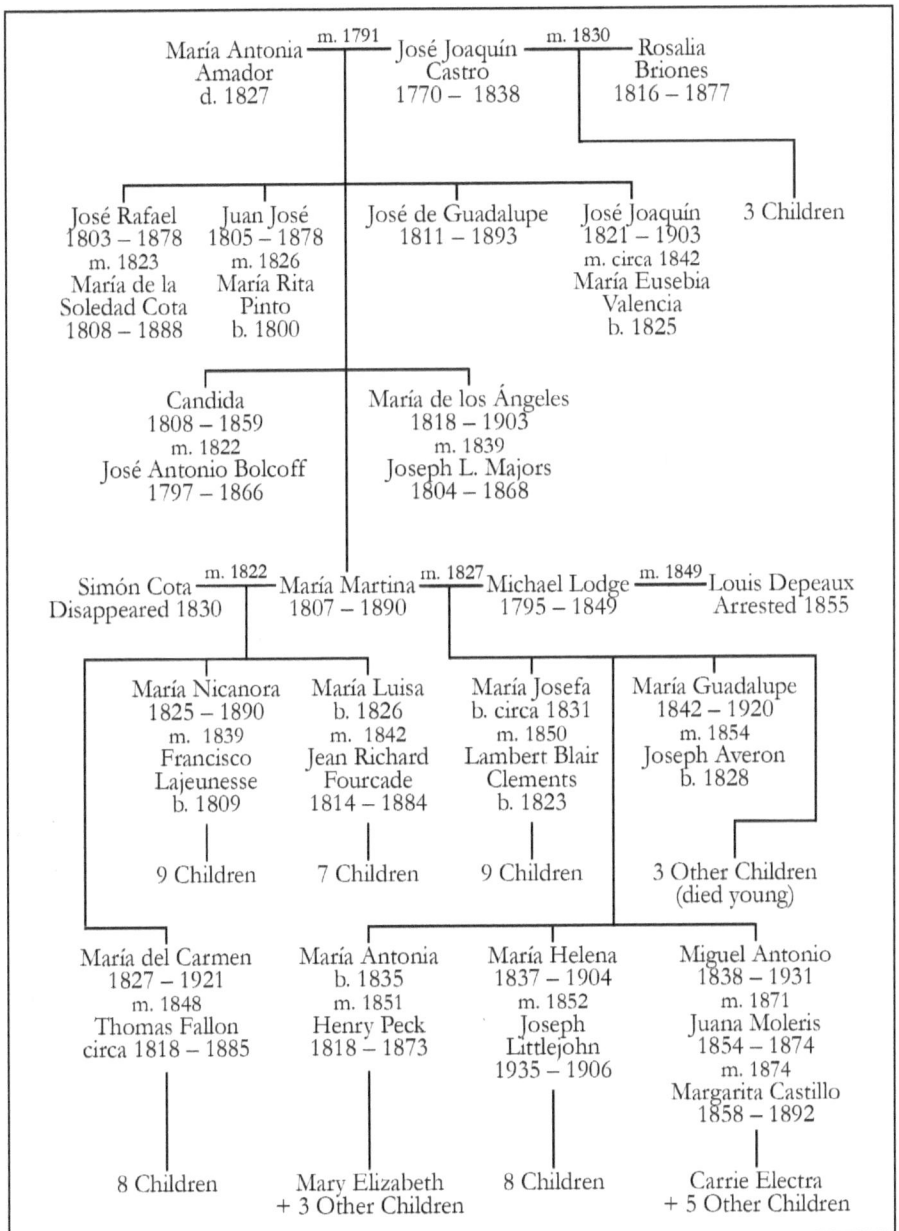

Figure 1.2 The José Joaquín Castro Family

The three most prominent *invalidos* at Branciforte were Juan José Peralta, José Antonio Rodriquez, and José Joaquín Castro. Peralta was from a well-known family and did not remain in Branciforte long, but rather headed out to claim lands elsewhere in Alta California. Rodriquez had first entered Alta California as a member of an *escolta* (a military escort) at Soledad in 1787. His sons would also serve in the military and be granted ranchos. Today, there are literally hundreds of his descendants living in Santa Cruz and Monterey counties. Castro has already been introduced as the son of Joaquín Isidro Castro. The less prominent *invalidos* were Marcelino Bravo, Marcos Villela, and Marcos Briones, the latter of whom also has many descendants in California and whose name appears many times throughout the early history of the Central Coast.

Branciforte, which was supposed to be a civil town, was for all but two years of its existence under the military administration of the Presidio of Monterey. Pueblos were intended to be the first line of defense for the missions against foreign invasion and domestic conflict, but as Branciforte grew, it became a center of smuggling and illegal trade, while the nearby Mission Santa Cruz declined precipitously. By all standards, Branciforte was a disaster. Many of its settlers survived by stealing from the mission rather than by growing crops or raising livestock. They encroached on mission land, tormented the mission's neophytes, and caused trouble as far as Mission San José, where the larger Native American population meant that there were more women to harass than were available locally. As a result of protests from San José, the Branciforte residents were forbidden to travel, so they had to be content harassing the residents of the local mission. Things became so intolerable that 200 neophytes abandoned Santa Cruz in order to get away from the predatory settlers. Only thirty to forty neophytes could be persuaded to remain at the mission, presumably mostly women since a dormitory was erected for them in 1810.

Joaquín Castro remained in Branciforte and by 1818 was the majordomo (chief steward) of Mission Santa Cruz, a position he held for several years and that made him one of, if not the, most influential men living in the pueblo. During this time, Castro and his wife had thirteen more children:

3. *María Josefa*, baptized on December 30, 1799 at Mission

Santa Cruz, was buried on February 2, 1811 at the Mission Santa Cruz cemetery.

4. *María Rafaela Inocencia*, baptized on December 30, 1799 at Mission Santa Cruz, married Francisco Rodriguez, the son of José Antonio Rodriguez, one of the five *invalidos* who accompanied Castro when he settled at Branciforte. Rodriguez was the grantee of Rancho Arroyo del Rodeo (also known as San Vicente or Los Coyotes) in July 1834. María Rafaela died in 1841.

5. *José Rafael Antonio*, born on October 16, 1801 in Branciforte, was buried on February 10, 1811 at the Mission Santa Cruz cemetery.

6. *José Rafael de Jesús* was born on October 15, 1803 in Branciforte and baptized at Mission Santa Cruz. He married María de la Soledad Cota of Mission Santa Barbara while he was serving in the Spanish army. The highest rank he achieved during his ten years of service was corporal. He was granted Rancho Aptos in 1833 by Governor José Figueroa and it was increased to its final size of 6,680 acres in 1840 by Governor Juan Bautista Alvarado. Rafael died in Aptos on May 14, 1878 and is buried in the Our Lady of Mount Carmel cemetery.

7. *Juan José*, baptized on June 19, 1805 at Mission Santa Cruz, married twice and was the *regidor* (magistrate) of Branciforte in 1833 and again in 1845. The date of his death is unknown.

8. *María Martina* was baptized on March 17, 1807, although the exact date of her birth is not recorded. After searching all known records, including Branciforte's pre-statehood records (translated by Star Girky), very little was discovered

regarding Martina's early years. It is known that she lived with her family in Branciforte, who pampered her as a child. Several articles have described her as being short, handsome, dark-skinned, and having long black hair. It is unfortunate to posterity that the only known picture of her was taken late in life, when she was obese and had lost most of her front teeth. Her story is chronicled throughout this book.

9. *Candida*, baptized on December 14, 1808 at Mission Santa Cruz, married the Russian-born settler José Antonio Bolcoff in 1822. She was one of the grantees of Rancho Refugio, located to the northwest of Santa Cruz. It was registered as one square league to Candida and two of her sisters, María de los Ángeles and María Antonia Jacinta.

10. *Francisco*, baptized on September 7, 1810 at Mission Santa Cruz, died on January 12, 1811 and is buried in the Mission Santa Cruz cemetery.

12. *José de Guadalupe*, baptized on September 17, 1811 at Mission Santa Cruz, served as the *juez suplente* (substitute judge) in 1841 at Branciforte, a Justice of the Peace in 1851, and a claimant to his father's Rancho San Andrés after Joaquín's death. He died a bachelor on August 15, 1893 at the home of his sister, María de los Ángeles.

13. *María Antonia Jacinta*, baptized on January 29, 1815 at Mission Santa Cruz, relinquished her share in Rancho Refugio when she became a nun in Monterey.

14. *José Ignacio*, born in 1817 at Branciforte, married Ricarda Rodriguez.

15. *María de los Ángeles*, baptized on September 12, 1818 at Mission Santa Cruz, married Joseph Ladd Majors on

December 19, 1839. That same year, she was made a grantee of Rancho Refugio. After Majors died on May 25, 1868, María lived another thirty-five years, long enough to enter the twentieth century. She died in 1903 at the age of 85.

16. *José Joaquín*, born around 1820, was the fifteenth and presumably youngest child of José Joaquín and María Antonia. His existence was discovered through court testimony given in a deposition on June 6, 1896, where he lists his age as about seventy-eight. Because their names are identical, he has often been conflated with his father. The younger Joaquín lived on his father's Rancho San Andrés for many years, where he built a home alongside a lagoon for himself and his wife. He finally left the property in 1882 and moved to Gilroy.

On June 30, 1827, Castro's beloved wife of thirty-six years died. Three years later, he married the seventeen-year-old Rosalia Briones, the daughter of Manuel Briones and María Antonia Vásquez. Castro fathered three more children with his second wife: María Ignacia Ángela de Fulgencia, Juan Bautista, and Juan. Shortly afterwards, he moved to Branciforte and became *alcalde* in 1831. When the Act of Secularization became law in 1833, Castro was the first to apply for land in what would become Santa Cruz County. He was granted a 13,000-acre property on November 26, 1833 that he named Rancho San Andrés. He died five years later at the age of sixty-eight in Santa Cruz. His property was divided between his surviving children while the core of the ranch had already been taken over by his three living sons, Guadalupe, Ignacio, and Joaquín.[23]

The presidio at Monterey is captured

In November 1818, at the height of México's revolutionary fervor against Spain by Latin American patriots, the Franco-Argentine revolutionary and pirate Hippolyte Bouchard along with 350 sailors captured the Presidio of Monterey after an exchange of cannon fire with its forty defenders. The revolutionaries, claiming to represent the Republic of Buenos, burned the fort and town, then California's capital, and proceeded to occupy it for a week, exhorting the local populace to join their cause. Spanish subjects all around Monterey Bay fled to the interior, and when Bouchard threatened to descend upon the interior, Governor Pablo Vicente de Solá ordered Father Ramón Olbes, the priest in charge of Mission Santa Cruz, to remove all valuables and take them to Mission Soledad until the danger had passed.

The padres obeyed the governor's order after asking the residents of Branciforte to help protect the mission from the pirates, who, as it happened, never came. While Mission Santa Cruz escaped the attentions of Bouchard, the good citizens of Branciforte seized the opportunity to loot the mission to the point that when Olbes returned, he was so discouraged that he asked permission to abandon it as a lost cause.[24]

México achieves its independence from Spain

As the war with Spain turned in favor of México, the Spanish Crown gave out its last land grants to settlers in New Spain. Throughout the period of Spanish control over Alta California, nine governors, plus two interim governors, ruled the province, including:

1. Gaspar de Portolá (1769 – 1770)
2. Pedro Fages (1770 – 1774)
3. Fernando Rivera (1774 – 1777)
4. Felipe de Neve (1777 – 1782)
5. Pedro Fages (1782 – 1791)
6. José Antonio Roméu (1791 – 1792)
    Interim: José Joaquín de Arrillaga (1792 – 1794)
7. Diego de Borica (1794 – 1800)
8. José Joaquín de Arrillaga (1800 – 1814)
    Interim: José Darío Argüello (1814 – 1815)
9. Pablo Vicente de Solá (1815 – 1822)[25]

On August 24, 1821, Spain finally accepted the cession of the First Mexican Empire via the Treaty of Córdoba. It began a twenty-seven-year transitional period in Alta California, where the power of the Catholic

Church and military declined, and the native-born Californios assumed supremacy over the province. It also saw the first significant influx of foreign immigrants.[26]

José Antonio Bolcoff settles in Branciforte and marries Candida Castro

Osip Volkov, born in 1797 in Kamchatka, Russia, was a trader for the Russian American Company when he was either captured by the Spanish or deserted at Point Conception near Mission Santa Barbara around 1815. He went to Mission Soledad, where he had his Greek Orthodox Church baptism ratified. Over the next five years, Volkov learned Spanish and became a translator for Governor Pablo Vicente de Solá, during which time he adopted the name José Antonio Bolcoff. In 1822, he moved to Branciforte and married Candida Castro. Bolcoff was later granted Rancho San Agustin in 1833. This property included most of modern-day Scotts Valley. Later, in 1839, his wife was granted a one-third interest in Rancho Refugio, which sat along the coast north of the future city of Santa Cruz. Bolcoff became involved in local politics and served as *alcalde* of Branciforte three times.[27]

Alta California becomes a province of the Mexican Empire

Eight months after the Treaty of Córdoba was signed between Spain and México, news finally reached Pablo Vicente de Solá, the last Spanish governor of Alta California, on April 11, 1822. Rather than resisting the change, he requested that all members of his staff take an oath of allegiance to the new government. Soon afterwards, a radical anticlerical movement arose across México. The Catholic missions were viewed as the most tangible and dangerous representation of Spanish colonial control. Consequently, they were stripped of their vast landholdings and entered a period of limbo for the next decade while the government contemplated their fate. Many Native Americans and some friars continued to reside at some of the missions during these years even though government and church support for them was limited.[28]

Rafael Castro marries María de la Soledad Cota and Simón Cota y Romero marries Martina Castro

During the early 1820s, two marriages of importance occurred: that of Rafael Castro and María de la Soledad Cota, and that of María's brother, Simón Cota y Romero, to Rafael's sister, Martina. Simón and María were the children of Manuel Antonio de Cota and Gertrudis Romero of Santa Barbara.

Simón was born on October 28, 1803 in Santa Barbara and became a corporal in either the Spanish or Mexican army—it is unclear which. He was stationed at the Presidio of Monterey when he married Martina. After their vows were exchanged, Martina moved to Monterey to live with Simón.

It is from this point that a clearer picture of the complex personality of Martina, as well as that of her brother Rafael, can be pieced together. Several historians have described both siblings as having a strong sense of pride in their families and marriages. Both were also purportedly quick of temper but open minded as far as generosity was concerned. Nonetheless, they stubbornly and fiercely clung to old Spanish traditions. Indeed, these traits were strongly entrenched in the Castro family as a whole, especially by the men.

Other traits also ran in the family. Many in the second generation refused to speak English and pretended not to understand it, even when they did. While Rafael possessed the somewhat rare ability to read and write, this ability eluded his sister completely. Both were very religiously devout, especially Martina. Whenever she needed guidance, she would turn to the Church and the padres at Mission Santa Cruz and, while she lived in Monterey, Mission Carmel.[29]

General Colonization Law passed by México

The General Colonization Law was passed by the Provisional Government of Mexico on August 18, 1824. It established the requirements that a person or persons must meet in order to request land from the government, as well as the requirements that the land itself must meet, such as its condition, location, whether or not it can be irrigated, or if it is poor for agriculture. Before the requested land could be granted, the government determined whether it originally belonged to a private individual, a corporation, or the government. This law was amended and new regulations added four years later on November 21, 1828.[30]

Martina Castro gives birth to Nicanora Cota in Monterey

Martina Castro and Simón Cota's first child was born in 1825 at Monterey. She was baptized María Nicanora Cota, but she dropped the final letter of her name following her marriage to Francisco Lajeunesse and was afterwards known as Nicanor.[31]

Michael Lodge arrives in Monterey and marries Josefa Luz

Michael Lodge, born around 1795 in County Cork, Ireland, arrived in Monterey in 1826. Among Lodge's talents were carpentry and a love for the sea. Shortly after his arrival, he met Josefa Luz, the daughter of García Luz, an *invalido* who had settled with his wife in Branciforte. Another of Luz's daughters, María Ramona de la Luz Carrillo y Lopez, eventually married John D. Wilson, who briefly served as an Indian Agent in San Francisco in 1849. Wilson was born in Scotland in 1790 and served in the United States Navy for approximately two years along the California coast before opening a private law practice in Santa Cruz in 1852. The marriage of the two men into the Luz family created a common bond between them, although they likely never met, and Martina Castro would later call upon Wilson's services to help her in several lawsuits.[32]

Martina Castro gives birth to María Luisa Cota in Monterey

In 1826, Martina Castro and Simón Cota's second child, María Luisa, was born.[33]

Josefa Luz gives birth to a daughter

A daughter was born to Michael Lodge and his wife, Josefa Luz, in 1827, while they were residents of Monterey.[34]

Martina Castro gives birth to María del Carmen

Martina Castro's third child, María del Carmen Juana Josefa Adelayda, was born in Monterey on July 12, 1827. Her father has been a point of debate among historians. Castro may have begun an affair with Michael Lodge while they both lived in Monterey. Throughout her life, Carmen went by Carmelita and Carmel.[35]

Michael and Josefa Lodge move to Branciforte

After Michael Lodge had lived in California for two years, he became a naturalized citizen of México and was given the Spanish name Miguel Loche. After their daughter was born, she, Michael, and Josefa moved from Monterey to Branciforte. Upon their arrival, he became the fifth foreigner to take up residence in the pueblo. Shortly after their arrival, the daughter was baptized at Mission Santa Cruz.[36]

Martina Castro gives birth to son

Around 1828, Martina Castro gave birth to a son who died a month later.[37]

Josefa Lodge and daughter die in Branciforte

Sometime in 1829, Michael Lodge's wife, Josefa Luz, and their daughter died of an unknown ailment in Branciforte.[38]

Simón Cota disappears mysteriously

Martina Castro's husband, Simón Cota, disappeared under mysterious circumstances around the month of March, 1830. Several historians have argued that he was assassinated and his body disposed of. At the time of his disappearance, he was serving as secretary of the military junta that was attempting to have the governor, Vicente de Solá, removed from office. While his assassination may explain his disappearance, the birth of a third child, María del

Carmen Juana Josefa Adelayda, on July 12, 1827, and her questionable parentage may also be a factor. Soon after Cota's disappearance, Martina moved to Branciforte with her three daughters—Nicanor, Luisa, and Carmel.[39]

Martina Castro marries Michael Lodge and gives birth to María Josefa at Branciforte

When did Martina Castro marry Michael Lodge: was it in 1831 or 1833? These are the dates in which two historians of note say it occurred. Leon Rowland in his book, *Santa Cruz County: The Early Years*, places the event in 1831, while Kenneth M. Castro and his sister Doris in their book, *Castros of California*, places the event in 1833. One piece of evidence to support Rowland's date is the fact that Martina gave birth to her fifth child, María Josefa, around 1831. However, this date is speculative since it is based on court testimony given in 1895, where Josefa stated her age was about sixty-four years. It should also be noted that both Nicanor and Luisa retained their father's surname, Cota, while Carmel and Josefa used Lodge's name.

Whether Castro and Lodge met in Monterey is also open to question, but both were living in Branciforte when they married. They settled on a small parcel of land and began raising crops and various animals.[40]

México begins granting land in Alta California

The majority of Mexican land grants were made after January 1832 under the General Colonization Law of 1824 and from the regulations added to the law in 1828. Except for the grants of pueblo lots and perhaps some grants located north of San Francisco Bay, most grants were made by the territorial governors. A total of eleven men served as elected governors of Alta California during the Mexican period, as well as four interim governors. After 1836, the governors ruled both Alta and Baja California, which formed the territory of the Californias. The governors were:

Provisional: Pablo Vicente de Solá (1822)
1. Luis Antonio Argüello (1823 – 1825)
2. José María de Echeandía (1825 – 1831)

3. Manuel Victoria (1831 – 1832)
4. Pío Pico (1832)
5. *In the South:* José María de Echeandía (1832 – 1833)
6. *In the North:* Agustín Vicente Zamorano (1832 – 1833)
7. José Figueroa (1833 – 1835)
   Interim: José Antonio Castro (1835 – 1836)
   Interim: Nicolás Gutiérrez (1836)
8. Mariano Chico (1836)
   Interim: Nicolás Gutiérrez (1836)
9. Juan Bautista Alvarado (1836 – 1842)
   Disputed by Carlos Antonio Carrillo (1837 – 1838)
10. Manuel Micheltorena (1842 – 1845)
11. Pío Pico (1845 – 1846)

Anyone desiring a grant from the Mexican government could present a petition to the governor, stating his or her age, nationality, and vocation, along with the quantity and, as nearly as possible, a description of the desired land. The petition was usually accompanied by a *diseño* (sketched map). After the governor reviewed the petition, he would make a marginal notation on it directing the prefect or local officer to examine and report whether the land was vacant and could be granted without injury to third persons or the public. The official's statement regarding the land was called the *informe* and was attached to the grantees' partition. All of the documents would then be returned to the governor.

If the governor was satisfied with the *informe*, he would issue a grant to the petitioner, who became the grantee. The petition, *diseño*, and *informe*, together with a copy of the grant, were collected together to form the evidence of the title, which was called the *expediente*. This was filed by the governor's secretary in the territorial archives at Monterey.

The final step in the process was to obtain formal approval for the grant from the territorial deputation or departmental assembly. The governor took care of this step by communicating his desires with the legislative body, which were referred to a committee which, in turn, made its own report on the matter. If the legislative body did not concur with the governor, the governor had the option to appeal to the Mexican federal government.[41]

Rafael Castro is granted Rancho Aptos and begins to develop the Aptos area

On August 13, 1833, Rafael Castro submitted a *diseño* for what would soon be called Rancho Aptos. Shortly afterwards, his petition was received by the governor and, before the year was over, he was granted his requested land. It was listed by the Mexican government as one square league in size (4,410 acres) extending from the Zanjón de Borregas (meaning "Lamb Gulch," today called Borregas Gulch) in the north to his father's Rancho San Andrés in the south. The government would later increase the rancho to an unknown size which the United States ultimately patented as 6,680 acres.

Castro built his first home on the shelf overlooking the confluence of Aptos and Valencia Creeks. When a flood damaged the home in 1840, he abandoned the site and rebuilt on the hill just to the west of the present bridge that spans Aptos Creek on Soquel Drive. His second home was so large that it extended from Soquel Drive to Highway 1, a distance of some 300 feet. As the 1850s approached, Castro began to lease his lands to individuals interested in its redwoods and minerals, always keeping an eye on future profitable ventures.

There were three year-round creeks that cut a path across his land, the largest being Aptos Creek. This was joined by Valencia Creek just prior to reaching the Monterey Bay, while this was joined by Trout Gulch Creek (alternatively called Ricardo Gulch) before meeting Aptos Creek. Along the coastline, there were steep bluffs and almost four miles of sandy beach, which quickly ascended into steep mountainous terrain. Much of the remainder of Rancho Aptos was thickly covered with tall redwood trees that increased in density and size further inland.

After acquiring his land, Castro's first thought was to raise cattle, which was foremost in the day's thinking among Mexican colonists. But he soon realized the value of the redwoods that covered his land, an awareness that was only beginning to enter the minds of his countrymen. The primary reason that the Spanish and Mexican colonists did not consider the redwood's value as a building material was because they had little need for timber, except to support the roofs of their adobe structures. They did not need much lumber for fencing, either, since there were so few settlers and most of their animals herded on open ranges. And redwood is not a good firewood since it is moist and relatively soft, so they used oak and madrone instead. But the situation began to change in the 1830s as more Americans arrived. Along with his father and several other settlers who lived along Corralitos Creek, Castro began cutting redwood commercially, ultimately producing the majority of lumber cut in the region at the time.

The method used to cut lumber at this early date was called whip-sawing. A small- to medium-sized tree was selected for cutting to make it manageable. Beside it, a pit at least eight feet deep was dug. After the tree

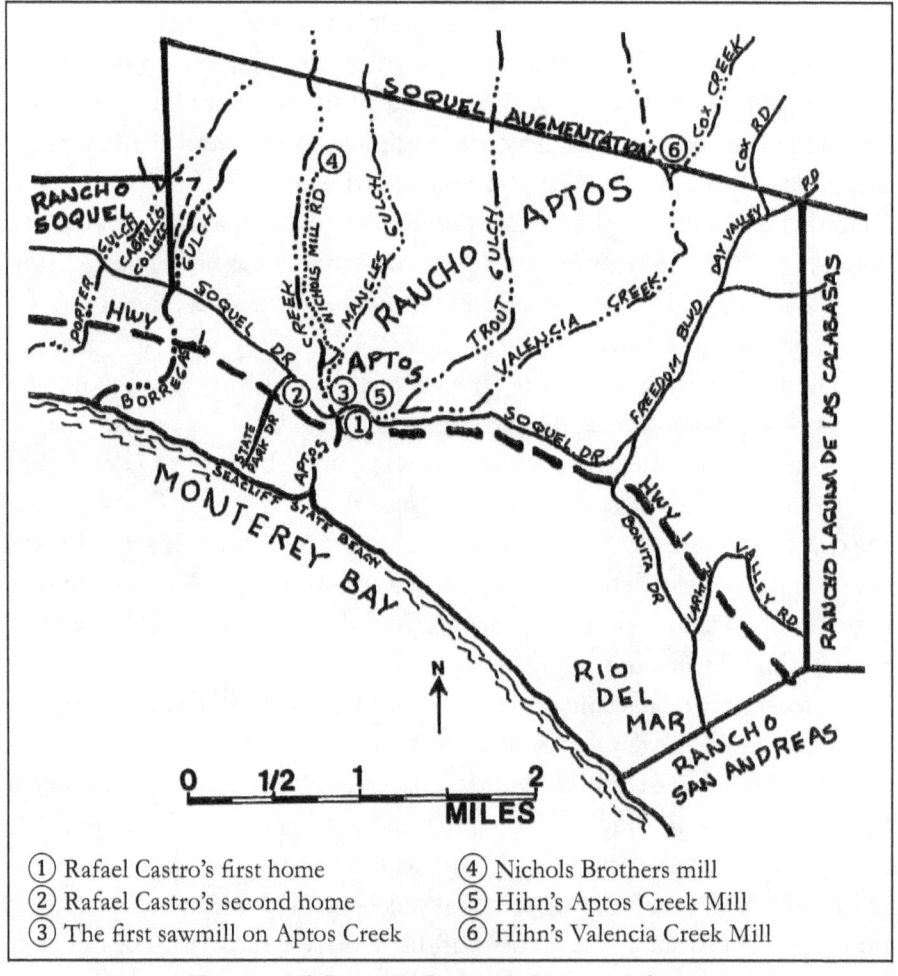

① Rafael Castro's first home
② Rafael Castro's second home
③ The first sawmill on Aptos Creek
④ Nichols Brothers mill
⑤ Hihn's Aptos Creek Mill
⑥ Hihn's Valencia Creek Mill

FIGURE 1.3 RAFAEL CASTRO'S RANCHO APTOS

was felled, it was stripped of its bark and limbs and cut into logs. Each log was then dragged and suspended over the pit. Two men used a long, thin, flexible saw with handles on both ends and began cutting—one man stood in the pit under the log and the other stood on top of the log, each alternating in the up-and-down motion of the saw. It was brutal work, but the method produced lumber that sold for $100 per 1,000 board feet. It should be noted that this method of producing lumber was both extremely difficult and unhealthy, especially for the man in the pit who had to breathe sawdust while the log was cut into strips of lumber.[42]

Secularization law concerning missions enacted

On August 17, 1933, the Mexican congress passed the Act for the Secularization of the Missions of California, which allowed mission land to be sold, granted, or annexed by the Mexican government without compensation to the Catholic Church. This changed the previously established process by which land could only be granted from areas outside the authority of the missions, such as in the case of Joaquín, Rafael, and Martina Castro, all of whom received grants for government-owned land.

With secularization, the Catholic Church was left with the land occupied by the mission buildings, the cemetery, and the land surrounding the buildings that were under the direct cultivation of the padres. The rest of the land from Mission Santa Cruz eventually passed to the residents of Branciforte, who, even before the act had been passed, took mission land to carve out their own family empires. As a result of this law, Mission Santa Cruz began to fall into decline, a process initiated several years earlier in 1825 when an earthquake severely damaged the structures.[43]

Martina Castro requests grant of Rancho Soquel

On September 7, 1833, Michael Lodge sent a petition to José Figueroa, brigadier general of the Mexican Army, commandant, inspector, and Superior Political Chief of Alta California. It was probably written by the *alcalde* of Branciforte, José Antonio Robles, and is translated as follows:

> *Michael Lodge, a native of Ireland under the Dominance of the King of England, before your Excellency, appears as best the law allows me informing your Excellency that having settled in the Town of Branciforte and married to a native of this soil with whom he has two children, and two step children, and having formed the resolution of remaining in the territory, to which effect and to make the acquisition of a place for cultivation and building a house for the season of sowing.*
>
> *I appear before your honor duly making the manifestation of the designs I have of establishing myself in the Country, so that your honor having the goodness to allow me to do what I have expressed in the place of the SANJIN of the RIVER SOQUEL.*
>
> *Considered in the class of an auxiliary of this town without detriment to any other party, and that I may make said sowing and house, acknowledging that said place belongs to the community of said town, and in as much as I beg of your Honor humbly what you may deem.*

The following day, Robles gave the Lodge family permission to move onto the land to begin building a home and cultivating the land.

On November 16, Martina Castro sent the following petition to Governor Figueroa, also probably written by Robles and translated as follows:

> *To: The Commander General and Superior Political Chief*
>
> *Martina Castro, a resident of the Town of Branciforte, daughter of the invalid Joaquin Castro, one of the founders of said town, married to the Irish man Michael Lodge, a carpenter by trade and farmer, with due respect and submission appears and says: "That being the owner of some cattle and some yoke of oxen and her husband having been granted by the alcalde of said town the place of the SAN JON of the RIVER of SOQUEL to settle therein said property as it is provided by the documents that I respectively accompany to your Excellency."*
>
> *Your petitioner applied anew to your Excellency as a daughter of this said [Joaquin Castro] and granddaughter of settlers in this Province, in order that in virtue of your fa-*

cility you may have the kindness of granting her the said place, from the River Soquel to the SAN JON *de las* BORREGAS. *One mile and a half in breath and two in length, to put in said cattle, sow the land and build a house and supply the wants of her family that consists of four children. The children are Nicanor and Luisa Cota and Carmel and Josefa Lodge.*

It is not without experience, Sir, of the well-known benevolence of your Excellency towards the poor, and your profundity to make happy ones that your petitioner under the belief that you will have the kindness to make her happy with this concession accompanying with the map of said place in as much I ask and beg your Excellency to have the goodness of granting by an effect of your great charity as I have petitioned your Excellency, remaining assured that this concession will be to the detriment of no one, and that I well...grace and mercy.

✗ [Martina Castro's mark]

The same day, Governor Figueroa wrote an *expediente* to the Father-

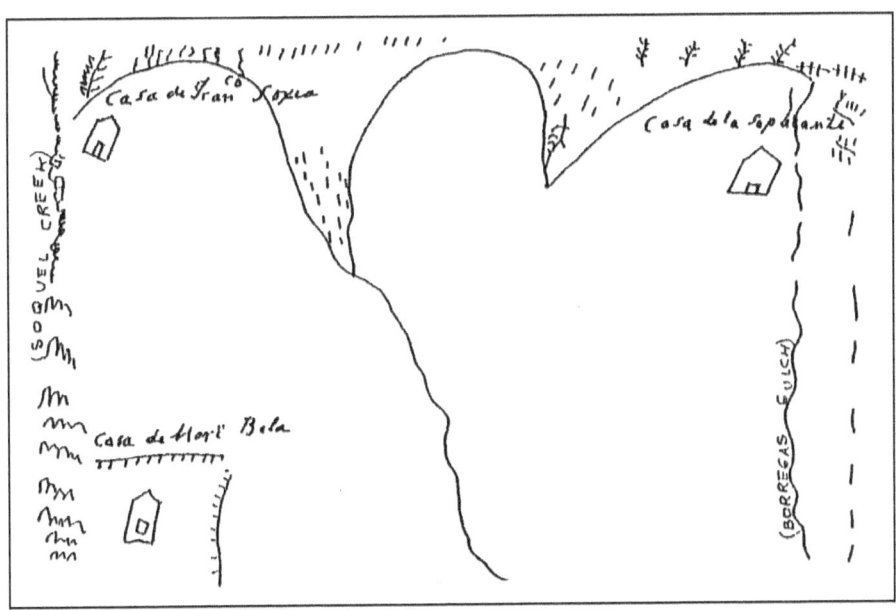

FIGURE 1.4 DISEÑO OF RANCHO SOQUEL COMMISSIONED BY MARTINA CASTRO

Minister of Mission Santa Cruz, which reads:

> *In conformity with the laws upon this matter let the farmers of the Town of Branciforte give information if the interested party in this petition has the necessary requirements to be attended to in her request. If the land petitioned for is within the twenty boundary leagues of the ten littoral ones, expressed in the Law of the 18th of August 1824. If it is ineligible land, temporary or uncultivable or if it belongs to a private individual, corporation or to the government. After the performance of which this Expediente will be sent to the Father Minister of the Mission of Santa Cruz so that he may oppose what he may think proper.*
>
> Governor José Figueroa
>
> *The Political Chief of the Territory Don José Figueroa so ordered, decreed and signed it. To which I certify.*
>
> Agustin V. Zamorano, Secretary

Three days later, an *informe* was sent from the Town of Branciforte and Mission Santa Cruz to Governor Figueroa, which states:

> *In the fulfillment of the order given to the Agriculturalist in a decree of the 16th of November of the present year, that your Excellency has deemed proper to address this agriculturalist in order to get information in accordance to said decree, I must say to your Excellency that the petitioner has all the necessary requirements to be listened to in her petition. But the petition she makes is of the place most occupied with the property of these residents as well as the place where they are settling, with their lands cultivated very near the town, they are the legitimate shelters of all the cattle, it has very little land fit for tillage that is not cultivated, and those are damp and the property of this town, for she was granted only one house and privilege to saw with the assent of all the neighbors...I inform your Excellency of, is for your knowledge and*

determination.
God and Liberty, Town of Branciforte

Jose Maria Salasan
Jose Robles

The place mentioned of Soquel does not belong to this Mission under my charge.

Friar Antonio Real

On November 22, Governor Figueroa sent Martina Castro his *expediente*, which concludes:

Having seen the petition with which this Expediente begins, the information of the municipal of the Town of Branciforte that of the Reverend Father, Minister of the Mission of Santa Cruz, and all that has been expedient to examine in conformity with what is decreed by the Laws and Regulations upon that matter. Martina Castro is declared to be the legitimate owner of the land known by the name of "Soquel" adjoining the river of that name and the Sanjan de las Borregas, and, if it happened to fall under the aegis of the Town of Branciforte, she will be subject to pay the Canon [clergyman] *or, that may be, to her when the boundaries may be fixed, subject to the other conditions that may be stipulated, give her the corresponding dispatch, recorded in the corresponding Book, and address this Expedient for its due approval to the Most Excellent Territorial Deputation to which case the interested party to whom this decree will be made known....*
Don Jose Figueroa, Commander General Inspector and Superior Political Chief of the Territory of Alta California, do order, decree, and agree, to which I certify.

Jose Figueroa
Augustin V. Zamarano

The following day, Governor Figueroa and his secretary, Zamarano, signed the following document:

> *Whereas Martina de Castro, wife of Miguel Lodge, has solicited for her personal benefit and that of her family the land known by the name of "Soquel" bounded by the river of said name and the Sanjon de las Borregas....having previously compiled with the preceding and investigations and in conformity with the laws and regulations of the subject, by virtue of the powers conferred on me in the name of the Mexican Nation, I have by decree issued yesterday, November 22, 1833, granted her the above mentioned land, and declared it to be her property by these presents, this grant being understood in entire conformity with the provisions of the laws and without prejudice to the use that the village of Branciforte may make in respect to the pastures, water, firewood, and lumber subject to pay the rent to the church which may be imposed on said land if it belongs to the commons of said village when its boundaries be marked out and subject to the approval or disapproval of the Executive, the Territorial Assembly, and to the Supreme Government under the following conditions:*
>
> *1. That she shall submit to the conditions established by the Regulations to be formed for the distribution of vacant lands. Meanwhile, neither the grantee nor her heirs can divide or cultivate the land adjudicated to them; impose on it any terse, entail, bond, mortgage, or any other incumbrance, even for purpose, nor convey it to mortmain [a corporate body, such as a religious or charitable organization].*
>
> *2. She may fence it without detriments to the crossings, roads and servitudes; She shall enjoy it freely and exclusively approbating it to the use or cultivation that it may best suit her, but within a year at most she shall build a house and it shall be inhabited.*
>
> *3. When the ownership is confirmed unto her, she shall petition the respective judge to give her juridical possession in virtue of this decree, by whom the boundaries shall be marked out, at which limits she shall put besides the landmarks some*

fruit trees or wild trees of some usefulness.

4. The land of which the donation is made consists of two miles longitude, a little more or less as exhibited by the sketch accompanying the Expediente. The judge who should give the possession shall have it measured conformably to Ordinance in order to mark the boundaries. The surplus which may result belonging to the Nation for the convenient purposes.

5. If she contravenes these conditions, she shall lose her right to the land and it shall be denounceable by another person.

In consequence, I order that this title serving her as a patent and being held as form and valid, be entered in the corresponding book and delivered to the interested party for his security and other ends.

Given in Monterey on the 23rd of November 1833.

José Figueroa
Agustin V. Zamorano, Secretary

It has been entered in the Book of Entries of titles in adjudication of lands, folio No. 11, filed in the Archives of the Secretary under my charge.

Agustin V. Zamorano

On November 23, Zamorano added the following notation to the *expediente*: "On the 23rd of November 1833, at this secretary's office appeared the interested party to whom the Grant by the Political Superior Chief was made known and informed of it. She said that she heard it and was satisfied and signed it with a cross for due proof."[44]

Rancho San Andrés is awarded to Joaquín Castro

On November 26, 1833, Joaquín Castro, the father of Martina, was awarded Rancho San Andrés by Governor Figueroa. When it was later patented by the United States, it consisted of 13,000 acres. When Castro died in 1838, the rancho was patented to his son Guadalupe.[45]

Rancho Soquel is awarded to Martina Castro by the Committee of Colonization

On May 10, 1834, the Committee of Colonization sent an *expediente* to Martina Castro concerning her request for Rancho Soquel:

> *The Committee of Colonization and vacant lands before whom is this Expediente, the formation of which was provoked by the petition made by Martina Castro of the place called 'Soquel,' have examined it with due circumspect, taking into consideration the Law of the 18th of August 1824, its rules and regulations and the general disposition on the 24th of November 1828 were dictated by the Supreme Government of Mexico for the best fulfillment of the first, by the examination of the Expediente, the Committee is fully aware of the opinion that is already had of the scrupulousness and tact with which the Political Chief ordered it to be formed, so much that neither in its formation is it lacking any essential matters nor in those practiced by what is said, the Committee ends offering to the deliberation of this Most Excellent Deputation the following proposition:*
>
> *That the concession made to Martina de Castro of the place called 'Soquel' granted the 23rd of November 1833 is approved in full conformity with what is decreed by the Law of the 18th of August 1824 and the regulations of the 21st of November 1828 in the 5th Article.*
>
> Jose Francisco Ortega
Jose Antonio Estudillo
Carlos Camello
José Castro

On May 17, another *expediente* was sent to Castro granting approval of her request for Rancho Soquel by Governor José Figueroa:

> *In session of this day, it was approved by the most excellent*

Deputation the proposition of the preceding opinion ordering Martina Castro to return the Expediente to the Supreme Political Chief for the proper purposes.

Governor Jose Figueroa
Juan B. Alvarado, Secretary

The grant for Rancho Soquel was given to Castro by Governor Figueroa on August 2:

The approved Grant made to Martina de Castro of the land called 'Soquel' granted on the 23rd of November 1833 in entire conformity with the provisions of the Law of the 18th of August 1824 and Article 5 of the Regulations of the 21st of November 1828. On the 17th of May 1834 in Monterey, the most Excellent Deputation of the Assembly approved the possession of the foregoing opinion and ordered the Expediente to be returned to the Superior Political Chief for its further ends.

Jose Figueroa
Juan Bautista Alverado, Secretary

In view of the approval issued on the 17th of May 1834 by the most Excellent Deputation Territorial Assembly and... testimony thereof and of this decree be delivered to the party of Martina de Castro, in confirmation to the grant of land called 'Soquel' which she obtained on the 22nd of November 1833 from Jose Figueroa, Inspector and Superior Political Chief of the Territory of Alta California, thus did order, decree, and sign, to which I certify.

Jose Figueroa
Agustin V. Zamorano, Secretary

It agrees literally with the original from which I ordered the present testimony to be taken for the secretary of the party of Martina Castro at Monterey on the 2nd of August

> *1834, being witnessed by citizens Navarete and Bonifaciode Madariaja of this neighborhood.*

> signed in witness whereof by the same
> Jose Figueroa
> Agustin V. Zamorano, Secretary[46]

Boundaries of Rancho Soquel are established

Between August 13 and 14, 1834, a survey party headed by José Antonio Bolcoff and assisted by Miguel Ramirez, Joaquín Castro, Juan José Castro, and Rafael Robles established the boundaries of Rancho Soquel. The four men that assisted Bolcoff also witnessed the *diseño*:

> *At the Rancho de Soquel at two o'clock in the afternoon, I, the present judge* [Bolcoff], *ordered the measurements to proceed. They began on the west, where we placed a landmark, and measured towards the east.*

The landmark would have been placed at or near the point where today's Bates Creek joins Soquel Creek and then measured eastward until a point was reached within the upper headwaters of Borregas Gulch. After landmarks were placed at each end and the sketch was drawn according to the measurements taken, the surveyor declared that the distance between the two points embraced one square league from point to point.

> *At the said Rancho de Soquel, Martina Castro, a resident of the village of Branciforte, accompanied by me, the judge of first instance of the said place, and the witnesses having previously measured the lands of said rancho as it appears in the foregoing acts, took the time...and real possessions of the said square league of...half a league longitude and ten miles latitude a little more or less; such land belongs to her by title of concession she obtained on the 23rd of November from the Superior Political Chief by virtue of the powers conferred on him by a decree of 31st January and by the approval of the*

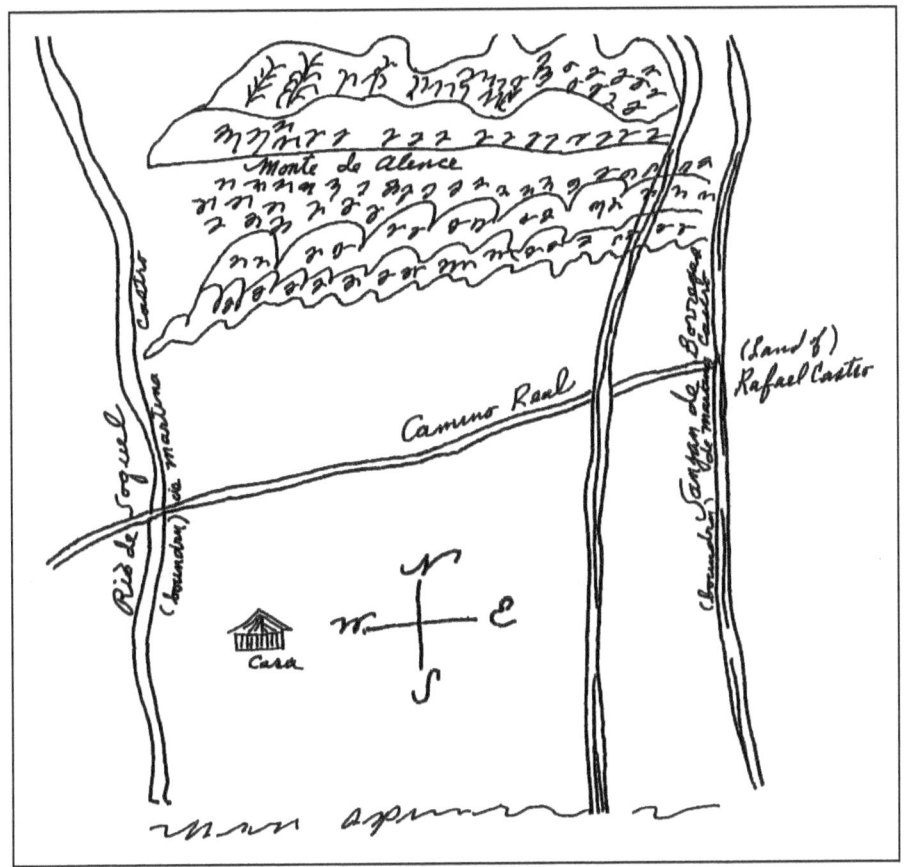

FIGURE 1.5 DISEÑO OF RANCHO SOQUEL DRAWN BY JOSÉ BOLCOFF

most Excellent Deposition assembly on the 14th of May of the present year; she entered and walked on said land, pulled up grass, threw away handfuls of earth, broke off branches of trees, threw away stones to the four winds and performed other ceremonies and acts of [joy] in sign of which the said [Martina Castro], she took and did take in of said land. The aforesaid judge of first instance ordered that said Martina Castro should be acknowledged hereafter as the true owner and possessor of the aforesaid land; and she asked me that in remembrance and preservation of her rights in future, I, the aforesaid judge, should deliver her a testimony whereof, which I did by virtue of my authority and that of the assisting witnesses with whom I act according to law in lieu of a Notary Public, there not being any here, which I certify.

Jose Antonio Bolcoff and witnesses[47]

Martina Castro begins to develop Rancho Soquel

While legal affairs were being settled by the government, construction began on the home Martina Castro had agreed to build when she placed her mark on the grant of November 23, 1833. The first structure was a temporary building that could house the family while a more permanent building was erected.

For the site of their permanent home, Michael Lodge chose a plateau that overlooked the beach to the south and Soquel Creek to the west (just to the west of where Capitola Avenue crosses Noble Gulch). Noble Gulch had a year-round water source from a spring that was plentiful enough to provide water for both the home and the surrounding garden. The completed building was a three-room adobe structure with a depth of thirty feet and fifty feet across. The largest of the three rooms was in the middle, which had a large fireplace and board floor. It served as the general living and reception area. The beams that supported the roof were rough-cut and covered with horsehide that was tanned with the hair left on.

The house and garden were surrounded by a fence made of redwood pickets driven into the ground. Nearby, the family built an ox-powered flour mill. These structures were probably the first permanent Western-style buildings constructed in the Soquel area. Later, after deeds and titles were established between Martina and her children, the home and garden encompassed approximately 219 acres.

Life at this time in the wilderness of Soquel was far different from today's setting and pace. The family's existence was an isolated life that provided challenges and problems that required immediate solutions in order to survive. It was a daily struggle to make a profit from the land so they could pay their bills and their employees. But the family was required to cultivate the land as a provision of their grant, which meant overcoming nature's obstacles. Growing helter-skelter throughout the entire area were large redwoods that had to be removed in order to make room for planting. Cutting down the trees was not enough—the stumps also had to be removed, which required the use of dynamite. Then, after the fields were plowed and planted, there was a constant battle to keep out nature's encroachment. Furthermore, there was the constant threat posed by local predators such as grizzly bears, mountain lions, and wildcats, all of which endangered the ranch's stock of cattle, sheep, pigs, and oxen.

While not noted for her business qualities, Castro more than made up for this by instilling in her children the necessary traits to both survive in their harsh and rugged environment and later provide for families of their own. For her daughters, Castro was a hard taskmaster who taught them the necessary skills that they would need as homemakers. They were forced to cook outdoors in crude clay ovens—bread and other necessary foods had to be made daily. And with no local stores around—the nearest was in Monterey forty-five miles away—family members had to be ready to innovate, accept compromises, and create workarounds to make up for missing supplies and foodstuffs. For example, clothes were washed in Soquel Creek and the family used river rocks to pound the dirt out. All of the girls were also well-trained in horse riding and shooting in order to fend off Native Americans and bandits, although they also usually worked in pairs to better protect themselves.

Meanwhile, Lodge and his hired hands were often out in the forest cutting down unwanted trees, hunting for the family's next meal, or stripping the tan oak trees of their bark and tying it into bundles for shipment to the nearest tannery. He was also a talented carpenter and produced furniture and other wood products for use on the ranch. In the fall, Michael used the family's small boat to transport surplus fruits and vegetables to Monterey. If not performing any of these tasks, he either tended the fields or watched over the herds. The ranch's pastureland was on what the family called the Palo de la Yesca.

The name Palo de la Yesca has confused historians since it first appeared in official government documents in 1859. The entire name of the location was given as the "stake at the spot of the Palo de la Yesca or Pink Tree." But the name itself has appeared on several documents over the years, including being written as "Yeska." Jean Fourcade was the first to write the name in a letter to the governor dated January 7, 1844.

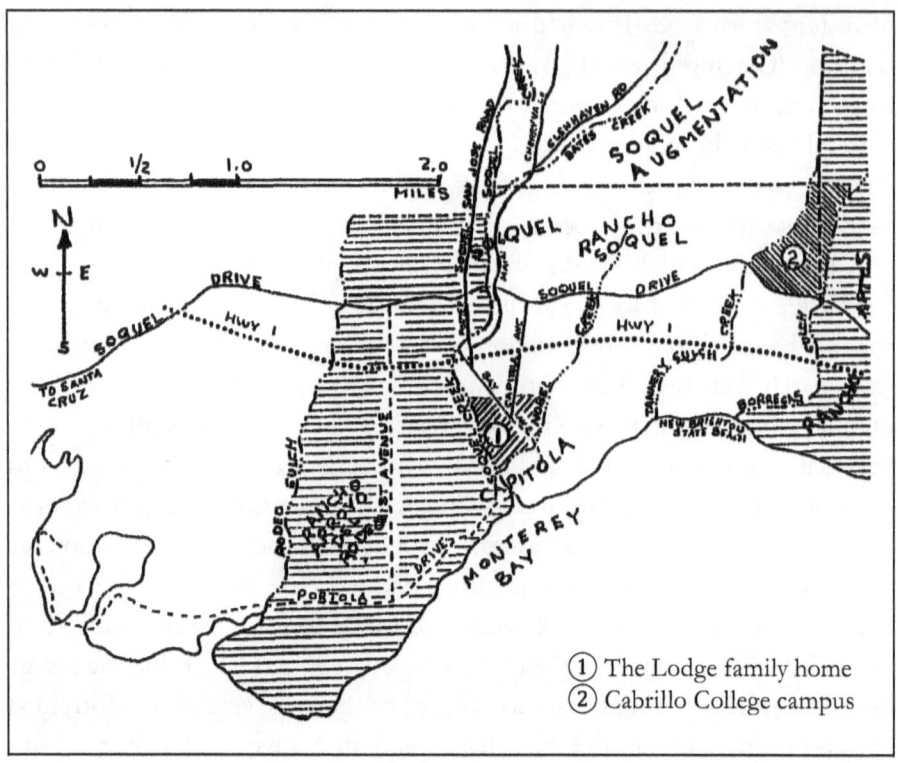

FIGURE 1.6 THE LODGE HOUSE WITHIN RANCHO SOQUEL

In *Santa Cruz County Place Names*, Donald T. Clark explains that *palo* means either "stick" or "piece of wood," while *yesca* means either "touchwood," "tinder," or "punk." *Touchwood* is a dried, decayed wood used as tinder, *tinder* being any flammable material that can be used for starting a fire. *Punk* is any substance that smolders when ignited and can therefore be used as tinder. Clark clarified, though, that the government name was "apparently named because of the prominence of a particular tree (*palo*) known for its pink (*yesca*) color." This was likely a mistake made by a court translator. One of Martina Castro's brothers, Juan José, revealed what Palo de la Yesca really meant in a deposition made before the Land Claims Commission on May 16, 1855: "Palo de la Yesca was so called from an oak tree that formerly stood there from which punk was obtained." He translated the term directly as "punk stick" or "punk wood" and located the titular tree in the modern-day vicinity of Soquel Cemetery on Soquel-San Jose Road.

Although the Mexican government did not tax its California colonists, Rancho Soquel still had several bills that had to be paid yearly, such as a fee paid to Mission Santa Cruz and wages owed to servants and field laborers. Because they were not rich, the family were often in financial trouble and Lodge took unusual measures to ensure bills were paid. Being a sailor at heart, he hated horse-riding and preferred to walk. On more than one occasion, local Native Americans raided the ranch but only took the horses. In order to restock, Lodge walked to Monterey, built several wagons on site, sold them, and then returned home with the profits, which he used to buy new horses from his neighbors.

Rancho Soquel was only a shallow ditch away from Rancho Aptos, which was four times larger. Size was not the only advantage that Rafael Castro had over his sister, Martina—his rancho was far more profitable, which allowed him to keep a larger herd of cattle. The bigger problem, though, was that Rafael allowed his herds to roam freely, and they often crossed Borregas Gulch into Rancho Soquel. When Rafael wanted his cattle to return, he simply sent some of his helpers on horseback to bring them back. These constant intrusions onto Martina's land meant that they could not cultivate the eastern half of the ranch.

Martina and Michael complained on several occasions to the local judicial authority, but to no avail. The law favored Rafael. Under Mexican law, it was not the responsibility of the owner of the intruding animals to keep them on their land. Rather, the landowners who were being infringed upon had to find a solution to keep their neighbor's animals off their property. Rafael was not willing to negotiate and made no effort to stop his cattle from grazing onto his sister's property. The problem began shortly after Martina was granted the land and continued for eight years.[48]

Martina Castro gives birth to María Antonia

María Antonia, Martina's sixth child, fifth daughter, and the second child fathered by Michael Lodge, was born in Soquel in 1835.[49]

The Republic of Texas declares independence from México

For several years, Americans had been allowed to settle in the northern borderlands of México, especially the state of Coahuila y Tejas that sat along the southwest border of the United States. The General Colonization Law outlined the conditions for settlement, implicitly stating that settlers be Roman Catholic and strongly recommending that they be citizens. Since a great number of the settlers were from Irish families, they already met the first condition, and men found that the easiest way to become a citizen was to wed a Mexican woman.

Despite the seeming success of the law, conflict between naturalized citizens and the Mexican government increased between 1824 and 1835 to the point that Texas declared independence from México on March 2, 1836 following six months of intermittent warfare. Although treaties were signed at Velasco, Texas on May 14, a cold war continued for nine years between México and the Republic of Texas until the United States granted statehood to Texas on December 29, 1845, prompting a military response from México, which led to the Mexican–American War.

The conflict in Texas caused Mexican officials in the Californias and other border territories to increasingly mistrust naturalized citizens and American settlers, and the United States government did nothing to calm these fears.[50]

Martina Castro gives birth to María Helena

María Helena, Martina Castro's seventh child, sixth daughter, and the third child fathered by Michael Lodge, was born in Soquel in 1837.

Martina Castro gives birth to Miguel Antonio

Martina Castro's first son to reach adulthood was born on Rancho Soquel in August 1838. Miguel was her eighth child, second son, and the first son born to Michael Lodge, after whom he was named.[51]

Nicanor Cota marries Francisco Lajeunesse

In 1839, Martina Castro's oldest daughter, Nicanor Cota, married a Canadian trapper named Francisco Lajeunesse. Lajeunesse was born in the French-speaking part of Canada in 1809 and entered California in 1833 as a part of the Joseph Walker party.

After his arrival in California, Lajeunesse began using an English translation of his surname, Young, although he continued to use both indiscriminately. In later years, he was also associated with another surname: Moss. Like Lajeunesse in French, the word *mozo* simply means 'young' in Spanish. At some point, however, a translator misheard the name and wrote it as 'Moss,' and both Lajeunesse and Cota used this contrived name permanently beginning in the 1860s.

Little is written about the years between Lajeunesse and Cota's marriage and 1852 except that they lived on Rancho Soquel alongside Nicanor's siblings and mother.[52]

María de los Ángeles Castro marries Joseph Ladd Majors

Born near Nashville, Tennessee on May 26, 1804, Joseph Ladd Majors arrived in Los Angeles via the Santa Fe Trail alongside Isaac Graham, Henry Neale, and several others in November 1834. Once there, he joined with other foreigners to protest México's policy of forcing foreigners to serve a term in its military. He arrived in Branciforte in 1835 and shortly afterwards applied for Mexican citizenship, adopting the name Juan José Crisóstomo Mayor (or Mechas).

Majors married María de los Ángeles Castro, one of Martina Castro's sisters, on December 19, 1839. They settled in the San Lorenzo Valley just north of the future townsite of Felton, where together they had twenty-two children. María lived to see the twentieth century, passing away at the age of eighty-five in 1903.[53]

Earthquake destroys Mission Santa Cruz's bell tower

Earlier, in 1825, an earthquake had begun the destruction of Mission Santa Cruz. But another quake on January 16, 1840 destroyed its bell tower and expedited the decline of its walls. The only remaining undamaged section of the mission collapsed during another earthquake in 1857.[54]

Henry Winegar Peck settles on Rancho Soquel

Henry Peck was born in New York State on April 16, 1818. He arrived in the Soquel area in 1840 and settled on Martina Castro's Rancho Soquel, where he built a small unfinished home of rough-hewn boards for himself. After the home was erected, he fenced in about one hundred acres, testifying later that it was one of the best fences that existed in the county at the time. He initially shared pastureland with Joshua Parrish and later Augustus Noble. The approximate location of Peck's acreage is along both sides of Fairway Drive heading north from Soquel Drive, ending near the boundary of the Forest of Nisene Marks State Park.[55]

Joseph Majors and Job Dye build a grist mill on Zayante Creek

In the spring of 1840, Joseph Majors and his partner, Job Dye, started a grist mill on Zayante Creek to the northeast of modern-day Felton. Shortly afterwards, California authorities decided to rid the territory of *extranjeros* (foreigners) who had not been naturalized. They rounded up a number of trouble-making foreigners and sent them to the Monterey area, then sent forty-one of them to San Blas in México.

Of the men sent to San Blas that were living in and around Branciforte, several would later return, including Albert Morris, Francisco Lajeunesse, William Chard, William Anderson, Charles Henry Cooper, and partners Henry Neale and Isaac Graham. Both Majors and Dye, while arrested and sent to Monterey, were not sent to San Blas because they were naturalized citizens and both had married Mexican citizens.

When the prisoners arrived in México, the government quickly repudiated the action taken in California and sent most home. Upon their return, Neale and Graham settled in the Zayante area and showed an interest in acquiring Rancho Zayante, formerly granted to Joaquín Buelna in 1834. Buelna was a former *alcalde* of Branciforte who, after conferring timber rights in 1835 to Ambrose Tomlinson and Job Dye, let his claim lapse. In 1839, Lajeunesse applied for the Rancho Zayante grant but was sent to San Blas and unable to assert his claim, despite the fact that he was married to a Mexican woman. The next to apply for the rancho was Majors, who on April 22, 1841 was given both Zayante and the adjoining Rancho San Agustín (today comprising most of the city of Scotts Valley).

Graham, Majors, Frederick Hoegar, and Peter Lassen are credited with building the first water-powered sawmill of any kind in the Santa Cruz area. It was erected around the time that Majors took over the land and situated at the confluence of Bean and Zayante Creeks. Tradition states that Graham purchased Rancho Zayante from his good friend Majors and then hired Lassen to build the mill, paying him one hundred mules for the task. However, an article in *Hutchings' California Magazine*, dated September 1859, suggests that it was Lassen who both purchased the rancho and built the mill. After he had cut between 40,000 and 50,000 board feet of lumber, he sold the property to Graham in exchange for the mules, intending to take them to the United States with him. In reality, Majors retained possession of the land on behalf of Graham, to whom the *alcalde* of Branciforte refused to grant the rancho.

Majors soon built a large home on what was once known as Allegro Heights and later as Escalona Heights. Below the home, he built a substantial grist mill at the upper end of Walnut Avenue that was powered by a huge undershot water wheel. The flat area on top of the hill surrounding his home was planted with grain for the mill. This mill was not completed until California was taken over by the United States in February of 1848.[56]

Martina Castro gives birth to María Guadalupe

In 1842, Martina Castro gave birth to her last surviving child, María Guadalupe Lodge, on Rancho Soquel. She was Castro's ninth child, seventh daughter, and the fifth child born by Michael Lodge.[57]

Luisa Cota and Jean Richard Fourcade marry in Carmel

On August 8, 1842, Luisa Cota married a Frenchman named Jean Richard Fourcade at Mission San Carlos Borromeo de Carmelo. Born outside Paris in 1814, Fourcade arrived by ship at Monterey in 1840. After his arrival, he was joined by at least three brothers. Fourcade soon entered into several industries, including the sale of lumber and farm products. Because he wanted to blend in with the local Mexican population, he changed his name to Ricardo Juan, a Spanish translation and inversion of his birth name. Following his marriage to Cota, he moved onto Rancho Soquel and served as a farm hand for eighteen months.[58]

Complaint from Martina Castro to Governor Micheltorena concerning problems caused by Rafael Castro

On October 26, 1843, the newly appointed Governor of the Californias, Manuel Micheltorena, received the following petition from Martina Castro:

> *Martina Castro, resident of Branciforte, presents herself before your Excellency with the most profound submission, informing you of the great trouble and considerable damage that she experienced in her rural property, that is to say of cattle and horses. The true cause is this: that Don Rafael Castro has most of his own property mixed with mine, from which it results that whenever they want to take hold of a head of cattle they harass and disturb my own, from which causes more or less damage.*
>
>   *Sir: I have not been able to prevent this for the space of eight years notice [despite] complaints made to the judges near the place. Therefore, I beg of your excellency to have the goodness to hear what I ask with Justice, for which I hope to receive grace and mercy.*
>
>  [Martina Castro's mark]

After reading the petition, the governor added the following note: "Let the Secretary of the Government report on this subject."[59]

Report by Governor Micheltorena's secretary concerning Martina Castro's complaint

On December 2, 1843, the governor's secretary, Manuel Jimeno, gave Micheltorena the following *informe*:

> *The land occupied by Martina Castro has never been cultivated by the community nor by any private individual of the Town of Branciforte, and when there were some settlers their cattle did not extend to the place of Soquel and now the few remaining residents have a few tame cattle that they maintain in the neighborhood of their houses, but if in the course of time they happen to increase their property and the number of settlers grew, there is yet in the place of the Town about three leagues, and the balance of the land destined to the commons of the settlers of Branciforte will be of four sites, that it is deemed difficult and conveniently established in the town for the respective persons.*
>
> *In virtue of this Expediente, I don't see any inconvenience to relieve Martina Castro of the trouble to which she is subject, and to free her of the great damages that she is sustaining. For the above reasons, she has not formed the formal resolutions of establishing herself and consequently the land is not as cultivated as it might be owning to the uncertainty in which she finds herself. Notwithstanding this Expediente, the determination of Your Excellency will be the most convenient.*
>
> Manuel Jimeno, Secretary[60]

Petition from Jean Richard Fourcade to Governor Micheltorena concerning Martina Castro's complaint

After reading the *informe* that his secretary Manuel Jimeno wrote on December 2, 1843, Governor Micheltorena added the following note to the document: "In conformity with the information of the Secretary, the judge will administer justice as petitioned for."

1843 – 1844 — The Tragedy of Martina Castro

On January 7, 1844, Jean Fourcade, acting on behalf of Martina Castro, sent a second petition to the governor. At this point, Castro only asked for the land that extends northward from Rancho Soquel to within the vicinity of where Bates and Soquel Creeks converge opposite the cemetery on Soquel-San Jose Road—land that her family could cultivate in place of the eastern half of her

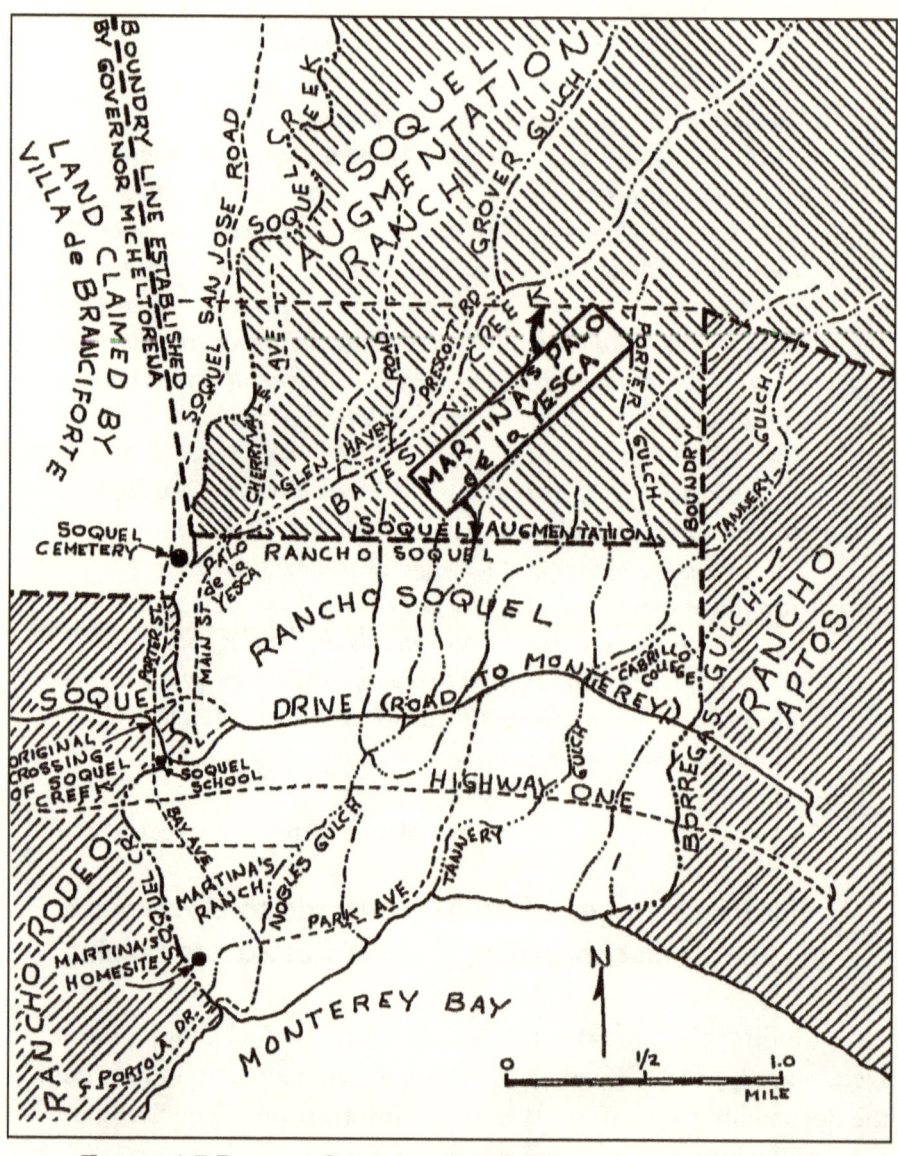

FIGURE 1.7 RANCHO SOQUEL AND THE PALO DE LA YESCA LAND

rancho that Rafael Castro's cattle and horses had made unusable. He wrote:

> *Most Excellent Governor:*
> *Martina Castro, inhabitant of the town of Branciforte, before the justification of Your Excellency...that having...of your goodness your decree of the date in conformity with the information of the secretary of the Government, to the end that I should be freed from the [burden] to which the condition of my title subjected me, I ask of your Excellency to have the goodness in conformity with your superior decree to order to give me a new title ever it be under the condition of neither transforming or settling, but not of subjecting myself at present that it should be for the benefit of all on the subject of pasture and woods as it is explained in the one I actually have, for that is what has caused my lien... [A]nd at the same time, I beg of your Excellency to have the goodness to order to add to the new title that I ask the Mountain Ridge immediate to the ranch that actually passes, known by the name of Palo de la Yesca, that is actually unoccupied in as much I pray your Excellency, that taking compassion on this poor woman with a large family, you may do her the grace of decreeing as she petitions....*
>
> At the request of the interested party,
> her son-in-law, Ricardo Juan[61]

Governor Micheltorena issues directives concerning Martina Castro's complaint

On January 11, 1844, Governor Micheltorena sent an *expediente* to Manuel Jimeno as follows:

> *Let the Secretary of the Government inform me taking personally the necessary information.*

He also sent the following *expediente* to Francisco Alviso, the new *alcalde* of Branciforte:

> *As it is ordered by the Most Excellent Governor, pass the proceeding petition to the second alcalde so that he may give information upon its contents and return it to this Secretary's office to report accordingly.*

Manuel Jimeno,
Secretary to the Governor of
Alta and Baja California[62]

Answer by Francisco Alviso to the directive concerning Martina Castro's complaint

On January 23, 1844, Francisco Alviso sent the following *informe* to Manuel Jimeno:

> *The land solicited by the interested party cannot be granted with the conditions that she requests because it is distant about a league and a few varas; besides, in the mountains, several settlers employ themselves in the working of timber for the subsistence of their families and I believe it cannot be granted the extent. It is all that I can inform upon this subject.*

Francisco Alviso

For some unknown reason, this *informe* was not properly filed in the government archives at Monterey but rather fell into the hands of Castro's son-in-law, Jean Fourcade.[63]

Secretary's report to Governor Micheltorena concerning Martina Castro's complaint

On February 8, 1844, Manuel Jimeno sent the following *informe* to Governor Michaeltorena:

> *The title of Martina Castro is drawn subjected to the conditions that were instituted in many other titles during the time*

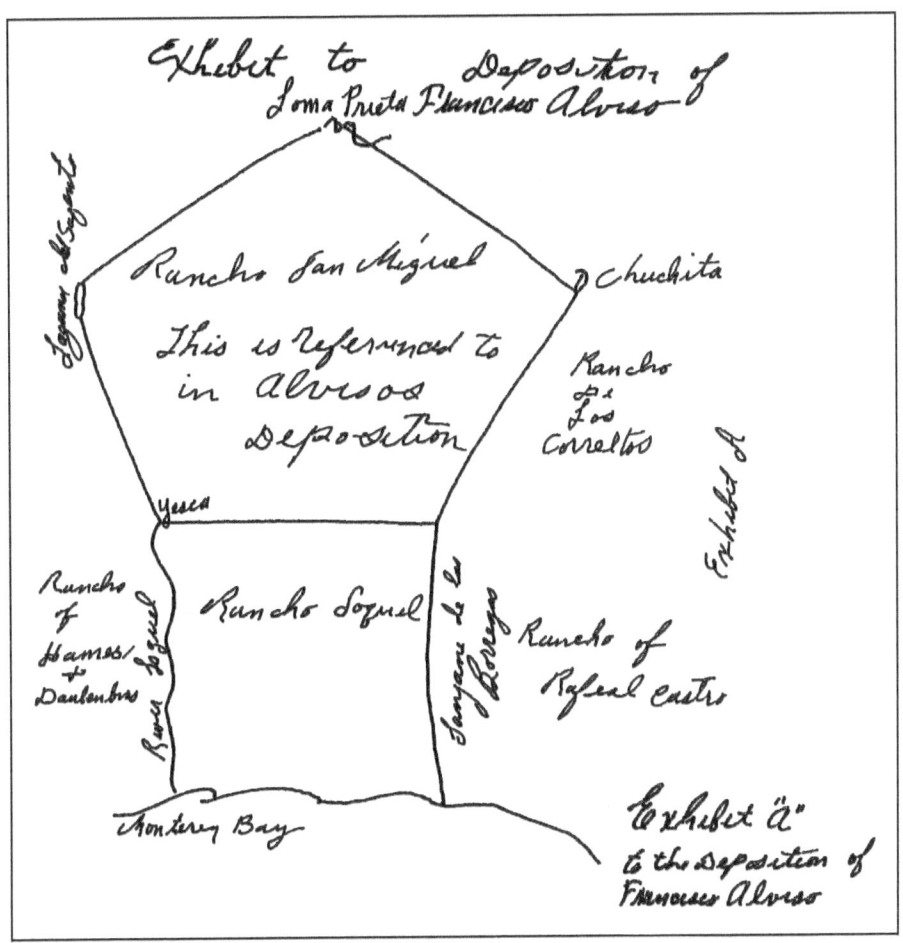

FIGURE 1.8 RANCHO SOQUEL AND RANCHO SAN MIGUEL

of General Figueroa in which they subjected the parties to pay censo [tax based on the census] *if the land proved to belong to the Town of Branciforte.*

I understand that the Town of Branciforte is to have for its population four square leagues in conformity to its existing law..., in which it mentions that to the new towns that extent may be marked, to which effect it should be consented that your Excellency should commission two persons desiring your confidence, in order that, accompanied by the Judge of the town, the measurement indicated may be made and it may declared for the town the four square leagues, leaving to the deliberation of your Excellency to find...of the grantees of the conditions to which they are subjected.

The Supreme judgments of your Excellency will resolve as it may deem it convenient.

Manuel Jimeno,
secretary to the governor[64]

Directives from Governor Micheltorena and Manuel Jimeno to Martina Castro concerning her complaint

On February 9, 1844, both Governor Micheltorena and Manuel Jimeno sent the following *expedientes* to Martina Castro:

In conformity with the preceding information, give the necessary orders so that dividing the expenses among all the residents of the Town of Branciforte may be made by Henry Cambustan, the judge, and another person that will be appointed by the secretary of the government.

Manuel Micheltorena,
Governor of Alta and Baja California

In the aforesaid date and in conformity with what has been decreed by his Excellency the Governor, let the interested party apply to the judge of Branciforte, to whom it is ordered to put Martina Castro in possession of all the extent that she selects from the Ridge de la Yesca to the Laguna del Sargento y la Chuchita, including la Loma Prieta, the interested party remaining engaging all without the conditions of the title which is returned with this writing for his safety.

Manuel Jimeno,
secretary to the governor

If Martina wanted the area that Alviso's sketch shows, her new property would be 32,000 acres—but it was soon proven that the sketch represents a total area of more than 70,000 acres. During testimony taken during the Land Claims Commission's hearings beginning in January 1852, it was stated several times that one name that Castro called the land was "San Miguel." Being deeply religious, she had selected St. Michael the Archangel as her patron saint and she named her only son to grow to adulthood after him. While the name was never substantiated during Land Claims Commission testimony, her use of it makes sense.

From the testimony, it appears that Cambustan was to survey only the area that Jean Fourcade mentioned in his petition. According to Fourcade, the area was known locally as "Palo de la Yesca," or simply as "Palo Yesca." "Ridge de la Yesca" is the small rise of hills along the south side of Bates Creek that lined the northwest corner of Rancho Soquel. During this period, Bates Creek was called "Arroyo de la Ballena" meaning "Creek of the Whale." Within the area where it joined Soquel Creek, opposite the cemetery, there was a large body of water they called "Laguna de la Ballena," (Lake of the Whale).

In the directive above, the governor informed Castro that Cambustan was going to survey and establish the official boundaries of Branciforte. This was important to Castro because, once the survey was completed, Rancho Soquel would not lie within the town's limits, which would release her from having to pay tithe to the mission fathers, as agreed to in her earlier grant. According to Francisco Alviso in testimony given in 1853, Jimeno allowed Castro to select her additional land from an area defined later. But neither she nor Michael Lodge wanted the entire area defined by Jimeno in his *expediente* and later by Alviso in his deposition.

The area established by the governor was already under consideration as a future land grant in whole or in part—from later testimony it is clear that several persons living in Branciforte, José Robles to name one, were under consideration as the grantee. Because of this, it is important to examine the individual boundaries set out by Alviso in his survey and illustrated in his sketch of the grant. Since the Palo de la Yesca has been discussed above, it will not be included in this summary. Each boundary point is examined below with a brief explanation as to its importance to the region.

Laguna del Sargento: The northwest corner of the land is a small body of water found on many early maps. The spelling has varied over the years—many of the variations have replaced the "g" in Sargento with a "j" (Sarjento), especially after California became a state.

Several historians, including Donald Clark, when discussing the small body of water, state that it is dry today. This is incorrect. Today, it lies full of water one mile south of Summit Road, just off Mountain Charley Road west of Highway 17. It lies within the confines of Mountain Charley's Christmas Tree Farm. Access to the lagoon is restricted by a chain-link fence, except during the Christmas season when the farm is selling trees.

Situated as it is near the lowest point along the crest of the mountains between Santa Cruz and San José, Laguna del Sargento was one of the few points of importance to both local Native Americans and early Spanish travelers. According to legend, Native Americans settled around its banks long before the Spanish entered Alta California. This has been borne out by the many artifacts that have been found around the lagoon. Charles McKiernan settled on its west bank in the early 1850s and found several mortars, pestles, and flint arrows in the area. The Spanish found solace there and used it as a resting area on the difficult journey from Santa Cruz to Santa Clara.

In his book, Clark writes of the name: "So far, I have only a hunch concerning the origin of the name. I think it may have been named for Sergeant Pedro Amador who was ordered by Governor de Borica to improve the so-called road between Santa Cruz and the Mission at Santa Clara. His 'improved' road passed by what was later called Laguna del Sargento."

Mexican and Unites States surveyors established the lagoon as the northwest corner of the contested area, but later, for the convenience of future surveyors, the point of

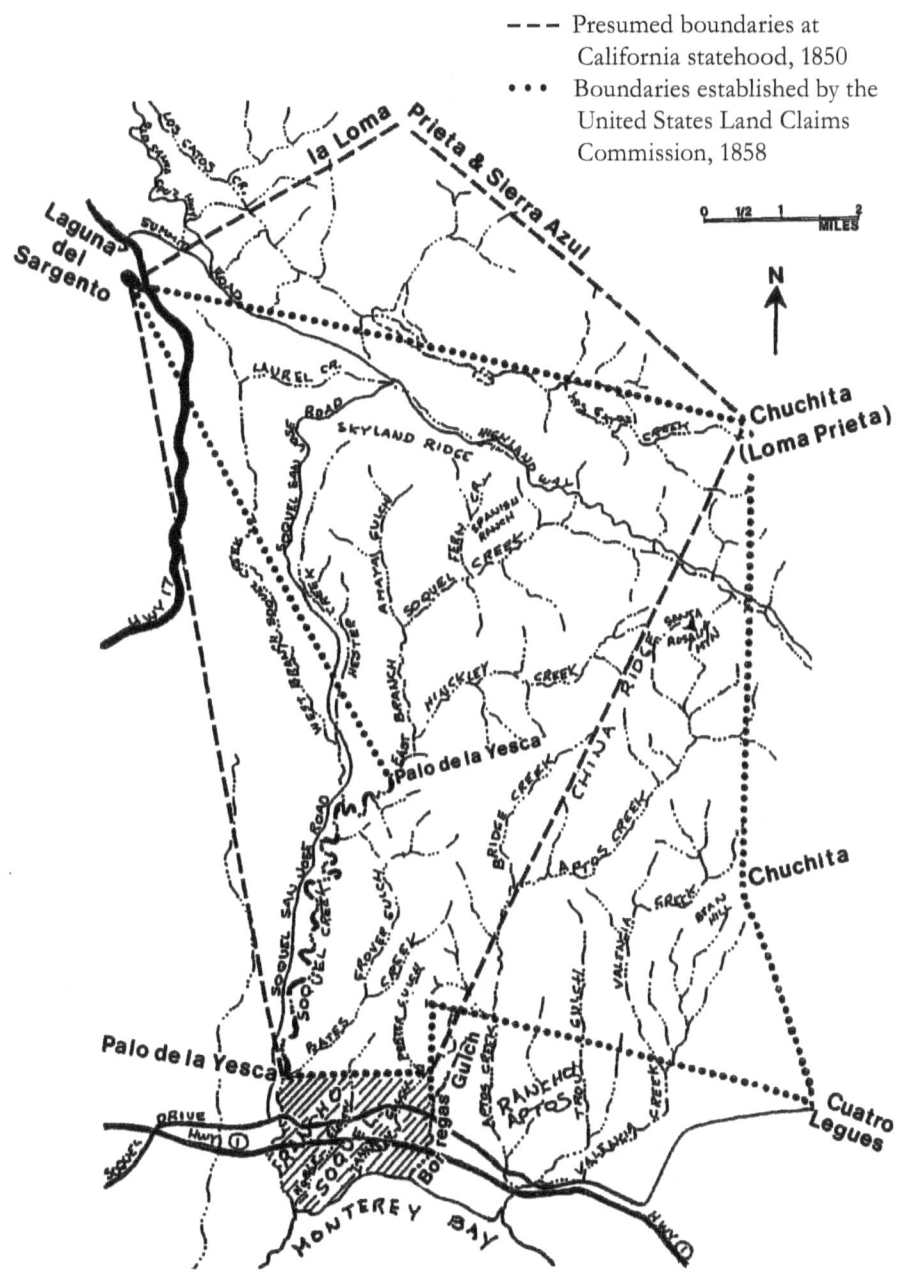

Figure 1.9 The boundaries of Rancho Soquel's augmentation

reference was moved a short distance to the southeast of the lagoon. It is this point that today serves as the northwest corner of Shoquel Augmentation.

LOMA PRIETA AND SIERRA AZUL: Today, Loma Prieta is the name given to the highest peak in the ninety-two-mile-long Santa Cruz Mountain chain at 3,791 feet, while Sierra Azul is the twelve-mile section as viewed from Santa Clara Valley that lies along the north side of Los Gatos Creek, extending from Lexington Reservoir southeast to Loma Prieta, and contains the highest peaks in the entire range. To the west of Loma Prieta, it includes Mount Thayer (3,483 feet), Mount Umunhum (3,486 feet), and Mount Elizabeth (3,004 feet), and to the east stands Mount Chual (3,562 feet). From Mount Chual, the range continues as a narrow ridge heading southeast for another twenty miles, gradually decreasing in elevation until reaching the Pajaro River, where the range ends abruptly. Today, the river serves as the boundary between Santa Cruz, Monterey, and San Benito Counties.

Loma Prieta means dark or black-looking ridge, while *Sierra Azul* means bluish mountain range. When the range is viewed from the ocean side, it has a dark cast because of the low-growing vegetation, while viewed from Santa Clara County, it appears to be slightly bluish.

Francisco Alviso on his sketch called the northernmost point of the area Loma Prieta. A question that he never answered in his testimony was his definition of "Loma Prieta." Was it the entire twelve-mile section of the range, or was it a specific point on the range? Just from the meaning of "Loma Prieta," he probably referred to the entire range. Another question that was not answered: if he meant the entire range, did it include both sides—from Los Gatos Creek to the top and then down the south side until the Guadalupe River was reached just north of San José? These unanswered scenarios seem unlikely. In both court testimony and testimony given before the Land Claims Commission, the range was called either "Loma Prieta," "Sierra Azul de la Loma Prieta," or "Sierra Azul y Loma Prieta," but it was always in reference to the ocean side.

For a brief time, Loma Prieta was known as Mount Bache, after Alexander D. Bache, a grandson of Benjamin Franklin. Bache was superintendent of the Coast Survey Department between 1843 and 1867 and was in charge when the team surveyed Shoquel Augmentation in 1858. Today, the only remnant of this name is in the short Mount Bache Road between Highland Way and Loma Prieta Avenue on the Summit.

CHUCHITA: The word *chuchita* is a female diminutive of the Spanish word *chucho*, but historians have been uncertain as to its meaning and why it was chosen to describe this location. Clark states that this "place has frequently been cited in deeds and in the notes kept by surveyors. For example, Frederick Hihn says in a document, 'southerly to the Chuchitas....,' and the *Survey of the Rancho de los Corralitos and Surrounding Claims* bears the note: 'Oak Tree L. C. No. 7, Place Called Chuchita.' The Township Plat Map, 1858-1883 of the U. S. Surveyor General for California for T10S, R1E shows the location (in Section 34) of Chuchita and (Thomas Wilson Wright's map of 1864) shows the location of Chuchitas. The Santa Cruz *Sentinel,* June 13, 1862, reported a 'Valuable Discovery—A coal mine has been discovered at a place called Chuchitas, situated in the mountains about twelve miles to the eastward of [Santa Cruz]...,' and the *Sentinel* of February 19, 1870, refers to a point on a map of Rancho Aptos 'called the chuchitas.'"

Clark goes on to explain that "Leon Rowland mentions a Chuchita Creek, which he translates as Little Opossum Creek. But, why so named? It is true that *chucha* is Spanish for opossum, but opossums were not introduced into this area until around 1910.... There is a Mexican word *chuchito* which is their name for a species of Nightshade.... 'Chuchita' is also one of the many diminutive forms of the personal name 'Jesus.' But again, why the name?" Variants of the word found in official documents also include Cuchita and Chachita. Today, the word is mostly used in Central and South America and used as slang for 'dog,' in which case a translation may mean 'little female mutt,' or its less polite variant.

To find this location, I decided to look into the name of the area located at the upper end of today's Rider Road on or near Bean Hill. I had no success until I was given a copy of Alviso's sketch by Stanley Stevens, who was at that time in charge of the Map Room at the University of California, Santa Cruz. The sketch places Chuchita not at the upper end of Rider Road but on top of the peak today called Loma Prieta. This revelation caused me to intensify my research. I gathered all my data and took it to a person that had friends knowledgeable with older Spanish words and their meaning, especially colloquialisms. They determined that *chuchita* was a slang word that could mean either 'hideout' or 'lookout point.'

Regardless, it is clear that Alviso called Loma Prieta 'Chuchita,' and if a line is extended from that peak to the northeast corner of Rancho Soquel located in Borregas Gulch, the line follows almost exactly a path down the center of China Ridge, today located within the Forest of Nisene Marks State Park. This proves that early Mexican surveyors knew the mountainous terrain better than they are given credit.

ZANJÓN DE LAS BORREGAS: This short, 9,000-foot-long gulch trends mostly in a southerly direction from its headwaters at 400 feet elevation located in Rancho Aptos just to the northeast of Cabrillo College's campus. The gulch's creek makes a sharp southwesterly turn just south of Highway 1. From the top of the campus until it reaches Monterey Bay, the creek forms the boundary between Ranchos Soquel and Aptos. The origin of its name and its possible meanings have been discussed previously.

Cuatro Leguas: The final boundary point for Rancho Soquel's augmentation was *Cuatro Leguas*, which, according to Clark, was "such a well known landmark that it gave its name to two roads: Valencia Road to Quatro Legues (now called Day Valley Road), and Quatro Legues to Corralitos Road (now called Hames Road). This boundary point was probably so named because it was four leagues from Mission Santa Cruz. It marked the southeast corner of the Augmentation and the northeast corner of Rancho la Laguna de la Calabases. This boundary point did not become a part of the Augmentation land until included in the plat issued by the United States Surveyor General for California on June 4, 1859.

So, what was the area that Alviso intended to include in the sketch that he presented to the Land Claims Commission when he testified on August 14, 1853? He knew that Loma Prieta was not a mountain peak but a dark-looking ridge that extends along the north side of Los Gatos Creek. But this ridge does not only lie in a general northwest direction heading away from Chuchita—today's Loma Prieta peak—it also follows Los Gatos Creek as it makes its turn at today's Lexington Reservoir to head almost directly north until reaching Guadalupe Creek, a creek with its headwaters high up Loma Prieta or, rather, Chuchita.

Testimony taken by the Land Claims Commission of several witnesses concerning the augmentation grant in 1853 revealed that at least some witnesses believed the Loma Prieta boundary included both sides of the ridge. But, did the ridge as a boundary end ten to twelve miles northwest of Chuchita, or did it continue along Los Gatos Creek until reaching Guadalupe Creek? Both options were potential boundaries that Castro could use to establish her augmentation boundaries.

Why was over 40,000 acres of land in Santa Clara County sought in addition to the over 32,000 acres that were already included in the augmented boundaries on Alviso's sketch? This question can be answered quite easily. In the fall of 1845, Captain Andres Castillo of the Mexican Army discovered cinnabar deposits in the Almaden Valley. He quickly filed a claim and Antonio María Pico, *alcalde* of San José, granted him 3,000 *varas* of land in the area on December 30. The captain immediately founded a company and began mining the ore, which was refined into substantial quantities of commercial quicksilver (mercury). The discovery of quicksilver inspired Castro to extend the northeast boundaries of the augmentation to encompass the Almaden Valley and the cinnabar deposits within it.

What is still unanswered is why Jimeno allowed Castro to choose additional land in the vicinity of Palo de la Yesca at this time, nearly two years before the quicksilver deposits were discovered within the proposed boundaries. And did he intend to grant Castro the whole 70,000 acres? When considering possible answers to these questions, it is important to note that the commercial value of redwood was becoming clear to Mexican authorities at this time, and that they were also aware of the abundant water supply emanating from the area, and its potential in mineral wealth.[65]

┬µ

CHAPTER 2

~

Echoes from the East

United States Army Captain John Frémont leads a group of soldiers into California

In mid-February 1844, Captain John Charles Frémont of the United States Army arrived in California from Oregon with sixty-two men, including Kit Carson as a scout. Also accompanying the troops were six Native Americans from Delaware. While claiming that the visit was peaceful and for scientific exploration, the captain was actually under orders to make maps of the routes that an invading army could choose to take. After spending a year exploring Oregon, California, and the Great Basin, Frémont returned to St. Louis, Missouri and prepared for his next expedition.

On June 1, 1845, Frémont and a party set out on his third expedition to the West with a moderate party of soldiers and mountaineers. Following a brief stop at Sutter's Fort near Sacramento, he took a small party to Monterey, where he received permission to winter his men from General José Castro, the military commander of Alta California. Castro added the condition that his group must keep away from settled areas along the coast, so Frémont took his men to today's Fremont Peak, around twenty-five miles from Monterey. Here, they built a log fortification and raised the American flag. Shortly afterwards, Castro sent him a warning letter and, realizing that Castro was prepared to back his threats with force, Frémont and his men packed up and retreated to Oregon. Along the way, the party was overtaken by Lieutenant Archibald H. Gillespie, a United States Marines officer, who presented Frémont with secret dispatches from Washington. The party turned back toward California on May 9, 1846.[66]

The Bear Flag Revolt begins

Captain Frémont's return to California under orders from the United States government further antagonized relations with the Mexican authorities and local Californios population. The annexation of Texas and the Mexican–American War, which had broken out on April 25, 1846, further spread fears of an American uprising in California. On June 10, 1846, a group of American settlers intercepted a herd of horses destined for General Castro and turned them over to Captain Frémont.

Four days later, under the leadership of William B. Ide and Ezekiel Merritt, several American settlers captured General Mariano Guadalupe Vallejo at his rancho in Sonoma. Vallejo was one of the most respected citizens in all California. He and some of his officers were taken to Sutter's Fort as prisoners, but Frémont refused to accept them without orders to do so from Washington. Lacking any other option, Ide, Merritt, and other rebels quickly had a flag sewn with the image of a grizzly bear beside a red star and hoisted it up a flagpole in Sonoma, declaring California a republic free from Mexican rule.[67]

Commander Sloat's warship anchors at Monterey

On July 2, 1846, an American warship, the USS *Savannah*, under the command of Commodore John D. Sloat, sailed into Monterey Harbor and dropped anchor. Five days later, on July 7, Sloat sent a company of United States Marines ashore where they quickly captured Monterey, hoisting the American flag over the customs house. After the flag was raised, the commodore turned over command of the areas captured to Commodore Robert F. Stockton, who served as *de facto* military governor of the areas under American control for the next ten months. With the capture of Monterey and the replacement of the Bear Flag at Sonoma with the Stars and Stripes on July 9, the Bear Flag Revolt came to an end and California became the western theater of the Mexican–American War.[68]

Captain Frémont proceeds under orders to capture California for the United States of America

Having solidified his position in Monterey, Commodore Stockton ordered Captain Frémont to march through California with his California Battalion made up of regulars and volunteers to capture it for the United States. People traveled from all over to join and Frémont established Monterey as their muster point.

From the Branciforte area, Frémont was joined by such notables as Thomas Fallon, William Blackburn, Alfred Baldwin, P. W. Waggoner, Billy Wears, Otis Ashley, Winston and Jackson Bennett, William Dickey, Robert Francis Peckham, John Hames, Pruett Sinclair, and John Daubenbiss. Daubenbiss had been working in San José, helping to build a flour mill for Mariano Vallejo. Wanting to assist in the cause, he served Frémont's by carrying dispatches between Stockton, stationed in Monterey, and Frémont, who was travelling throughout California to rally support.[69]

John Hames contracts to build a sawmill on Rancho Soquel

In an agreement signed by Michael Lodge and John Hames on November 1, 1846, Lodge paid Hames $5,000 to build a sawmill on Soquel Creek just to the north of his homesite and slightly south of the main road between Branciforte and Monterey (today's Soquel Drive). Hames was a native of New York State, born in 1811. He arrived in California in 1843. Under the contract, he built a mill, drying and lumber-storage yards, millpond, and worker cabins, all along the west side of Soquel Creek. One of the workers that Hames hired to help in the construction was John Daubenbiss, who had just arrived from San José.

Daubenbiss was born in Bavaria in 1816. He arrived in New York in 1835 but left for Oregon six years later. After spending a year there, he joined the Hastings party that was heading to California. The party reached Bodega Bay in today's Sonoma County in 1843. While there, Daubenbiss decided to leave the party to help Stephen Smith build a sawmill. After the mill was running, he moved to San José, where he was hired by Maríano Vallejo to build a flour mill. He stayed in the San José area until early 1847, when he moved to Soquel to help Hames build Lodge's mill.

Just as construction of the mill was nearing completion, the Bear Flag Revolt began. Both Hames and Daubenbiss left to join Captain Frémont's California Battalion, leaving the mill not quite able to produce lumber. Although Hames had agreed to operate the mill after it was finished, his sudden departure meant that Lodge had to hire someone else to operate the facility once spring arrived and the ground was dry enough to pull logs to and from the millpond.

It is unclear how Lodge's sawmill was powered. In all likelihood, it was water powered with its source located high above the mill on the ridge at an elevation such that the water pressure could power the saws. Water with such requirements, though, was three to four miles away to the north. The other possibility is that the mill was steam powered, making Lodge's lumber mill the first such powered sawmill in Santa Cruz County. At the moment, this mystery has yet to be solved.[70]

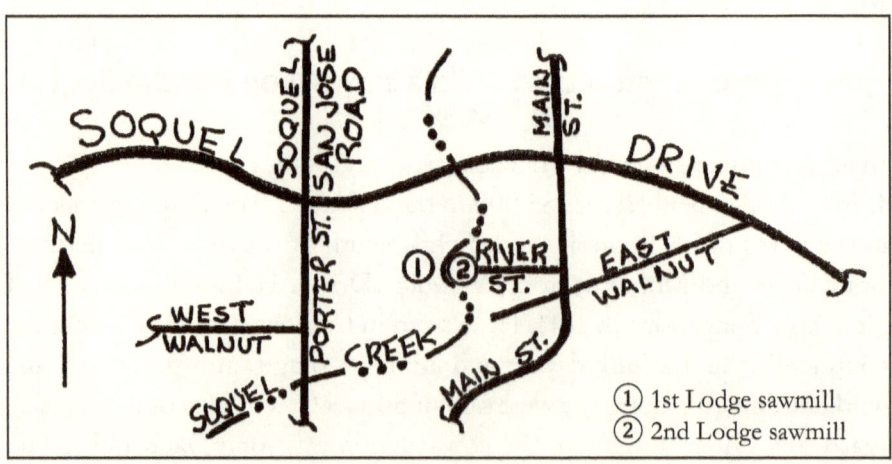

FIGURE 2.1 THE LODGE SAWMILLS

The only American casualties on the Central Coast during the Mexican–American War occur near Monterey

During Frémont's campaign in California, one of his foraging parties of thirty-five men and 500 horses was ambushed by Mexican soldiers under the command of General Manuel Castro at Natividad near Monterey, north of the mouth of the Salinas River, on November 16, 1846. The battle was brief and there were less than a dozen total casualties, but it was the only actual military engagement between Americans and Mexicans fought in Northern California and produced the only American casualties in the region.[71]

Martina Castro gives birth to Elejenia, Dolores, and Joaquín

Between 1844 and 1846, Martina Castro and Michael Lodge produced three more children named Efejenia, Dolores, and Joaquín. Because none of them survived to adulthood, almost nothing is known about their lives.[72]

The Battle of Santa Clara

In late 1846, after crossing overland and entering California, the Aram-Imus party of fifty-seven American colonists went to Mission Santa Clara and barricaded themselves inside. Over the next few months, over 175 more Americans took refuge at the mission. At the urging of Captain Frémont, a militia company of around thirty-five able-bodied men was formed from the group and placed under the command of Joseph Aram. The Mexican soldiers at the San José pueblo were content to keep them besieged in the mission rather than suffering losses from a direct attack. At the same time, friendly Californios such as Ignacio Alviso supplied the group with food. Adna Hecox, whose family was in the mission, wrote in his memoirs that fourteen people died of an illness during the months-long siege.

Finally, on January 2, 1847, a band of Californios led by Captain Francisco Sánchez, acting commandant of Yerba Buena (San Francisco), led a garrison of around 200 troops against the Americans. A mixed force including Aram's militia and thirty-three volunteers led by James Frazier

Reed of the Donner Party, numbering less than 100 men in total, defended the mission from a nearby mustard field. After skirmishing all day, only four Mexican soldiers were killed and both sides agreed to an armistice. Six days later, Sánchez surrendered his troops to a contingent of United States Marines who had been called to help. The action effectively ended the western theater of the Mexican–American War, although the war itself would not end for another eighteen months.[73]

General Stephen Kearney is appointed military governor of Alta California

Following the Battle of Santa Clara, Commodore Stockton was replaced as military governor of California by General Stephen Watts Kearney of the United States Army. His appointment began on February 13, 1847 and only lasted three months.[74]

Michael Lodge hires Henry Hill to operate his sawmill

With John Daubenbiss and John Hames fighting alongside Captain Frémont, Michael Lodge hired Henry Hill in March 1847 to run his mill. Hill was of German extraction and had entered Alta California in 1834 with the Hijar-Padres party from México. Lodge also hired Guadalupe Castro, his wife's bachelor brother. After the rains ceased and the ground was dry enough to drag the logs over, lumber production at the mill finally began.[75]

The Hecox family settles on Rancho Soquel

Shortly after the end of the Mission Santa Clara siege, the Hecox family crossed the Santa Cruz Mountains and settled on Rancho Soquel. Adna Andres Hexoc was a native of Detroit, Michigan, born on January 2, 1806. He married Margaret M. on April 1, 1846 and soon afterwards they left their home in Illinois for California by wagon train. They arrived in the Sacramento Valley on October 1, 1846, rested for a few days, and then headed for Santa Clara.

The family probably had no inkling of what was occurring in California between the American settlers, native Californios, and Mexican military. Upon their arrival at Santa Clara on December 15, 1846, they holed up within the confines of Mission Santa Clara alongside around 100 others who wanted nothing to do with the conflict. Hecox preached that day before the masses in what he believed to be the first Protestant sermon in Alta California. As soon as the fighting ended, the family departed for Branciforte and settled on Rancho Soquel in April

The earliest known English-language description of the Soquel area was written by Margaret in June 1847. In a letter, she describes the journey by wagon from Mission Santa Clara to Soquel and her perspectives on the rancho:

> *We traveled by the way of Gilroy and the Pajaro Valley. It took us eight days to reach Soquel near Branciforte, where we decided to remain for a while, at least.*
>
> *Never will I forget the kindness of the Spanish people along the way. Particularly the Spanish women, who came to us as we traveled along or camped in the slushy mud, for it rained most of the way, bringing us offers of homemade cheese, milk, and other appetizing food. Spanish men, whom we met on the way, told us that we would be more than welcome to help ourselves to beehives, when necessary, as that was a well established custom of the country. They informed us that all that was necessary was to hang the plainly branded hide on a tree (after butchering the steer), which could easily be identified by its owner. We took them at their word and helped ourselves to two beehives along the way.*
>
> *When we reached the little village of Soquel, spring had arrived, and I never could make you realize the heavenly beauty and charm of that place. Many of its attractions have since been destroyed by civilization. But at that time it was almost an earthly paradise.*
>
> *Mr. Hecox found an unused cabin in which we camped for awhile. He almost immediately secured work with a genial and well-to-do Irish gentleman named Michael Lodge, who had an attractive Spanish wife. My husband's job was to superintend the building operations of a new lumber mill and several other men were engaged to work the project.*

> There were no stores in either Soquel or the nearby larger town of Santa Cruz. All of our supplies had to come from Monterey. My husband had organized a protestant church soon after our arrival. The Sunday meetings were held at our home for some time. He also was occasionally called to Santa Cruz to deliver a sermon.[76]

Colonel Richard B. Mason replaces General Kearney as military governor of Alta California

General Kearney was replaced as military governor of Alta California by Colonel Richard B. Mason on May 31, 1847. Mason's tenure lasted for two years, the longest of the seven military governors of California.[77]

Francisco Alviso resigns as *alcalde* of Branciforte and William F. Blackburn is appointed interim mayor of Santa Cruz

During California's short tenure as a military province, Francisco Alviso resigned his position as *alcalde* of Branciforte. Perhaps unintentionally, he was the last *alcalde*. Traditionally, the area west of the San Lorenzo River had been under the direct control of Mission Santa Cruz. After secularization, a scattered settlement began to form near the mission and became known as Santa Cruz. Across the river to the east, the old pueblo of Branciforte continued to exist as the secular heart of the community. American control of Alta California changed this long-standing status quo. The Santa Cruz settlement was the first community in California to be reorganized under the military government, and it became the seat for a new county. Although Branciforte officially lingered as a town until 1905, it lost its independence and quickly became simply a suburb of Santa Cruz. The resignation of Alviso allowed Colonel Mason to appoint William F. Blackburn as the first mayor of Santa Cruz on June 21, 1847.[78]

Colonel Frémont charged with mutiny and arrested

Despite leading the army that captured California from México, Colonel

Frémont had been told to transfer his troops to General Kearney, who was acting as military governor. Frémont refused the order and requested instead that he be appointed governor of Alta California. When Kearney refused, Frémont went to Commodore Stockton and received the appointment despite Stockton not actually having the authority to do so. The end result was that on August 22, 1847, Frémont was charged with mutiny against the United States government and Kearney in particular. He turned himself in on September 17.

After a hotly contested trial, during which affairs in California were vividly illuminated, Frémont was found guilty on all twenty-three charges made against him. He was sentenced to dismissal from the army. President Polk accepted the verdict but remitted the sentence, offering to reinstate Frémont as a lieutenant colonel in the United State Army. Frémont declined and was permitted to resign.[79]

Carmel Cota and Thomas Fallon marry

At some point in 1848, Martina Castro's fourth daughter, Carmel Cota, married a mysterious Irishman named Thomas Fallon. Few things are known about Fallon with certainty, including his origins and where he lived prior to moving to Branciforte around 1844. He was probably born around 1818 in County Cork, Ireland, the same county as Michael Lodge and Peter Tracy. Castro's granddaughter, Carrie Electra Lodge, a daughter of Miguel Lodge, recounts in an interview recorded in 1965 that "Fallon was an actor whose company went broke in New Orleans, and after the company disbanded, he packed his bags and headed west. Along the way, he picked up the trade of making saddles, a trade he would soon practice in the vicinity of and in Branciforte. He arrived on the local scene in the mid 1840s." It was in Branciforte that Fallon first met Lodge and Castro, as well as Cota.

Evidence for the marriage of Fallon and Cota is found in a deposition made by Fallon before the Land Claims Commission on March 31, 1856 where he was asked: "Have you in any way been connected in interest with this tract of land [Rancho Soquel's augmentation] and, if so, how and when?" He replied: "Yes, I was interested in it, first in 1848 on account of marrying one of the daughters of Martina Castro." Fallon and Cota later moved to San José, where he became the city's mayor in 1859.

It must be reemphasized that the early life of Thomas Fallon is lost in rumor and hearsay. This murkiness was made no less clear by the publication in 1978 of *California Cavalier: The Journal of Captain Thomas Fallon* by future San José mayor Thomas McEnery. At first considered a genuine work of history based on a real document, it was later revealed by McEnery's daughter that no original source for the book exists and that her father, while well-versed in Fallon's life, made up anything he could not answer.[80]

Gold discovered at Sutter's Fort

In what Brian D. Dillon describes in his book, *Archaeological and Historical Survey of the Soquel Demonstration State Forest, Santa Cruz County, California*, as one of the most remarkable coincidences in world history, gold was discovered at Sutter's Mill in the Sierra foothills on January 24, 1848, only a week before a peace treaty was signed ending the Mexican–American War. The find rocked the world and, later, the fortunes of many, including Martina Castro and her family.[81]

Treaty of Guadalupe Hidalgo ends the Mexican–American War

The Treaty of Peace, Friendship, Limits, and Settlement between the United States of America and the Republic of México, commonly known as the Treaty of Guadalupe Hidalgo, was signed on February 2, 1848, setting a schedule and conditions for ending the war. The treaty went into full effect when President James K. Polk proclaimed it on July 4, 1848. Through the treaty, the annexation of Texas was confirmed and most of the Southwest, including California, became territories of the United States.

The treaty included several important promises regarding the property rights of those holding Spanish and Mexican land grants. Article VIII outlines the rights of individuals who chose to remain in ceded territory:

Mexicans now established in territories previously belonging

> to Mexico, and which remain for the future within the limits of the United States, as defined by the present treaty, shall be free to continue where they now reside, or to remove at any time to the Mexican Republic, retaining the property which they possess in the said territories, or disposing thereof, and removing the proceeds wherever they please, without their being subjected, on this account, to any contribution, tax, or charge whatever....
>
> In the said territories, property of every kind, now belonging to Mexicans not established there, shall be inviolably respected. The present owners, the heirs of these, and all Mexicans who may hereafter acquire said property by contract, shall enjoy with respect to it guarantees equally ample as if the same belonged to citizens of the United States.

Meanwhile, Article IX establishes the ceded land as United States territory and extends protection over its residents in the same manner as all other citizens and residents living within the United States:

> The Mexicans who, in the territories aforesaid, shall not preserve the character of citizens of the Mexican Republic, conformably with what is stipulated in the preceding article, shall be incorporated into the Union of the United States, and be admitted at the proper time (to be judged of by the Congress of the United States) to the enjoyment of all the rights of citizens of the United States, according to the principles of the Constitution; and in the mean time, shall be maintained and protected in the free enjoyment of their liberty and property, and secured in the free exercise of their religion without restriction.[82]

Agreement between Michael Lodge and John Hames concerning the Rancho Soquel sawmill

After he left Captain Frémont's California Battalion, John Hames approached Michael Lodge and demanded the $5,000 that he was promised when he built the sawmill and its supporting facilities along the Soquel Creek. Around this same time, news of the gold discovery in the Sierra Nevada had reached Soquel and fired the imagination of both Lodge and Martina Castro. In order to satisfy Hames' demands, Lodge granted him title to all of his cattle and sheep, plus all of the sawmill's output, for however long he and Castro were away. When this agreement was reached on February 16, 1848, the mill was inoperable due to the damage caused by the previous winter's storms. Lodge likely assured Hames that the mill would be rebuilt shortly, and production would begin soon.

Besides the problem of rebuilding the mill, Lodge had a potato crop worth at least $20,000 that was nearly ready for harvesting. After a brief search, he hired someone who was willing to bring in the harvest and handle its sale, but the identity of this person has never been found. The next year, Hames and John Daubenbiss conducted an experiment on Rancho Soquel: they grew $8,000 worth of potatoes on fewer than four acres. While these retailed for only twenty-five cents per pound in San José and Monterey, they could sell them for a dollar per pound in the Gold Country. But by 1850, the rate outside the Gold Country had dropped to eight cents per pound due to increasing investment in the potato industry. The rate further dropped to just four cents per pound in 1851. The bottom fell out of the potato market entirely the next year, when a 120-pound bag could be purchased for only ten cents. This crash prompted a short depression beginning in 1853.[83]

Lodge hires Adna Hecox to rebuild his mill

Owing to the fact that John Hames built Michael Lodge's sawmill too close to Soquel Creek, it was washed away by winter storms in the winter of 1847-1848. Wanting to rebuild the mill, Lodge looked for a qualified person to perform the task and settled upon Adna Hecox, who had recently moved into a cabin on Rancho Soquel and had worked as a carpenter at the mill. Hecox decided to move the mill site from its previous location along the west bank of Soquel Creek to the east bank.[84]

Jean Fourcade delivers missing documents to the government archives in Monterey

Shortly after the United States took control of the government archives at Monterey, William E. P. Hartnell, a government translator assigned to the archives, noticed that the petition from Martina Castro to Governor Micheltorena, dated October 26, 1843, and Francisco Alviso's *informe*, dated January 23, 1844, were missing from the files. Immediately, he issued a request that the two documents be delivered to the archives.

On March 7, 1848, Jean Fourcade, Castro's son-in-law, delivered the two missing documents. The next day, Hartnell affixed the following note to the *informe*: "This document was not found in the Archives but was delivered to me on March 7, 1848 by Ricardo Juan, son-in-law of the party interested, and retained by order of the Governor."

Upon examination, Hartnell discovered that two instances of the word 'cannot' were crudely erased and replaced with '*si*' (yes). This poor editing reversed the meaning of the statement and was later critical to proving the legitimacy of Castro's augmentation grant. Anticipating this, Hartnell requested that Alviso be subpoenaed to give testimony concerning the meaning and originator of these altered words.[85]

Francisco Alviso makes a statement in regard to the *informe* he wrote in 1844

On March 14, 1848, before William Blackburn, the last *alcalde* of Branciforte, the following statement was given by Francisco Alviso regarding his *informe* of January 23, 1844:

> *In the matter of Dona Martina Castro's situation in the Mountain "de la Yesca bordering on the Laguna del Sargento la Chuchita."*
>
> *Francisco Alviso, an inhabitant of Santa Cruz, Alta California, whose name appears in said title, being duly sworn, disposes and says...that he was acting for a period of time both before and after.*

> *Alviso continues that at the date aforesaid to the order of the then acting Governor, to wit, Manuel Micheltorena, he gave the information pursuant of Law relative to said land there partitioned for by the said Dona Martina Castro, that the second Alcalde, being advised by the first alcalde and several other persons, all residents in said Pueblo, reported that the said lands so petitioned for as aforesaid could not be granted to the petitioner, but that afterwards, to wit, on the foresaid date of January 1844 being in Monterey and the office of the government and conversing with Don Manuel Jimeno, who was well acquainted with the lands so petitioned for as aforesaid, I became convinced that the information, so given as aforesaid unfavorable to the said petitioner Dona Martina Castro for the grant of the lands aforesaid was erroneous and therefore went with the said Martina to the presence of his Excellency the Governor and there committed the same, as well appear...reference to said title papers, and my letters written to the Government on or about the dates as aforesaid.*

Francisco Alviso

Sworn to and subscribed before
this 14th day of March 1848,
William Blackburn,
Mayor of Santa Cruz[86]

Letters from the French consul in Monterey to France's Minister of Foreign Affairs concerning the gold frenzy and the Fourcade brothers

On August 17, 1848, the French consul in Monterey, J. A. Moerenhout, wrote a letter to the French Minister of Foreign Affairs regarding the discovery of gold in California and the frenzy it sparked worldwide:

> *On the morning of the 15th I left the Pueblo for Monterey, but it was a day's journey to the Mission of San Juan. The 16th*

I continued on my way over the Sierra de San Juan, a difficult, long and extremely tiresome climb for the horses. In the 'Plaine de la Nation' [Rancho Nacional] *I found the farms and the villages almost entirely abandoned—the only inhabitants were a few women and children—and on entering Monterey I was struck by the silence that reigned there. Not a ship was in the port, not a soul was to be seen in the streets, and I soon learned that all the men, Californians and foreigners, had left for the gold regions, and the Governor alone remained with a few officers, that the soldiers had deserted, and that there remained hardly enough to mount guard at the fort.*

On October 15, Moerenhout followed with a second letter to the minister:

On the 17th of last August I had the honor of addressing to Your Excellency a report on the journey that I had just made in the northern part of Alta California, the principal object of which was to visit the gold regions that had recently been discovered in this country. These discoveries, far from decreasing, are constantly extending both to the north and to the south, but the spots most noted now for their richness and to which most people are going are the rivers Cosumnes, Mokelumne, Stanislaus, Merced and the source of the San Joaquin, together with the hills and gulches that separate or lie between these rivers.

Just as I was writing this, two Frenchmen, the Messrs. Fourcade presented themselves at the Consulate on their return from the Placer with seventy pounds of gold. Two other Frenchmen who were working with them but who have remained at the Pueblo of San Jose have a like sum; that is to say, one of them, named Cinquantin, has forty pounds, and the other one, whose name I do not know, twenty-eight pounds.

Nearly all his gold comes from a single gulch, about four-hundred yards long located about four leagues north of the Stanislaus. It has produced more than $150,000. The *most extraordinary thing is that this gold has been obtained without washing the dirt, for as water is entirely lacking there at this season they gathered nothing but the large pieces and the grains that are visible and easy to pick up.*

J. A. Moerenhout
Consul for France

The two Fourcades mentioned in the above letter are: Jean Richard Fourcade, husband to Luisa Cota, and a brother, who probably went by the name Jean Albert Fourcade.[87]

The activities of Thomas Fallon in Branciforte, Rancho Soquel, and the Gold Country

Before he joined Captain John Frémont's California Battalion and marched south, Thomas Fallon lived near the mission plaza in Santa Cruz. After leaving the battalion, he settled in San José where he set up a shop making saddle trees. In late 1847, he entered business with Elihu Anthony and returned to Santa Cruz, continuing his profession there, probably in conjunction with Anthony's blacksmith shop and foundry. It was during this period that he met Carmel Lodge and they were married.

When news of the gold strike in the Sierra Nevada reached the area, Fallon took some of his own product plus eight dozen picks that Anthony had made from ships' bolts and headed for Hangtown (now Georgetown), located just to the north of Placerville.

In an interview, Robert Peckham recounted that, in October 1848, he and a partner had purchased $2,000 worth of goods in Sacramento to sell in the gold fields. They hired a two-mule wagon to take them and the supplies to what is now called Big Bar on the Mokelumne River. After crossing the river, they headed up its south side for about thirty miles, reaching the summit of a high hill overlooking a deep valley where they observed the blue, curling smoke of campfires. Descending the hill, they found, besides a number of Native Americans collecting gold in the river, Thomas Fallon with his stock of goods in the river. He had been there but a few months and had already made a fortune. Three days later, Fallon received a message from his brother-in-law, Jean Fourcade, that he had discovered a gulch of fabulous richness only sixteen miles away. It should be noted that this places both Fallon and Fourcade in close proximity to Michael Lodge.[88]

The activities of the Lodge family in the Gold Country

The precise date when Martina Castro and Michael Lodge left their ranch and arrived in the Sierra foothills is not known, but several sources suggest it was in early 1849. Lodge and Castro were smart investors and knew that looking for precious metals by digging was a difficult and time-consuming task. Instead, they decided to establish a mercantile store from which they could sell supplies to eager gold miners. Lodge and Castro purchased several wagonloads of supplies and moved to the Carson Hill gold strike in Calaveras County along the Stanislaus River. Their children did not accompany them initially—Henry Hill, who was hired to run the sawmill while they were away, took care of them for the first few months.

The couple opened their store just to the southeast of Angel's Camp and entered into a partnership with Balo Reed, who operated a freight business. After they were settled, they sent for the children, whom Hill brought a short time later. These included Antonia, Helena, Miguel, Guadalupe, Efejenia, Dolores, and Joaquín. Josefa, who was seventeen at the time, probably remained on Rancho Soquel since she married Lambert Clements the next year.

Lodge and Castro's granddaughter, Carrie Lodge, recounted some of her grandparents' history while in the Gold Country. Her father, Miguel Lodge, had traveled there with his parents in 1849 and passed his memories on to her. Carrie herself may have also learned some information firsthand from Castro since she was nine years old when her grandmother died. The following are some pertinent excerpts taken from the interview:

Q: Would you tell me about the incident you mentioned earlier when the Indians came to your grandmother's store?
A: Oh yes. That was in Calaveras. That was when they had the store. Two ornery whites, oh boy, they were tough ones,

came a rushing to the store. Grandpa was there, and one of them says, "you're the only one that understands English here, and we are Americans, and we're being chased by the tribe of Indians. We killed an Indian and they're after us." He says, "you've got to hide us." I suppose they were armed. They must have been if they killed an Indian. Well, so Grandma was brought up among the Indians, and she knew their ways. And so sure enough, towards the evening, the band of Indians was all in paraphernalia and painted faces, they made a big bonfire on the other side of the river. They danced around on their haunches, and boy, it was a big powwow. Then it was quiet for about a few minutes, and then two squaws came over. Maybe they were thinking it over, wondering if the people in the store were to blame. Maybe they's been thinking. Anyway, they came over, and Grandma went to the door to welcome them. Of course, they understood Spanish, and she spoke to them in Spanish. She took them inside and combed their hair and made two big braids and put some ribbon on them you know. She'd get things like that from the big ships that'd come into the port in San Francisco from the Orient. They's get those wonderful silk shawls, boy, $800 and $900, my oh my. So the Indians, they were all taking it in. They liked that. Then Grandma took those great big, like the girls have now, the silk handkerchiefs you know. In Spanish we call them *mascadas*. They used to be very pretty and all silk. And Grandma put penuche in their hands. We's have penuche candy, but it was hard penuche see; it would last a long time. That's what the Indians would like.

    And so she had nuts and raisins and cookies, and things like that which she thought they would like, so that they wouldn't get in a hurry. Well, then she gave both of them the same treatment, each one the same, and then ushered them to the door. And they went across back and there was silence.

Then two bucks came, and they got the same treatment. Yes, they got the same treatment. Then they went back. Well, they knew that Grandma and Grandpa weren't to blame, that these were different people, so Grandma wasn't worried any more. So, in the morning Grandma and Grandpa got up early, and sure enough, they went to feel the ashes you know, and they were warm yet. But that's warm country anyway up there. But if it wasn't for Grandma knowing about the Indians and their ways, those Indians could have assassinated the whole brood and bunch. Oh, it was terrible dangerous. And, one time, Aunt Mary [Guadalupe] told us: "You know, we don't know how well off we are. Oh, we have everything at the point of our fingers. They used to take their washing and go to the creek."

When Grandma and Grandpa went up to the mining country, Calaveras, they left Henry Hill here. Henry Hill took care of the two boys, Papa and his brother Joaquín, until Grandma and Grandpa would call for them. And when they got settled up there then Henry was to take the boys up. And when they were ready to go up, they did. And you know, Papa almost lost his life there. It just seemed as though some bad luck was on the heels of the family over there. It's too bad. They never should have gone up there.

Q: When was that, Carrie, that they went up there?

A: Forty-nine. Grandpa got the gold fever. And they left a crop of potatoes down here that brought $20,000 to whoever harvested them. I don't know who did it, whether it was Grandpa or he sold the crop to someone, but they got $20,000. See what a good landslide that was for that time. And instead of getting that, they lost everything, and Grandpa lost his life.

Q: The accounts I've read about it say that people think he was attacked by robbers. Is that what your family thought?

A: Oh, that's the only thing, but it could also have been the treachery of his partner, because Grandpa never got five cents from a freighting outfit [that] he was a half partner in. He owned half the freighting outfit and half of the store that carried pretty near everything, the way they do in the little country stores. Those stores have to carry what they get calls for, in clothes and country tools, and grain, and things like that. But there were some awful rough people there.

Q: If the whole family went to Calaveras, how was it that your grandfather was coming home alone when he was killed?

A: There was sickness. They lost three children; they had typhoid fever from conditions. Sometimes they'd find an Indian half in the water and half out of the water see, and conditions brought on that typhoid and with the heat and all.

Q: Was it the three youngest children who died?

A. Yes, that was Joaquínito, Dolores, and Efejenia. So, Grandpa got scared, and he said, "Martina, take all the children and go home, and I'll follow right away, as quick as I settle the business here." And that's the last.

Q: So, she came home ahead of him?

A: Yes. He sent Grandma because he was scared that this sickness would get the other children.

Q: That's how he happened to be coming back alone?

A: Yes. But as I told you, Grandpa used to walk a lot. Aunt Mary says there was plenty of horses, but he never would take a horse. He would walk. He was born a sailor, a born sailor. But you know, Aunt Mary told us something. She said that Grandma and Grandpa had an understanding that the first one that would die away from each other, they'd let the other know.

Carrie continued that, after Castro returned from the gold fields on April 20, 1849, she woke up one night, then awakened the daughter sleeping with her, seven-year-old Guadalupe, and told her to get the rest of the children because they should all pray—their father had just been killed.

Two weeks later, a Native American runner came to Rancho Soquel and informed the family of Lodge's passing. He was buried in the same graveyard as their three youngest children, located just to the southeast of their former store near Angel's Camp. It should be noted that this place cannot be accessed today: when construction of the New Melones dam began, because it would be sitting directly on top of the graveyard, all the bodies were exhumed and reinterred in a nearby mass grave dug above the waterline.

The lingering question remains, however: who killed Michael Lodge? Was it his freighting partner Balo Reed? Was he killed during a holdup before he could shut down the store? Was he murdered by robbers on his way home? This latter option seems unlikely since he was buried so close to his store. Is it possible that he was the target of a plot that arose within his own family? It must be remembered that, thanks to Robert Peckham, both Thomas Fallon and Jean Fourcade, along with at least one of the latter's brothers, were near Angel's Camp at this same time. Both had much to gain from Lodge's death.[89]

General Bennet Riley replaces Colonel Richard B. Mason as military governor of California

On April 13, 1849, General Bennet C. Riley was appointed to replace Colonel Richard B. Mason as military governor of California. He was the last military governor to rule before democratic elections were held at the end of the year.

William Carey Jones arrives in Monterey from Washington to examine Spanish and Mexican land grant records

On a quiet night in September 1849, twenty days out of Panama, the steamship *Oregon* arrived in the pleasant, but nearly deserted, port of Monterey, most residents having gone to the Sierras to seek their fortune. The ship that brought attorney William Carey Jones dropped anchor without difficulty, allowing the confidential agent of the United States government to walk ashore.

Jones was the son-in-law of Senator Thomas H. Benton of Missouri and had been chosen for this role in California due to his skills with the Spanish language and knowledge of Spanish and Mexican land law. He carried with

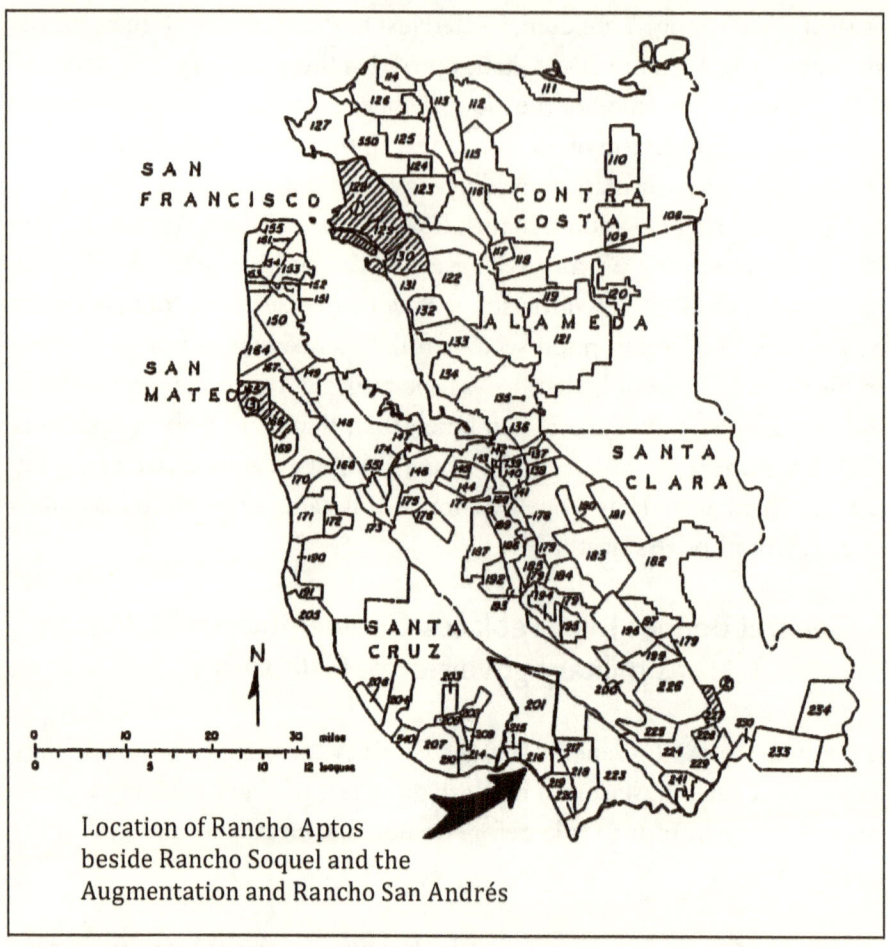

FIGURE 2.2 SPANISH AND MEXICAN LAND GRANTS IN THE BAY AREA

him detailed instructions from the Commissioner of the General Land Office, Justin Butterfield, plus others from the Secretary of the Interior, Thomas Ewing, wishing him success in this "arduous undertaking."

He came to California to examine the records of Spanish and Mexican land titles and was told to classify all grants or claims derived and to list separately those originating from the period of the Mexican–American War. It was later decided by the Supreme Court that all grants made after July 7, 1846—the date that Commodore John C. Sloat took possession of Monterey—would not be valid. This date was later upheld by the United States Supreme Court in *Botiller v. Dominguez* (1889). Jones was to collect all the legal forms, from petition to grant, that had been used in California, and to prepare a table of land measurements. Furthermore, he was instructed to investigate mission lands and their source of title, to report on mining titles, to check on claims to islands, and to look into Native American rights. The purpose of all of this was to gather reliable information about the whole landholding system of the former governments of California and to get the report to Congress before the end of the next session.

Almost immediately after stepping ashore, the archives at Monterey were thrown open to him. He found the records of land titles imperfect and confused. Those dated prior to 1839 seemed to be missing, and no book had been started for the year 1846. Even with the missing records, he was impressed with the size of the individual grants under Mexican law—as large as eleven square leagues (nearly 50,000 acres)—which he felt would require a liberal attitude on the part of Congress.[90]

Convention held to establish a constitution for California

After General Bennet Riley assumed military control of California in April 1848, he realized that something had to be done to end the chaos in the territory. The feeling of unrest and dissatisfaction that had been growing among the populace for a government finally crystallized into a convention, which was held in Colton Hall in Monterey on September 3, 1849.

A body of men representing all sections of the territory gathered there, wholly on their own initiative, for the purpose of forming a state. Dr. Robert Semple, who had taken such an active part in the Bear Flag Revolt, was selected as chairman. The men reflected a wide range of professions, including lawyers, doctors, merchants, bankers, printers, and farmers, yet nearly all were or had recently engaged in mining for gold. It was a collection of individuals who, by the very nature of their lives, were endowed with self-reliance, courage, and intelligence. After the convention convened, members gave little thought toward organizing a territory and instead began framing a constitution.[91]

Third District Court holds first session in Branciforte

One of the first acts performed by the military when it took control of California was to establish a court system. The first suit brought before the Third District in what would become Santa Cruz County was a suit against Louis Depeaux as defendant on September 15, 1849. Depeaux was a Frenchman born either in New York City or France in 1823. Other than the fact that he was small in stature, little is known about him prior to his arrival in Monterey in 1847. Later evidence makes clear that he was a deserter from the United States Navy, although the name of the vessel from which he deserted is unknown. He established himself on Rancho Soquel while Martina Castro and Michael Lodge were in the Gold Country and, not long after Castro's return, he moved into her home and took over management of the property.

Ennis Lodge had likewise moved onto Rancho Soquel while Castro and Lodge were away, even building a home, but he did so without the permission of the family. After repeated demands that Lodge vacate the rancho, Depeaux destroyed Lodge's home. Although Depeaux won the case against Lodge, forcing the latter off the property, he was required to pay Lodge's court expenses and reimburse him for the destroyed structure. [92]

California's constitution is signed in Monterey

The constitution that was framed by the members of the convention that met in Monterey on September 3 was signed on October 13, 1849. Its most important provision declared that the Territory of California was against slavery and would remain so if it joined the Union. The constitution also established the territory's boundaries. As soon as possible, copies of the constitution were distributed throughout California, with November 13 fixed as the day to allow the electorate to either accept or reject the proposed constitution. [93]

Martina Castro marries Louis Depeaux

On October 14, 1849, forty-two-year-old Martina Castro married twenty-six-year-old Louis Depeaux at Mission San Juan Bautista. Because Depeaux was of French origin and two of Castro's sons-in-law—Francisco Lajeunesse and Jean Fourcade—were also of this extraction, as well as the fact that there were other prominent Frenchmen living in the vicinity of Rancho Soquel at the time, several historians have commented that there may have been a conspiracy that led to this marriage. Although never proven, the marriage of such a young man to Castro so soon after Michael Lodge's murder certainly appears suspicious.

During his short tenure in the area, Depeaux was not a popular figure and the public in general distrusted and disliked him. Later testimony given by several residents of Soquel concluded that Depeaux was neither a man to trust nor believe, even under oath. He was also known to have made several indecent advances toward his wife's unmarried daughters. This may have been the primary reason most of them married at such young ages: they wanted to get out of the house. Josefa Lodge married in 1850 at around age eighteen, Antonia Lodge married in 1851 at age sixteen, Helena Lodge married in 1852 at age fifteen, and Guadalupe Lodge married in 1854, no older than twelve.[94]

The new constitution is ratified by voters and Peter H. Burnett is elected governor

In spite of heavy rains throughout most of the territory, there were enough votes cast by the electorate on November 13, 1849 to ratify the constitution that was agreed the previous month. Peter H. Burnett was elected governor and John McDougall lieutenant governor. During this same election, the first four federal congresspeople were elected, although they would not take their seats until after California was admitted into the Union in September 1850. William M. Gwin and John Frémont, both Democrats, were elected to the Senate, while Edward Gilbert, a Democrat, and George W. Wright, an Independent, were elected to the House of Representatives. The congressional delegation was not warmly received in Washington, especially by Southerners, since the territory had voted against slavery and all four congresspeople were opposed to it. Frémont, meanwhile, had drawn the short straw and was selected as the junior senator. As such, and because of the timing when California was granted statehood, he was only able to serve for seven months before his term was over.⁹⁵

Theron Per Lee elected to the California Legislature

In January 1847, Theron Rudd Per Lee arrived in California as a member of Colonel Jonathan D. Stevenson's regiment of New York Volunteers to help free the area from Mexican rule. At the end of the war, Per Lee was made Justice of the Peace, but he sought political office and was elected to the territorial assembly of California for the Monterey district on November 13, 1849. However, he soon was proclaimed the first Adjutant General of California—head of the state's National Guard—by the governor. On September 31, 1850, he was appointed a Santa Cruz County judge, replacing William Blackburn, who had resigned the position. When his term ended in 1854, he opened a private practice in Santa Cruz, which he ran until 1870, after which he returned to New York.⁹⁶

First state legislature meets in San José

On December 15, 1849, the newly elected legislature met for the first time in the new capital of the territory, San José. Five days later, military rule over California officially ended when the newly elected governor, Peter Burnett, and lieutenant governor, John McDougall, assumed their offices. However, the military remained to maintain law and order until local sheriffs could be appointed or voted into office.⁹⁷

Branciforte County established

On February 8, 1850, the California territorial legislature accepted twenty-seven areas as counties, of which one was Branciforte County. Geographically, it was the smallest county in the state until San Francisco County was created, although it was not the least populated. On April 5, the county was renamed Santa Cruz County.⁹⁸

Peter Tracy is appointed County Recorder

Peter Tracy, born in 1816 in Cork County, Ireland, arrived in Branciforte from México in 1849. While in México, he learned Mexican law and became fluent in Spanish. Once Santa Cruz County was organized in 1850, Tracy became its combined Clerk of the Court, County Recorder, and County Auditor, taking office in March.[99]

William Jones submits his report to Congress concerning mission lands and Spanish and Mexican land claims

Upon its completion, the report written by William Jones concerning mission lands and Spanish and Mexican land claims was submitted on April 10, 1850 to Secretary of the Interior Thomas Ewing, who passed it on to President Millard Fillmore, who in turn sent it to Congress for consideration. After California was accepted into the Union, Congress began drafting legislation for the settlement of private land claims in the state based on the Jones Report.

The Jones Report was remarkable in its scope and detail, as well as being a model of clarity and direct writing, and it was a landmark in the history of land titles in California. It affected legislation that Congress passed, and its liberal viewpoint found continuing expression in later court decrees ruling upon the ownership of California land.

The final laws that were to affect Mexican citizens concerning land grants in California were the result of several independent sources, including Jones' report; an exhaustive report produced by Secretary of the State Henry Halleck, which was turned over to Governor Mason on March 1, 1849; and bills offered by both of California's first senators, John Frémont and William Gwin, who intended to settle private land claims.

During a debate between Senators Thomas H. Benton and Gwin, the latter stated: "Our titles in California are equities.... We call upon you to examine them in a liberal and beneficial spirit, and confirm all that are just. We ask the interposition of a board to collect the evidence, and then the right to bring our titles before our own court. Then, as a final resort, and forever to settle the question, we claim a right of appeal to that power at Washington 'which has neither guards, nor palaces, nor treasures.'" The Webster Dictionary defines *Equity in Law* as "a resort to general principles of fairness and justice whenever existing law is inadequate; a system of rules and doctrines, as in the U.S., supplementing common and statute law and superseding such law when it proves inadequate for just settlement; a right or claim recognized in a court of equity." The debate continued in Congress until March 3, 1851, when the report was finally accepted into the Congressional record.[100]

Laws passed by California establishing rights of spouses

As California approached statehood, it found itself in a dilemma just as Texas had several years earlier. Women were considered more or less second-class citizens—especially in the business world, which included the purchase and sale of land—California had women who were landowners through Spanish and Mexican land grants, many of which were large estates. While a few claiming lands were unwed—they were usually widows—the majority were married. To compound the problem, most could not either read or write in any language, or for that matter understand the territory's new language, English.

The state legislature debated the problem and passed on April 16 and 17, 1850 two acts to protect the rights of female landowners, especially when a domineering husband was involved. Both of these acts had far-reaching effects on Martina Castro and her family. Several early transactions between Castro's daughters and their husbands would be voided because the rules and regulations established by these acts were not followed. Several times a grantee would have to appeal all the way to the California Supreme Court because one or more of the established rules were not followed properly. Both the lower and upper courts debated whether property owned before the acts were enacted came under these rules. The Supreme Court never considered this, however, due to the clever manipulation of Robert Peckham.

The first of the two acts, An Act Concerning Conveyances, established rules and regulations concerning deeds and the sale of land. It set laws for transactions by married couples, by husbands alone, and by wives alone.

This act also stated who could acknowledge a deed signed by a woman and set procedures that the person acknowledging the deed must follow and that it must be confirmed that the deed reflected the wishes of the woman, free from the husband's influence. Owing to its importance to this story, this act is included in full as follows:

AN ACT CONCERNING CONVEYANCES

The People of the State of California, represented in Senate and Assembly, do enact as follows:

§ 1. Conveyances of lands, or of any estates or interest therein, may be made by deed, signed by the person from whom the estate or interest is intended to pass, being of lawful age, or by his lawful agent or attorney, and acknowledged or proved and recorded as hereinafter directed.

§ 2. A husband and wife may, by their joint deed, convey the real estate of the wife in like manner as she might do by her separate deed if she were unmarried.

§ 3. Every conveyance in writing whereby any real estate is conveyed or may be affected, shall be acknowledged, or proved and certified, in the manner hereinafter provided.

§ 4. The proof or acknowledgement of every conveyance affecting any real estate shall be taken by some one of the following officers: 1st. If acknowledged or proved within this State, by some Judge or Clerk of a Court having a seal, or some Notary Public, or Justice of the Peace of the proper county: 2d. If acknowledged or proved without this State, and within the United States, by some Judge or Clerk of any Court of the United States, or of any State or Territory having a seal, or by any Commissioner appointed by the government of this State for that purpose: 3d. If acknowledged or proved without the United States, by some Judge or Clerk of any court of any State, Kingdom, or Empire, having a seal, or by any Notary Public therein, or by any Minister, Commissioner, or Consul of the United States appointed to reside therein.

§ 5. Every officer that shall take the proof or acknowledgement of any conveyance affecting any real estate shall grant a certificate thereof, and cause such certificate to be endorsed

or annexed to such conveyance; such certificate shall be: 1st. When granted by any Judge or Clerk, under the hand of such Judge or Clerk, and the seal of the court: 2d. When granted by an officer who has a seal of office, under the hand and official seal of such officer.

§ 6. No acknowledgment of any conveyance whereby any real estate is conveyed or may be affected, shall be taken, unless the person offering to make such acknowledgement shall be personally known to the officer taking the same, to be the person whose name is subscribed to such conveyance as a party thereto, or shall be proved to be such by the oath and affirmation of a credible witness.

§ 7. The certificate of such acknowledgement shall state the fact of acknowledgement, and that the person making the same was personally known to the officer granting the certificate, to be the person whose name is subscribed to the conveyance as a party thereto, or was proved to be such, by the oath or affirmation of a credible witness, whose name shall be inserted in the certificate.

§ 8. Such certificate shall be substantially in the following form, to wit: "State of California, County of ———, on this —— day of——, A. D. ——, personally appeared before me, a Notary Public (or Judge, or officer, as the case may be) in and for the said county, A. B., known to me to be the person described in, and who executed the foregoing instrument, who acknowledged to me that he executed the same freely and voluntarily, and for the uses and purposes therein mentioned."

§ 9. When the grantor is unknown to the court or officer taking the acknowledgment, the certificate may be in the following form, to wit: "State of California, County of ———, on this —— day of——, A. D. ——, personally appeared before me, a Notary Public (or Judge, or officer, as the case may be) in and for said county, A. B., satisfactorily proved to me to be the person described in, and who executed the within conveyance, by the oath of C. D., a competent and credible witness for that purpose, by me duly sworn, and he, the said A. B., acknowledged that he executed the same freely and vol-

untarily, for the uses and purposes therein mentioned."

§ 10. *The proof of the execution of any conveyance whereby any real estate is conveyed or may be affected, shall be, 1st, by the testimony of a subscribing witness, or 2d, when all the subscribing witnesses are dead, or cannot be had by evidence of the handwriting of the party, and of at least one subscribing witness, given by a credible witness to each signature.*

§ 11. *No proof by a subscribing witness shall be taken, unless such witness shall be personally known to the officer taking the proof, to be the person whose name is subscribed to the conveyance as a witness thereto, or shall be proved to be such by the oath or affirmation of a credible witness.*

§ 12. *No certificate of such proof shall be granted, unless such subscribing witness shall prove the person whose name is subscribed thereto as a party, is the person described in, and who executed the same; that such person executed the conveyance, and that such witness subscribed his name thereto as a witness thereof.*

§ 13. *The certificate of such proof shall set forth the following matters: 1st. The fact that such subscribing witness was personally known to the officer granting the certificate, to be the person whose name is subscribed to such conveyance as a witness thereto, or was proved to be such by oath or affirmation of a witness, whose name shall be inserted in the certificate. 2d. The proof given by such witness of the execution of such conveyance, and of the facts, that the person whose name is subscribed to such conveyance as a party thereto is the person who executed the same, and that such witness subscribed his name to such conveyance as a witness thereof.*

§ 14. *No proof by evidence of the handwriting of the party and of a subscribing witness shall be taken, unless the officer taking the same shall be satisfied that all the subscribing witnesses to such conveyance are dead, or cannot be had to prove the execution thereof.*

§ 15. *No certificate of any such proof shall be granted, unless a competent and credible witness shall state on oath, or affirmation, that he personally knew the person whose name is subscribed thereto as a party, well knew his signature (stating his means of knowledge), and believes the name of the person subscribed thereto as a party was subscribed by such person; nor unless a competent and credible witness shall in like manner state that he personally knew the person whose name is subscribed to such conveyance as a witness, well knew his signature (stating his means of knowledge), and believes the name subscribed thereto as a witness was thereto subscribed by such person.*

§ 16. Upon the application of any grantee in any conveyance required by this act to be recorded, or by any person claiming under such grantee, verified under the oath of the applicant, that any witness to such conveyance residing in the county where such application is made, refuses to appear and testify touching the execution thereof, and that such conveyance cannot be proved without his evidence, any officer authorized to take the acknowledgment or proof of such conveyance, may issue a subpoena requiring such witness to appear before such officer and testify touching the execution thereof.

§ 17. Every person who being served with a subpoena shall, without reasonable cause, refuse or neglect to appear, or appearing, shall refuse to answer upon oath touching the matters aforesaid, shall be liable to the party injured in the sum of one hundred dollars, and for such damages as may be sustained by him on account of such neglect or refusal, and may also be committed to prison by the Judge of some Court of record, there to remain without bail until he shall submit to answer upon oath as aforesaid; but no person shall be required to attend who resides out of the county in which the proof is to be taken, nor unless his reasonable expenses shall have been first tendered to him.

§ 18. A certificate of the acknowledgment of any conveyances, or of the proof of the execution thereof, as provided in this Act, signed by the officer taking the same, and under the seal of the officer, shall entitle such conveyance, with the certificate or certificates as aforesaid, to be recorded in the office

of the Recorder of any county in this State.

§ 19. A married woman may convey any of her real estate by any conveyance thereof, executed and acknowledged by herself and her husband, and certified in the manner hereinafter provided, by the proper officer taking the acknowledgment.

§ 20. No covenant expressed or implied in any such conveyance shall bind such married woman or her heirs, except so far as may be necessary effectually to convey from such married woman and her heirs, all her rights and interest expressed to be conveyed in such conveyance.

§ 21. Any officer authorized by this Act to take the proof or acknowledgment of any conveyance whereby any real estate is conveyed or may be affected, may take and certify the acknowledgment of a married woman to any such conveyance of real estate.

§ 22. No such acknowledgment shall be taken, unless such married woman shall be personally known to the officer taking the same, to be the person whose name is subscribed to such conveyance as a party thereto, or shall be proved to be such by a credible witness; nor, unless such married woman shall be made acquainted with the contents of such conveyance, and shall acknowledge on an examination, apart from and without the hearing of her husband, that she executed the same freely and voluntarily, without fear or compulsion, or undue influence of her husband, and that she does not wish to retract the execution of the same.

§ 23. The certificate shall be in the form heretofore given, and shall set forth that such married woman was personally known to the officer granting the same, to be the person whose name is subscribed to such conveyance as a party thereto, or was proved to be such by a credible witness, whose name shall be inserted in the certificate, and that she was made acquainted with the contents of such conveyance, and acknowledged, on examination apart from and without the hearing of her husband, that she executed the same freely and voluntarily, without fear or compulsion, or undue influence of her husband, and that she does not wish to retract the execution of *the same. Every certificate which substantially conforms to the requirements of this Act shall be valid.*

§ 24. Every conveyance whereby any real estate is conveyed, or may be affected, proved or acknowledged, and certified in the manner prescribed in this Act, to operate as notice to third persons, shall be recorded in the office of the Recorder of the county in which such real estate is situated, but shall be valid and binding between the parties thereto without such record.

§ 25. Every such conveyance, certified and recorded in the manner prescribed in this Act, shall, from the time of filing the same with the Recorder for record, impart notice to all persons of the contents thereof, and all subsequent purchasers and mortgagees shall be deemed to purchase with notice.

§ 26. Every conveyance of real estate within this State, hereafter made, which shall not be recorded as provided in this Act, shall be void as against any subsequent purchaser, in good faith and for a valuable consideration, of the same real estate, or any portion thereof, where his own conveyance shall be first duly recorded.

§ 27. Every power of attorney, or other instrument in writing containing the power to convey any real estate as agent or attorney for the owner thereof, or to execute as agent or attorney for another, any conveyance whereby any real estate is conveyed or may be affected, shall be acknowledged or proved, and certified and recorded as other conveyances whereby real estate is conveyed or affected, are required to be acknowledged or proved, and certified and recorded.

§ 28. No such power of attorney or other instrument, certified and recorded in the manner prescribed in the preceding section, shall be deemed to be revoked by any act of the party by whom it was executed, until the instrument containing such revocation shall be deposited for record in the same office in which the instrument containing the power is recorded.

§ 29. Every conveyance or other instrument, conveying or affecting real estate, which shall be acknowledged or proved and certified, as hereinafter prescribed, may, together with

the certificate of acknowledgment or proof, be read in evidence without further proof.

§ 30. When any such conveyance or instrument is acknowledged or proved, certified and recorded in the manner hereinafter prescribed, and it shall be shown to the Court that such conveyance or instrument is lost, or not within the power of the party wishing to use the same, the record thereof, or the transcript of such record, certified by the Recorder under the seal of his office, may be read in evidence without further proof.

§ 31. Neither the certificate of the acknowledgment, nor of the proof of any such conveyance or instrument, nor the record, nor the transcript of the record of such conveyance or instrument, shall be conclusive, but the same may be rebutted.

§ 32. If the party contesting the proof of any such conveyance or instrument, shall make it appear that any such proof was taken upon the oath of an incompetent witness, neither such conveyance or instrument, nor the record thereof, shall be received in evidence until established by other competent proof.

§ 33. If any person shall convey any real estate, by conveyance purporting to convey the same in fee simple absolute, and shall not at the time of such conveyance have the legal estate in such real estate, but shall afterwards acquire the same, the legal estate subsequently acquired shall immediately pass to the grantee, and such conveyance shall be valid as if such legal estate had been in the grantor at the time of the conveyance.

§ 34. Any person claiming title to any real estate may, notwithstanding there may be an adverse possession thereof, sell and convey his interest therein in the same manner and with the same effect as if he was in actual possession thereof.

§ 35. The term "real estate," as used in this Act, shall be construed as co-extensive in meaning with lands, tenements, and hereditaments.

§ 36. The term "conveyance," as used in this Act, shall be construed to embrace every instrument in writing by which any real estate or interest in real estate is created, aliened,

mortgaged, or assigned, except wills, leases for a term not exceeding one year, executory contracts for the sale or purchase of lands, and powers of attorney.

§ 37. Any mortgage that has been, or may hereafter be, recorded, may be discharged by an entry in the margin of the record thereof, signed by the mortgagee, or his personal representative or assignee, acknowledging the satisfaction of the mortgage, in the presence of the Recorder or his Deputy, who shall subscribe the same as a witness, and such entry shall have the same effect as a deed of release duly acknowledged and recorded.

§ 38. Any mortgage shall also be discharged upon the record thereof by the Recorder in whose custody it shall be, whenever there shall be presented to him a certificate executed by the mortgagee, his personal representative or assignee, acknowledged, or proved and certified as hereinbefore prescribed to entitle conveyances to be recorded, specifying that such mortgage has been paid, or otherwise satisfied or discharged.

§ 39. Every such certificate, and the proof or acknowledgment thereof, shall be recorded at full length, and a reference shall be made to the book containing such record, in the minutes of the discharge of such mortgage, made by the Recorder upon the record thereof.

§ 40. If any mortgagee, or his personal representative or assignee, as the case may be, after a full performance of the conditions of the mortgage, whether before or after a breach thereof, shall, for the space of seven days after being thereto requested, and after tender of his reasonable charges, refuse or neglect to execute and acknowledge a certificate of discharge or release thereof, he shall be liable to the mortgagor, his heirs or assigns, in the sum of one hundred dollars, and also for all actual damages occasioned by such neglect or refusal.

§ 41. All conveyances of real estate heretofore made, and acknowledged or proved [according] to the laws in force at the time of such making and acknowledgment of proof, shall have the same force as evidence, and be recorded in the same manner and with the like effect as conveyances executed and *acknowledged in pursuance of this Act.*

§ 42. The legality of the execution, acknowledgment, proof, form, or record of any conveyance or other instrument heretofore made, executed, acknowledged, proved, or recorded, shall not be affected by anything contained in this Act, but shall depend for its validity or legality upon the laws then existing and in force.

The second of the two acts was An Act Defining the Rights of Husband and Wife, and more specifically defined the rights for husbands and wives acting alone or together, as well as establishing the rights of a married woman concerning her separate estate and property. Again, the act is included in full due to its importance to this story:

An Act Defining the Rights of Husband and Wife

The People of the State of California, represented in Senate and Assembly, do enact as follows:

§ 1. All property, both real and personal, of the wife, owned by her before marriage, and that acquired afterwards by gift, bequest, devise, or descent, shall be her separate property; and all property both real and personal, owned by the husband before marriage; and that acquired by him afterwards by gift, bequest, devise, or descent, shall be his separate property.

§ 2. All property acquired after the marriage by either husband or wife, except such as may be acquired by gift, bequest, devise, or descent, shall be common property.

§ 3. A full and complete inventory of the separate property of the wife shall be made out and signed by the wife, acknowledged or proved in the manner required by law for the acknowledgment or proof of a conveyance of land, and recorded in the office of the Recorder of the county in which the parties reside.

§ 4. If there be included in the inventory any real estate lying in other counties, the inventory shall also be recorded in such counties.

§ 5. The filing of the inventory in the Recorder's office shall be notice of the title of the wife, and all property belonging to

her, included in the inventory, shall be exempt from seizure or execution for the debts of her husband.

§ 6. The husband shall have the management and control of the separate property of the wife, during the continuance of the marriage; but no sale or other alienation of any part of such property can be made, nor any lien or incumbrance created thereon, unless by an instrument in writing, signed by the husband and wife, and acknowledged by her upon an examination separate and apart from her husband, before a Justice of the Supreme Court, Judge of the District Court, County Judge, or Notary Public, or if executed out of State, then so acknowledged before some Judge of a Court of Record, or before a Commissioner, appointed under the authority of this State to take acknowledgment of deeds.

§ 7. When any sale shall be made by the wife of any of her separate property, for the benefit of her husband, or when he shall have used the proceeds of such sale with her consent in writing, it shall be deemed a gift, and neither she nor those claiming under her shall have any right to recover the same.

§ 8. If the wife has just cause to apprehend that her husband has mismanaged or wasted, or will mismanage or waste, her separate property, she, or any other person in her behalf, may apply to the District Court for the appointment of a trustee, to take charge of and manage her separate estate: such trustee may, for good cause shown, be from time to time removed by the Court, and another appointed in his place. Before entering upon the discharge of his trust, he shall execute a bond, with sufficient surety or sureties, to be approved by the Court, for the proper performance of his duties. In case of the appointment of a trustee for the wife, he shall account for and pay over to the husband and wife, or either of them, the income and profits of the wife's estate, in such manner and proportion as the Court may direct.

§ 9. The husband shall have the entire management and control of the common property, with the like absolute power of disposition as of his own separate estate. The rents and profits of the separate property of either husband or wife shall be deemed common property.

§ 10. No estate shall be allowed to the husband as tenant by courtesy upon the decease of his wife, nor any estate in dower be allotted to the wife upon the decease of her husband.

§ 11. Upon the dissolution of the community by the death of either husband or wife, one half of the common property shall go to the survivor, and the other half to the descendants of the deceased husband or wife, subject to the payment of the debts of the deceased. If there be no descendants of the deceased husband or wife, the whole shall go to the survivor, subject to such payment.

§ 12. In case of the dissolution of the marriage, by decree of any Court of competent jurisdiction, the common property shall be equally divided between the parties, and the Court granting the decree shall make such order for the division of the common property, or the sale and equal distribution of the proceeds thereof, as the nature of the case may require.

§ 13. The separate property of the husband shall not be liable for the debts of wife contracted before the marriage, but the separate property of the wife shall be and continue liable for all such debts.

§ 14. In every marriage hereafter contracted in this State, the rights of husband and wife shall be governed by this Act, unless there is a marriage contract, containing stipulations contrary thereto.

§ 15. The rights of husband and wife, married in this State prior to passage of this Act, or married out of this State, who shall reside and acquire property herein, shall also be determined by the provisions of this Act, with respect to such property as shall be hereafter acquired, unless so far as such provisions may be in conflict with the stipulations of any marriage contract.

Marriage Contracts

§ 16. All marriage contracts shall be in writing, and executed and acknowledged or proved, in like manner as a conveyance of land is required to be executed and acknowl-

edged or proved.

§ 17. When a marriage contract shall be acknowledged or proved, it shall be recorded in the office of the Recorder of the County in which the parties reside, and also in the office of the Recorder of every county in which any real estate may be situated, which is conveyed or affected by such marriage contract.

§ 18. When any marriage contract is deposited in the Recorder's office for record, it shall, as to all property affected thereby, in the county where the same is deposited, impart full notice to all persons of the contents thereof.

§ 19. No marriage contract shall be valid, or affect any property, except between the parties thereto, until it shall be deposited for record with the Recorder of the County where the parties reside, and if it relates to real estate in other counties, with the Recorder of the County wherein such property is situated.

§ 20. A minor, capable of contracting matrimony, may enter into a marriage contract, and the same shall be as valid as if he was of full age: Provided, it be assented to, in writing, by the person or persons whose consent is necessary to his marriage.

§ 21. A marriage contract may be altered at any time before the celebration of the marriage, but not afterwards.

§ 22. The parties to any marriage contract shall enter into no agreement, the object of which shall be to alter the legal order of descent, either with respect to themselves in what concerns the inheritance of their children or posterity, or with respect to their children between themselves, nor derogate from the rights given by law to the husband, as to the head of the family, or to the surviving husband or wife as the guardian of their children.

§ 23. No stipulation of any marriage contract shall be valid, which shall derogate from the rights given by law to the husband, over the persons of his wife and children, or which belong to the husband, as the head of the family, or to the surviving husband or wife, as the guardian of their children.[101]

Josefa Lodge marries Lambert Clements

Sometime in 1850, Josefa Lodge married Lambert Blair Clements. Born on July 6, 1823 and raised in Philadelphia, Clements departed New York as a member of Captain Nathaniel Crosby Jr.'s crew on January 10, 1845. After sailing around Cape Horn, his ship stopped at Valparaiso, Chile before continuing to Honolulu. It arrived at its final destination of Portland, Oregon around November, at which time Clements joined a crew that shuttled cargo between Portland and San Francisco. He remained in this job for seventeen months before jumping ship at San Francisco. He arrived in Branciforte on April 22, 1847 and settled on Rancho Soquel, where he met Josefa Lodge, Martina Castro's fourth daughter.[102]

Daniel Post settles on the Summit

Daniel Post (also known as Thomas Doakes) arrived in California in 1816 aboard the schooner *Albatross* and settled in Branciforte. He is credited with being the first European to settle along the Summit of the Santa Cruz Mountains beginning in 1850. Professionally, he was a hunter and trapper and lived along the west side of Laguna del Sargento, one mile south of the future Mountain Charley Road. Because Post neglected to file a claim for his land with authorities, the land that his cabin occupied was eventually lost. As a result, he moved to Santa Cruz, where he spent the rest of his days.[103]

Thomas Wright replaces Edmund Kellogg as County Surveyor

In 1850, Edmund B. Kellogg was elected the county's first surveyor. He served in this position for only a few months before being replaced by Thomas Wilson Wright in August 1850. Wright was a native of Minden, Louisiana, born on October 29, 1824, but he was raised in western Arkansas where he studied to be a surveyor. When the Mexican–American War broke out, he joined G Company of the Arkansas Volunteers, in which he reached the rank of sergeant. He fought in General John E. Wool's battalion during the Battle of Buena Vista on February 23, 1847. After serving a year in the quartermaster's department, he returned to Arkansas and then headed for California, arriving in Santa Cruz on December 31, 1849.

Wright held the position of county surveyor until 1890, except for a collective total of eight years. He is credited with laying out most of the county's roads and its first railroad. He also surveyed the wild back country many times, making him one of the most knowledgeable people concerning the county's mountainous regions. He became one of the most trusted men in the county and was often called upon to testify when land disputes were involved.

Since his duties did not take all of his time, he also often served as a deputy to Peter Tracy, the county recorder. In an interview conducted in 1892, Wright recounted that, when he arrived, there were only two houses where the main business part of Santa Cruz is now situated. One of them was a big log house near where City Hall now stands, owned by Eli Moore. The other was a store of boards belonging to Elihu Anthony. All the other buildings were adobes, located on the hill in the vicinity of the mission, where the Catholic church now stands. At the time, there were not more than a dozen American children in the town.[104]

Agreement between Martina Castro and her sons-in-law

The following article of agreement, signed on August 28, 1850, between Martina Castro, Louis Depeaux, Jean Fourcade, and Francisco Lajeunesse went missing, although over the next sixteen years its contents would be referred to in several lawsuits despite its disappearance. In a deposition made by Depeaux on July 11, 1856, he quoted the document from memory. But because the wording of the agreement depended solely on Depeaux, its exact wording was questioned by his opponents.

Depeaux's record was filed away in the transcript of the appeal held in the Third District Court, Santa Cruz County, in the Thomas Courtis v. Frederick Hihn case file, which sought to overturn the ruling in the partitioning suit for Rancho Soquel. It is now held in the Map Room at the McHenry Library at the University of California, Santa Cruz. It was prepared for presentation to the California Supreme Court by M. D. Carr & Company, based in San Francisco, in 1865. In 1993, Stanley Stevens, curator of the Map Room, discovered the document filed in Leon Rowland's archives in Special Collections, seemingly displaced from the rest of the court transcript. It was mixed with documents that concerned Castro's father, Joaquín, but the names on the agreement were those of Castro, Depeaux, Fourcade, and Lajeunesse, proving it was the original document signed on August 28, 1850.

The following is the exact wording of the agreement found by Stevens:

Article of Agreement

This article of Agreement made and entered into this twenty-eighth day of August A.D. 1850 between Donna Martina Castro of the first part and Francisco Young, Ricardo Juan, Thomas Fallon and Lambert B. Clements, sons in law of the aforesaid Donna Martina Castro, all of Santa Cruz County of Santa Cruz, state of California, on behalf of the wives, daughters of the aforesaid Donna Martina Castro, legal heirs to the Rancho now in possession of the aforesaid Donna Martina Castro, and for the better security of the right of their wives, have entered into the following agreement at Soquel at the house of Donna Martina Castro in the county of Santa Cruz, state as aforesaid, witnesseth:

The aforesaid Donna Martina Castro, of the county and state as aforesaid, hereby agrees and by these presents does give to give unto her children named, Nicanor Cota wife of Francisco Young, Maria Luisa Cota wife of Ricardo Juan, Carmen Lodge wife of Thomas Fallon, and Maria Josefa wife of Lambert B. Clements, also Maria Antonia Lodge not married, Maria Helena Lodge not married, Miguel Antonio Lodge, and Maria Guadalupe Lodge not married, free and equal portions of the Rancho now in possession of Donna Martina Castro, to be equally divided alike among all the heirs in accordance with title held by Donna Martina Castro, respecting the boundaries of said mentioned Rancho, reserving for the benefit of herself and family, which includes Louis Depeaux, her husband, at the present time one son named Miguel Antonio Lodge and one daughter named Maria Guadalupe Lodge now being with her to embrace all that piece of that land where her house now stands from the river Soquel running across to a gulch back of the house including all between those two mentioned boundaries from the house to the water's edge of the Pacific Ocean until such time as the Rancho shall be properly surveyed.

Now the aforesaid Donna Martina Castro hereby agrees to give and by these presents does give to each of the heirs permission to build a house upon said mentioned Rancho for the benefit of themselves and families and to make such other improvements as they may think proper, and by this binds herself not to molest them giving them the same privileges as herself in regard to the use of timber for building purposes, firewood, fencing etc.

Be it also understood that Donna Martina Castro hereby binds herself not to sell or otherwise dispose of any part of the within mentioned Rancho. And be it further understood that within named sons-in-law hereby agree and by these presents do bind themselves to protect and defend the rights of said Rancho against all invaders and squatters.

In witness whereof we have hereunto affixed our names and seals, the day and date herein mentioned.

X [Martina Castro's mark]
Francisco Young
Ricardo Juan
Thomas Fallon
Lambert B. Clements

Witness at signing: Louis Depeaux
Endorsed: Donna M Castro Depeaux,
agt. with her children, August 1850

Orrin Bailey, Notary Public

Notice that the agreement above was intended to give land to Castro's children within Rancho Soquel only. When she put her mark on the paper, Castro considered her property to be composed only of Rancho Soquel and the Palo de la Yesca land, not the larger area that would eventually become Shoquel Augmentation.[105]

Land transfer by Martina Castro to her children

On August 29, 1850, the day after making her agreement with her children, Martina Castro was convinced by her son-in-law Thomas Fallon to sign a document prepared by Durrell Gregory that would ensure that the earlier agreement was legal. As before, she did not write the document, but rather had it composed for her and in her presence. After the document was written, Castro insisted that the two underlined phrases below be emphasized before she agreed to sign the document. Later testimony regarding this document suggests that Castro intended it to simply be a legal version of the agreement of the previous day, but what transpired was that Castro formally transferred title to eight-ninths of her land to her eight children and sons-in-law. The text of the deed reads:

> *This indenture, made and entered into this twenty ninth day of August, eighteen hundred and fifty, between Donna Martina Castro, of Santa Cruz County, wife of Louis Depeaux, and her children, Nicanor Cota, wife of Francisco Lajeunesse, Maria Luisa Cota, wife of Ricardo Juan, Carmel Lodge, wife of Thomas Fallon, Maria Josefa, wife of Lambert Blair Clements, Maria Antonia Lodge, a daughter, not married, Maria Helena Lodge, a daughter, not married, Maria Guadalupe Lodge, a daughter, not married, and Miguel Antonio Lodge, a son, all of said county of Santa Cruz, witnesseth;*
>
> *That whereas, on the twenty-third day of November, eighteen hundred and thirty-three, the said Donna Martina Castro received from J. Figueroa, the Governor of Upper California, a grant to herself and family of a tract of land two miles in length by a half league in breadth, a little more or less, with certain conditions, which have been performed, and limitations that have since been released; and whereas, also, the said Donna Martina Castro afterwards petitioned*

Micheltorena, the then Governor of both Californias, for the removal of the limitations and restrictions under the above mentioned ranch or tract of land was held, and in addition for a new title to said ranch, and for another tract of land on [the] mountain, which new title was granted to her and to her family to an extent of territory extending as far as the Laguna del Sarjento and La Chuchita, including the Loma Prieta, which grant was made to me and family by Micheltoreno, through an <u>order to his Secretary, Manuel Jimeno</u>, without any conditions or limitations.

There are, therefore, to knowledge that my beforementioned children have each an interest of one undivided ninth part of each of said ranchos, both of which are embraced in the last mentioned grant, and are entitled, under each of the said grants, to the enjoyment of the same in common with me. And this indenture further witnesseth, that, in order to secure fully to my said children the aforesaid interest in the above mentioned grants, I, the said Martina Castro, for and in consideration of the natural love and affection which I have and bear to my said children, and for the further sum of five dollars, to me in hand at and before the sealing and delivery of these presents, the receipt whereof is hereby acknowledged, have granted, bargained, sold, and conveyed, and do by these presents grant, bargain, sell, and convey, unto the said Nicanor Cota, Maria Luisa Cota, Carmel Lodge, Maria Josepha Lodge, Maria Antonia Lodge, Maria Helena Lodge, Maria Guadalupe Lodge, and Antonio Miguel Lodge, and <u>to each of them</u>, and to their heirs and assigns, the one undivided ninth part each, (I retaining the other ninth part), of the entire rancho embraced in the two above mentioned grants, extending from the Pacific Ocean to the Laguna del Sarjento and the Chuchitas, with all the rights, members, and appurtenances belonging – the said children holding each an undivided ninth part of said rancho, and I one undivided ninth part of the same; to have and to hold the said above granted premises of each of them, my said children, and their heirs and assigns, and to their own proper use, benefit, and behoof forever.

And the said Martina Castro, her heirs, executors, and administrators, will forever warrant and defend the title thereof to her said children. And this indenture further witnesseth, that the said Martina Castro does at one and immediately give to all her said children the enjoyment and possession of the said rancho, in common with her, and the use of the timber thereon for building, fencing, fires, etc., reserving to herself, however, for the use of herself and husband Louis Depeaux, her son, Miguel Antonio Lodge, and her daughter, Maria Guadalupe Lodge, the sole and uninterrupted possession of so much of said rancho—and on which her house now stands*—as is included in the boundaries to commence at the mouth of the Soquel River; thence up to the main crossing place below the old sawmill; thence, in a straight line to a gulch in the rear of the house; down said gulch to the ocean; thence back to the place of beginning; to retain the possession of said tract of land until such time as the rancho may be partitioned off to the joint owners, according to law.

In witness whereof, I have hereunto set my hand and seal, the day and year above written.

* *Mrs. Martina Depeaux objects to the last condition concerning where her house stands, and it is to be understood that the ranch is to be in common, until a final division be made.*

Signed by Peter Tracy for Martina Castro
✗ [Martina Castro's mark]

signed in the presence of
T. R. Per Lee
Peter Tracy

STATE OF CALIFORNIA
County of Santa Cruz

On the 29th day of August, A. D. 1850, personally appeared before me, Peter Tracy, County Clerk in and for said county,

Martina Castro, known to me to be the person described in and who on being made duly acquainted with the contents of the within instrument, and who declared, on examination apart from her husband, and without his hearing, that she executed the same, freely and voluntarily, without fear or compulsion, or under influence of her husband, and that she does not wish to retract the execution of the same.

In testimony whereof, I have hereunto set my hand and affixed my private seal, there being no official seal provided at office.

Peter Tracy, Clerk

I have read the foregoing, and fully agree with the conveyance therein made by my wife.

Louis Depeaux

Witnesses:
T. R. Per Lee
Peter Tracy

STATE OF CALIFORNIA
County of Santa Cruz

On this 29th day of August, A.D. 1850, personally appeared before me, Peter Tracy, County Clerk in and for said county, Louis Depeaux known to me to be the person described in and who executed the foregoing instrument, freely and voluntarily, and for the uses and purposes therein mentioned.

In testimony whereof, I have hereunto set my hand and affixed my private seal, there being no official seal provided at office.

Peter Tracy, Clerk

Recorded August the 30th, A.D. 1859, in Book A, pages 38,

39, and 40, among the records for Santa Cruz County, State of California

C. P. Stevenson, Recorder[106]

Casimero and Dario Amayo settle on the Summit

At some point in 1850, Casimero and Dario Amayo, two native Californios and brothers, settled on Rancho Soquel's augmentation with their families near the headwaters of the creek that would later bear their name. Their homes were erected just to the west of where Lyman Burrell would later build Mountain Home (today, across Summit Road almost directly opposite the Burrell Schoolhouse, to the west of Loma Prieta Avenue). Because the brothers settled in the back country among the many giant redwood trees, several historians assume that they settled there to log. In actuality, the two were more active in homesteading and farming, cutting down a redwood tree only when it was in the way or if its wood was needed for something on the farm. Little of the two families' activities are known except that they were some of the first to settle in the Summit area.[107]

California is admitted into the United States

After two years as a territory following the conclusion of the Mexican–American War, California became the thirty-first state of the United States of America on September 9, 1850.[108]

Chapter 3

~

In Defense of My Own

A tax bill is issued to Martina Castro for her land, forcing her to borrow from Thomas Fallon to pay

On November 27, 1850, Martina Castro and Louis Depeaux received from the county a tax bill in the amount of $300. It is not known if this was for Rancho Soquel only or if Rancho Soquel Augmentation was included, but the latter is doubtful because the area had never been surveyed. Because the couple did not have this amount of money on hand, they approached Thomas Fallon, who agreed to loan them the money. But the loan was not made without conditions agreed to by both. After the note was written, it was signed by Depeaux while Castro put her mark to it. Because the note was never found, the conditions that Fallon demanded can only be derived from the deed signed in the office of Theron Per Lee on November 29, 1850.

It will be remembered that Per Lee accompanied Peter Tracy on the night of August 29, 1850 when the deed was brought to Castro's house for her to mark. After both Castro and Depeaux signed the deed, only Tracy acknowledged it. On November 28, in the office of Per Lee, the judge acknowledged the deed in front of both Castro and Depeaux. The acknowledgement was filed separately in the county's record books.

In the deed, Fallon agreed to loan Castro and Depeaux the necessary $300 to pay the county's tax bill, while as collateral Castro agreed to pass title to a certain part of her land if the terms agreed upon by all parties were not satisfactorily met. Castro used as collateral her entire homestead totaling some 219 acres in Rancho Soquel, her 1/9th claim to land in the "upper ranch" (lies between Rancho Soquel and a line drawn from the Laguna del Sargento to Loma Prieta), and all of the land that was situated north of the upper ranch. The loan was due in six months, with a penalty of ten percent of the balance due each month until the total balance was repaid. Without incurring a penalty, the full amount was due May 27, 1851.

Because the deed was written in English and Castro was illiterate, it is unclear whether she was aware at the time of the difference between the Article of Agreement and the deed signed the following day. Based on the events that followed, she probably was not aware. The full text of the deed follows:

STATE of CALIFORNIA
County of Santa Cruz

Know all men by these presents that we, Louis Depeaux and Martina Castro, both of said county, for and in consideration of the sum of $300, to us paid by Thomas Fallon. The receipt whereof is hereby acknowledged, do hereby give, grant, bargain, sell, and convey unto the said Thomas Fallon, his heirs and assigns forever, the one undivided ninth part of the following described piece of land situated in the county afore said, one of which said pieces of land lies on the Bay of Monterey and embraces two miles in length by half a league breath, a little more or less, said tract of land being known as the SOQUEL FARM, of said tracts of land adjoining the above described piece of land commonly known as the NEW GRANT, extending from said first described piece of land to the Laguna del Sarjento...and to the Chichutos...and the said undivided north part of the above mentioned piece of land, being the entire interest that we, the said Depeaux and

Castro, or either of us in anywise have therein together, with all the privileges and appurtenances to the same, in anywise belonging. To have and to hold the said tract of land to him, the said Thomas Fallon, his heirs, and assigns to their own use and behoof forever. And we, the said Louis Depeaux and Martina Castro, his wife, for ourselves, our heirs, executors, and administrators, do covenant with the said Thomas Fallon, his heirs, and assigns, that we are lawfully seized in fee of the afore mentioned premises, that they are free from all incumbrances that we have a good right to sell and convey the same to the said Fallon, as aforesaid, and that we will, and our executors and administrators shall, warrant and defend the same unto the said Thomas Fallon, his heirs, and assigns, forever against the unlawful claim of all persons.

Provided nevertheless that, if the said Louis Depeaux and Martina Castro, their heirs, executors, or administrators, shall pay unto the said Thomas Fallon, his heirs, executors, administrators, or assigns, the said sum of $300 on or before the 27th of May, 1851, then this deed shall be absolutely void to all intents and purposes, as also a certain promissory note bearing even date with these presents signed by the said Louis Depeaux and Martina Castro, whereby for value received, their promise to pay to the said Thomas Fallon, or order six months after date, sum of $300, with interest thereon, after the first six months, at the rate of ten percent per month until paid, said note bears no interest for the first six months after the date thereof.

On testimony whereof, we have hereunto set our hands and seals this 27th day of November, 1850.

Louis Depeaux
X [Martina Castro's mark]

Signed sealed and delivered in the presence of:

Peter Tracy
T. R. Per Lee

STATE OF CALIFORNIA
County of Santa Cruz

On this, the 28th day of November, 1850, personally appeared before me, T. R. Per Lee, County Judge of said county, Louis Depeaux and Martina Castro, known to me to be the persons described in the foregoing deed and whose names are subscribed there, and the said Louis Depeaux acknowledged to me that he executed the same freely and voluntarily, and for the purposes therein mentioned.

And the said Martina Castro, having been made acquainted with the contents of such deed of conveyance, on an examination apart from and without the hearing of her husband, acknowledged that she executed the same freely and voluntarily, without fear or compulsion or under influence of her husband, and that she does not wish to retract the execution of the same.

In testimony whereof, I have hereunto set my hand and affixed my private seal, the day and year above written.

T. R. Per Lee, County Judge,
Santa Cruz County[109]

Bishop Joseph Sadoc Alemany arrives in Monterey

Born in Vic, Spain on July 13, 1814, Joseph Sadoc Alemany studied for the priesthood at Viterbo, Italy and completed his studies in Rome in 1837 as a priest of the Dominican Order. In 1840, he moved to the Ohio River Valley, where he perfected his skills in the English language, becoming an American citizen in 1845. In 1849, he travelled back to Rome to attend a general chapter meeting, where he was appointed the first Bishop of Monterey. Although he argued against this appointment, he accepted it and was consecrated a bishop on June 30, 1850 at the Church of San Carlo al Corso in Rome.

Alemany arrived in San Francisco in December 1850 and assumed his post in Monterey shortly afterwards. Jurisdiction over Baja California, which remained part of México after the end of the Mexican–American War, was disputed when Alta California became part of the United States. Alemany attempted to spread his authority over the entirety of his mandate—Baja California, the state of California, and the territories that would become Nevada, Utah, and Arizona—but México fiercely protested his authority and the United States government did not appreciate him interfering in Mexican affairs. Church officials in México refused to deliver tithes and other funds gathered from its congregations to the diocese of Monterey, which further slowed his ability to unify the churches under his authority. Nonetheless, he still reported some progress during the first plenary council meeting in Baltimore in 1852.[110]

Dr. John Vandenberg arrives in Santa Cruz from San José

Dr. John P. P. Van den Berg was born in Aachen on the River Rhine (now in Germany) in 1815. He received his early education in his native city before entering the University of Bonn, where he received a doctorate in medicine in 1831. After graduation, he went to Brussels where he was engaged in medical practice. He was next commissioned as Assistant Surgeon to the British Army in eastern India, but through the influence of a medical friend, he resigned his commission and remained in the hospital service in England for three years.

In 1839, he came to the United States, where he engaged in the practice of medicine first in Lancaster, Pennsylvania and then later in Richland, Ohio. It was during this time that his surname became Vandenberg. He moved to Iowa in 1847 but soon crossed the plains for California in 1850, arriving in the San José area around August. He opened a mercantile shop in town but quickly became dissatisfied. The allure of Santa Cruz County drew him away from San José in mid-1851.[111]

Mount Diablo established as principal point for Northern California's meridian

In order to properly subdivide the state, establish county and municipal boundaries, and attend to the several land claim disputes that had arisen since the United States had acquired California, a principal point was established at Mount Diablo from which a meridian and base lines could be drawn throughout Northern California and Nevada. United States Deputy Surveyor General for California Leander Ransom established this point in 1851 and Richard Howe drew the principal meridian the following year.[112]

Congress passes an act concerning the settlement of Spanish and Mexican land grants

The debate that began in Congress with the submission of William Jones' report to Secretary Ewing on April 10, 1850 ended with the enactment of a bill submitted by Senator William McKendree Gwin on March 3, 1851. The bill passed in spite of provisions in Articles VIII and IX of the Treaty of Guadalupe Hidalgo that guaranteed protection for all property rights of Mexican citizens, in effect throwing the burden of proof on anyone who claimed lands granted by the Spanish and Mexican governments.

Each and every person claiming land in California by virtue of any right or title derived from the Spanish or Mexican government had to present the same to a board of three commissioners alongside any documentary evidence and testimony of as many witnesses as the claimant could gather to support their claims. This commission was appointed by the president to serve a three-year term, although that term was ultimately extended by two years. Provision was made for a secretary skilled in Spanish and English and up to five clerks to be selected by the commissioners. The secretary's primary duties were to act as interpreter and keep records of all proceedings.

After hearing arguments in favor of a claim, the commissioners proceeded to examine the evidence "and to decide upon the validity of the said claim, and, within thirty days after such decision is rendered, to certify the same, with the reasons on which it is founded, to the district attorney of the United States in and for the district in which such decision shall be rendered."

When a claim was rejected, an appeal could be made to the district court for review. The petition from the commission to the district court had to be accompanied by a full statement of the claim and a transcript of the commissioners' report. If the district attorney decided against the claimant, the claimant could appeal to the Supreme Court of the United States.[113]

Father Llebaria is appointed head priest of Mission Dolores in San Francisco

In 1849, Father Juan Francisco Llebaria, vice rector of the Ecclesiastical Diocesan Seminary of St. Vincent de Paul (now Notre Dame Seminary) in New Orleans, was sent to Panama. But soon after his arrival, his health began to deteriorate, and he was allowed to leave to take up a post in California. Once in San Francisco, he was appointed head priest of Mission Dolores and anglicized his name to John Francis Llebaria to better suit the English-speaking laity.

He soon met the head of the diocese, Bishop Alemany, who elevated Llebaria to the rank of vicar general. Shortly afterwards, the bishop sent him to Marysville in Northern California to establish a church.[114]

Antonia Lodge marries Henry Winegar Peck

On May 12, 1851, Henry Peck married Martina Castro's fifth daughter, Antonia Lodge. She was sixteen and he was thirty-three. The difference in age, while not uncommon for the time or place, may have led to Peck making several poor decisions regarding his wife and his business throughout his life. These ultimately resulted in his divorce from the former and the collapse of the latter. Nonetheless, Peck played an important role in the history of the Soquel ranchos until his death on September 14, 1873.[115]

Helena Lodge marries Joseph David Littlejohn

Joseph (José) David Littlejohn was probably born near Monterey in 1835. Although he was of Scottish descent, he was born a Mexican citizen since his father, David Littlejohn, had received citizenship several years earlier in order to qualify for a land grant. David was granted Rancho Los Careros in what would become Monterey County in 1834.

Joseph was no older than sixteen when he married Martina Castro's sixth daughter, Helena Lodge, on May 21, 1851. She was around fourteen at the time. Among Martina's children, Helena was the only to marry a man close to her own age. Neither of them could read or write, and with

Helena almost constantly pregnant—she gave birth to fourteen children in a span of sixteen years—they had few opportunities to better themselves.

Helena's niece Carrie Lodge recalled that "Joseph knew quite a lot outside work. He knew horses like his hands. He knew how to drive, knew outside work, but that's about all." Little else is known about their lives.[116]

Money borrowed from Thomas Fallon by Martina Castro and Louis Depeaux to pay county tax bill is due

On May 29, 1851, the $300 that Louis Depeaux and Martina Castro had borrowed from Thomas Fallon to pay their property tax came due. It is unknown whether the amount was repaid; during the Rancho Soquel Partitioning Suit that followed, Fallon claimed that it was not paid, while Castro claimed that it was. The agreement itself disappeared and was never found.[117]

Charles McKiernan settles on the Summit

Charles Henry McKiernan was born in County Leitrim, Ireland on March 22, 1830. According to most accounts, he joined the British Army in 1848 to avoid the terrible famine in Ireland. He was sent to serve in either Australia or New Zealand. But after gold was discovered in California, he joined the crew of *El Dorado* bound for San Francisco. When the ship arrived on January 15, 1850, he fled without paying his fare and headed for Trinidad in Humboldt County and then went on to the gold fields in the Sierra Nevada. He quickly amassed $12,000 in gold dust at the mines at Rose's Bar on the Yuba River. Using his small fortune, he bought thirty-two mules and four horses and organized a pack train to supply the miners with provisions. He charged $1.00 a pound for anything from sugar to bacon, turning a quick profit on his first trip to the mines.

McKiernan returned to Marysville where he bought ten additional mules and hired three helpers to assist him in the three-day journey to the mines. But hostile Native Americans attacked, and McKiernan escaped with nothing but his life. He tried panning for gold once again. He recounts: "I went to work again in the mines of the Feather River at Rich's and Smith's bars, and continued there until I had spent the balance of my money, becoming 'strapped,' as the miners used to say when a man had lost all of his money. Arriving in Santa Cruz via San Francisco and finding that there was nothing for me to do there, I started for Oregon over the Santa Cruz Mountains." Stories told that there was good farming land in the Santa Clara Valley, but because the valley was hopelessly clogged with rival land claimants and squatters waiting for the Land Claims Commission to establish ownership, McKiernan decided to head to Oregon and avoid the court battles entirely.

Stories of "Mountain" Charlie McKiernan differ. Some state that he attempted to settle in the Santa Clara Valley before coming to Santa Cruz, while others claim he started in Santa Cruz and moved away. The second seems the most likely since it establishes the reason why he settled on the Summit: he had been there before. Presumably, he took the Franciscan Trail between Santa Cruz and Santa Clara, pausing at the Laguna del Sargento near the top of the ridge. He spent approximately seven months living on the Summit in a hollowed-out redwood tree or a cave beginning in June 1851. He was helped by at least one other man, who sawed enough wood for McKiernan to build a cabin.

The location of this cabin was lost for some time and was frequently confused with his second cabin, which was situated on the west side of the lagoon, south of today's Summit Road on land that he later purchased. McKiernan eventually hired a gardener to tend his land and the gardener lived in the first cabin, which later passed into the family of Diana C. Larson. It has been greatly expanded upon and improved but still sits at 22196 Summit Road, halfway between Mountain Charlie Road and Stagecoach Road.[118]

Frederick Augustus Hihn settles in Santa Cruz

From his arrival in Santa Cruz on September 20, 1851 at the age of twenty-two until his death on August 23, 1913 at eighty-four, Frederick Augustus Hihn was the most prominent pioneer of the county, the man with the greatest land holdings, the one who paid the greatest amount in property taxes, and the county's first millionaire.

On August 16, 1829, Friedrich August Ludewig Hühn, as he was originally known, was born in Holzminden, Brunswick (now in Germany).

In addition to his mother and father, the latter of whom was a merchant, Hühn's family consisted of six brothers and two sisters.

After graduating from the gymnasium (high school) in Holzminden at age fifteen, Hühn entered the mercantile house of A. Hoffman in Schöningen as an apprentice merchant. Three years later, at the age of eighteen, he entered into the business of collecting medicinal herbs and preparing them for sale. During this time, his dislike of his country's government began to create within him a yearning for political liberty. Just as he was preparing to depart for Wisconsin, news arrived of the gold discovery in California. He could not resist the temptation and decided to join the great throng leaving in search of gold.

He booked passage on the brig *Reform* on April 20, 1849 with about sixty others and sailed out of Bremen, heading for San Francisco via Cape Horn. Two months later, the brig reached Rio de Janeiro. To Hühn, the land seemed like paradise—the beauties of the tropical scenery and vegetation and the balmy air, filled with the delicious odor of orange blossoms, entranced him. But they were disenchanted by the large gangs of overburdened slaves. After five days of rest, the ship set sail again. Opposite the La Plata River, they endured a terrific storm. Not long afterwards, they passed through the Straits of la Maire and came into view of Cape Horn, a tall cliff jutting boldly into the ocean. It was midwinter and the thermometer was low, but all thronged to see the great column and bid adieu to the Atlantic Ocean. It seemed to them as if they were entering a new world.

Two weeks later, they landed at Valparaíso and, after resting for four days, they sailed off again. At last, on October 12, 1849, after passing through the Golden Gate, the ship entered San Francisco Bay. The harbor was full of ships, most having brought gold seekers. *Reform* docked near the foot of Washington Street not far from Montgomery Street. San Francisco was then just a small town, but every nationality seemed to be represented. After a short stay, Hühn in the company of several companions from *Reform* headed for Sacramento.

Friedrich Gerstaecker, one of Hühn's companions, documented his travels in California. He explains:

We started on the 27th of October in good earnest for the

> *mines; but the reader ought to have seen us. Our little party consisted of seven souls, and a motley company it was, three of them being merchants' clerks, one an apothecary, one a sailor, one a locksmith (the locksmith and one of the merchants' clerks were brothers), and myself.*

Gerstaecker describes Hühn as "a stout young fellow, of about twenty years of age, with a green hunting-cap, yellow overcoat, trowsers [sic], and half boots, a striped bag over one shoulder, a rolled-up blanket over the other, and a double-barreled gun in his hand." The apothecary was Johan Ernest Kunitz, who later came to Santa Cruz and became Hühn's neighbor.

After encountering and overcoming several obstacles in Sacramento, Hühn's party finally reached the South Fork of the Feather River in early November 1849. They bought a mining claim and prepared to establish a camp for the winter, but soon after arriving, it began to rain, and it kept raining. The Feather River rose and washed away their tools and they had to subsist for a while on manzanita berries. The flooding prompted several debates over land rights and gold claims, prompting the party to pack up and return to Sutter's Fort on November 18. After a short rest, they continued to Sacramento, where they arrived on December 1, and the party disbanded.

Hühn and Johan E. Kunitz remained in Sacramento and opened a confectionery, which proved very popular. They did a good amount of business for a few weeks in December, but then disaster struck suddenly. Around Christmas, the American River overflowed its banks, destroying their little candy factory. With few financial resources at his disposal, Hühn headed for the mines at Long Ear on the American River near Auburn.[119]

While in Auburn, Hühn took his first step toward becoming a United States citizen and submitted his naturalization papers on June 6, 1850. It was probably at this time that he Americanized his name to Frederick Augustus Hihn. After moderate success in the mines, Hihn returned to Sacramento in August 1850 and became the proprietor of two hotels on K Street named the Uncle Sam Mouse and the Mechanics Exchange. But a year later, he noted in his diary that "times were getting very dull." He soon sold both houses and headed for San Francisco, where he opened a drug store on Washington Street near Maguire's Opera House.

On May 5, 1851, a fire broke out in San Francisco and burned down much of the city that had developed over the preceding three years. Hihn was heavily impacted by this disaster. Over the next five months, he wrote almost daily in a private diary about his struggle living in San Francisco and his attempts to make a profit in frontier California:

> May 5: The great fire swept down Washington Street to the Bay; my drug store with nearly all its contents gone. I had a lot of goods in Hutton's Auction Store on Washington, below Montgomery, found it abandoned and everything in confusion; before I could find my goods, the house became full of smoke, nearly killing me, got out the back door. Had saved a few things out of the drug store, which I sat up with during the night.
>
> May 6: Woke up at the house of my partner; he said he found me asleep with the goods and took me to the house. I looked up and saw a microscope I had missed for some time, felt in my pocket and found my purse with $500 gone. Swore vengeance.
>
> May 7: Went to live in a room in an alley off Clay Street, north of Dupont: collected small sums due me and invested all in buying ticking and hay to make mattresses.
>
> May 8: Made mattresses.
>
> June 20: Mattresses, dull sale; placed them for sale on commission.
>
> June 29: Great fire this morning; burnt out again, lost all my mattresses and all my stock. Down to bedrock again.[120]
>
> June 30: Discouraged. Made up my mind to go back to my fatherland. Was on my way to ship as a sailor to work my

passage. Passed by where my drug store was on Washington Street, found my old neighbor Brown clearing the coals from his place and some new lumber on the street. 'What are you doing, Brown,' says I. 'Getting ready to put up a shanty,' says he. 'What,' says I. 'Start your own shop again? I was burnt out twice in two months and I have given it up.' 'Well,' says he, 'someone has got to do business. It might just as well be someone else.' I pulled my hat down over my eyes, saying, 'What a coward I am.' I did not look any further for a vessel to go home on.[121]

July 3: Took the agency of the Sacramento Soap Factory.

July 4: Am selling soap to dealers and buying tallow, soda, and rosin for the soap factory.

August 12: Soap selling slow. Agreed with Hintch, a cigar dealer, who was also burnt out in the May and June fires, to buy out a lot of mules, pack them with goods and go to settle at Mission San Antonio of which I had read in Germany as having a fine climate and rich lands.[122]

August 14: We bought five mules with pack saddles and two horses, one for Hintch's wife, who is to go along. Commenced to buy the goods.

August 16: Am 22 years old today. How different from my last birthday at home, three years ago. There I had presents and good wishes from my dear parents and brothers and sisters, a beautiful wreath of flowers, and a fine cake. I have had to rough it ever since I left home and now all I have is $300, invested in a few pack mules and a little merchandise. But never mind. I was a boy then and am a strong man now, and I won't give up. My father and mother are getting old and they need my assistance.[123]

August 17: This morning we started for San Antonio. We had some trouble to pack the mules, but we got a fair start at 8 o'clock, arrived at San Mateo late in the evening, and camped under the oaks. The roan mare got away with the saddle on.

August 18: Could not find the mare. A Spaniard came along with a lot of horses, mules, and jacks. I bought a fine yellow mule and a jack from him for $90, my partner's money.

August 19: Hunted the mare again. Was riding Mrs. Hintch's horse with a side-saddle. Found a man riding the mare towards the City; claimed the mare. He says, 'All right, I picked the mare up; my team is right ahead, let us overhaul it and you can take the mare.' 'Allright,' says I, and so we went ahead, but the mare was fast and my old plug slow and the sidesaddle hard to ride on, so I could not keep up with him and he would not go slow. He soon got out of my sight, but I followed him, passed his team, and found him at Sanchez's fixing the saddle. I jumped off my horse and tried to get hold of the mare, but he said, 'Hold on, Sonnie, the mare is too good for you. I will keep her myself and you can go to h—!' He was a big powerful man and I a boy, but I did not mean to let him get away with the mare. So I drew my revolver and told him I must have the mare. 'You darsn't fire,' said he, and jumped at me, and struck the pistol out of my hand; it went off but did not hit him. He threw me down and held me, saying, 'My teamster will be here soon, and then we will finish you.' I heard the team coming.[124]

The next moment I was on top, with my hand on his throat. He had to let go, but only just in time before the teamster could get hold of me. He picked up my pistol, and I ran for the house. Three times the hammer clicked, but the barrels were empty. I had emptied them early in the morning, shooting at squirrels. I got into the house, the two men close after me. The Frenchman, who kept the house, took my pistol away from them as they entered. I smashed an old chair, took hold of a leg, got into a corner and kept the men off. The big man told the teamster, 'You hold him here, and I will get away with the mare.' No sooner had he gone than I drove the teamster away and followed the big man. I overtook him in a willow grove; he was fixing the saddle again. I jumped from my horse and took hold of the mare, while he grabbed a butcher knife which I had in a sheath on my side. 'Ah,' he said, 'now I will rip you open.'

I don't know how I managed to get the knife away from him, but I grabbed his hand and the knife was in my hand again. 'Well,' said he, 'my teamster will be here soon and that will settle your hash.' 'Yes,' said I, 'but you will die before he comes, unless you let that mare go.' It was awful for me to make up my mind to kill him—I was thinking of my folks at home and of God.

The team coming, and yet some distance off, I said to him, 'I will call for help three times, and if none comes, you die.' I called loudly, 'Help, help, help,' and just as the team stopped close by us and I was ready to drive my knife into his heart, three men came out through the bushes. I asked them to help me arrest the thief. He told them that he did not claim the mare, but that he had found her and wanted $10.00 for his trouble, but that I refused to pay him. The teamster backed him up in his statement, and the men decided that the mare should be given up to me and I should pay him $5.00. I hated to do so, but did it. The man went away on the team. I cursed the men for refusing to help arrest the man. They said, 'That man is the leader of a band of thieves; we are poor, and live close by here with our families; if we had helped to arrest him our houses would probably be burned and we would be murdered before daylight tomorrow. I went back to Sanchez and found that the teamster had got my pistol. Went back to camp.

August 20: Started anew on our voyage. Camped in the evening near Santa Clara Mission.

August 21: Passed through San Jose; was astonished to find such a fine large town. Camped 18 miles south of San José.[125]

August 22: Arrived at San Juan at noon. Our mules' backs had got sore. Decided to rest them for a few days. Hired a room in an old adobe near McMahon's store and displayed our goods.[126]

August 24: Mr. Breen and his family were about the only white settlers there, except McMahon and a French baker.[127] All the others were Californians; they flocked into our store as soon as we opened. Neither my partner nor I could speak Spanish, so I tried to make use of what I could remember of Latin. They would say, *'Es un padre.'*

August 25: Had picked up some Spanish and tried it for the first time. A senorita came in to buy a handkerchief. 'Un peso,' I ought to have said, but I did say, *'Un beso.'* She took the handkerchief and I took *un beso* [a kiss].

August 30: Nearly all the goods sold. It was decided that I should start the next day, take the horses, mules and jack, and go to the City, keep the yellow mule and roan mare and sell the other stock, buy a wagon and a load of goods, and come back to San Juan.

    Two Spanish gamblers had been watching me. I gave out that I was going to the City the next day, but I quietly started at supper time, got to the river about dark, turned down the river and then back again up the river above the crossing, tied my animals in the willows, had a few crackers and water for supper, and waited until near day break, when I started again on my trip. When about 20 miles from San

José, I met these two gamblers on horseback going towards San Juan. They must have followed me and finally returned, giving up the chase. I had $1,400.00 in my belt.

I greeted them, having my pistol in my hand on the pommel of my saddle, pointed at them, saying, '*Buenos dios, caballeros, como lo va.*'

They saw I was prepared and went on without troubling me.

Arrived at San José in the afternoon, stopped at the Mariposa Store.

Sold the jack and the mules, kept the yellow mule.

Fearing that the Spanish gamblers might have followed me, and it being a moonlit night, I went towards San Francisco. About midnight I arrived amongst the oaks on the Pulgas Ranch, when I fell from my horse fainting. I laid there about two hours before I became conscious, took the saddle off the mare, tied the horse to the fence, and had a good sleep until morning.[128]

September 1: Arrived in San Francisco last night, sold the old horse, bought an old wagon and harness.

September 6: Have bought a fine assortment of goods, intend to start for San Juan tomorrow. As I have never harnessed, hitched up or drove a horse, I hired Holm to assist me and to go to San Juan with me.

September 7: This morning early, Holm and I hitched up buckskin and roan and drove them to Commercial Street, where part of my goods was stored.

Holm could not drive, it took the whole street for him to get along, and he could not get to the front of the store, where the goods were. So we had to pack them to where the wagon was.

We then started to finish loading on Kearny Street,

finally got all loaded. I thought I had better drive, started, and ran into a cart.

The cartman swore great big blue oaths. I told him not to swear so hard, that I had never driven before, and that I was trying my best to get along.

Says he, 'Don't mind my swearing, youngster, a fellow has got to say something when he gets mad.'

'Here Jack,' he said, calling to a man who was standing nearby; 'Take care of my cart while I get this boy out of the scrape.' Then he got on and started the horses up. Then he started in again answering 'H—— & D——, who has harnessed up this team, the lines are wrong, everything is wrong.'

So he changed the lines and loosened the harness on top, and drove until we got out of the crowd near California Street. He would not take any pay, said he had taken it out in swearing.

September 8: Passed through San José, and got along all right, until we came to Fisher's when the tire came off the hind-wheel, and the wheel went down with two spokes broken.[129]

September 9: Made spokes out of oak saplings, got a raw-hide, cut it into strips, put the tire on, and wrapped it with the strips.

September 10: Started for San Juan, driving slowly. Holm had to walk behind the wagon and keep the tire on.

Arrived at San Juan in a dilapidated condition, but everybody turned out and welcomed us. I asked what was the matter. Then my partner told me that he never expected to see me alive again; that the evening I had left for the City the two Mexican gamblers inquired for me and, finding I had gone, they started late in the evening on horseback after me and returned the next morning, and then left the town, no one knew where to.

September 11: Wanted to unpack the goods I bought, but my partner said 'No. Let us go back to San Antonio.'

September 12: Started for San Antonio, team heavily loaded, went slowly

September 13: Arrived in Monterey, a dead town. Tresconi kept the Washington House, a fine hotel, had the best billiard table I ever saw. The U.S. Custom House a shabby affair. Joe Boston kept a store near the hotel, no customers, bought shoes from him much cheaper than in the City, also bought some goods of a German house very cheap.[130]

September 14: Started out again for San Antonio.

September 15: Camped last night in the Salinas Valley. Saw a big herd of antelopes early this morning.

September 16: Arrived at Mission Soledad. Only one inhabitant. Had a sign 'Tienda' [store] over his door.
'What have you got to sell,' I asked him.
'Barley,' said he. 'What else?' 'Lemonade.'
'Who buys?' *'De Repente Algunos,'* meaning occasionally a few.
The whole country looks indeed like a solitude. Am getting discouraged.

September 17: On our way for San Antonio. Got into deep sand, horses could not pull the load. My partner wanted me to whip them. I refused. Got off the wagon and said I would not go any further. He drew his pistol and said he would kill me. 'No, you won't,' said I, walking towards him; 'Put down that pistol or I'll knock you down,' showing him the butt end of the whip. He put the pistol down, and I took it away from him. 'Now,' said I, 'it is time for us to divide.'

He said he had the most money and wanted the team. 'All right,' said I, 'You take the team and enough more to make us even, and then let us make two piles out of the balance and throw up for choice.'

The piles were made, but by that time my partner wanted to know what I was going to do with my things. I told him that I expected to try to take them to Santa Cruz and sell them there and go back by schooner to the City.

As I had never before heard of Santa Cruz, except once casually in Monterey, I don't know how I came to select the place.

'Let us go to Santa Cruz together,' my partner said; at first I refused, but he begged so hard and I did not know how I could possibly get my goods out of this wilderness without a team, so at last I consented. The goods were packed again into the wagon, and the horses headed north towards Santa Cruz.

September 18: Stopped for lunch near the foot-hills. I went out to prospect for a road, found it. As I was coming back, I found both my partner and his wife in great agony and vomiting, and a terrible smell. I asked him what was the matter. He pointed to a small spotted animal that was hopping about, about the size of a cat. 'Chase it away, it is killing us.' I went after the animal, threw my riatta over it, dragged it until it was dead, and then brought it back to camp. 'Take it away, for God's sake, take it away,' my partner and his wife cried, and they commenced vomiting again.

I took it away and when I came back they told me that Mrs. Hintsch saw this animal hopping about in the grass, and thinking it was a rare animal, she threw her shawl over it to capture it, but the shawl went too far and the animal gave her a dose all over such as she will never forget. Hintsch came to her assistance and got a good dose too. That night I took their clothes, and the only ones they had, and buried them in a hole. The next morning the smell was all gone.

September 19: Crossed the Pajaro River, bought a fine water melon from an Indian, who has a little garden on the banks of the river. The melon was very fine.

September 20: Arrived on bank of San Lorenzo. The axle of our wagon broke. Saddled buckskin and rode over to the town to get a team to take our goods across and to get a place to stop in. The first man I met was Andy Trust. I asked him about team and a place, but he looked at the yellow mule and did not pay any attention to what I said. I went up the street and met Jim Prewitt.[131]

He did the same as Trust. But finally he told me that the place next door was vacant, and that Mr. Case had charge of it. So I went to see and hired the place from him, got Fairchild's team to haul the goods over, and before evening we were housed in the *chaloupe*, as the Spaniards called it, at the junction of Front and Willow Streets [Pacific Avenue], and our mare and mule were in the back yard.[132]

While we were eating our supper, I heard a good many people, and went out into the yard to find what was the matter. 'Good evening, gentlemen,' I said. 'Am glad to meet you, but would like to know what I have here that makes you laugh so much.' That made them laugh more. Finally, one man spoke up, saying, 'Where did you get that yellow mule from?' 'I bought him,' I said, 'over a month ago over near San Mateo.'

'That is my mule,' said Captain Whiting, 'he was stolen from me in this town about that long ago.'[133]

'Prove that,' said I, 'and you can have the mule.' 'Everybody knows my mule, what say ye people?' 'Yes,' they all said laughing. So I had to give up the yellow mule.

Many times I had refused to sell or swap him off, but it was all right anyhow, he must have inspired me to bring him home.

After his arrival in Santa Cruz, Hihn discontinued making entries in his diary. Reflecting on the above events several years later is a Santa Cruz local item published on May 11, 1877 entitled "Judge Lynch Not Always Right":

> *A correspondent sends us the following instance of dangers of lynch law, showing the narrow escape one of our now prominent citizens had here in the early days:*
>
> *In 1852 a very respectable and intelligent looking Spaniard was hanged here, and not by fathers and families, for stealing a horse, as it was charged, but there was not one iota of proof against him. He said he had bought the horse at Pajaro, and his appearance was greatly in his favor. F.A. Hihn first entered this town with a mule, which had been stolen from captain Whitney, and which Mr. Hihn had exchanged a poor horse for, at Gilroy, giving $50 to boot. Mr. Hihn at that time was not fluent with his English, but his word was taken, just as the poor Spaniard's should have been. I fear the example set lately. Every hoodlum may think himself equal to administering the law. Let us proceed with the lawyers if criminals escape after this.*

Hihn established himself in a residence at the junction of Pacific Avenue and Front Street, while Hintch and his wife returned to San Francisco.[134]

Lambert Blair Clements and John S. Mattison elected Justices of the Peace

Two residents of Soquel ran for the position of Justice of the Peace in the October 1851 election: John S. Mattison and Lambert B. Clements. Both men were elected, and then reelected the following fall. Besides serving as a Justice of the Peace, Clements was in partnership with Asa C. Sanford, running a mercantile store in Santa Cruz along the San Lorenzo River near Water Street.[135]

Father Llebaria appointed head priest of Mission Santa Cruz

After Father John Llebaria returned from his assignment near Marysville, he reported to Bishop Alemany in Monterey. He was soon afterwards given the post of head priest at Mission Santa Cruz. He remained in this position until mid-1853.[136]

Land Claims Commission convenes in San Francisco

The first meeting of the Northern California unit of the Land Claims Commission convened in San Francisco in January 1852, while its parallel board in Southern California met in Los Angeles at the same time. Notices from both commissions for grantees and landholders to appear before the panel were sent out immediately, although the first ruling in California was not issued until August.

The exact date that Martina Castro was notified that she was to appear before the Land Claims Commissioners to present proof of her claim to Rancho Soquel is unknown, but she was told to present her petition on April 17. Castro and Louis Depeaux hired Durrell Stokes Gregory to represent them before the commission, and he immediately began gathering the necessary evidence to support her claim.

In order to pay Gregory, Castro and Depeaux decided to lease Rancho Soquel to Gervis Hammond for a period of five years. Hammond moved to the county in mid-1849, where he worked in several timber operations within Rancho Zayante. The next year, he was elected as the county's first Assessor. He moved to Soquel in 1851, where he built a home overlooking Soquel Creek. He partnered with Hugh Pablo McCall, a French Canadian that had come over the Santa Fe Trail in the mid-1830s, to harvest timber within Rancho Soquel.

The agreement signed by Castro and Depeaux gave Hammond and McCall the right to cut timber for five years, while the partners agreed to pay the couple $1,500 for the first year and $2,500 for each subsequent year.

It needs to be emphasized here that this agreement completely contradicts both the Article of Agreement signed on August 28, 1850, and the deed signed the next day, in which Castro agreed not to sell or otherwise dispose of any part of the ranch that her children lived on. The agreement with Hammond ended unexpectedly in 1854 when Hammond died at his home.[137]

Martina Castro is abandoned by husband Louis Depeaux

Sometime in March 1852, Louis Depeaux deserted Martina Castro. In an agreement signed on October 28, Castro stated that "he has deserted me and I don't know if he will ever return." By this point, only ten-year-old Guadalupe Lodge still lived in the family home. Even fourteen-year-old Miguel Antonio Lodge had moved out and was probably living with his sister, Antonia, and her husband, Henry Peck. This meant that Castro had to face her first meeting with the Land Claims Commission alone. She was also dealing with two lawsuits: one by I. Belden & Company and another by John Hames, who wanted to recover the $5,000 that Michael Lodge owed him for building the first sawmill on Soquel Creek in 1846.[138]

Land transfer from Lambert and Josefa Clements to Pruett Sinclair and Jones Hoy

In the first transfer based on Martina Castro's deed of August 29, 1850, the Clements sold Josefa Lodge's one-ninth land claim in Rancho Soquel and the augmentation for $2,000 on March 30, 1852. The couple had plans to move to San Francisco and start a business and wanted to relieve themselves of their responsibilities in Soquel. However, by demanding her portion, Josefa also forced Martina Castro into partitioning her land, something she had been reluctant to do despite the previous agreement. With the land divided, Thomas Fallon could use the language of the deed, which was written by Lambert Clements, as well as the loan agreement he had made with Castro and Depeaux on November 29, 1850 to acquire all of Rancho Soquel.

Not much is known about either of the men who purchased the Clements' land. Pruett Sinclair was a Frenchman who changed his surname after arriving in the country from 'Saint Claire' to Sinclair. Many years later, one of his sons married a daughter of Carmel Cota and Thomas Fallon. Jones Hoy, meanwhile, was a forty-niner who afterwards took up a job at Isaac Graham's lumbermill in 1850. Sinclair and Hoy set up a small lumbermill in 1853 in the hills above Corralitos and logged the redwoods in the area for several years before selling their land to Benjamin Hames, a brother of John Hames.

With their sale finalized, the Clements moved away, although they returned in 1860 following several failed business ventures in San Francisco. Clements was also dragged back to Santa Cruz on several occasions both to aid Fallon in his plots and to support his in-laws during the Soquel Partitioning Suits.[139]

Martina Castro presents her proof of ownership for Rancho Soquel to the Land Claims Commission

On April 19, 1852, Durrell Gregory officially submitted proof of ownership of Rancho Soquel to the Land Claims Commission on behalf of Martina Castro, his client. His petition reads:

> *Petition to the Board of Land Claims Commission for ascertaining and settling private Land Claims within the State of California, from Durrell S. Gregory, attorney for Martina Castro Depeaux concerning her Rancho Soquel.*
>
> *Your Petitioner, Martina Castro, a resident of Branciforte of the County of Santa Cruz in the State of California, respectively presents to your Honorable Board that she claims a certain tract of land called Soquel, containing ten miles longitude by half a league more or less, situated in the County of Santa Cruz in said State of California. That she claims the same in fee, virtue of a grant made to Martina Castro under the authority of the Mexican Government by José Figueroa, Governor of the Territory of Upper California, bearing date, Monterey, 23rd of November 1833, and approved by the Territorial Deputation on the 17th of May 1834.*
>
> *Your petitioner further presents, that the said grantee of the 5th of February 1852 transferred her right in said land to Gervis Hammond in a lease for five years.*
>
> *Your petitioner would further represent that the mea-*

sured possession of said tract of land was given to the said grantee on the 14th day of August, 1834, and the boundaries thereof designated and defined, and she has been in the legal possession thereof ever since; and that she has no knowledge of any interfering claim.

Your petitioner presents here with the original grant of said land in the Spanish language, together with a translation of the same, and will make further proof of title if required by the Board.

Your petitioner prays your Honorable Board to take into consideration her claim to said tract of land and decree her title to be valid, and confirm the same.

And your petitioner will ever pray,
Durrell S. Gregory, attorney for claimant[140]

Plank and Turnpike Act passed by State Legislature

On April 20, 1852, the California state legislature passed the Plank and Turnpike Act, which allowed private groups to organize joint stock companies in order to build private toll roads, stipulating that, after twenty years, the roads would become public property.[141]

Route of Principal Meridian for Northern California surveyed from Mount Diablo through Santa Cruz County

Since the earliest United States surveys, townships and sections have been located and planned in respect to principal axes which pass through an origin called an initial point. The north-south axis is called the principal meridian, while the east-west axis is the base line.

Public lands, at least in the American West, are divided into townships, sections, and quarter sections. Further subdivisions are made after the land has passed into the hands of private owners. Townships are generally measured as six square miles and are divided into thirty-six sections, each approximately one square mile in size. Because of the uneven terrain in

California, though, the actual sizes of townships and sections can vary significantly and few along the coast are actual six-mile squares.

Richard Howe was contracted in 1852 to run the Principal Meridian for Northern California and Nevada, called the Mount Diablo Meridian. This line would be used to triangulate the boundaries for all townships and sections in the region.

Howe began his survey at the summit of Mount Diablo and intended to run it straight south to its intersection with the Pacific Ocean. But because of the difficult terrain in the Santa Cruz Mountains, he elected to meander through the Santa Clara Valley by means of offsets along section lines of several miles, entering Santa Cruz County through Pajaro Gap and then down the Pajaro Valley, ending just to the west of the present town of Aptos, which he calculated was due south of Mount Diablo. He then ran the meridian south to the top of a bluff in what is today Seacliff State Beach Park. From there, he ran the line north again to the top of the first ridge above what is now known as Aptos Terrace, thereby completing his assignment as best as was possible at the time. No changes would be made to this initial alignment for six years.[142]

Land sold by the United States government to fund public schools in California

On May 13, 1852, California was given a total of 500,000 acres of public land to sell through an act of Congress in order to fund a statewide public school system. Within the provisions of the law, it was made clear that only public land could be used—no land from within the boundaries of a Spanish or Mexican land grant was eligible.

Government land in the United States dates back to the end of the American Revolution, when the United Kingdom gave 451 million acres to the newly independent country as part of the Treaty of Paris in 1783. From that date forward, any land acquired through conquest, cession, or purchase, with the exception of Texas and Hawaii, that was not otherwise privately held fell under the control of the Bureau of Land Management or its predecessors. When California was annexed to the United States in 1848, all unowned land became government land and it fell within its purview to decide what to do with that land. This is one of the reasons why the Land Claims Commission was so important—with such vague boundaries between grants and unclaimed land, it was vital to establish ownership. While the Commission did its work, surveyors mapped the new state to discover what would become government land.

As townships were plotted in California, Sections 16 and 36, assuming they had no mineral value, were set aside for school land warrants. Under state law, this land could be purchased for as little as $1.25 per acre but could not exceed 640 acres by one applicant. Once the land was purchased, it could be used for speculation or as collateral for the purchase of other properties, a practice often used by buyers.

The confusion of the early years, when the Land Claims Commission was still settling grant boundaries and establishing ownership, meant that many townships were plotted without setting aside Sections 16 and 36, while others placed those two sections within land that was later determined to be a grant. When either of these situations happened, the purchaser was granted public land of equal value. This procedure became so common that it was known as "floating the warrant," and the purchaser often had no choice other than to float to the new land's location.[143]

John Watson and Durrell Gregory lay out Watsonville on and Watson builds an illegal shingle mill on Rancho Aptos

Born in Georgia in 1814, John Howard Watson attended West Point to become an officer in the United States Army but never graduated. He moved to Texas in 1840 where he studied some law, may have gotten married, and possibly killed a man. This final act may have been what prompted him to leave and head to California. He arrived in San José in 1850 and, shortly afterwards, was elected a judge of the Third District Court, which included Contra Costa, Branciforte, and Monterey Counties. He only remained in this position for a year before resigning the position to Craven P. Hester.

Watson settled in the Pajaro Valley in 1852 and became active in the local community. He joined in partnership with Durrell Gregory, who was Martina Castro's attorney before the Land Claims Commission, and the two moved onto the 5,496-acre Rancho Bolsa del Pajaro. Once there, they began to lay out a town. The illegality of this action does not seem to have bothered either man. Even though Sebastian Rodriguez had been granted the land by the Mexican government in 1837, it was only in 1860 that the grant was patented, by which time the settlement was already established.

The naming of the town did not fall to Watson, but rather to a British-born forty-niner named Henry Fell Parsons who was serving as deputy sheriff. While filing paperwork, he scribbled the name 'Watsonville' on a map to describe Watson and Gregory's township. He resigned as deputy in late 1854 and took a position in the County Recorders' Office under Peter Tracy, where he later became involved in the Rancho Soquel lawsuits.

While Watson and Gregory were laying out Watsonville, Watson also built a shingle mill on Aptos Creek in 1853. It was located about two miles north of today's Soquel Road and was complete with a flume, millpond, and support facilities. Whether he knew that the land was claimed by Rafael Castro and ignored that fact or honestly thought that the land was public is not known, but based on his actions in the Pajaro Valley, he likely knew he was acting illegally. In any case, Castro soon discovered the mill and forced Watson to relinquish the facilities to him.

Watson only remained in Santa Cruz County until 1855, at which time he became Collector of the Port of Monterey. During these years, he travelled to the Nevada Territory regularly in search of gold, almost being killed at one point in a skirmish with Native Americans. He was elected to the California State Senate in 1859 but resigned in 1861, leaving California permanently and becoming a lawyer in Nevada. He briefly moved to the Idaho Territory in 1865 but returned to Nevada where he served as Justice of the Peace in Mountain City. He fell ill in 1881 and died in Elko, Nevada, on August 2, 1882.[144]

Peter Tracy applies for School Land Warrant

Peter Tracy applied for the first School Land Warrant in Santa Cruz County on June 28, 1852. Warrant No. 228 was for 160 acres of land just below the headwaters of Bates Creek within land that would later be determined to be within Rancho Soquel's augmentation land.[145]

Benjamin, Uriah, and Merritt Nichols arrive in Santa Cruz

Benjamin Cahoon Nichols was born in New York in 1830 and, along with his brothers Uriah and Merritt, came to California in 1852. Little is known of the brothers except that they moved to Santa Cruz soon after arriving in the state and worked at a sawmill in Branciforte Gulch together.[146]

John Vandenberg moves to Rancho Soquel

In 1852, Francisco and Nicanor Lajeunesse ran a small rural general store from a building 500 yards from their home on Rancho Soquel. John Vandenberg, who had settled in Santa Cruz, liked the area around the Lajeunesse home and soon relocated to an eighty-acre tract nearby, where he built an expansive home. After settling into his new property, he opened a new medical practice in Soquel.[147]

The Schultheis family settles on the Summit

John Martin Schultheis was born in Bavaria in 1826. In his youth, he learned cabinet making and farming. He moved to the United States as a young adult and settled in Ohio, where he married Susan Byerly. Soon after their marriage, they decided to head west and arrived in the Santa Clara Valley in 1852 but found the political situation of the ranchos difficult to navigate. Therefore, they decided to settle on the summit of the Santa Cruz Mountains.

It took John and Susan Schultheis three days to bring all of their belongings to the summit with them, using an oxen team to haul the wagon. They were forced to drive their oxen team through thick brush in several places to make it to the top of the ridge. Once there, the couple chose a site beside a small lagoon that was located near the corner of today's Old Santa Cruz Highway and Summit Road. The indentation of the lagoon is still visible, although it has since been plowed over and used for growing crops.

After the Schultheis settled, they planted several orchards, a vineyard, and fields of grain to feed their livestock. John and Susan had a total of four children, all born on the Summit. Susan became well known in the area as a nurse and midwife and often traveled as far as Boulder Creek to see patients.

The Schultheis home still stands today at 22748 Summit Road. It is believed to be the oldest building in the Santa Cruz Mountains, although it has been covered with new lumber to preserve its integrity.[148]

Suit filed by Thomas Fallon against Martina Castro regarding the partition of Rancho Soquel

On August 2, 1852, Thomas Fallon filed Case No. 74 with the Third District Court against Martina Castro regarding her inaction in partitioning Rancho Soquel and the Augmentation. In addition to him, the plaintiffs were his wife, Carmel Cota, Jones Hoy, and Pruett Sinclair. Their attorney was Henry Richardson. The defendants in the suit were Castro, Nicanor and Francisco Lajeunesse, Luisa and Jean Fourcade, Antonia and Henry Peck, Helena and Joseph Littlejohn, Guadalupe Lodge, and Miguel Lodge. Their attorney was Durrell Gregory. The complaint was filed as follows:

> *Thomas Fallon and Carmel Lodge, his wife, Jones Hoy and Pruitt Sinclair, residents of the county of Santa Cruz and plaintiffs in this suit, represented by Henry Richardson, their attorney, come into this court and complain that they hold and are in possession of certain real estate situated in the County of Santa Cruz, State of California...which they hold as tenants in common with the defendants, named herein, and they now file their complaint to obtain partition of the said lands and real estate according to the respective rights of the parties interested therein in, pursuant of the statute in which case made and provided.*
>
> *And the said plaintiffs further show that the said Martina Castro Depeaux has seized and possessed in her own right by...a tract of land...known as the Rancho of Soquel, containing an area of land two miles in length by a half league in breath, more or less as laid down on the map, which accompanies the said grant and which is bounded on the west by the Soquel River, on the south by the Bay of Monterey, on the east*

by the Sanjon de los Borregas, and in the north by the Laguna Biena, and being also seized and possessed of a certain other tract of land adjoining the last mentioned premises, comprising an area extending from the Biena de las Yesca as far as the Laguna del Sargento and la Chuchita, including the Loma Prieta, which said mountain grant of land was made to the said Martina Castro by Manual Micheltorena, Governor of Alta California, on the 9th day of February 1844.

And the said Martina Castro Depeaux, so seized and possessed of the afore premises, and on the 29th day of August 1850, by a certain deed, executed by herself and her then husband Louis Depeaux, and acknowledged signature by him, did convey unto each of her children one-ninth of the premises....

And the said plaintiffs further state that on the 30th day of March 1852, Josefa, the wife of Lambert B. Clements, joined in a deed with her husband and conveyed all her rights in the said estate onto the said plaintiffs, Jones Hoy and Pruitt Sinclair, who now hold and possess the same; and the said plaintiff Thomas Fallon and Carmel, his wife, still hold and possess the individual one-ninth part thereof, and that each of the defendants are seized and possessed of an individual ninth part of the said estate as tenants in common with the other parties of this suit.

And the said plaintiffs allege that the interests of the said plaintiff, as well as those of the said parties hereto named as defendants, would be greatly [enhanced] by a union and [combining] of the said estate of Rancho Soquel with the area added by Manual Micheltorena (and since this added land is comprised chiefly of mountainous terrain not acceptable of cultivation, which the plaintiffs allege could not properly be set off in farms; therefore, this upper added land should be sold and the proceeds thereof be divided among the parties).[149]

Gervis Hammond, Thomas Wright, Montgomery Shackleford, and Craven Hester apply for School Land Warrants

On August 3, 1852, Gervis Hammond, Montgomery Bell Shackleford, and

Thomas Wright applied for School Land Warrant No. 90, which comprised 160 acres just to the north of the warrant granted to Peter Tracy two months earlier. Meanwhile, newly appointed District Judge Craven Hester applied for two adjacent 160-acre plots—Warrant No. 37—in the far north below Summit Road and along Amayo Creek. He settled on this land and led a relatively quiet life for the next six years.[150]

Land transfer from Jean and Luisa Fourcade to Montgomery Shackleford

On September 10, 1852, two deeds were signed between Montgomery Shackleford and Jean and Luisa Fourcade. In the first, the Fourcades agreed to sell Luisa's one-ninth claim to Rancho Soquel and the Augmentation to Shackleford in exchange for $6,000, with $1,000 paid up front and a mortgage deed agreed to settle the remainder. In the mortgage deed, Shackleford was to pay the remaining balance in two installments, the first of another $1,000 and the second the full $4,000, but no date was specified for either payment. Both deeds were received and acknowledged by Thomas Wright, who was serving as Peter Tracy's assistant at the County Recorders' Office.[151]

Transfer of part of Nicanor Cota's land to Thomas Wright, Peter Tracy, and Montgomery Shackleford

In a deed signed September 19, 1852, Nicanor Cota and Francisco Lajeunesse sold 878 acres of their one-ninth claim in Rancho Soquel's augmentation to Thomas Wright, Peter Tracy, and Montgomery Shackleford. The section was located north of Rancho Soquel, from the junction of Soquel and Bates Creeks north to the junction of Grover Gulch and Bates Creek (at the end of today's Prescott Road). This deed was later misrepresented by the grantees, who insisted that all of Cota's claim was sold to them. This meant that Wright, Tracy, and Shackleford claimed 1,211 acres in total.[152]

Agreement between Martina Castro, Durrell Gregory, and John Wilson

In an attempt to settle her growing legal problems, Martina Castro made an agreement with Durrell Gregory and John Wilson on October 28, 1852 for the two attorneys to provide legal services for her in exchange for profits derived from Rancho Soquel. Wilson likely joined the case due to his indirect relationship to Castro. Wilson's wife, Maria Ramona de Luz Carrillo y Lopez, was a sister of Michael Lodge's first wife, and it may have been through this relationship that Wilson first came into contact with Castro. His and Gregory's agreement with Castro reads:

> *That the same Martina Castro owns and possesses in her own right and separate property two ranches in Santa Cruz County, one called Soquel, on which she resides, and the other called "San Miguel," of which is in the possession, both of which granted in her own name and as her separate property many years ago by the Mexican Government.*
>
> *That she is the wife of Louis Depeaux, who has abandoned her and left her without his aid to manage her property, and she knows not whether he will ever return to aid therein in the management thereof.*
>
> *That it is necessary to have the titles of these ranches confirmed before the United States Land Commission and that she is wholly incapable of doing so herself.*
>
> *That she is sued by one John Hames and also by J. Belden & Company and these suits need defending, which she is unable to do.*
>
> *She also expects other suits to be brought against her and has difficulties to settle with tenants and others. Also some of her children have by fraud and unfair dealing pretended to have obtained from her a conveyance of part of the said Rancho, which pretended conveyance she is desirous to have set aside by suit in court, which she desires to have brought immediately and to recover rents and profits and damages of them for taking possession and occupying portions of the same under this fraudulent transaction.*

She also desires to bring a suit against one John Hames for rents and profits and damages for unlawfully occupying a portion of the said Rancho and for cutting timber thereon, and she expects other legal difficulties in all of which she needs the aid of attorneys' counsel to attend for her these several matters and has no ready money to pay them; she therefore proposes to said Durrell S. Gregory and John Wilson to employ them as her attorney in all of these matters and to give them one undivided half part of the said ranches, therein rents and profits and all that may be recovered from said John Hames, and also what may be received from those who pretended to hold and possess under the before named fraudulent contract, in part payment for their legal services in all her matters; till the several matters are ended [and] by me abandoned, each of them, the said Durrell S. Gregory and John Wilson, to have a share and share alike in the said undivided one half of whatever shall finally be mine therein.

It is agreed that Durrell S. Gregory has brought the suit now pending against me by John Hames before this agreement is made and that one of the points likely to arrive in the suit by J. Belden & Company as the same as well arise in the John Hames suit now pending, and therefore Durrell S. Gregory is released from appearing for me therein by the said John Wilson is to do in all the other matters, above named, except as the above expected, and are to have half the rents issues and profits of all that is finally obtained or recovered in the same, except so far as the Soquel Ranch is concerned, by a lease and contract the said Martina Castro and her husband made on or about the 5th day of February 1852. The rents, profits and issues arising under the same is reserved out of the contract, and the said Durrell S. Gregory and John Wilson agree to and accept the above proposition, the said Martina Castro paying the legal costs and expenses of the afore proceedings.

Therefore, it is hereby agreed mutually between the parties fully and entirely to adhere to and abide by the said proposition and acceptance, and the said Martina Castro covenants to convey to the said Durrell S. Gregory and John Wilson their several shares as above stated, in accordance with this agreement, and the said Durrell S. Gregory and John Wilson each for himself agrees and covenants to do and faithfully perform the above agreement on their part, the said Durrell S. Gregory reserving the right not to appear in the suit to be brought against John Hames and, if he does so, the benefit of the results to the said John Wilson.

In witness, our hands and seals this day of October 28, 1852.

Witnessed by:
Gervis Hammond
Joseph Ladd Majors
[Martina Castro's seal]
John Wilson
Durrell S. Gregory

STATE OF CALIFORNIA
COUNTY OF SANTA CRUZ

On this 28th day of October A.D. 1852, before me, B. C. Whiting, Notary Public in and for the County of Santa Cruz, aforesaid, personally came Durrell S. Gregory, John Wilson and Martina Castro Depeaux, to me known to be the persons as described, and who executed the within conveyance or contract and acknowledged (the said Martina Castro Depeaux acknowledging separate and apart from her husband) that they severally executed the same freely and voluntarily and for the uses and purposes therein mentioned.

Witness my hand and private seal. The day and year first above written, having no National Seal at present.

B. C. Whiting, Notary Public

Both Gregory and Wilson initially answered the Land Claims Commission summons concerning Rancho Soquel's augmentation, but Gregory later withdrew. Wilson remained invested in Castro's defense, possibly out of familial solidarity.[153]

In Defense of My Own   1852

Peter Tracy applies for additional School Land Warrants

Peter Tracy added to his School Land Warrant holdings on November 19, 1852 when he applied for Warrant Nos. 327 and 329, both located north of Prescott Road along Bates and Grover Creeks and immediately south of his previous warrant land. All three were registered by the state on December 20.[154]

Thomas Fallon applies for School Land Warrants

Thomas Fallon applied for three School Land Warrants on November 27, 1852, totaling one square mile and forming a square. Warrant No. 108 was twice the normal grant size, measuring 320 acres, while Warrant Nos. 353 and 354, located directly to the north of No. 108, each totaled 160 acres. The three warrants were located within Rancho Soquel's augmentation, along the east side of Soquel Creek just north of the rancho's original southern boundary. They were registered by the state on December 20.[155]

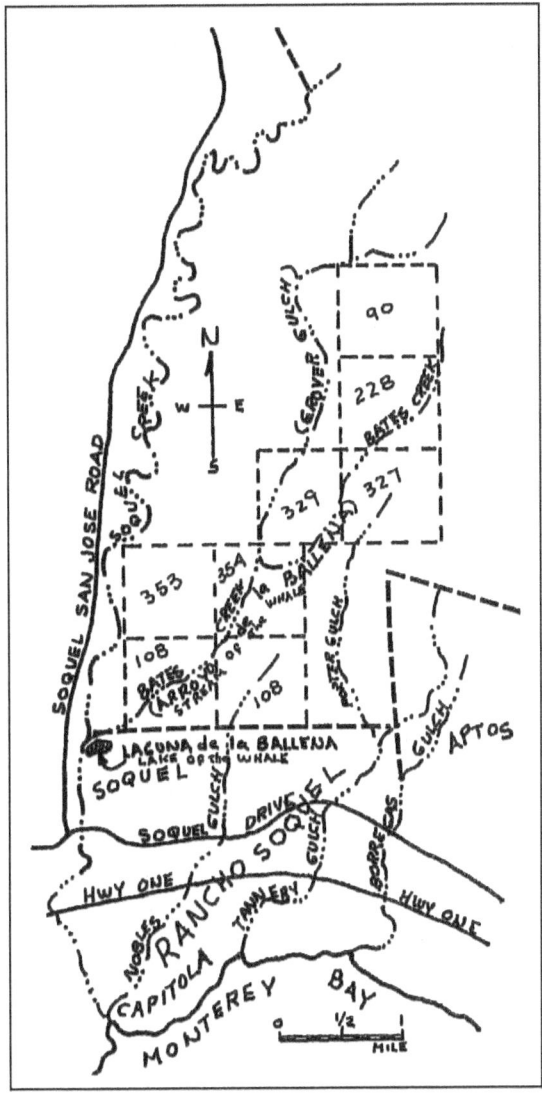

FIGURE 3.1 SCHOOL LAND WARRANTS ALONG RANCHO SOQUEL'S NORTHERN BOUNDARY

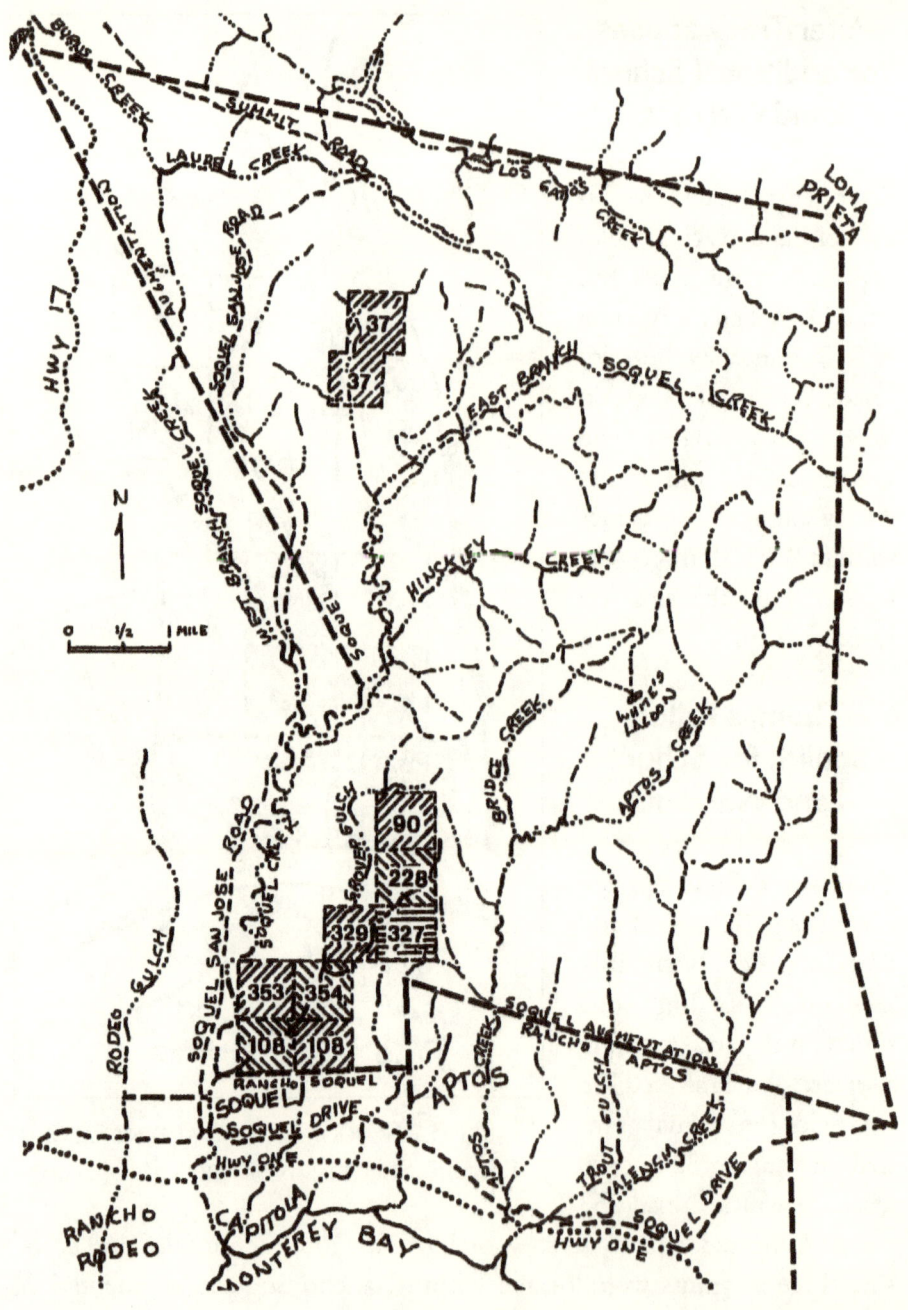

FIGURE 3.2 SCHOOL LAND WARRANTS IN RANCHO SOQUEL'S AUGMENTATION

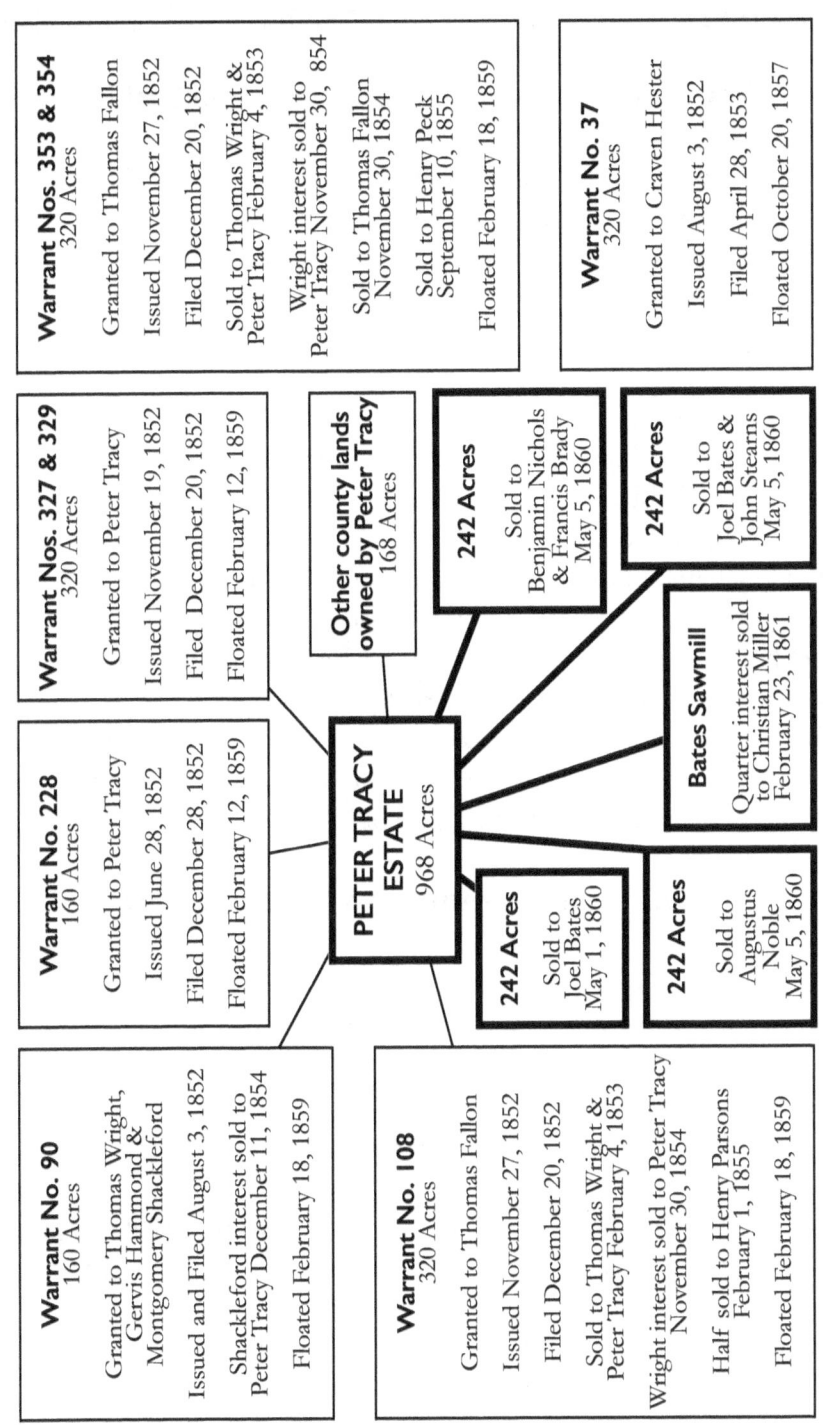

FIGURE 3.3 SCHOOL LAND WARRANT PURCHASES AND TRANSFERS

Frederick Hihn reenters the mercantile business

Around the end of 1852, Frederick Hihn decided to reenter the mercantile business and opened a general-purpose store that soon began to prosper. As his business grew, he erected what was then considered a fine two-story building, with his business occupying the first floor and his living quarters the second.

After this structure was built, hard times hit Santa Cruz County. Wheat, potatoes, and lumber—the principal products of the region—were rendered almost worthless. Wheat sold for a cent a pound, potatoes rotted in the fields, and lumber went down from $55 to $12 per thousand board feet. Faced with customers who could not afford to pay cash—and he could not afford to sell his goods on credit—Hihn decided to exchange his goods for the products of his customers when they did not have cash available. The wheat he received he ground into flour, while lumber, shingles, and flour were shipped to more lucrative markets, such as Los Angeles, Monterey, and San Francisco. Some days, more than $500 worth of eggs and chickens were received and shipped to San Francisco. Fresh butter was put in barrels and sold in the fall and winter in place of imported butter.[156]

Louis Depeaux returns to Martina Castro

Based on a letter dated July 22, 1853, Louis Depeaux returned home to Martina Castro in early- to mid-1853. Why he left and where he went is not known.

Robert Peckham is elected District Attorney

Robert Francis Peckham was born in Charleston, Rhode Island on January 30, 1827. He was the oldest of a family of nine children and they were poor and depended on the income provided by their father, which did not average fifty cents a day. Peckham's education was confined to what he could get at a common country school for less than three months in a year, between the ages of four to sixteen. Early in life, he developed a taste for

In Defense of My Own 1853

books and a proficiency for learning that gave him, even as a mere child, a widespread reputation. He also enjoyed machinery and mechanics and had a love for the sea.

At the age of twelve, Peckham learned the multiplication table and within three months he was master of all the rules and problems in Nathan Daboll's *Arithmetic* and, the following winter, he mastered Columbus's *Algebra* and the mathematical part of surveying and navigation. Two years later, he went before the examining board and was granted a certificate authorizing him to teach at any public school in the county. Shortly afterwards, he began teaching in the same schoolhouse where he had received his education.

After serving in various positions in his home state, Peckham answered the call of the sea and signed on as a green hand on a whaling ship in 1845 at the age of eighteen. Apparently, the romance of a seafaring life had worn off when the vessel docked in San Francisco. He jumped ship with only the clothes on his back, four sea biscuits, and a plan to hide out until his ship sailed.

After four days, starving and thirsty, Peckham headed south, hoping to find someone who could at least let him know if the ship had departed. He found two Mormons, victims of persecution of the time, who were living at Mission Dolores in San Francisco. They shared their food with him, and the next morning one of them went to check on the whaler. It was still in port.

Peckham stayed with the Mormons for ten days waiting for the whaler to leave. Restless, he headed south to San José, selling his boots to a Californio he met along the way, and continuing barefoot over the clover burrs and prickly grass.

During the next few years, Peckham worked washing wheat, farming, soldering, shop clerking, and looking for gold in the Sierra foothills. It was in this final capacity that he met Thomas Fallon and Jean Fourcade, sons-in-law of Martina Castro, while prospecting on the Stanislaus River. He was present around the time of the murder of Michael Lodge and he was one of the few witnesses aware of the fact that all four people were in the same place at that time.

Not long after his encounter with Fallon and Fourcade, Peckham turned away from the gold fields for Sacramento. Along the way, he met a party of immigrants who had crossed the mountains that year from the Mississippi Valley. In the party was a young lady, Ann E. Smith, to whom he was married in San Francisco on January 14, 1849. After the marriage, he moved to San José, where he opened a mercantile establishment in a tent. In 1850, he was viewed as a potential candidate for district attorney, but in order to qualify he had to become a lawyer and he had only studied during his leisure time for about four months. Under the mentorship of the lawyer Augustas A. Heslup, and after a grueling and extensive examination, his answers were found to be as intelligent as those of a candidate applying for admission to the State Supreme Court. He was soon admitted to the bar, which allowed him to run for District Attorney. He lost the election.

Undaunted by his defeat, Peckham applied for a seat when the District Court opened in San José. He was admitted to the bar of the court on motion and without examination. He hung a new sign on the old blue cloth tent that his mercantile business occupied formally announcing himself as "attorney at law." But business did not come. At this early period in California history, most looked upon an attorney as a rather ridiculous sight. But as legal problems and lawsuits began to compound, especially those relating to the Land Claims Commission, the situation quickly changed.

Peckham decided to leave San José in 1850 and moved to Monterey, where he remained for a year. After his move, clients began to appear. His income only averaged about $25 a month while his cost of living continued to climb. He took up farming, concentrating on growing potatoes. When the bottom of the market fell out in 1851, Peckham began to despair of not being able to make a living in law. Though he had kept up his studies, he was driven by sheer necessity to turn his attention to something else.

In fall 1851, Peckham moved to Salinas, deciding to continue his farming there, and he took up a quarter section of what was represented to him by adjoining ranchers as being public land. After he settled, his neighbors managed to have his land surveyed and included in a grant. Thus, he became the first successful squatter in the Salinas Valley. He fenced his forty acres and sowed it with grain, but the year had been dry and very little grew. However, he made his house into a stage stop on the route between

San José and Monterey, and he subsisted primarily on lending horses and providing goods, such as beef, bread, sugar, and coffee. Meanwhile, he kept up with his study of law in the hope of one day achieving a higher position.

In 1853, Peckham moved again, this time to Santa Cruz, where he joined with George W. Crane to open a legal office downtown. He was elected District Attorney for Santa Cruz County in the fall and served in this position for three years while also attending to his own cases through his law firm. In both capacities, he handled several important cases that earned him both acclaim and undue attention. After his term ended, he remained in Santa Cruz County for nine more years, providing legal services for many including Frederick Hihn, Thomas Fallon, and Martina Castro.[157]

Lyman Burrell and his family settle on the Summit

Lyman John Burrell was born in Sheffield, Massachusetts on September 4, 1801 and settled in the Summit area in 1853. Burrell wrote several articles when he was in his eighties for the *Mountain Echoes*, a newsletter published for the Summit Literary Society by Mary B. Smith. Only ten issues were ever released between December 31, 1881 and November 25, 1882, and in them, Lyman proposed "to offer from time to time autobiographical notes, which shall form a series of profiles, the first of which we herewith present, and which we have styled Recollections of an Octogenarian by Col. Lyman John Burrell." His articles were aggregated into four extended pieces, the first two of which follow:

> *I was one of a family of eight children. We were brought up as New England farmers' children generally were in those days, with habits of industry, economy, and plain wholesome living.... I began to go to school at the age of two years and nine months, and walked a mile and a quarter to our schoolhouse. I learned easily and progressed so rapidly the first season, that I gained the enviable reputation of being a child of great promise. With a change of teachers the next season, I lost my interest in the lessons and became so fond of play that for several years I made but very little progress in book learning. I*

believe I learned more during my first school year than I did for several years after, because I had not then learned to play.

The old-fashioned schoolmasters of New England were generally good disciplinarians. Whatever other good qualifications they might have had, they were considered as trifling compared to this. They [believed like] Solomon, that to "spare the rod would spoil the child." Being a little, delicate, flaxen-haired boy, not able to make any formidable resistance, they regularly selected me as a good subject to practice upon. They seemed to consider it a duty as well as a pleasure to honor me in this way, and I soon became so accustomed to such honors that I looked for them as a matter of course and as a necessary part of my education. In those early days, it was considered a heinous offense to even smile in school.

I had an elder brother who used to enjoy seeing me in trouble. Instead of kindly trying to hide my faults and shield me, as a brother should, he would sometimes make faces and do funny things to make me laugh, that he might have the fun of seeing me so whipped. When I became old enough to be useful on the farm, I was kept at work during the summers, and went to school only in winter. Thus passed the first fifteen years of my life. On the whole, my early boyhood was a happy one, for I did not lay my little troubles much to heart.

About this time [1816], our family moved to [Lorain County] Ohio to make a new home in that vast wilderness. Here my pioneering commenced. Here all of my energies were put forth to fell and burn the forest trees, to dig up the roots, to plow, and to plant. I took real pleasure in subduing the land. But I still went to school in the winters for several years, and then my father sent me away from home to attend a seminary, where I stayed three terms and finished my school education.

At this time of my life, I was uncommonly fond of all kinds of sport, but fishing was my favorite. After a hard day's work with my axe, I have spent many a night in fishing; sometimes wading half of a night in cold water and catching so many fish that a wagon had to be sent in the morning to bring them home.

At the age of twenty one years, my father gave me one hundred acres of land. It was partly covered with beautiful black walnut trees. He fitted me out as well as he was able, and I started forth to fight life's battles alone. I was full of courage, strong, and hopeful. He gave me a cow, a horse, a colt, a pair of oxen, a wagon, an axe, and a good supply of provisions. My horse had one lame foot caused by the bite of a rattlesnake, and he was not much account. I depended chiefly on my oxen for help and used to drive them into town with my wagon when necessary. I soon built a house and brought home my young wife.

Previous to my marriage, I had been quite ill with chills and fever. I did not entirely recover from this for several years; and sometimes did not feel strong enough for very hard work. About this time, I taught school in winter.

I discovered too late, that in cutting down my black walnut trees and burning them, I had made a great mistake. If I had left them standing and worked elsewhere for a few years, I should have had a good fortune in them. But by industry and economy, I prospered. My farm was put under good cultivation and produced well. Then, when everything was complete and in good order, I became tired of the monotonous round of farming. I was a natural pioneer. I loved the excitement of it. I soon rented my farm, moved into town, and went to work in a stone quarry. I enjoyed this for a time, then turned my attention to buying cattle and selling meal. I also manufactured lard oil, tallow oil, soap, and candles.

I served my county two years as Treasurer. During all these years, I had many ups and downs, many joys and sorrows. Altogether, I had failed to become rich. I was not very well satisfied with my success in business.

In 1849, being then forty-eight years old, I was taken with the California fever. I thought "surely this is my road to wealth." I left my wife and three young children in Elyria, Ohio, where we had been living several years, joined a small party, and came with them overland to California. We were six months on the journey. It was a long and tiresome journey.

We were not molested by Indians or wild herds. Nothing of much consequence occurred to me on the trip except one accident which happened on the plains, being tempted away from my train by wild beasts, I shot a mature animal. The shot of my gun took off one of my fingers. I had plenty to time to nurse it. I soon recovered; because it came from my left hand, I did not considerate of so much consequence. I was able to work as soon as we reached our destination. I engaged in mining at once. It suited me. I became interested in it, and really enjoyed it. I still think there is no work I ever did that I liked as well.

After working about a year and a half, I returned home, having been absent two years. I carried home over $2,000 which I had saved. I went home by steamer. Unfortunately, I took the Panama fever and was only just able to reach home. I was very sick for a long time. I was able to do nothing for a year. I began to think that nothing but the climate of California would cure me; and, feeling a little better, I once more left my family and came to California. I came this time by steamer, and was only a month on the way. My lost health came back to me at once. I settled down in Santa Clara Valley near Alviso, with the intention of there making a permanent home for my family.

I commenced by taking land on shares, but an entire failure of crops resulted. I then worked for wages on a farm for a short time.

My family joined me the next year. We soon learned that the valley climate did not suit my wife. Her health was not good when she came, but instead of growing stronger as we had hoped, she continued to grow weaker. I then, for the first time, came to the Santa Cruz Mountains to look for a spot to make a "Mountain Home." I selected this ridge where I now live, and where my three children are settled around me. I then thought it was Government land. It seemed a vast, solitary wilderness, no houses and no roads. I knew that bears and lions dwell here, but I feared them not.

About this time, I had a very promising crop of potatoes growing in the valley. Wild cattle broke into the enclosure and *totally destroyed them. I considered this a great misfortune at the time, but I afterwards saw that it was all for the best. Though I had paid 12 1/2 cents a pound for the potato seed and had put in my time and labor, the loss of the crop set me free to leave home and come to the mountains.*

Other men in the valley whose crops were not injured by cattle had the satisfaction of harvesting, putting into sacks, and carting their potatoes to the "embarcadero," where they lay, for want of market, until they were dumped into the bay.

To quote from Leon Rowland: "Potatoes were worth a bit [12.5¢] a pound in 1851 and 1852. The flat lower valley of the Soquel was planted to them. By 1853, everyone in California who could was raising potatoes, and the price bubble burst." This was the situation that Burrell faced.

I returned to my home, put up a supply of provisions and tools, and with my son, then about thirteen years old, came back to the mountains to build a house. We camped out of doors, in company with another man who was building a house, about a mile from our location. We commenced by cutting down redwood trees, cutting them into proper lengths, and splitting them into bolts. We then hitched these bolts to the horse and dragged them up to the spot where our house was to stand, which was near the place where Mr. Sears' house now stands.

Here we split them into boards and built the house. Even the window casings and sashes were made of split lumber. As soon as the outside and the roof were on, we slept in the house, without doors or windows.

A bear's trail ran near the house. Every morning we could see their tracks as they had been passing back and forth in the night. They might have looked in upon us as we slept, but they never troubled us. For several years after, this seemed to be a favorite resort for bears. When the house was finished, we returned to the valley and made preparations for moving. I purchased enough flour to last a year and carried it to the house of a Mr. Forbes, who lived near where Los Gatos now stands. This was the man who afterwards built the stone mill

> *now known as "Roger's Mill" [Forbes Mill]. From there, we were to pack it on horseback in small quantities as we needed it.*

At this point in Burrell's story, some additional information by Stephen Payne in *A Howling Wilderness* must be added. Firstly, Burrell was actually married three times. His first wife, Mary Amelia Stillman, died a few years after their marriage leaving behind a young daughter, Eliza M. It was after Mary's death that Burrell moved to Elyria, Ohio, and there he married as his second wife Clarissa Wright. Clarissa produced one son, James Birney, born on August 4, 1840, and two daughters, Martha A. and Clarissa. Clarissa, too, died relatively young and Burrell took as his third wife Philomela Thurston Reed, whom he married as her second husband on February 19, 1876.

In the Santa Clara Valley, Burrell led an uneventful life near the future town of Alviso, but in his recollections above, he neglected to mention that he rented his land from James Lick, later of Lick Observatory fame. After his potato crop failed, he leased a different plot between Alviso and Santa Clara after his family arrived, but the marshy conditions in the area had an ill effect on Clarissa's health, prompting their move to the mountains. Near the Summit, the man who built his cabin at the same time as Burrell was probably James Taylor, who settled in the area at around the same time.

Burrell continues in his second article:

> *I have heretofore given you a brief sketch of my early life, my two trips to California, my selection of a home on the Santa Cruz Mountains, and of building a home here for my family. At that time, there was no one living in this vicinity. It might truly have been called a "howling wilderness:" for these beautiful hills and valleys, now covered with orchards and vineyards, comfortable houses, school houses, good roads, with all kinds of improvements going on, and everywhere teeming with busy life, were then the abode of fierce and dangerous animals. They made their homes in the thickets and hollow trees, and went forth both day and night to seek food for themselves and for their young. Wildcats and lions were often seen prowling about while the sun was shining; and the night was*

often made hideous by the howling of the coyote. There were a few wild cattle here, also deer and other game; but no roads or fences. The road from Los Gatos to Lexington was tolerably fair. From there to the top of the hill now known as the "Evans place," there was a very poor logging road; and from this hill to Mountain Charley's cabin was a foot trail which led down the southern slope of the mountains towards Santa Cruz. From Mountain Charley's cabin to our house there was not even a foot trail. No man had ever been known to drive over the summit with a wagon. It was considered not only a difficult, but a rather dangerous undertaking. In those days, a man could not safely travel very far alone, unless he was well armed, because bears were not infrequently seen on the trails, and they had not always the politeness to turn out for a man; but, on the contrary, they would, so inclined, dispute his passage.

There was, however, a brave and fearless woman living in Santa Cruz and having perhaps more courage than discretion, who resolved to go to San Jose by way of these mountains. For her to resolve to do a thing was to do it. She took her horse and buggy and an axe, and made her way alone, through thick and thin, over the hills, and across the canyons, from Santa Cruz to San Jose without harm. This was the notable Mrs. Farnham, a practical farmer and a natural pioneer, whom some of you will probably remember.

When we were ready to move up to our "Mountain Home," my wife was in very delicate health. It was feared that the journey would be too hard for her. A lady friend in Santa Clara kindly drove with her in a buggy across the valley to where the town of Los Gatos now stands. Here she rested in the house of a Spanish family. I hired four yoke of oxen and two wagons. An old friend, who had formerly been my partner in business, kindly offered to accompany and assist us on the journey. We packed our household goods on the wagons, also one little pig, which was put into a box, and a few chickens. The three children went along with us, riding or walking as they chose. We also took a saddle horse with us, on which my *wife was to ride. Towards evening, we reached the town of Los Gatos, then known as "Jones Creek," and here my wife joined our company. We made a good fire, ate supper, spread our blankets on the ground, and slept on feathers and in a palace.*

After an early breakfast, we began our second day's journey. The ascent of the mountains was not as easy in those days as it is now. We had no graded turnpike. The road we were to travel had been made for the purpose of getting down logs. It was very rough and steep, and sometimes very sideling. In some places, we found it difficult to keep the cattle from sliding off the lower side. We first went over Jones' Hill, a distance of about four miles, on the east side of the creek, then we crossed over and went to the top of another hill on the north side of Moody's Gulch, now known as the "Evans Place." We selected the top of this hill for our second camping ground. On climbing these hills, we had to double our team and carry up only one load at a time. Here we were all glad to rest. We made our fire, fed our cattle, and laid our supper on the tablecloth, which was spread on the ground. I well remember a little incident that occurred here, which gave us all a surprise: as we sat around the table on the ground, eating our supper, an inquisitive little snake, belonging to the Racer family [probably a western yellow-bellied racer (*Coluber constrictor mormon*)], *with more curiosity than politeness, quietly crawled across the lap of one of our little daughters, and then glided along the tablecloth gracefully curving his body around and between the dishes, peeping into this and that as he went along. Then suddenly he disappeared on the opposite side, before we had time to recover ourselves or to offer him any hospitality. This was our first introduction to the native inhabitants. We began to get some idea of the kind of neighbors that would be likely to call on us. We expected hardships and had prepared ourselves to meet them, but I fear we had not brought with us sufficient grace to take kindly to such company as this. We have since met with many of the same family, but never been able to feel any great friendship for them.*

We slept soundly the second night. We already began to feel

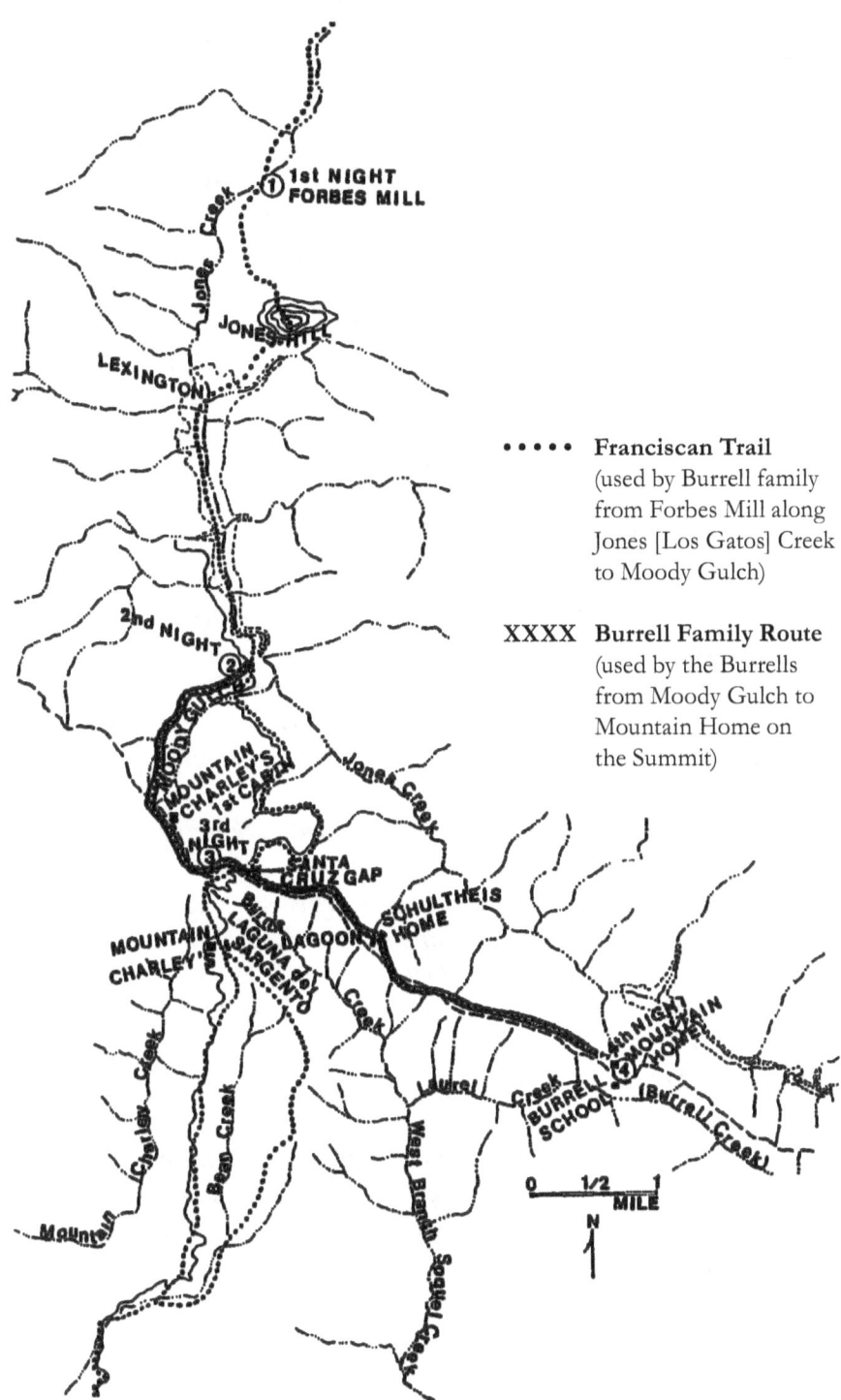

FIGURE 3.4 BURRELL'S ROUTE FROM FORBES MILL TO MOUNTAIN HOME

the benefit of the pure and invigorating mountain air. On the third day, we followed trails or made our way as best we could to the top of a hill near Mountain Charley's. It was so rough and steep that we had to partly unload our wagons and take up only a part of a load at a time, thus making several trips. After a hard day's work, and having made but very little progress, we camped near a large rock. The next day we had no trails at all to follow, but we finally reached our home in safety. We unpacked our goods and took supper in our own house. We all were pleased with our new home and its surroundings. We enjoyed the fine view of those magnificent old mountains to the north. We were delighted to see the waters of the Pacific on the south, nearly fifteen-hundred feet below us, and it seemed as if we had never seen such gorgeous sunsets as we then saw here. We laid many plans for beautifying and improving our place and then christened it "Mountain Home."

Even little piggy looked pleased when released from his long confinement. He seemed to enjoy his pen as well as we did our house—at least he found no fault with it. The chickens also seemed to appreciate their new home.

The next morning, our friend started back to the valley with the oxen and empty wagons. No other wagon, with one exception, came to these hills for the next five years. Everything and everybody went and came on horseback. We brought with us a supply of flour and other groceries, but we brought no meat. I depended on my rifle for that. I made it a rule to go out every Saturday afternoon and hunt for the ensuing week. I found plenty of deer, ducks, quail, and squirrels. I hunted, not for sport, but for support. The children were fond of trapping quails and were quite successful. In this way, we had a good variety of meat and plenty of it. Mountain Charley lived alone in a cabin about three miles from us. He was a famous hunter, especially among the bears. He killed many, but at last he was almost killed by one of them.

The next year, another family came. They lived in the house that was built the summer previous, about a mile from us. My family did not feel quite as lonesome after they came.

In those days, we kept a large dog which was a protection against the ravages of the smaller wild animals. He used to sleep on our doorstep. I recollect of being awakened one night by screechings and strugglings near our door. I sprang from my bed, seized my rifle and opened the door. It was too dark to take aim. I could see nothing at all. I knew by the sounds I heard that some animals had made an attack on the dog and that he was fighting for his life. I shouted but did not fire. The dog soon got the best of the fight and his enemy left. He was not badly wounded. He seemed greatly pleased with his victory. He was so excited over it that he sat on the steps and barked all the rest of the night. The next morning, I examined the spot and found plenty of lion's hair and tracks.

Soon after this, I brought another pig from Santa Clara and put it in the pen with the first one. We fed them mostly wild oats. They thrived well and soon gained a weight of 150 pounds each. One night, a lion went into the pen, took one of them out, and carried it off alive into the hills on the other side of the creek. We could hear it squeal for a long distance. In the morning, we saw where its feet brushed the dew from the grass it was dragged along. We thought the lion must have been uncommonly large to be able to take such a heavy pig over a high fence and carry it so far. Such was the fate of poor piggy! After a while, the other had a family of little ones. A hungry bear came along and robbed her of every one. At last, the poor mother herself met with a sad fate. Like many of the human family, she fell into temptation. She killed and ate a young lamb. As a penalty, she was lunched and packed in a barrel of salt the next day.

The bears were quite neighborly about our house, after coming in the evening or early morning, but never molesting the family. One night, when I was absent from home, a large bear came into the yard, examined everything about the place, licked the troughs where the hogs had been fed, and then went away. He was closely watched through the windows by the folks at home, but they thought it imprudent to fire upon him.

I once put up a large gate between the two oak trees now

standing in our school yard. There was a fence running north and south connecting with this gate. There had formerly been a trail leading between these trees, on which bears were accustomed to travel. We had often seen their tracks here. One night, a bear came along and found the gate in his path. He could easily have jumped over the fence on either side, but he scorned to do this, He turned not to right or left, but took hold of it, wrenched it from its fastenings, and laid it on the ground, thinking no doubt, that he was lord of the forest and always would be. A similar circumstance occurred near the sub spring in my son's vineyard, where also we had put up a gate. A bear unceremoniously removed it in the same manner. Sometime after this, I had a very unfortunate experience with two bears, and came very near losing my life by one of them.[158]

James Taylor with family settles on the Summit

Shortly after the Burrell family settled on the Summit, James Taylor arrived with his family in 1853. Taylor and his wife, Margaret, settled on the north side of the future Summit Road near today's junction of Morrell Road and Morrell Cutoff. After building his home, Taylor planted several orchards and fields of grain.

John Young writes that Taylor was well-known in the Summit District. "'Uncle Jimmy' and 'Aunt Margaret' Taylor, who attended all weddings and funerals in the region for nearly forty years. Kindly and benevolent, they were loved throughout the mountains…. [Taylor] had married 'Aunt Margaret' Higgins several years before. They had no children of their own, but adopted William Dennis."[159]

Jean Fourcade builds a tannery in Porter Gulch

Probably in late 1853, Jean Fourcade, in partnership with an older brother, began constructing a tannery near his home within Rancho Soquel on what is today the Cabrillo College campus. The first buildings were constructed just to the north of the County Road to Watsonville (today's Soquel Drive) on the east side of Porter Gulch. The site is visible from Porter Gulch Road heading north away from Soquel Drive on the right. Until Fourcade sold the facility to Benjamin Franklin Porter on January 1, 1858, it was constantly expanded until it occupied five acres, all enclosed with a fence. At that time, it consisted of a tannery, vats, flumes, aqueducts, three worker houses, outhouses, a barn, hen houses, machinery, and some fruit trees.[160]

Thomas Fallon sells School Land Warrants to Peter Tracy and Thomas Wright

For reasons unknown, Thomas Fallon sold his School Land Warrants to Peter Tracy and Thomas Wright on February 4, 1853. Wright was likely involved in this transaction because he was assisting Tracy in the Recorder's office and they saw an opportunity to turn a profit.[161]

Martina Castro presents to the Land Claims Commission her claim to Rancho Soquel's augmentation

On February 6, 1853, Durrell Gregory and John Wilson formally presented their claim for Rancho Soquel's augmentation to the Land Claims Commission on behalf of Martina Castro. Both men had much to gain from the ruling because they would each receive a quarter of the total acreage in payment for their services. Gregory also was involved in the division agreement in August 1850 and knew that the documentation concerning the legitimacy of the grant was questionable.

> PETITION TO: *The Board of Land Claims Commission from Durrell S. Gregory and John Wilson, attorneys for Martina Castro Depeaux concerning Soquel Augmentation Ranch.*
>
> *TO: The Board of Commissioners for ascertaining and settling private land claims within the State of California.*
>
> *Your petitioner Martina Castro states to the Honorable Board that on the 22nd of November 1833, she obtained a grant of land from Governor Figueroa, the Governor of*

Upper California, who had full powers to grant the same for a tract of land of about one league square lying there near the Town of Branciforte in the County of Santa Cruz and State of California. Which grant was called "Shoquel or Soquel" and reached on the sea coast from the Soquel River to the "Sangua de los Borregas," being more or less one mile and a half and two miles more or less back from the sea coast. Which grant afterwards was duly confirmed and allowed by the Departmental Assembly of the Republic of Mexico.

On the 17th of May 1834 and on the 2nd of August 1834, the said Governor Jose Figueroa, having full power and authority, confirmed the same and issued a final grant for the same. To your petitioner thusly vesting a full fee...thereto in your petitions.

That she was residing thereon before the date of the grant and has ever since and is still residing thereon, having complied with all the conditions required of her. There was no judicial...lien given her because the same was unnecessary, as she had long lived on and possessed the same before, as the records and papers now remaining of record as part of her [petition] fully appears. She shows here to the Board the record of her petition all the [evidence] thereon up to the final grant inclusive as part of this Petition marked "A" and a translation thereof marked "B." [The paper marked "A" is Francisco Alviso's EXHIBIT "A" of Rancho San Miguel submitted with his deposition dated August 14, 1853 and included with the February 9, 1844 Directive.]

Your petitioner also states to this Honorable Board that afterwards...and about the year 1844, when the cattle and sheep and other animals of your petitioner had greatly increased, as her family had doubled, so also the said tract of land being near the said Town of Branciforte and therefore much of the stock of the citizens of the place grazed and passed upon the land so granted to your petitioner, the same became entirely inadequate to support the stock. She owned and it was of the profits of her stock that she mainly supported her family...it became and was the policy of the Mexican Government *to give to citizens ample lands to any family in proportion to the amount of stock they possessed, and to increase the same from time to time as the stock and means of the Ranchero increased, because in the [wealth] and increase of the people was to be found the wealth and power of the government.*

...Therefore, she asked for an additional grant lying at an adjoining on the back of the others, from the sea shore, extending from the ridge to which her other grant extended called the "de la Yesca," up to the "Laguna del Sarjento" and "la Chuchita," including "la Loma Prieta," which place was called "Palo de la Yesca," of which land she had taken possession of before she so petitioned for the same, grazing her stock on it, cutting wood, etc., and has ever since...been in possession and has cultivated parts thereof, and she states that after due proper inquiries were made by Governor Micheltorena, who was then and thus Governor of Upper California and possessed the usual and ordinary powers of Governor, but was also clothed with the extraordinary powers as such, and on the 7th of January 1844, the said governor made a grant to the extent of the boundaries named in the petition, of which your petitioner obtained a full right to the same and has ever since occupied the same, and has fully on her part complied with all the conditions of the same as the law requires.

She also shows her petitions that the proceeding thereon and the grant of a second taken from the Archives of the Government.... Therefore, she prays that each of the said grants be fully confirmed to her and whatever else may be proper in the premises.

John Wilson
Durrell S. Gregory,
attorneys for the Plaintiff Martina Castro Depeaux

Filed in office February 16, 1853 by George Fisher, Secretary and Recorded in Volume No. 1 of Petitions on pages 578, 579 and 580

Land transfer from Henry and Antonia Peck to Montgomery Shackleford

On February 13, 1853, the Pecks agreed to sell Antonia Lodge's one-ninth claim to Rancho Soquel's augmentation to Montgomery Shackleford. It was Shackleford's third tract of land purchased within the Augmentation in six months but, like the previous two, it was incorrectly registered by Peter Tracy in the County Records office.[162]

Santa Clara County authorizes a turnpike from San José to the Santa Cruz County line

In 1853, there was a rough road from Los Gatos that ran up Los Gatos Creek and for the most part followed the old Franciscan Trail. The portion of the route to Lexington (a former town now under Lexington Reservoir near the James J. Lenihan Dam) had been improved by Zachariah "Buffalo" Jones, who lived nearby and operated a sawmill in the valley. Jones had settled in the area shortly after he arrived in the region around 1846 and he began charging a toll for every person that wanted to cross his land.

It was through Jones' land that John Frémont crossed later in 1846, and it was crisscrossed with skid roads to transport cut timber from the hillsides down to the mill. Although Frémont called these pathways roads, Jones viewed them as little more than bear trails. He later said: "Steep, rough, and in the summertime a wonderous place for dust, the trail in wintertime was a dangerous place for pack-trains and men alike. The bull teams that followed and the stagecoach that came later, with their iron-shod wheels, did little toward improving the route, simply transforming it into a pair of parallel ruts that provided a hair-raising ride for venturesome travelers."

When Charles McKiernan arrived on the scene in the early 1850s, he also improved portions of the Franciscan Trail and added new trails and roads. He primarily focused on the route between his home on the Laguna del Sargento to the south, toward modern-day Scotts Valley. He may have also tried to improve the route to San José, but the part of the trail to Los Gatos Creek displeased him, so he usually bypassed it by following the ridge to the top of Moody Gulch and then following that down to the creek, where he rejoined the Franciscan Trail. This is the route the Burrells took when they moved up to the Summit.

As the pressure to have a useable wagon road between San José and Santa Cruz increased, the Santa Clara County Supervisors relented and sent a party of explorers under the leadership of Sheriff John M. Murphy to examine the situation and report back. Murphy followed the Franciscan Trail from Los Gatos over the section that Jones had improved and then continued along the old trail until they reached McKiernan's bypass up Moody Gulch. They continued up this trail until they reached McKiernan's home, where they were delighted to find that they could continue on horseback to Santa Cruz along a route that could, with difficulty, support wagons. Murphy reported that, due to Jones' and McKiernan's efforts, it would only cost $10,000 to construct a wagon road from Lexington to the county line, a distance of about eight miles.

On March 12, 1853, the supervisors authorized the building of a turnpike from San José to the Summit according to the provisions of the Plank and Turnpike Act of April 1852. However, because the authorization did not specify the tolls and the county was unwilling to actually build the road, nothing immediately came of this authorization.[163]

Craven Hester files for additional School Land Warrant

School Land Warrant No. 37, which consisted of two separate sections of 160 acres each, was filed by Craven Hester on April 28, 1853. It must be noted that Hester, a district judge, knowingly purchased land in a contested Mexican land grant that fell within his jurisdiction, meaning that it was likely any process regarding the legality of the grant or school land warrants would reach his bench.[164]

Peter Tracy and Thomas Wright sign a lease granting Joel Bates access to their School Land Warrant properties

On June 16, 1853, Peter Tracy and Thomas Wright signed a lease with Joel Bates for the latter to cut lumber, mill, and graze livestock upon School

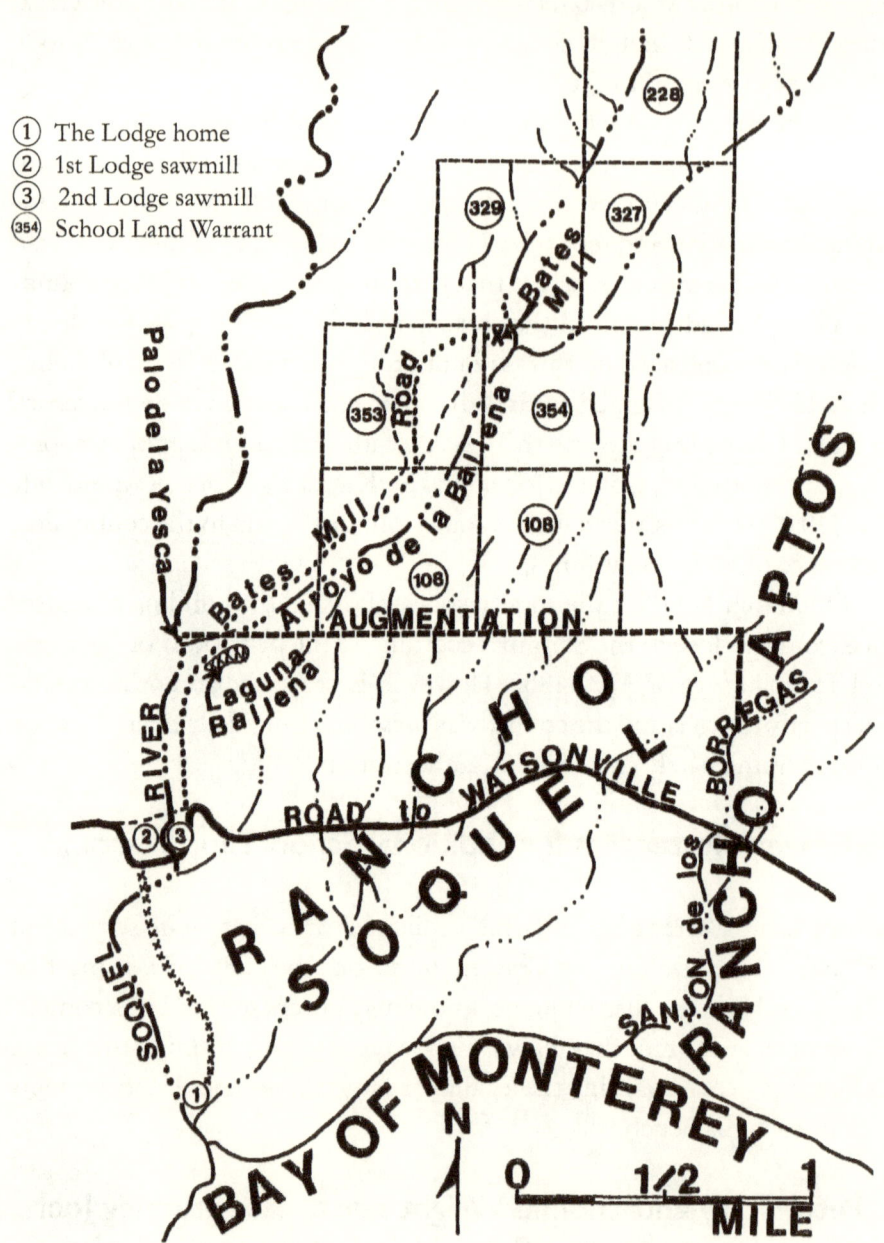

FIGURE 3.5 BATES SAWMILL AND BATES MILL ROAD

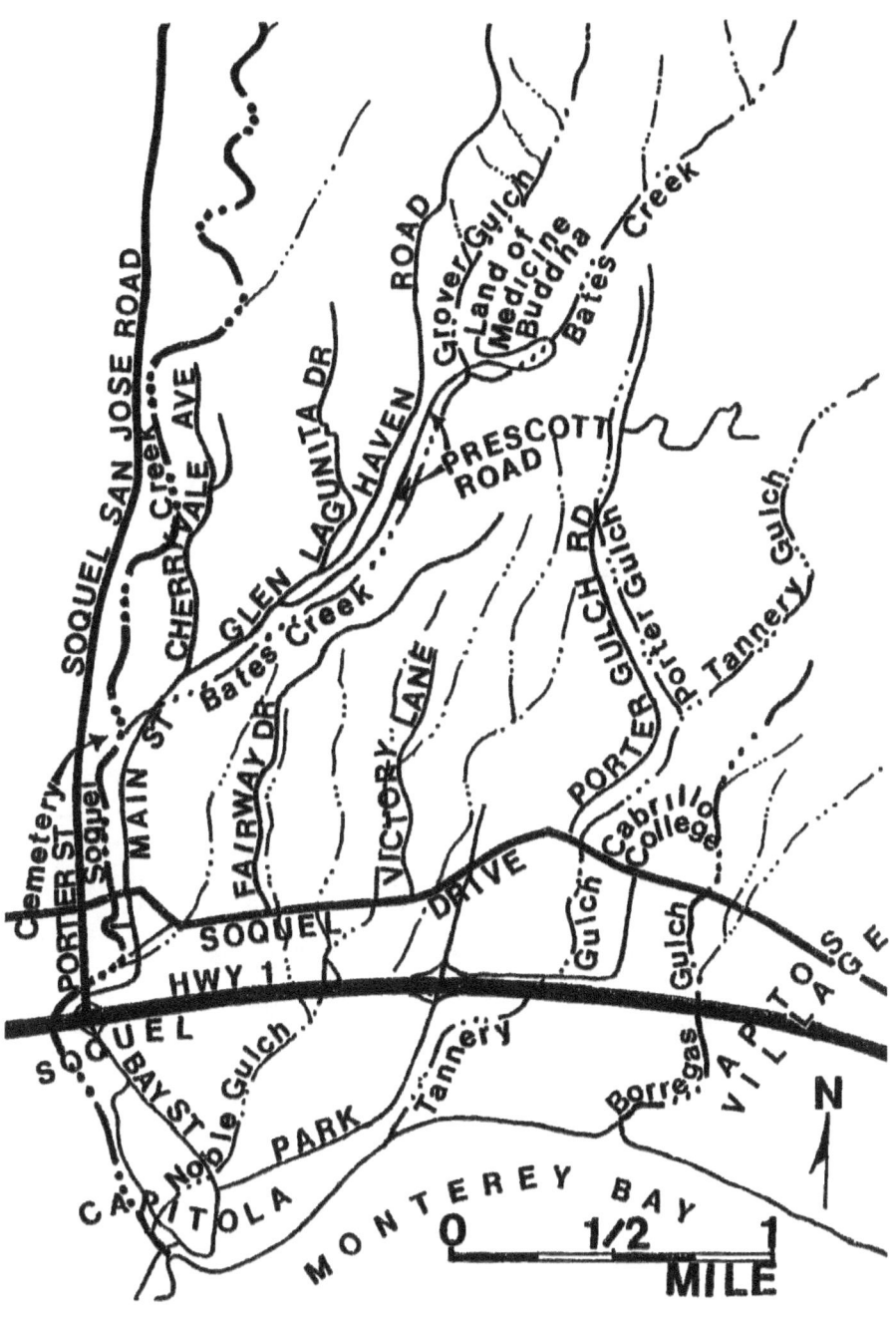

FIGURE 3.6 BATES CREEK AND TANNERY GULCH WATERSHEDS

Land Warrant Nos. 108, 353, and 354 for a period of two years, with an offer to renew the lease on a yearly basis for up to ten years.

Bates was a native of New Jersey and was born in 1806, but his forty-seven years before moving to Santa Cruz County remain largely a mystery. After signing the lease, he brought on two partners, Wilson K. Herrick and George K. Gluyas, and together they built the first steam-powered sawmill in Rancho Soquel. The mill itself was small compared to later mills on the property—its daily output was only about 15,000 board feet. It was located near the end of today's Prescott Road, where Grover Gulch meets Bates Creek.[165]

Letter from Louis Depeaux to John Wilson concerning Martina Castro's lands

On July 22, 1853, Louis Depeaux sent a letter to his and Martina Castro's lead attorney, John Wilson, concerning Rancho Soquel and its augmentation. It reads:

> *Dear Sir,*
> *I arrived here about 12 o'clock today. Tomorrow I will leave for Alviso and I think by Tuesday 1 will [be] in your city* [San Francisco] *with my witness* [probably Francisco Alviso] *and my wife and daughter to be ready by Wednesday to take the testimony of the witnesses before the Commissioners.*
> *I have been talking with the U. S. Surveyor and also with Mr. Gregory and they both think that it would be a good idea to have the Rancho surveyed and if you think it is of any use I wish you would get the order from the Surveyor General so I can bring it down with me and have it done immediately.*
> *Excuse my short letter but I hope that we can talk face to face within a few days.*
>
> Yours with respect,
> Louis Depeaux[166]

Land transfer from Jones Hoy to Joseph Majors

On July 25, 1853, two deeds were signed between Jones Hoy and Joseph Majors. In the first, Hoy sold his half of the one-ninth part of Rancho Soquel that he had purchased from Josefa Lodge in March 1852 to Majors. In exchange, Majors agreed to pay $4,000 for the property with $500 paid upfront and the remainder due by an unspecified date via a mortgage deed, with reversion of the property to Hoy if Majors failed to pay.[167]

Joseph Alemany ordained archbishop of Northern California

Three years after becoming bishop of Monterey, on July 29, 1853, Joseph Alemany became the first Archbishop of San Francisco. This new archbishopric covered an area that encompassed all of California north of Monterey as well as most of Nevada and Utah. He had an immense area to rule but few available funds or resources to build churches, create new parishes, establish an independent school system, or fund the recruitment of new priests.

Indeed, this final point proved to be especially problematic. An underpaid person, whether they are dedicated to the work of God or to some other interest, must eat and pay for the necessary items they need to survive. Because priestly work was demanding and the pay was so low, many priests were forced to find other ways to augment their income. But since a priest could not become involved in a commercial business, he had to find other means of making a profit, such as in real estate.[168]

Land transfer from Carmel Lodge to Joshua Parrish

On August 1, 1853, Carmel and Thomas Fallon sold Carmel's one-ninth part of Rancho Soquel for $800 to Joshua Parrish. According to Donald Clark, Parrish was "a forty-niner from Ohio, who took up farming in Soquel.... In 1853 Parrish made a trip back to Ohio; here he married Narcissa Dell. In 1854 he was elected road supervisor for Soquel. In 1870, the Parrish family helped establish the Soquel Congregational Church (the 'Little White Church') which was built on land donated by them." The hill to the east of the church was named after him. Parrish built a home, barns, fences, and several other buildings and planted an orchard on his property. His home was in the vicinity of today's junction of Capitola Avenue and Soquel Drive.[169]

Rafael Castro begins leasing land in Rancho Aptos

In the early 1850s, Rafael Castro began leasing parts of Rancho Aptos to individuals attracted to its redwoods, its minerals, and its farming potential. On August 1, 1853, he entered into an agreement with four men: Sosthène Maximilian Driard, Fortune Chevalier, Joseph Silvera Sr., and Peter Tracy. The agreement gave the four men several rights on Rancho Aptos, including allowing them to build a sawmill along the east bank of Aptos Creek within the vicinity of today's Aptos Village shopping center.

After the mill was completed and operating, Castro seized control of it and established the Cascade Grist Mill. Undeterred, the four men then built a second mill farther up Aptos Creek and resumed converting redwood timber into lumber. This operation continued until 1873, when several of the partners abandoned operations to search for gold in Australia.[170]

Thomas Fallon asserts his claim to all of Rancho Soquel, and Louis Depeaux and Durrell Gregory are added as defendants

Because Thomas Fallon claimed that the $300 he had loaned to Martina Castro and Louis Depeaux was overdue, he laid claim to all of Castro's land on August 12, 1853. Before the Third District Court, he argued that, according to the provisions of the agreement made on November 29, 1850, whereby her property was pledged as collateral for the amount borrowed, she had defaulted on her loan and her land was thereby forfeit to him. He brought on Robert Peckham as his attorney for the matter of acquiring the ranch, while Henry Richardson remained his lawyer for the matter of the ranch's partitioning. His formal complaint was written by Peter Tracy on August 25 and reads as follows:

Whereas Thomas Fallon has filed in my office a complaint

> *claiming of you, Louis Depeaux, the sum of $300 together with interest thereon at the rate of ten percent per month from the 27th day of May in 1851. Secured by a certain mortgage on certain real estate and praying of the court a decree for the sale of the said mortgage premises and also for the foreclosing of all encumbrances on the mortgaged premises subsequent to the mortgage aforesaid as is more fully set forth in said complaint, a copy of which is hereinto presented.*
>
> *You are therefore commanded to appear and answer said complaint within ten days from the day of service on this unit if service be made on you in the county; within twenty days if service be made on you out of the county but in this district; and within forty days if elsewhere.*
>
> *And you are hereby notified that, in case of your failure to answer as above specified, the plaintiff will apply to the court for the relief demanded in his said complaint.*
>
> *In testimony whereof, I, Peter Tracy, Clerk of the Court of the District Court aforesaid, have hereunto set my hand and affix the seal of the said District Court, the 25th day of August in 1853.*
>
> Peter Tracy, Clerk of the Court

After it was filed, Peckham asked Tracy to reissue the original complaint combined with the new complaint and also asked for the summons to be reissued, which the sheriff delivered on September 6 to Castro, Depeaux, and Durrell Gregory. Depeaux, who had only just returned from having abandoned his wife, was brought on as a defendant. Likewise, Gregory became a defendant due to his undefined interest in Rancho Soquel through the agreement he had signed in November 1850.

In his response to the complaint filed the following day, Gregory appears to deny that he was party to the promissory note in which Castro and Depeaux were loaned $300. He also appears to argue that the loan was not related to the mortgage clauses in the November 1850 deed and, therefore, the deed and note must be judged separately. There could be more information in this note, but poor penmanship and deterioration from time have rendered the document nearly impossible to decipher further.

With Gregory now drawn into the case, Castro hired the law firm of Wilson, Russell, and Williams to help defend against Fallon's attempt to seize her land, although Gregory remained her attorney on the matter of the partitioning suit.[171]

Francisco Alviso testifies before the Land Claims Commission concerning Rancho Soquel and its augmentation

In the office of Alfred Felch, one of the five Land Claims Commissioners, Francisco Alviso testified on August 4, 1853 as a witness for Martina Castro in defense of her claims to Rancho Soquel and its augmentation. Alviso testified in Spanish, which was translated by George Hughes, secretary for the Board of Commissioners. The deposition was filed on August 11 and presented to the commissioners on August 14.

The following questions were asked by John Wilson, attorney for Martina Castro:

Q: What is your name, age, and place of residence?
A: My name is Francisco Alviso, my age is 64 years, and I reside in Santa Clara County.
Q: Were you ever alcalde at Santa Cruz, California, and, if so when?
A: I was alcalde there in 1844.
Q: Was the petition of Martina Castro for a grant of the Rancho San Miguel referred to you? And, if so, state all you know about it.
A: The petition of Martina Castro was referred to me in 1844 while I was alcalde. The land described in it was called "Palo de la Yesca." It was an augmentation to the rancho which she had before, but I do not know the name of the Rancho. I made thereon that the land might be granted to her.
Q: Did you or not make two reports on said petition?
A: I made two reports on two petitions. The first was about

a month after I went there to live, where I knew but little about the country. I then made an unfavorable report. I was induced by some people there who had evil designs to report against it. On the second petition, I made a favorable report. I had at the time more knowledge of the subject and knew that the land was vacant and inhabited only by bears.

Q: Look at the paper here presented and hereto annexed marked "Exhibit A" and say whether it represents the ranchos of which you speak.

A: I have looked at it. It does represent the land described in the petition referred to.

The following questions were asked by the Land Claims Commission law agent, Mr. Greenhower:

Q: Did you ever know the lands of which you speak by the name Rancho de San Miguel?

A: I have not.

Q: Have you ever known Mrs. Martina Castro in occupation of the land?

A: I have known her to occupy it with cattle, to live on it, and to cultivate a portion of it. This was after I made the report in 1844.[172]

Fourcade family at home in Rancho Soquel

On September 11 and 12, 1853, Christophe-Ernest de Massey and a few of his associates, all Frenchmen, visited Santa Cruz County. In a letter to the French Minister of Foreign Affairs, De Massey wrote:

> *Upon going to see Mr. Thomas Fallon, who knew the purpose of our visit, he sent us over to see his brother, Mr. Fourcade, a Frenchman from Bordeaux, who married the daughter of a 'ranchero' and who owned property about two leagues from here.*

On the morning of September eleventh, we left Santa Cruz to visit the rancho. Toward four o'clock we reached our destination. Mr. Fourcade, the owner and manager, it appears, was formerly a sailor whose ship was confiscated or deserted by the crew when the placers [gold deposits] was discovered in California.

Fourcade stayed in California and tried his luck at the mines, where he had remarkable success; within three months, he took out nuggets valued at $30,000. Then, since he had been one of the first to reach and exploit these particular placers, the mines were named after him. These diggings are famous as far south as this. To cap the climax he had his heart, fortune, and hand accepted by a rich Californian.

The rancho contains between eight and eleven square leagues of land. Just now, it is in litigation over a boundary dispute; the case is still pending.

We noticed, as we walked around, that it looked like a fine piece of property; it has three kilometers of seacoast, running water on it, not to mention fields suitable for pasturage, meadows, woods, and soil adaptable for use in making bricks. He has offered us a certain number of animals, access to the ocean, and an acre of land on the shore for a landing. As all this seemed like an attractive proposal, we were about ready to sign an agreement.

While we were discussing all these points with Mr. Fourcade, he graciously invited us to spend the evening with his family. We accepted his invitation without ceremony, hoping in this way to settle all minor points during the course of the evening.

Orders to kill a two-year old steer were immediately given with as much unconcern as a French farmer would show in ordering chickens dressed for extra guests. A Mexican servant mounted on horseback started off, lasso in hand, after an animal. He brought it down at a distance of thirty feet, turned around, and returned dragging his victim, tied by the horns, behind him. He then severed the animal's head with one blow, threw it away, then cut the remaining into quarters.

All this did not take more than twenty minutes.

After quickly grilling some steaks, our meal was ready. The menu was simple: red beans, which were fairly good, an abundance of meat, tortillas, and fresh water. Tea, coffee, wine, and brandy may occasionally be used here, but of this I am not certain. At all events, they are reserved for state occasions.

The senora, the mistress of the house, is young, pretty, and in an interesting condition [she was pregnant]. *She did not dine at the table with her husband and brother-in-law. Five of us, counting Fourcade and his brothers, enjoyed the feast; the fifth was a relation of the woman* [her brother, Miguel Lodge].

In the course of the conversation, the purpose of our visit was again broached. It was then that a number of difficulties and obstacles put in an appearance. They were quite willing, it seemed, to rent us part of the rancho, but first of all it was necessary to have the rancho divided among the eight co-owners and to obtain the consent of the grandmother [Martina Castro].

Neither did they care to rent for over three years and we wanted a six years' lease, with the privilege of buying at a price fixed in advance to be applied against the rental, for we hoped eventually to make the lands valuable. Our host, without refusing our proposition, asked permission to defer his reply until next December, hoping, so he said, that the property would by that time be divided.

In this country, a deal delayed is a deal lost. This was our conviction when, toward nine o'clock, our host escorted us to the apartment reserved for us. It was a dirty, untidy place close to the ground and with mud walls thickly covered with dust, a door that refused to close, and broken panes of glass.

The hides of a few horses were spread on the floor and were used to sit or sleep on. Everything was primitive and extremely simple; I understand the owners' quarters are equally uncomfortable, and yet they are considered to be wealthy rancheros. Moreover, I do not think the Fourcades are like so many local ranch-owners, who do not know any better way of living.

Had we not been afraid of offending these people, we would have camped out in the open, but such a move might have seemed like repaying courtesy with rudeness. So we resigned ourselves to the situation and with a clear conscience lay down to sleep of the just.

First of all, however, here is some gossip about the household...true or false as it may be...that is being circulated around the country. On the surface it seems far from charitable, and what surprises me is that it is known as there is little visiting out here between families because of the great distances. It concerns the domestic life of my hospitable hosts, the Fourcades.

Now, when anyone speaks of them, they are mentioned in disparaging tones as small, blunt men, and if anyone asks whether they are married, there is an embarrassing silence, for theirs is a three-cornered establishment and no one knows what the status of the one woman is. Perhaps in California, there is a sacrament that blesses such a union, but it does not meet with local approval.

In France, there is a constant visiting back and forth between neighbors. But in California, this country with the future, it is possible to travel forty kilometers without meeting a solitary person. It is barely.

Early on the morning of September the 12th, we left our hosts and returned to Santa Cruz. As the day was a fêteday, we joined in the singing of mass, accompanied by violins and other discordant instruments.... [A]fter an exceptionally good dinner, we left for San Juan.

For three hours, our route followed the coast. We passed one fine rancho, owned by a rich Californian, who, like most of his associates, is uneducated and unable to read or write. Riding, gambling, playing, drinking, swaggering, and brutality take the place of this elementary knowledge and seem essential to the happiness of these isolated ranch owners.

There appears to be some confusion in the letter above. Luisa Cota married Jean Fourcade in 1842, six years before gold was discovered, so the match had nothing to do with Fourcade's wealth. The second Fourcade brother at the dinner was likely Albert Fourcade, who traveled to the Gold Country with Jean and seems to have been living with Jean and Luisa on Rancho Soquel in 1853. The rancho mentioned by De Massey in the final paragraph was most likely Rancho San Andrés, owned by one of José Joaquín Castro's sons at the time, since Rafael Castro, owner of Rancho Aptos, was literate.[173]

Suit filed by John Hames versus Martina Castro regarding unfulfilled payment for a sawmill

On September 19, 1853, Durrell Gregory filed a complaint with the Third District Court (Case No. 78) on behalf of his client, John Hames, stating: "On or about the 1st of November in 1846 that I, John Hames, did enter into an Agreement in which I would be paid the sum of $5,000 for building a sawmill, storage yard, millpond dam, and additional supporting facilities for Michael Lodge. I completed the mill and its supporting facilities and began to produce lumber but was never paid by Martina Castro's second husband Michael Lodge, today deceased."

It is interesting to note here that Gregory, as predicted by the agreement of October 28, 1852, remains Castro's representative before the Land Claims Commission as well as her lawyer in the Thomas Fallon lawsuit. Meanwhile, the attorney Castro hired for the Hames sawmill case, Robert Peckham, otherwise represents her opponent in the Fallon case.[174]

Decision regarding the promissory note of November 29, 1850 left to the court

Perhaps realizing that a vital piece of evidence was missing from his argument in Third District Court, Case No. 74, Robert Peckham, representing Thomas Fallon, requested on September 29, 1853 that a search be conducted for the promissory note signed by Martina Castro and Louis Depeaux documenting the details of the $300 loan.

The next day, Castro's attorneys, Wilson, Russell & Williams responded to Fallon's new complaint by stating that the borrowed $300 was repaid in full according to the terms of the agreement of November 29, 1850. In addition, they argued that since the agreement was between Fallon and Depeaux and Rancho Soquel belonged solely to Castro, Depeaux had no legal claim to any portion of the property and, therefore, could not legally offer it as collateral. At this same time, the lawyers lodged a counterclaim that Thomas and Carmel Fallon owed Castro $2,000 for room, board, and other expenses incurred over an undefined period.

Four days later, on October 3, Peckham entered several motions claiming that Castro and Depeaux were still liable for the $300, despite lacking the evidence. Since he refused to drop the matter, the decision regarding the loan and its role in the Rancho Soquel partitioning suit was left to the court.[175]

Land transfer from Martina Castro to Jane Smith

Because Martina Castro was in need of money to pay expenses that were beginning to accumulate, she sold her one-thirteenth part of Rancho San Andrés that she had inherited from her father, José Joaquín Castro, in 1838 to Jane Smith on October 21, 1853.[176]

Frederick Hihn marries Therese Paggen in Santa Cruz

A native of France, Therese Paggan, born on May 17, 1836, was raised in Paris and México City. Her family relocated to San Francisco in 1849 and it was there that she likely met Frederick Hihn. She was only around thirteen when they met but Hihn courted her off-and-on for four years until finally marrying her on November 23, 1853. They were wed on the second floor of Hihn's building in Santa Cruz, where they established their home and started their family.[177]

Montgomery Shackleford pays outstanding mortage to Luisa Cota

On December 30, 1853, Montgomery Shackleford paid the $5,000 that he owed for Luisa Cota's one-ninth claim to Rancho Soquel, thereby completing the terms of the mortgage.[178]

That same day, Louis Depeaux wrote a letter to John Wilson concerning the ongoing Land Claims Commission case:

> *Sir, we have not heard anything about our land title for some time, but knowing that we had to prove judicial possession and we can do it. Next week Jose Bolcoff is coming up to the City to give testimony as regards the possession and you will please take his testimony as regards the judicial possession of the Rancho Soquel for he was alcalde at the time my wife got possession and he gave it. Also take his testimony on the Rancho de San Miguel on the upper grant, the land that Francisco Alviso gave testimony of. Mr. Gregory and myself have made arrangements about the cattle and, as soon as I can sell, I will pay you some money in ten days at most. I can send you $500 at the start of the week.*
>
> I remain yours truly,
> Louis Depeaux

The Land Claims Commission was moving exceptionally slowly regarding the issue of Rancho Soquel not because they questioned the legitimacy of the original grant, but that many questions remained regarding the augmentation grant. To better understand the sequence of events, the Commission combined the evidence for both grants in chronological order from 1833 through 1844.[179]

Benjamin and Edward Porter settle in the Aptos area

Benjamin Franklin Porter was born in Vermont on April 20, 1823 and arrived in San Francisco in 1854 alongside his brother, Edward. In 1857, he settled along Aptos Creek within Rancho Aptos while Edward opened the first general store and post office in the Soquel township on July 5.

Land transfer from Nicanor Cota to John Vandenberg

On January 21, 1854, John Vandenberg purchased from Francisco and Nicanor Lajeunesse the eighty acres of land within Rancho Soquel that he had leased for the previous two years. His purchase included his home, the Lajeunesse home, and the local general store. After finalizing the purchase, Vandenberg leased his land and its structures and moved to Santa Cruz, where he built a large mansion.[180]

Robert Peckham demands proof of Thomas Fallon's debt to the Depeaux family

On February 17, 1854, the attorney for Thomas Fallon, Robert Peckham, in Third District Court, Case No. 74, demanded that proof be supplied by Martina Castro and Louis Depeaux that Fallon and his wife owed the sum of $2,000 for room and board.[181]

Henry Cambustan testifies before the Land Claims Commission on behalf of Martina Castro

On March 1, 1854 in the office of R. Aug Thompson, one of the Land Claims Commissioners, Henry Cambustan testified in defense of Martina Castro. The following questions were asked of him by John Wilson:

- Q: Please state your name, age, and place of residence.
- A: My name is Henry Cambustan, my age is thirty seven, and I reside in the County of Monterey, California.
- Q: State what you know of Martina Castro having obtained from Governor Micheltorena a grant of land in the Soquel Augmentation Ranch...made to her in the present County of Santa Cruz. State also where it is situated and what you know of its boundaries.
- A: About the beginning of the year 1844, Governor Micheltorena gave me a written order to go and mark out the

boundaries of the town of Branciforte. I was there acting in the capacity of Surveyor General.

The order above mentioned directed me to commence at the center of the Mission of Santa Cruz and measure one league in north, south, east and west direction in the company of the judge of the Pueblo of Branciforte.

The said order further directed me, after marking out the boundaries of the pueblo, to mark out those of the rancho of Martina Castro where the judge should give the juridical possession. I did not comply with the said order because my other business was extensive and difficult and the rivers at that time were high and there were no boats for crossing them and, as the order specified no particular time for its execution, I deferred it. It was also in the wintertime and the roads were in an almost impassable state. I never afterwards executed the said order.

The order did not specify the boundaries but referred to the title. I saw the title at the time, but as I did not go to measure it, I did not examine it particularly. The said rancho is situated in the County of Santa Cruz. I have seen the house—it is about five or six miles from the town of Santa Cruz. I know one of the boundaries: it is the Loma Prieta, situated six or eight miles from the north of the house of the rancho. I was informed that it was one of the boundaries. The rancho house in which Martina Castro lives is situated about half a mile to the east of the arroyo Soquel and I believe the rancho is known of the same name. I was there a few months after I came to the county in the year of 1840. She was living there then and has continued to reside there ever since. I have frequently passed there over the years and have seen canals on the land and herds of cattle and horses and also portions of the land enclosed and under cultivation.

The following questions were asked by the Land Claims Commission's

Law Agent Greenhower.

> Q: Who told you that the Loma Prieta was a boundary of the said rancho?
> A: I do not know who told me. I learned it when I was at Santa Cruz.
> Q: Is there a place known as the Laguna del Sargento; if so, state how far it is from the sea and in what direction?
> A: There is such a place—it is about four or five miles from the bay and about the same distance from the said Rancho house in a northwesterly direction.
>
> Enrique Cambustan[182]

Land transfer by Martina Castro and Louis Depeaux to Henry Cambustan

For services rendered that were not specified in the deed, Martina Castro and Louis Depeaux sold Henry Cambustan one quarter of all the lands claimed in both Rancho Soquel and the Augmentation in exchange for one peso on March 7, 1854. The reason for this transfer is obvious: the Depeaux were rewarding Cambustan for not revealing the whole truth to the Land Claims Commission regarding the status of the Augmentation.[183]

Third District Court issues ruling on Hames v. Castro case

On April 5, 1854, the Third District Court handed down its decision regarding Case No. 78, John Hames v. Martina Castro, et al. The judge decided that the record did not disclose any benefit to the defendant, Martina Castro, arising from the contract entered into on November 1, 1846 between Hames and Michael Lodge, but he agreed that she was nonetheless liable, being the survivor of her husband, for one-half of the community debts.

The judge came to this decision through several declarations, namely:

- That by Mexican law, all property acquired during marriage

was ruled common property, and the wife could neither be bound as security for her husband, nor liable as a joint contractor, except where it was shown that the contract was advantageous to the wife;
- That to establish that a contract is advantageous to the wife, means that it accrued to the benefit of her separate estate;
- And that under Mexican law, where the wife is the survivor of the husband, she is liable for one-half of the community debts, but, to affix this liability, it must be shown that a fruitless effort has been made to obtain payment through an administration of the community assets, or that there is no common property and that the community is insolvent.

To recoup costs for the trial, Martina presented a bill of costs to Hames for the amount of $63.50, and included a pledge that:

> *I, Martina Castro, defendant in the above entitled cause, do solemnly swear, that the items in the above memorandum are correct to the best of my knowledge, information, and [...] that the disbursements have been necessarily smaller in the action.*
>
> [Castro's mark]
>
> *Sworn and subscribed before me this April 5, 1854.*
>
> [name unreadable],
> Justice of the Peace, Soquel

As instructed by Hames, Durrell Gregory immediately began preparing an appeal to the California Supreme Court, which he submitted in January 1855.[184]

Charles McKiernan meets a grizzly bear on the Summit

After settling on the Summit in June 1851, Charles McKiernan began working his land. On May 8, 1854, he had an ill-fated encounter with a grizzly bear. The following is from an interview he gave regarding the incident in 1878:

> *From the Summit, I hunted for a living, making little for two or three years, when a man by the name of William Dearing proposed to form a co-partnership with him and kill deer for the San Francisco market. We killed 1,000 deer that year, and sold them from $5 to $10 a head, making $7,000, and killed besides quite a number of bear.*
>
> *I next bought a flock of sheep and kept them on the mountain when one night a lion got among them and killed 70 head. It is astonishing how destructive these animals are to sheep. They will jump into a corral when undisturbed, for they are great cowards, and kill large number of them, and then leave their prey until the next night, when they will come to the feast. After this failure, I realized that speculating on sheep in the mountains was wrong; therefore, I sold out the balance, which totaled about 700 head.*
>
> *I began hunting bear after I parted with the sheep. One day I was hunting about three miles from my house, not far from where Lyman Burrell lives, down in a bottom near a little pond, when I discovered a large grizzly bear lying on its haunches with its head turned from me. I approached the bear within 10 steps, dismounted from my mule, and having a good shot in my rifle, I gave her a shot just in back of the head, supposing from the falling of her head that I had killed her. I began reloading, and after I had put in the powder and about to ram down the ball, she made a rush at me. I grabbed the pommel of the saddle, but the mule was so frightened that she jumped and finally jerked away and ran home. When the mule turned to run off, she threw me some distance from the spot where I fired at the bear. The bear in the meantime had returned back to her nest, where she had two cubs. When I released the reins of the mule, I sprang to my feet, dropping my gun, then looking back at the bear, I saw that she was making another charge at me. I turned and ran, and never was there*

a man that ran as I did until I reached my home. The bear got pretty close at times and would doubtless have caught me had she not been mortally wounded. The next day, I returned to the place and found the bear dead. I caught the cubs and brought them home. I kept them for four months, then they began killing my hogs, so I had to kill them.

My next encounter with a bear came very near putting "my chunk out." I had been hunting all day with James Taylor and we had killed five deer. While we were engaged in packing two of them out of a gulch, I saw a bear 400 yards below, feeding. We attempted to get around and ahead of him to get a good shot. As we neared, we saw that he was a very large one. While attempting to get around the bear, unbeknown to us, he was preceding in the same direction, and as we were climbing a small mound and had reached the top, there was the bear, looking at us face to face. Meeting us so suddenly, the bear gave a snort and plunged at us. Taylor fired the first shot and missed. By this time, the bear was within three jumps of me and rapidly approaching.... Taylor headed for a near tree while I drew a bead on him and fired. The ball struck him over the eye and glanced but so stunned him as he made his last spring that he fell by my side. I struck his head with my gun, breaking the barrel. All of this had occurred in but a moment. Next, the bear arose, with his tremendous jaws wide open, and made a snap at me, catching me over the left eye and forehead, crushing my skull and tearing out about five by three inches of it. I then threw up my arms in front of my face in a locked position which the bear grabbed in his mouth, crushing down with his grinders upon one arm, while his tusks passed entirely through the other, missing the bone. The bear, after taking his revenge on me, left the scene. Still conscious, I could hear him rolling and snapping down the mountain through the brush, but I could not see him because I had lost my sight.

Following the attack, Doctors A. W. Bell and T. J. Ingersoll attended McKiernan personally. Ingersoll recorded in his notes:

My partner, Dr. A. W. Bell, went out and found him next morning about sunrise, with the front part of his head terribly mangled and some wounds on both arms, but rational. When the bear sprang on Charley and bit him, [he took] out a piece of the frontis bone over the left eye and nose, triangular shaped, and about 3 3/4 inches on every side....

The piece of skull taken out by the animal was sent in with a request that I should have a plate of silver made and come out immediately to assist in dressing the wound. Making all necessary preparation, I hastened to the patient, getting there about 9 o'clock P.M., when I found that the piece of the frontis bone sent in was only about half of the bone taken out.

On the next morning, [I] returned to San Jose to have another plate made, sufficiently large to cover the brain...getting back to the patient the same day at 8 o'clock P.M. Dr. Bell and myself proceeded to apply the plate and dress the wounds; [we] got through [at] about 11 o'clock P.M.

The part of the bone detached was all that portion of the frontis bone, above the left eye and nose, and in the orbit about 3/4ths of an inch...taking a portion of the zygomatic process, ranging up about four inches parallel with the coronal suture, from that point, irregularly to the right of the root of the nose, about 3 3/4 inches on each of the three sides. The muscles and instruments were brought together and secured with sutures...soon closed by first intention, with the exception of two or three points for the matter to flow, and where the parts would not meet.

By general bleeding and cold applications to the head, very little disturbance took place. After the expiration of a week, I found that the plate was irritating the parts so much that it was impossible for them to become sound and immediately took it out, very much against the wishes of the patient. I would here mention that it was at the urgent solicitation of the patient that the plate was used in the first place.

Notwithstanding the expostulations of his physicians, the wound healed kindly, with the exception of two points on each side of the nose. There were some spicula of bone, which kept up an irritation and discharging of matter. The left eyeball, in consequence of the muscles above it contracting, not having sufficient support, turned up about eight degrees. General health good.

Some twelve months after the events above related, the patient, having suffered from an intolerable pain in the head, came into town, and consulted Dr. Spencer and myself. It was decided to perform an operation. Accordingly, we, with some others, waited upon him at the National Hotel, where, after administering chloroform, the operation took place.

We cut down and found a deep-seated abscess under the anterior lobe of the brain at least two inches deep, above and behind the nasal process, which was discharging through the small sinus above the right eye. The operation had the desired effect. The abscess soon got well and the patient was relieved of the pain he had been suffering some time before.

His health is good, but as a matter of course, his face is much disfigured. He does not think his mind or memory has been affected by the injury he received from the bear, but sometimes complains of a dull sensation in the region of the brain.[185]

Guadalupe Lodge marries Joseph Averon

Joseph Averon was born in France in 1828 into a family alleged to be of nobility. While Averon's father loved the army life, Joseph wanted to get away and joined the navy. Averon was serving as a cook aboard Commodore Sloat's ship, the USS *Savannah*, in Monterey when the American flag was raised over the custom house on July 7, 1846. He took the opportunity to jump ship and made his way to Branciforte, where he chose to settle.[186]

In October 1854, Averon married the twelve-year-old María Guadalupe Lodge, Martina Castro's seventh and youngest surviving daughter. According to Carrie Lodge, Guadalupe's niece, Guadalupe likely married Averon to get away from her stepfather, Louis Depeaux. The situation was not especially unusual in any case—the high ratio of single men to women in California in the 1850s was terrible, so men often took girls in their early teenage years as brides.[187]

Livestock sale by Joseph Majors to Charles Watson

In order to compensate Charles Watson for the $1,634 that he borrowed in order to pay Jones Hoy for his 1/18 share of Rancho Soquel, on October 4, 1854 Joseph Majors signed over all of his livestock, including his entire cattle and oxen herd and all of his horses, to Watson. The livestock was placed in the custody of the sheriff, who in turn placed it in the custody of Hoy.[188]

Third District Court orders Pruett Sinclair to pay amount owed to Charles Stevenson

On October 8, 1854, the Third District Court supported a claim made by Charles Stevenson that Pruett Sinclair owed him $674. Sinclair was ordered to pay the debt in full.[189]

José Bolcoff testifies before the Land Claims Commission on behalf of Martina Castro

In San Francisco on October 14, 1854, José Bolcoff gave a deposition on behalf of Martina Castro before Land Claims Commissioner Peter Lott. Castro's attorney, Durrell Gregory, asked the questions. Bolcoff's testimony was taken in Spanish and translated by an interpreter as follows:

> Q: What is your name, age, and place of residence?
> A: My name is Jose Bolcoff, my age is 57 years, and I reside in Santa Cruz County, California.
> Q: Look at the document now shown to you marked "A.P.L." [the map of Rancho Soquel drawn by Bolcoff on August 13-14, 1834] exhibited in this deposition and herefore filed in this case, and state whether you are acquainted with the handwriting of the persons whose signatures appear therein. If yes, your means of knowledge, and whether their signatures in said document are genuine.
> A: The rubrics of Jose Figueroa and Rafael Gonzales, at the

beginning of this document, were their genuine rubrics. I have seen them both affix them to documents and am well acquainted with them. I was the alcalde who gave the juridical possession to Martina Castro in this case, and this Jose Antonio Bolcoff is my genuine signature. I wrote the names of Martina Castro, Miguel Ramirez, Joaquin Castro, Juan Jose Castro and Rafael Robles respectively. They were all present and requested me to do so and they each made a mark. Here in my presence, except said Robles, whose father was dying that day and he left without making his mark. I am acquainted with the handwriting of Francisco Rodriquez. I have seen him write and this is his genuine signature.

Q: Look at the document now shown to you marked "B.P.L." [the grant for Rancho Soquel, dated August 2, 1834], as exhibited in this deposition, and herefore filed in this case, and state whether you are acquainted with the handwriting of the persons whose signatures appear therein. If you state yes, state your means of knowledge and whether their signatures in said document are genuine.

A: The rubrics of Jose Figueroa here are genuine at the beginning of this document, I have seen them respectively affix them to documents [and] am well acquainted with them. The signature of said Figueroa on the third page is also genuine, and also of Agustin D. Zamorano. I have seen them both write and know their handwriting well, and wherever they occur in this document, they are genuine.

Q: Are you acquainted with the land in question called Soquel? If yes, state whether the diseño in the document first exhibited to you marked "A. P. L." is a correct delineation thereof and whether the boundaries of said land are conspicuous and well-known objects?

A: I am acquainted with the said tract of land and this diseño is a correct presentation of it and the boundaries are well known and easily ascertained objects.

Q: State the boundaries of said tract of land.

A: It is bounded on the east by a "ditch," which divides this land from that of Rafael Castro; on the west by the Arroyo de Soquel, which separates it from the land of Francisco Rodriquez; on the north by hills, a redwood stake was driven at the northern boundary; and on the south by the sea. These were the boundaries established by me as alcalde when I gave the juridical possession in this case.

Q: State what you know of the occupancy of the tract of land in question by Martina Castro.

A: In 1833, Martina Castro lived on the place. She had a house, corrals, and some of the land enclosed and cultivated, about 140 acres. She had horses, cattle, and sheep on the place, and she has continued ever since then to occupy the place till the present time.

A few questions were also asked by Law Agent Greenhower:

Q: How were the boundaries established when you gave the juridical possession?

A: We measured all around the rancho with a cord of 50 *vares* in length. Actually, they placed a stake at the northwest corner and supposedly measured heading eastward.

Q: Were there any other artificial marks placed in the boundaries besides the stake you mentioned?

A: There were not—there was no necessity for it. The Arroyo and the ditch, the sea were distinct boundaries.

Jose Bolcoff

Filed October 16, 1854,
George Fisher, Secretary[190]

Land transfers from Thomas Wright to Peter Tracy and from Tracy to Thomas Fallon

In a pair of unusual land transfers, Thomas Wright sold his half interest in School Land Warrant Nos. 108, 353, and 354 on November 30, 1854 to Peter Tracy, who then possessed the entirety of the three sections. Tracy then turned around and immediately sold Warrant Nos. 353 and 354 to Thomas Fallon, from whom he had originally purchased the sections, retaining for himself Warrant No. 108.[191]

Cornello Perez testifies before the Land Claims Commission on behalf of Martina Castro

In San Francisco on December 8, 1854, Cornelio Perez gave a deposition before Peter Lott. Perez, born in 1810, had served as the second *juez de campo* in Santa Cruz County after statehood. The primary role of the *juez* was to inspect cattle brands and resolve title disputes regarding roving livestock. He was the second American *juez*, serving alongside Juan Gonzales, succeeding to the position after José de la Cruz Rodriguez stepped down in 1851. Perez was acting as a witness on behalf of Martina Castro in regard to Land Claims Commission Case No. 184. Castro's attorney, Durrell Gregory, asked the questions. His testimony was taken in Spanish and translated by an interpreter as follows:

> Q: What is your name, age, and residence?
> A: My name is Cornelio Perez, my age is 44, and my residence is Santa Cruz County, California.
> Q: Are you acquainted with the rancho called Soquel, claimed in this case, and, if so, state what you know of the occupancy and cultivation of said rancho by the original grantee?
> A: I know said rancho. I have known it to be in the occupation of Martina Castro before it was granted to her some 19 or 20 years. She had a house—a modern house—before the grant, and corral, horse and cattle. She had two large fields enclosed and cultivated, and before the grant and after the grant she

built a large adobe house, and she has continued in such occupancy till the present time and is still living there. She gave permission to some men to build a mill on one corner of the place, a sawmill, and that remained there as her property.

The following question was asked by Law Agent Greenhower:

Q: How do you know when said grant was made?
A: I know it because I knew that one Francisco [Girien] had some stock on the place and he refused to move them off and then I saw an order from Governor Figueroa to said [Girien] requiring him to remove said stock because the land belonged to Martina Castro. And it was well known and publicly understood among the neighbors that she had received a grant of the place.

Cornelio Perez[192]

Land transfer from Montgomery Shackleford to Peter Tracy

On December 11, 1854, for $200, Montgomery Shackleford sold his one-third interest in School Land Warrant No. 90, which he shared with Gervis Hammond and Thomas Wright, to Peter Tracy.[193]

Letter from Louis Depeaux to John Wilson

On December 14, 1854, Louis Depeaux wrote the following letter to John Wilson concerning the ongoing assessment of Rancho Soquel and its augmentation by the Land Claims Commission:

Sir, as of November 16, if you look in the office of the Land Claims Commissioners, you will see testimony of Jose Bolcoff and by whom it is taken. Concerning the state of myself and wife, we are willing to pay for what value we have received and no more. Write and let us know what deduction you are willing to make as you say you are willing to deduct. I have had a talk with Durrell S. Gregory and he says what business he does for us he does on his own account, not in partnership with you. But yet I am willing to pay you what is right for I don't want anyone to work for me for nothing.

You need not devote any more of your time to our business as I wrote you before. Send me word how we can settle with you.

Louis Depeaux

This letter from Depeaux to Wilson is both enlightening and revealing. Wilson, it will be remembered, was an indirect relation to Castro through her second husband Michael Lodge's first marriage. He was hired based on his expertise in handling Mexican land claims. Depeaux fired him via this letter because he had not succeeded in the task that he was hired to do, namely to legitimize the Augmentation grant.[194]

Martina Castro makes plans to move to México

At this point, it is necessary to summarize and conclude the story of Martina Castro and Louis Depeaux's efforts to establish the legitimacy of Rancho Soquel and the Augmentation through the end of 1854

The first documented contract between Castro and John Wilson was during the period that Depeaux had deserted her. On October 28, 1852, Castro entered into an agreement with both Wilson and Durrell Gregory, in which they agreed to represent her in several lawsuits that she expected to be brought against her. One of these was the John Hames sawmill suit. Another was brought against her by several of her sons-in-law, who wished to partition or outright seize her properties. She also brought suits against her sons-in-law in order to recover the profits that they made by the sale of her land through the deed of November 29, 1850. Furthermore, she asked for the attorneys to represent her before the Land Claims Commission concerning her two land grants. Because Wilson claimed expertise in this area, it was decided that Gregory would handle the simpler Rancho Soquel grant claim, while both would work on the augmentation grant, with Wilson handling the majority of the effort.

Because Castro could not afford to pay the two, she agreed to give them a total of one-half of the land and monies that they recovered from her sons-in-law and their grantees, plus half of all the land that they were able to convince the Land Claims Commission to accept as legitimate and award to her. In the aforementioned agreement, a clause stated that if either attorney chose to act against Castro in court, he would forfeit his half of both land and monies. In the end, Gregory chose to represent Hames in the sawmill case and, as a result, gave up his claims to any property.

On August 2, 1852, Thomas and Carmel Fallon, Pruett Sinclair, and Jones Hoy brought suit against Castro in order to force her to partition or sell Rancho Soquel and the augmentation in order to divide the land and proceeds among herself and her heirs. Gregory represented Castro at the time, but when Fallon claimed that Castro and Depeaux were in default of $300 he had loaned them to pay county property taxes—an allegation the latter denied—Gregory was brought into the case as a defendant and Wilson, Russell & Williams were hired to settle the matter of the unpaid debt. Fallon hoped to prove that Castro defaulted, which would have allowed him to claim ownership of all her lands according to the original loan agreement signed on August 29, 1850.

When Depeaux dismissed John Wilson in the letter of December 14, 1854, he knew that the Land Claims Commission was prepared to acknowledge the grant of the Rancho Soquel but would reject the Augmentation grant. According to a later interview with Miguel Lodge, Castro began considering moving to México in April 1854 in order to leave behind the troubles that had plagued her for the previous four years. But the move was continuously postponed due to the ongoing lawsuits and her need to be available to the Land Claims Commission. However, with all the cases closed or nearly so at the end of the year, she resumed making plans to move.

The Archdiocese of San Francisco agrees to purchase Rancho Soquel from Martina Castro

Expecting Rancho Soquel's augmentation to be declared an illegitimate grant, Martina Castro hoped to sell Rancho Soquel and use the funds to pay her debts and finance her relocation to México. At the end of 1854, she began looking for buyers and found one in the head priest of Mission Santa Cruz, Father Llebaria. Through several exchanges, Castro and Louis Depeaux agreed to sell Rancho Soquel for $2,000 and her claim to any confirmed land in the augmentation for $500. With negotiations completed, Llebaria returned to Archbishop Alemany, head of the diocese in San Francisco, to draft the paperwork, leaving Father John Ingoldsby in Santa Cruz to examine the deeds and land claims at the County Recorders' Office.

Ingoldsby was born in 1819 near Chicago, Illinois. He was ordained a priest on August 18, 1844 by Saint Mary's Cathedral and remained a parish priest there until 1850. Poor health forced him to a better climate and he chose to move to California, where his cousin Charles McKiernan lived. He arrived in San Francisco on October 21, 1850 and, shortly afterwards, was appointed an assistant priest at Mission Dolores.

In 1852, Bishop Alemany sent Ingoldsby to the Sierra Nevada to perform church duties there. In the Gold Country, Ingoldsby became the leading advocate for the church in an area ranging from Sacramento to the Yuba River, preaching from camp to camp. While there, he established the first Catholic church in Placerville, better known at the time as Hangtown. Shortly after Alemany became Archbishop of San Francisco, he recalled Ingoldsby, who resumed his former position at Mission Dolores. But Llebaria often called Ingoldsby to serve as his proxy in Santa Cruz, meaning that he quickly learned of the land disputes on Rancho Soquel.

According to later testimony given by Deputy County Recorder Henry Parsons, during the month of December 1854 and into January 1855, Ingoldsby was frequently found in the Santa Cruz County Recorders' Office examining the records relating to Rancho Soquel and its augmentation. He paid particular attention to the deed of August 29, 1850 from Castro to her children. Parsons recalled that "He and I frequently spoke of the informality of the acknowledgment of Martina, as recorded therewith." Ingoldsby also closely examined the acknowledgment recorded by Judge T. R. Per Lee on November 29, 1850.

Meanwhile, Miguel Lodge recalled that, as the church finalized its purchase of his mother's property, Castro and Depeaux began selling their furniture to Ingoldsby. By this time, Miguel was the only child still living in Martina's house and he was given into the care of his sister, Antonia Peck.

This being done, Castro and Depeaux left for San Francisco, where John Wilson was preparing the transfer deeds with church officials.[195]

Land transfer from Martina Castro to the Catholic Church

Around January 7, 1855, Martina Castro and Louis Depeaux arrived in San Francisco, where they stayed at the home of Castro's sister Candida and her husband, José Bolcoff.

Roughly two weeks later, on January 22, Castro sold all 1,668 acres of Rancho Soquel, including her home and the rights to any land granted to her within the Augmentation, to the Catholic Church for the sum of $2,000. Fathers Llebaria and Ingoldsby were allowed to purchase Rancho Soquel because the impending results from the Land Claims Commission were expected to validate the grant. At the same time, the priests knew that it was unlikely any land in the Augmentation would be legitimized by the commission.

Indeed, in light of the near certainty that the Augmentation grant would be declared invalid, John Wilson and Father Llebaria came to the conclusion that its transfer to a prominent individual within the Catholic Church could breathe new life into the case. Their eyes immediately fell upon Archbishop Alemany, the senior-most church official in Northern California. With his name and support, they hoped to overturn or appeal the pending rejection by the commission. Whether Alemany was aware of the anticipated rejection of the grant when he joined the plot is unknown. If he did not know, he likely joined because Castro wished to sell all of the contested land to the church. If he did know, then he was one of the plotters from the beginning and hoped to use his influence to coerce the commissioners or courts into reversing their decision.

Two deeds of sale were drawn up for Castro to sign, one for Rancho Soquel, in which Alemany was not listed as a beneficiary, and another for the augmentation, in which he was. Both deeds are included below in full owing to the importance of their contents to the ongoing story.

DEED OF SALE: RANCHO SOQUEL
This Indenture, made the 22nd day of January, A.D. 1855,

between Louis Depeaux and Martina Castro Depeaux, his wife, parties of the first part, and John Francis Llebaria and John Ingoldsby of the city of San Francisco, parties of the second part, witnesseth:

That the said parties of the first part, for and in consideration of the sum of two thousand dollars, lawful money of the United States of America, to them in hand paid by the said parties of the second part, at and before the ensealing and delivery of these presents, the receipt whereof is hereby acknowledged, have granted, bargained, sold, aliened, remissed, conveyed, and confirmed, and by these presents do grant, bargain, sell, alien, remiss, convey, and confirm, unto the said parties of the second part, and their heirs and assigns, forever, all that piece or parcel of land lying and being in the county of Santa Cruz, and described as follows, to wit:

Commencing at the blazed oak tree standing on the side of the hill north of the dwelling of the parties of the first part, on the Soquel Ranch, and east of the fence of Mr. [Joshua] Parrish and the river Soquel; thence running eastwardly to the corner of the field owned by Henry Peck; thence running southwardly to a large oak tree on the line with an old fence, between the lands of said parties of the first part and one Pruett Sinclair; thence running westwardly to the Soquel River; and thence northerly along the margin of said river to the point of beginning; containing about two hundred and nineteen acres of land.

And also all the estate, right, title, interest and property of them, the said parties of the first part, in and to the remaining portion of the Soquel Ranch, not above particularly described, together with all and singular the tenements, hereditaments, and appurtenances thereto belonging or in anywise appertaining, and the revision and revisions remaining, rents, issues and profits, thereof; and also the estate, right, title, interest, property, possession, claim, and demand whatsoever, as well in law as in equity, of the said parties of the first part, of, in, and to the above described premises and every part and parcel thereof, with the appurtenances, to have and to hold, *all and singular, the above mentioned and described premises, together with the appurtenances, unto the said parties of the second part, their heirs and assigns, forever.*

And the said parties of the first part, for themselves, their heirs, executors, and administrators, do hereby covenant, promise, and agree to, and with the said parties of the second part, their heirs and assigns, that they have not made, done, committed, executed, or suffered any act or acts, thing or things whatsoever, whereby or by means whereof, the above mentioned and described premises, or any part or parcel thereof now are, or at any time hereafter shall or may be, impeached, charged, or encumbered in any manner or way whatever.

In witness whereof, the said parties of the first part, have hereunto set their hands and seals, the day and year first above written.

Sealed and delivered in the presence of:
C. Morgan
Char. M. C. Delany

Louis Depeaux
✗ [Martina Castro's mark]

STATE OF CALIFORNIA
COUNTY OF SAN FRANCISCO

On this 22nd day of January, A.D. 1855, before me, George T. Knox, a Notary Public in and for said county, personally appeared Louis Depeaux and Martina Castro Depeaux, his wife, to me known to the individuals described in and who executed the annexed instrument, and acknowledged that they executed the same freely and voluntarily, for the uses and purposes therein mentioned.

And the said Martina Castro Depeaux, being by me made acquainted with the contents of said instrument, and on an examination made apart from and without hearing of her husband, acknowledged that she executed the same freely and voluntarily, without fear or compulsion, or under influence of her husband, and that she does not wish to retract the execution of the same.

In witness whereof, I have hereunto set my hand and affixed my official seal, the day and year first above written.

George T. Knox, Notary Public

Filed for record,
January 25, 1855, at 9 o'clock A.M.
Peter Tracy, County Recorder

Deed of Sale: Augmentation Ranch

This Indenture, made the 22nd day of January, A.D. 1855, between Louis Depeaux and Martina Castro Depeaux, his wife, of the County of Santa Cruz, State of California, parties of the first part, and the most Reverend Joseph Sadoc Alemany and Reverend John Francis Llebaria of the City of San Francisco, parties of the second part, witnesseth:

That the said parties of the first part, for the consideration of the sum of $500, lawful money of the United States of America, to them in hand paid by the parties of the second part at or before the ensealing and delivery of these presents the receipt whereof, is hereby acknowledged, have granted, bargained, sold, aliened, remissed, released, conveyed, and confirmed, and by these presents do grant, bargain, sell, alien, remiss, release, convey, and confirm unto the said parties of the second part, and to their heirs and assigns, forever all the right, title, interest, and estate of the said parties of the first part in and to the Rancho situated in the county of Santa Cruz and known as the Augmentation Ranch, adjoining the Soquel Ranch in said county.

Together with all the singular the tenements, hereditaments, and appurtenances thereto belonging or in any wise appertaining, and the revision and revisions, remainder and remainders, rents, issues, and profits thereof; and also all the estate, right, title, interest, property, possession, claim, and de-

mand whatsoever, as well as in law as in equity, of the said parties of the first part, of, in, and to the above described premises and every part and parcel thereof, with the appurtenances, to have and hold, all and singular, the above mentioned and described premises, together with the appurtenances, unto the said parties of the second part, their heirs and assigns, forever.

And the parties of the first part, for themselves, their heirs, executors, and administrators, do hereby, covenant, promise, and agree to and with the said parties of the second part, their heirs and assigns, that they have not made, done, committed, executed, or suffered any act or acts, thing or things, whatsoever, whereby or by means whereof, the above mentioned and described premises, or any part or parcel thereof, now are, or at any time hereafter shall or may be, impeached, charged, or encumbered in any manner or way whatever.

In witness whereof, the said parties of the first part, have hereunto set their hands and seals, the day and year first above written.

Sealed and delivered in the presence of:
C. Morgan
Char. M. C. Delany

Louis Depeaux
✗ [Martina Castro's mark]

STATE OF CALIFORNIA
COUNTY OF SAN FRANCISCO

On this 22nd day of January, A.D. 1855, before me, George T. Knox, a Notary Public in and for said county, personally appeared Louis Depeaux and Martina Castro Depeaux, his wife, to me known to be the individuals described in and who executed the annexed instrument, and acknowledged that they executed the same freely and voluntarily, for the uses and purpose therein mentioned.

And the said Martina Castro Depeaux, being by me

made acquainted with the contents of said instrument, and on an examination made apart from and without hearing of her husband, acknowledged that she executed the same freely and voluntarily, without fear or compulsion, or under influence of her husband, and that she does not wish to retract the execution of the same.

In witness whereof, I have hereunto set my hand and affixed my official seal, the day and year first above written.

George T. Knox, Notary Public

Filed for record,
January 25, 1855, at 1/2 hours, two o'clock P.M.
Peter Tracy, County Recorder[196]

Confirmation of Rancho Soquel grant by the Land Claims Commission

On January 23, 1855, the Land Claims Commission officially announced its opinion regarding Martina Castro's grant of Rancho Soquel:

This is a claim for a tract of land situated in the present County of Santa Cruz, two miles in length by a league in width, a little more or less as explained by the sketch attached to the Expediente. The Expediente consists of the original petition, informe, and a copy of the grant, if given, that were all filed in the archives. The original copy of the grant was delivered to the grantee.

It was founded on a grant made by Governor Jose Figueroa on the 23rd day of November 1833, which was duly approved by the Committee of Colonization on the 17th of May, 1834, and a testimonial of such approval by the governor and secretary and dated August 2, 1834, delivered for her security.

Individual possession of the premises was given by the proper officer on the 14th of August 1834, and the boundaries established. The originals of all these documents are filed in the case and their genuine authenticity is established by this testimony.

The grantee is known to have occupied and cultivated the land extensively from the approval to the grant to the present time, and still continues to reside on it. The validity of the claim is fully proved, and a decree of confirmation will be entered.

filed in the office January 23, 1855,
George Fisher, Secretary

Decree of Confirmation by the Board of Commissioners for the Land Claims Commission for defendant Martina Castro for Rancho Soquel.

In this case, we having the proofs and allegations, it is adjudged by the Commission that the claim of the petitioner is valid, and it is therefore decreed that the same be confirmed.

The land of which confirmation is made is situated in the County of Santa Cruz and is known by the name of "Soquel," being the same which was granted to the claimant by Governor Jose Figueroa on the 23rd day of November 1833, and which has been held and occupied ever since, and is bounded as follows: on the west by the river Arroyo de Soquel; on the east by the Sanjon de las Borregas; on the south by the sea; and on the north by the hills, where a stake was driven to mark the boundary; being two miles in length by half a league in breadth. For a more particular description, reference to be had to the original grant, map, and record of juridical possession filed in the case.

Alpheus Gelch, R. Thompson, Commissioners

filed in office January 23, 1855,
George Fisher, Secretary

Motion to send a transcript to both the Northern and Southern Districts for the reason that the land claimed in

this case lies in both districts.

McKune, Law Agent

filed in office, March 6, 1855,
George Fisher, Secretary

recorded in Journal Volume 4, page 225,
George Fisher, Secretary[197]

Land transfer by Montgomery Shackleford to George Hinckley Kirby

On January 29, 1855, Montgomery Shackleford sold his 1/27 claim to Rancho Soquel's augmentation, which he had obtained from Nicanor and Francisco Lajeunesse in September 1852, to George Hinckley Kirby. After the purchase, Kirby moved into Shackleford's former home and immediately began making improvements by adding a commercial tree nursery, increasing the amount of land devoted to crops, and building several more structures within the property. To better secure his land from unwanted visitors, he also extended the fencing to enclose all of his new features.[198]

The Depeaux family departs for the Hawaiian Islands

After Martina Castro put her mark on the two deeds in late January 1855, Louis Depeaux informed the Catholic priests that she would no longer be available as a witness before the Land Claims Commission. About two weeks later, Depeaux, Castro, and her son Miguel Lodge boarded a ship for the Hawaiian Islands. Why the destination was changed from México and who decided to change it is unknown, but it seems likely that it was done by Depeaux to keep Castro aloof of news regarding the appeal of the Land Claims Commission's decision. With Castro removed from the scene, Father Llebaria and John Wilson could operate safely without worrying that she might testify and reveal their scheme.

The priest and lawyer planned to make a plea to the commission that they had new witnesses: Castro's two brothers, Guadalupe and Juan José, as well as Henry Cambustan. With help from Archbishop Alemany, whose name was on the recently signed deed, the political pressure would be such that the commission would have to reconsider its decision.

In testimony taken in 1896, Lodge recounts his memories of the days leading up to the departure and the ship that they hired to take them overseas:

> *When Martina (my mother) and stepfather, Louis, left for San Francisco planning to board a ship that would take them to Mexico, they left me behind at home with guardians. I was not living at home with my mother for the past several years or so. I was instructed to wait two weeks, then join them in San Francisco, which I did. We spent another two weeks there preparing for the trip, which mother had changed from Mexico to the Sandwich Islands* [Hawaiian Islands].
>
> *When I arrived, I found mother still unstable, as unstable as she was at home. She claimed that the captain of the ship we were to sail on was a pirate ship and they wanted to kill her.*

At this point, Lodge describes his mother as short and weighing about 200 pounds. He also stated that she stubbornly refused instructions and ignored people when they called her. The family sailed aboard the *Leveret*, bound for Honolulu, under Captain Warner, at a cost of $50. It should be emphasized that, while this testimony seems straightforward, it is not entirely reliable because it was taken in order to prove that Castro was mentally ill at the time, a tactic that her descendants hoped would void all of the subsequent land transfers and restore to them their lost heritage.[199]

Land transfer from Peter Tracy to Henry Parsons

With the news that the Augmentation grant was about to be rejected, Henry Parsons, assistant to Peter Tracy in the Recorders' Office, convinced his boss to sell him an interest in Tracy's School Land Warrants on February 1, 1855. Tracy agreed and sold him an undisclosed percentage—probably half (80 acres)—of Warrant No. 108.[200]

Depeaux family arrives in Honolulu

The Depeaux family arrived on O'ahu on February 23, 1855 and moved onto the Hillman Ranch. The property was likely owned by Samuel Charles Hillman, who operated an imported magazine and journal subscription service in downtown Honolulu. Hillman traveled to San Francisco somewhat regularly to purchase products and Depeaux probably met him during one such trip. Hillman lost his store in 1857 and later moved to the Pajaro Valley, where he lived in the late 1860s before relocating to Southern California around 1870. Miguel Lodge notes in his testimony in 1896 that, during this time, his mother was often "unsound of mind," appearing unsteady and hitting things. She also used a strange language that nobody could understand.[201]

Chapter 4

~

Soquel in the Balance

Land Claims Commission declares Rancho Soquel's augmentation grant invalid

On April 17, 1855, the Land Claims Commission formally rejected Martina Castro's grant of the augmentation to Rancho Soquel. The commission stated that the claimant offered in evidence a traced copy of an *expediente* and what was purported to be a traced copy of a grant in pursuance of said *expediente*. She also provided a subsequent *expediente* for an extension of the former grant, together with traced copies of what were purported to be a portion of an intermediate proceedings therein, and a traced copy of what was purported to be a grant in pursuance of the last *expediente*. The *expediente* consisted of the original petition and the *informe*.

The commission continued: "but no proof whatever is offered to establish the existence of the originals, or what purports to be copies are copies of the originals. We are of opinion that the proofs in the case are insufficient to entitle the claimant to be a confirmation, a decree therefore will be granted rejecting the same."

Opinion by the Board of Commissioners concerning the rejection of the Soquel Augmentation grant request.

In this case, on hearing the proofs and allegations, it is agreed by the commission that the claim of said petitioner is not valid, and it is therefore decreed that the application for the confirmation is thereof denied.

The commissioners also declared that the Soquel Augmentation Ranch is located within the Southern District of California; therefore, the transcripts of the proceedings and decisions shall be sent to the United States District Court for the Southern District of California for further consideration.

The transcripts of the proceeding documents, testimony, and decisions for Rancho Soquel, which is an accepted legitimate grant to Martina Castro, is transmitted to the Attorney General of the United States for the Northern District of California for further consideration.

R. Aug. Thompson
S. B. Farewell

filed in office on the 17th of April 1855
George Fisher Secretary[202]

Affidavits and depositions submitted to the Land Claims Commission regarding Rancho Soquel's augmentation grant

Over a two-day period in May 1855, the Land Claims Commission received two affidavits and four depositions regarding the validity of the grant of Rancho Soquel's augmentation. The two affidavits were received on May 15, one submitted by John Wilson, the other by Father Llebaria, both on behalf of the Catholic Church. The first states simply that:

Martina Castro moves the court for leave to set aside the decree of rejection entered in this case and for leave to give new evidence to support the claim upon the following affidavit to show cause why the same should be so set aside once rehearing begins.

The second affidavit is more detailed:

> *I, John Francis Llebaria, state that in the case of Martina Castro for the Augmentation to the Soquel Rancho, being case No. 593, that this affiant has been since about the month of January last, has had the entire control of management of the case for the claimant and for this affiant, and then he applied sometime in the month of February 1855 to John Wilson, one of the attorneys who had charge of the case before the board, to know what testimony was further wanting to prove the case, so as the same could be confirmed, and the said lands of the grant of this affiant.*

The next portion of the second affidavit is unreadable, but it appears to state that whatever is necessary to confirm the augmentation grant to him will be done to prove the boundaries, the occupation, and also the genuineness of the papers of the grant. It continues:

> *This affiant sent to Santa Cruz, where the land lies, and engaged Juan Jose Castro and Guadalupe Castro, who live adjacent to the land claimed, who had seen the original grant, and who knew all about the occupation and boundaries of the land claimed, and they promised further to be in the City of San Francisco about the first of April 1855, and about that day, this affiant is informed and believes the information to be true, that the said Juan Jose Castro became sick and was unable to attend before the board on the claim. But the same Juan Jose Castro is here now and is prepared to give testimony. This affiant has also been informed and believes the same to be true, then the same Guadalupe Castro was wholly unable to attend at the above named time because of private business which he cannot leave, but he is here now, and this is the earliest that this affiant has been able to procure their attendance, and they are both prepared to show the validity of the claim and therefore be opened and a new hearing granted upon this case.*
>
> Father John Francis Llebaria

On May 16, Guadalupe and Juan José Castro came together to present to the Land Claims Commission the following deposition:

> *We, the undersigned, say that they have had the foregoing affidavit read to them and interpreted to them, being the affidavit of Father John Francis Llebaria as above, and so far as the facts are there stated, which relate to them, they are true, and they failed to appear because they could not, as stated in said affidavit.*
>
> Guadalupe Castro
Juan José Castro

The same day, Guadalupe Castro gave a more thorough deposition before R. Aug. Thompson of the Land Claims Commission on behalf of his sister. After being duly sworn in, he replied to the following questions asked by Wilson:

Q: What is your name, age, and place of residence?
A: My name is Guadalupe Castro, my age is thirty-nine years, and I reside at San Andres in the County of Santa Cruz.
Q: Are you acquainted with the tract of land claimed by your sister Martina Castro, in this case lying in Santa Cruz County and known as the augmentation to the Rancho de Soquel? If you do, do you know the boundaries of the said augmentation and, if yes, please state them?
A: I am acquainted with the said tract of land and I know the boundaries of the said augmentation. They are commencing at the boundary of the Rancho de Soquel and thence to the Laguna del Sargento, the said boundary being designated by the place known as "Palo de la Yesca." From the said Laguna del Sargento to the Loma Prieta, thence to the point known by the name of Chuchita, and thence to the land of the Rancho de Soquel and adjoining the land of Don Rafael Castro and that of the said Rancho de Soquel.
Q: Do you know whether the land *aumento* has been occupied?

If yes, when, by whom, and state the kind of occupancy?

A: Martina Castro has occupied the said *aumento* ever since previous to the grant of it to her pasturing thereupon her stock. She had her house and improvements upon the Rancho de Soquel and lived there.

Q: Are you acquainted with the handwriting of Ricardo Juan, Francisco Alviso, Manual Jimeno, and Manual Micheltorena? If so, state your means of knowledge and look upon the documents now shown you marked "RAF Exhibit No. 1" to this deposition, purporting to be a certified copy from the office of the Surveyor General of the United States of an original *expediente* on file in the archives of said office, and state whether the signatures of the above named persons, where they therein occur, are then genuine signatures on the said original. Also, look at document marked "RAF No. 2 Exhibit" to this deposition and answer the same question, reference to the part thereof, continued on pages 16 (LDK) to 23 (LDK) inclusive? And have you or have you not examined in the office of the United States Surveyor General the original papers of which the same exhibits purport to be copies?

A: I am acquainted with the hand writing and signatures of the above mentioned persons. I have this day examined the original papers referred to in the preceding interrogation in the office of the United States Surveyor General and can state that I believe the signatures of Ricardo Juan, Francisco Alviso, Manual Jimeno, and Manual Micheltorena, where they occur therein, to be their true genuine signatures, having seen them all write.

Q: After the grant of the augmentation to Martina Castro, have you ever seen any paper in her possession purporting to be such grant, and, if yes, state whether the different signatures to it were known by you, and, if yes, were they the same as those in the original document referenced to in your previous answer in the office of the United States

Surveyor General? And state if you know what became of the copy which you saw in Martina Castro's hand?

A: I saw in the possession of the said Martina Castro about the year 1844 the grant from Manual Micheltorena for the same *aumento* and also the previous grant by Figueroa of the Rancho de Soquel. I believe they were the identical papers which I this morning saw in the office of the United States Surveyor General, on these at least contain the matter.

It should be noted that Guadalupe Castro could neither read nor write, yet he seems confident enough in this deposition to claim that he recognized indisputably the signatures of four men on a document signed ten years earlier.

Guadalupe's brother, Juan José, was also interrogated by Wilson before Thompson, which then created the third deposition of the day. He required the translation services of a Mr. Beancing, an associate officer under Law Agent Greenhower.

Q: What is your name, age, and place of residence?

A: My name is Juan Jose Castro, my age is fifty-three years, and I reside adjoining the Town of Watsonville in the County of Santa Cruz in California.

Q: Are you acquainted with the tract of land claimed in this case, lying in Santa Cruz County and known as the augmentation to the Rancho de Soquel? If yes, do you know the boundaries of the augmentation and, if yes, please state them?

A: I am acquainted with the augmentation to the Rancho de Soquel and I also know the boundaries of the same. The boundaries are on one side, the place known as "Palo de la Yesca," so called from an oak tree that formerly stood there from which punk was obtained. On another side, the Laguna del Sargento, on another side the Loma Prieta de la Sierra Azul, which Loma is the highest point of the Sierra, and on the other side, a place called "la Chuchita," and on the said last side it adjoins the lands of Rafael Castro, and on the side towards the sea, that of the original Rancho de

Soquel, on the side of the Palo de la Yesca, it adjoins the lands of the Pueblo of Santa Cruz, or Branciforte.

Q: Do you know whether the land *aumento* has been occupied? If yes, when, by whom, and state the kind of occupancy?

A: Yes, the said *aumento* has been occupied by Martina Castro, who owned the Rancho de Soquel on which she grazed and pastured her stock on the said *aumento* from the date of the grant thereof to her. Both the *aumento* and the Rancho de Soquel I consider one and the same property.

Lastly, Wilson interviewed Henry Cambustan, the former surveyor general of Branciforte in 1844, who had given testimony in March 1854 regarding his knowledge of the boundaries of both Soquel grants.

Q: What is your name, age, and place of residence?

A: My name is Enrique Cambustan, my age is thirty-eight years, and I reside at Monterey, California.

Q: State whether you have examined the original papers now on file in the United States Surveyor General's office pertaining to the grant to Martina Castro for the Rancho de Soquel and the augmentation to the same, of which the papers now here shown you and marked "RAF Exhibit No. 1," to deposition of Guadalupe Castro May 16, 1855, and herein exhibited. If yes, are you acquainted with the signatures to the same and state your means of knowledge and are they or not genuine?

A: I have this morning examined the original papers of which the said document marked "RAF Exhibit No. 1" purports to be a certified traced copy from the office of the United States Surveyor General, and I am acquainted with the signatures of Manual Micheltorena, Ricardo Juan, and Manual Jimeno, having seen them write and sign their names often, whose signatures where they appear in and upon the aforesaid original papers I believe to be their genuine signatures.[203]

John Wilson requests an addendum to the agreement of October 28, 1852

On May 21, 1855, John Wilson requested an addendum to the agreement made between Martina Castro, Durrell Gregory, and Wilson on October 28, 1852. Namely, he wanted to add an acknowledgement by Archbishop Alemany to the terms of the agreement and a further promise to sign a deed confirming said terms once Wilson and Gregory did the same. This was necessary to ensure the terms of the agreement remained after the transfer of Rancho Soquel to the Catholic Church. Due to ongoing lawsuits, appeals by various parties, and resistance from Gregory, the addendum would not actually be added to the agreement until May 20, 1861.[204]

Martina Castro and Miguel Lodge are sent back to San Francisco

According to testimony given by Miguel Lodge in 1896, Martina Castro continued to act strangely after the Depeaux family moved to the Hillman Ranch on O'ahu. She became increasingly erratic and claimed to see witches, but she also had more lucid moments and befriended several Native Hawaiians, who visited her daily at the ranch. Nonetheless, her behavior finally pushed Depeaux over the edge and he began to beat his wife in late April 1855. Lodge quickly jumped in to defend his mother and Depeaux decided at that moment that his wife and stepson needed to go back to San Francisco. They set sail from Honolulu aboard *Yankee*, captained by James Smith, on May 5.

During the voyage, Lodge claimed that he tried to keep his mother with him at all times, but he failed once, and the results were almost disastrous. He heard someone shout, "woman overboard," and the ship was brought around. The captain lowered a launch and crewmembers picked the forty-six-year-old woman out of the Pacific Ocean, rescuing her before she drowned, which possibly was her goal. No corroborating evidence exists for this story, so Lodge's potentially unreliable testimony serves as the only source.

After they arrived back in San Francisco in June, they rested for about two weeks at the home of José and Candida Bolcoff. On their return home, Lodge left his mother in order to work for a Mrs. Freeman in Redwood City, with whom he remained for approximately eight months.[205]

Northern District of the Land Claims Commission accepts the validity of Shoquel Augmentation

On April 17, 1855, the Land Claims Commission had declared that Rancho Soquel's augmentation was located outside of the Northern District's jurisdiction. On June 26, John Wilson formally appealed this ruling on Martina Castro's behalf, stating "that the land claimed in this case is situated north of parallel 37 degrees north latitude; therefore, it is located in the Northern District of California."

The Northern District the same day confirmed Wilson's statements and accepted the validity of the land grant, ruling:

> *In this case, on hearing the proofs and allegations, it is adjudged by the commission that the claim of the said Petitioner is valid, and it is therefore decreed that her application for the confirmation thereof be allowed.*
>
> *The land of which confirmation is hereby situated in the County of Santa Cruz, and is called "Shoquel," with an addition, a ridge called "Paloui," to be located agreeably to the calls of the grants, and the map accompanying the Expediente on file in this case, with reference to the depositions, also on file herein.*

Aug. Thompson
S. B. Farwell
Commissioners

This is the first instance where the name "Shoquel" was used to refer to the augmentation grant, and this name was used inconsistently in the several lawsuits that followed the grant's confirmation. For this reason, and to differentiate it from Rancho Soquel and the earlier iterations of the augmentation, the confirmed property will henceforth be named Shoquel

Augmentation in this book. Their ruling continues:

> *The claimant in this case has offered in evidence in support of her claim a traced copy of an Expediente dated the 16th day of November 1833 addressed to Governor Figueroa for a grant of the place in question, in a Petition of which Figueroa issued an Expediente, a provincial grant on the 22nd day of November 1833. On the 17th day of May 1834, the preceding received that approval from the Departmental Assembly. On the same day, Governor Figueroa replied to the petition a final time. On the 7th day of January 1844, the petitioner presented another Expediente for an extension of the grant, so as to include an adjoining ridge called "Palacie," in a Petition of which in February following Governor Micheltorena in an Expediente issued a grant to the extension asked for. The document establishing the foregoing facts are on file once proven to be genuine.*
>
> *The petitioner has also proven that she was in possession of the place and being at the time of the issuing of the grant, and that she has continued to live on the place ever since. We think also that the boundaries are so well settled by the proof that there will be no difficulty in locating the same. We think this a valid grant and a decree of confirmation will accordingly be entered. The grant is confirmed.*

The commission ordered that all material, evidence, transcripts, and proceedings that were to be sent to the Southern District be retained for use in the case, and that copies of all such material also be filed with the Third District Court and sent to the United States Attorney General.[206]

Frederick Hihn is sworn in as a U.S. citizen

While Frederick Hihn was adjusting to married life with Therese, attempting to expand his general store's clientele, and becoming involved in local Santa Cruz affairs, he received notice that he was finally naturalized as a citizen of the United States on July 2, 1855.[207]

Occupants of Rancho Soquel and Shoquel Augmentation served eviction notices

In the aftermath of the Land Claim Commission's ruling, the Catholic Church moved to seize the land that they had purchased from Martina Castro, triggering a cascade of lawsuits. As of August 1855, several individuals and families claimed to own or lease land and lived within the boundaries of the properties, some legally, some as squatters.

Among Martina Castro's family, Luisa and Jean Fourcade, Helena and Joseph Littlejohn, Guadalupe and Joseph Averon, Antonia and Henry Peck, Josefa and Lambert Clements, and Nicanor and Francisco Lajeunesse all lived on Rancho Soquel. Carmel and Thomas Fallon also owned property but did not live there. Outside the family, Joshua Parrish, Pruett Sinclair, John Vandenberg, and George Kirby all lived within one of the grants' boundaries.

In addition, several people claimed ownership of a portion of the grants, either through quitclaims or School Land Warrants, including Montgomery Shackleford, Peter Tracy, Thomas Wright, Joseph Majors, Joel Bates, Henry Parsons, and Craven Hester.

After the eviction notices were served, a few obeyed and departed, but the majority decided to stay and fight. While several hired attorneys of their choice, the Castro family put aside their differences and hired Robert Peckham to represent them.

Immediately, Peckham claimed that when Martina Castro signed the two deeds in San Francisco, she owned only one ninth of each ranch; therefore, she could have only sold this portion of land to the Catholic priests. Thus was laid the legal foundation between attorneys Peckham and John Wilson for the next twelve years as the case progressed from the local district court to the California Supreme Court.

Land transfers from Josefa, Guadalupe, and Luisa Lodge, Joseph Majors, and Pruett Sinclair to Durrell Gregory

On August 11, 1855, several landowners in Rancho Soquel and Shoquel Augmentation, including the Clements, Averons, Fourcades, Joseph Majors, and Pruett Sinclair, sold Durrell Gregory one-third of their tracts within their lands for $1.00 each. This made Gregory the owner of 4/27 of both properties, although he had overlooked the fact that the Clements had sold their entire property to Sinclair and Jones Hoy in March 1852 (Hoy had subsequently sold his portion to Joseph Ladd in July 1853). The owners did this in order to give Gregory a personal interest in the land which he was defending before the Land Claims Commission and courts.[208]

Frederick Hihn acquires land in Rancho Soquel and Shoquel Augmentation

On October 8, 1854, the Third District Court had ruled that Pruett Sinclair owed Charles Stevenson $674, with the sheriff holding Sinclair's 1/18 part of Rancho Soquel and Shoquel Augmentation as collateral until the amount was paid. On June 25, 1855, the amount came due, but Sinclair had still not paid, so the land was sold at auction. The auction was held on August 21 and the highest bidder, purchasing the land for $450, was Frederick Hihn, who thus began his career as a real estate investor while simultaneously entering into the confusing and unstable legal battle over the fate of Martina Castro's land grants.[209]

Land transfer from Thomas Fallon to Henry Peck

On September 10, 1855, Thomas Fallon sold School Land Warrant Nos. 353 and 354—comprising 320 acres—to his close friend Henry Peck.[210]

Land transfer from Father Llebaria and Archbishop Alemany to Father Ingoldsby

Before the suit against Martina Castro's heirs could be brought, ownership of the two ranches had to be reduced from three to just one. With only one owner, the suit would be greatly simplified, thus saving both time and costs. The three priests decided that ownership of both ranches should be placed with Father Ingoldsby, the lowest ranking of the three, and, besides, Ingoldsby reported to Father Llebaria, the archbishop's Vicar-General, the

Soquel in the Balance 1855

number two man in Alemany's Northern California diocese. The transfer deeds were drawn up and signed on September 10, 1855 in the office of John Wilson in San Francisco and read as follows:

> *This indenture made and executed that 10th day of September 1855 between the most Reverend Joseph Sadoc Alemany and John Francis Llebaria, parties of the first part, and the Reverend John Ingoldsby, party of the second part, all of the City of San Francisco, State of California, witness to wit:*
>
> *That the said parties of the first part for the sum of one dollar in hand paid of the second party and acknowledge the conveyance to said Ingoldsby all their right and title and interest which they or either of them has or holds in a Ranch lying in the county of Santa Cruz and called and known there by the name of the Soquel Ranch and the Augmentation, thereto both granted to one Martina Castro by the Mexican nation and whereon she lately resided, and which said Ranch and the Augmentation thereto, the said Martina Castro, under the name and style of Martina Castro Depeaux, joined by her husband Louis Depeaux, conveyed by deeds to the said parties of the first part with all the appurtenances thereto belonging. To have and to hold to the said Ingoldsby and his heirs forever all the interests which both or either of said parties of the first part have in and to the said described Soquel Ranch and the Augmentation grant thereto attached free from the claims or demands of the said parties of the first part, their heirs or assigns, forever given our hands and seals the day and year first above written.*
>
> Joseph S. Alemany
John Francis Llebaria

State of California
County of San Francisco

On this 12th day of September 1855, before me personally came Joseph S. Alemany and John Francis Llebaria, to me severally known to be the persons described in and who executed the foregoing instrument, and severally acknowledged that they executed the same freely and voluntarily for the uses and purposes therein mentioned. In witness whereof, I have hereunto set my hand and seal the day and year last aforesaid.

E. R. Carpenter, Notary Public

Recorded in Book of Records Volume 3rd and upon pages 110 and 111 of the records of the Recorders Office, Santa Cruz County, California, September 14, 1855.

Peter Tracy, Recorder
Henry F. Parsons, Deputy Recorder

The day after, the three priests made a compact to ensure that they and the fate of the two land grants were protected and that their lawyers, Wilson and newly hired James W. Scarborough, were paid. The agreement was as follows:

This Agreement is made this 11th day of September 1855, between the Reverend John Ingoldsby of the first part, by the most Reverend Joseph Sadoc Alemany and the Reverend John Francis Llebaria of the second part, all of the City of San Francisco, State of California, witnesseth:

That the said parties of the second part, on the 10th day of September 1855, conveyed their deed bearing that date certain interests in the Soquel Ranch and the Augmentation, thereto the title to which is now fully vested in the said John Ingoldsby, by a regular chain of conveyances from Martina Castro Depeaux and Louis Depeaux, her husband, to the said Ingoldsby, which said land is before the Board of Commissioners for the settlement of Martina's land claims in California, and with the Soquel and Augmentation tracts have been confirmed by said board but have yet to be further contested, and as there are persons on the same land as trespassers who refuse to give up the same, therefore it becomes necessary to have land suits and law-

yers to attend to it, and in consequence thereof, the said first and second parties to this agreement, have made arrangements with John Wilson and James W. Scarborough to attend thereto all this litigation as their attorneys, by a written agreement for the terms of which reference is made for the particulars thereof of these parties, being further advised that it was doubtful whether the whole three first and second parties owning as they did common interests could bring a joint suit, and therefore the parties of the second part in this contract, for the consideration aforesaid, have by deed as before as cited conveyed all their interest to the party of the first part, and the parties of the second part of this agreement agree to aid the said Ingoldsby in attending to the same and to pay each an equal share of the expenses that may be necessary to be incurred in the prosecuting the right of title of the said land till the same is complete, and to give an equal share of time as they shall agree to do from time to time and have alike power to council in the whole affair till the same is fully completed or they agree to abandon the same, and whenever the same is hereafter demanded by either of the second parties to this agreement, the said party of the first part shall reconvey to each of the parties of the second part one equal third part of the land now held by the said Ingoldsby as before subject to their equal share of the expenses necessarily expanded, which may incur and subject to the claim of the said Wilson and Scarborough, as per the agreement before referred to in this agreement.

witness our hands and seals the day
and year first aforesaid
Joseph S. Alemany
John Francis Llebaria
John Ingoldsby

State of California
County of San Francisco

On this 12th day of September 1855, before me personally appeared Joseph S. Alemany, John Francis Llebaria, and John

Ingoldsby, to me severally known to be the persons described in and who executed the foregoing instrument, and severally acknowledged that they executed the same freely and voluntarily for the uses and purposes therein mentioned. In witness whereof, I have hereto affixed my hand and official seal the day and year past aforesaid.

E. R. Carpenter, Notary public

As compensation for their successful efforts, Wilson and Scarborough were each to receive one quarter of both grants in payment, continuing the offer made by Castro earlier with Scarborough replacing Durrell Gregory, who had left the case to defend John Hames. Wilson and Scarborough, in turn, promised to sell half of their properties to grantees who were agreeable to all parties. The money derived from these sales would be donated to the Catholic Church.[211]

Judge rules in favor of Martina Castro against claims of John Hames

On September 14, 1855, the California Supreme Court handed down its decision concerning the appeal of the Third District Court's ruling by John Hames in his case against Martina Castro—Case No. 78—regarding the contract her second husband, Michael Lodge, entered into with Hames to build a sawmill on Soquel Creek. Justice Solomon Heydenfeldt delivered the following opinion, which Chief Justice Hugh Murray concurred:

This action is upon a contract made during the Mexican dominion and must have its effect and construction to the laws then prevailing.

Several interesting questions entered into the consideration of the case at the bar and were argued with an ability which displayed much erudition and research on the part of the counsel engaged on both sides. But from the view we take of the case, only one question is necessary to be considered. The proof shows that at the time of making the contract, she was a married woman and entered into it jointly with her husband. By giving to the evidence the construction most unfavorable to the wife, the contract would appear to have been a joint purchase for the joint benefit of husband and wife.

By the Mexican laws, all property acquired during marriage is common property. By the 61st Law of Toro, the wife can neither be bound as security for her husband, nor liable as a joint contractor, except it be shown that the contract has been advantageous to the wife. Schmidt's Law of Spain and Mexico, sec 4, ch. 2.

To establish that the contract was advantageous to the wife means necessarily that it accrued to the benefit of her separate estate, for whatever the husband is bound to furnish is expressly excluded from the qualification of advantage to her, and there would be no use for the rule, if her advantage was referred to some new acquisition to the common property. In this case, the record does not disclose any benefit to the defendant arising from the contract. But it is urged that she is liable, being the survivor of her husband, under the rule of the Mexican law, for one-half of the community debts. To fix this liability, however, it must be shown that a fruitless effort has been made to obtain payment through an administration of the community assets, or that there is no common property, and that the community is insolvent. Until this is done, the defendant cannot be made to answer personally for any part of the debt.

It results from these views of the rules under the Mexican system of jurisprudence that the Court was correct in ordering a nonsuit and the judgment is affirmed.[212]

Land Claims Commission submits decision regarding Rancho Soquel for approval by the Attorney General

On September 26, 1855, Land Claims Commission secretary George Fisher received the transcript of the proceedings and decision regarding Martina Castro's claim on Rancho Soquel. Fisher forwarded the documents to the clerk of the United States District Court for the Northern District of California, who received them on October 4 and forwarded them on to the Attorney General, who would make the final ruling regarding the case.

Land transfer from Rafael Castro to Nicholas Valencia

On November 8, 1855, Rafael Castro sold an unknown portion of Rancho Aptos to Nicholas Valencia. The area included the mostly seasonal "Arroyo de Novillos," which loosely translates as "Creek of the Young Bulls (or Oxen)," undoubtedly a reference to Castro's cattle herds. Following Valencia's acquisition of the land, the stream became known as Valencia Creek.[213]

Land Claims Commission submits decision regarding Shoquel Augmentation for approval by the Attorney General

On November 21, 1855, Land Claims Commission secretary George Fisher received the transcript of the proceedings and decision regarding Martina Castro's claim on Shoquel Augmentation. Fisher forwarded the documents to the clerk of the United States District Court for the Northern District of California, who received them on December 1 and forwarded them on to the Attorney General, who would make the final ruling regarding the case.[214]

Attorney General rejects Shoquel Augmentation grant and Martina Castro is sent to the Stockton Insane Asylum

On December 31, 1855, John Wilson, as the representative for Father Ingoldsby, who was the sole owner of Rancho Soquel and Shoquel Augmentation at the time according to the deed of January, received the following notice by United States Attorney General John Y. Mason:

> *You will please take notice in the above case, decided by the Commissioners to ascertain and settle private land claims in the State of California in favor of the claimant, and a transcript of the proceedings in which was received in this office on the 18th day of December 1855, the appeal in the District Court of the United States for the Northern District of California will be presented by the United States.*

The court assigned the appeal Case No. 343 and, shortly after sending this notice, began calling witnesses to testify regarding their knowledge of Martina Castro and the Soquel land grants. Castro's husband and attorneys had ensured that she was unable to testify before the Land Claims Commission in 1855, but it would be much more difficult for her to avoid appearing in court. At the time the notice was given, Castro was living on Rancho Soquel in the home of one of her daughters. Thus, an insidious scheme was hatched to ensure she would avoid the witness stand a second time. Just days after receiving notice of the new trial, Castro was admitted to the newly opened Insane Asylum of California in Stockton.

All the information historians have concerning Castro's time in Stockton is secondhand, derived from Carrie Lodge's 1965 interviews, which clearly drew on Miguel Lodge's version of events. Carrie recalls that Martina appeared at the church in San Francisco after her return from the Hawaiian Islands seeking a piece of luggage that she had left there before departing in early 1855. Because no one remembered or recognized her and she seemed disoriented, the priests or local authorities sent her to the nearest facility that could handle persons in her state.

Of course, this cannot be correct since Castro was living with one of her daughters in Soquel a few weeks after returning from San Francisco. And if she was suffering from a mental illness, Lodge certainly would have accompanied his mother home.

After reading Carrie's interview and the testimony of Lodge and his sisters, I decided that I had to contact the Stockton Development Center, the successor to the original asylum. Under the provisions of Section 5328 of the Welfare and Institutions Code, no information about a former patient, however long ago the case, could be released without the approval of the close relative of the patient. I finally found the descendent I needed in the person of Mr. Charles V. Kieffer, who descended from Castro's sister María de los Angeles and Joseph Majors. Kieffer wrote the necessary letter, resulting in a return letter from the Supervisor of Client Records, who stated that "during the period of Martina Castro's stay at the facility, the only information we have is a very limited entry in an admissions ledger: 'Mexican, about 35 years old, simple dementia, history unknown.' And the date of her discharge is November 8, 1856."

At the conclusion of the discussion, I was invited to visit the medical center and read the personal journals of Dr. Robert K. Reide, the head doctor during the period of Castro's stay there. The doctor's journals consisted of three books, but none of them mentioned Castro. This was unusual since the doctor recorded the name and date that each of his patients entered into and were released from the asylum, adding comments concerning the patient's status at each date.

My contact at the center was somewhat knowledgeable of the rules, regulations, and the laws in existence during the period that Castro was admitted, and he stated that both a doctor's analysis and a court order were required to put a person in an asylum. But she could have entered the asylum through two other avenues. First, she could have been delivered by a group of sufficiently high authority or status, such as the Catholic Church. Or she could have been temporarily transferred from the hospital wing to the asylum to undergo examination of her "simple dementia." Since she was clearly sent to the hospital in a state that the doctors judged to be dementia, and since she was only fluent in Spanish, it is quite possible that her period of examination and observation lasted the better part of a year.

Who placed Castro in the asylum is a mystery. It seems unlikely that her family sent her there—at least they did not do it directly. Had they done so, they would have gone through the proper authorities and there would be records to document her admission into the facility. The people that would benefit most from committing her were Father Ingoldsby and the Catholic Church, who wanted at all costs to keep her from testifying in the impending trial in order to uphold the validity of her land grants and transfers. They also potentially had the power and clout to have Castro committed through back channels. The truth of the matter remains unknown.[215]

Augustus Noble settles on Rancho Soquel

Augustus Noble was born on December 28, 1823 in Baltimore, Maryland, where he worked for several years as a cooper. The allure of gold drew him to California, where he arrived on July 19, 1849. He spent some time looking for the elusive mineral but, failing that, moved to Maine, where he settled down and started a family. He and his family returned to California sometime in 1855. From that point on, he divided his business activities between San Francisco and Sacramento. This brought him into contact with John Wilson and James Scarborough, as well as Thomas Courtis, who will enter this story shortly. He also counted among his friends Father Ingoldsby, Father Llebaria, and Archbishop Alemany. Because of these friendships, Noble was recruited as a courier for the priests and their attorneys. In 1856, Noble and his family settled in Soquel on land sold to him by the Catholic Church, thereby drawing him into the legal battle over Rancho Soquel and Shoquel Augmentation.[216]

District Attorney announces his intention to review the Rancho Soquel and Shoquel Augmentation grants

On February 28, 1856, United States District Attorney S. W. Ingr sent a petition to the District Court for the Northern California District concerning Rancho Soquel:

> *This Petition of the United States by their attorney represents; that this cause is an application for a review of the decision of the Board of Commissioners whereby the claim Appellee and confirmed as appears by reference to the records in the case; that a transcript of the said records was filed in this court on the 1st day of May in 1833: that a notice of appeal was filed on the 1st day of May, 1834; and that the land claimed lies in the said District; that the said claim is invalid. Wherefore, appellants pray that the said decision of the Board be reversed and that this Court decide the said decision to be invalid.*
>
> S. W. Ingr, United States District Attorney

The following day, Ingr submitted a second petition for Shoquel Augmentation:

> *This Petition of the United States by the attorney represents; that this cause is an application for a review of the decision of the Board of Commissioners whereby the claim of the said*

appellant by reference to the names in this case; that a transcript of the said Recorder was filed in this court on the first day of August in 1854; that a notice of appeal was filed on the 1st day of August 1854; and that the land claimed lies in the Northern District; that the said claim is invalid. Wherefore, appellants pray that the said decision of the Board be reversed and that this Court determine the said title to be invalid.

S. W. Ingr, United States District Attorney[217]

John Wilson petitions Third District Court regarding jurisdictional boundaries

On March 3, 1856, John Wilson, on behalf of Martina Castro, sent a petition to the United States District Court for the Northern California District concerning the jurisdiction under which Shoquel Augmentation fell:

And the said Martina Castro for answer to the Petition filed in this court in Case No. 343 on the docket of the Court, says she admits the case was confirmed by the Board of Private Land Claims and that the land lies within the Northern District of California and that it is within the jurisdiction of this Court, but she denies all other facts stated in their Petition of the said United States that the decree of confirmation entered by the Board of Private Land Claims be confirmed and whatsoever else may be just in the premises.

John Wilson, Attorney for the Plaintiff

Two days later, Wilson also wrote a petition to the court regarding Rancho Soquel:

And the said Martina Castro for answer to the Petition filed by the United States in Case No. 295, on the docket of the Court, says she admits the claim was confirmed to her by the Board of Private Land Claims and that the land claimed in her original petition before said Board lies within the Northern District of California and is within the jurisdiction of this Court, but she denies all other allegations made by the United States in her said Petition and prays the decree of the Board of Private Land Claims confirming the land to this claimant and prays be affirmed and whatsoever case is just and proper in the premises.

John Wilson, Attorney for the Claimant[218]

Deposition given by John Hames to the District Attorney concerning Shoquel Augmentation

On March 5, 1856, John Hames came before the acting United States District Attorney Andrew Glassell to answer questions concerning his knowledge of Shoquel Augmentation.

Q: What is your name, age, and place of residence?
A: My name is John Hames. I am forty-one and reside in Santa Cruz County.
Q: Are you acquainted with Martina Castro, the claimant in this case and, if so, how long have you known her, and if you have had any conversation with her about her title to the land in the above entitled claim? If so, state that conversation particularly according to your best recollection.
A: I am acquainted with Martina Castro, known her since the spring of 1845, have had a conversation with her about her title to the land. She has spoken to me several times about it, first time in 1845 or '46. She told me she put in a petition for what she called the "Yesca," same now known by the name "Aument." She gave it no other name than "Yesca." She told me that owing to the people living in the village of Branciforte and the alcalde, she was unable to obtain the grant.
Q: Did you ever have a conversation with Francisco Alviso

about a report he had made in this case?

A: In the spring of 1848, I went to him and asked him if he had been to Monterey and agreed that this tract of land could be granted to Martina Castro. He said no and I asked him if he could testify to that, and he said yes. He went with me before Justice Blackburn in the spring of 1848 at Santa Cruz. He was sworn and he stated on oath that he never agreed that the "Yesca" could be granted.[219]

Deposition given by Thomas Fallon to the District Attorney concerning Shoquel Augmentation

On March 31, 1856, before the acting United States District Attorney Andrew Glassell, Thomas Fallon answered questions concerning his knowledge of Shoquel Augmentation. He was sworn in by George Johnstone, a commissioner of the United States District Court for the Northern California District.

> *Being duly authorized to administer oaths, in San Francisco, on March 31, 1856, before me, came Thomas Fallon, a witness jurat on behalf of the United States in Case No. 343, being an appeal from the Board of Commissioners to ascertain and settle Private Land Claims in the State of California in case No. 593, on the docket of the said Board of Commissioners, and was duly sworn and testified as follows:*

Q: What is your name, age, and place of residence?
A: Thomas Fallon, I am thirty-three years of age, and I reside at San Jose, Santa Clara County.
Q: Are you acquainted with Martina Castro, the claimant of the place called "la Yesca?"
A: I am, but it is better known by the name of the "Aumento."
Q: To what is it, the Aumento?
A: To the Soquel Ranch.
Q: How long have you known the claimant Martina Castro?

A: For about ten years.

Q: Have you in any way been connected in interest with this tract of land and, if so, how and when?

A: Yes, I was interested in it, first in 1848 on account of marrying one of the daughters of Martina Castro, and afterwards in 1852 by deed from Martina Castro to one ninth of the whole tract.

Q: Have you ever taken any steps in connection with the prosecution of the claim of Martina Castro to the ranch?

A: In the fall of 1849, I went and saw Mr. Hartnell, who was then the translator for the government. On account of being interested, I applied to him for copies of all papers related to this ranch that were in the archives at Monterey.

Hartnell gave me copies of the petition from Martina Castro to Manuel Micheltorena for this ranch called the "Yesca." Also a copy of the report from the alcalde of Santa Cruz, named Francisco Alviso, and also a copy of a paper signed by Manual Jimeno. These were all the documents in the archives which he said related to this property and certified to this fact and also to the correctness of the translation.

I noticed where there was a note written in the margin of the originals in the archives changing the words "no" to "si," and in the copy that Hartnell gave me of the report of the alcalde it read "no," and I asked Hartnell why it was so and he observed to me that it was right that it should be so, for it was changed. I was a little angry with him at the time, for I was interested, and I finally asked him what he thought about the matter, and he told me there was no title—there was nothing that I could base a title upon except the paper with Jimeno's name upon it and that he did not consider it worth anything.

At this moment, John Wilson, who was present during the testimony to represent Castro and the Catholic Church's interests, objected to all that was said to or by Hartnell. Hartnell continued:

Q: Are the papers which you saw in the archives at Monterey on the occasion to which you refer the original title papers which have been filed before the Board of the Land Commission in this case?

A: I believe they are. In fact, I am almost positive of it, because in 1852, I examined with my attorney, Judge Ord, the same documents referred to and he pronounced them as absolutely of no account.

Q: Where were those papers when you examined them with Judge Ord?

A: I think it was in Palmer Cook Company's building on Kearny Street in San Francisco.

Q: How came they to be there?

A: I cannot tell.

Q: In whose possession were they?

A: I do not know. Judge Ord informed me before we went in that he would apply to the Law Agent to see them.

Wilson objects to the conversation between Fallon and Ord.

Q: Have you ever seen those papers since?

A: No, I think not.

Q: How came you to go to this place when you last saw the papers?

A: I wished to engage Judge Ord to prosecute this claim before the Law commission.

Wilson objected to this question as irrelevant.

Q: Why did you go to the place on Kearny Street now than to any other place to see these papers?

A: Judge Ord informed me that this was the place where the archives were kept.

Wilson objected to this answer as improper evidence.

Q: What time was this?
A: Sometime late in the summer of 1852.
Q: Did you ever take any further steps in connection with those papers and, if so, what?
A: After that, I never took any steps towards a confirmation as I looked upon it as hopeless.

Wilson objected to this answer as improper evidence.

Q: Did you ever take any other steps in regard to this claim between the time that you had the conversation with Mr. Hartnell at Monterey and the time that you went with Judge Ord to see the papers on Kearny Street?

Wilson objected to this question as irrelevant.

A: I did—from the time I spoke to Hartnell until 1852, I did all I could towards the confirmation by inquiring and trying to find out evidence in favor of the claim. I spoke to Manual Jimeno himself upon the subject, and I showed Jimeno the copies of all the papers that Hartnell had given me. I explained the contents of the papers to Jimeno and asked him if he knew anything more about it. He said that was all he knew about it.

Wilson objected to this answer as improper evidence.

Q: Of what did these papers that you explained to Jimeno purport to be copies?
A: They were copies of all the papers relating to the Ranch of la Yesca, which Hartnell gave me. There was a petition from Martina Castro to Manual Micheltorena asking for the ranch; a report of the alcalde of Santa Cruz, Francisco Alviso, saying it cannot be granted; a paper signed by Jimeno himself—these were about all the papers.

Wilson objected to this answer as improper evidence.

Q: Do you know positively whether these were all the papers which you explained to Jimeno or not?
A: These were all the papers that I could find relating to the ranch.
Q: What were the dates respectively on these papers, if any?
A: I think all the papers were dated in 1844, but I can't be positive.
Q: What were the contents of the petition of Martina Castro which you saw in the archives at Monterey?

Wilson objected to this question as improper evidence.

A: In the first place, it complained about her brother's cattle on her ranch and afterwards asking for the "Sierra la Yeska," but I do not think the quantity of land was mentioned, nor the boundaries.
Q: Did you not, after the abandonment of the prosecution, claim by yourself and in connection with others, procure and cause to be created some School Warrants upon this tract of land?
A: After I gave up all hopes of getting it through the commission, by the advice of my attorney, I considered it government land and I had 640 acres of School Land Warrants located upon it. I have now got no interest in it.
Q: How have you ceased to have an interest in the said tract?
A: I sold out my interest in the lower Soquel Ranch and I afterwards sold out my interest in the School Land Warrants, and when I sold the School Land Warrants the parties wanted me to add in daily interest, which I might have in the ranch of the de Yeska, and I did so, although neither of us considered it worth anything.
Q: To whom did you sell said interest, and when?
A: I sold the School Land Warrants in 1853 to Thomas W.

Wright and Peter Tracy, and I afterwards got back one half into my own hands and I then sold them to Henry W. Peck in 1855, so that now I have no interest. I gave quitclaims in every instance.

sworn to and subscribed before me
this 28th day of March 1856
George Pen Johnstone, U.S. Commissioner
filed March 31, 1856 in office[220]

Charles Bruce Younger opens branch office in Santa Cruz

Charles Bruce Younger was born on December 10, 1831 in Liberty, Missouri and studied law at Central College in Danville, Kentucky. He was admitted to the bar in 1855 and soon afterwards left for San José, California, arriving in December. He opened a law office in town and began investing in local mining and transportation projects. His success led him to open a branch office in Santa Cruz on April 1, 1856.[221]

Deposition given by Francisco Alviso to the District Attorney concerning Shoquel Augmentation

On April 12, 1856, Francisco Alviso, former *alcalde* of Branciforte at the time Martina Castro claimed to receive the augmentation to Rancho Soquel, gave his testimony before the acting United States District Attorney Andrew Glassell. John Wilson, attorney for Martina Castro and the Catholic Church, asked the questions while George Johnstone observed as the court commissioner:

Q: What is your name, age, and place of residence?
A: My name is Francisco Alviso, I am sixty-three years of age, and I live at Little Panola in Contra Costa County, California.
Q: Did you ever have any conversation with one John Hames in regard to the augmentation grant of Martina Castro in Santa Cruz County, California?

A: I never had.

Q: Do you know John Hames?

A: I do not.

Q: Did you ever make oath before Squire Blackburn of Santa Cruz County or Judge Blackburn of said county about this grant of Martina Castro?

A: I never made any oath concerning this grant before that judge.

Q: Were you ever alcalde of Santa Cruz County? If yes, when?

A: I was once alcalde of Santa Cruz, but I do not recollect exactly when. Figueroa was governor at the time, I believe, or Micheltorena. I forgot which, but on reflection, I am justly positive that Micheltorena was governor. It was about 1846.

Q: Were you ever called upon by the governor while you were alcalde for information as to whether the augmentation grant should be made to Martina Castro?

A: The governor did call upon me for such information. I made one, the first report upon the representation of persons living in the neighborhood of the land, who were hostile to the grant, and I reported adversely to the grant at that time; but afterwards, finding the land was vacant and no good reason existing against the grant, on the application of Martina Castro I reported a second time and then in favor of the grant.

Glassell then cross-examined Alviso:

Q: Do you recollect the date of the grant report you made?

A: I do not recollect the date.

Q: What did you do with that grant report?

A: I sent it to the governor and don't know what he did with it.

Q: Have you ever seen that report since you sent it to the governor?

A: I have never seen it since.

Q: What did you do with your second report?

A: I sent it to the commandant general, Micheltorena.
Q: Have you ever seen that report since you sent it to the commandant general?
A: I have never seen it since.
Q: Did you ever alter by erasure or otherwise any of the words in your first report to which you have referred?
A: I never did, either in my first or second report.
Q: In the spring of the year of 1848, before Alcalde William Blackburn and John Hames and others, did you not state in substance that you never had reported that the said Augment could be granted?
A: I never made any such statement at the time or to the parties named in the question.
Q: Are you interested either directly or indirectly in the event of the confirmation of the claim?
A: I have no interest in the event of the confirmation of this claim.

At this point, Wilson resumed questioning:

Q: Were you ever sworn before Judge Blackburn on any occasion? If yes, what year and what was it about?
A: I was sworn once before Judge Blackburn in relation to the suit concerning some timber.
Q: Do you know whether this augmentation grant was ever made to Martina Castro?
A: I know that it was made.

Glassell again cross-examined Alviso:

Q: How do you know this grant was made to Martina Castro?
A: She told me her title had been confirmed.
Q: Did you ever see this grant?
A: I never did.[222]

Charles H. Willson claims ownership of half of Joseph Major's land in Rancho Soquel and Shoquel Augmentation

In October 1854, Joseph Majors had mortgaged one eighteenth of Rancho Soquel and Shoquel Augmentation as well as most of his livestock to Charles Watson, who in turn sold this land and livestock to Charles H. Willson of San Mateo County. Over the following eighteen months, Majors made several payments to first Watson and later Willson, eventually amassing enough funds to repay the entire remaining balance on the debt. On April 15, 1856, he offered to pay off the final $688.18, but Willson refused, stating that he wanted to keep the animals because he could sell them for more money. Willson sold the livestock and, due to possessing one eighteenth of the Soquel grants as collateral, claimed that the land was his as well despite never giving Majors an opportunity to purchase it back.[223]

Several land transfers occur within Rancho Soquel and Shoquel Augmentation

On May 3, 1856, several tracts of land were sold to Augustus Noble, William Otis Andrews, and Benjamin P. Green. John Wilson and James Scarborough sold each of the men one twelfth of their combined claims to Rancho Soquel and Shoquel Augmentation for $1.00. Following the sales, Wilson and Scarborough were left with one eighth of each land grant. However, ownership of the properties was contested, so the three buyers also purchased the same land from Father Ingoldsby for $2,000 each since Ingoldsby had the better claim. This negated any contest over the land transfer and ensured that Noble, Andrews, and Green were in full possession of their properties. Andrews was unable to pay the entire amount to Ingoldsby so was in debt to the priest for $916.

Following the purchases, ownership of Rancho Soquel and Shoquel Augmentation according to Martina Castro's sale of January 1850 was divided between:

- Father Ingoldsby, who owned one half of each ranch
- John Wilson, who owned one eighth of each ranch

- James Scarborough, who owned one eighth of each ranch
- Augustus Noble, who owned one twelfth of each ranch
- William Andrews, who owned one twelfth of each ranch
- Benjamin Green, who owned one twelfth of each ranch

This breakdown does not account for competing claims by Martina Castro's children, their grantees, and School Land Warrant owners. By this point, the situation had become very confusing and the attorneys on all sides of the dispute were seeking remedies.

To complicate matters further, Green turned around and subdivided his property, selling it to four new owners. On May 5, he sold Charles Plum of Santa Cruz a small tract that amounted to 1/120 of Rancho Soquel and Shoquel Augmentation for $500. He sold the same amount of land also to Adolph F. Branda, but for the much higher price of $1,500. To Mary E. J. Slade of San Francisco, he sold a much larger portion amounting to 1/48 of the land of the combined grants for $500. Lastly, on May 13, Green sold Henry Lawrence of San Francisco a 1/120 part of the grants for $500. After these sales, Green was still left with just under half of his recently purchased land, which amounted to 3/80 of Rancho Soquel and Shoquel Augmentation. Through the sales, he made a total of $3,000, which amounted in a profit of $1,000.[224]

Land transfer from Pruett Sinclair to Frederick Hihn

On May 29, 1856, Frederick Hihn signed the deed that he won in a sheriff's auction for a 1/54 portion of Rancho Soquel and Shoquel Augmentation. While recording the deed at the Recorder's Office, the clerk made a mistake that would later void the Augmentation part of the purchase, leaving Hihn with a 1/54 claim to Rancho Soquel.[225]

Father Ingoldsby requests change of venue to San Francisco

The purpose of Father Ingoldsby's suit against Martina Castro's family was to prove that Castro's deed of August 29, 1850 was obtained through a fraudulent misrepresentation of facts. If the deed was accepted as being fraudulent, then Castro's sale of Rancho Soquel and Shoquel Augmentation to Archbishop Alemany and Fathers Ingoldsby and Llebaria on January 22, 1855 was legitimate. John Wilson represented the plaintiff, Father Ingoldsby, while Robert Peckham and Gregory Yale represented Castro's family, which sought to prove that the deed was legitimate in order to validify their own rights to own property on the two grants.

The list of defendants was large and encompassed nearly all of Castro's family, as well as several other claimants within the two grants, including Luisa and Jean Fourcade (the suit's named defendants under their alias, the Juans), Helena and Joseph Littlejohn, Guadalupe and Joseph Averon, Antonia and Henry Peck, Nicanor and Francisco Lajeunesse, Joshua Parrish, Montgomery Shackleford, Peter Tracy, Thomas Wright, Durrell Gregory, Joseph Majors, Pruett Sinclair, Jones Hoy, John Vandenberg, Joel Bates, George Kirby, Frederick Hihn, Henry Parsons, Craven Hester, and Carmel and Thomas Fallon.

The attorneys for both sides faced problems that seemed insurmountable. Wilson's success or failure depended largely on Louis Depeaux, who sought revenge against his stepchildren and their spouses. Peckham's case, meanwhile, relied heavily on the testimony of Peter Tracy. However, neither of these witnesses was overly trustworthy.

Tracy's position was compromised due to the fact that he owned land within Shoquel Augmentation. More problematic was that this land was almost entirely composed of School Land Warrants, some of which he had leased to Joel Bates for the purpose of logging and grazing. Therefore, Tracy had a financial interest in the land, which could potentially taint his testimony.

The challenge facing Wilson regarding Depeaux was a bit more daunting. After Castro left Depeaux in O'ahu in late 1855, Depeaux was taken prisoner by the crew of USS *Decatur* on charges of desertion. It must be remembered that Depeaux first arrived in California after having fled an unknown United States naval vessel in 1847. *Decatur* anchored at Mare Island in San Francisco Bay in early June 1856, just as the trial was set to begin. The captain of the ship refused to allow Depeaux to testify in Santa Cruz County. Therefore, Wilson requested the trial be moved to San Francisco so that Depeaux could give his deposition. Due to Depeaux's situation and the uncertainty regarding how long *Decatur* would remain in port, Depeaux's testimony came early in the trial.

Wilson also faced the added difficulty that his client, Ingoldsby, would not be personally present for much of the trial. Just prior to the start of the trial, Archbishop Alemany assigned Ingoldsby to a new post in the Gold Country and the priest was preparing to relocate when the trial began. In lieu of a deposition, a brief statement was made by Ingoldsby on June 25 that would introduce Depeaux's deposition when it was entered as evidence. The statement, notarized by Robert C. Rodgers in San Francisco, follows:

> *I, John Ingoldsby, the plaintiff in the Ingoldsby versus Ricardo Juan, et al., suit, being sworn, says that one Louis Depeaux is, as this affiant is informed and believes, a material witness for him in the above cause, in the issues joined in said cause, and this affiant also says he has what he expects to prove by said witness, to his counsel, in the above cause, and he advises me that his statement is material to be used for this affiant in the above case.*
>
> *This affiant also states that the said Louis Depeaux is an enlisted sailor on board the United States vessel of war Decatur, now in the Bay of San Francisco, in this state, and does not reside in the county of Santa Cruz, where this cause is now pending, and will not, as this affiant believes, be present when the cause shall be tried, and, in fact, this affiant believes he will continue to be absent when his testimony is required, and therefore this affiant desires to take his deposition, to be read in the above case, on trial thereof.*
>
> Reverend John Ingoldsby

The above statement was delivered to Peckham at his home in Santa Cruz on June 28, accompanied by the request to change the venue from Santa Cruz to San Francisco.[226]

Letter from Louis Depeaux to John Wilson

On July 5, 1856, Louis Depeaux wrote to John Wilson concerning the impending trial and his current status aboard USS *Decatur*:

> *I wish to drop a few lines informing you that through your influence, the captain told me that he would write to the Secretary of the Navy for my discharge. I also wish you to write me a note requesting me to be down by the 14th to attend to our...business, for I am ashamed to go to him and ask for permission without having something to show as regards the truth. Please state it as very important and I will show it to him when I ask for his permission.*
>
> *I wish you would write to the keeper of the lunatic asylum at Stockton to see if my wife has my papers up there, for if she has, she may have some of great importance. One in particular which is an obligation in our behalf with the heirs. Write as soon and oblige your friends and servant.*
>
> Louis Depeaux
>
> *P.S. If any one speaks to you about my testimony, don't say that you intend to put much [trust?] on it, but let me [be alone] and I will make a case for you to tell you all I can [ever] that the entire deed to the children was a fraud and one of them told me that it was their intention to commit a fraud when they drew it up. I have thought it all over since I saw you last.*
>
> Yours,
Louis Depeaux

It is apparent, if not obvious based on his letter, that Depeaux was not a witness that Wilson had to convince to testify. How much he participated in the plot to commit fraud against his wife both before and after his disappearance in 1852 is debatable. It is obvious that both Depeaux and Martina Castro were aware of the fraud by the time the agreement was signed by Castro, Wilson, and Durrell Gregory on October 28, 1852. However, no action was taken against the fraud, probably because of Thomas Fallon's partitioning suit and his attempt to acquire the entirety of Castro's land in 1852.

In spite of his disappearance, after Depeaux returned, he remained with Castro through the Fallon partitioning suit, the John Hames sawmill suit, and through the anguish caused by having to present to the Land Claims Commission evidence for the legitimacy of Rancho Soquel and the Augmentation. By the end of 1854, Depeaux was deeply involved in the plot with the Catholic priests to appeal the rejection of the Augmentation grant. What Depeaux was not prepared for was Castro leaving the Hawaiian Islands early or himself being imprisoned by the United States Navy aboard the *Decatur*. But even in this instance, he was able to submit his deposition to the court.[227]

Deposition given by Louis Depeaux

On July 14, 1856, Louis Depeaux was escorted under naval custody and in chains to the office of Robert C. Rodgers, a notary public in San Francisco, to testify in regards to Seventh District Court Case No. 131. Present in the office besides Rodgers and Depeaux was another notary, Orrin Baily, as well as John Wilson, James Scarborough, and Robert Peckham. Wilson asked the initial series of questions:

Q: What is your name and place of residence?
A: My name is Louis Depeaux and I am a resident of the city of San Francisco in California.
Q: Do you know the parties, plaintiff and defendants, to this suit?
A: I do know all except one or two of the defendants.
Q: The defendants have set up in their answer in the case above a deed from Martina Castro to some of the defendants, dated about the 29th of August 1850—do you know anything about the execution of that instrument? And, if you do, state all you know about it.
A: I do know that there was a paper or deed drawn up by the heirs of Martina Castro, about the latter part of August 1850, which was supposed to convey the privilege of occupancy of the place, which she, Martina Castro signed; and

before the paper was put on record, Thomas Fallon came to me and said he wished to have it changed to another form, which I consented to him to do, if the other should be a conveyance of the same meaning and purport of the first. He had a paper drawn up afterwards. I read a part of it sometime afterwards, at Santa Cruz, and found it was not of the same purport as the first. He sent the paper by Peter Tracy, who was County Clerk, who requested me to sign it; my wife declined signing it, as it was written in English, and not properly translated. And said Tracy declined to translate it for her, but assured her it was the same as the first; his excuse was that he had not time to translate it; at last I took the pen myself, and asked her if she was willing to sign; she said she was, provided it was the same as the first paper, and I signed it for her, because she cannot write; she did not touch the pen, or make any mark on the paper: the paper was then taken away to be recorded at the Mission, without giving us an opportunity of knowing the contents. I did not sign it myself at that time, not thinking it was necessary to be signed by me at all.

I had the original paper in my possession from the time it was executed in August 1850 to the year 1855, and then sent it by my wife from Honolulu to San Francisco. I have examined all my papers since and cannot find that one; this paper which is now exhibited [marked "A"] I believe to be a copy of the first document alluded to; I never had a copy of the second document in my possession. About six or eight weeks after signing for my wife, the second document was presented to me in the Clerk's office at the Mission, by Peter Tracy, the Clerk, who requested me to sign it: Thomas Fallon took me there for the purpose. I signed it under the belief that it was the same as the first conveyance alluded to; at the time of my signing in the Clerk's Office, there were present Peter Tracy, Thomas Fallon, and I think Robert King.[228] When I signed for my wife the first instrument, Peter Tracy, my wife, and two children, Miguel and Guadalupe, were present.

The only way we found out that the second instrument conveyed away any more than the first was through Antonia Lodge, and the wife of Henry Peck. She came home to her mother's, Martina Castro's, and asked her mother what she had been doing. Her mother asked, why she asked that? She said that Fallon had told her that they all had an equal right in the ranch and that he said she had given a paper, giving the right to them. Martina Castro then asked me if it was so. I told her I believed the second paper to be the same as the first. She told me to go and examine it. I neglected doing so, and do not know to this day the entire substance of that paper.

Q: State whether you know of any agreement on the part of Martina Castro's children or their husbands, binding themselves to do or perform certain things if she would give them the first agreement? And if you know, state what it is.

A: The husbands of the children then married agreed to assist in paying taxes, defending in lawsuits, and to keep off squatters. They were Thomas Fallon, Lambert B. Clements, Ricardo Juan, and Francisco Young. The latter did not sign the agreement, but agreed to do so, the others did sign it in my presence. The first year they paid no taxes. I had to borrow the money of Thomas Fallon, for which I paid interest, and paid the taxes myself. They did not, any of them, assist against squatters, but I believe Fallon laid a School Warrant on and squatted himself. They did nothing towards complying with the agreement except to pay their taxes after the first year, but were an incumbrance in the lawsuit, which was then pending and they were to assist in.

At this point, Peckham asked Depeaux several questions:

Q: Did you sign the paper for Martina Castro at her request

and in her presence?

A: I did sign it by her consent, provided, as she said, it was the same as the first paper. Peter Tracy said to her, "How, in the name of God, do you suppose your husband would deceive you?" I said, "here goes it," and signed it. We both supposed at the time it was the same as the first. The name was written with ink made of gunpowder and vinegar and had a yellow cast. I was the husband of Martina Castro at that time and am yet.

Q: In whose handwriting was the paper above spoken of by you?

A: It was in the writing of Lambert B. Clements.

Q: Was the first paper read to you?

A: Yes, and myself and Martina, my wife, were present when it was drawn up.

Q: How long was it from that time until the time that Thomas Fallon came and told you he wanted it changed to another form?

A: Some three or four days.

Q: Did he or did he not explain to you the alterations which he wished to make?

A: He did not tell me of any material alterations, but said he wanted to conform to the law. I told him it must contain the same substance as the other.

Q: Where were you when Peter Tracy came and requested you to sign that document?

A: At my own house. He did not request me to sign it; he wanted my wife to sign it.

Q: Have you seen your wife since your return from Honolulu?

A: I have not.

Q: What had you or your wife, to your knowledge, told them [the three Catholic priests] in relation to the existence of the deed above spoken of by you, from Martina Castro to her children?

A: We told them that a paper was existing whereby the children claimed the right of occupancy of equal shares of the ranch, and we also told them [that the children] said they had another paper, whereby they had a right to the property, but that we denied the existence of any such paper, that we had never intended to make any such a conveyance or paper.

Q: Did you or did you not tell them that the children of Martina Castro had a paper under which they claimed to own eight-ninths of the property?

A: I told them there was such a paper in existence by which the children intended to claim eight-ninths of the ranch, but we denied that it was legally executed.

Q: Is that paper the second paper spoken of in your testimony?

A: I believe it is, but cannot say positively, as I never read it. I told these persons very much the same as I have sworn to in my testimony now taken.

Louis Depeaux[229]

Land transfer from John Vandenberg to Frederick Hihn

On September 5, 1856, John Vandenberg sold half of his one ninth part of Rancho Soquel, which he had purchased from Nicanor and Francisco Lajeunesse in 1854, to Frederick Hihn for $1,850.[230]

Castro family prepares to bring Martina Castro home from Stockton

During her 1965 interviews, Carrie Lodge revealed that her family knew where Martina Castro was being held, "and the way they knew where grandma was through Thomas Fallon, and it was just the good Lord that made it so that Fallon found out she was there. I think he was mayor of San Jose at the time."[231] So he was going out on the street and a man saw him, and he says, 'Say Fallon, do you know where your mother-in-law is?'

"And he says, 'Well, I suppose she's down home with the folks.'

"'Well,' he says, 'she isn't. I went up to see my son, who's in the same place that she's in, in the state hospital in Stockton, and I saw your mother-in-law there.'

"So, Fallon got in touch with the family here and they sent Maria Helena Littlejohn, and she was high [pregnant] already, but they had a spring wagon, and it took them three months to go and come."

While Lodge's story may be true in part, it lacks some important details. For instance, in a letter by Louis Depeaux to John Wilson, it is revealed that he already knew that she was in a "lunatic asylum." Indeed, as the attorney for Father Ingoldsby, the man likely responsible for Castro's confinement, Wilson almost certainly knew of her whereabouts.

It was probably through Depeaux's letter that Robert Peckham learned of her location, and he quickly had the proper paperwork drawn up to retrieve Castro. He, Helena and Joseph Littlejohn, Jean and Luisa Fourcade, and Antonia Peck set off for Stockton on September 23, 1856.[232]

Land transfer from William Andrews to Adolph Branda

On September 29, 1856, William Andrews sold three tenths of his one twelfth part of Rancho Soquel and Shoquel Augmentation to Adolph Branda for $1,000. This was the second purchase by Branda within Martina Castro's two land grants and with it, he came to own one thirtieth of each grant.[233]

Robert Peckham requests change of venue to Contra Costa County

On November 1, 1856, Robert Peckham requested that the venue for Case No. 131 be moved to Contra Costa County from San Francisco. This was done to make it easier to gather the testimony of Peter Tracy. Peckham also wrote to the district attorney for Contra Costa County to request that the deed signed by Martina Castro on August 29, 1850 be made available for Tracy to review.[234]

Santa Cruz Gap Joint Stock Company announces sale of stock to build a turnpike from San José to the Summit

Over four years after the passage of the Plank and Turnpike Act and three years after Santa Clara County authorized the construction of a turnpike between San José and the Summit of the Santa Cruz Mountains, the Santa Cruz Gap Joint Stock Company was incorporated to finally build the proposed route.

At this time, the only direct route between San José and Santa Cruz was the ungraded but lightly maintained remnant of the old Franciscan Trail, which followed Los Gatos Creek for much of its length before heading up Moody Gulch and reaching the stage stop at Charles McKiernan's Laguna del Sargento. From his ranch, McKiernan ran a toll road down to Santa Cruz via a route that passed through Scotts Valley. A survey done by Santa Clara County in 1853 had found a viable route, but there were no available funds to build it.

On November 1, 1856, the Santa Cruz Gap Joint Stock Company announced that they intended to sell $20,000 worth of stock to build a toll road from Los Gatos to the top of the Santa Cruz Mountains, ending at the county line. Within a short time, investors from both Santa Cruz and Santa Clara Counties subscribed to the requisite stock. The company stated that it would build and maintain the road while Santa Clara County would set the amount for the tolls.

The board of directors were Adolph Pfister (president), David Bacon Moody (secretary), Lyttleton Albert Whitehurst, Alexander S. Logan, E. H. Evans, R. S. Smith, and J. Y. McMillan. The company appointed six viewers (surveyors) to plan the road, three from each county. The three appointed from Santa Clara County were Sheriff John M. Murphy, L. B. Healy, and W. M. Hoy. The three from Santa Cruz County were Harry Rice, George Evans, and Henry Peck. The latter's job was to plan the extension of the road from the Summit to Soquel.

A special person of note among the board of directors was David Moody. Born in Michigan City, Indiana on March 14, 1837, Moody arrived with his parents and siblings in San José on Christmas Day, 1847. At the age of twenty-one, he entered into the flour-milling business with his father and two brothers, Charles and Volney D. The business occupied most of Moody's working career right up to his retirement. The family's mills were known as the Moody Mills and comprised eleven units at their peak, distributing flour throughout the state. Later, their mills combined with several others and became known as the Sperry Flour Company, which included a mill on Pacific Avenue in Santa Cruz. Moody served as secretary and auditor of the new company for eighteen years, eventually moving to the company's headquarters in San Francisco. In 1861, he married Jeannette G. Wright. The couple had two daughters: Nettie and Anna L.

In addition to working in the flour industry, Moody served as president of the San José Woolen Mills for sixteen years and, during this period, he was also promoter of the Vendome Hotel. He served as San José City treasurer in 1862 and as Santa Clara County treasurer in 1867. From 1867 to 1871, he was chairman of the Republican Central Committee and in 1886, he helped organize the California State Board of Trade, which later became the California Chamber of Commerce. He was elected their president and held this office until moving to San Francisco. Notably, Moody owned the major gulch up which the turnpike to Santa Cruz ran and this gave him the leverage to become one of the company's first board members.[235]

Martina Castro released from insane asylum in Stockton

After spending around eleven months at the insane asylum in Stockton, Martina Castro was finally released on November 8, 1856. Carrie Lodge explains that "it took them three months to go and come. She said she stopped there, and grandma knew her daughter Helena right away. She said 'Helena, take me home.' It was all in Spanish, you know. And the Sisters [presumably the asylum's staff], they didn't want to let her go, and Grandma says, 'look, they took all my clothes away.' She just had little shoes on and a long chemise...they didn't want her to run away, and that's the way they [the patients] do sometimes. Well, so they [the staff] told my aunt Helena that they wouldn't let her have her. So Helena says 'I'm going to sit right here until I take my mother home.' And she didn't have to wait long. They gave grandma her clothes and she came home."

Lodge overlooks some important technicalities that must have occurred prior to this final moment of release. It seems unlikely that the asylum would simply release Castro without prior arrangement. It was likely Robert Peckham who notified the asylum in advance of their arrival and submitted paperwork in order to regain custody. The alternative explanation is that Castro was there voluntarily, or at least not being forcibly held at the asylum.[236]

Deposition given by Peter Tracy on behalf of defendants

The following deposition by former Santa Cruz County Clerk Peter Tracy was taken before his successor, J. C. Wilson, in Contra Costa County between November 21 and 27, 1856 in regard to Case No. 131. Robert Peckham prepared questions on behalf of the defendants with the assistance of Mr. Coult, while John Wilson and James Scarborough cross-examined Tracy on behalf of Father Ingoldsby. On hand was the deed dated August 29, 1850, which Tracy had access to throughout his testimony. Peckham began:

Q: How old are you, where do you reside, and how long have you resided there?
A: I am in my fortieth year, reside in Santa Cruz. I have resided there since August 1849.
Q: What public positions have you held in the county?
A: I have been County Clerk a fraction less than six years.
Q: Were you present during the taking of the deposition of Thomas W. Wright this morning?
A: Yes, during a portion of the time.
Q: Look at this document and say whether your name as it appears there as a subscribing witness to the signature of Martina Castro is your genuine signature?
A: That is my signature.
Q: Look upon the [deed] and say whether you recognize any signature upon that document as being your signature and, if so, where is it upon the document?
A: I find my signature twice on page four and three times on page five.
Q: What was the object of your first signature on page four?
A: As a witness to Martina's signature.
Q: Examine that document and state whether or not you recognize the handwriting in which the name Martina Castro

appears upon the fourth page accompanied by a cross and, if so, whose is it?

A: It is my handwriting and Martina Castro's cross.

Q: State when and where that instrument was executed, and all the circumstances attending its execution.

A: This document was executed on the old adobe house on the lower Soquel Ranch in Santa Cruz County on the 29th day of August, 1850. Louis Depeaux and Judge Per Lee were present, and I think that Maria Guadalupe was present. Judge Per Lee and I went down at the request of Mr. Thomas Fallon to get the signature and acknowledgment to this instrument of Martina Castro.

When we arrived at the house, we found Martina Castro a little unwell. She was sitting on the sofa and Louis Depeaux at the side of her with his arm around her neck. I read this instrument to her in Spanish. She appeared to be aware of the meaning of the document before I translated it to her. In the course of the translation, when we came to the words heirs and assigns, she remarked, "I have got no heirs—I want my children just to take their share of the ranch and pay their share of the taxes and fight the squatters." She made an objection subsequently, which is written on the bottom of the fourth page in my handwriting and signed by me at her request and for her.

Q: State what means your seal and signature on the fifth page?

A: After Martina Castro had signed the deed, I wrote out the acknowledgment, and I then thought, though very little acquainted with law at that time, that the husband's signature should be on the deed, and I made a note under the acknowledgment, on the fifth page, and which Louis Depeaux signed, after he had read the deed himself. I then took his acknowledgment.

Q: When and where did that signing by Louis Depeaux take place?

A: At the same place and at the same time that Martina Castro signed, to wit, the 29th of August 1850.

Q: What means the two seals opposite your signatures on the fifth page?

A: I placed them there as seals. I had just come from Mexico and it was the custom there.

Q: You state that the cross on the fourth page annexed to your signature of Martina Castro was her cross; are you sure that it was not made by Louis Depeaux?

A: I am positive, because I made the cross myself and she held the top of the pen.

After the above testimony was given, the following indemnification bond was written and signed by Henry Peck and witnessed by Lambert Clements. The purpose of this document was to protect Tracy against loss or damage caused by his testimony, and to give him a legal exception from penalties or liabilities incurred by his later actions regarding his School Land Warrants within Shoquel Augmentation.

> *Whereas, Peter Tracy, of the County of Santa Cruz, together with Thomas W. Wright, signed, sealed, and delivered to Joel Bates, Wilson K. Herrick, and George L. Gluyas, on the 16th of June 1853, a certain indenture of lease by which they leased to said Joel Bates etc. the privilege of lumbering, milling, and grazing on the land on which state School Land Warrants Nos. 353 and 354 for a total of 320 acres, and No. 108 for 320 acres, for the term of two years, and therefore from year to year for ten years, at the option of the said Joel Bates etc.*
>
> *Now, therefore, we the undersigned undertake and promise to save harmless and indemnify the said Peter Tracy (but not his assigns), against all manner of actions which may be brought against him in any manner whatever, upon covenant in said indenture, either expressed or implied, for the quiet enjoyment or possession of said Joel Bates etc., or either of them, or by any of their assigns, to the demised premises during the term or existence of said indentures or lease.*
>
> *Given under our hands and seals at the County of Santa*

Cruz, on the 24th day of November 1856.

Henry W. Peck
J. C. Wilson

witnessed by
Lambert B. Clements

After the indemnification bond was signed by Peck and Wilson, Tracy was asked by Wilson if it was sufficient to protect him against any liability that he may incur upon said lease. Tracy answered: "I look upon it as sufficient."

Tracy continued his testimony on November 24 as before, with Wilson resuming his questioning:

Q: State whether you ever owned any interest in the Augmentation Ranch and, if so, from whom you obtained it, and when you obtained it, and the extent of that interest.

A: I had and have an interest in the Augmento. I acquired one half of one ninth from Thomas Fallon, and one third of one ninth from Francisco Lajeunesse and his wife. He is sometimes called Francisco Young. He is best known as if his name was Elisha Moss. I have four School Land Warrants located between the two ranches, as I think.

Q: State the description of your School Land Warrants' location, as in regards the lines of the two ranches, and state if you know the line which divides the two ranches.

A: I know the line which divides the two ranches. I know a tract of land which is between them.

Q: State the differences it will be to you if the plaintiff recovers in this suit or if the defendants recover.

A: I can't say exactly. I never saw the complaint and do not know what they claim.

Q: If the plaintiff Ingoldsby should recover the Ranch of Soquel and the Augmentation as one tract of land, what would you lose?

A: I suppose I would lose my interest in the Augmentation, as before stated, and would have to float my land warrants.

Q: What are the lands considered worth upon which you have located your land warrants?

A: They are valued by the assessor at two dollars per acre. If I had a patent for the land and a complete title, I think it would be worth $25 per acre.

Q: How many acres have you located there?

A: I have now 640 acres.[237]

Q: If the defendants should recover in this action, would you not consider your title good?

A: I should not consider my title good under the Land Warrants until I got a patent for them.

Q: Would you not consider it that your interest would be advanced in the School Land property and also in the other interest in the augmentation by the success of the defendants in this suit?

A: If they got the land as the plaintiff claims it, joined together, it would be to my advantage that they should win the suit. But, as I said before stated, I believe those warrants are located on public land lying between the two ranches.

Q: Have you any agreement or understanding with any of the defendants in this suit, whereby it is understood or agreed, between you and them or any of them, that, if they recover in this suit, they are not to claim the land that you have located by school warrants?

A: I have not. None of them would dare make such a proposition to me to affect my testimony, even if they felt so inclined.

At this point, Peckham cross-examined Tracy:

Q: Are you a party to this suit?

A: I don't know that I am. I never had any papers served on me.

Q: Suppose the plaintiff Ingoldsby succeeds in this action and gets a judgment against the defendants—would not he still be compelled to bring his action against you to determine your rights?

A: Certainly.

Q: Then the only interest you have in this controversy is in having the question of law decided favorably to your interest, with a view to any action which may hereafter be brought against you to determine your rights?

A: My interests are altogether included in the questions of law and in the boundaries of the two ranches, excepting the interest in the Augmentation.

Q: Suppose the boundaries should be established as they claim it in this action, would you not have a right to contest that those were the true boundaries in an action brought against you?

A: I should contest it.

Q: Then you would not consider your rights bound by the judgment in this action any further than the questions of law, which may arise on this trial, may be determined against in an action to be brought against you?

A: I would not.

Peckham then resumed his questioning:

Q: Have you possession of any part of the lands of the Augmentation or on which you have located school warrants?

A: I think I have possession of the land on which I have located school warrants, by virtue of the location, and also by a portion of it being leased to Lewis Herrick and Bates, and upon which they have erected a steam sawmill.

Q: What is Mr. Bates' name?

A: Joel Bates.

Q: Is not now Joel Bates a party to this suit?

A: I don't know.

At this prompt, Wilson asked a final question:

Q: State whether you have or have not had indemnification against any liability that you might be made or become made to Joel Bates, Wilson Herrick, and George L. Gluyas, or either of them, upon any covenants in your lease to them for quiet enjoyment and possession?

A: Yes, sir, I have an indemnification bond, of which the following is a copy.[238]

United States Justice Department announces Martina Castro's Rancho Soquel grant will not be contested

On November 22, 1856, the United States Department of Justice issued its decision regarding the fate of Rancho Soquel:

> *In the case of the claim of Martina Castro, confirmed to the claimant by the Commission, Case No. 184, appeal will not be prosecuted by the United States.*
>
> I am respectively William Blanding, Esq.,
> United States Attorney in San Francisco[239]

Martina Castro returns to Rancho Soquel, where she lives for the remainder of her life

With her home sold and under the control of the Catholic Church and her husband a prisoner aboard *Decatur*, Martina Castro relied on her daughters for both care and shelter. Carrie Lodge reflected in an interview in 1965: "Just think of the misery that grandma went through. Enough to make anybody lose their mind." When the interviewer asked if she ever recovered from her mental condition, Carrie answered:

> *Well, to a certain extent. But there was something in grandma that you didn't try to find out anything at all. You respected*

> her and let her have her peace and quiet. If she talked to you, you talked. But grandma never really recovered good, see.
>
> One lady who lived on the place where grandma's old house was told me about the time that grandma came to visit her. Papa's third wife took her to see the lady. They then took grandma to see her old home, and she thought that she was coming to see her own home. You see her mind wasn't thinking clearly, so they had to be careful with grandma.

Castro continued to live in the Averon house for the next four decades but quickly faded from society. The fate of Louis Depeaux is unknown—he may have been executed for desertion in a time of war, he may have been imprisoned briefly and then released to an unknown fate, or he may have been cleared of his crimes and simply left. The truth of the matter may never be discovered, although it is relatively certain that he left San Francisco aboard *Decatur* in mid-February 1857, never seeing his wife again. Castro found herself shunned by many members of her family as well as citizens of the county for her reckless actions regarding her land. Indeed, the repercussions of her deeds were felt to the end of the century and beyond. But her active role in the history of Santa Cruz County came to an end with the confirmation of her property sale to the Catholic Church at the end of 1856.[240]

Attorney General agrees not to appeal Land Claims Commission award of Rancho Soquel to Martina Castro

On January 22, 1857, the office of Caleb Cushing, Attorney General for the United States, issued both a stipulation and an order concerning Rancho Soquel:

> *In pursuance of the notice from the Attorney of the United States, hereunto announced, it is hereby stipulated and agreed that the appeal heretofore taken in this case from the decision of the United States Land Commission to ascertain and settle private land claims in California be dismissed, and the notice*

of intention to prosecute said appeal filed in this Court by the Attorney General of the United States, be withdrawn, and that the claimant have leave to proceed under the decree of said Land Commission in her favor as under final decree.

signed by the District Attorney
and John Wilson for Martina Castro

The Attorney General of the United States having given notice that no appeal will be further prosecuted in this case and a stipulation having been entered by the United States District Attorney for the dismissal of the appeal from the decision of the Board of the United States Land Commission heretofore rendered in her favor: on the motion of the District Attorney, it is ordered, adjudged, and decreed that the appeal pending in this Court be dismissed and that the claimant have leave to proceed under the decree of the Land Commission heretofore rendered in her favor, as under final decree.

[Ogden] Hoffman, United States District Judge[241]

Archbishop Alemany sends Father Ingoldsby to Weaverville to serve as priest

For unknown reasons, Archbishop Alemany sent Father Ingoldsby to Weaverville on February 1, 1857 to serve as a priest for the Catholic community there.[242]

Attorney General agrees not to appeal Land Claims Commission award of Shoquel Augmentation to Martina Castro

On February 2, 1857, the United States Attorney General's office issued an official statement concerning Shoquel Augmentation:

In the case of the claim of Martina Castro, confined to the claimant by the Commission, Case No. 593, appeal will not be prosecuted by the United States.

W. H. Chevers, Deputy[243]

Letter from Augustus Noble to John Wilson

From his home in Soquel, Augustus Noble wrote to John Wilson on February 10, 1857:

> *I did not see you in the city when there last, which I should have been glad to have done although I might [have] had nothing very important to communicate. The heirs are pretty quiet. I have little to say. Young Miguel I have not been able to see. He lives with the Pecks, who keep a sharp eye upon him.*
>
> *In regard to the Depeaux character, the padre* [probably Archbishop Alemany] *showed me a long list of names who I understand would believe him under oath. If his evidence is sustained, I don't see but that we are all right. Should anything occur which would help our case, I will communicate. Remember me to the Padre.*[244]

Letter from Robert Peckham to John Wilson

On February 12, 1857, Robert Peckham, the attorney for the defense, wrote to John Wilson, the attorney for the plaintiff. Because Peckham's penmanship is extremely poor, much of the letter's intent is lost. But after careful scrutiny, these sections of interest can be interpreted for the most part:

> *Your note of the 6th has been received. I am not aware that the clerk in Santa Cruz has received notice to send Peter Tracy's deposition to the clerk in Contra Costa County. I think the record has not yet been trans switched [sic].*
>
> *Our Peter Tracy deposition, since it has not yet arrived and cannot do so by our course of time before the steamer [the USS Decatur] sails before the 15th. Of course, neither of us can know whether it has arrived before the time of the meeting of the court.*

The next paragraph is too poorly written to read word-for-word, but it seems to read: "I will allow your Depeaux deposition if you allow my Tracy deposition, which you object to. It seems that we both have incompetent witnesses, but my incompetent witness's testimony seems to contradict your witness."

In the next paragraph Peckham appears to say: "...that the long trip to Contra Costa at that time of the year is imprudent because of the character of my witness, but the personal trust put in me by my clients comes first."

Peckham ends the letter by stating that he feels that neither of them have a case of merit, but "we can doubtless be able to make a trial of this case." The letter ends with Peckham asking Wilson if he is willing to accept the suggestions he made in the letter and, if so, drop him a line.

This letter makes it clear that Peckham knows he has a weak case and expects to lose in the lower court, putting his hope in winning an appeal in the state Supreme Court.[245]

United States Justice Department announces Martina Castro's Shoquel Augmentation grant will not be contested

On March 20, 1857, the United States District Attorney issued a stipulation and an order concerning Shoquel Augmentation:

> *The Attorney of the United States, having given notice that the appeal in this case will not be prosecuted as per notice hereunto annexed, it is hereby stipulated and agreed that the appeal taken from the decision of the United States Land Commission to this court be dismissed; that the notice of intention to prosecute said appeal be withdrawn; and that claimant have leave to proceed under the decree of the said Land Commission heretofore entered in her favor, as under final decree.*
>
> William Blanding, District Attorney
>
> John Wilson,
> Attorney for claimant
> Martina Castro in San Francisco

The Attorney General of the United States, having given notice that appeal will not be prosecuted in this case, and a stipulation to that effect having been entered into by the United States Attorney: on motion of the District Attorney, it is ordered, adjudged, and decreed that claimant have leave to proceed under the decree of the United States Land Commission heretofore rendered in her favor, as final decree.

Honorable Ogden Hoffman, District Judge[246]

Santa Cruz Gap Turnpike construction begins

With all the stock sold and Santa Clara County amending the 1853 law in early 1857 to favor the new route, construction on the Santa Cruz Gap Turnpike began in March 1857. The road's width was planned to be from twelve to twenty feet from the toll house in Los Gatos along Los Gatos Creek, up and over Jones Hill (St. Joseph Hill), and then continue until Moody Gulch was reached. From here, the trail that McKiernan pioneered would be widened until the county line was reached. From this point, until an extension was later constructed to Soquel, McKiernan's route from his home to Santa Cruz would serve as the main thoroughfare.[247]

Letters from Father Ingoldsby to John Wilson

Two letters from Father Ingoldsby to John Wilson were found in the Wilson file at the Bancroft Library that date to his tenure in Weaverville. The first was written on April 4, 1857:

Dear Friend,
Your favor of the 24th of last month has been duly received, and in reply I have only to say that the matter is entirely in your hands. If you can find a surveyor in whom you can place implicit confidence, and who is at the same time willing to do the work for the amount allowed by the government, and binding himself to ask or demand nothing from us, I think that it would be well to have him go on and do the work as soon

as possible. If there is not a priest sent here to take my place, I do not think that I can leave before the 15th of next month. If you need me very much, please call on Father Llebaria and present the matter to him and get him to go and see the archbishop on the subject. At all events, I can be down before that portion of the line about which there is, or can be, no difficulty. That is the line from the Laguna del Sargento to the Aloma Alta, and thence to Chuchita.[248] *This part can be surveyed without any trouble, since all agree on those landmarks.*

My respects to your family, and to Judge Scarborough. I remain yours, respectfully,

John Ingoldsby

P.S. I have written a letter to cousin Charles [McKiernan] telling him that the survey may be commenced before I get down, and [telling] him to give whatever assistance may be in his power, which I am satisfied he will simply do. He will see that there will be no obstruction to running the line in his neighborhood.

The second letter was written as a reply to a now lost letter by Wilson. The letter sent by Ingoldsby is dated April 16:

To: General John Wilson from Weaverville, California

Your letter of the 9th last has just reached me, and in reply I have only to state that my early arrival in San Francisco will, I might say entirely, depend on the action which Father Llebaria and his Grace, the most Reverend Archbishop Alemany, will take in this matter. If the archbishop either sends a priest here or tells me that I am wanted there, I will start for San Francisco as soon after as possible.

Please see Father Llebaria on this subject. If they take no action in the matter, you may expect a call from me early in the next month. So I have nothing further to say, I will conclude by asking you to remember me to Judge Scarborough

and to your son.
  I remain yours respectively,

John Ingoldsby[249]

Archbishop Alemany reassigns Father Llebaria from Santa Cruz to San Francisco and strips Father Ingoldsby of his license to preach in California

On May 5, 1857, Archbishop Alemany reassigned Father Llebaria from Mission Santa Cruz to Saint Patrick's Church in San Francisco.

Around the same time, Alemany sent notice to Father Ingoldsby in Weaverville recalling him to San Francisco. Upon his return on May 20, the archbishop issued a Removal of Facilities decree, canceling Ingoldsby's license to function as a priest for the Catholic Church in the Archdiocese of Northern California. Six weeks later, on July 2, Alemany issued a decree of Permanent Exeat to Ingoldsby, thereby allowing the priest to preach in other dioceses. With these two decrees, Alemany removed Ingoldsby from his archdiocese using established canon law, and he was under no obligation nor gave any to justify his reasons for doing so.[250]

Letter from Charles McKiernan to John Wilson

Charles McKiernan was no scholar, nor did he have good penmanship. However, the biggest problem with his letter to John Wilson, dated July 24, 1857, is that his grammar is atrocious to the point of near incomprehensibility. The following is an attempt to transcribe this letter, with all spelling and grammatical errors retained:

> *Dear Sir, I had the sumons served on Godalope Castro on this day he fild a complant or ansor and served me which I send to you he has been to see Father lebara and brought letters from him stating he had arranged matters with him and to send him the note now I give you a copy of the receat I gave Lleberea I promise to pay $450 or return the note now if you think you can recover the face of the note I want you to do it now castro*

> *says he paid $100 he got no credit for I dont wat to be made afool of between them when I make an agreement I want to stick to it rite to me to san jose and let me now what to do I shall be in on Tuesday mere and like to have your answer.*
> *Remans yours truly*
>
> Charles McKiernan[251]

Peter Tracy passes away in Santa Cruz

On August 7, 1857, Peter Tracy died at his home in Santa Cruz. To quote Leon Rowland, "if it were not for his death at age 41, he would undoubtedly have become one of the county's wealthiest men." When he died, his estate included land up the coast, around Soquel, and 968 acres of School Land Warrant land within Shoquel Augmentation. He also had a quarter interest in Joel Bates' sawmill.[252]

Agreement between Archbishop Alemany and Father Ingoldsby

On September 2, 1857, Archbishop Alemany and Father Ingoldsby made the following agreement:

> *This agreement made this second day of September in the year of our Lord one thousand eight hundred and fifty seven between the Reverend John Ingoldsby of the first part and the most Reverend Joseph S. Alemany, Archbishop of San Francisco, of the second part, witnesseth...*
> *That the said John Ingoldsby, party of the first part, for and in consideration of the sum of one dollar to him in hand paid by the said Joseph S. Alemany, party of the second part, at and before the ensealing and delivery of these presents to the receipt whereof, hereby acknowledge and of the further sum of one dollar to be paid as hereinafter mentioned both for himself and his successors by these presents, covenant, promise, and agree with the said Joseph S. Alemany, his successors and assigns, that he, the said John Ingoldsby or his successors or assigns, shall and*

will upon the request and at the proper cost and charge of the said Joseph S. Alemany, his successors and assigns, grant, sell, and convey unto the said Joseph S. Alemany, his successors or assigns, and make, execute, acknowledge, and deliver to the said Joseph S. Alemany, his successors or assigns, a good and sufficient deed of conveyance of the one undivided one third of all the right title and interest of the said Ingoldsby of, in, and to all that certain Rancho situated, lying, and being in the county of Santa Cruz, state of California and about three miles from the town of Santa Cruz, known as the Soquel Ranch and of the Augmentation, later thereto subject known to the claims of Messrs. John Wilson and James W. Scarborough, according to a certain written agreement referred to in an agreement executed on or about the Eleventh day of September, A.D. 1855, by and between the said Ingoldsby and Alemany and the Reverend John Francis Llebaria, and also to the said Alemany, and share being the one third of the necessary expenses incurred in prosecuting certain litigations in said last mentioned agreement referred to bring the land and premises specified in the said last mentioned agreement to which reference is hereby made.

In consideration whereof, the said Joseph S. Alemany, for himself, his successors, and assigns, hereby covenants and agrees to and with the said John Ingoldsby and his successors to pay his as them to said sum of one dollar on the execution and delivery of said deed as aforesaid.

In witness whereof, the said parties have hereunto set their hands and seals the day and year first above written.

signed and sealed in presence of David Bisler,
witness as to Joseph S. Alemany, John Ingoldsby,
by his attorney in part, Charles McKiernan

Joseph S. Alemany,
by his attorney David Bisler

State of California
City and County of San Francisco

On this second day of September, A.D. 1857, before me, F. J. Thibault, a Notary Public in and for said county, duly accompanied and sworn, personally appeared Charles McKiernan, personally known to me to be the same person described in and who executed by Power of Attorney the annexed instrument as the attorney in fact of John Ingoldsby, named in the annexed instrument as party thereto and therein described as the party execution the same by his said attorney and the said Charles McKiernan, acknowledged to me that he executed the same freely and voluntarily, and for the act and deed of the said John Ingoldsby and for the uses and purposes therein mentioned.

In witness thereof, I have unto set my hand and affixed my official seal the day and year last above written.

J. F. Thibault, Notary Public

State of California
City and County of San Francisco

On the twenty sixth day of September, A.D. 1857, before me, J. F. Thibault, a Notary Public in and for said county, personally appeared the within named David Bisler personally known to me to be the subscribed to the annexed instrument as a witness thereto, who being by me duly sworn, disposed and said that he resides in the city and county of San Francisco, state of California, that he was present and saw Joseph S. Alemany, personally known to him to be the same person described in and who executed the annexed instrument freely and solemnly sign, seal, and deliver the same, and that he, the defendant, thereupon subscribed his name and as a witness thereto.

In witness thereof, I have hereunto set my hand and affixed my official seal the day and year last above written.

J. F. Thibault, Notary Public

This agreement, in other words, stripped Ingoldsby of his direct involvement in Rancho Soquel and Shoquel Augmentation, thereby allowing him the freedom to leave California. He promptly left for the East Coast while Alemany took full possession of Martina Castro's land, although it is unclear whether he pushed Ingoldsby out so the Catholic Church could profit from the property or so he could.

Over the next two years, Ingoldsby travelled to New York before returning to his home near Chicago. He died around the end of 1859 and was buried in Saint Patrick's Cemetery in Joliet, Illinois. In his *History of the Catholic Church in California*, William Gleeson notes that Ingoldsby "was one of the pioneers of the Church in the post-Hispanic period." Henry L. Walsh, meanwhile, emphasizes how important Ingoldsby was to the Catholic Church establishing itself in the Gold Country. Walsh explains that he travelled from one mining camp to another, a zone covering nearly 200 square miles. He built the first Catholic Church in Sacramento, worked in Placerville and Weaverville, and had a close personal relationship with Archbishop Alemany. In a short time, Ingoldsby accomplished more than many did in a lifetime.

Following Ingoldsby's death, Thomas Courtis was appointed administrator of his estate and took possession of his claims in Rancho Soquel and Shoquel Augmentation, which amounted to a one-sixth claim to each.[253]

John Thomas Porter elected Santa Cruz County Sheriff

Born on July 17, 1830 in Duxbury, Massachusetts, John Thomas Porter arrived in California aboard *Herculaneum* in the early 1850s in search of gold. Determined to remain in the mines until he had accumulated $10,000, he soon found life boring and decided to try some other means of earning his fortune. He secured the contract of loading a hay bark at Stockton, then worked as a buyer of supplies for several stores in San Francisco. He soon relocated to Monterey, where he served as the port's collector, before entering the drying business, where after two years he obtained enough capital to open a mercantile store in Santa Cruz. In 1855, he quit the retail business and took up farming in the Pajaro Valley. Once settled, he entered local politics and was elected the sheriff of Santa Cruz

County on October 5, 1857. He was reelected in 1859 but resigned before the end of his term on October 1, 1861.

Craven Hester's School Land Warrant is floated

On October 20, 1857, Craven Hester's 320-acre School Land Warrant No. 37 within Shoquel Augmentation became the first warrant section to be floated to a valid location elsewhere in California. Unlike other tracts within Shoquel Augmentation further south, Hester's property on Amaya Creek was indisputably within Martina Castro's grant boundaries as established by Francisco Alviso. Because of this, the United States government mandated it be vacated and assigned Hester a similar section elsewhere.[254]

Letter from Charles McKiernan to John Wilson

Charles McKiernan wrote to John Wilson again on November 1, 1857. As before, this transcription reflects original grammar and spelling and may contain minor transcription errors:

> *Dear sir the note I got from father Llibera which we have dued on he has settled with castro giving him any note and a receat in full of all demands receat and note he has left with the county clark I been to see castrou and offrd to takak my expences and with draw the suit and give him up his note he says he has paid all to the padre*
>
> *I got a man to prove that was by when he acknowledged the note was good except he had paid some on it and had not got credit for it you should have no other bissness down heer next cort I should not ask you to come down to attend to it alone there is severals on the soquel ho wish to make arangment to rent land the want to make arangment in case we should get posseshon before the should get there crop of to have it by paying us the rent the agrees to pay for it the ushale rent is a forth and fifth of the crop I think it would be advisable for us to make such arangement as we may not be able to get posseshion before it is to late to put in a crop and a years rent*

is a big item the ears will not plant much if any thing nor no one will rent from them if the are not seguerd by paying us the rent if you should not have to com down to the next cort and above of renting the land as I have stated heer I wish you would send me down a coppy of a lace or agreement that I could make with them that the could take no advantage of plase rite to me as soon as you get this and let me know if you shall be down and what to as about the soquel if you do not con Direct to Santa Cruz.
Remans yours truly

Charles McKiernan

To summarize this letter, McKiernan is in the process of assisting the surveyors who are establishing the boundaries of Shoquel Augmentation. At the same time, he is collecting rent money from the defendants, who are squatting or trespassing on Archbishop Alemany's land. McKiernan specifically wants to gather rent money before the new harvest is planted since a lot of money is involved, but some of the renters want to pay the entire year's rent upfront while others are refusing to pay entirely. In response, he asks Wilson to assist him the next time he is in Santa Cruz and to send him relevant paperwork in the meantime.[255]

Final arguments regarding the validity of Martina Castro's deed of August 29, 1850

Beginning in December 1857 and carrying over into January 1858, final arguments were made before the Seventh District Court in Contra Costa County concerning Case No. 131: the validity of Martina Castro's deed of August 29, 1850. The records for this suit are on file in Martinez and I have over the years made several attempts to acquire a copy of them with no success. The information below is based on several letters sent to John Wilson, the California Supreme Court's report of the appeal, and testimony given during the two partitioning suits of the 1860s. Besides the depositions given by Louis Depeaux and Peter Tracy, several additional depositions were entered as testimony, including ones by Thomas Wright, Lambert Clements, and Castro's brothers Juan José and Guadalupe.

John Wilson, now representing Father Llebaria since Father Ingoldsby had been stripped of his property and sent away, argued that the deed in question was obtained under false pretenses. He also argued that it included several mistakes, falsehoods, and misrepresentations. The following items were accepted as valid facts by the court:

- The document entered into evidence in this case is not a joint deed of conveyance from Castro and Depeaux, but rather a deed from Castro alone;
- Castro and Depeaux were present together at the signing of the deed but did not join in its execution;
- The endorsement by Depeaux on the back of the deed does not include a seal, is undated, contains no words of conveyance, and is therefore invalid;
- The provisions included in the deed were not approved by Castro;
- The signatures of Castro cannot be proven;
- The deed does not include proper acknowledgement of consent by a married woman taken by an authorized officer;
- The acknowledgement that is on the deed is not in the correct form, being incorrectly endorsed or annexed and not sealed with the seal of his office;
- The deed was gained from Castro through fraud and a gross misrepresentation of facts.

With the expected decision to be made in favor of Father Llebaria, Robert Peckham returned to Soquel and met with the defendants. They agreed to a payment of $1,000 for his services thus far and he asked them if they wanted to appeal the expected decision to the California Supreme Court. After discussing all aspects of the case, the heirs decided to proceed with an appeal. Peckham had already begun making preparations for such a decision and had contacted several justices of the Supreme Court to discuss the merits of their case. Receiving positive support from the justices,

Peckham assured his clients that the upper court would likely reverse the lower court's decision.[256]

Frederick Hihn sells his general store to his brother Hugo

Frederick Hihn filed the following notice in the *Pacific Sentinel* on December 18, 1857:

> *The undersigned would respectively inform his friends and the public of Santa Cruz and vicinity, that he has sold out his stock of merchandise to his brother, Hugo Frederick Hihn, who will continue to carry on business under his own name, at the old stand.*
>
> *All persons knowing themselves indebted to the old firm, will please call and settle their accounts.*

Several reasons for this sale have been suggested, but the most likely is that he wanted to shift his focus to real estate. Hihn's first acquisitions in Rancho Soquel and Shoquel Augmentation were tenuous and he needed to concentrate all of his efforts on keeping these lands and expanding elsewhere, such as into neighboring Rancho Aptos.[257]

تمّ

Chapter 5

~

Enter the King

Preliminary sale of Rancho Soquel tannery to Benjamin Porter

Probably in late 1857, talks began between Jean Fourcade and Benjamin Porter concerning the sale by Fourcade of his tannery located in Tannery Gulch. It was agreed on January 1, 1858 that Porter would pay Fourcade $600 for the five-acre facility. This included the tannery itself and all facilities necessary to conduct leather tanning such as vats, flumes, aqueducts, worker houses, mules for hauling bark, hen houses, machinery, and several fruit trees, all of which was surrounded by a fence.[258]

Letter from Charles McKiernan to John Wilson concerning the arrival of government surveyors in the Soquel area

On January 2, 1858, a concerned Charles McKiernan wrote to John Wilson regarding the arrival of surveyors and their plans for Rancho Soquel and Shoquel Augmentation. As before, his letter is transcribed here verbatim:

Dear general I received your letter on yesterday I had sent to

> *the post office before whether the theim I sent with neglected enquireing I do not know the surveyors got heer on fryday last I understand the comminst suring the north line of the souquel. likewais the south line of the agmentation on Saterday last I understand there directions is to run the souwest line of the agmentation from the soutwest corner of the Souquel ranch to the laguna I am goint down to where the are to day I shall stop with them if the require me until the get true I send you the fifty dolars you require by wells fargoes express which will lave in the morning if there should be any difacoulty with regard to the boundries I shall lit you now direcly with regard to the judge selling out hisenterest I cannot sine or make a deed withoud Father John rites to me to do so for he told me on no condishions to sine a deed until the lawsuite is finely dissideed and remined no of it in his leter.*

To summarize McKiernan's letter, he pledged to assist the surveyors and already volunteered information to them regarding one corner of Shoquel Augmentation: the Laguna del Sargento beside his home on the Summit. McKiernan also says that the $50 he had presumably collected from tenants is being sent to Wilson via Wells Fargo. Lastly, McKiernan makes clear that he will not facilitate any land transfers until the appeal of the Soquel suit is resolved.

The judge to whom McKiernan refers is probably Craven Hester, who owned 320 acres in School Land Warrant No. 37. Although Hester had been informed that his warrant grant would be floated to an appropriate new section elsewhere in the state, it appears that he was still attempting to recoup some of his losses from the structures he had built on the property.

The surveyors whom McKiernan discusses arrived in Santa Cruz County in November 1857 but did not begin any actual survey work until late December. According to McKiernan, they arrived on the Summit on Christmas Day 1857, which was the previous Friday. The federal Surveyor General of California, who led the surveying party, was former California state assemblyman and senator James W. Mandeville.[259]

Seventh District Court rules in favor of Father Ingoldsby

In early January 1858, the Seventh District Court of California in Contra Costa County decided in favor of the plaintiff, Father Llebaria (acting in the stead of Father Ingoldsby), agreeing that the deed of August 29, 1850 was made under suspicious circumstances and was therefore invalid. As a result, Martina Castro's sale of both Rancho Soquel and Shoquel Augmentation on January 22, 185 to Llebaria, Ingoldsby, and Archbishop Alemany was considered a valid and proper transaction, with the men obtaining full possession.

Robert Peckham, on behalf of the defendants, immediately began preparing his appeal to this decision.[260]

Land transfer from Helena Lodge to Frederick Hihn

On January 8, 1858, Helena and Joseph Littlejohn agreed to sell 1/27 of both Rancho Soquel and Shoquel Augmentation to Frederick Hihn for $2,000. As an incentive, Hihn also promised to pay all of the court expenses for the Littlejohns in the upcoming California Supreme Court case, regardless of the result.

This deed is interesting in that it is the first that describes the controversial western boundary of Shoquel Augmentation. According to the deed, the boundary extended from the northwest corner of Rancho Soquel, where Bates Creek converges with Soquel Creek, along a straight line until it reached Rancho San Agustín in Scotts Valley. After following this rancho's eastern side, it continued in a northwest line until Laguna del Sargento was reached. The deed also established the size of Shoquel Augmentation as encompassing 70,000 acres.[261]

Letter from Charles McKiernan to John Wilson

Charles McKiernan wrote to John Wilson again on January 17, 1858 to ask him for clarity regarding the ongoing lawsuit and also to update Wilson on the progress of the Santa Cruz Gap Turnpike. As before, all original grammar, spelling, and punctuation has been retained:

> *Dear general I have been looking for a letter from you since I came home from Sanfrancisco I went to see you when I was down but you had gone to martiness I had several horses and boys with me and I could not well wate as my expences was prety heavy your son told me you would rite to me when you came home I have received to letters from father Ingoldsby since I seen you meerly of the same nature as the one you received which your son shown me when I was down plase rite to me as soon as you get this and let me know all the particulars about father Johns case if the have takeing an appeal and when the triel is likely to come on as I want to rite to Father John and let him know all I can about it*
>
> *there has been only Hean and vandenburg asked for leases from me the rode across the mountains is progreson rapiedly on Santaclara side of the mountain the have let the contract to bild it to the county line and have it finished the 1st of April. Santacruz sede is makeing up a company to make there side*
>
> *I have nothing more worth spakeing about I hope to heer from you soon as I want to rite to Father John.*
>
> *Remains yours truly*
>
> Charles McKiernan

In the end, McKiernan confesses, only John Vandenberg and Frederick Hihn have agreed to sign lease agreements with Wilson. And with so much uncertainty regarding the lawsuit, even McKiernan seems conflicted and confused. On the matter of the turnpike, McKiernan reports that the route from Santa Clara to the Summit is scheduled for completion to the Summit on April 1 but that construction on the Santa Cruz side has yet to begin.[262]

Santa Cruz residents discuss the potential of a turnpike through the Santa Cruz Mountains via Branciforte Creek

Movement by Santa Cruz County residents to fund a second road between Santa Cruz and the Summit began on January 30, 1858 under the direction of Judge Henry Rice and Frederick Hihn. Construction of the Santa

Cruz Gap Turnpike had already begun by this time but a new route up Branciforte Creek was favorable to many locals. A committee was formed to investigate the potential and practicality of such a route, composed of Elihu Anthony, Samuel A. Bartlett, Nathaniel Holcomb, John Hames, and Hihn. Their primary task was to survey the route, estimate costs, and gather other relevant statistics so that a joint stock company could be formed at the next meeting, if such was deemed appropriate.

Two days later, Anthony presented a petition to the Santa Cruz County Board of Supervisors signed by several citizens of Santa Cruz demanding that a highway be built between downtown and the Summit. The route that was proposed went up Branciforte Creek to Blackburn Gulch near William Blackburn's sawmill and then continued until reaching the west branch of Soquel Creek in the adjacent watershed. From this point, it would continue to follow the creek until the Summit was reached. For the most part, this proposed route paralleled today's Highway 17 slightly to the east. The supervisors agreed to a survey of the route under the direction of the county surveyor, Thomas Wright, with a report to be presented at the next meeting.[263]

Louis Depeaux confirms land transfer from Martina Castro to Henry Cambustan

Sitting before a notary public in San Francisco on February 5, 1858, Louis Depeaux confirmed that the deed Martina Castro had signed on March 7, 1854, granting Henry Cambustan one quarter of Rancho Soquel and Shoquel Augmentation, was legitimate. Since Castro's mark on the deed had not been properly acknowledged by Depeaux prior to this point, the deed had remained invalid.

This action serves as one of only two references to Depeaux's ongoing presence in Santa Cruz County after his arrest by the United States Navy in 1855. In 1865, Depeaux testified in an unrelated court case that he had been a resident of Soquel since 1847. The sources never name him again after this and his ultimate fate remains unknown.[264]

Letter from Augustus Noble to John Wilson

On February 5, 1858, Augustus Noble wrote to update John Wilson on the progress made by the surveyors mapping Rancho Soquel:

> *The surveyors arrived and commenced on Saturday last and completed the survey of the Soquel Ranch. They have taken all that the grant called for and have bounded on the east by Rafael Castro's ranch, giving us a fine stick of land there which has been in possession of squatters for six years who called it government land.*
>
> *We are to have a new road to Santa Clara Valley up the Soquel River. I expect to start tomorrow with a party to lay it out, from Nathaniel Holcomb's with Craven P. Hester's. This road will add to the value of our property as well as be a great advantage for the traveling public.*
>
> *Robert Francis Peckham has returned from the Supreme Court. He told the heirs that the judge assured him that Martina Castro's deed would be pronounced 'good.' He says he intended to bring forward another point in case the deed was not allowed, but the judges told him there was no need of it. You have this for what it is worth. The heirs gave him $1,000 for going to Sacramento. The point he was to bring up was that Martina could only convey a part, or one-ninth of the estate, the balance belonged to her children.*
>
> *Mountain Charley was here yesterday and went to see the surveyors. They will have a bad job on the Aumento. I hope they will not fail in the matter. Give my best wishes to Mr. Thomas Courtis and Irene.*[265]

Probate court in San Francisco confirms the death of Adolph Branda

A dramatic turn of events occurred on January 20, 1858, when Adolph Branda committed suicide in a remote suburb of San Francisco. The *Alexandria Gazette* in Virginia reported on March 3:

From the California papers we learn that Adolph F. Branda, a native of Norfolk, Va., and employed as a confidential clerk by the house of Macondray & Co., of San Francisco, committed suicide on the 20th of January. He hired a horse, went to the Lone Mountain Cemetery, wrote a letter, directed it to Mr. Macondray, placed it together with a ten dollar piece in a handkerchief, and tied the bundle to the horn of the saddle.—He then turned the horse loose and it returned to the stable in the city, where the bundle was opened, the letter found and sent to Macondray. In it he confessed he had wronged his employers by embezzling the funds and avowed his intention to commit suicide. His body was afterwards found in the Cemetery. By his side was found a small vial, containing about four grains of strychnine, and scatt red on the ground were scraps of paper torn from a memorandum book. On these pieces of paper the deceased wrote disjointed sentences with a pencil, expressive of his feelings and the thoughts uppermost in his mind after swallowing the deadly substance. The character of his handwriting as the time passed and as the poison operated on the system grew more tremulous and indistinct. Both sides of the paper are written on, except the last scrap, which contains only these words, "I am dy"—probably put there at the moment deceased fell into the first paroxysm. The sad fate of Branda presents one of the most singular cases of suicide on record.

On the first piece of paper deceased wrote:

"Yet the thoughts of my poor mother keep my heart warm, or rather hot, for I feel I am her murderer. God help me.

How slowly time passes; it seems to me nearly half an hour since I took the fatal dose, yet I do not suffer. How chilly it is! I feel stiff from the cold."

Number two:—

"It is fearful to die thus alone—to look around, see the hills, hear the roar of the ocean. See your fellow-beings moving in the distance, yet die alone.

"Just after my third dose a man passed and told his friend I was crazy. God forgive me. I hope I am. What terrible sus-

pense this waiting for death."
Number three:—
"—For science—half of the bottle I have taken, four doses of the starch—at intervals of about three minutes, yet do not suffer. I feel nervous, but will note the time on the back of this."
"—I think it has been fifteen minutes since I took the first. I am cold and chilly. May some good result from my death."
On the fourth piece the writing is without any order. The words are spread irregularly over the paper lengthwise and diagonally. They are as follows:
"—fully half an hour. I am dying. God help me. A. T. B."
Number five: *"I am dy—"*

On February 13, the probate court in San Francisco ordered that Branda's land, which totaled 1/30 of Rancho Soquel and Shoquel Augmentation, be auctioned to the highest bidder since Branda had left no will or heirs.[266]

Wesley and William P. Burnett purchase land adjacent to Shoquel Augmentation

Wesley Burnett & Company was an enterprise that was involved mostly in business transactions involving trading and selling from a small mercantile store located along the San Lorenzo River just north of Santa Cruz. The company was jointly owned by the Burnett brothers, Wesley and William P. Around the beginning of 1858, through a transaction of which I have not been able to find any record, the two came into ownership of about 600 acres of timberland along the west bank of Soquel Creek within the vicinity of today's Soquel-San Jose and Laurel Glen Roads. About 600 feet south of the junction of the latter two roads, they built a small sawmill on Soquel Creek that they ran for two seasons. They sold most of the products at their store.[267]

Editorial proclaims the benefits of a road to San José

The following editorial appeared in the *Pacific Sentinel* on February 13, 1858:

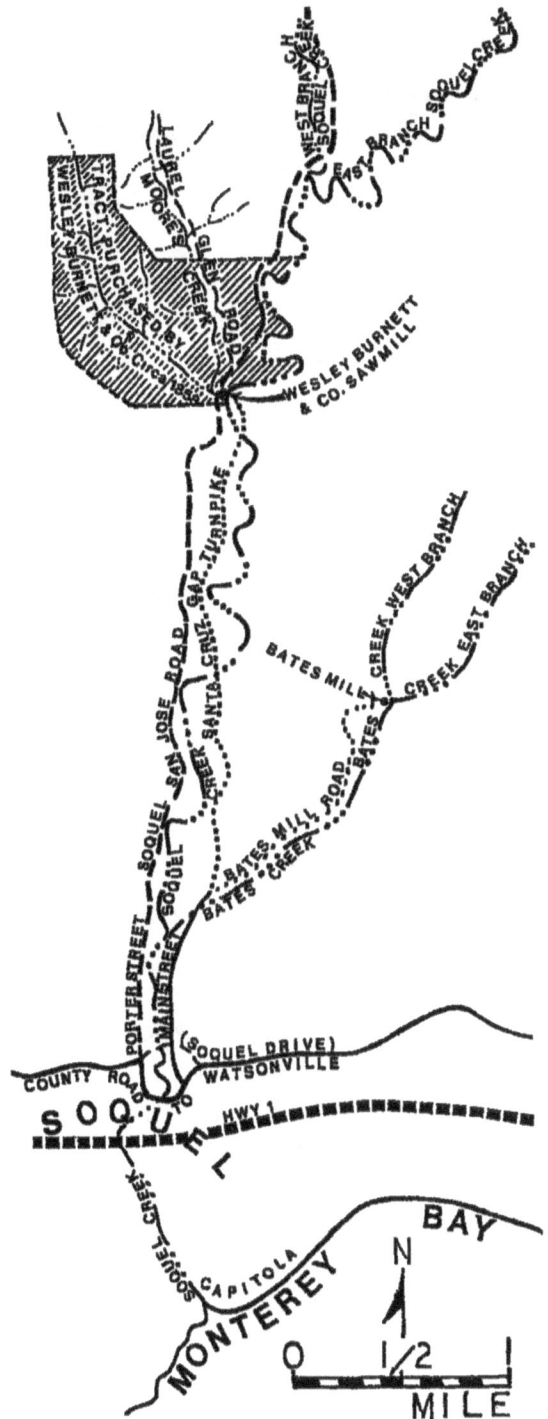

FIGURE 5.1 BURNETT & COMPANY LAND AND SAWMILL ON SOQUEL CREEK

> *The proposed road from San Jose to Santa Cruz, if constructed, can scarcely fail to be of great benefit to this place. It will open a way to redwood forests of vast extent, where hundreds can find profit in getting out lumber, it will reduce the traveling fare and bring more strangers here, and thus render our town more known. And Santa Cruz only needs to be known to be appreciated. We challenge the state to beat us in health and pleasantness of climate, beauty of scenery, etc. Had we the means of intercourse with San Francisco, in as cheap and speedy a manner as San Jose, we would soon leave that village clear behind. So, fellow-citizens, walk up and put that road through the mountains.*[268]

Benjamin Nichols and Francis R. Brady form partnership

Sometime in 1858, Benjamin Nichols joined in a partnership with Francis R. Brady. Little is known of Brady before this time, but the two men worked together to build a tannery somewhere in the vicinity of Soquel. However, shortly after opening, the tannery shut down for unknown reasons.[269]

Notice given of a public meeting to discuss the construction of a turnpike from Santa Cruz to the Summit

On March 8, 1858, a meeting was convened at the courthouse in Santa Cruz. In the days prior, the following notice was published in the *Pacific Sentinel*:

> TO ALL WHOM IT MAY CONCERN: *Take notice that it is our intention to form a Joint Stock Company for the purpose of building a turnpike road, commencing at or near Jacob Blackburn's place and Nathaniel Holcomb's place, and running from each place towards the divide, so as to intersect the road of the Santa Clara and Santa Cruz Gap Turnpike road on the summit of the mountains, and that there will be held a meeting on March 8 at the Court House in Santa Cruz for the purpose of a preliminary organization of such company. Samuel A. Barlett; Nathaniel Holcomb; John Daubenbiss;*

George Parsons; Henry Rice; John Elder; Asa W. Rawson; and Francis M. Kittridge.[270]

Letter from Augustus Noble to John Wilson

Augustus Noble sent a second letter to John Wilson on March 20, 1858 explaining his strategy to deal with squatters living on Rancho Soquel:

> *We have concluded to do nothing in regard to getting an injunction [against] the squatters on the Augmento Ranch at present, or while the survey is in progress. We think we can make an argument with the squatters on the Soquel Ranch to leave in the fall and also prevent them from cutting timber and wood, providing that you get the survey of the Soquel Ranch affirmed by the Surveyor General. You can then direct Mountain Charley to meet with myself and their heirs so that we may give authority to someone of the party to make arguments, collect rents, and commission suits. At present, outside parties are taking advantage of the matter and lawsuits between us to "stick" the ranch and it is better for us to join together and save what we can.*[271]

Construction on the Santa Cruz Gap Turnpike continues

On March 27, 1858, the following update on the progress of the Santa Cruz Gap Turnpike was published in the *San Jose Tribune:*

> *The work upon this important improvement is progressing favorably. The different parties are energetically pushing the construction of their respective sections. And although most of the contractors have discovered upon taking active hold of the job that they had somewhat underrated the difficulties to be overcome and labor to be performed, and that in consequence of these miscalculations they will probably, for the present, be anything but gainers by the operation, they have no idea of retiring from the work, but will finish their portions,*

according to contract. The road on this side is expected to be finished, with the exception of certain bridges, by the first day of April.[272]

Santa Cruz citizens declare their intention to form a company to build a turnpike from Santa Cruz to the Summit

With the turnpike from Santa Clara to the Summit nearing completion, the working group in Santa Cruz decided to move on forming a joint stock company. On April 24, 1858, they announced their intention to hold a meeting on May 4:

> *We, the undersigned, intend to organize a joint stock company for the purpose of constructing a turnpike road to commence near Edward Scott's house, running through the Bean Gulch to the divide, so as to intersect the Santa Cruz Turnpike road. A meeting to organize will be held on the 4th of May 1858, at 2 o'clock P.M. at the Courthouse in Santa Cruz.*
>
> *Signed by Frederick A. Hihn; Adna A. Hecox; John Elden; George W. Inskeep; Lambert B. Clements; James Skene; Richard C. Kirby; Asa W. Rawson; George Otto; L. Farnham; Hiram David Scott; George E. Scott; Elihu Anthony; G. Q. Russell; J. C. Watham; Hiram Imus; Henry Rice; Charles Mckiernan; Alexander McPherson; and Samuel A. Bartlett.*[273]

Letter from Charles McKiernan to John Wilson

The quality of writing and style makes clear that the letter written by Charles McKiernan on April 25, 1858 was done with the assistance of Frederick Hihn. McKiernan once again was informing John Wilson of the situation in Rancho Soquel, specifically his and Hihn's plan to deal with the squatters:

> *All parties interested in the Soquel Ranch have agreed to join to eject the squatters if necessary and Augustus Noble and*

Enter the King 1858

> *Joshua Parrish are going to try to make arrangements with the squatters by which they either pay rent or agree to leave the land this year. Let us know if that will suit you and if you will sign a lease to them (or advise them to sign). Enclosed we send you a petition to the Surveyor General to have the Aptos Rancho surveyed. Rafael Castro is willing at present to call the Borregas Gulch his eastern boundary and we think it best to have this matter settled now before he changes his mind. We all are very anxious to have the survey of the Soquel Ranch and Augmento completed, which will enable us to better sustain injunction or ejectment suits if they are needed.*

This letter and Augustus Noble's letter of a month earlier reveal that those who owned land within Rancho Soquel and Shoquel Augmentation and wanted to keep their land were in desperate need of a leader who would champion their cause in ejecting squatters and demanding rent be paid. It appears from this letter that Hihn stepped up to the challenge.[274]

Santa Cruz Gap Turnpike completed

Another *San Jose Tribune* article published on May 1, 1858 revealed the completion of the route from Santa Clara to the Summit:

> *The road through the Santa Cruz Gap is now completed as far as the company at this end is concerned. The drive from town [San Jose] to the mouth of the gap by the upper road is one which cannot be equaled in beauty by any in the vicinity, and we expect to see the same extensively traveled this summer.*

On May 5, Joseph Johnson and Peter Davidson drove a wagon to the Summit from San José. The *Alta California* described the road in 1860 as having a moderate grade that allowed horses to trot the seven miles to the Summit. The road was cut into the side of steep hills and was so narrow and crooked that turnouts were provided to allow wagons to pass. Although these turnouts were an improvement, "many accidents...occurred with unmanageable horses and careless drivers," resulting in the loss of both horses

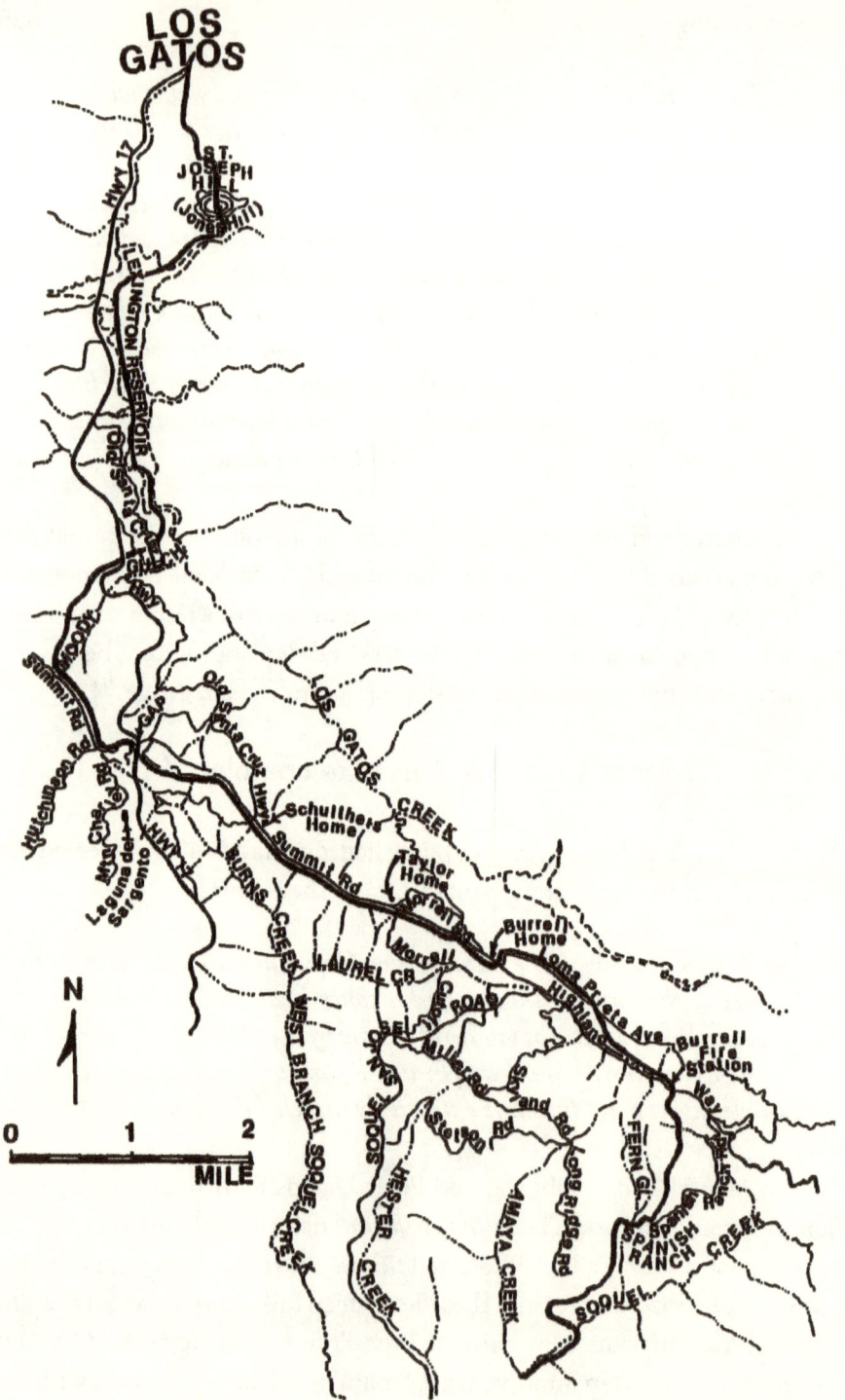

FIGURE 5.2 SANTA CRUZ GAP TURNPIKE – LOS GATOS TO THE SUMMIT

and wagons. To make matters worse, Zachariah "Buffalo" Jones continued to charge tolls on his section of the route until lawsuits forced him to abandon his claim to 180 acres in the foothills above Los Gatos.

Although a tremendous sum of money was spent on the building of the road, it was annually in danger of being washed out by winter storms. The tolls that were collected were hardly enough to cover the damage caused by these storms. In its first year, floods and rockslides caused so much damage that it cost more to repair the road than it had to build it. A newspaper records that "More than six feet of rain has fallen in these mountains, and streams have swollen so tremendously in consequence that trees along the banks were uprooted, fences and sheds washed away, and deep inroads made into bordering ranches."[275]

Status of the Santa Cruz turnpikes

With the completion of the Santa Cruz Gap Turnpike, citizens of Santa Cruz County redoubled their efforts to begin construction of a similar route from the ocean side of the mountains, with projects in Santa Cruz and Soquel moving forward. The *Pacific Sentinel* published this short editorial on May 8, 1858:

> *Road matters seem to be engrossing the attention of our citizens very considerably. Soquel and Santa Cruz are earnestly at work, surveying and subscribing stock for their respective roads. Both the rival roads are said to be excellent, both running through well timbered district of country, and both are zealously advocated by their adherents. The result probably will be two superior turnpikes to the summit, one by Scott's and thence up the creek to Beans' and Mountain Charley's. The other up the divide between Soquel and Branciforte Creeks, intersecting the road at the Santa Clara boundary. So pitch in Soquel, and hurrah for Santa Cruz.*

The newspaper also had this to say regarding funding for the Santa Cruz Turnpike:

> *The stock in the Santa Cruz turnpike is nearly all taken, and*

> *we are informed the company will probably commence work in a few days.*

On May 12, an advertisement was released in the *Pacific Sentinel* for contractors:

> *To Contractors! Contracts on the Santa Cruz Turnpike Road will be let on Monday the 24th instant. The lettings to commence at the house of George E. Scott, at 11 o'clock A.M., and to continue until all the contracts are taken.*
>
> signed by Elihu Anthony, President
> Frederick A. Hihn, Secretary
> Santa Cruz, May 12, 1858[276]

Letter from Augustus Noble to John Wilson

Augustus Noble wrote once again to John Wilson on May 13, 1858, revealing issues he had been having with the survey crews working in Shoquel Augmentation:

> *The surveyors have finished the survey of the Augmento Ranch. We tried to get them to adjust the first or lower line of the northwest boundary to the northwest corner of the Soquel Ranch as you will see in the plot [enclosed with the letter]. But they say that the case must be argued before Mr. Mandeville, the surveyor general who will decide which is the proper boundary. In the plot you will see two lines that they have run. We want the lower line adopted running from the corner of the Soquel Ranch and taking Nathaniel Holcomb's place. The tract of land around Holcomb's was known as the 'Palo Yeska Ranch' just as the tract between the Soquel River and Borregas Gulch was known as the Soquel Ranch 'or tract,' and it was this 'Palo Yeska Ranch' or tract of land that the old woman [Martina Castro] asked for. Near Holcomb's house in a field stood a 'Palo Yeska' or 'punk tree,' and near it were several trees and away was the*

Enter the King   1858

river where they have formed the upper line, and in the plot stood another, and perhaps forty more between them, but the old woman asked for the 'Palo Yeska Rancho tract,' because it was the 'only vacant' land adjoining her ranch.

Rafael Castro is now in the city. If I could find him here, I would try and get his affidavit. I understand he will sign what I have stated, and if he comes back in [a reasonable time] I will

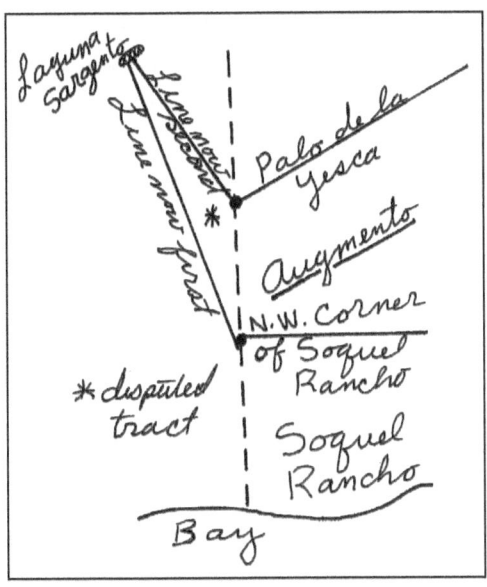

FIGURE 5.3 DISPUTED TRACT IN SHOQUEL AUGUMENTATION

get his affidavit and send it to you. He is in the city most of the time lately attending to his lawsuit and I understand he is dissatisfied with the survey of his ranch. Jose Bolcoff will say the same. If I can find any others I will try and get their affidavits and send them to you next week. Should they adopt the other line, we shall lose one third of the value of the Augmento Ranch.

We now have a road over the mountains, and another from Santa Cruz. Give my regards to Mr. Courtis, and I am truly,

Augustus Noble[277]

Construction begins on the Santa Cruz Turnpike

As part of its now-regular update on the progress of the Santa Cruz Turnpike, the *Pacific Sentinel* reported the following on May 15, 1858:

> With pleasure we announce the important fact, for Santa Cruz County, the primary organization of the Santa Cruz

Turnpike Company met pursuant to notice on the 12th of May, with the stockholders at the court house, and reported the entire stock taken in one day by reliable parties. All the legal steps having been completed within the primary movement, the president, Elihu Anthony, then announced, that the next legal business in order for the stock holders to elect by ballot the officers of the permanent organization of the company for one year. The results of the balloting showed almost a unanimous choice of Elihu Anthony, President; William F. Cooper, Treasurer; Frederick A. Hihn, Secretary; and as Directors: Charles McKiernan, Hiram D. Scott, Hiram Imas, J. B. Arcan, and A. W. Ramon. On motion a committee was appointed to draft a code of by-laws for the company and report instanter, which report was received and adopted article by article with amendments. The Directors were then instructed by the stock-holders to proceed with a definite survey upon which the lettings of contracts could be made on the 24th of May.

Much spirit and manly enterprise was evidenced in the speeches, and a determined feeling of the stock-holders to have every article of the by-laws or the resolutions to express what they meant so as to secure the grand object of building the road without the least possible difficulties in the future to connect us with San Jose by stage in four hours. The stockholders then empowered the directors to proceed with the work, stipulating the assessments for three months.

We are happy to say truthfully that the meeting conducted its business in the most spirited manner, it being composed of our best reliable citizens, every stockholder being present but two.

To be enthusiastic in such a movement cannot be deemed a divergence from the highest interests of our county or State, because we lessen the toil of a two days fatiguing ride from San Francisco to that of less than one; it will also render ease of access, vast forests of redwoods; and offers to the traveler a mountain view, on the top of the dividing ridge unsurpassed in the world; and one that has been visited by hundreds, climb-

> *ing over ragged cliffs and through thick brush, to enjoy its grandeur; for the want of the easy and natural route now selected up the gentle ascent on the survey adopted by the company, where a horse with a buggy can easily trot the entire distance from Santa Cruz to that truly commanding and delightful mountain view.*

The same issue of the *Sentinel* included this tidbit on a later page:

> *Subscribers to stock in the Santa Cruz Turnpike are hereby notified that the books of said company are now made up and that an assessment of ten percent as prescribed by law has been levied on each share, and you are required to pay the first assessment within the present month to the undersigned.*
>
> William F. Cooper, Treasurer[278]

Letter from Charles McKiernan to John Wilson

In an effort to define the boundaries of Shoquel Augmentation according to its wider dimensions, Charles McKiernan attempted to sway the surveyors in various ways. He described some of these methods in a letter to John Wilson on May 23, 1858:

> *Dear general I received your note on thursday last requesting me to see noble and peck about haveing the lines of the ranch run wheare the aught to be the lines has been run I believe right at first I been with the surveyors when the run the first line comminceing at the northwest corner of the Soquel ranch and running a direct line to the lagoon after that line was run Holkam got a drunkin spainard to swear that the palia de lieska was the corner of the ranch a mile and a half up the souquel creek from the corner of the souquel ranch and got them to run aline from there to the lagoon send you a scetch of the land in desfute and the lines as the are run I had a talk with noble peck and Haihn peck said that the surveyors told*

him that both lines run would sent to the survey general and it would be for him to say which was the right on likeways the said what ever proof we might offer would have to be before the surveyor general also peck has told me that rafell castro has run his line and takeing a third of the soquel ranch comineing at the mouth of the boregas gulch and running due north which will com over on the soquel to the tanery and takes bates is mill our line folowes the bed of the boregas gulch I expect we will have to prove our boundrys I expect you will have to get bolcof he may know of som others which will prove to them if you think he had better comdown I will send you you an order for his pasky the lines is all run and he now contery and if the proof hasto be before the surveyor general I do not know how he il figures any thing heer if you send him down right to Haihn and let us know what to dow I am so busy I could not go after the rock No more at present but Remains yours truly

Charles McKiernan

Rafael Castro claimed that his western boundary extended directly north from the mouth of Borragas Gulch instead of following the twist and turns of the gulch to a point where the County Road (Soquel Drive) crossed it. If the Surveyor General accepted Castro's claim, then Benjamin Porter's tannery fell within Castro's Rancho Aptos rather than in Rancho Soquel.[279]

Land transfer from James Scarborough to Cyrus Coe

On May 24, 1858, James Scarborough sold his remaining claim to one eighth of Rancho Soquel and Shoquel Augmentation to Cyrus Coe of San Francisco for $3,000. With this sale, Scarborough was entirely divested of his stake in Martina Castro's properties.

Two days later, Coe sold two-thirds of his claim to Thomas Courtis for $2,000, with an option to purchase the remainder at an unspecified future date.[280]

Letter from Augustus Noble to John Wilson

Augustus Noble sent two short letters, the second enclosed within the first, to John Wilson on May 25, 1858, updating him on Soquel gossip:

> *Your letter of March 25, 1858 was duly received. I would have answered it before this if I had not expected to see you and Father Llebaria here. The several questions that you have asked have required much time for consideration. The first question regarding the boundary of the Soquel Ranch will be shown to Jose Bolcoff, the man that put her* [Martina Castro] *in possession. The heirs have all got their information from him. They have had the ranch surveyed by Thomas Wilson Wright, the County Surveyor, who has promised a deposition if one is necessary.*
>
> *The old woman, Martina Castro is living with the Jean Richard Fourcade family. She is said to be as 'sound' of mind as she has been for several years. This I have from a friend who sees her often and has known her for some three years.*

The second letter reads:

> *I met Charley* [McKiernan] *in Santa Cruz on Saturday together with Frederick A. Hihn. You have probably received Charley's letter by this time. Send Jose Bolcoff down and when he arrives I will have him explain the boundary between Rancho Soquel and Rafael's Rancho Aptos to Rafael. Also, with Jose Bolcoff's assistance I hope we will be able to establish the lower line of the Aumento as the correct one.*[281]

Land transfer from Joseph Majors to Charles H. Willson

On May 26, 1858, an auction was held in which Joseph Majors sold a 1/18 claim to Rancho Soquel and Shoquel Augmentation, as well as the land that he owned in Ranchos Refugio and San Agustín, to the highest bidder. The winning bid was from Charles H. Willson of Marin County, who bid $1,250 for the combined properties, $300 of which was for Martina Castro's former land. It should be noted here that when the court ordered Majors to sell his claims in Soquel, it failed to take into consideration the error that occurred in the deed of July 25, 1853, in which Jones Hoy only sold his land in Rancho Soquel to Majors. A second copy of this deed was signed on November 1.[282]

Land transfer from Benjamin Green to William Ireland

In a deed signed on June 9, 1858, Benjamin Green sold three-tenths of his remaining 1/12 part of Rancho Soquel and Shoquel Augmentation to William Ireland of San Francisco for $900. For some unknown reason, the deed was not filed with the County Clerk until March 18, 1859.[283]

Land transfer from Jean Fourcade to Benjamin Porter

After waiting nearly six months, the sale by Jean Fourcade to Benjamin Porter of the tannery and its surrounding land along the Country Road to Watsonville was finalized and approved on June 11, 1858.[284]

Land transfer from Augustus Noble to Roger Hinckley and John Shelby

On June 19, 1858, Augustus Noble sold half of his 1/12 claim to Shoquel Augmentation to Roger Gibson Hinckley and his son-in-law, John Lafayette Shelby, for $750. Hinckley and Shelby are listed in several publications as millwrights, but nothing could be further from the truth. When the two men purchased the property, they used the redwood timber to repay all—or a good part of—the money owed to Noble for the land. The rest was used to purchase cattle and build a homestead for Shelby. According to later court testimony, Shelby settled on the property with his family, where he raised cattle and sheep. Hinckley does not appear to have lived on the property or been associated with it in the years after the purchase.

The land in question is located just to the south of Sugarloaf Mountain and west of the junction of Hinckley Creek and the East Branch of Soquel

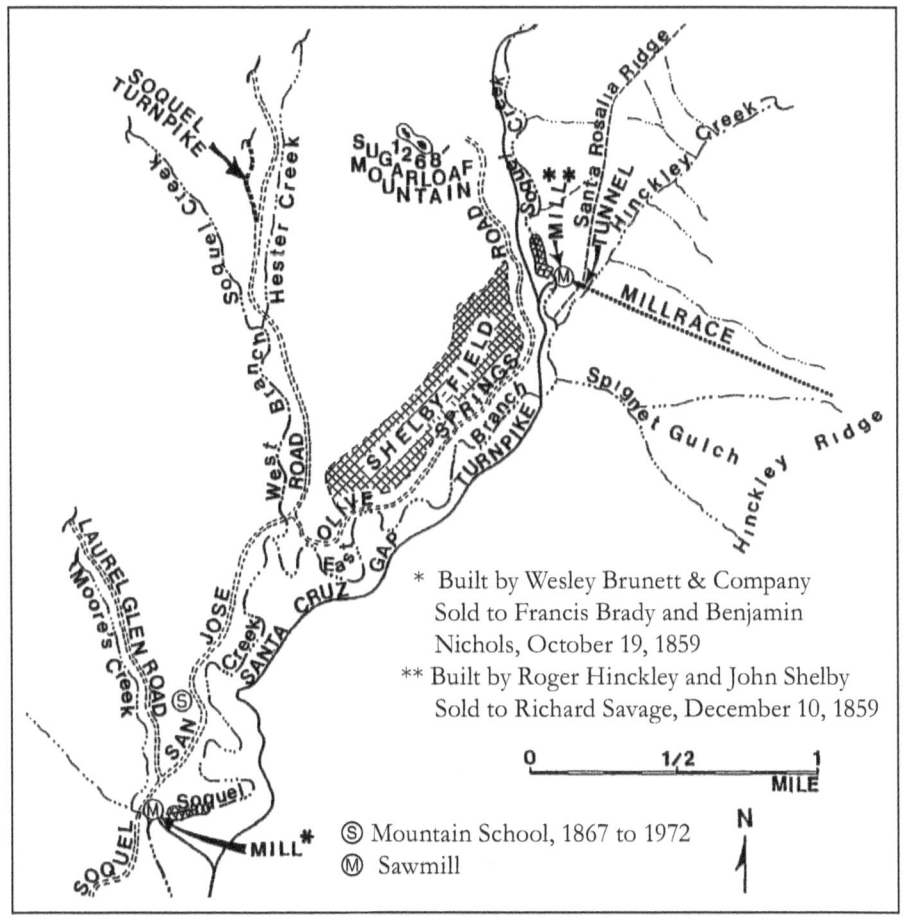

FIGURE 5.4 BURNETT COMPANY AND HINCKLEY & SHELBY SAWMILLS

Creek, within the vicinity of Olive Springs. The 1,268-foot-high Sugarloaf Mountain is located one third of a mile northwest of the Olive Springs Quarry's main yard—the mountain itself provides the ore that is taken from the area—one third of a mile directly east of the Soquel-San Jose Road, and halfway between Hester Creek and the East Branch Soquel Creek. For many years, it served as one of the better-known natural landmarks in the area and was mentioned in early Spanish diaries and referenced frequently in newspapers.

Sugarloaf is named for its shape, although the east side has since eroded and been quarried so it no longer looks like a sugar loaf. In the nineteenth century, sugar was not sold in boxes or bags but rather was delivered to the grocer in hardened dome-shaped cakes that were called loaves. These were then broken into pieces with a sugar nip and sold to the public by the pound. Because many mountains resembled these sugar cakes, 'sugarloaf' became a common name applied to them by settlers. California has some hundred orographic features so named. When used as a descriptive term, the name is usually spelled in two words, but when the term is used with a hill, mountain, peak, or butte, it is usually spelled as one word. Regarding Sugarloaf Mountain above Soquel Creek, it also went by the name San Francisco Mountain in the 1860s into the 1890s. This name was due to the claim that the city of San Francisco could be seen from the mountain's summit. Some locals also called the mountain 'Ingerloaf,' which was simply a popular sugar loaf brand.

Shelby's farm sat in the southern shadow of Sugarloaf on a small floodplain created by the confluence of Spignet Gulch Creek and Hinckley Creek. Because Hinckley and Shelby did not possess the financial means to develop the land, they decided to build a sawmill and use the water from the creeks to drive the saws. The hoped to sell the mill and the 1/96 part of Shoquel Augmentation that it and its facilities occupied to an interested buyer once enough wood was cut to repay Noble for the land. The mill was erected on the East Branch of Soquel Creek just to the north of its confluence with Hinckley Creek. Hinckley Creek and the divide between the two watersheds soon became associated with Hinckley, who was the senior partner in the venture.

Because a water-powered sawmill needs fast-running water to operate its saws, water has to be delivered with sufficient velocity. To accomplish this, Hinckley and Shelby rerouted the small creek that ran down Spignet Gulch. The word 'spignet' is a corruption of the word 'spikenard,' which is a species of herb that grows along the West Coast from the Bay Area to Oregon (*Aralia californica*). From this gulch, Hinckley and Shelby built a wooden mill race to the waterwheel at the mill. As the race approached the mill, the flume became increasingly narrow to increase the water's speed and create more force against the wheel blades. To overcome Hinckley Divide (today's Santa Rosalia Ridge), a tunnel was dug through the hillside, which still exists in part to this day.

Besides the mill and mill race, several other support buildings were erected for the mill, including a cookhouse and bunkhouses for workers, storage buildings, and a dam across the East Branch of Soquel Creek in order to create a mill pond to soak the log prior to cutting.[285]

Land transfer from Joseph Majors to Frederick Hihn

Once again, Joseph Majors was forced to sell some of his land to pay his debts. On July 3, 1858, the court required him to sell his 1/18 claim to Rancho Soquel and Shoquel Augmentation. Frederick Hihn was the highest bidder at $175. Unbeknownst to both Hihn and the court, Majors had already auctioned this land to Charles Willson six weeks earlier. In addition, Majors did not actually own any land in Shoquel Augmentation, having only purchased a claim to Rancho Soquel in 1853. Regardless, Majors formally passed the title to Hihn on August 6. It did not take long for Hihn and Willson to become aware of these discrepancies and rival claims.

After this sale, Majors disappears from the history of Santa Cruz County. He and his wife, María de los Ángeles Castro, had a total of nineteen children together. Majors died on May 26, 1868 at the age of sixty-four. His wife lived for almost another fifty years, passing away at the age of eighty-five in 1903.[286]

Judgment made in favor of Father Ingoldsby

On behalf of his absent client, Father Ingoldsby, who now resided in Chicago, John Wilson brought suit against William Andrews to recover the $916 that he still owed the Catholic Church for the purchase of 1/12 of Rancho Soquel and Shoquel Augmentation. On July 22, 1858, the Third District Court, in Case No. 219, ruled in favor of Ingoldsby and ordered Andrews to pay the amount owed.[287]

Letter from Augustus Noble to John Wilson

In yet another letter to John Wilson, dated July 24, 1858, Augustus Noble expresses serious concerns regarding the survey just completed by James Mandeville:

Jose Bolcoff has been here. He showed us the boundaries of the Augmento. He knows nothing about the Palo Yeska, but shows a pine tree in back of Nathaniel Holcomb's house which was to be a boundary. From there the line ran to and took in Bean's place. If this is so, it would be better to have a new survey providing there is no danger of the squatters raising a mess and carrying back our case to the United States District Court. If we can get the Surveyor General to adopt the lower line, namely commencing at the northwest corner of the Soquel Ranch as it is already surveyed and run in a direct line to Sargents lake. According to the enclosed plot we should be as well off as to have a new survey.

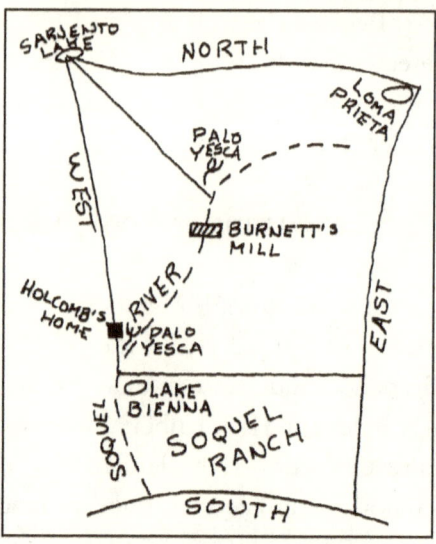

FIGURE 5.5 THE LOCATION OF NATHANIEL HOLCOMB'S HOME WITHIN SHOQUEL AUGMENTATION

You will see on the accompanying map there are two lines on the northwest boundary. We want the lower line adopted. This will be about as well for us as to have a new survey. But, in case a new survey is done, Jose Bolcoff had better come down with the surveyors. Unless the surveyors are given instructions which they cannot depart from, because they can easily be misled by any squatter that they meet in the hills.

P.S. I shall be in the city in two or three weeks and I will show you what we should lose or could gain by a new survey.[288]

Land transfer from Augustus Noble to Craven Hester

For some unknown reason, Augustus Noble sold his remaining 1/24 claim to Rancho Soquel and Shoquel Augmentation, which he had previously purchased from the Catholic Church, to Craven Hester on August 7, 1858. Hester undoubtedly purchased this land to compensate for the School

Land Warrant which had been floated to some other location in the state. By purchasing the property, he was able to remain legally on the land that he already occupied and on which he had made several improvements.[289]

William Andrews dies before repaying his debt to Father Ingoldsby

William Andrews died suddenly on August 14, 1858 before paying the court-ordered amount that he owed Father Ingoldsby for the land he had purchased in Rancho Soquel and Shoquel Augmentation. Since his estate did not have enough money to make this payment, the court ordered that a portion of Andrews' land be sold at auction.[290]

Location of toll gate for Santa Cruz Turnpike established

The *Pacific Sentinel* published the following update regarding the Santa Cruz Turnpike on August 14, 1858:

> *At the Board of Supervisors meeting an order was passed [in which it] was stated that at the last meeting a toll gate was established at or near Bean's house, and the company was empowered to erect the gate at or near George Edwin Scott's house, on the western terminus of the turnpike road.*
>
> *A petition was then presented asking that a road be laid off from the Santa Cruz Turnpike at or near Bean's house to the highest accessible point of timber land on the so called Bean's Creek. Charles McKiernan and Hiram D. Scott were appointed to view out the road's route.*[291]

Letter from Augustus Noble to John Wilson

On August 26, 1858, Augustus Noble, now divested of his land in the Soquel area, wrote to John Wilson to give him the latest news on the survey and the turnpikes:

> *I should have answered your letter sooner, but we have been*

expecting to see those surveyors, but we got tired of waiting. On Saturday we had a meeting. Present were Frederick A. Hihn, Joshua Parrish, Henry Peck and myself. We drew up a petition to the Surveyor General which we want you to present to him. We feel that you should get the survey of the Soquel Ranch adopted as soon as possible for the following reason: Rafael Castro, who owns the Ranch adjoining to the east of us called Aptos Ranch, says that his western boundary calls for a line to run due north from the mouth of Borrages Gulch. If the boundary line is as such, he would take off a third of the Soquel Ranch though he admits to be still trying to get his ranch surveyed. I am afraid that he may be trying to spring a trick on us. I wish you would look at his grant and see what his boundaries are and let me know as soon as possible.

If the surveyor came down, we think you had better send Jose Bolcoff. Henry Peck is afraid that [Camlison?] will not speak hospitingly enough, but we can get old Rafael Castro. He says the "Palo de la Yeska" was near Nathaniel Holcomb's house, and I think we can find others who will say the same. Have Juan [Castro] get the surveyors back here, but with the head man gone and the others scattered over the state, it would be better if we could have a new set sent down. We would try to have the survey finished in a confused manner as much as possible.

The new road will pass through the territory in dispute. We want as soon as the Rancho Soquel area is approved to have the squatters clear out, and if they refuse, commence suits of ejection against them.

Give my regards to Mr. Courtis and Irene

Augustus Noble[292]

Samuel McKee defeats Craven Hester as judge for Third District Court

Samuel Bell McKee, born in Ireland in 1821, arrived in the United States with his family at an early age. They settled in Georgia and McKee spent his early education there before pursuing a law degree in Alabama under the mentorship of Judge Collier of Tuscaloosa. He later moved to Mississippi, where he married and opened a law practice. In 1853, the attraction of California proved too strong to ignore and McKee and his family moved to Oakland, where he began a new law practice. His professional card, copied from the advertising columns of the first newspaper published in Alameda County in 1854, made the following announcement: "Samuel McKee, Attorney-at-law and General Collecting Agent, Cal., will give prompt attention to all business entrusted to his care in the Courts of Alameda County and the counties adjoining. Office on the east side of Broadway, near the Plaza."

In November 1856, he was elected an Alameda County judge. Two years later, he was nominated by the Democratic Party for the position of judge for the Third District. His opponent was the incumbent, Craven Hester. McKee won the race handily on September 1, 1858. He retained this position through 1875. It was later said of McKee that "few men possess the rare qualities that win admiration and respect alike from rich and poor, Democrats and Republicans, advocates and clients, as does Judge McKee. His decisions are nearly always conclusive, and seldom or never set aside. His profound knowledge of the law, his kindly manner, amiable qualities and happy manner of treating both clients and attorneys, prevent any unfounded objections or unreasonable criticisms of his conduct. He is, indeed, a model judge, and the Third District is justly proud that its laws are administered by such a man." McKee left a deep impact on Santa Cruz County that is still felt today.[293]

Letter from Augustus Noble to John Wilson

By September 15, 1858, Augustus Noble was becoming upset with the decisions being made by the surveyors and also frustrated with his own inability to intervene. He summarized these complaints to John Wilson in the following letter:

> *Juan Jose Castro has been here and he says that the Palo Yesca was where the surveyors put it, so his deposition will not help us at all. He wanted $60 to go and show it [to the Surveyor*

> *General at the northwest corner of Rancho Soquel].*
> *Thomas Wilson Wright will give his affidavit in regard to the Loma Prieta, but it will not help us any as he says if we take in all the hill we should be three miles from where the miners are at work. This is confirmed also by several that live near there.*

The mines that Noble mentions were the quicksilver mines located about three miles to the north of Loma Prieta and Mount Thayer along the Guadalupe Creek. Their mention here provides insight into the desire by those claiming ownership of Shoquel Augmentation to extend the northern boundary as close to the mines as possible. In addition, by changing the location of the "Palo de la Yesca" from the northwest corner of Rancho Soquel to its present location opposite Spignet Gulch just to the south of Hinckley Creek, James Mandeville deprived the Augmentation of many acres of valuable land.

The quicksilver mines are now closed after having polluted the ground and Guadalupe Creek for decades. They form a part of the Almaden Quicksilver County Park.[294]

Land transfer from Craven Hester to Benjamin Farley

On September 28, 1858, Craven Hester sold 1/48 of his claim in Shoquel Augmentation to his friend Benjamin Farley, a resident of Santa Clara County, for $375. Hester had made several improvements to the land since buying it in early August, and its close proximity to the Soquel Turnpike meant that he and Farley had much to gain by maintaining the land. Over the next two years, the men planted orchards and vineyards and laid the groundwork of the Redwood Lodge, which would become a popular stage stop on the road to San José.[295]

First three miles of the Soquel Turnpike open to traffic

The *Pacific Sentinel* reported on October 2, 1858 that all work on the Soquel Turnpike had been suspended due to unexpected delays. Two weeks later, on October 16, the *Sentinel* corrected its original notice and clarified that work had stopped on a portion of the route due partially to heavy rains. It explained further that, once the rains ceased, work to improve this troublesome section would resume. The first three miles were already open to the public, with eleven miles left to go to reach the Summit. The goal of the turnpike company was for their road to accommodate four-horse coaches operating at full speed across the entire route.[296]

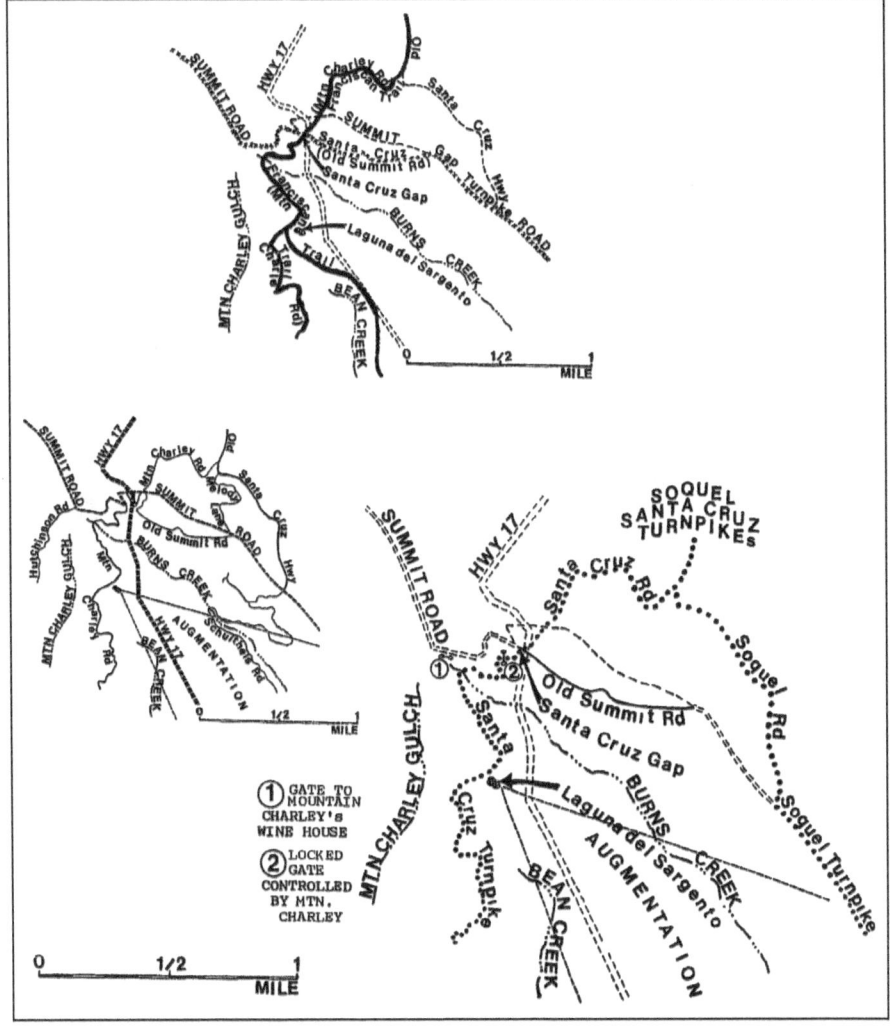

FIGURE 5.6 EARLY ROUTES ACROSS THE SANTA CRUZ MOUNTAINS

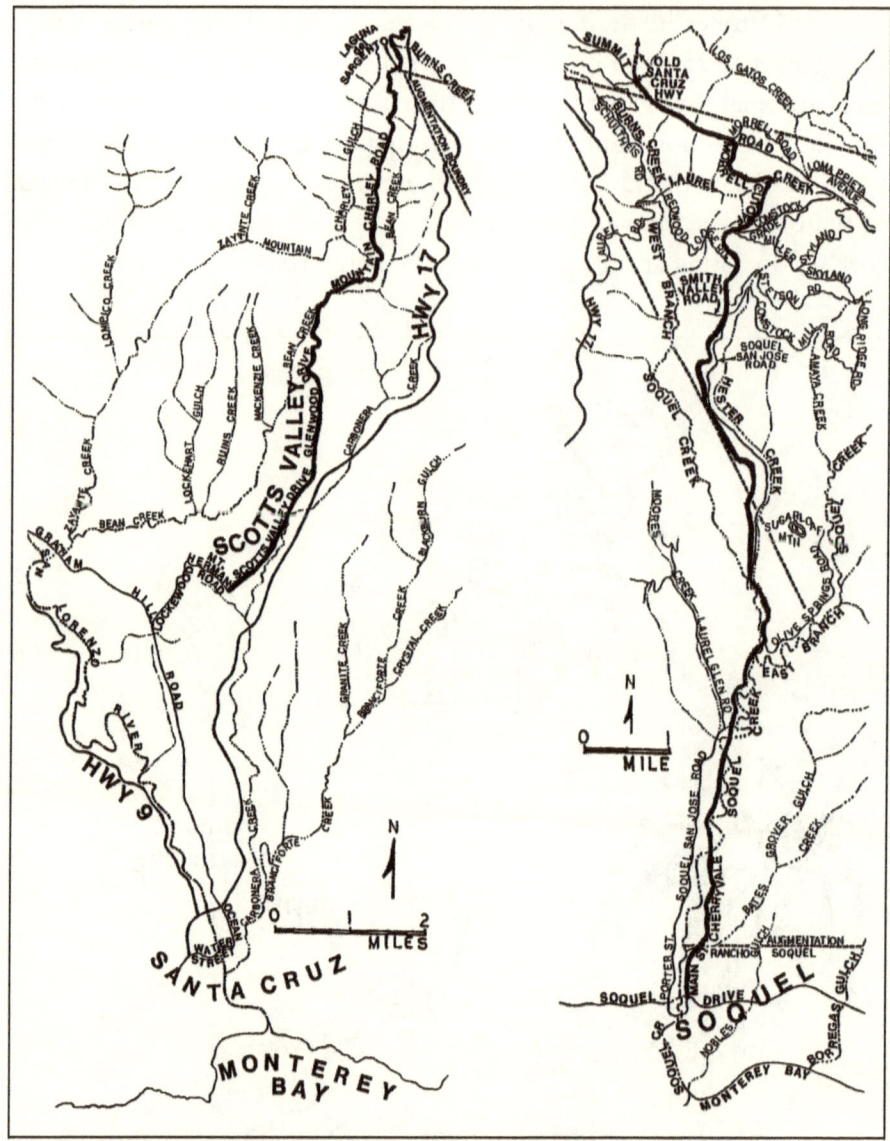

Figure 5.7 Santa Cruz and Soquel Turnpikes

Santa Cruz Turnpike opened to the public

As slow progress was being made on the Soquel Turnpike, the rival Santa Cruz Turnpike opened to the public on October 16, 1858. The *Pacific*

Enter the King   1858

Sentinel announced:

> *A Glorious Triumph of Industrial Improvement. We can announce to the world, or more especially to the citizens of Santa Cruz and Santa Clara counties, the completion of the Santa Cruz Turnpike, as far as contracted for, by the industry of Charles McKiernan and Hiram Scott, who have nobly finished, by strong effort, a road up to the dividing summit, and made it passable and safe for carriages and teams, with ordinary prudence on mountain roads, and we have the satisfaction of announcing that stage coaches run tri-weekly over the road.*

McKiernan and Scott were paid $6,000 to construct the road from Scott's home to the Summit Road. Shortly after the first tolls were collected, it became known as the McKiernan Toll Road. For twenty years, a toll was collected to use the turnpike in either direction. Afterwards, according to the act passed in 1852, the county took over the road. This occurred on August 27, 1878.

The road had its origins in downtown Santa Cruz, where it departed town by crossing the San Lorenzo River at Water Street and turning up Ocean Street to the north. The route then followed Graham's Grade (Graham Hill Road) to somewhere in the vicinity of Sims Road or Lockewood Road—it is not entirely certain since the clearest map of the route is Thomas Wright's 1880 county map. In any case, the route then continued down modern Scotts Valley Drive, where Scott installed a gate so that he could collect the toll to use the road. It is from here that the turnpike formally began.

Near Scott's house was the Hendrick's place, where extra horses could be borrowed for the ride up to the Summit. After the gate was opened and the toll paid, the first part of the journey up the mountain led to Charles Martin's ranch on Bean Creek. From there, it was on up to McKiernan's home beside the Laguna del Sargento, where any borrowed horses were returned. About a mile beyond McKiernan's house, the other end of the turnpike was reached, where travelers journeying to Santa Cruz would pay their toll.[297]

John Wallace establishes Mount Diablo Meridian through the Santa Cruz Mountains

On October 16, 1858, James Mandeville, the United States Surveyor General for California, directed John Wallace to complete the survey through the Santa Cruz Mountains, thereby finishing the task left only partially done by Richard Howe six years earlier. However, rather than starting from the point where Howe deviated in the Santa Clara Valley, Wallace began in Aptos and worked his way north. While this accomplished the task satisfactorily, in 1980, George N. Darling was hired by the United States Geological Survey to retrace Wallace's steps and finally survey Sections 3, 4, and 5 of the Soquel Township. Most of it was within Shoquel Augmentation but small portions sat outside and therefore required surveying.[298]

Martina Castro's children appeal decision awarding Rancho Soquel and Shoquel Augmentation to the Catholic Church

In late 1858, Robert Peckham, acting alongside Gregory Yale on behalf of the Castro children and their spouses in appealing the decision to award all of Rancho Soquel and Shoquel Augmentation to the Catholic Church, presented his clients' appeal to Case No. 131 before the Seventh District Court in Contra Costa County:

> *Appeal from the Seventh District, County of Contra Costa. This is an action of ejectment* [an action to secure or recover possession of real property by the true owner]. *The facts are stated in the opinion of the court, but will, probably, be better understood by setting forth the amended answer of the defendants, which presents the question upon which the opinion of the court is based. It is as follows:*
> "*That all the right, title, or interest which Martina Castro had in any part of the demanded premises was held by her before her marriage with Louis Depeaux in 1849 and before the adoption of the constitution of the State, and that the same was her separate property; that she, in August, A.D. 1850,*

with the knowledge, consent, and concurrence of her husband, made a deed to her children, for a valuable consideration, purporting to convey to them eight-ninths of the demanded premises, which conveyed an equitable title and conveyed her into a trustee for their use and benefit; that all the rights which the children took under that deed, had, by divers conveyances, vested in the defendants; that the children entered into possession of the property, after the execution of the aforesaid deed, with the consent of the aforesaid Martina and her husband; and that they and the defendants had made improvements to the amount of $18,700, which were now on the premises demanded; that plaintiff and his co-tenant subsequently purchased the demanded premises of the said Martina and her husband, with reference to her said deed to her children, and with full and actual notice thereof, and that the price paid by them was about one-half of the ninth part of the demanded premises, which she, in said deed to her children, reserved to herself; and that they purchased with full and actual notice of the rights of the defendants of their possession and of the value of their improvements; and defendants deny any interference with the said Martina or plaintiff, in the enjoyment of the remaining one-ninth part of the land sought to be recovered." This answer was sworn to.

Plaintiff moved to strike out the amended answer upon the following grounds:

1st: Because the same was irrelevant.

2nd: Because the same set up a sham defense.

The court ruled that the amendment should be stricken out, unless defendants should elect to rely on such amendment to the exclusion of the original answer; and defendants refusing so to elect, the amendment was stricken out, and the defendants excepted.

What Peckham achieved by allowing John Wilson to strike out the amendment was to shift the debate from the last incriminating argument accepted by the lower court, that the "said pretended deed was obtained from Martina Castro by fraud and fraudulent misrepresentations of facts."

This in effect removed the Augmentation from the appeal (thereby awarding it to the Catholic Church) and concentrated all attention on Rancho Soquel, where Castro's children had made the most investments.[299]

United States Surveyor General completes survey of Rancho Soquel and Shoquel Augmentation

The field surveys of Rancho Soquel and Shoquel Augmentation conducted by a team led by James Mandeville, the Surveyor General for California, were completed sometime in late 1858 or early 1859. For reasons never specified, Mandeville decided against including all of the Sierra Azul within the boundaries of the Augmentation. His reasoning is obvious when the range is viewed from Monterey Bay: it appears barren and of little practical interest to anyone living on the ocean side. Therefore, when the surveyors reached the Laguna del Sargento, they were instructed to head straight towards the peak that Francisco Alviso called "Chuchita."

By establishing the north boundary as a line from the lagoon to Chuchita, they created two new problems. First, they had eliminated the Loma Prieta range. And second, they had renamed Chuchita "Mt. Bache." If the peak's name were to remain Mt. Bache, all of the deeds written to date were incorrect. Therefore, Alexander Bache's name was sacrificed and the peak was renamed "Loma Prieta," thereby turning the range into a single peak.

With Loma Prieta established, more problems arose. First, there was now no point along the Augmentation's boundary called Chuchita, a point referenced in every deed written to date concerning the area. And second, by moving the location of the Palo de la Yesca five miles to the north, away from Soquel Creek, between 7,000 and 8,000 acres of land were lost. The solution to both problems was to move Chuchita to its present location at the end of Rider Road on Bean Hill. This move brought almost the entire Valencia Creek watershed into the Augmentation.

Through these changes, Governor Micheltorena's original description of the Augmentation still matched, even if the actual boundary points had changed. And every reference to these boundary points after this date officially referred to these new points. This inevitably caused more disputes over the ensuing years, especially regarding the location of the Palo de la Yesca.[300]

Enter the King 1859

Frederick Hihn shifts his business interests

Not long after Frederick Hihn sold his store to his brother Hugo in 1857, he contracted with the Pacific Coast Steamship Company to rebuild the pier at Soquel Landing (where the Capitola Wharf now sits). In 1859, he formed a partnership with Elihu Anthony and built a reservoir at the end of School Street just below the mission which provided water to downtown Santa Cruz via redwood piping. These ventures proved profitable and Hihn had amassed around $30,000 by the end of the year.

It was later revealed in 1867 during a deposition taken for two lawsuits against him led by Antonia Peck and Benjamin F. Bayley that Hihn transitioned slowly into the real estate business during this time. When giving his testimony, Robert Peckham asked if he was ever a moneylender, to which Hihn replied that he had once been, but not for several years, implying he had ceased lending money around 1859. Peckham followed with several more questions, including:

> PECKHAM: How have you employed your capital?
> HIHN: In buying land and gas stocks in San Francisco.
> P: What have you done with your properties in Rancho Soquel and in the Soquel Augmentation Ranch to date?
> H: I have sold parts of it in both ranches. The balance of it I have tried to put it into shape, brought it into cultivation, most of it, cleared it up, and went to considerable trouble to have the boundaries fixed up, and I have built two houses on it, improved the roads leading to it and from it, and helped to build bridges, and paid taxes on it.

Some of these acquisitions in Rancho Soquel and Shoquel Augmentation have already been documented above, while others are still forthcoming. But Hihn's business focus made a decisive shift in 1859 that cannot be overlooked. From this point forward, real estate became Hihn's driving interest in Santa Cruz County.[301]

Judgment made in favor of Martina Castro's deed of 1850

After the upper court struck out the amendment offered by Robert Peckham in Case No. 131 before the Seventh District Court, arguments on the remaining nine points of contention began. The lower court in Contra Costa County accepted these points, and the Supreme Court of California ruled upon them as follows:

1. The document in question was not a joint deed of conveyance by Martina Castro and Louis Depeaux as man and wife, drafted in order to transfer the right of Castro in the property named in the deed. The court ruled that a deed which recites the title of the wife and then declares that the husband unites in the conveyance, in pursuance of the statute, is sufficient.

2. That Castro and Depeaux were at the pretended date and execution of the signing of the deed husband and wife and did not join in the execution. The court ruled that, in such case, the joining of the husband in the conveyance is not the purpose of passing title, for he has none to convey, it is only as a precaution against imposition, or to afford her his protection, or similar reasons of policy, or to evidence his renunciation of the right to manage or control it.

3. That the deed on its face only purports to be the deed of Castro and not the joint deed of her and her husband. The court explained that it was a familiar rule, recognized by this and all other courts, that where several papers concerning the same subject matter were executed by or between the same parties at the same time, all are to be construed as one instrument.

4. That the pretended consent endorsed on the back of the same by Depeaux is not under seal, has no date to it, con-

tained no words of conveyance, and is without consideration and is utterly void. On this point, the court stated that a deed properly executed and acknowledged by the wife, of her separate property, with the assent of her husband underwritten, not under seal, but properly acknowledged, is sufficient to pass the title.

5. That Castro, whose mark was on the deed, being a married woman when the same was executed and delivered, therefore her execution thereof cannot be proved in any other manner than that found in the statutes of conveyance and those defining the rights of husband and wife. However, the court decided that lands acquired by a married woman under Mexican laws, and which were her separate estate, might be conveyed before the adoption of our stature with the bare assent of the husband, by many informal instruments or possibly without writing. By the California state constitution, property thus acquired was the separate estate of the wife; she did not, therefore, look to the statute respecting conveyances as the source of her authority to sell or dispose of her property. On the contrary, the statutes were a limitation upon her power, prescribing a new and distinct mode of conveying the land or evidencing the sale or disposition of it. It disabled her from disposing of her property as she could have done before. Therefore, she retained all her original rights and powers over the subject, except such as were expressly taken away.

6. That it appears upon the face of the paper offered in evidence that the same was not the deed of Castro, because there was evidence on the paper itself that she did not assent to all the provisions therein set forth. On this formality, the court ruled that literal conformity with the statute concerning conveyances of the separate property of the wife, as a general rule was not required—a substantial compliance was all that was necessary.

7. That there was no acknowledgment of the paper offered before any proper officer authorized to take acknowledgments of a married woman. The court directed attention to the sixth section of the act concerning husband and wife, which related only to separate property acquired after the passage of the act. No retrospective operation was intended, or perhaps, could have been given to it. In such cases, the statute only operated upon future transactions and matters.

8. That the pretended acknowledgment endorsed on the paper offered was not in due form. This pedantic technicality was promptly discarded by the court, which stated that there was no peculiar form for the signing of a deed. Any writing which clearly showed that a party had adopted a sealed instrument as his own, intended to be bound by the contents of it, was, if not a formal, at least a sufficient execution to satisfy the statute.

9. And lastly, that the pretended acknowledgment before Peter Tracy was not endorsed or annexed to the pretended deed and it was not shown he used the seal of the court. On this point, the court clarified that a county clerk may take and certify an acknowledgment to a deed, although he had no seal of office. His general phrase, "having a seal," was only intended to denote a court of record, which was defined to be a court having a seal. The power of the clerk was never intended to be made to depend upon the fact of his having procured this article or the care with which he preserved it.

In the end, Justice Joseph Glover Baldwin made the opinion on the case and Chief Justice David Smith Terry concurred. Baldwin concluded:

We have avoided the expression of any opinion upon many

questions presented by the record and have assumed some positions more for the purpose of argument than with a view to decide them, the real question passed upon being the validity of the deed from Martina and Depeaux. We expressly leave open the question whether a grant, made in the usual form and with the usual conditions, by the Mexican authorities, to a married person, creates a separate estate or common property. The court erred in striking out the answer setting up this defense.

The error of excluding this defense, founded on this deed, is sufficient to reverse the judgment below, and, probably, decides the entire controversy.

Judgment reversed and cause remanded for further proceedings, in pursuance of this opinion.

In summary, the opinion of the Supreme Court on January 1, 1859 confirmed Castro's deed of August 1850 in which she gifted 8/9 of her two land grants to her children and their spouses. This had the effect of nullifying her later deed of January 1855 with the Catholic Church, except for the 1/9 remaining portion of her property that she retained for herself. The decision by the court was based entirely on the points made by John Wilson, but it left one important question unanswered: was the deed of 1850 obtained through fraud or the misrepresentation of facts? This question has never been satisfactorily answered.[302]

School Land Warrants floated to other locations in California

Because a School Land Warrant could not be located within the confines of a Spanish or Mexican land grant, and Shoquel Augmentation was judged to be a legitimate grant to Martina Castro, Warrant Nos. 90, 228, 327, 329, and half of 108, all owned by Peter Tracy's estate, and the other half of No. 108, owned by Henry Parsons, were floated to eligible locations elsewhere in California on February 12, 1859. A week later, on February 18, Warrant Nos. 353 and 354 claimed by Henry Peck were also floated. Of the seven warrants, the last two were floated to the Pajaro Valley along the west bank of the creek that runs through Rancho Cañada de los Osos. I have been unable to discover the fates of the remaining five warrants.[303]

Land transfer from Antonia Lodge to Lyman Burrell

When the Burrell family moved to the Summit, their land was considered available for settlement. But when James Mandeville completed his survey of Shoquel Augmentation, Burrell's home fell within the boundaries of the land grant. To ensure that he retained his land and home, Burrell entered into an agreement with Henry and Antonia Peck on April 13, 1859, who offered Burrell one third of their claim to the Augmentation (1/27 of the total area) in exchange for $1,500. Burrell paid a down payment of $1,000 and signed a promissory note for the balance. An identical deed was signed again on October 2, 1860, although on this date, no money was exchanged. The due date for the remaining amount was not mentioned in either deed, which proved to be a point of contention later.

Burrell discusses these points and life on the Summit in the third part of his series, "Recollections of an Octogenarian by Col. Lyman John Burrell," edited by Mary Smith for the newspaper *Mountain Echoes* in 1882:

> *I settled in the Santa Cruz Mountains in the fall of 1852. I came as a pioneer, knowing nothing about the capabilities of the soil. I had everything to learn by experience. I made many experiments and several failures before I discovered that the land was better adapted to fruit growing than to anything else. From a financial point of view, I was a very poor man when I came, but I was rich in health and strength, rich in hope and courage, with a good will to work and a determination to bring order out of chaos and make a good living for my family. For want of means, I was obliged to commence in a small way and to go on step by step. I first broke up four acres of open land and sowed wheat. It resulted in a small crop of only fifteen or twenty bushels to the acre. I counted this a failure. Next I took a stock of pigs to buy on shares. The two little pigs that we first brought from the valley grew so well on the wild oats that I felt sure a good success. But I was disappointed. As the oats became ripe and sunburst, the pigs grew poor and sick. The sharp, stiff beard of the oats injured them, and I was obliged to remove them to the valley. I set out a few fruit trees*

the first year, and added a few more every year, but not very many. It was quite a long job to make the necessary pickets and fences for enclosing land for an orchard and vineyard, having no one to help me excepting my son.

One day while the pigs were here, we had an encounter with grizzly bears. We were at work making a fence near the spot where neighbor Sears' house now stands, and the pigs were feeding on the hill nearby, when we heard an unusual noise among them, as if they were frightened. I took an axe in my hand, got over the fence, and went up the trail to see what troubled them. There was thick brush on one side of the trail and a picket fence on the other. When about halfway up, I saw an old bear at the top, with a cub behind her, coming down at full speed on the trail. I shouted and swung my axe, hoping to make her turn back, but she paid no attention whatsoever to me. Seeing that a collision was inevitable, and that she would be upon me before I could get over the fence or out of her way in the brush, I turned back and ran as fast as possible on the trail, with the bear and cub behind me. I soon came to a short turn in the trail, where I stumbled and fell flat on the ground, a little outside of the trail. The old bear instantly took one of my limbs between her jaws. She gave one good, strong bite. Meanwhile, the cub, which was close behind, ran by us and turned down the trail. The mother, seeing this, followed it a few steps, turned again and looked at me, and then ran on after her cub. I sprang up and got over the fence. My wife and daughters came running towards me, having been alarmed by my shouting, and my son came running from another direction with his gun to rescue me. But he was too late to shoot the bear. They helped me into the house and took care of my wounds. This misfortune disabled me for about six weeks. Until this happened, I had never felt any fear for wild animals, but after this, I never had the least desire to meet a bear.

Another day, when I was alone hunting for deer, I came to a clump of redwoods where one large tree was surrounded by many small ones. I was on the point of creeping through the brush when I heard the hoarse growl of a bear within. I took the hint at once and departed as rapidly as I could till I was out of sight and hearing, thinking that, in this case at least, "the better part of valor was discretion." The bear did not follow me. I presume that she had a nest of young bears concealed there.

I next tried the experiment of keeping cows. A. S. Waylund had brought up a stock of cattle from the valley and kept them in our neighborhood through the winter and spring. At harvest time, he took his family to the valley and left the cows in our care. My wife and one of the daughters went over to their place every day to milk them and make butter for our own use, until after harvest, when the family returned. We then took about seventy cows on shares. We hired an experienced man to help us for the first three months at sixty-five dollars per month and board. He helped milk the cows, took care of the calves, helped about fence making. I did the churning and corralled the cows at night. When he left, we did all the work ourselves and we made it a paying business.

When the feed dried upon the open land, the cattle troubled us by straying away into the woods and scattering in different directions. Two of us were generally obliged to go after them towards night on horseback. It took us two or three hours to gather them in, and then we did not always find them all. My two daughters, then nine and eleven years of age, would sometimes milk twelve cows each, while we were away hunting for a few stray ones. I remember one cow being lost for nearly a week. At last we found her quite near home, down on her knees, with her head caught in a hole at the foot of a tree. I suppose she was trying to get water and, in some way, got fastened. Her head was swelled so much that I had to chop away a part of the tree before I could release her. She must have suffered dreadfully. She could hardly walk; but after a long time, she recovered. We kept these cows only eight months, and we made enough in that time to buy twelve cows with calves, and horse, besides our living, and paying one hired man. We packed the butter to the valley on horseback and sold it in San Jose. When we drove up from the valley, the twelve cows and calves that we had bought, we brought with them thirteen heifers that we had contracted to keep for three years on shares. I was to have the use of them and half of the increase.

One of my best cows died on the journey, in consequence of drinking too much water. Two of them proved so wild that I fatted and sold them to a butcher. Our little daughters were very active and courageous in those days. I well remember some things that used to astonish us. One day, when my son and I were very busy at some work, the two girls went to gather in the cows. They met Mountain Charley, who informed them that he had seen two cows at some distance away, feeding with his wild cattle, and that they could not possibly separate them. But they went on. They found ours by themselves and had no trouble in gathering them together, but they also found a young calf. It followed on for a short distance, but soon tired out. The eldest girl then dismounted, lifted the calf, and placed it on the horse in front of the youngest, who held it on and rode home with it; while the eldest remounted her horse and drove home the others.

Another time, we had a young cow that had been lost two or three days. She came home one morning, but soon turned and went away again. Our youngest daughter, seeing this, followed her some distance into the woods till she came to a dead calf, torn up by lions. She came home and told us. I put a bottle of strychnine in my pocket and she led me to the place. I poisoned the calf, and the next morning had the satisfaction of finding a very large lion lying dead beside it.

We used to make traps for catching bears. One day, this daughter was riding horseback, when she took it into her head to ride down to the trap and see if any were caught. She galloped home very much excited, saying that one had been caught and had just got away. We went to the trap and found that the logs were still wet where he had been gnawing his way out. We afterwards caught a bear in that trap which we shot and dressed for our table.

The lions used to trouble us a great deal about our calves.

> We kept them in a pen. One night, a lion took one of them over the fence and carried it away. We had a spirited little Spanish cow which was plucky and spiteful. The next night, we put her into the pen with the calves. The lion came again as we expected, but he found his match. The cow pushed him against one of the fence boards with so such force that it broke, and then she thrust him through this aperture to the outside, leaving many locks of his hair to testify to his inglorious defeat. He came no more. We lost no more calves from that pen.
>
> All this time, our few fruit trees and vines were growing well. We had a good garden every year and had plenty of vegetables and melons. We also raised little grain every year for family use. Thus, things went without much change for about three years, when a sorrow came upon us. My beloved wife again grew feeble and gradually declined until I was left alone with the children.

To quote from Steven Payne's book *A Howling Wilderness*: "In 1857 Clarissa's health began to worsen and she died of consumption. There is no record of the date of her death and her last letters to her relatives back East remain undated. The only reference is in Birney Burrell's diary on Tuesday, February 10, 1857: 'Mother is going to stay down in the valley for several weeks to go through a course of medicine.' The diary is blank from May 28th to October 25th, 1857. Probably she died during this period. She was buried on the ranch." Burrell continued:

> I had found out that I was not on government land as I had supposed when I first settled here. The time at length came when I must either buy in or sacrifice all of my improvements. To do this, I sold off nearly all of my stock to raise the money. I bought an undivided twenty seventh part of the Soquel Augmentation Rancho, paying $1,000 down and giving my note for $500 more.
>
> The signing of the deed with the Pecks was a great setback to me, but I had a little stock left. My children were now well grown. As we had no school on the mountains, they had all been to school in San Jose and the youngest a part of the time

in Soquel. My son and I now went to work making shakes and pickets which we carried to San Jose and sold. Fortunately for us, the turnpike road was made. It was so much better than the old way of packing everything up and down the hills on horseback, that we never felt like grumbling at the toll (we had to pay to use the "Soquel Turnpike").

And now we began to put in more fruit trees and grape vines. But our troubles were not at an end. There were many owners of the Augmentation Rancho, some owning a much larger share than others, and it was still undivided. Some of the larger owners wished to have it all sold at public auction, and the money divided among the owners pro rata. The smaller owners, who had made themselves good homes and made many improvements, did not wish to be sold out in this way but wanted the land divided. They believed that some of the large owners had designs upon the land, and as there was likely to be no competition, in case of an auction sale, they would bid it in at very low figures. They commenced a suit and we had to defend ourselves at great trouble and expense.[304]

Letter from Frederick Hihn to John Wilson

On April 19, 1859, Frederick Hihn wrote again to John Wilson in San Francisco, apparently still on the side of Wilson's clients, the Catholic Church:

Your favor of the 9th just came duly to hand. I thank you for the granting of extension of time for answering. I have seen several of the owners of the Soquel Rancho and they seem to think favorably of securing your services in the survey of the Augmento. I called a meeting of the owners for next Saturday and I would pray you to inform me by that time on what terms you would be willing to attend to the alteration of the survey, so that we could consider and ponder upon your offer then. You will please to state if you wish to have the money paid down or how much of it you would require for your expenses in case you would have to come here to take testimony. I would state here that several parties who claim several deeds from you and the Reverend John Ingoldsby will probably join with us in this matter.[305]

Land transfer from Andrews Estate to George Porter

Born in Massachusetts in 1823, George Keating Porter had three brothers and two cousins, the latter both born in Vermont. On April 21, 1859, Porter placed the highest bid in a sheriff's auction of a 7/120 claim to Rancho Soquel and Shoquel Augmentation. This land was originally owned by the late William Andrews, who had died still in debt to the Catholic Church in the amount of $916. Porter's bid for the property was $740.[306]

Land transfer from Luisa Cota to Frederick Hihn

After several negotiations, Luisa Cota and Jean Fourcade agreed to sell one-third of Cota's one-ninth claim (1/27 of the total property) to Rancho Soquel and Shoquel Augmentation to Frederick Hihn for $1,100 on April 29, 1859. Hihn paid them $375 upfront, with a payment scheduled for November 1 and another on the same day the following year. In addition, Hihn agreed to pay for all of the expenses incurred by the Fourcades to have the property confirmed by the Surveyor General, as well as any costs associated with making corrections to the said survey or dividing the land equally between the rightful owners. As a part of this, he also pledged to defend the Fourcades against anyone whatsoever who sought to claim or recover possession of their interest in either grant land.

This deed is interesting for several reasons. When it was signed, the Surveyor General for California had completed his survey of both properties. While the plats had not yet been officially released, the boundaries and acreage for both land grants were known. The acreage for Rancho Soquel was established at 1,668 acres, while that of the Augmentation was set at 32,702 acres. The boundary between the two was a line that extended due east from the junction of Bates and Soquel Creeks to a point in Borragas Gulch.

Despite the boundaries being fully known by both parties, Hihn nonetheless set the size of Rancho Soquel at approximately 2,500 acres and that of Shoquel Augmentation at nearly 70,400 acres. Soquel's boundaries were described thusly: "Commencing on the mouth of the Soquel River, thence running northerly along said river about three miles [it was about two miles to the junction of Bates and Soquel Creeks] to a cottonwood tree which stands on the eastern bank of the river nearly opposite the house formerly occupied by one Highmore, thence running easterly, passing near the Bates sawmill to the northwest corner of the Aptos Rancho, thence southerly along the west side of Rancho Aptos and along Borregas Gulch to the mouth of the said gulch." The boundaries of the Augmentation were described as: "Commencing at the northwest corner of Rancho Soquel, thence running northwesterly including the la Yesca tract and along the eastern line of the San Augustine Rancho to the Laguna Sarjento, thence running easterly including the Loma Prieta, then to the Chuchitos, thence southerly to a bunch of redwood trees known as the quatro leguas, thence westerly along the north line of Rancho Aptos to the northeast corner of Rancho Soquel."[307]

Letter from Frederick Hihn to John Wilson

On June 3, 1859, Frederick Hihn wrote a brief letter to John Wilson:

Dear Sir: Messrs. Reynolis and Clarke have authorized me somewhat conditionally to draw on them of $20.00 as part of the expenses to be insured in correcting the survey of the Augmentation of the Soquel Rancho. I have explained to them the circumstances and advised them that I had drawn on them in your favor for $20.00. You will please to have the enclosed order presented to them and I think they will pay it....

I am trying to collect the balance for you and though I have not yet surrendered they all promise fair and I think you will get your money when the two months are out. Please let us know what you are doing in the survey matter we would like to have it settled. The squatters are making serious inroads into the timber on the Rancho.

Yours Respectively, F. A. Hihn[308]

Plats establishing boundaries for Rancho Soquel and Shoquel Augmentation signed by United States Surveyor General

The two plats for Martina Castro's Mexican land grants were signed by the United States Surveyor General, James Mandeville, in San Francisco on June 4, 1859, although the survey had been completed six months earlier. The reason for the delay was due to attempts by John Wilson on behalf of the Catholic Church and many in Santa Cruz County to have the "Palo de la Yesca" boundary point remain at the northwest corner of Rancho Soquel, while Mandeville wanted it farther up Soquel Creek. Eventually, it was decided to set it opposite Spignet Gulch Creek along the East Branch of Soquel Creek.

When the plats were signed, two identical notes were added to each

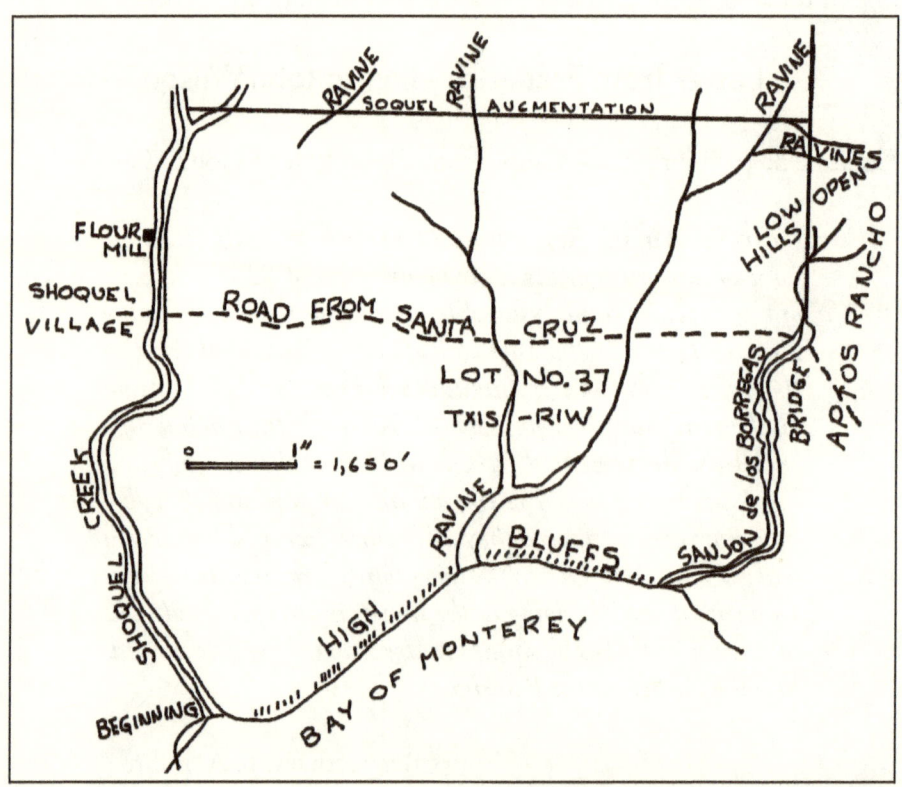

Figure 5.8 Plat of Rancho Soquel signed by the United States Survyeor General of California, June 4, 1859

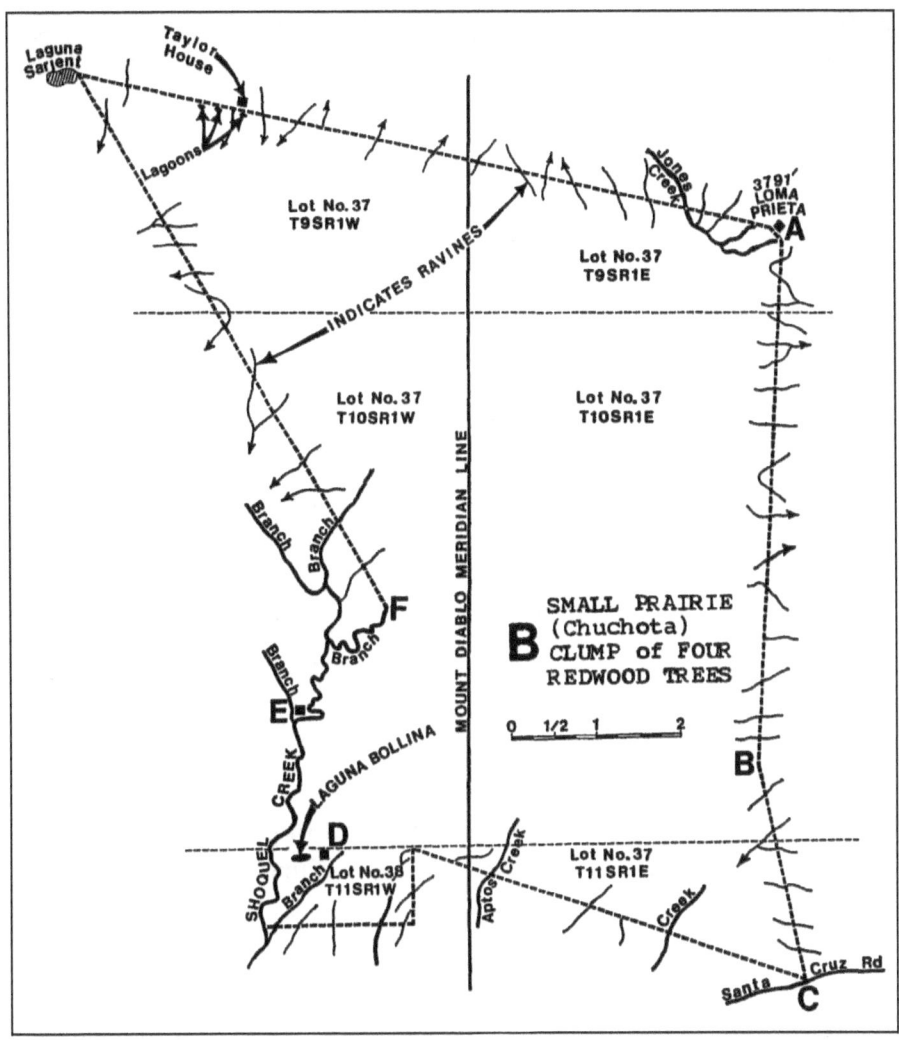

FIGURE 5.9 PLAT OF SHOQUEL AUGMENTATION AS SURVEYED BY JOHN WALLACE

stating: "the fieldnotes from which this plat has been made out have been examined and approved and are on file in this Office [of the United States Surveyor General in San Francisco]." The filing of the plats finally put to rest attempts by the Catholic Church, Castro's heirs, and other landowners to expand the size of Shoquel Augmentation by adding 7,000 acres to the northwest corner. Keeping the Palo de la Yesca survey point where Francisco Alviso had placed it was important for both Ingoldsby and Hihn because the entire route of the Soquel Turnpike was planned so that it remained within the confines of Rancho Soquel and Shoquel Augmentation all the way to the Summit.

In addition to losing the valuable acreage along the Augmentation's western edge, thousands of acres were also lost along the northern boundary, in the area that Alviso had marked "Loma Prieta." It was here that the original survey passed into Santa Clara County following along the north side of Los Gatos Creek to a point near the cinnabar deposits south of San José. Mandeville's survey opened this area to settlement and commercial use, but not to the Augmentation's claimants.

On a more positive note for the claimants, the survey increased acreage in the Valencia Creek watershed along the Augmentation's eastern border. This also resolved the long-standing dispute with Rafael Castro over the boundaries between Rancho Soquel, Rancho Aptos, and Shoquel Augmentation.

Father Llebaria given Removal of Facilities and Permanent Exeat decrees by Archbishop Alemany

At some point near the end of the Supreme Court case in June 1859, Archbishop Alemany issued a Removal of Facilities decree to Father Llebaria, effectively depriving him of his status of priest within the archdiocese of Northern California and forcing him into exile if he wished to preach. While there was no official reason given for this expulsion, it was likely the direct result of Llebaria's role in Martina Castro's incarceration at the Stockton Insane Asylum and his subsequent failure to win the appeal before the Supreme Court. While Alemany undoubtedly wished to defrock and excommunicate both Llebaria and Ingoldsby for bungling the Castro land purchase so completely, he was unable to do so without drawing the attention of his superiors in the Catholic Church, which would immediately draw undue attention to his own role in the failed scheme. Instead, as with Ingoldsby, a decree of Permanent Exeat was issued to Llebaria. Shortly after the trial ended, Llebaria left California and became a priest in México.

Alemany remained archbishop in San Francisco for another twenty-five years, retiring on December 28, 1884 and returning to Spain the next year. He died in Valencia on April 14, 1888.[309]

Land transfer from Branda Estate to Frederick Hihn

Because the estate of Adolphe Branda was delinquent in paying its taxes for the one thirtieth claim to Rancho Soquel and Shoquel Augmentation for 1858, the county's tax office ordered that the land be auctioned to the highest bidder. Frederick Hihn had the highest bid and took possession of the property on June 28, 1859.[310]

Frederick Hihn plans lawsuits to establish claims in Rancho Soquel and Shoquel Augmentation

With the two plats signed in June 1859, along with a favorable decision by the California Supreme Court, Hihn turned his attention from supporting the Catholic Church to advancing his own agenda in Soquel. More specifically, he turned his attention toward securing ownership claims to both properties at the expense of people who had acquired land from the Catholic Church and Castro's heirs.

In an 1867 deposition, Robert Peckham revealed that Rancho Soquel and Shoquel Augmentation in the lawsuit were considered to be a "franchise title." That meant that, if Father Ingoldsby and his beneficiaries had won the case, the entirety of the properties would go to them without Martina Castro's children and beneficiaries receiving anything. The same was true in the reverse. However, despite the law being on his side, Peckham had his doubts, stating: "I always thought the case of Ingoldsby vs. Ricardo Juan was law, but I had my doubts that the Supreme Court would think so!"

Regardless of the law, it is obvious from the many letters sent to John Wilson that several important people in Santa Cruz County accepted that the properties were owned by the Catholic Church after 1855. By the end of 1858, Joshua Parrish, Augustus Noble, Charles McKiernan, Henry Peck, and Hihn were some of the church's strongest supporters. But with the Supreme Court siding with Castro's heirs, Hihn decided that the time had arrived to conclusively settle the matter of land ownership in the two properties. Hihn calculated that he owned approximately twenty-seven percent of Rancho Soquel and twenty-two percent of Shoquel Augmentation. But these percentages depended upon a successful partitioning suit where the Catholic Church only received one ninth of each ranch.

Hihn decided to adopt two separate approaches regarding each land grant. For Rancho Soquel, he sought to establish ownership percentages and allocate plots relative to each portion claimed. But in the Augmentation, he wanted to sell the land at auction and divide the proceeds between the owners according to their percentages claimed. He later claimed that this option was ideal to address the rugged terrain of the Augmentation and to avoid further conflict with people living within the property or along its disputed borders. The fact that Hihn could benefit tremendously through an auction by buying the best sections of land was an additional benefit of this option.

Around July, Hihn approached Peckham and hired him as his attorney in two lawsuits that he hoped would force the partition of the two properties. Separate lawsuits were necessary since both the Land Claims Commission and the state courts had decided to treat the properties as separate. Peckham accepted the offer and set his fee at $1,500 for both suits. Hihn then asked Henry and Antonia Peck to serve as plaintiffs in the Rancho Soquel suit, while Hihn himself took the role of plaintiff in the Augmentation suit, with the two plaintiffs each taking responsibility for half of Peckham's fee. At the time, the Pecks were in debt to William M. Moore for $1,400, which they had borrowed on April 2, 1854, using their home as collateral. Unable to pay Peckham's fee, they took out a second mortgage, which was held by Peckham.[311]

San Francisco probate court grants Adolphe Branda's land to Frederick Macondray

On July 18, 1859, the San Francisco County Tax Collector's Office placed for auction the one thirtieth claims to Rancho Soquel and Shoquel Augmentation held by the late Adolphe Branda. The highest bidder with a bid of $1,500 was Frederick W. Macondray, a resident of San Francisco. At the time, the court and Macondray were unaware that Frederick Hihn had recently been granted the same property via a separate court-mandated auction in Santa Cruz County.[312]

Frederick Hihn and John Garber are hired to compare Santa Cruz County's recorded deeds against its index books

Around the beginning of August 1859, Santa Cruz County hired Frederick Hihn and John Garber to examine the books of deeds and indexes to ascertain whether the two agreed. According to later testimony by Israel Wilson, their examination was both thorough and complete. Hihn certainly benefited personally from the position, which granted him unrestricted access to many of the disputed deeds in question.[313]

Land transfer from Durrell Gregory to Benjamin Porter

On August 13, 1859, Benjamin Porter purchased what he believed was a 4/27 claim to Rancho Soquel and Shoquel Augmentation from Durrell Gregory. Gregory had received this land four years earlier from the Fourcades, Clements, Averons, Majors, and Pruett Sinclair in exchange for representing the families before the Land Claims Commission. Gregory did not realize at the time that their payment was only for land in Rancho Soquel and that he had grossly miscalculated the size of their payment.[314]

Land transfer from Miguel Lodge to Henry Cambustan

At some point in August 1859, Miguel Lodge finally reached the age of twenty-one, allowing him to enter political and public life, including the signing of deeds. The first deed to which he agreed was encouraged by Jean Fourcade and was in compensation to Henry Cambustan for "services rendered"— likely his testimony before the Land Claims Commission in 1854. It was the same one fourth claim to Rancho Soquel and Shoquel Augmentation that Martina Castro and Louis Depeaux had given Cambustan but that Lodge likely had to consent to upon reaching his majority.[315]

Land transfer from Frederick Hihn to Frederick Macondray

It seems that Frederick Hihn and Frederick Macondray reached an agreement concerning their conflicting ownership of the same parts of Rancho Soquel and Shoquel Augmentation. On August 26, 1859, Hihn sold 45.8 acres of land that sat on the border of both properties to Macondray for $1,500. The deed confirming this purchase and the property boundaries was signed on February 25, 1860.[316]

Land transfer from Miguel Lodge to Henry Peck

On August 29, 1859, Miguel Lodge sold the entirety of his claims to Rancho Soquel and Shoquel Augmentation to his brother-in-law Henry Peck for $500. This action drove a wedge between Martina Castro's children but provided Hihn with potentially easier access to the land since he was close friends with the Pecks. On June 18, 1895, Hihn recalled publicly and in Lodge's presence that:

> *Michael Lodge, the only son of the proud Martina Castro, is still living on the ranch, but instead of being the owner of thousands of acres, his present possessions are but a little more than one acre.*
>
> *Michael had the misfortune of being of rich parents and receiving little or no education. On the day he arrived at the age of twenty-one, he was tricked into signing a paper which swept away all his inheritance. The paper was voidable in law but required money and experience to make it void. He had neither. The result was he conveyed his interest, thus incumbered, to his brother-in-law for what he could get for it, which was but little. It would have been much better for him to have been poor and to have received a fair education. Since then, he has labored faithfully at common labor to make a living for himself and family.*

In her interviews, Carrie Lodge reported that Henry Peck, while on his deathbed in 1873, called for Miguel and asked for his forgiveness. Carrie did not disclose or know whether such forgiveness was given by her father.[317]

Land transfer from Antonia and Henry Peck to William and Wesley Burnett

On September 14, 1859, Antonia and Henry Peck sold a 1/54 claim to Shoquel Augmentation to Wesley and William Burnett for $750. The location of the land in question is not mentioned in the deed but it must have been opposite the Wesley Burnett & Company sawmill on Soquel Creek near the junction of today's Soquel San José and Laurel Glen Roads.[318]

Land transfer from John Hames and Pruett Sinclair to Frederick Hihn

Once again, on September 29, 1859, the court ordered Pruett Sinclair and John Hames to sell land that they owned in Shoquel Augmentation in order to repay a debt. At the time, the pair owned a 3/54 claim in Shoquel Augmentation as well as properties in downtown Santa Cruz and along Corralitos Creek in Eureka Canyon. They offered all of these properties at auction, which was won by Frederick Hihn, who bid $1,425. Sinclair and Hames used the money to pay off their outstanding $925. It is unclear if they actually owned a 3/54 claim to the Augmentation, but because the sheriff's office made a mistake when it approved the deed, the matter went to court.[319]

Letter from Craven Hester to John Wilson

On October 13, 1859, Craven Hester wrote to John Wilson regarding the future of the legal debates surrounding the Soquel land grants:

> *Since I saw you, Judge Hoffman has decided the Soquel Augmentation Ranch's boundary question; and from the decision, if objections are made to the survey, the District Court will entertain jurisdiction and establish the boundary.*
>
> *I desire to know what you have done in the Augmentation of the Martina Castro claim. Perhaps you should file the survey and make the necessary objections to the boundary if you*

think it should be contested, that the proper testimony may be heard and the boundary finally established so that a patent may be issued.

Let me know by return mail what you have done and what you intend doing in regard to it. The parties interested desire the matter closed as soon as possible.[320]

Land transfer from Wesley and William Burnett to Francis Brady and Benjamin Nichols

Wesley and William Burnett sold the sawmill they had built in 1858 on Soquel Creek as well as the surrounding land, totaling 500 to 600 acres, to Francis Brady and Benjamin Nichols for $4,000 on October 19, 1859. The included land sat on the west bank of the creek, directly opposite the tract of timberland in Shoquel Augmentation that the Burnetts had purchased a month earlier.[321]

Frederick Hihn pays part of Jean Fourcade's debt

On November 1, 1859, Frederick Hihn met a condition outlined in the deed he had made with Luisa and Jean Fourcade on April 29 by making the first of two payments to Fourcade's creditors.[322]

Land transfer from Roger Hinckley and John Shelby to Richard Savage

On November 14, 1859, an agreement was made by Richard Savage to purchase a 1/96 claim to Shoquel Augmentation for $1,800 from Roger Hinckley and John Shelby. The land ran north for about a half mile from the confluence of Hinckley Creek with Soquel Creek. The purchase included a water-powered sawmill, its millrace, a millpond, and several outbuildings including worker shanties. Savage agreed to pay what he owed in monthly installments of unspecified amounts. The deed was signed on December 10. After the land transfer, Hinckley and Shelby continued to own a contiguous 1/32 claim in Shoquel Augmentation.[323]

Land transfer from Antonia and Henry Peck to Joel Bates

Antonia and Henry Peck signed a deed on November 21, 1859 wherein they sold a 1/27 claim to Shoquel Augmentation to Joel Bates. This property covered an area that included parts of former School Land Warrant Nos. 108, 353, and 354, in which Bates had already been cutting timber for several years until the warrants were floated to Watsonville and elsewhere due to the decisions made in the Ingoldsby lawsuit.[324]

Land transfer from Wesley and William Burnett to Francis Brady and Benjamin Nichols

Following their purchase of the Burnett sawmill on Soquel Creek a month earlier, Francis Brady and Benjamin Nichols purchased the Burnett Brothers' 1/54 claim to Shoquel Augmentation for $750 on November 23, 1859. This land was located directly to the east of the mill, just south of the intersection of today's Laurel Glen and Soquel San Jose Roads.[325]

Land transfer from Benjamin Porter to James Taylor

After James Mandeville established the boundaries for Shoquel Augmentation, James Taylor discovered that part of his land was situated within its boundaries. He approached Benjamin Porter hoping to solve his dilemma. Porter agreed to sell him a 1/54 claim to the Augmentation for $500 on January 20, 1860.[326]

CHAPTER 6

~

Road to Partition

Complaint filed by Henry and Antonia Peck

On February 13, 1860, a formal complaint was filed with the Third District Court by Henry and Antonia Peck to twenty-eight individuals living at the time on Rancho Soquel. The complaint reads:

> *The plaintiffs Henry W. Peck and Maria Antonia Peck, his wife, residents of the County of Santa Cruz, complain of Frederick A. Hihn, Joseph Averon, Maria Guadalupe Averon, his wife, Jose David Littlejohn, Maria Helena Littlejohn, his wife, Ricardo Fourcade Juan, Maria Luisa Juan, his wife, Joshua Parrish, Miguel Antonio Lodge, Benjamin F. Porter, Francisco Young, Nicanor Young, his wife, Pruett Sinclair, Augustus Noble, George K. Porter, and George H. Kirby, all residents of the county of Santa Cruz, and Dr. John P. P. Vandenberg, J. S. Reed, Thomas Fallon, Carmel Fallon, his wife, all residents of the County of Santa Clara, and Charles H. Willson, William Ireland, Frederick. W. Macondray, Thomas Courtis (in his own right), and*

Thomas Courtis (as administrator of the Benjamin P. Green, William Otis Andrews, and John Ingoldsby), all residents of the County of San Francisco, all defendants, and show to the court that they, the said plaintiffs and said defendants, are seized of in free simple, and hold together and undivided a certain tract of land situated in the County of Santa Cruz, and State of California, known as the Rancho Soquel, bounded on the southwest by the Bay of Monterey, on the northwest by the Soquel River, on the southeast by the Borregas Gulch, and on the northwest by the Upper Soquel Ranch, containing about 2,800 acres, more or less, being the same as surveyed under instructions from the United States Surveyor General for California, as the land called Soquel, confirmed to Martina Castro, of which tract of land as described, it belongs as follows:

Plaintiffs:
  Henry Winegar Peck (360/3240)
  Maria Antonia Peck (360/3240)

Defendants:
  Frederick A. Hihn (708/3240)
  Maria Guadalupe Averon (360/3240)
  Maria Luisa Juan (240/3240)
  Maria Helena Littlejohn (240/3240)
  Dr. John P. P. Vandenberg (360/3240)
  Joshua Parrish (360/3240)
  Augustus Noble (120/3240)
  George K. Porter (39/3240)
  William Ireland (93/3240)

It is also stated that the following defendants claim to have some interest in common with the plaintiffs, the nature and extent of which is unknown to the plaintiffs; and whereof, they the said defendants, and each and every of them deny partition to be made, though often requested by plaintiffs, through said lands and tenements as so situated as to be susceptible to such partition among all the respective owners thereof, with-

out injury to any of them:

Miguel Antonio
Benjamin F. Porter
Francisco Young
Pruett Sinclair
Charles Plum
J. S. Reed
Charles H. Willson
George H. Kirby
Frederick W. Macondray
Thomas Fallon
Carmel Fallon
Thomas Courtis (in his own right)
Thomas Courtis (as administrator for Benjamin P. Green, William Otis Andrews, and John Ingoldsby)

Said plaintiffs, therefore, in order that they may justly apportion themselves in severalty of the respective portions of said lands and tenements belonging to them, and that each of said defendants may severally apportion themselves of their respective shares, pray this Honorable Court, that a summons may be issued to each and every of the said defendants, commanding them to appear and answer this bill or complaint, and that the rights of each and every of these parties, plaintiffs and defendants, may be ascertained and determined by the judgment and decree of this court, and that partition of said lands and tenements may there be made, under the direction of and by referees appointed by this court, among the parties, plaintiffs and defendants, according as they are respectively entitled, and that the share of the plaintiffs may be assigned and set off to them jointly, and that the costs may be apportioned among the parties, and for whatever other and further relief may be legal, equitable, and just.

> And they will ever pray, etc.
> signed by Robert F. Peckham,
> attorney for the plaintiffs

The court responded to the request promptly by registering it as Case No. 280, which became known as the Rancho Soquel Partitioning Suit. It

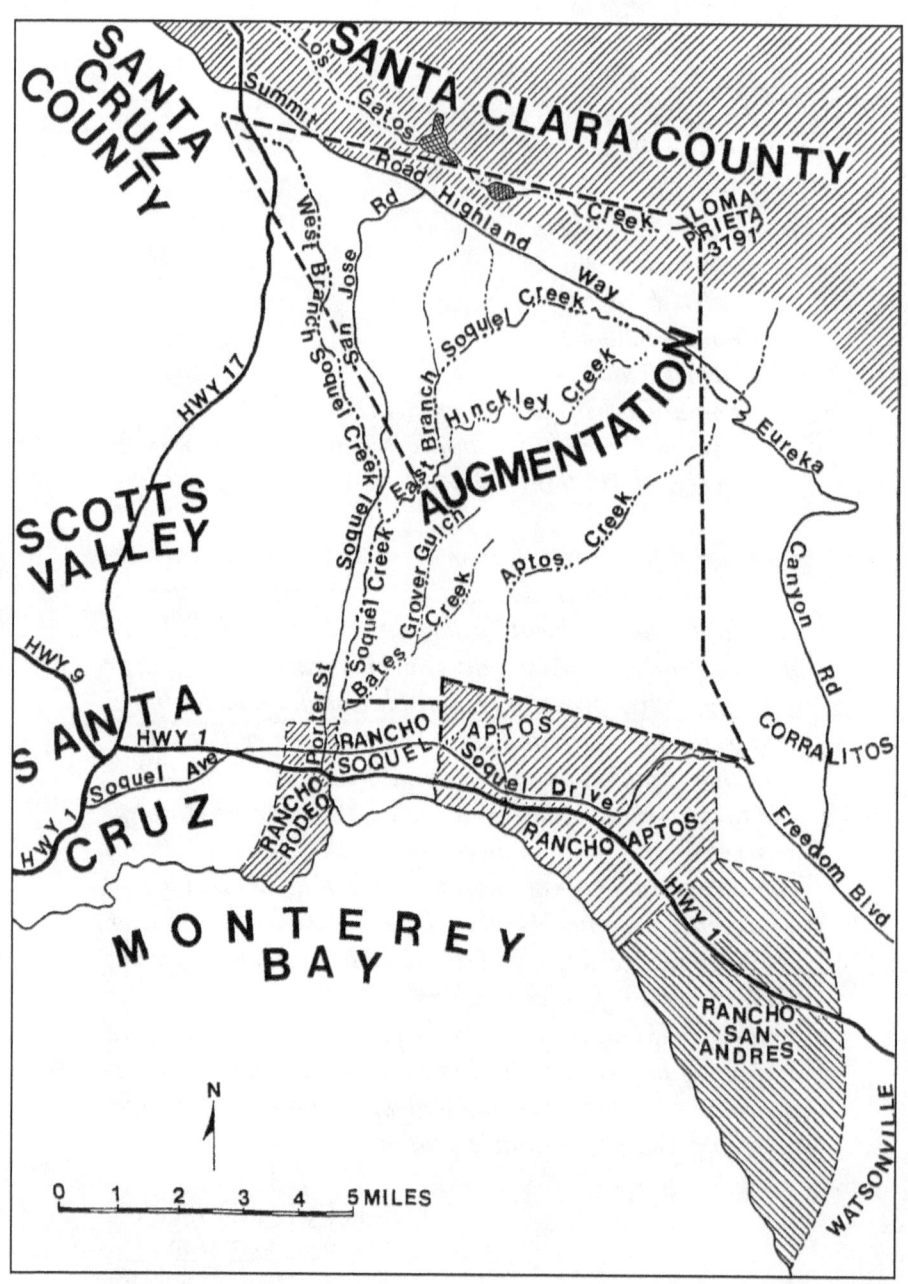

FIGURE 6.1 RANCHO SOQUEL AND SHOQUEL AUGMENTATION

issued a summons the same day to all of the parties listed as defendants by the Pecks. The summons reads:

> *You are hereby required to appear in an action brought against you by the above named plaintiffs in the District Court of the Third Judicial District of the State of California, in and for the County of Santa Cruz, and to answer the complaint filed herein, a copy which accompanies this summons, within ten days (exclusive of the day of service), after the service on you of this summons, if served in the county; or, if served out of this county, but within this Judicial District, within twenty days; or, if served out of said district, then within forty days, or judgment by default will be taken against you according to the prayer of said complaint....*
>
> *And you are hereby notified that if you fail to appear and answer the said complaint as the above required, the said plaintiffs will apply to the court for the relief demanded in the Complaint.*
>
> Given under my hand and the Seal of the Third Judicial District of the State of California, in and for the said County of Santa Cruz, this 13th day of February in the year of our Lord One Thousand Eight Hundred and sixty. signed by David J. Haslam, Clerk of the court

A review of the above two documents prompts two questions. The first concerns the acreage of Rancho Soquel: the plat signed by James Mandeville clearly states that its total acreage is 1,668.03 acres, while both the complaint and the summons state it is 2,800 acres. Why? The answer becomes clear once the objectives of Hihn are taken into account. When Hihn and Peckham prepared these documents, they included within Rancho Soquel the Palo de la Yesca immediately to the north of Rancho Soquel. Because this land was important to Hihn for his future plans in the area, and because he wanted the Augmentation sold at auction to the highest bidder, he was willing to have this section annexed to Rancho Soquel.

The second question concerns the denominator used in designating the fractions of Rancho Soquel that were owned by the various parties: 3,240. The reason this was used is that it was the lowest common denominator for George Porter's 7/270 claim and Augustus Noble's 1/12 claim to the property. When the two numbers are multiplied together, 3,240 is the result. This number was also conveniently divisible by nine, which was the smallest denominator claimed by a party in the partitioning suit.

One final note is that Father Ingoldsby was one of the defendants in this case, implying that his (or rather Archbishop Alemany's) ownership of the rancho was in doubt. Had the Catholic Church initiated the partitioning suit, the property claims would have been:

John Ingoldsby (540/3240)
Joseph Alemany (540/3240)
John Llebaria (540/3240)
John Wilson (405/3240)
Augustus Noble (270/3240)
Thomas Courtis (270/3240)
William Andrews (189/3240)
Cyrus Coe (135/3240)
William Ireland (81/3240)
Mary E. J. Slade (67.5/3240)
Henry Lawrence (40.5/3240)
Benjamin Green (27/3240)
Charles Plum (27/3240)
Adolphe Branda (108/3240), which was contested between Hihn and Macondray[327]

Land transfer by Frederick Hihn to Frederick Macondray

On February 26, 1860, the first deed was filed in the Rancho Soquel Partitioning Suit. Its purpose was to resolve a conflicting 1/30 claim to Rancho Soquel and Shoquel Augmentation purchased at auction by both Frederick Hihn and Frederick Macondray, who had bought the land on June 28 and July 18, 1859 respectively. Because Hihn's deed was earlier, it was agreed that he had acquired the land. However, to avoid further conflict, Hihn agreed to sell the 48.5-acre portion of land located in Rancho Soquel to Macondray on August 26, 1859. In February 1860, after being served his summons in the partitioning suit, Macondray realized that Hihn had neglected to transfer to him 9.8 acres that were also part of Adolphe Branda's original 1/30 claim. To correct the error, Hihn signed over the overlooked acreage, but created a new error when he accidentally stated that the land came from both Rancho Soquel and the Augmentation.[328]

Patents signed by President James Buchanan for Rancho Soquel and Shoquel Augmentation

On March 19, 1860, President James Buchanan passed title for Rancho Soquel and Shoquel Augmentation to Martina Castro Depeaux. This formally ended the debate over the external boundaries of the two land grants but did not resolve the issue of ownership or internal boundaries between private properties.[329]

Frederick Macondray and John Vandenberg answer complaint

In the Rancho Soquel Partitioning Suit, on April 2, 1860, Frederick Macondray claimed that he owned a 23/600 claim to Rancho Soquel, while on April 7, John Vandenberg claimed that he was the owner of a one ninth claim. Vandenberg stated that he was currently and had for the past six years occupied a portion of his rightful claim, making improvements including houses and fences, which were permanent and could not be removed except at great expense.[330]

Santa Cruz County probate court sets the value of Peter Tracy's Soquel properties

On April 5, 1860, the Santa Cruz County Probate Court fixed the amount of the executor's bond that was required to sell the School Land Warrants owned by the Peter Tracy Estate in Shoquel Augmentation. Before his death on August 7, 1857, Tracy had appointed Asa W. Rawson and Francis

M. Kittridge executors of his estate. The two attorneys had Tracy's will probated and then petitioned the court for letters of administration. As executors of the will, Rawson and Kittridge secured two bonds in the sum of $1,000 each on April 14. The two executors took oaths, as required by an act passed by the California government on March 8, 1860, and then they were authorized to sell Tracy's real estate by public or private sale.

The 968 acres of land were divided into four sections and sold at auction. Joel Bates successfully purchased the first quarter (amounting to 242 acres) on May 1 for $360. On May 5, the remaining three quarters were sold at auction. Francis Brady and Benjamin Nichols purchased one section for $350. Augustus Noble purchased another for $359. And Joel Bates and John Stearns bid $375 for the final section. What none of these purchasers realized—and indeed the judge himself may not have been aware of—was that all of these School Land Warrants had been floated elsewhere in the state on March 20, 1857. Regardless, all of the new owners took possession of their properties promptly and began to improve the land.[331]

Hiram Morrell arrives in Santa Clara County

Born in Waterville, Maine on April 25, 1835, Hiram Clifford Morrell arrived in California in 1854 with the hope of striking gold and becoming rich. He spent six years searching for the elusive metal before finally giving up. Most of this time was spent in the area of the North Fork of the American River in Placer County, although he also worked in various sawmills in Sugar Pine. Afterwards, he headed for the greener pastures of the Santa Clara Valley, arriving around 1860. Upon arrival, he joined a lumber crew in Aldercroft Canyon off Los Gatos Creek, working for Howe & Weldon. The next year, he joined McMurtry & McMillin, which operated a mill along the creek, and remained with the company for four years. During this time, he established his home in the Summit area of the Santa Cruz Mountains, where he met Lyman Burrell's youngest daughter, Clara. After two years of courtship, he married her on November 15, 1864. Burrell sold the couple sixty acres of land on the Summit and they immediately began to cultivate it.[332]

Land transfer from William Ireland to Augustus Noble

On June 4, 1860, William Ireland sold to Augustus Noble for $900 the land he had purchased within Rancho Soquel and Shoquel Augmentation two years earlier. In total, it included 41.7 acres in the former and 817.5 acres in the latter.[333]

The Santa Clara Turnpike Company changes management

As construction of the Soquel Turnpike neared completion, Frederick Hihn withdrew his support for the road. Hihn feared that the completion of the road would draw attention away from the areas where his investments were located. At the same time, Soquel was attempting to take the county seat away from Santa Cruz, which troubled Hihn who viewed Santa Cruz as the heart of his planned transportation network.

Without Hihn's financial help, the turnpike was now in need of additional financing and took in new backers. This allowed construction to continue. As a part of this change of focus, the corporate name was changed to the Santa Clara and Soquel Turnpike Company. The new entity reported on June 8, 1860 that work was progressing fast and the road would be ready for use in four weeks.

On schedule, the road was completed in mid-July. Competition with the Santa Cruz Turnpike began at once, while improvements were made and accommodations arose along the route. The first such hostelry, the Hotel de Redwoods, was situated about nine miles north of Soquel directly to the west of the turnpike and, more importantly, just beside the long meandering access road to Hester's Sulphur Springs. The springs were the first attraction made accessible by the turnpike and were located near the headwaters of Hester Creek, just to the north of today's Stetson Road eight miles north of Soquel. The attraction featured several sulfur-enriched springs and was named after the property's owner, Craven Hester. It is unclear whether Hester discovered the springs himself or they were already known, but regardless, access to them was geographically restricted until the turnpike reached such a point that an access road could be established.

For several years, it was the combination of both the springs and the hotel that attracted visitors to the area, with the springs providing the stronger enticement. But as the popularity of the redwoods increased, the general area became known for both features. Eventually, the name Hotel de Redwoods became synonymous with the springs.

The area's unique features attracted people from around the world, as this contemporary description shows:

> *On the confines of civilization on the lonely summit dividing the valleys of the coast from those of the eastward slope, where the stage stops to water the animals from a cool, clear, crystal spring, a specimen of the irrepressible Yankee has...well, he has either pitched a tent, or reared a habitation, nature has done more for him than she performs for most mortals; each monster tree of the group has been hollowed out by decay and fire, in one of them he resides, with ample room; in another, the largest, some thirty or forty feet in circumstance, he has opened a refreshment stand, dispensing fruit, milk, cakes, beer, and other liquids and edibles for the hungry and thirsty passengers. It is a lovely spot, and not one of us but wishes we could camp there for the season.*
>
> *We received a hearty welcome from the proprietor, and were soon under the cooling shade of the hotel, which is composed of a half a dozen large redwood trees. The largest one is devoted to the bar. It is about 350 feet high and 45 feet in circumference. Here the travelers congregate, while the stage stops to water the horses and drink their soda water. Ed Bowker, the proprietor, is a lively Yankee, and when he hears the stage approaching, he rushes out and advertises his establishment in the auctioneer's style. The springs come bubbling out from the foot of the mountain. The water is cool and refreshing, with just sulphur enough to make the taste pleasant. All the rooms of the hotel are hollowed out from the trunks of the trees, and make very good sleeping apartments.*

As the popularity of the hotel grew, attracting an ever-increasing number of guests, a village developed around it. Land within easy reach was sold and homes constructed, a free-standing general store was built, and

Road to Partition 1860

then a post office was added to the store that operated between June 3, 1879 and October 16, 1882. With the increase in traffic, Bowker decided that the time had arrived to expand the available accommodations. A two-story building was erected that supplemented the tree rooms with ten additional guestrooms. Unfortunately, it burned to the ground in 1885. The new hotel built in its place had enough room for 110 guests but burned down in 1903. A third hotel was built shortly afterwards but was damaged extensively by the 1906 San Francisco Earthquake. Repairs revived the structure and additional cottages were installed around it. The general store was enlarged as well. As automobiles came into vogue in the 1930s, a service station was added and the hotel was renamed Redwood Lodge. However, another fire destroyed almost the entire community in 1953, leaving little evidence that a settlement ever existed there. Today, the only remnant is a solitary concrete gas pump island.

The Hotel de Redwood was not the only overnight accommodation in the area. Also attempting to compete for customers of the sulphur springs was the Bonny Blink (or Blink Bonny) Hotel. The

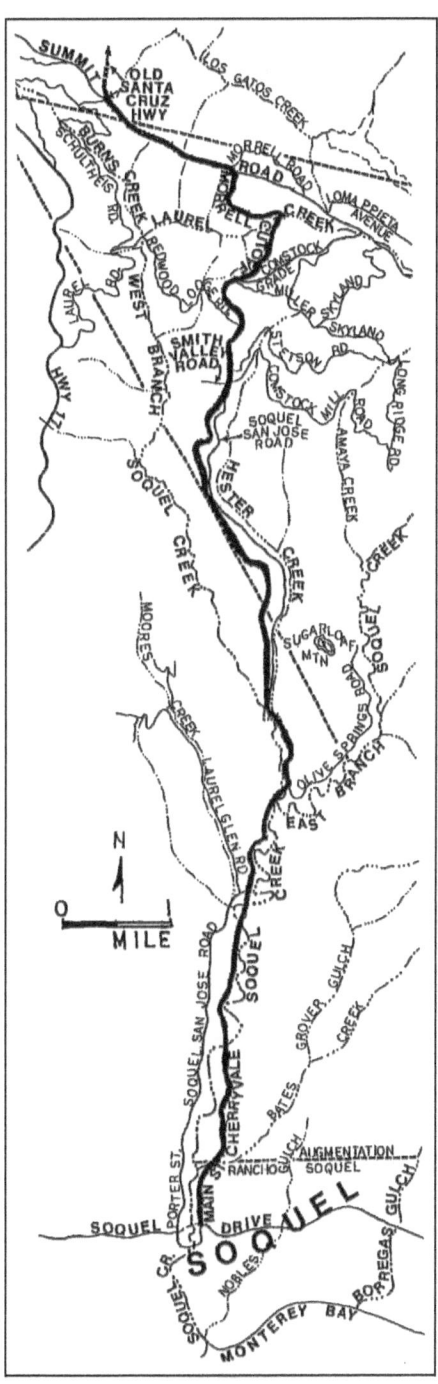

FIGURE 6.2 SOQUEL TURNPIKE

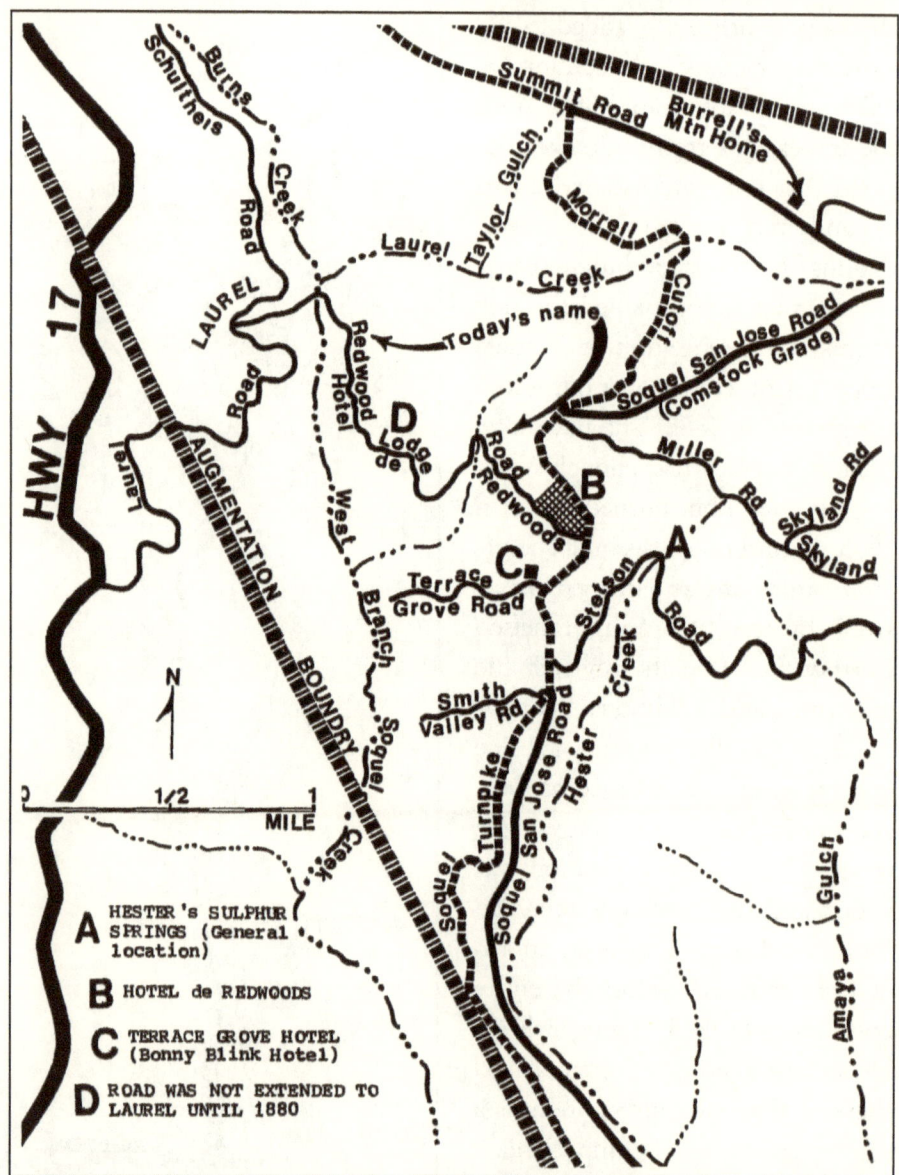

FIGURE 6.3 SOQUEL TURNPIKE NEAR THE SUMMIT

strange Scottish-influenced name derived from the broad panoramic view provided by the facility's windows that overlooked the Monterey Bay. The view was *bonny* (pretty) and made one *blink*. To quote from the *Santa Cruz Surf*, dated May 1, 1889: "At one point the turnpike road sweeps grandly around a grassy spur upon the hither on which Blink Bonny's pretty cottage is placed. Where the windows can look out and down on the undulating hills, the bits of clearing on their slopes, the pine-filled glens and intervals, and...far away...the dim ocean mingled with the grey sky beyond."

The hotel was located south of the Hotel de Redwood and just north of Stetson Road and served as a stage stop for travelers. As it became clear that the building's features were popular, the owner renamed it the Terrace Grove Hotel to give it a more elegant flair. The original structure was only two stories, with a large basement capable of housing horses and supplies. After the 1906 earthquake, the building was renovated, the basement was refurbished, and a third story was added.[334]

Land transfer by Nicanor Cota and Frederick Hihn

It seems that Frederick Hihn used the time he spent in the Santa Cruz County Recorder's Office in 1859 to his advantage. It is likely that during his review of property indexes and books of deeds he noticed that the Lajeunesses' two deeds were improperly acknowledged. The first deed signed by Nicanor Cota and her husband, Francisco Lajeunesse, was dated September 19, 1852, in which they sold around 1,000 acres in the Augmentation to Peter Tracy, Thomas Wright, and Montgomery Shackleford. The second deed was signed on January 21, 1854, in which they sold the entirety of Nicanor's claim in Rancho Soquel to John Vandenberg. During the Shoquel Augmentation Partitioning Suit, it was revealed that Henry Peck had alerted Hihn to this discrepancy, but Hihn's activities in the Recorder's Office likely brought this vulnerability to his attention earlier.

In early June 1860, Hihn sent letters to Joel Bates, Francis Brady, Benjamin Nichols, John Stearns, and George Kirby, demanding that they contribute to paying for legal counsel in the Shoquel Augmentation Partitioning Suit. The first four men had acquired an interest in the Augmentation when they purchased sections from the Peter Tracy Estate, while Kirby had purchased a separate stake in 1855. These men all occupied land, some 1,132 acres total, within the area of the Augmentation that Hihn had transferred to Rancho Soquel in order to increase its acreage to the surveyed total. At the time this was done, Hihn recognized their rights and acknowledged their claims.

Hihn also sent a separate letter to Cota in which he agreed to support her desire to divorce her husband by hiring a lawyer on her behalf and paying all the related expenses in order to secure her divorce. In exchange, she would sell to him her one-ninth claim to Rancho Soquel and Shoquel Augmentation, which due to the error above, Hihn calculated was still legally owned by Cota. Shortly afterwards, John Stearns was hired to act as her attorney. Stearns later testified that it was Henry Peck who had paid him his fee, and that he could not recall if Hihn manifested a lively interest in the divorce suit, having only mentioned it briefly on several occasions. Stearns also testified that Hihn paid Peck $20 or $25 in Cota's divorce suit. Also, when it came time to have the papers served on Cota's husband, the deputy sheriff refused to deliver them unless his fee was secured. Stearns told the deputy that Peck told him that he would pay the costs. Shortly after, Hihn stated "If Henry had agreed to pay the costs, I suppose he will, but if he doesn't, I will." When Deputy Sheriff Samuel Duncan later testified, he stated: "Frederick A. Hihn paid the fees. I don't know how he came to pay them, he volunteered to pay them."

The sale of Cota's property to Hihn was finalized on July 23 in the office of Notary Public James FitzJames Bennett. The price for the properties was set at $500. Lajeunesse was not present at the signing of the deed, although Bennett, Peck, and Lambert Clements were all witness to it. After putting her mark on the deed, Cota asked for assurances from Hihn that he would do what he had promised to in his letter. She also asked for some flour to feed her family. Hihn asked Bennett to give her what she requested.

The next day, Lajeunesse joined the others mentioned above in Bennett's office and signed and sealed the deed in exchange for a $50 gold coin paid by Hihn. Immediately afterwards, Hihn sold half of Cota's land in the Augmentation to Peck for $250. It is unclear why Hihn made this sale—was it in repayment for something unspecified or simply a friendly agreement? In any case, this added to his purchase of Miguel Lodge's one-ninth interest in the Augmentation gave Peck more land than Hihn: a full one-sixth of the grant land.

Hihn also made a separate acquisition that same day in Bennett's offices from Helena and Joseph Littlejohn. Helena had held back a 2/27 claim to the Augmentation when she had sold the remainder to Hihn in 1858. But legal troubles had caught up to the Littlejohns and they agreed to sell their remaining claim to Hihn, in exchange for which Hihn agreed to pay all legal fees in the two partitioning suits. A clause in the agreement, however, restricted Hihn from entering into possession of the land until after the successful conclusion of both suits. Thus, the Littlejohns retained full ownership of their claim to Rancho Soquel.[335]

Charles Willson answers complaint

On July 25, 1860, Charles Willson answered the complaint served to him in the Rancho Soquel Partitioning Suit, claiming that he owned 1/18 of the rancho due to a deed signed on May 26, 1858.[336]

Nicanor Cota and Francisco Lajeunesse divorce

On July 26, 1860, Francisco Lajeunesse was served a summons and complaint by Deputy Sheriff Samuel Duncan. It stated that, while living with Nicanor Cota, Lajeunesse had nine children, four of whom were adults and five minors, and that he was totally incapable of providing for their sustenance and education. It stated further that Lajeunesse treated Cota in a cruel and inhuman manner during fits of drunkenness by striking her with his hands and fist, beating her with a stick, and cruelly and inhumanely expelling her from his residence and refusing to permit her to return. Furthermore, he committed acts of cruelty and violence upon his children. It concludes by stating: "wherefore this plaintiff demands judgment of divorce from the defendant, and that said marriage and bonds of matrimony may be dissolved. This plaintiff further prays relief and demands judgment against the defendant that she may have the care, custody, and education of the children."

Lajeunesse answered the complaint by denying all of his wife's charges and, moreover, asserting that she committed adultery with one Venturo Ruida. He said that she did so at Ruida's house in January 1859, and then again on June 20, 1860 at her own residence in Santa Cruz. And she continued to do so to the present, for which reason Lajeunesse had not cohabitated with his wife for the previous month. Lajeunesse concluded his defense by asserting that Cota "is a woman of gross immoral character and conduct; that she is in all respects unfit to have the charge and custody of the children; that her conduct is of evil example to them, and calculated to bring disgrace and ruin upon them."

Cota answered her husband's charges by denying them outright. She added that on November 1, 1858, Lajeunesse used violence in an attempt to compel her to sell her body as a prostitute in order to earn him money. This is why Lajeunesse had expelled her from the house. Cota ended by revealing that Lajeunesse had threatened to kill her as soon as such an opportunity arose that would not implicate him.

Unable to determine the truth, District Judge Samuel McKee assigned a referee to interview witnesses for the plaintiff and defendant, asking him to report his findings on September 28.[337]

Benjamin Porter, George Porter, and Joshua Parrish answer complaint

On July 27, 1860, Benjamin and George Porter answered the complaint in the Rancho Soquel Partitioning Suit. Benjamin claimed that he was the owner of five acres, on which was a tannery, including vats and buildings for the manufacture of leather. George claimed ownership of a 7/270 part of the rancho through a winning bid made on April 21, 1859. Both men claimed that they had made valuable improvements to the part occupied by the tannery.

Meanwhile, Joshua Parrish also answered the complaint by claiming that he owned one ninth of the rancho by purchase from Carmel and Thomas Fallon on August 1, 1853. Furthermore, he had made valuable improvements by adding an orchard, houses, barns, and fences, all of which were permanent and could not be removed except at great expense.[338]

Antonia and Henry Peck respond to Charles Willson's claim

On July 31, 1860, Henry and Antonia Peck responded to Charles Willson's claim in the Rancho Soquel Partitioning Suit that he owned 1/18 of Rancho

Soquel. In contrast, they asserted that Willson held no claim to the ranch nor to Shoquel Augmentation.[339]

Frederick Hihn answers complaint

In the Rancho Soquel Partitioning Suit, Frederick Hihn backed the claims of the Pecks on August 4, 1860, stating that Charles Willson held no claim to Rancho Soquel and adding that John Vandenberg also had no share in the property. However, Hihn asserted that he was in personal possession of 8/27 of the rancho and had the proof that would verify this claim.[340]

Antonia and Henry Peck respond to the Porters' claim

On August 4, 1860, in the Rancho Soquel Partitioning Suit, Antonia and Henry Peck denied the claims made by the Porters, stating that they had no right to any land in Rancho Soquel, including to the land upon which stood the tannery.[341]

More summons issued in the Rancho Soquel suit

Robert Peckham issued fresh summons for the Rancho Soquel Partitioning Suit on August 10, 1860 to Mary Slade, Henry Lawrence, and Thomas Courtis, in his role as administrator for the estates of Benjamin Green, William Andrews, and John Ingoldsby.[342]

Charles Willson withdraws from the Rancho Soquel suit

On August 14, 1860, only ten days after the Pecks responded to his claims, Charles Willson filed a deposition via his attorneys, John Reynolds and David Clarke, that requested all matters hitherto presented by him and his attorneys to the court be withdrawn from the Rancho Soquel Partitioning Suit.[343]

Complaint filed by Frederick Hihn

On August 14, 1860, exactly four months after the Pecks issued their formal complaints regarding Rancho Soquel, Frederick Hihn filed his own complaint with the Third District Court, requesting summons be sent to the forty-three people who claimed land within Shoquel Augmentation. The complaint read:

> *The following defendants live in Santa Cruz County:*
> *Henry Winegar Peck*
> *Antonia Peck*
> *Jose Littlejohn*
> *Helena Littlejohn*
> *Ricardo Fourcade Juan*
> *Luisa Juan*
> *Joseph Averon*
> *Guadalupe Averon*
> *Frederick C. Hihn*[344]
> *Augustus Noble*
> *John Lafayette Shelby*
> *Roger Gibson Hinckley*
> *George K. Porter*
> *Cyrus Coe*
> *Richard Savage*
> *Christian Miller*
> *George H. Kirby*
> *Henry F. Parsons*
> *Francis R. Brady*
> *Benjamin C. Nichols*
> *Joel Bates*
> *John P. Stearns*
> *Francis M. Kittridge*
> *Asa W. Rawson*
> *H. B. Holmes*
> *Benjamin F. Porter*
> *Charles Plum*
>
> *The following defendants live in Monterey County:*
> *Henry Cambustan*
> *Joaquin Boledo*

The following defendants live in San Francisco County:
   John Wilson
   Frederick W. Macondray
   Joseph Sadoc Alemany
   Thomas Courtis (in his own right)
   Thomas Courtis (as administrator for John Ingoldsby,
      William Otis Andrew, and Benjamin P. Green)

The following defendants live in Santa Clara County:
   Craven P. Hester
   James Taylor
   Thomas Fallon
   Carmel Fallon
   Benjamin Farley
   Lyman John Burrell

The following defendant lives in Marin County:
   Charles H. Wilson

The above plaintiff, Frederick A. Hihn, complains of the above named defendants, and shows to the court that he, the plaintiff, and the said defendants, together with divers persons unknown to the plaintiff, are in possession of and hold together and undivided, the following described lands and tenements, situated in the State of California, County of Santa Cruz and County of Santa Clara, known as the Augmentation to the Soquel Ranch, bounded by a line commencing at the northwest corner of the Soquel Ranch, so called, and running up the Soquel River to a place known as Palo de la Yeska; thence to the Laguna Sarjenta; thence to, and including the Loma Prieta; thence to the Chuchitas; thence to the Cuatro Leguas; thence to the northwest corner of the Aptos Ranch; thence to the northeast corner of the Soquel Ranch and from thence to the place of beginning, containing thirty-two thousand seven hundred and two acres, more or less.

And the plaintiff further shows, that the said lands and tenements above described, it belongs to him to have thirteen fifty-fourth parts thereof in fee and in severalty; and that as to the remaining forty-one fifty fourth parts thereof, the plaintiff is unable to state or to inform the court who is the owner thereof, or entitled to have the same the owner, or owners thereof, being unknown to plaintiff.

Plaintiff further shows, that of the lands and tenements above described, the defendants above named, and each and every one of them, claim to have some title, claim, or interest in common with the plaintiff, but the nature extent, and validity of which claims, plaintiff has no knowledge, and cannot inform this Honorable Court.

Plaintiff further avers and shows to the court, that said land is so situated, that the same cannot be divided and the respective shares set off, and assigned to the respective owners thereof, without injury in a great degree to the several parties in interest.

Plaintiff further shows that said lands discovered with a large, extensive, and valuable growth of redwood timber, and that the chief value of said land is in its timber and the cutting and waste of said timber trees is destructive to the chief and principal value of said estate.

Plaintiff further shows, that the defendants, Francis R. Brady and partner Benjamin Cahoon Nichols, Richard Savage and Joel Bates, are now, and for a long time have been, engaging in cutting down, wasting, and destroying the timber trees growing on the land above described, and by doing so, are wasting and destroying the value of the said estate; and that said defendants above named, if unrestricted, will continue to cut said timber and destroy said premises, and by so doing commit great and irreparable injury to plaintiff and interest in said estate.

Wherefore plaintiff prays, that each and every one of the defendants may be summoned before the court to answer this Bill of Complaint, and show this court the respective interest which each of them have in the land and tenements above described; and that a summons may be addressed to, and served by publication, on the persons who have, or claim any interest

> *in said lands and tenements, and the ownership and responsibility in said lands and tenements, may be ascertained by this court; and that a sale of said lands and tenements be had under the direction of this court, and proceeds thereof divided among the several parties in interest they shall be found entitled by the judgment of this court; and in the meantime, that said defendants Francis R. Brady and his partner Benjamin Cahoon Nichols, Richard Savage and Joel Bates, may be enjoined from cutting and wasting the timber growing and standing on said premises; and for such further and other relief as may be according to law, equity, and good conscience.*

Robert F. Peckham,
attorney for the plaintiff Frederick A. Hihn

The court immediately approved of the complaint and registered it as Case No. 308, better known as the Shoquel Augmentation Partitioning Suit. It then duly issued the summons, as requested. The statement sent by the court to the forty-three claimants read:

> *You are hereby required to appear in the action brought against you by the above named plaintiff in the District Court of the third Judicial District of the State of California, in and for the County of Santa Cruz, and to answer the complaint filed herein (a copy of which accompanies this summons) within ten days (exclusive of the day of service). After the service on you of this summons, if served in the county, or if served out of this county but within this Judicial District, within twenty days; or if served out of said district, then within forty days; or judgment by default will be taken against you according to the prayer of said complaint:*
>
> *The said action is brought to procure a sale and a division of the proceeds among the respective owners thereof, of the following described lands and tenements, situated in the State of California, County of Santa Cruz and County of Santa Clara, and known there as the Augmentation of the Soquel Ranch…and in the meantime, to procure an injunc-*

tion against the defendants Francis R. Brady and partner Benjamin Cahoon Nichols, Richard Savage and Joel Bates, to prevent them from cutting timber and committing waste on said premises.

And you are hereby notified that if you fail to appear and answer the said complaint as above required, the said plaintiff will apply to the court for the relief demanded in the complaint.

Given under my hand and the seal of the Third Judicial District Court, of the State of California, in and for the said County of Santa Cruz, this 14th day of August, in the year of our Lord One Thousand, Eight Hundred and sixty.

David J. Haslam, Clerk[345]

Activities along Whitewash Alley

Loma Prieta Avenue along the Summit began as an extension of the Santa Cruz Gap Turnpike. As time passed and Lyman Burrell began selling land to persons that wanted to settle along the Summit, many chose to live along the Turnpike. As a result, it continued to be extended until it reached the turnoff to Loma Prieta around 1860. For a number of years after the Santa Cruz Turnpike was completed, Loma Prieta Avenue was known as Whitewash Alley. John Young reports that it earned this name "because of its double row of white-washed fences bordering it for miles."[346]

Augustus Noble answers the Complaint

On August 20, 1860, Augustus Noble answered the complaint regarding his claims in Rancho Soquel, stating that he owned 67/1080 of the rancho through deeds purchased from Father Ingoldsby and William Ireland in 1856 and 1860 respectively. Since acquiring the land, Noble had lived on his property and made permanent, substantial, and valuable improvements including a home, outhouses, and fences.[347]

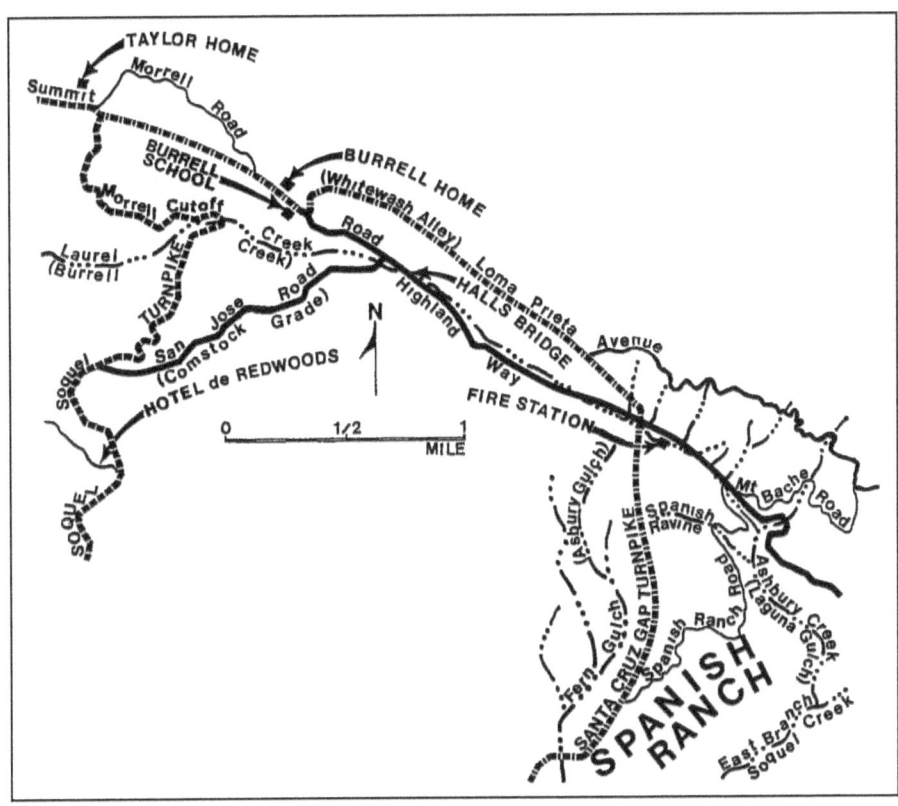

FIGURE 6.4 WHITEWASH ALLEY AND SUMMIT ROAD

Anti-logging agreement reached between Frederick Hihn, Benjamin Nichols, Francis Brady, and Richard Savage

Frederick Hihn approached Richard Savage, Francis Brady, and Benjamin Nichols on August 20, 1860 with an offer: he would not serve them with an anti-logging injunction to stop their logging activities within Shoquel Augmentation if they agreed to cease all cutting for the next eight months. All three men agreed to the terms.

The next day, Hihn went to Judge McKee and requested that an injunction be served to Joel Bates, stopping his logging activity within the Augmentation. Bates was probably approached at the same time as the previous three but refused to stop. Judge McKee approved and the injunction was served the next day.

With this serving and the previous agreement, Hihn achieved his goal of stopping all logging activities within the Augmentation until the sale or partitioning of the land was completed.[348]

Lien placed on Richard Savage's land by Roger Hinckley and John Shelby

On September 1, 1860, Roger Hinckley and John Shelby placed a lien on Richard Savage's land, claiming that the latter had not been keeping up with the agreed monthly payments that were in the original deed. And since Savage could no longer make a profit from his sawmill due to the agreement with Hihn, it was unlikely that he could make his payments or repay his debt until the mill reopened. The lien included everything Savage owned in Shoquel Augmentation, including his land, the sawmill, and all of its support facilities located along Soquel Creek.[349]

Judge McKee calls first session in the Shoquel Augmentation Partitioning Suit and and Joel Bates answers complaint

On September 6, 1860, District Judge Samuel McKee called to order the first session for the Shoquel Augmentation Partitioning Suit (Third District Court, Case No. 308). McKee was also the presiding judge in the Rancho Soquel partitioning suit and both trials would run concurrently in the same courtroom, often on the same day, and with Robert Peckham representing the plaintiffs in both suits. Similarly, since the majority of defendants were involved with both suits, their attorneys were also often in the courtroom or nearby.

The same day, Joel Bates responded to the complaint against him in the trial, claiming to own 1/27 of Shoquel Augmentation through a deed signed with Antonia and Henry Peck in 1859. This amount did not include the 484 acres of School Land Warrant land he had purchased in May 1860. In his defense, Bates stated that he had erected expensive and permanent improvements along the west side of Bates Creek consisting of a dwelling house, a steam-powered sawmill, a barn, fencing and other improvements,

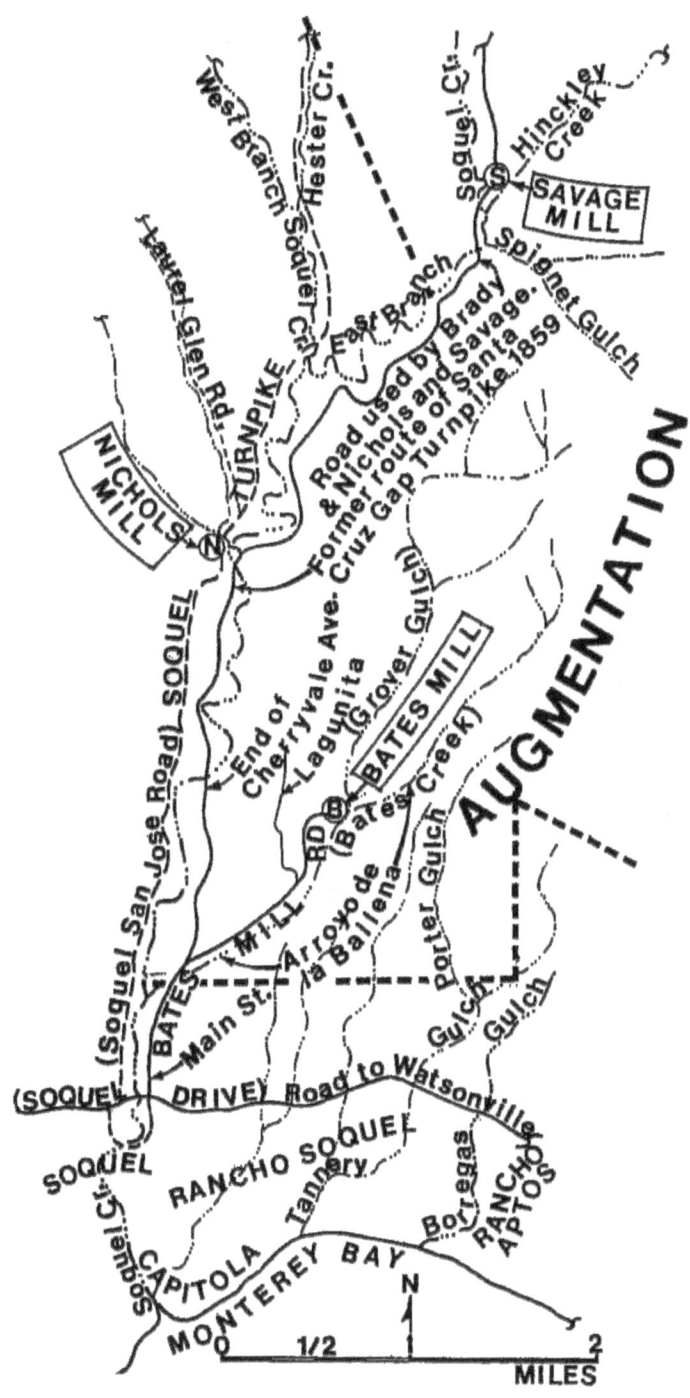

Figure 6.5 The locations of the Bates, Brady & Nichols, and Savage mills within Shoquel Augmentation

all of which could be set apart from the lands of the plaintiff and other defendants. He further rejected the assertion that the Augmentation must be divided among its proper owners and that its value was timber, arguing that he had caused no irreparable injury to the plaintiff and his co-tenants or devaluation of the land by felling the trees. In fact, he contended that by cutting the timber, he has actually increased the land's value by allowing roads to be built through the cleared land.[350]

Land transfer from Archbishop Alemany to Thomas Courtis

In a deed signed on September 7, 1860, Archbishop Alemany sold to Thomas Courtis his claim to land in both Rancho Soquel and Shoquel Augmentation for $250. The amount of land sold was not mentioned, but according to the deed dated September 10, 1855, Alemany owned a one sixth claim to both land grants. Courtis already administered Father Ingoldsby's one sixth claim and Benjamin Green's 1/120 claim, as well as a 1/27 claim that he owned himself. This meant that he owned up to forty-three percent of each grant—717 acres in Rancho Soquel and 14,062 acres in the Augmentation—in accordance with the Catholic Church claim.[351]

Joel Bates appeals Frederick Hihn's anti-logging injunction to California Supreme Court

On September 8, 1860, Joel Bates submitted his appeal to the California Supreme Court to overturn Frederick Hihn's injunction to stop his logging activities in Shoquel Augmentation during the duration of the partitioning suit.[352]

Francis Brady and Benjamin Nichols answer the complaint

On September 10, 1860, Francis Brady and Benjamin Nichols answered Frederick Hihn's complaint in the Shoquel Augmentation Partitioning Suit by claiming a total of 1/54 of Shoquel Augmentation. The partners claimed that they had constructed on their land a dwelling house, fencing, a millpond dam, and other improvements, all of which could be set apart from the land of others. Their land also included their sawmill, which had a few additional structures. Brady and Nichols did include their claims to 242 acres of the School Land Warrants they had purchased in May.[353]

Frederick Hihn answers the response by Joel Bates, Francis Brady, and Benjamin Nichols

On September 21, 1860, Frederick Hihn answered the response issued by Joel Bates, Francis Brady, and Benjamin Nichols in the Shoquel Augmentation Partitioning Suit. He stated that the School Land Warrants claimed were illegal and, therefore, they could only claim land purchased through their deeds of November 21 and November 23, 1859. He further disputed the claim that logging activity increased the value of the land and that the land owned by the three could be set off without injury to himself and to others.[354]

Lyman Burrell, Roger Hinckley, and John Shelby answer the complaint

On September 22, 1860, Lyman Burrell, Roger Hinckley, and John Shelby answered Frederick Hihn's complaint in the Shoquel Augmentation Partitioning Suit. Burrell stated that if Hihn claimed ownership of 13/54 part of Shoquel Augmentation, then there was plenty remaining from which his 1/27 claim could be taken. He also denied that the Augmentation was so situated that it could not be divided and his share established without injury to a great degree to the plaintiff and other defendants. Hinckley and Shelby made a similar answer, claiming that they owned 1/36 of the Augmentation upon which they had constructed at great expense improvements consisting of a water-powered sawmill, a millpond dam, a flume and mill race, a tunnel for a feeder line, a house, and additional support buildings, all of which were enclosed with fences. The two also contended that their land was so situated that a partition of the Augmentation could be made without prejudice to any of the other owners therein.[355]

George Kirby answers the complaint

On September 25, 1860 George Kirby answered Frederick Hihn's complaint in the Shoquel Augmentation Partitioning Suit, stating that since his deed of January 29, 1855 with Montgomery Shackleford, he had occupied land in the southwest corner of Shoquel Augmentation, upon which he had erected lasting and valuable improvements. Both Kirby and his attorney, John Stearns, himself a defendant, denied that the Augmentation could not be divided and the respective shares set off and assigned to the proper owners without injury to those with interest.[356]

Nicanor Cota and Francisco Lajeunesse divorce referee reports his findings

On September 28, 1860, the court-appointed referee, A. W. Blair, reported back to Judge McKee concerning his findings in the divorce suit filed by Nicanor Cota against her husband, Francisco Lajeunesse. Cota and several other witnesses, including her son Thomas Young, Henry Peck, Jean Fourcade, Ventura Ruida, and Miguel Lodge, all testified in her favor and Ruida denied all charges of adultery. Lajeunesse refused to testify. This weighted the results of the inquiry heavily on the side of Cota.[357]

Richard Savage answers the complaint and Frederick Hihn responds to answers by George Kirby and Lyman Burrell

On September 29, 1860, Richard Savage answered the complaint issued by Frederick Hihn in the Shoquel Augmentation Partitioning Suit. He stated that his land was situated such that it could be set off from other lands without injury either to the plaintiff or other defendants. By so responding, he also ignored the lien placed on his land by Roger Hinckley and John Shelby.

On the same day, Hihn responded to the answers submitted by George Kirby and Lyman Burrell, denying that they were entitled to the 1/27 parts of Shoquel Augmentation that they each claimed.[358]

Land transfer from Antonia and Henry Peck to Joel Bates and Lyman Burrell

On October 2, 1860, two deeds signed earlier by Henry and Antonia Peck were signed again. The first was originally signed on April 13, 1859 and granted Lyman Burrell a 1/27 part of Shoquel Augmentation. The second, signed on November 21, 1859, gave the same amount of land to Joel Bates. The likely reason that these deeds were reissued is that the claimed portions were originally derived from Antonia Peck's part of the land grant. However, with Henry Peck's acquisition of a massive percentage of the Augmentation from Frederick Hihn and Miguel Lodge, it made sense to transfer Burrell's and Bates' claims from Antonia's smaller percentage of the Augmentation to Henry's portion, from which several claims already derived.[359]

Amended complaints and summons served to defendants

On October 3, 1860, complaints and summons for both the Rancho Soquel and Shoquel Augmentation Partitioning Suits were reissued after being amended to include the previously overlooked defendants, Mary Slade and Henry Lawrence. Both became potential owners in the properties through Catholic Church deeds in which Benjamin Green was the grantor.[360]

Benjamin and George Porter answer second complaint

Benjamin and George Porter answered the second complaint from Frederick Hihn in the Rancho Soquel Partitioning Suit on October 11, 1860, with the same answer that they gave for the first complaint in July.[361]

James Taylor answers the complaint

James Taylor answered Frederick Hihn's complaint in the Shoquel Augmentation Partitioning Suit on October 15, 1860, claiming that there appeared to be plenty of land available for his 1/54 claim. He also joined the other defendants in arguing that his land in no way caused injury to the other parties.[362]

John Vandenberg answers second complaint

On October 17, 1860, John Vandenberg answered Frederick Hihn's second complaint in the Rancho Soquel Partitioning Suit nearly identically as his first answer given in April. However, there was one important difference: he had signed his deed with Nicanor and Francisco Lajeunesse on January 21, 1854, but Hihn had purchased the same one-ninth portion of Rancho Soquel from the Lajeunesses on July 24, 1860. In his new complaint, Hihn questioned the validity of the first deed, claiming it was not properly notarized, an accusation that Vandenberg refuted.[363]

Land transfer from Luisa Lodge to Casimero and Dario Amayo

In a deed signed on October 17, 1860, Luisa and Jean Fourcade sold a 1/27 claim to Shoquel Augmentation to Casimero and Dario Amayo. The purpose of this deed was to ensure that the brothers and their families retained possession of the land that they had occupied for over ten years.[364]

Thomas Courtis, Mary Slade, Henry Lawrence, and Charles Plum answer the complaint

On October 30, 1860, Thomas Courtis, Mary Slade, Henry Lawrence, and Charles Plum answered the complaint issued to them regarding the Shoquel Augmentation Partitioning Suit. All four, as well as the estates that Courtis administered, concluded that the plaintiff or any other defendants were seized in fees simple for any portion of their lands and therefore their lands did not qualify for partitioning.[365]

Frederick Hihn honors agreement made to the Fourcades

On November 1, 1860, Frederick Hihn paid the remaining $350 in debt that Luisa and Jean Fourcade owed to Philip Shephard, Samuel Holloday, and James Cary. This was part of an agreement made the previous year in exchange for purchasing 1/27 claims to Rancho Soquel and Shoquel Augmentation.[366]

John Wilson requests that the agreement between Archbishop Alemany, Father Llebaria, and Father Ingoldsby be recorded

On November 8, 1860, the agreement signed by Archbishop Alemany, Father Llebaria, and Father Ingoldsby on September 11, 1855 was entered into the public record by request of John Wilson. This was done in order to establish the conditions under which the three men intended to partition Rancho Soquel and Shoquel Augmentation. Although Ingoldsby had died the previous year in Chicago and Alemany had sold his claim, several others had purchased land from the three men and needed their claims to be declared legitimate in order to participate in the partitioning suits.[367]

Subpoenas served to resolve the property dispute between Frederick Hihn and Charles Willson

On November 24, 1860, Sheriff John Porter served subpoenas to witnesses in order to resolve the rival land claims of Frederick Hihn and Charles Willson over property purchased from Joseph Majors. Subpoenas were served by Deputy Sheriff Samuel Dunnan to Miguel Lodge, Lambert Clements, O. K. Stampley, James Murphy, I. C. Wilson, Majors, and Porter. They were ordered to appear in court on December 17.[368]

Thomas Courtis is accepted as the administrator of the Ingoldsby Estate

In December 1860, the probate court in Santa Cruz granted the final Letters of Administration to Thomas Courtis for the estate of the late Father Ingoldsby.[369]

Benjamin Farley, Craven Hester, and Charles Willson answer complaint

On December 14, 1860, Benjamin Farley answered the complaint issued to him by Frederick Hihn regarding his claims to Shoquel Augmentation.

His attorney, Craven Hester, also claimed ownership of 1/48 of the Augmentation and submitted his own response three days later.

That same day, December 17, Charles Willson answered the complaint as well concerning his 1/18 claim to the Augmentation. He asserted that his property could not be partitioned between all of the owners without disadvantaging all of them. This statement reflected an agreement with Hihn that resolved their ongoing property dispute. Willson accepted that Joseph Majors had only sold him a claim to Rancho Soquel in 1858. Since Willson had signed his deed first, Hihn withdrew his objections and allowed Willson to take possession. In exchange, Willson abandoned his claim in the Augmentation to Hihn.[370]

Land transfer by Jones Hoy to George Evans

On December 16, 1860, Jones Hoy sold half of his one ninth claim to Shoquel Augmentation to George W. Evans. Immediately afterwards, Frederick Hihn contested the sale, claiming that this property had already been sold by Hoy to Joseph Majors, who had in turn sold it to Hihn.[371]

Nicanor Cota and Francisco Lajeunesse finalize divorce

After twenty-two years of marriage to Francisco Lajeunesse, Nicanor Cota was given her final divorce papers on December 18, 1860. As discussed above, she moved to San Luis Obispo and changed her name to Nicanor Moss. Meanwhile, Lajeunesse, after relocating to Ventura, also adopted the surname Moss.[372]

Frederick Macondray answers the complaint

On December 19, 1860, Frederick Macondray answered Frederick Hihn's complaint in the Shoquel Augmentation Partitioning Suit by claiming through his deed dated July 18, 1859 that he owned a 1/30 claim to Shoquel Augmentation. Like most of the other defendants in the case, he argued that his land could be partitioned off without injury to the claims of other defendants.[373]

George Evans, and Benjamin and George Porter answer the complaint, while Frederick Hihn responds to answers

On January 2, 1861, George Evans answered the complaint issued by Frederick Hihn regarding Shoquel Augmentation, stating that he owned a 1/18 claim to the Augmentation.

Three days later, on January 5, Hihn responded to the answers given by George Evans, Frederick Macondray, and Charles Willson. He denied outright that Evans or Willson had any claim to land in the Augmentation, while he asserted that Macondray only had a 1/120 claim to the property rather than the 1/30 that Macondray asserted.

On January 9, Benjamin and George Porter answered the complaint by charging that Joel Bates, Francis Brady, Benjamin Nichols, and Richard Savage had caused waste and spoliation within the area by cutting valuable trees.[374]

Frederick Hihn and the Pecks answer second complaint

On January 15, 1861, Frederick Hihn answered the amended complaint in the Rancho Soquel Partitioning Suit by reasserting that he claimed 8/27 of Rancho Soquel. Next, Henry and Antonia Peck answered Joshua Parrish by rejecting his claim that he owned 1/9 of the rancho through his deed signed in August 1853. The Pecks also denied that Benjamin Porter was the owner of the five acres on which the tannery sat and that George Porter was the owner of the 7/270 of the property through his deed of April 1859.[375]

Several more defendants answer complaint

On January 18, 1861, Frederick Hihn responded to the claims of Benjamin and George Porter in the Shoquel Augmentation Partitioning Suit with the simple answer that neither had any claim, legal or otherwise, to land in Shoquel Augmentation.

Three days later, on January 21, Henry Peck answered the complaint by first explaining that George Kirby, Henry Parsons, Augustus Noble, Francis Kittridge, Asa Rawson, John Stearns, and Henry Cambustan did not have the right or title to land in the Augmentation via their floated

School Land Warrants. Peck added that Joel Bates, Francis Brady, and Benjamin Nichols also could not claim land from the warrants, meaning that their remaining lands were significantly smaller than what they claimed. Peck concluded by outlining the land that he owned via his wife and that he had purchased from Miguel Lodge and Hihn. However, he conceded that he had sold 1/27 to Lyman Burrell, 1/27 to Joel Bates, and 1/54 to Wesley Burnett & Company, meaning that the Pecks' total claim to the Augmentation was 5/27 of the land grant, making them the second largest claimants after Hihn. The next day, Antonia Peck answered the complaint in the same manner as her husband.

On January 23, several more answers to the complaint were given. Carmel Fallon's response closely mimicked that of Antonia's. Luisa Fourcade, meanwhile, stated that Christian Miller, Joaquin Boledo, and James Taylor had no claim to the land that they occupied in the Augmentation and that she was entitled to 2/27 of the grant land, despite having sold 1/27 to Hihn in April 1859 and another 1/27 to the Amayo brothers in October 1860. On the latter sale, Fourcade claimed that the sale was made by her husband without her consent. She concluded by asserting that her husband had no claim to the Augmentation, thereby hinting at their marital problems. Jean Fourcade ignored his wife's answer and personally claimed 2/27 of the Augmentation, although he did agree that Miller, Boledo, and Taylor had no claim to the property.

Thomas Courtis and John Wilson, meanwhile, acting on behalf of themselves and several other individuals and estates including Mary Slade, Charles Plum, Henry Lawrence, Father Llebaria, and the estates of Benjamin Green and Father Ingoldsby, asserted strongly that Hihn had no right to any grant land since Martina Castro and Louis Depeaux had sold the entire Shoquel Augmentation to representatives of the Catholic Church.

At the time of this suit, the portions of the property claimed within Shoquel Augmentation via transactions with the Catholic Church or subsequent sales were:

Ingoldsby Estate: 1/6 (16.7%)
Green Estate: 1/120 (0.8%)
Thomas Courtis: 1/4 (25.0%)

Father Llebaria: 1/6 (16.7%)
John Wilson: 1/8 (12.5%)
Cyrus Coe: 1/24 (4.2%)
Mary Slade: 1/48 (2.1%)
Charles Plum: 1/120 (0.8%)
Henry Lawrence: 1/80 (1.3%)
Roger Hinckley and John Shelby: 1/32 (3.1%)
Richard Savage: 1/96 (1.0%)
Craven Hester: 1/48 (2.1%)
Benjamin Farley: 1/48 (2.1%)
George Porter: 7/270 (2.6%)
Frederick Macondray: 1/30 (3.3%) (contested with Hihn)[376]

Thomas Courtis, John Wilson, Mary Slade, Charles Plum, and Henry Lawrence answer the complaint

On January 28, 1861, Thomas Courtis, John Wilson, Mary Slade, Charles Plum, and Henry Lawrence answered Frederick Hihn's complaint in the Rancho Soquel suit. As with their answer to the Shoquel Augmentation suit, the group asserted that they had acquired the land from the Catholic Church, which had purchased it from Martina Castro and Louis Depeaux. Therefore, Hihn had no right to any of the land in the rancho.

At the time of this suit, the portions of the property claimed within Rancho Soquel via transactions with the Catholic Church and subsequent sales were:

Ingoldsby Estate: 1/6 (16.7%)
Green Estate: 1/120 (0.8%)
Thomas Courtis: 1/4 (25.0%)
Father Llebaria: 1/6 (16.7%)
John Wilson: 1/8 (12.5%)
Cyrus Coe: 1/24 (4.2%)
Mary Slade: 1/48 (2.1%)
Charles Plum: 1/120 (0.8%)
Henry Lawrence: 1/80 (1.3%)

John Porter: 7/270 (2.6%)
Benjamin Porter: 1/648 (0.2%)
Frederick Macondray: 1/30 (3.3%) (contested with Hihn)[377]

Richard Savage's debts satisfied through court-ordered sale of land to Benjamin Cahoon

Earlier, a summons had been served to Richard Savage that ordered him to appear in court because of a past due debt of $810.61 owed to Benjamin Nichols. Because there was already a lien placed on Savage from past due payments owed to Roger Hinckley and John Shelby, the court combined the two debts and ordered that a public auction be held for Savage's 1/96 claim to Shoquel Augmentation and his water-powered sawmill in Hinckley Gulch. On February 4, 1861, Benjamin Cahoon, the uncle of Nichols, made the winning bid of $1,100.

Cahoon was born in Fairfields, New York in 1798, the son of an American patriot who had fought in the Revolutionary War alongside his brothers. When he arrived in California during the Gold Rush, he was already wealthy from working and investing in sawmills in New England and running a successful mercantile store and distillery.

On the journey west, Cahoon became the leader of a group of forty-niners who hired a ship to travel around Cape Horn. They arrived in San Francisco sometime in late 1850 or early 1851. In the company of several members of his party, Cahoon headed for Sacramento where his talent for business came to the forefront. He made several shrewd business transactions, but soon tired of the hectic life, being so close to the gold fields. He began to look around for a more quiet place to spend the rest of his years. He finally settled on the peaceful surroundings he found in Santa Cruz County in the early 1860s, where soon after he purchased Savage's land.[378]

Antonia and Henry Peck respond to the statements made by Thomas Courtis and John Wilson

On February 4, 1861, Henry and Antonia Peck replied to the statement Thomas Courtis made on October 30, 1860 and the combined statements

Courtis and John Wilson made on January 28 regarding the Rancho Soquel Partitioning Suit, arguing that they were all untrue since Martina Castro could only claim 1/9 of Rancho Soquel when she signed her land over to the Catholic Church in 1855. Therefore, Courtis held no claim to the rancho while Father Llebaria and the Ingoldsby Estate each could claim no more than 1/18 of the rancho.[379]

Helena Littlejohn and Guadalupe Averon answer complaint

On February 7, 1861, Helena Littlejohn and Guadalupe Averon answered Frederick Hihn's complaint in the Shoquel Augmentation Partitioning Suit by jointly stating that Hihn, Benjamin Porter, Christian Miller, Joaquin Boledo, Archbishop Alemany, and James Taylor, held no claim within Shoquel Augmentation. Littlejohn's list also included John Wilson and Cyrus Coe, while Averon's had Augustus Noble and Charles Willson. The former claimed a 2/27 part of the Augmentation and the latter 1/9, and both asserted their right to a portion of any profits made from the sale of Augmentation land.[380]

Sale of Peter Tracy's School Land Warrants to John Stearns confirmed and Stearns answers complaint

It will be remembered that on May 5, 1860, John Stearns and Joel Bates successfully bid on 242 acres of former School Land Warrant land sold by the Peter Tracy Estate from within Shoquel Augmentation. Despite the land having been floated, Stearns successfully confirmed his purchase and ownership of the land and had it entered into the county record books on February 14, 1861.

Having confirmed his purchase, Stearns finally answered the complaint issued to him on February 21 regarding the Shoquel Augmentation Partitioning Suit, agreeing with Frederick Hihn that the Augmentation could not be divided. Furthermore, he announced his claim as 1/27 of the grant land, an amount that could only be achieved by also claiming the entirety of the land that Joel Bates had purchased from both School Land Warrants and Antonia Peck.

In any case, Stearns and Bates sold their 242 acres as well as the steam-powered sawmill located upon it to Christian Miller and his associates for $500 on February 2.[381]

Land transfer from Father Llebaria to Thomas Courtis

On February 28, 1861, Father Llebaria signed a deed in which he sold his 1/6 claim that he still held to both Rancho Soquel and Shoquel Augmentation to the administrator of his estate, Thomas Courtis, for $250 in gold coin. Llebaria was in México at the time and the deed was presented to him by a local consul of the United States. This gave Courtis a substantial claim to the properties, especially since he also administered the estates of Father Ingoldsby and Benjamin Green.[382]

Thomas Fallon answers complaint

On April 9, 1861, Thomas Fallon answered Frederick Hihn's complaint in the Shoquel Augmentation Partitioning Suit by stating that Henry Parsons, Augustus Noble, John Stearns, Francis Kittridge and Asa Rawson, through their association with Peter Tracy's School Land Warrants, had no right to land in Shoquel Augmentation, while Francis Brady, Benjamin Nichols, and Joel Bates were entitled to the 242 acres claimed in warrants. This acreage was in addition to the two deeds they entered into with Henry and Antonia Peck. Fallon concluded by stating that he was entitled to 1/9 of the remaining land in the Augmentation after 1,120 acres of School Land Warrant parcels were removed from the Augmentation's total area and conveyed to Rancho Soquel.[383]

Frederick Hihn denies statement made by John Stearns

On April 11, 1861, Frederick Hihn stated that John Stearns was not entitled to a 1/27 claim to Shoquel Augmentation as he had argued in February.[384]

Augustus Noble answers complaint

On April 13, 1861, Augustus Noble answered the complaint regarding Shoquel Augmentation by stating that Frederick Hihn did not have a claim to 13/54 of the Augmentation and, therefore, it could be partitioned between the rightful claimants without injury in a great degree to the interested parties.[385]

Charles Younger is made referee to determine ownership claims in Rancho Soquel and Shoquel Augmentation

On April 15, 1861, Judge Samuel McKee issued the following decision regarding both the Rancho Soquel and Shoquel Augmentation partitioning suits:

> *It appearing to the court from the pleadings in both the Rancho Soquel and Augmentation cases that the rights of the respective parties thereto are in issue, and that it is a proper case for a reference, it is ordered that it be referred to Charles Bruce Younger with assistance from Samuel Drennan and David J. Haslam to hear the proofs and interests of the respective parties to try the same, and all the issues therein and report his findings thereon together with the evidence taken therein, to this court, on or before the first day of the next term thereof.*

Both sides in the cases had submitted a motion to appoint a referee to assist the judge in making decisions concerning the rival ownership claims. However, it was due to the influence of Frederick Hihn that Younger was chosen. Younger lived in San José at the time but maintained an office in Santa Cruz. Younger, Drennan, and Haslam were only to determine the percentage claims of each claimant—it was left to McKee to assign the actual land to the claimants.[386]

Charles Willson withdraws answers to both complaints

On April 17, 1861, Charles Willson withdrew his answer to the complaints in both partitioning suits. He authorized the clerk to enter a default for want of answer, but with no costs or damages attached. The request was signed by his attorney, Daniel Black.[387]

Charles Younger serves notice requesting proof of ownership in Rancho Soquel and Shoquel Augmentation

On April 22, 1861, Charles Younger issued the following notice regarding the Rancho Soquel and Shoquel Augmentation partitioning suits:

> *Take notice that Thursday the 2nd day of May, 1861 at 10 O'clock A.M. has been and is hereby set as the time, and the Court House in the town of Santa Cruz, as the place for the hearing and trial of the above entitled cause, before the undersigned referee herein appointed by the Third District Court.*
>
> *Charles B. Younger*[388]

Frederick Hihn denies Augustus Noble's answer

On April 23, 1861, Frederick Hihn responded to the answer in the Shoquel Augmentation Partitioning Suit given by Augustus Noble ten days earlier, stating that when Martina Castro signed the deed on January 22, 1855 to Archbishop Alemany and Father Llebaria, she was in possession of no more than 1/9 of Shoquel Augmentation. Therefore, Noble was not entitled to any part since all of the land he claimed was outside Castro's portion.[389]

Land transfer from Charles Willson to Frederick Hihn

On April 25, 1861, Frederick Hihn purchased a 1/18 claim to both Rancho Soquel and Shoquel Augmentation from Charles Willson. This specific claim had been disputed between the two men for several years, with Hihn claiming he had purchased it from Joseph Majors. By this sale, the battle over the claim was ended and Hihn came into full undisputed possession of it.[390]

Frederick Macondray hires a new attorney to represent him against Frederick Hihn concerning the Branda Estate

On April 30, 1861, Frederick Macondray fired his attorneys and then hired Selden S. Wright to represent him. Macondray made this change because he felt that Wright would be better able to represent him before the probate court in San Francisco regarding Adolphe Branda's lands in Rancho Soquel and Shoquel Augmentation, which Macondray had purchased from the Catholic Church. The conflict between Macondray and Frederick Hihn was over who had a better claim, since they had both purchased the land through court auctions held in two different cities two weeks apart.[391]

Frederick "C." Hihn answers complaint

On April 30, 1861, Frederick Hihn, via his obligatory alias of Frederick C. Hihn, answered his own complaint in the Shoquel Augmentation Partitioning Suit by stating that he had no right, title, claim, or entrust to any portion of the land in Shoquel Augmentation.[392]

Thomas Courtis requests the property he purchased from Father Llebaria be added to his claim

On May 2, 1861, Thomas Courtis requested that the 1/6 claim to Rancho Soquel and Shoquel Augmentation that he had purchased from Father Llebaria in México be added to his claim of ownership in the Rancho Soquel and Shoquel Augmentation partitioning suits. Robert Peckham accepted the claims on behalf of the plaintiff.[393]

John Wilson asserts his claim to half of Rancho Soquel and Shoquel Augmentation

On May 20, 1861, John Wilson requested that the sale made by Martina Castro to Archbishop Alemany on May 21, 1855 be added to the earlier agreement made between Castro and her attorneys, Wilson and Durrell Gregory, on October 28, 1852. This was to make clear that the two attorneys had a right to half of all her land once all the litigation over its fate was decided, a situation that remained unresolved in 1855 and, indeed, at the time of Wilson's request in 1861. In effect, this claim added a fourth unique aspect to the partitioning suits since Wilson's claim sat separate from the Catholic Church claims, the claims of Castro's children, and the floated School Land Warrants.[394]

Henry Parsons answers complaint

On May 23, 1861, Henry Parsons answered the complaint regarding Shoquel Augmentation by stating that Frederick Hihn could claim no more than 1/27 of the Augmentation, and he denied that it could not be divided among the legal owners without injury to a great degree to the interested parties and that its chief value was in timber.[395]

Land transfer from Luisa Lodge to Casimero and Dario Amayo

The deed signed on June 12, 1861 by Luisa and Jean Fourcade was identical to the deed they had signed on October 17, 1860, in which 1/27 of Luisa's claim to Shoquel Augmentation was sold to Casimero and Dario Amayo.[396]

Casimero and Dario Amayo answer complaint

On June 13, 1861, Casimero and Dario Amayo answered the complaint regarding Shoquel Augmentation by agreeing that Frederick Hihn owned a 13/54 claim and that the area could not be divided and fairly partitioned among the respective owners. Since they had purchased their property the previous October, the Amayos had erected permanent structures including a house, corrals, fences, and other improvements situated about a half mile to the west of the portion of land occupied by Lyman Burrell.[397]

Frederick Hihn responds to answer given by Thomas Courtis

On July 4, 1861, Frederick Hihn responded to Thomas Courtis's answer to the complaint regarding Shoquel Augmentation by stating that, based on the facts that Martina Castro only owned 1/9 of the Augmentation when she and her husband signed the deed on January 22, 1855 with Archbishop Alemany and Father Llebaria, and that she had earlier passed title to the other 8/9 of the Augmentation to her children in the deed dated August 29, 1850, all of Thomas Courtis's claims were unfounded.[398]

Charles Younger releases his report regarding ownership claims in Rancho Soquel

On August 17, 1861, Charles Younger, in his role as referee for the Third District Court in the matter of the partitioning of Rancho Soquel between its various claimants, submitted his report to Judge McKee. Due to a later decision by the County of Santa Cruz to film and destroy most of the original records, however, the actual findings have been lost. In every place where the court ordered that the referee's findings be read into the record, there is only a simple statement on the surviving document: "insert referee findings here." In order to arrive at the findings below, extensive research and evaluation of many ambiguous statements was necessary. The following is a reconstruction of the report, based on a blank template and information found elsewhere:

> *Charles B. Younger, appointed Referee by this Court, states to the Court that he has now herein completed his findings of facts, herein, together with the under taken, and is ready to file the same on the payment of his fee for his services as Referee herein, and in appearing to the Court that the parties herein have by agreement and stipulation in writing passed to the hands of Charles B. Younger for his services as Referee herein $500.*

FINDINGS OF REFEREE

<u>JOSHUA PARRISH</u> *is the owner in fee, and entitled to partition in severalty of the 1/9th part of the ranch.*

<u>MARIA GUADALUPE AVERON</u> *is the owner in fee (as of her separate estate), and entitled to partition in severalty of the 1/9th part of the ranch.*

MARIA ANTONIA PECK *is the owner in fee simple (as of her separate estate), and entitled to partition of the 1/9th part of the ranch.*

HENRY W. PECK *is the owner in fee, and entitled to partition of the 1/9th part of the ranch.*

MARIA HELENA LITTLEJOHN *is the owner in fee (as of her separate estate), and entitled to partition of the 2/27th parts of the ranch.*

MARIA LUISA JUAN *is the owner in fee (as of her separate estate), and entitled to partition of the 2/27th parts of the ranch, except as to that certain five acres thereof including within a certain fence, separating the land a tannery.*

BENJAMIN F. PORTER *is the owner in fee and entitled to partition of the 1/9th part of all that certain five acres of the ranch included within a certain fence, separating the land whereon stands a certain tannery and buildings for the manufactory of leather. The five acres, on the north, east, and west is separated from land occupied by defendant Ricardo Fourcade Juan, and on the south by the road between Santa Cruz and Watsonville. The defendant Benjamin F. Porter (and others) have been in possession of the five acres since 1858, and while so in possession have at own proper costs and expense, made useful, valuable, and permanent improvements on said premises, consisting of a tannery, vats, flumes, aqueducts, three dwelling houses, out-houses, barn, hen-houses, machinery, and some fruit trees, all now upon the said five acres last aforesaid.*

GEORGE K. PORTER *is the owner in fee, and entitled to partition of the 7/270th parts of the ranch.*

FREDERICK W. MACONDRAY, *and that of the lands and tenements herein first described, and described in the Complaint, the defendant William Macondray and James Otis, as executors of the last will and testament of Frederick W. Macondray, deceased, and the heirs and devisees of Frederick W. Macondray, deceased, whose names are unknown, are the owners in fee simple, and entitled to have set off and assigned to them 19/540th parts of the same, in severalty.*

AUGUSTUS NOBLE *is the owner in fee, and entitled to parti-*

tion of the 1/12th part of the ranch.

FREDERICK A. HIHN *is the owner in fee, and entitled to partition of the 71/270th parts of the ranch.*

And it is further considered, adjudged and decreed, that the defendants Benjamin F. Porter, George K. Porter, the plaintiffs Henry W. Peck and Maria Antonia Peck, the defendants Frederick A. Hihn, Joshua Parrish, Maria Luisa Juan, Maria Guadalupe Averon, Maria Helena Littlejohn, and Augustus Noble, have each at their own proper costs and expense, made useful, permanent, and valuable improvements on said lands above described.

And it is further considered, adjudged, and decreed, that neither of the defendants, Joseph Averon, Jose David Littlejohn, Ricardo Fourcade Juan, John P. P. Vandenberg, Miguel Lodge, Thomas Fallon, Carmel Fallon, Francisco Young, Nicanor Young, Pruitt Sinclair, Charles H. Willson, William Ireland, William Otis Andrews, Charles W. Plum, J. S. Reed, George H. Kirby, Thomas Courtis in his own right, or Thomas Courtis as Administrator of Benjamin P. Green, deceased, Mary E. J. Slade, Henry Lawrence, Thomas Courtis as Administrator of John Ingoldsby, deceased, John Francis Llebaria, John Wilson, or Cyrus Coe, have any title right, claim, or interest in the lands and tenements described in the Complaint, or any part thereof.

Charles B. Younger,
Court assigned Referee[399]

Charles Younger releases his report regarding ownership claims in Shoquel Augmentation

On August 22, 1861, five days after submitting his report on Rancho Soquel, Charles Younger submitted his report on Shoquel Augmentation to Judge McKee. As with the previous report, all of the actual percentages were blank in the report and had to be derived through alternate sources. The following is a summation of the report using the original incomplete document as a template:

> *Charles B. Younger, appointed Referee by this Court herein, states to the Court that he has now herein completed his findings of facts, herein, together with the under taken, and is ready to file the same on the payment of his fee for his service as Referee herein, and in appearing to the Court that the parties herein have by agreement and stipulation in writing passed to the hands of Charles B. Younger for his services as Referee herein $1,000, and the Court having each and inasmuch the said findings of facts of said Referee.*

CARMEL FALLON is the owner in fee, and entitled to partition severalty of 1/9th part of the ranch.
MARIA GUADALUPE AVERON is the owner in fee, and entitled to partition severalty of 1/9th part of the ranch.
MARIA ANTONIA PECK is the owner in fee, and entitled to partition severalty of 1/9th part of the ranch.
MARIA HELENA LITTLEJOHN is the owner in fee, and entitled to partition severalty of 2/27th parts of the ranch.
MARIA LUISA JUAN is the owner in fee, and entitled to partition severalty of 1/27th part of the ranch.
HENRY W. PECK is the owner in fee, and entitled to partition severalty of 2/27th parts of the ranch.
LYMAN JOHN BURRELL is the owner in fee, and entitled to partition severalty of 1/27th part of the ranch.
JOEL BATES is the owner in fee, and entitled to partition severalty of 1/27th part of the ranch.
GEORGE W. EVANS is the owner in fee, and entitled to partition severalty of 1/18th part of the ranch.
CRAVEN P. HESTER is the owner in fee, and entitled to partition severalty of 1/48th part of the ranch.
BENJAMIN FARLEY is the owner in fee, and entitled to partition severalty of 1/48th part of the ranch.
JAMES TAYLOR is the owner in fee, and entitled to partition severalty of 1/54th part of the ranch.
GEORGE K. PORTER is the owner in fee, and entitled to parti-

tion severalty of 7/270th parts of the ranch.

<u>FREDERICK W. MACONDRAY</u> *is the owner in fee, and entitled to partition severalty of 1/30th part of the ranch.*

<u>AUGUSTUS NOBLE</u> *is the owner in fee, and entitled to partition severalty to 1/540th part and 1/280th part of the ranch.*

<u>CASIMERO & DARIO AMAYO</u> *are the owner in fee, and entitled jointly to partition severalty to 1/27th part of the ranch.*

<u>FRANCIS R. BRADY & BENJAMIN C. NICHOLS</u> *are the owner in fee, and entitled jointly to partition severalty to 1/54th part of the ranch.*

<u>ROGER G. HINCKLEY & JOHN L. SHELBY</u> *are the owner in fee, and entitled jointly to partition severalty to 1/36th part of the ranch.*

<u>RICHARD SAVAGE</u> *is the owner in fee, and entitled to partition severalty to 1/96th part of the ranch.*

<u>FREDERICK A. HIHN</u> *is the owner in fee, and entitled to partition severalty to 12/90th undivided parts of the ranch.*

When Judge McKee issued his order that Younger be assigned referee to partition the Augmentation, he made it clear that each of the defendant's and the plaintiff's claim to land would not be filed until their portion of Younger's bill was paid in full. Only when their portion was paid, would their finding be filed officially with the court. Thus, for example, it was entered into the court records on October 8, 1861 that James Taylor, Craven Hester, Maria Luisa Juan, Maria Guadalupe Averon, Frederick W. Macondray, George Evans, and Camel Fallon had paid Younger their portion of his bill. Therefore, their findings were allowed to be filed with the court.

Younger also agreed with the majority of the defendants that the Augmentation was not suitable to partition and that only the lands of Lyman Burrell and James Taylor could be partitioned and set off by water and bounds. He concluded that the balance ought to be sold and the profits divided among the remaining claimants.

Later that day, after reading the report, John Wilson, Thomas Courtis, Mary Slade, Charles Plum, Henry Lawrence, and Augustus Noble notified the court that they took exception to the conclusions, which did not favor the claims of the Catholic Church, and that they would seek a second opinion.[400]

Land transfer from Richard Savage to Benjamin Cahoon

After having won the property at auction seven months earlier, Benjamin Cahoon finally came into possession of his 1/96 claim in Shoquel Augmentation and its accompanying sawmill on August 26, 1861. Cahoon never reopened the mill, however, and it eventually passed to his daughter, Lucy, who sold it and the surrounding land in 1868.[401]

Frederick Hihn is elected to the Santa Cruz County Board of Supervisors

On September 4, 1861, Frederick Hihn received 400 of the 573 votes cast in the Third Supervisor District, centered on the town of Pescadero, securing for him a position on the Santa Cruz County Board of Supervisors. His opponent in the election was former mayor William Blackburn. Hihn's term began on May 5, 1862.[402]

Anti-logging injunction served on Joel Bates overturned by California Supreme Court

In September 1860, Joel Bates appealed an injunction issued to him on behalf of Frederick Hihn ordering him to cease logging activities within Shoquel Augmentation while the partitioning suit was in progress. The California Supreme Court agreed with Bates' stance and overturned the injunction on September 11, 1861, thereby allowing Bates to resume logging activities on the land that he claimed in the Augmentation. In reality, Bates, Francis Brady, Benjamin Nichols, and Richard Savage had been able to cut the timber on their properties since May, when the eight-month injunction expired. Bates waited until his appeal resolved to resume logging activities, but Savage was too occupied with the partition suit to cut timber and then sold the land to Benjamin Cahoon, who also chose not to cut timber at this time. It is unknown if Brady and Nichols resumed logging at this time or earlier, but it seems doubtful.[403]

John Porter resigns as sheriff

Despite a possible theft of county revenue in 1859, John Porter remained the Santa Cruz County Sheriff until resigning from the post on October 1, 1861. He was soon appointed the Collector for the Port of Monterey by President Abraham Lincoln, a position that he retained until early 1866. The statute of limitations on his possible crime expired in 1863, a fact noted by County Supervisors Frederick Hihn and Adna Hecox in a report to the board on August 5, 1863.[404]

John Vandenberg objects to the Younger Report

On October 3, 1861, John Vandenberg stated that the Younger Report should show that he was the owner in fee and entitled to 1/9 of Rancho Soquel. In addition, he argued that the report should be put aside due to incorrect statements made by Henry Peck and Frederick Hihn. On October 5, Vandenberg repeated his objections to the and requested that the report be set aside and a new report prepared during the January term.[405]

Craven Hester and Benjamin Farley object to the Younger Report

On October 8, 1861, Craven Hester on behalf of Benjamin Farley and himself objected to the Younger Report's finding that Shoquel Augmentation was not suitable for partition between the claimants without great prejudice to their interest, except for the lands of Lyman Burrell and James Taylor. In contrast, Hester argued that his and Farley's land could be set off by water and bounds. Concerning the remainder of the Augmentation, he agreed that it should be sold and the profits divided accordingly among the various claimants.[406]

Thomas Courtis and John Wilson petition for a new report

On October 14, 1861, Thomas Courtis, speaking for the Ingoldsby Estate and himself, John Wilson, Mary Slade, Cyrus Coe, Charles Plum, and Henry Lawrence requested that the Younger Report be set aside and that a new report be drafted. They argued that the report and findings did not reflect actual facts and were contrary to established laws.

This group of defendants was joined by the Macondray Estate's attorney and representatives for Archbishop Alemany and Father Llebaria, who entered into evidence Martina Castro's deed signed in August 1850. Wilson objected to this entry, however, questioning the validity of the deed.

The next day, Courtis requested a second time that the report be dismissed and a new report be produced by Charles Younger.[407]

Lien placed on Lyman Burrell's property by Antonia and Henry Peck at the request of Robert Peckham

On October 18, 1861, Robert Peckham on behalf of Frederick Hihn placed a lien on the property of Lyman Burrell for $500. When Henry and Antonia Peck signed the deed on April 13, 1859 in which Burrell purchased a 1/27 claim to Shoquel Augmentation, Burrell gave them $1,000 in gold coin and a promissory note for $500. Burrell later recalled that "Henry Peck, whom I had purchased my 1/27th undivided part from, decided to foreclose on the property note of $500 that I had given him and his wife Antonia. The lien that Henry Peck placed on my property attached my land as well as all of my stock. Henry was refusing me permission to sell a flock of sheep which were ready for market and whose proceeds could have paid the debt in full. The agreements between Henry and Hihn was, that if [Peck] could gain control of my land, then he, Hihn would take over my 1/27th claim."[408]

Arguments for and against the partition of Shoquel Augmentation

On October 18, 1861, Frederick Hihn responded to the defendants who wanted Shoquel Augmentation partitioned rather than auctioned. He testified before Judge McKee that the Augmentation was so situated that partition could not be made without injury in a great degree to several interested parties. Robert Peckham then called several witnesses to testify on the matter. Thomas Wright, Samuel Drennan, John Daubenbiss, and John Hames each explained that they were well acquainted with the property and that it was so situated that a partition might be made without prejudice to the rights of any of the parties, and that improvements should be considered as added value to the land. John Porter, Lambert Clements, and Elihu Anthony then testified each in turn that the rival claims were such that it could not be partitioned without prejudice to the interested parties. It is interesting to note here that these latter three men were all leaders in the county's financial world in one way or another and potentially had something to gain through the auctioning of the Augmentation.

Following the testimony of Hihn and his allies, several of the defendants in favor of partitioning the Augmentation testified before the court. These included Joel Bates, Francis Brady, Benjamin Nichols, John Stearns, George Kirby, and Richard Savage, who also called as witnesses Birney James Burrell (John Burrell's son), Henry Hill, Otis Straton, and Henry Clay White. These claimants and their witnesses all argued that the Augmentation could be justly and equally partitioned without prejudice to any of the interested parties, and that those who had improved their land could retain it in such a way that they would receive no injury to their interests. Charles Younger went on record to deny that the property could be partitioned, except for the claims of Lyman Burrell and James Taylor.

The sudden appearance of White in the Shoquel Augmentation partitioning suit necessitates an explanation regarding his role in this story. On his 1863 map of the Augmentation, Thomas Wright shows a "Lacuna" (Webster's Dictionary defines this word to mean "ditch, hole, or pool") with a "U" figure along its south side, which he calls a cabin. Research into these maps revealed a meticulously detailed journal by Wright which he maintained throughout his years as county surveyor. Surveyors today often cannot decipher Wright's notes, especially those relating to the Augmentation's backcountry, because the terrain has changed so much in the ensuing years. In several entries, Wright mentions a "White's Home" or "White's cabin" near the lagoon. However, he never explains who White was or if he was still alive or living in the home at the time of his surveys. At the time of the surveys, there were several Whites living in Santa Cruz County, but none could definitively be linked to the home beside the lagoon until the discovery of the court transcripts regarding people knowledgeable concerning the Augmentation. It seems certain that Henry White was the person in question, but nothing else is known about him.

The history of the lagoon itself, though, is more important to this story since it sits almost at the center of the Augmentation. White's Lagoon is a narrow 500-foot long sag pond lying today in an ecologically sensitive area oriented in a general east-to-west direction at about 1,400-foot elevation on China Ridge. During periods of overflow, the lagoon empties eastward into White's Lagoon Gulch. The lagoon is usually very shallow, partially covered with reeds, grass, and willows, which over the next few decades will have enough sediment deposited into it to complete its transformation from a lagoon into a meadow.

Before the 1906 earthquake, White's Lagoon was about half today's size. This is confirmed by explorations along the north side of the lagoon, where there are remains of a skid road that was used by the Loma Prieta Lumber Company in the mid- to late-1890s. The road heads directly into the lagoon from the west and then its traces can be found leaving the lagoon's east side toward White's Lagoon Gulch. From these indications, it is obvious that logs were pulled along a path that passed by the north side of a smaller body of water in order to reach the gulch, and from there, the road continued to the railroad line below along Aptos Creek.

The effect of the earthquake on White's Lagoon was profound. An article in the *Santa Cruz Surf* published on October 20, 1906 revealed some drastic changes to the area:

> *Up here, known to a few hunters and woodsmen, was a body of water, covering between two and three acres, called "White's Lagoon." IT IS DRY! Its bottom was cracked by the earthquake as a kettle might be. Augmented by the hunter, our party of seven sat midday on a promontory full forty feet above the former bed of the creek [White's Lagoon Gulch] and quietly surveyed the work of thirty seconds, which had completely transformed the face of Nature in this locality.*
>
> *A little to the left was a huge clump of bushes, with wonderfully broad leaves for a bush. Ah! Ha! Not a bush, but the*

> *top of a great maple tree, roots, trunk and branches all down below, imbedded in the oozy earth, its more slender branches and topmost twigs visible. Closer inspection showed that the apparent shrubbery in sight was simply tops of trees. As at Deer Creek, the camera fails to catch an adequate conception. It is beyond the scope of any lens; it is beyond the range of physical vision. It is only the eye of the imagination aided by the full view of the locality that can comprehend the magnitude and majesty of the instantaneous movement which wrought these results.*

Returning to the arguments against the Younger Report, the specific complaints made by several of the overlooked defendants, all beneficiaries of the Catholic Church or the School Land Warrants, are presented here in their entirety to better outline their claims, assertions, and desires:

> *Joel Bates answers the plaintiff Hihn by calling several witnesses that testify on his behalf that tend to show that he has erected and has permanent and valuable improvements on his premises consisting of a steam-powered sawmill, houses, buildings, fences, cleared and cultivated land and a flume, all of the present value of $6,000 to $7,000, and that such improvements have added to the permanent value of the premises.*
>
> *Francis R. Brady and Benjamin Cahoon Nichols answer Hihn by calling several witnesses that testify that the partners have erected and have on the property permanent and valuable improvements consisting of houses, fences, a dam and crops all totaling $525, which add to the value of the premises.*
>
> *George Kirby answers Hihn by calling several witnesses that state that both Kirby and his grantor, Montgomery Bell Shackleford, have erected and made in the southwest corner of the Soquel Augmentation Ranch valuable improvements increasing the value of the premises consisting of houses, fences, orchards, nursery and clearing and cultivated lands, and the present value is $1,000.*
>
> *Richard Savage answers by calling several witnesses that*

> *testify that he, and his two grantors, Roger Gibson Hinckley and son-in-law John Shelby, have made valuable improvements on the premises now standing and adding to the value thereof. The improvements consist of a water-powered sawmill, houses, fences, flumes, a tunnel and mill race, plus roads, all valued at $5,250.*

After the above objections were entered into the record, the defendants requested that the Younger Report be set aside and a new report be produced. Savage objected to the report on the grounds that he was no longer the legal owner of the 1/96 claim to the Augmentation and, therefore, was no longer liable for the fees he had been ordered by the court to pay. He stated that the reason he was no longer liable was that the court had ordered him to sell his sawmill and land to Benjamin Cahoon. Meanwhile, Brady, Nichols, Kirby, and Stearns objected because the Younger Report failed to recognize their ownership of and claims to former School Land Warrant lands.

Robert Peckham, the Pecks, the Fourcades, the Littlejohns, and the Averons entered into evidence the deed dated September 19, 1852 in which the Lajeunesses sold 1,000 acres total to Thomas Wright, Peter Tracy, and Montgomery Shackleford. This deed misrepresented the 333 1/3 acres each was to receive as 1/27 of the total Augmentation each, or 1,211 acres per person. Kirby then entered into evidence a deed dated January 29, 1855 in which Shackleford sold to Kirby his share of the Augmentation, which both assumed was a claim to 1/27 of the total property.

Bates, Brady, Nichols, and Stearns then entered into evidence a deed dated February 4, 1853 in which Thomas Fallon sold Wright and Tracy School Land Warrant Nos. 108, 353, and 354, a total of 640 acres. Wright then was called to testify on their behalf. He stated:

> *I am one of the grantees of the latter deed and I know where the Warrants are located that are mentioned in the deed. They were located between Rancho Soquel and the Soquel Augmentation Ranch, stretching from the west boundary of the two areas on the Soquel River east to the east boundary at Borregas Creek.*

> *The enclosed area encompassed approximately 950 acres, or 1/33rd part of the entire Augmentation. The purpose of this deed was intended to convey Thomas Fallon's interest in all the land between the eastern and western lines of the ranch, and extending from one to the other, and north of the southern line of the locations.*

The four defendants also entered another deed, dated November 30, 1854, into the record, in which Wright sold his half interest in School Land Warrants Nos. 108, 353, and 354 to Tracy.

After Tracy died, the administrators of his estate, Asa Warson and Francis Kittridge, petitioned to sell Tracy's real estate in a public auction. The winning bidders for the estate were Bates, Brady, Nichols, Noble, and Stearns, each of whom submitted their deeds to the record.

Several more deeds overlooked by Younger were entered as evidence at this time, as well, including a deed from September 1859 in which the Pecks sold Wesley Burnett & Company a 1/54 claim in the Augmentation; a deed signed in November 1859 where Burnett sold that claim to Brady and Nichols; and a deed signed in that same month in which Bates purchased 1/27 of the Augmentation from the Pecks.

After these deeds were entered, Brady and Nichols called Stearns to testify concerning Wesley Burnett & Company. Stearns stated that he knew the firm and the owners, Wesley and William Burnett, from April 1, 1857 to January 1, 1860, during which time they performed as traders.[409]

Frederick Hihn and Martina Castro's daughters request that the Younger Report be accepted

On October 18, 1861, Luisa Juan, Helena Littlejohn, and Guadalupe Averon joined Frederick Hihn in requesting that the deeds and agreements submitted to the court by Thomas Courtis regarding Rancho Soquel be removed from evidence and his request for a new report be denied.

However, Robert Peckham, on behalf of Hihn, advised Judge McKee that the Younger Report had indeed made an error in stating that Hihn had a legitimate claim to 71/270 of Rancho Soquel. Peckham claimed that, instead, Hihn should have an 8/27 claim, which amounted to about fifty-six additional acres. Furthermore, Peckham clarified that Augustus Noble should only have a 1/27 claim, not the 1/12 in the report; that George Porter should have a 13/1018 claim, not 7/270; and that Frederick Macondray should have a claim to 18/243 of the ranch and not 19/540. All three of the revisions were because Martina Castro only sold her 1/9 portion of the ranch to the Catholic Church, so all of the claims to her property must be situated in that portion. Because of these errors, which Peckham claimed were against the law and contrary to the other evidence contained in the report, Peckham filed an objection to the report.[410]

Lyman Burrell pays off his debt to Antonia and Henry Peck

In desperate need of $500 to pay off the debt he owed to Henry and Antonia Peck and release the lien they had placed on his property, Lyman Burrell sent his son, Birney, to San Francisco on October 20, 1861 to borrow money from some friends. Birney returned with the money and Lyman repaid the Pecks, preventing Frederick Hihn from acquiring the Burrells' property through foreclosure. Hihn did not actually need the property, but rather sought the so-called Spanish Ranch, which was located to the south of the Burrells along the East Branch of Soquel Creek across from Sulphur Springs.[411]

Joel Bates dies in Santa Cruz

Joel Bates did not enjoy his victory over Frederick Hihn or his permission to resume logging activity in Shoquel Augmentation for long. On October 21, 1861, he died, only forty days after the injunction against him was lifted by the state Supreme Court. Bates' health had been declining for several years and curtailed his activities to a great extent. He and his heirs never reactivated the sawmill and it remained inactive for the next four years.[412]

Benjamin and George Porter petition for a new report and reject Thomas Courtis's claims

On October 24, 1861, Benjamin and George Porter objected to the statements made by Thomas Courtis nine days earlier regarding to the Younger Report and requested that a new report be commissioned. Their reasoning closely matched the reasons submitted by Robert Peckham, the Fourcades, the Littlejohns, and the Averons on October 18.[413]

Defendants petition for a new report and enter their deeds into the court record

On October 23, 1861, Francis Brady, Benjamin Nichols, Casimero and Dario Amayo, Benjamin and George Porter, Roger Hinckley, John Shelby, Henry Parsons, and the attorney representing the Bates Estate joined Frederick Hihn in requesting a new report be produced by Charles Younger regarding claims in Shoquel Augmentation. They specifically requested that the deeds by Father Ingoldsby, John Wilson, and James Scarborough entered into the record by Thomas Courtis be removed from evidence and only those accepted by Younger be considered, but that additional deeds also be included that had been overlooked or deemed void by Younger.

Judge McKee rejected the suggestion that a new report be drafted and accepted the Younger Report as it had been initially entered. Furthermore, he declared that both deeds sealed by Martina Castro, that to her children in August 1850 and that to the Catholic Church in January 1855, were valid, but that the latter deed only related to the remaining 1/9 interest Castro held in Shoquel Augmentation.

With this decision made by McKee, the defendants came forward to submit their deeds into evidence beginning on October 25. Several of the defendants included deeds that had either been invalidated by Younger or by other court cases. In these cases, the defendants provided justifications or explanations for why they felt the deed was valid or relevant.

Benjamin Porter provided the first set of deeds, most of which were accompanied with explanations and occasional witnesses:

> DEED *dated July 25, 1853, in which Jones Hoy sold his 1/18th claim in both ranches to Joseph L. Majors.*

Porter clarified that Younger had declared this deed for

land in Rancho Soquel only and, furthermore, that it was contested by Hihn.

DEED *dated August 11, 1855, in which the Juans* [Fourcades], *Clements and Averons, Pruett Sinclair and Joseph L. Majors each sold to Durrell S. Gregory 1/3rd of their claim in both ranches for services rendered.*

Porter claimed that Gregory received through this deed a total claim of 8/54 to both ranches, but Younger had decreed that only Sinclair passed title, and the amount of land was only a 1/54 claim to the Augmentation.

DEED *dated August 13, 1859, in which Durrell S. Gregory sold his claimed 8/54ths parts in both ranches to himself* [Porter].

DEED *dated January 20, 1860, in which he himself as grantor sold 1/54th of the Augmentation to James Taylor, which leaves him 7/54ths in the Augmentation and 8/54ths in Rancho Soquel.*

Younger claimed that Porter sold his entire claim to the Augmentation to Taylor, and his claim to Soquel was void. But Porter next pointed out to the court that Hihn was claiming Taylor's 1/54 part through another series of deeds.

Porter ended his testimony by calling as witnesses Luisa and Jean Fourcade, Josefa and Lambert Clements, and Joseph and Guadalupe Averon to testify that he had paid Gregory $1,000 for the claimed land. He rested his case by submitting his motion for a new report. Younger promptly denied these claims by Porter, insisting that he had sold all of his claims in the Augmentation to Taylor except for 1/54.

The next day, the Bates Estate, Brady, Nichols, John Stearns, George Kirby, and Richard Savage appeared before Judge McKee and made their case for why lands sold after 1850 outside of Martina Castro's personal claims should be considered as legitimate. The basis of their claims was the long-standing argument that the deed signed in 1850 was illegitimate and, therefore, none of Castro's children actually had claims to the Augmentation. Furthermore, claims to School Land Warrants should be considered valid since they were made in good faith:

> *The six defendants making this request jointly state that the rights, interests and estates to which the evidence shows that Joel Bates (deceased), Francis R. Brady and Benjamin Cahoon Nichols, and Augustus Noble and John Stearns through their School Land Warrants and George H. Kirby and John Stearns are respectively entitled to in the Augmentation, excluding the interests allowed to them by the referee, are, by the finding of the referee, allotted and given to other parties not entitled thereto.*
>
> *The evidence also shows that Joel Bates (deceased) has made improvements totaling $7,000 while the referee sets the value at only $5,600. The same holds for Richard Savage who has made improvements totaling $5,000, while the referee sets the value at $4,000. The evidence also shows that George Kirby has made improvements totaling $1,800, while the referee does not find that he has made any improvements.*
>
> *Also, the evidence presented to the referee clearly shows that the Augmentation is so situated that partition can be made without great prejudice to the owners thereof, while the referee finds that the premises is so situated that partition thereof cannot be made without great prejudice to the owners thereof, except as the interests therein of Lyman Burrell and James Taylor.*
>
> *The six defendants next present a joint statement, to wit: "We, the above defendants declare that the referee's findings and decisions are against the law as follows...."*

At this point, they submitted their deeds into the record with explanations as to why they should be considered:

> DEED dated February 4, 1853, in which Thomas Fallon sold to Peter Tracy and Thomas W. Wright School Land Warrant Nos. 108, 353 and 354 totaling 640 acres.

The defendants rejected the implication by Younger that School Land Warrants could not be transferred.

> DEED dated September 19, 1852, in which Nicanor Lajeunesse and her husband sold to Peter Tracy, Thomas W. Wright and Montgomery B. Shackleford valid land and the grantors did pass on valid and effectual title to the grantees for the undivided 1/9th part of the Augmentation.

> DEED dated July 23, 1860 and July 24, 1860, in which Nicanor Lajeunesse sold to Frederick A. Hihn her 1/9th claim to land in both ranches in spite of the valid objections to the admission of the deed in which it is stated that it was void and of no effect, to wit.

> Their evidence showed that Lajeunesse, when she signed the deed with Hihn, did not have any right to land in the Augmentation to convey and that she did not follow proper legal procedures for conveying land. Furthermore, they argued that the transaction between Lajeunesse and Hihn was contrary to public policy since it was linked to a divorce settlement that Hihn was funding to the detriment of Francisco Lajeunesse, who also could claim by rights a portion of the Augmentation due to his marriage to Nicanor.

The six defendants concluded by arguing that the land could and should be partitioned among the various claimants in as best a manner as possible so that everyone could enjoy the portions they had settled upon and improved. Therefore, the Younger Report should be disregarded and a new report prepared that takes into account equity between claims.[414]

Several defendants file their objections to the Younger Report and petition for a new report

On November 7, 1861, Thomas Courtis filed objections against the Younger Report, arguing that the report did not appropriately state all of the facts nor embrace all of the issues in the case. Notably, he objected to the finding that he and several other claimants held no interest in Rancho Soquel and Shoquel Augmentation, and argued instead that:

> THOMAS COURTIS *in his own right is entitled to 5/12th parts.*
> THOMAS COURTIS *as administrator of John Ingoldsby, deceased, is entitled to 1/5th parts in the Augmentation. In addition to the aforementioned claim, he holds legal title to 1/2 of both ranches, in fee, subject to the equitable claim of defendant John Wilson and one James Scarborough and their grantees to the whole amount of the 1/2, while the referee does not find that Courtis has any right in either ranch as administrator or that John Wilson and James Scarborough or their grantees have any interest therein either legal or equitable.*
> CYRUS COE *is entitled to 1/24th part.*
> MARY E. J. SLADE *is entitled to 1/48th part.*
> CHARLES H. PLUM *is entitled to 1/120th part.*
> HENRY W. LAWRENCE *is entitled to 1/80th part.*

In contrast, Courtis argued, it was the children of Martina Castro, as well as Joel Bates, James Taylor, Henry Peck, George Porter, John Daubeniss, Francis Brady, Benjamin Nichols, and Frederick Hihn, who held no interest based on the evidence. Courtis concluded by clarifying that:

> *The referee gave effect to and adjudges as valid and effectual, to pass title to the said premises to the parties claiming them under the pretended deed of Martina Castro to her children dated August 29, 1850, notwithstanding the objections of these defendants, as the same are stated in the minutes of the*

referee's report.

The findings and decision of the referee does not give effect to the deed from Martina Castro and Louis Depeaux to Father John Francis Llebaria and the Archbishop John Alemany dated January 22, 1855, offered and read in the evidence by the defendants, except so far as to convey title to 1/9th of the premises while the said deed is valid in law to pass title to the whole of the said premises to these defendants, and those claiming under said deed.

The errors of law occurring at the trial before the referee, and excepted to at the time by each and every of these defendants, for the particulars of which, reference is made here to the minutes of the referee, and the testimony taken by him, now on file in this court.

On December 14, Robert Peckham and Joseph H. Skirm, representing Frederick Hihn and Benjamin Porter respectively, filed a motion with the Third District Court for a new report to be conducted by Charles Younger. Antonia and Henry Peck, Helena and Joseph Littlejohn, Luisa and Jean Fourcade, Guadalupe and Joseph Averon, and Carmel and Thomas Fallon all joined in arguing for the Younger Report to be set aside and for a new report to be produced.

Two days later, Craven Hester and Benjamin Farley filed a similar motion, although their reasons were more detailed. Hester, on behalf of Farley and himself, argued that:

The referee reported that the Augmentation was not susceptible of partition and that the land be sold while the premises is susceptible of partition without prejudice to the owners thereof.

The referee improperly and illegally and without the knowledge or consent of Craven P. Hester and Benjamin Farley permitted to be withdrawn from the record of evidence made by the referee of one Augustus Noble, and made an order to the effect that the three following deeds were executed by John Ingoldsby on the same day for the same land that Craven P. Hester had paid Augustus Noble a consideration for, and that he had no notice of the other deeds, only the one made by John Ingoldsby to Augustus Noble.

On May 3, 1856, three deeds were entered into which John Ingoldsby stated that Augustus Noble, Benjamin P. Green and William Otis Andrews were paying $2,000 each for 1/12th of Rancho Soquel and the Augmentation. On the same day, three additional deeds were written, in which each grantee was sold by attorneys John Wilson and James Scarborough 1/24th of each ranch for one dollar paid in hand, which resulted in each grantee claiming 1/12th part of each ranch, while the two attorneys retained half of their original 1/4 claim to land in each ranch. After the previously discussed deeds were signed, the three Catholic priests claimed 1/6th parts in each ranch, while the two attorneys would claim 1/8th of each ranch.

DEED dated June 19, 1858, in which Augustus Noble and his wife sell to Roger Gibson Hinckley and John Shelby 1/2 of his 1/12th part of the Augmentation.

DEED, dated August 7, 1858, in which Augustus Noble and his wife sell to Craven P. Hester 1/2 of his 1/12th part in the Augmentation.

DEED dated September 28, 1858, in which Craven P. Hester sells 1/2 of his 1/24th part in the Augmentation to Benjamin Farley.

Also on December 16, Augustus Noble filed his own objection to the Younger Report. He argued that:

Because of the insufficiency of the evidence to justify the findings and decisions of the referee, the evidence does not show that Carmel Fallon, Antonia Peck and Frederick A. Hihn are the owner of a separate estate or otherwise, in fee simple or otherwise.

Because the findings and decision of the referee is against law when he would not allow the School Land Warrants in which Thomas Fallon, Peter Tracy, Gervis Hammond, Montgomery B. Shackleford and Thomas Wright purchased, or the grantees that they sold all or portions to.

It was against law when Charles B. Younger allowed the deed between Nicanor Lajeunesse and Frederick A. Hihn dated July 23, 1860 and July 24, 1860 to stand while declaring the deed between Thomas Wright, Peter Tracy, and Montgomery B. Shackleford dated September 19, 1852 void and invalid.

Hester concluded his objections by stating that it was against the law for Younger to disallow his 1/27 claim to the Augmentation that he had purchased on May 5, 1860 from the Tracy Estate (derived from School Land Warrants) and his 1/40 claim that he had purchased from William Ireland on June 4, 1860.

After hearing these objections and motions, Judge McKee overruled all of the objections and motions for a new report. He made his final decision regarding the partitioning of Rancho Soquel on December 19, and no further testimony or evidence was allowed to be submitted for the case.

In response, all of those who claimed land via the Catholic Church's claim to Shoquel Augmentation came forward to reiterate their desire for a new report. By so doing, they joined Hihn, Porter, and the Castro children—all of whom claimed land via Martina Castro's 1850 deed—in desiring a more equitable partition of the properties between claimants.[415]

Benjamin Farley pays debt to Craven Hester in full

On March 5, 1862, Benjamin Farley paid the remaining $162 that he owed Craven Hester for a 1/48 claim to Shoquel Augmentation. The amount had been outstanding since the original deed was signed on September 28, 1858.[416]

Several defendants file their acceptance of the Younger Report

On April 2, 1862, Richard Savage, Francis Brady, Benjamin Nichols, John Stearns, George Kirby, the Bates Estate, Luisa Fourcade, Helena Littlejohn, and Carmel Fallon filed their acceptance of the Younger Report, motioning that their previous request for a new report be deleted from the record.

With the acceptance of most of the beneficiaries of the Younger Report, Charles Younger requested his fee from the defendants who still owed him for conducting the report. Judge McKee had agreed that a $1,000 fee was appropriate for the task, and that defendants would pay Younger in direct proportion to the percentage of land they received. Furthermore, only defendants who paid their fee could have their claims filed with the court.

Thus, Younger produced the following amounts each defendant owed, except for those who had already paid in full:

Guadalupe Averon: 1/9th of $1,000, or $111.11
Antonia Peck: 1/9th of $1,000, or $111.11
Helena Littlejohn: 2/27ths of $1,000, or $74.00
Henry Peck: 2/27ths of $1,000, or $74.00
Lyman Burrell: 1/27th of $1,000, or $37.00
Richard Savage: 1/96th of $1,000, or $10.44
Benjamin Farley: 1/48th of $1,000, or $20.83
Casimero and Dario Amayo: 1/27th of $1,000, or $37.00
The Bates Estate: 1/27th of $1,000, or $37.00[417]

Agreement between Henry Peck and Frederick Hihn

Henry Peck was always on the lookout for new means to amass his fortune. But much to his chagrin, every endeavor ended in some degree of failure. When Peck heard of the discovery of gold up in Humboldt County, he saw yet another opportunity. Thus, on April 21, 1862, Peck approached Frederick Hihn and offered to sell him his 1/9 claim to Rancho Soquel as well as the 1/18 claim to Shoquel Augmentation that he had purchased from Hihn two years earlier. But Hihn turned down the offer. Several days later, Peck returned and offered the lands again, as well as Antonia Peck's 1/9 claim to Soquel and their combined 5/27 claim to the Augmentation, all for only $4,000. Peck was willing to bargain because he had debts to repay before he could travel north. Yet Hihn turned him down a second time.

Failing to find another local buyer for the land, Peck informed Hihn that he would have to go to San José or San Francisco to seek an interested party. Hihn took this to mean that Peck was going to sell the land to Thomas Courtis or John Wilson, who claimed the same land via the Catholic Church claim. Not wishing to further complicate matters, Hihn relented and agreed to buy the Pecks' claims. With the assistance of Robert Peckham, the two men agreed to the following deed and agreement:

> *This Indenture made and entered into this twenty first day of April A.D. 1862 by and between Frederick Augustus Hihn of the State of California and County of Santa Cruz, party of the first part, and Henry Winegar Peck of the same state and county, the party of the second part, WITNESSETH:*
>
> 1ST ARTICLE. *That the party of the first part for and in consideration of the price herein after mentioned and the covenants herein after contained on the part of the party of the second part, his heirs and assigns, to be well and faithfully kept and performed, doth hereby for himself, his heirs and assigns, covenant and agree to grant, bargain, and sell and convey unto the party of the second part, his heirs and assigns, all the right, title, and interest conveyed to him this day by the party of the second part and his wife, Maria Antonia Peck, in and to those certain tracts of land in the State of California, County of Santa Cruz, and mostly in the Township of Soquel, and known there as the Soquel Ranch and the Soquel Augmentation Rancho, and bounded by a line commencing on the Bay of Monterey at the mouth of the Soquel Creek and running thence up said Soquel Creek to the place called Palo de la Yeska; thence to the Laguna Sergento; thence to and including the Loma Prieta; thence to the place called Chuchitas; thence to the place called Cuarto Legues; thence to the Borregas Gulch at the northwest corner of the Aptos Rancho; thence down the Borregas Gulch to the Bay of Monterey; thence along the Bay of Monterey to the place of beginning, containing thirty four thousand three hundred and seventy acres.*
>
> 2ND ARTICLE. *The said party of the second part, for himself his heirs and assigns, doth covenant and agree with the party of the first part that he will, or his heirs or assigns*

shall, purchase of the party of the first part, his heirs or assigns, the aforesaid interest in the aforesaid tract of land on or before January 1, 1863, and to pay to him or them as a part of the consideration and purchase price of this tract on or before the day last aforesaid the sum of $4,850.

3RD ARTICLE. *The said party of the second part doth for himself and his heirs and assigns covenant and agree with the said party of the first part, his heirs and assigns, that he will or that they shall, as a further part of the consideration and purchase price of said interest in said tract of land, pay to the party of the first part, his heirs or assigns, a further sum of money equal to one half of all sums that H. E. Heriter may at any time finally recover upon any judgment now rendered or to be rendered before the said first day of January 1863 against John T. Porter in the suit now pending in the District Court of the County of Santa Cruz, wherein the said H. E. Heriter is plaintiff, John T. Porter defendant, and Frederick A. Hihn intervenor* [a third party to a suit to protect his interests], *and one half of all sums that may be necessarily expended by or on behalf of the said defendant, John T. Porter, and intervenor, Frederick A. Hihn, in counsel fees and other expenses and disbursements in defending said action, less one half of such balance of the net proceeds of the sale of the parts taken from said Heriter* [...] *of or by virtue of process in the suit of Frederick A. Hihn and others against the said Heriter, heretofore prosecuted to judgment in the District Court of the County of Santa Cruz as shall remain after paying all the costs and expenses of prosecuting said action.*

4TH ARTICLE. *And the said party of the second part for himself, his heirs and assigns, further covenants and agrees with the said party of the first part, his heirs and assigns, that in case the suit of H. E. Heriter against John T. Porter, defendant, and Frederick A. Hihn, intervenor, shall not be finally disposed of before the first day of January 1863, that the said party of the second part, his heirs and assigns, shall on said last named day execute and deliver to the said party of the first part, his heirs and assigns, a penal bond with* two good and sufficient securities in half the amount claimed by the said Heriter, conditioned for the payment to the said party of the first part, his heirs and assigns, of a sum of more or equal of all sums that the said H. E. Herter may at any time finally reserve upon any judgment rendered, or to be rendered in the aforesaid action, and one half of all that may be necessarily expended by or on behalf of the said defendant, John T. Porter, and intervenor, Frederick A. Hihn, in counsel fees and other expenses and disbursements in defending said action, less one half of such balance of the last proceeds of this sale of the parts taken from said Heriter under color of or by virtue of process of the suit of Frederick A. Hihn and others against the said Heriter, heretofore prosecuted to judgment in the District Court of Santa Cruz County as shall remain after paying all costs and expenses of prosecuting said action.

5TH ARTICLE. The said party of the second part for himself, his heirs and assigns, further covenants and agrees to pay to the party of the first part, his heirs and assigns, as a further part of the purchase price of said interest in the aforesaid tract of land, on or before the first day of January 1863, a sum of money equal to one half of all such sums of money as may be before the day last aforesaid recovered by representatives of Joel Bates, deceased, upon a certain injunction bond executed by the said Frederick A. Hihn and others and filed in the District Court of the County of Santa Cruz in the suit by Frederick A. Hihn, Joel Bates, and others for a partition of the Soquel Augmentation Ranch, and for an injunction against said Joel Bates and one half of all counsel fees and other expenses which may be necessarily expended in defending any suit that may be brought in said suit.

6TH ARTICLE. And the party of the second part for himself, his heirs and assigns, further covenants and agrees with the said party of the first part, his heirs and assigns, that in case no recovery be had on the aforesaid injunction bond before the first day of January 1863, that the said party of the part, his heirs and assigns, shall on said last named day execute and deliver to the said party of the first part, his heirs *and assigns, a penal bond in the sum of $1,500, with the good and sufficient sureties, condition for the payment to the said party of the first part, his heirs and assigns, one half of all such sums of money as may at any time received in said injunction bond and one half of all counsel fees and other expenses which may be necessarily incurred in defending any suit which may be brought on said bond.*

7TH ARTICLE. *And the said party of the second part for himself, his heirs and assigns, further covenants and agrees to pay to the said party of the first part, his heirs and assigns, as a further part of the purchase price of said interest in said tract of land, a sum equal to one half of all such sums, exclusive of counsel fees in the District Court as shall be expended by the party of the first part, his heirs and assigns, between this date and the first day of January 1863, in and about the litigation in the District Court in the County of Santa Cruz of the suits now pending for the partition of said Rancho Soquel and the sale of the Soquel Augmentation, and in the execution of the decrees of said Court in said action and of defending any appeals in either of said causes that may be taken to the Supreme Court by any party or parties claiming under John Ingoldsby, deceased, and in prosecuting and defending any appeal by any other party in which the interest in said land in this instrument agreed to be sold and conveyed is involved.*

8TH ARTICLE. *And it is further consented and agreed by and between the parties hereto that if the party of the second part, his heirs and assigns, shall at any time before the first day of January 1863 make the payment provided for in* ARTICLE No. 2 *of this Agreement, and the payment provided for in* ARTICLE No. 4, *so for as any expenditures shall then lie under in liabilities incurred. And the payments provided for in the 3rd* ARTICLE *and the 5th* ARTICLE, *if any of the recoveries provided for in said* ARTICLES *be then had, and if any said recoveries be not then had, then as to such recovery or recoveries be not then had given the causes pending bond as provided for in the 4th and 6th* ARTICLES. *The same shall be taken as a full performance by the party of* the second part for his part of this Agreement.

9TH ARTICLE. *That the party of the first part for himself, his heirs and assigns, covenants and agrees with the party of the second part, his heirs and assigns, that if he or they shall on or before the first day of January 1863, well and faithfully in all things comply with his part of this Agreement, that he will or that his heirs or assigns shall upon such performance execute, acknowledge, and deliver to him or them a good and sufficient conveyance by deed of grant, bargain, and sale for the interest in said tract of land in this Agreement.*

10TH ARTICLE. *It is further covenanted and agreed by and between the parties hereto that the time fixed for the performance of this Agreement by the party of the second part, to wit, the first day of January 1863, is an essential and material part thereof, and in case he, his heirs and assigns, shall fail to fully perform his part of the Agreement until after this day, the same shall become null and void, and neither party be further bound thereby.*

11TH ARTICLE. *It is further covenanted and agreed by and between the parties hereto that this Agreement is not intended as a mortgage, and shall not by itself, or in connection with the conveyance this day made by the party of the second part and his wife to the party of the first part, be construed as a mortgage, or as fixing to show said conveyance a mortgage in any sense whatsoever.*

12TH ARTICLE. *And it is further covenanted and agreed by and between the said parties that this instrument is not intended and shall not be construed to give to the party of the second part, his heirs or assigns, the right to enter upon or to possess any portion of the said lands until the conveyance provided for in ARTICLE No. 9 of this Agreement shall be executed, but that until such execution, the possession and rights of possession shall be and remain with the party of the first part, his heirs or assigns.*

In witness whereof the said parties have hereunto set their hands this day and year above written.

WITNESS:
Robert F. Peckham

SIGNED BY:
Frederick A. Hihn
Henry Winegar Peck

The mention of H. E. Heriter in the third and fourth articles concerned a suit that Hihn was pursuing against Heriter alongside the Pecks, Thomas and Carmel Fallon, and Benjamin Porter. Heriter had been discovered logging illegally within the Augmentation along the road between the Brady and Nichols mill and Benjamin Cahoon's mill at the mouth of Hinckley Gulch. Lying along the road between the two mills were a number of posts installed by the plaintiffs, who were claiming damages of about $400, in addition to court fees. They also wished to stop Heriter's logging activity on their lands. In the deed above, Peck agreed to assume half of any damages that could possibly be brought against Hihn in the suit or any countersuit. In the end, Heriter lost the case and paid the damages and court fees.

The deed above was signed at two different locations. Peck signed in front of Hihn in the home of Peckham in Santa Cruz. Afterwards, Peckham went to the home of Mr. Winterham in Santa Cruz, where Antonia was spending the evening. During testimony given in 1867, in which Antonia attempted to reclaim her lost property from Hihn, Peckham stated that he explained the contents of the deed to her in English, as required by California law, before she put her mark on it. However, Antonia responded that she was unable to understand even the simplest questions put to her in English, therefore an interpreter was provided. Through an interpreter, she testified that it was her understanding that, when she put her mark on the deed, she was signing a mortgage. Since she was the plaintiff in the case, she was not cross-examined.

The original agreement allowed Peck to pay the sale price of his land—$4,000—plus a $500 fee to buy back the land by a specified date. In the end, an extra $350 was added to the sale price for a forgotten debt that was due shortly, and therefore the total buy-back price for Peck was $4,850. The reason Peck negotiated this buy-back option in the first place was in the hope that he would strike it rich in Northern California and be able to reclaim everything he had sacrificed to hunt for gold. However, fearing that the deed could be construed as a mortgage, Hihn added several clauses and also made clear to Peckham that he would never loan money for such poor land.

During the 1867 trial, Peck claimed that he only received $300 from Hihn after he signed the deed. In contrast, Hihn testified that he gave Peck about $1,650, keeping the remainder to pay Peck's debts to William M. Moore ($1,400) and Peckham ($750), the latter to repay a second mortgage and for representing Peck in the two partitioning suits. The remaining $200 was retained by Hihn to pay back another unnamed debtor. Peckham backed up Hihn's claims in subsequent testimony. Peck also tried to argue that his 1/18 claim to Shoquel Augmentation was not a part of the agreement since he could not find evidence that he owned the property. This seems unlikely, though, since the deed is located exactly where it should be in the Santa Cruz County Book of Deeds.

After relieving the Pecks of their second mortgage, Hihn leased their home to a Mr. Christiansen. Shortly afterwards, Antonia approached Hihn and asked if she could continue to occupy her former home while Henry travelled to Humboldt County. Hihn declined, explaining to her that the home was already occupied by a new tenant. Nonetheless, Henry visited Hihn a few days later with the same request. Hihn decided to ask Christiansen if he would be willing to host Antonia and her four daughters in his home while Henry was away, and Christiansen agreed.[418]

Frederick Hihn sworn in as county supervisor

Elected to the position on September 4, 1861, Frederick Hihn was sworn in as a Santa Cruz County supervisor for the Pescadero area on May 5, 1862.[419]

Coal discovered along Valencia Creek

A *Santa Cruz Weekly Sentinel* article published on June 13, 1862 reported that coal had been discovered along the east branch of Valencia Creek (today called Cox Creek after Charles Cox, an early settler in the area). The reporter explained that a tunnel measuring six feet wide and ten feet high was being dug to reach the coal vein, with the tunnel widening as it bore deeper into the earth. Other outcroppings had also been found in the area but were not being worked at the time.[420]

Henry Peck sells buy-back rights for Rancho Soquel and Shoquel Augmentation to James Brennan

After having sold his property to Frederick Hihn in April 1862, Henry Peck departed for Humboldt County in search of gold, leaving his wife and four daughters as tenants of Mr. Christiansen, to whom Hihn had leased the Pecks' former home. After sending letters to his wife several times, Peck briefly returned in late August to negotiate the sale of his buy-back rights to Rancho Soquel and Shoquel Augmentation, since he needed more funds to continue his gold prospecting in the north. He sold his buy-back rights to Captain James Brennan, who paid Peck $1,150, which was $6,000 minus the actual cost of buying back the land from Hihn. Feeling satisfied with the sale, Peck returned north.[421]

Charles McKiernan marries Barbara Berrick and begins improving his property

On August 11, 1862, Charles McKiernan married Barbara Berrick, the nurse who tended his wounds after he fought a grizzly bear. Despite keeping several mistresses over the ensuing years, Charles produced seven children with Barbara. In fact, it was because of these children and the lack of secondary education opportunities on the Summit that the family eventually moved to San José.

By the 1860s, McKiernan had been operating on the Summit for over a decade and many of the early structures he had built were in disrepair. Marriage prompted him to finally improve these facilities, especially the toll gate on the Santa Cruz Turnpike, since traffic was increasing along the route. He made upgrades to his home, as well, adding a large farmhouse, a barn, and several outbuildings for stagecoach passengers. Further up the ridge toward Summit Road, he renovated the small cabin that was the first

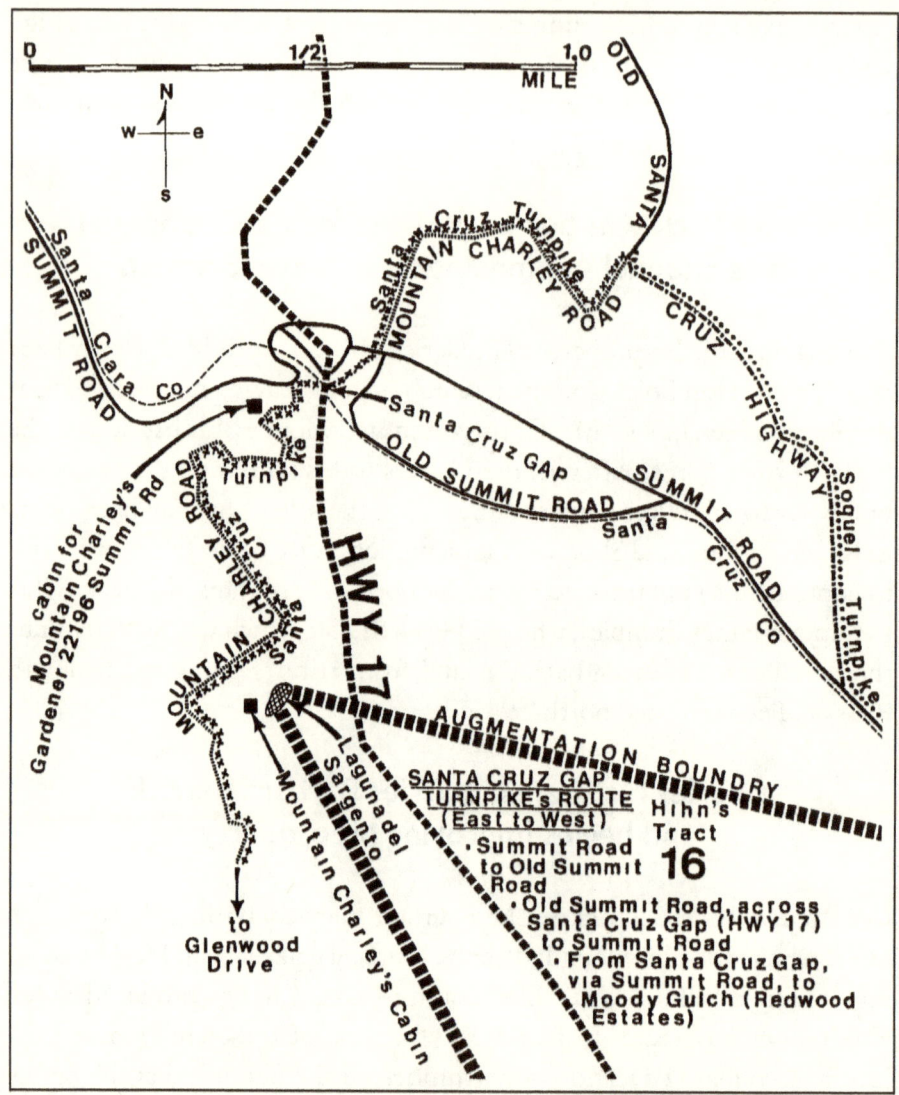

FIGURE 6.6 THE THREE TURNPIKES ON THE SUMMIT

house he lived in when he settled on the Summit in 1851. Since moving to the larger house, he had converted the cabin to a caretaker's cottage, but it had not been kept in good repair. Elsewhere on his property, he added orchards and vineyards.

Meanwhile, McKiernan removed most of the 3,000 acres of old-growth coast redwood that was scattered throughout his property. He generally cut these trees by leasing the land or granting stumpage rights to independent contractors, such as the Santa Clara Valley Mill & Lumber Company and the Morrell Brothers.[422]

Frederick Macondray dies in San Francisco

On August 27, 1862, Frederick Macondray died in San Francisco. The court assigned his brother William Macondray and attorney James Otis to act as the executors of his will. The two men were, therefore, responsible for carrying on the fight over Macondray's claims to Rancho Soquel and Shoquel Augmentation.[423]

Robert Peckham elected County Judge

In September 1862, Robert Peckham was elected a Santa Cruz County district judge. He took office in January 1863.[424]

Frederick Hihn signs lease allowing Antonia Peck to live in former home

In early October 1862, Henry Peck confronted Frederick Hihn regarding the living conditions of his wife and children in their former home on Rancho Soquel. He told Hihn that Mr. Christiansen, the landlord, had "treated his wife badly" and "that he had wronged her." Using these claims as a pretense, Peck then asked to be given his old home back. Confused, Hihn approached Christiansen to ask about his side of the story. Christiansen said that Antonia Peck had attacked and abused him, contradicting Henry's story.

Despite the contradictory statements, Hihn sided with his friend Henry and agreed to a new lease with the Pecks wherein Antonia and their children could remain in the home until October 20, 1863 for $250, made in two installments. Two clauses were added to the lease agreement to further benefit the family. If Henry bought back the property before January 1, 1863, he would not have to pay any rent. If the buy-back date lapsed but he made improvements to the property prior to October 20, he could avoid making the second payment.

Of course, Henry had already sold the buy-back rights to Rancho Soquel and Shoquel Augmentation to James Brennan. Shortly after Henry's deal with Hihn, Brennan approached Hihn to request an extension of the buy-back rights, stating that he did not have the money but would have it soon. Hihn acquiesced and allowed a sixty-day extension with an interest rate of 1.5 percent per month.[425]

Craven Hester, Benjamin Farley, James Taylor, and Lyman Burrell amend answers given earlier on the Younger Report

On December 12, 1862, Craven Hester on his own behalf and as attorney for Benjamin Farley amended his answers to the Younger Report by stating that, a long time before the beginning of this suit and since purchasing a portion of Shoquel Augmentation, both he and Farley made permanent and valuable improvements thereon, which continued to exist. The improvements consisted in part of an orchard of the value of $400. Hester prayed that he might be assigned both land and the value of the improvements jointly with Farley.

Three days later, on December 15, James Taylor amended his answer by highlighting that he had erected houses on his property, as well as a fence, which amounted to $600 in value. Lyman Burrell then came forward noting that improvements made to his property totaled $2,000. Hester and Farley then further amended their answers by clarifying that each of their properties was valued at $400.

Hester, who represented the other three individuals, concluded his amendments by petitioning the court to grant them their due interest in the land, either by granting them their fair allotments or compensating them for the value of the improvements that they made to their properties.

Hester's amendments were the last considered by Judge McKee in the Augmentation partitioning suit. The next day, McKee returned to his offices in Oakland and began preparing his final decisions regarding both the Augmentation suit and the Rancho Soquel partitioning suit.[426]

Henry Peck pays off lease and returns to Humboldt

On the first day of 1863, Henry Peck appeared at the home of Frederick

Hihn in Santa Cruz and handed him the $125 that was due according to the lease the two had signed on October 17, 1862. According to Hihn's testimony given during the Peck v. Hihn lawsuit in 1867, the following dialogue was exchanged between the two men after Peck paid Hihn:

HIHN: Henry, this is the last day to buy the ranches back.
PECK: I've made up my mind not to buy them back.
H: I don't like that on your part. You and I have fought that matter so hard and I want you to fight it out with me.
P: I have made up my mind not to buy them back. I've not got the means to do it. I don't care about it.
H: I was visited earlier by Capt. [James] Brennan and he asked me for an extension from the due date of January 1, 1863, which I gave him.
P: I know of the visit—the captain told me—but I have other uses for the money that the captain gave me. I have purchased a new homesite elsewhere.
H: I am sorry that you have come to that conclusion, and if you consider that you are paying too much to buy back the land, I am willing to take less. Instead of the $4,850, I am willing to reduce the amount by $500.
P: I don't care about buying the land back. I want to go back to the mines. I want to go back and make arrangements there to put up a mill, and there are other things I have seen there. I don't care about having anything to do with the land here. I don't like the people here, and they don't like me. I am sick of the partitioning suits, both of which carry the threat that I could lose everything to the John Ingoldsby backers if they win. You are in a better position to recover financially if they win than I am.

Shortly afterwards, Brennan found himself unable to secure the required funds to buy back the property from Hihn. Thus, Hihn found himself the owner of a claim to an additional twenty-six percent of Rancho Soquel and eighteen percent of Shoquel Augmentation.[427]

Land transfer by Lyman Burrell to Stephen and Joseph Chase

On April 18, 1863, Stephen Hall Chase and Josiah "Joseph" W. Chase purchased 1/24 of Lyman Burrell's 1/27 claim to Shoquel Augmentation on the Summit for $100. The cousins had arrived in San Francisco from Maine aboard the three-mast schooner *Golden Rucker* on May 18, 1859. Shortly afterwards, they headed south from San Francisco to San José and hired themselves out as laborers for a lumber camp near Lexington on Los Gatos Creek. The land they purchased from Burrell was a tiny tract of approximately fifty acres, but it would shortly afterwards be enlarged to 146 acres due to decisions in the partitioning suit.

The Chases built a sawmill near the junction of Highland Way and Summit Road, near where today's Soquel San Jose Road ends. The mill sat alongside Laurel Creek, which at the time was known as Burrell Creek. With the building of this mill, small as it was, Stephen and Joseph became the first to commercially produce lumber on the Summit. Prior to this time, most of the wood products made in the area was split stuff used locally by farmers and ranchers. The Chases transported their lumber to the Santa Clara Valley, where there was more profit, via the Soquel and Santa Cruz Gap Turnpikes.

In order to reach the Soquel Turnpike, a bridge had to be built over Burrell Creek. For some reason, it was named Hall's Bridge, likely after Stephen's middle name, and it remained a feature for several years along the route. Today, the bridge is gone and the creek has been redirected through a culvert.[428]

Decision and judgment by Judge McKee in the Rancho Soquel and Shoquel Augmentation Partitioning Suits

On April 20, 1863, Judge McKee released his decision regarding the partitioning of Rancho Soquel and Shoquel Augmentation. He released his decision through three judicial decrees, the first of which addressed Martina Castro's conflicting deeds:

> *Martina Castro, the grantee of the Mexican Government and patentee of the government of the United States of the*

> *ranches in controversy, on the 29th of August, 1850, by deed, conveyed to each of her eight children an undivided ninth part of these ranches, reserving to herself the remaining ninth part. In the deed, it is recited that she had received the ranches from the Government of Mexico for her own benefit and that of her family; and that from the time of receiving the grant, until execution of the deed, they had been bound in common with her on the ranches. This deed, by which she conveyed to each the undivided interest in the estate which she admitted she had obtained and held for all, was a gift. The testimony clearly established, that such was her intention.*
>
> *The consideration expressed was natural love and affection, and also five dollars in hand passed. But this cash consideration was merely nominal for no money, in fact, paid. The whole transaction constituted a donation from a mother to her children of that which she acknowledged she had received and held for them. Each of the daughters [and her son], therefore, took by that deed an undivided ninth part of the ranches in separate estate.*

In other words, the portion of land purchased by Father Ingoldsby on behalf of the Catholic Church in January 1855 was only Castro's personal one-ninth claim to both properties, not the entirety, as several claimants asserted.

McKee's second decree clarified how Charles Younger and himself arrived at the final partitioning percentages. Because it has already been addressed above, it will not be repeated here.

The third decree centered on the reasoning behind McKee's decision to have the area partitioned among the owners as established by Younger in his report rather than have the property auctioned in its entirety or in sections, as had been sought by both Frederick Hihn and Younger himself:

> *The Referee(s) have reported that the Augmentation is incapable of division except as to two of the claimants, namely Lyman John Burrell and James Taylor, and recommends that the shares of these two be set off to them and the remain-*

ing sold. There is no doubt of the power of the court to allot to such of the parties as can have their lands allotted to them their shares and to direct a sale of the residue which cannot be divided....

But we cannot, from the evidence, reach the conclusion that this property, a ranch containing about 32,702 acres, cannot be partitioned. And unless to be impracticable, or a sale will prove of greater benefit to the owner, the court will always decree a partition, and even where an equality of prejudice may exist to owner via partition and a sale, partition will be preferred.

Doubtless many difficulties will attend a partition of this ranch on account of the mountainous character of the property, but these cannot be allowed to control the legal and equitable right of the owners to have their respective interests segregated from each other.

A sale of so extensive a tract of country might prove advantageous to a few, but it might at the same time result with the prejudice of most and involve a sacrifice of the interests of some of the claimants. Apprehended difficulties of a partition may vanish or diminish before the reality of an effort, or be provided against or modified by the decree of the court, or for instance a right of way to portions where it may be impracticable to make roads may be decreed.

Some of the owners have made improvements before and since they acquired title; they are entitled to have their shares allotted to them so as to include their improvements if it can be done without prejudice to others; and this allotment might be made without taking these improvements or the value of them into consideration. If these improvements have been placed upon favorable localities of the ranch, shares, which have to be located so as to include them, will only have to be shown of their proportions to equalize them in the other shares, but these are matters for the Referee of Commissioners to be appointed to make partition, for it is them to take these things into consideration and determine the quantity and quality of the several shares into which the ranch is to be divided, and *equalize the shares. We therefore sustain the exceptions as to the sale and overrule the other exceptions filed to the report of the referee and order the same to be confirmed. And decrees of partition may be prepared accordingly.*

Two days after the release of his decision, on April 22, McKee entered into the record the following interlocutory decree regarding Rancho Soquel:

Henry W. Peck and Antonia Peck, his wife, as Plaintiffs, versus Frederick A. Hihn, Joseph Averon, Maria Guadalupe Averon, Joseph David Littlejohn, Ricardo Fourcade Juan, Maria Luisa Juan, Francisco Lajeunesse, Nicanor Lajeunesse, Joshua Parrish, Dr. John P. P. Vandenberg, Charles H. Willson, Miguel Lodge, Benjamin F. Porter, Thomas Fallon, Carmel Fallon, William Macondray and James Otis as Executor of the last will and testament of Frederick W. Macondray, and the heirs and devisees of Frederick W. Macondray, whose names are unknown, William Otis Andrews, Charles W. Plum, J. S. Reed, William Ireland, George H. Kirby, Thomas Courtis in his own right, Thomas Courtis as Administrator of Benjamin P. Green, deceased, Mary E. J. Slade, Henry Lawrence, Thomas Courtis as Administrator of John Ingoldsby, John Francis Llebaria, John Wilson, Cyrus Coe, George K. Porter, Pruitt Sinclair, [and] Augustus Noble, as Defendants.

The Report of Charles B. Younger, Referee in the above entitled cause, having been filed with the Clerk of the Court on the 17th day of August, 1861, and the several objections to the report of said Referee made by the defendants Frederick A. Hihn, Dr. John P. P. Vandenberg, Thomas Courtis in his individual right, Thomas Courtis, Administrator of John Ingoldsby, John Wilson, Mary E. J. Slade, Cyrus Coe, Henry W. Lawrence, and Charles Plum, having been argued and submitted at the December term of this court, A. D. 1861, and taken under advisement by the Court being sufficiently advised thereupon, it is considered, ordered, adjudged, and decreed by the Court that each and every of said objections be and the same are hereby overruled, and that said Report of the Referee be and the same are hereby in all things confirmed.

And it is further considered, adjudged, and decreed that the Plaintiffs Henry W. Peck and Antonia Peck, his wife, and the defendants Frederick A. Hihn, Joshua Parrish, Maria Guadalupe Averon, Maria Helena Littlejohn, Maria Luisa Juan, Benjamin F. Porter, George K. Porter, William Macondray and James Otis, as executors of the last will and testament of Frederick W. Macondray, deceased, and the heirs and devisees of Frederick W. Macondray, whose names are unknown, and Augustus Noble, are seized of in fee simple, and hold together and undivided, the tract of land described in the complaint, situated in the County of Santa Cruz, and State of California, known there as the Rancho Soquel, bounded on the southwest by the Bay of Monterey, on the northwest by the Soquel River, on the southeast by the Borregas Gulch, and on the northeast by the upper Soquel Ranch, so called, containing about 2,800 acres, more or less, being the same as surveyed under instructions from the United States Surveyor General for California, as the land called Soquel, confirmed to Martina Castro.

And it is further considered, adjudged, and decreed by the Court, that of the lands and tenements above described, the plaintiff Henry W. Peck is the owner of in fee simple, and is entitled to have set apart and assigned to him, one equal ninth part thereof, in severalty.

And that the plaintiff Maria Antonia Peck is the owner of in fee simple, as her own separate estate, and is entitled to have set apart and assigned to her, one equal ninth part thereof, in severalty.

And that the defendant Frederick A. Hihn is the owner of in fee simple, and is entitled to have set apart and assigned to him, 71/270th parts, in severalty.

And that the defendant Joshua Parrish is the owner of in fee simple, and is entitled to have set apart and assigned to him, one equal ninth part thereof, in severalty.

And that the defendant Maria Guadalupe Averon is the

owner of in fee simple, as of her own separate estate, and is entitled to have set off and assigned to her, one equal ninth part thereof, in severalty.

And that the defendant Maria Helena Littlejohn is the owner of in fee simple, as of her own separate estate, and is entitled to have set off and assigned to her, 2/27th parts thereof, in severalty.

And that the defendant Maria Luisa Juan is the owner of in fee simple, as of her own separate estate, and is entitled to have set apart and assigned to her, 2/27th parts of the said lands and tenements described in the Complaint, in severalty, and that of so much of the lands and tenements described in the Complaint as shall contain five acres, included within a certain fence separating the land whereon stands a certain tannery and buildings for the manufacture of leather on the north, east, and west from land occupied by the defendant Ricardo Fourcade Juan, on the south by the Santa Cruz and Watsonville road.

And that the defendant Benjamin F. Porter is the owner of in fee simple...and entitled to have set off and assigned to him, 1/9th part of the same, in severalty.

And that of the lands and tenements herein first described, and described in the Complaint, the defendants William Macondray and James Otis, as executors of the last will and testament of Frederick W. Macondray, deceased, and the heirs and devisees of Frederick W. Macondray, deceased, whose names are unknown, are the owners of in fee simple, and entitled to have set off and assigned to them, 19/540th parts of the same, in severalty.

And that the defendant Augustus Noble is the owner of in fee simple, and entitled to have set off and assigned to him, 1/12th part thereof, in severalty.

And that the defendant George K. Porter is the owner of in fee simple, and is entitled to have set off and assigned to him, 7/270th parts thereof, in severalty.

And it is further considered, adjudged, and decreed that the defendants Benjamin F. Porter, George K. Porter, the *plaintiffs Henry W. Peck and Antonia Peck, the defendants Frederick A. Hihn, Joshua Parrish, Luisa Juan, Guadalupe Averon, Helena Littlejohn, and Augustus Noble have each at their own proper costs and expense, made useful, permanent, and valuable improvements on said lands above described.*

And it is further considered, adjudged, and decreed that neither of the defendants, Joseph Averon, Joseph David Littlejohn, Ricardo Fourcade Juan, Dr. John P. P. Vandenberg, Miguel Lodge, Thomas Fallon, Carmel Fallon, Francisco Lajeunesse, Nicanor Lajeunesse, Pruit Sinclair, Charles H. Willson, William Ireland, William Otis Andrews, Charles W. Plum, J. S. Reed, George H. Kirby, Thomas Courtis in his own right, or Thomas Courtis as Administrator of Benjamin P. Green, deceased, Mary E. J. Slade, Henry Lawrence, Thomas Courtis as Administrator of John Ingoldsby, deceased, John Francis Llebaria, John Wilson, or Cyrus Coe, have any title, right, claim, or interest in the lands and tenements described in the Complaint, or any part thereof.

And it is further considered, adjudged, and decreed that all the lands so held in common between the plaintiffs and some of the defendants described in this decree, may be partitioned and divided without injury to the several rights and interests of the several owners thereof, and without the necessity of a sale thereof.

And it is further considered, adjudged, and decreed that partition and division of all of said lands described in this decree be made according to the respective rights of the parties therein, as the same have been ascertained and settled by this decree.

And it is further considered, adjudged, and decreed that Thomas W. Wright, of the County of Santa Cruz, Samuel Drennan, of the County of Santa Cruz, and Charles B. Younger, of the County of Santa Clara, be, and are hereby appointed and constituted Referees for the purpose of making such partition and division, that before proceeding to the execution of their duties as such, the said Referees shall be sev-

erally duly sworn before some officer authorized to administer oaths, honestly and impartially, to execute the trust reposed in them, and make partition and division as directed by this decree, and that such oath be filed with the Clerk of this Court.

And it is further considered, adjudged, and decreed that the said Referees shall partition and divide all of said lands described in the complaint and in this decree, and shall allot and set apart to the plaintiff Henry W. Peck, one equal 1/9th part thereof, quantity and quality relatively considered.

And to the plaintiff Maria Antonia Peck, one equal 1/9th part thereof, in the same manner.

And to the defendant Frederick A. Hihn, 71/270th parts thereof, in like manner.

And to the defendant Joshua Parrish, 1/9th part thereof, in like manner.

And to the defendant Maria Guadalupe Averon, 1/9th part thereof, in like manner.

And to the defendant Maria Helena Littlejohn, 2/27th parts thereof, in like manner.

And to the defendants William Macondray and James Otis, as executors of the last will and testament of Frederick W. Macondray, deceased, and the heirs and devisees of Frederick W. Macondray, deceased, whose names are unknown, 19/540th parts, thereof, in like manner.

And to the defendant Augustus Noble, 1/12th part thereof, in like manner.

And to the defendant George K. Porter, 7/270th parts thereof, in like manner.

And to the defendant Maria Luisa Juan, 2/27th parts thereof, in like manner, with the exception of five acres included, within a certain fence separating the lands whereof stands a certain tannery and buildings for the manufacture of leather, on the north, east, and west from land occupied by defendant Ricardo Juan, and on the south by the Santa Cruz and Watsonville road; and that the said five acres so excepted and described, that said Referees allot and set apart to the defendant Benjamin F. Porter, 1/9th part thereof, in *like manner.*

And it is further considered, adjudged, and decreed that in making such division and partition, the said Referee shall not take into consideration the value of any improvements erected, standing, or being on any portion of said lands and premises; and that so far as the same can be done without injustice to any of the parties..., the said Referees shall set apart and allot to each of the aforesaid parties, the lands on which each of them have permanent and valuable improvements, fences excepted.

And it is further considered, adjudged and decreed that the said Referees shall designate the parts and portions so allotted, and set apart to each of said parties, by proper description and monuments.

And it is further considered, adjudged, and decreed that said Referees all meet together in the making of said partition and division; and that they make a full and ample report of their doings and proceedings to this Court, at the next term thereof, or as soon thereafter as is practicable for them so to do, under their hands and seals, or under the hands and seals of any two of them, specifying therein the manner in which they shall have executed this deed, and describing the lots and shares allotted to each party, with the quantity, sources and distances of each, with the descriptions of the courses, stakes and moments thereof, and a map designating and delineating the lots and portions set apart to each by name, and the items of their charges and expenses in executing this decree. That the said Referees, or such two of them as shall execute said report acknowledge the same, or cause it to be proved in the manner conveyances are required to be acknowledged or proved by law, and that such report be filed in the office of the Clerk of this Court.

And it is further considered, adjudged, and decreed that the said Referees be authorized and directed to employ a surveyor, and to cause all necessary surveys and maps to be made, to execute this decree; and that all the parties to this cause shall produce to and have with the said Referees, for such time as the *said Referees shall deem reasonable, all deeds, writings, surveys or maps relating to the said premises, or any part thereof.*

And it is further considered, adjudged, and decreed that the Clerk of the Court issue to the said Referees, a certified copy of this decree, attached to a commission, directing them to execute the provisions thereof.

In witness whereof, I have hereunto set my hand in open Court this 22nd day of April, 1863.

District Judge Samuel B. McKee

The release of this decree was followed at the same time by a similar decree regarding the Augmentation:

Frederick A. Hihn, as Plaintiff, versus Henry W. Peck, Maria Antonia Peck, Joseph David Littlejohn, Maria Helena Littlejohn, Ricardo Fourcade Juan, Maria Luisa Juan, Joseph Averon, Maria Guadalupe Averon, Frederick C. Hihn, Augustus Noble, Roger Gibson Hinckley, John Lafayette Shelby, George K. Porter, Cyrus Coe, Richard Savage, Benjamin Farley, Craven P. Hester, Cassimero Amayo, Daria Amayo, Pruitt Sinclair, William Ireland, J. S. Reed, George H. Kirby, Henry F. Parsons, Francis R. Brady, Benjamin Cahoon Nichols, Luther Farnham as Administrator of the Estate of Joel Bates, John P. Stearns, Francis M. Kittridge, Asa W. Rawson, Lyman John Burrell, H. B. Holmes, Benjamin F. Porter, William Macondray and James Otis as Executor of the last will and testament of Frederick W. Macondray, and the heirs and devisees of Frederick W. Macondray, whose names are unknown, Christian Miller, Miguel Lodge, Nicanor Lajeunesse, Henry Cambustan, Joaquin Boledo, John Wilson, George W. Evans, James Taylor, Archbishop Joseph Sadoc Alemany, Thomas Fallon, Carmel Fallon, Charles H. Willson, John Francis Llebaria, Mary E. J. Slade, Charles W. Plum, Henry W. Lawrence, Thomas Courtis in his own right, Thomas Courtis as Administrator of Benjamin P. Green, Thomas Courtis as

Administrator of John Ingoldsby, John Wilson, William Otis Andrews, [and] Francisco Lajeunesse, as Defendants.

The Report of Charles B. Younger, Referee in the above entitled cause, having been filed with the Clerk of the Court on the 22nd day of August, 1861, and the several objections to the report of said Referee made by the plaintiff Frederick A. Hihn and by the defendants Richard Savage, Joel Bates (deceased), Francis R. Brady, Benjamin Cahoon Nichols, George H. Kirby, John P. Stearns, Thomas Courtis in his own right, Thomas Courtis as Administrator of the Benjamin P. Green and John Ingoldsby estates (both deceased), John Wilson, Mary E. K. Slade, Cyrus Coe, Henry W. Lawrence, Charles Plum, Augustus Noble, Craven P. Hester, and Benjamin Farley having been argued and submitted at the December term of this Court, A.D. 1861, and taken under advisement by the Court, being sufficiently advised thereupon, it is considered, ordered, adjudged, and decreed by the Court that each and every of said objections be and the same are hereby overruled, and that said Report of the Referee be and the same are hereby in all things confirmed.

And the objections, having been submitted at the April term of this court starting in 1862, and taken under advisement by the Court, being sufficiently advised, thereupon it is considered, ordered, adjudged, and decreed by the Court that the objections to the Report of the Referee Younger by the defendants Craven P. Hester and Benjamin Farley, that the said Referee should have found and reported by said Report, that the lands and testaments described in the complaint was and is susceptible of a partition. Whereas the Referee found and reported that the same should be sold.... And that so much of the report of the Referee as finds and reports to the Court the several titles, rights, and entrust of the respective parties to this suit in the lands described in the Complaint be and the same is surely confirmed.

And it is further considered, adjudged, and decreed that the Plaintiff Frederick A. Hihn and the defendants Carmel Fallon, Maria Antonia Peck, Maria Helena Littlejohn,

Maria Guadalupe Averon, Maria Luisa Juan, Henry Peck, George W. Evans, Cassimero Amayo, Dario Amayo, Lyman Burrell, Luther Farnham as Administrator of the estate of Joel Bates and the heirs of Joel Bates, Francis R. Brady, Benjamin Cahoon Nichols, Richard Savage, Roger Gibson Hinckley, John Lafayette Shelby, Craven P. Hester, Benjamin Farley, James Taylor, George K. Porter, William Macondray and James Otis as executors of the last will and testament of Frederick W. Macondray and his unknown heirs, [and] Augustus Noble are seized of in fee simple, and hold together and undivided, the tract of land described in the complaint, situated in the County of Santa Cruz, and State of California, known there as the Soquel Augmentation Rancho, bounded by a line commencing at the northwest corner of the Soquel Ranch, and running up the Soquel River to the place known as Palo de la Yeska; thence to the Laguna Sarjento; thence to and including the Loma Prieta; thence to the Chuchitas; thence to the Cuatro Leguas; thence to the northwest corner of Aptos Ranch; thence to the northeast corner of the Soquel Ranch; and thence to the place of beginning, containing thirty-two thousand seven hundred and two acres, more or less, being the same as surveyed under instructions from the United States Surveyor General for California, as the land called Shoquel, confirmed to Martina Castro.

And it is further considered, adjudged, and decreed by the Court, that of the lands and tenements above described, the plaintiff Frederick A. Hihn is the owner of in fee simple, and is entitled to have set apart and assigned to him, 12/90th parts thereof, in severalty.

And that the defendant Maria Antonia Peck is the owner of in fee simple, as her own separate estate, and is entitled to have set apart and assigned to her, one equal ninth part thereof, in severalty.

And that the defendant Maria Helena Littlejohn is the owner of in fee simple, as her own separate estate, and is entitled to have set apart and assigned to her, 2/27th parts thereof, in severalty.

And that the defendant Maria Guadalupe Averon is the owner of in fee simple, as her own separate estate, and is entitled to have set apart and assigned to her, one equal ninth part thereof, in severalty.

And that the defendant Carmel Fallon is the owner of in fee simple, as her own separate estate, and is entitled to have set apart and assigned to her, one equal ninth part thereof, in severalty.

And that the defendant Maria Luisa Juan is the owner of in fee simple, as her own separate estate, and is entitled to have set apart and assigned to her, 1/27th part thereof, in severalty.

And that the defendant Henry Peck is the owner of in fee simple, and is entitled to have set apart and assigned to him, 2/27th parts thereof, in severalty.

And that the defendant George W. Evans is the owner of in fee simple, and is entitled to have set apart and assigned to him, 1/18th part thereof, in severalty.

And that the defendants Casimero and Dario Amayo are the owners of in fee simple, and are entitled to have set apart and assigned to them, 1/27th part thereof, in severalty.

And that the defendant Lyman John Burrell is the owner of in fee simple, and is entitled to have set apart and assigned to him, 1/27th part thereof, in severalty.

And that the deceased defendant Joel Bates is the owner of in fee simple, and is entitled to have set apart and assigned to his estate, 1/27th part thereof, in severalty.

And that the defendants Francis R. Brady and Benjamin Cahoon Nichols are the owners of in fee simple, and are entitled to have set apart and assigned to them, 1/54th parts thereof, in severalty.

And that the defendant Richard Savage is the owner of in fee simple, and is entitled to have set apart and assigned to him, 1/96th part thereof, in severalty.

And that the defendants Roger Gibson Hinckley and John Lafayette Shelby are the owners of in fee simple, and are entitled to have set apart and assigned to them, 1/36th parts thereof, in severalty.

And that the defendant Craven P. Hester…is the owner of in fee simple, and is entitled to have set apart and assigned to his estate, 1/48th part thereof, in severalty.

And that the defendant Benjamin Farley is the owner of in fee simple, and is entitled to have set apart and assigned to him, 1/48th part thereof, in severalty.

And that the defendant James Taylor is the owner of in fee simple, and is entitled to have set apart and assigned to his estate, 1/54th part thereof, in severalty.

And that the defendant George K. Porter is the owner of in fee simple, and is entitled to have set apart and assigned to his estate 7/270th parts thereof, in severalty.

And that the defendant Augustus Noble is the owner of in fee simple, and is entitled to have set apart and assigned to his estate 1/540th and 1/288th parts thereof, in severalty.

And that the defendants William Macondray and James Otis, as executors of the last will and testament of Frederick W. Macondray, deceased, and the heirs and devisees of Frederick W. Macondray, deceased, whose names are unknown, are the owners of in fee simple, and are entitled to have set apart and assigned to their estate, 1/30th parts thereof, in severalty.

And it is further considered, adjudged, and decreed that neither of the defendants, Joseph David Littlejohn, Ricardo Fourcade Juan, Joseph Averon, Frederick C. Hihn, Cyrus Coe, George H. Kirby, Henry F. Parsons, John P. Stearns, Francis M. Kittridge, Asa W. Rawson, H. B. Holmes, Benjamin F. Porter, Christian Miller, Henry Cambustan, Joaquin Boledo, John Wilson, Father John Llebaria, Thomas Fallon, Charles H. Willson, Archbishop Joseph Sadoc Alemany, Mary E. J. Slade, Charles W. Plum, Henry W. Lawrence, Thomas Courtis in his own behalf, [or] Thomas Courtis as Administrator of the John Ingoldsby and Benjamin P. Green estates have any title right, claim, or entrust in the lands and tenements described in the Complaint or any part thereof.

And it is further considered, adjudged, and decreed that all the lands so held in common between the plaintiff and some of the defendants described in this decree, may be par-

titioned and divided without injury to the several rights and entrust of the several owners thereof or any of them, and without the necessity of a sale thereof.

And it is further considered, adjudged, and decreed that partition and division of all the lands in this decree be made according to the respective rights of the parties therein as the same has been ascertained and settled by this decree.

And it is further considered, adjudged, and decreed that Samuel Dunnan of this county of Santa Cruz, Charles B. Younger of the county of Santa Clara, and David J. Haslam of the county of Santa Cruz be and are hereby appointed and constituted referees for the purpose of making such partition and division before providing to the execution of this decree as such the said referees there by being duly sworn before some officer authorized to administer such oath honestly and impartially to execute the trust, respect in them and to make partition and division as directed by this decree, and that such oath be filed with the clerk of this Court.

And it is further considered, adjudged, and decreed that the referees shall partition and divide all of said lands described in the complaint and in this decree, and shall allot and set apart to the plaintiff Frederick A. Hihn 12/90th parts thereof, quantity and quality relatively considered.

And to the defendant Maria Antonia Peck, 1/9th part thereof, quantity and quality relatively considered.

And to the defendant Maria Helena Littlejohn, 2/27th parts thereof, quantity and quality _not_ relatively considered.

And to the defendant Maria Guadalupe Averon, 1/9th part thereof, quantity and quality relatively considered.

And to the defendant Carmel Fallon, 1/9th part thereof, quantity and quality relatively considered.

And to the defendant Maria Luisa Juan, 1/27th part thereof, quantity and quality relatively considered.

And to the defendant Henry Peck, 2/27th parts thereof, quantity and quality relatively considered.

And to the defendant George W. Evans, 1/18th part thereof, quantity and quality relatively considered.

And to the defendants Casimero and Daria Amayo, 1/27th part thereof, quantity and quality relatively considered.

And to the defendant Lyman John Burrell, 1/27th part thereof, quantity and quality relatively considered.

And to the defendant Joel Bates, deceased, 1/27th part thereof, quantity and quality not relatively considered.

And to the defendants Francis R. Brady and Benjamin Cahoon Nichols, 1/54th part thereof, quantity and quality relatively considered.

And to the defendant Richard Savage, 1/96th part thereof, quantity and quality relatively considered.

And to the defendants Roger Gibson Hinckley and John Lafayette Shelby, 1/36th part thereof, quantity and quality not relatively considered.

And to the defendant Craven P. Hester, 1/48th part thereof, quantity and quality relatively considered.

And to the defendant Benjamin Farley, 1/48th part thereof, quantity and quality relatively considered.

And to the defendant James Taylor, 1/54th part thereof, quantity and quality relatively considered.

And to the defendant George K. Porter, 7/270th parts thereof, quantity and quality relatively considered.

And to the defendant Augustus Noble, 1/540th and 1/288th parts thereof, quantity and quality relatively considered.

And to the defendants William Macondray and James Otis, as executors of the last will and testament of Frederick W. Macondray, deceased, and the heirs and devisees of Frederick W. Macondray, deceased, whose names are unknown, 1/30th part thereof, quantity and quality relatively considered.

That all of the above percentages shall be adhered to as close as possible in the opinion of the referees, that their decisions shall be done without prejudice to the entrust of any of the other of said parties' interests...but...if in the opinion of the referees, then entrust of all the parties who are found in said lands by this decree may be subserved by setting off to any and or other of said parties, a quantity of land greater than his equal proportion thereof quantity and quality relatively considered, as found and ascertained by the decree then the referees shall report to allot and set off to such party or parties so much of said lands as shall in the opinion of the referees be for the best interests of all the parties interests therein as found and ascertained by this decree.

And it is further considered, adjudged, and decreed that in making such division and partition the referees shall not take into consideration the value of any improvements erected standing or being on any portion of the lands and premises and that so far as the same can be done...injustice to any of the other parties interested. The referees shall set apart and allot to each of the aforesaid parties the lands upon which each of them has permanent and valuable improvements, roads and fences are excepted.

And it is further considered, adjudged, and decreed that the referees shall designate the parts and portions so awarded and set apart to each of the parties by proper descriptions and designations in order to identify the areas awarded to each individual.

And it is further considered, adjudged, and decreed that the referees all must take this in the making of said partition and division and that they make a full and ample report of their doings and proceedings to this Court at the next term thereof or as soon thereafter as is practicable for them so to do under these hands and seals or under the hands and seals of any two of them, specifying therein the manner in which they shall have executed this decree and describing the lots and shares assigned to each party.

And it is further considered, adjudged, and decreed that the said Referees be authorized and directed to employ a surveyor, and to cause all necessary surveys and maps to be made, to execute this decree; and that all the parties to this cause shall produce to and have with the said Referees, for such time as the said Referees shall deem reasonable, all deeds, writings, sur-

veys or maps relating to the said premises, or any part thereof.

And it is further considered, adjudged, and decreed that the Clerk of the Court issue to the said Referees a certified copy of this decree, attached to a commission, directing them to execute the provisions thereof.

In witness whereof, I have hereunto set my hand in open Court this 22nd day of April, 1863.

District Judge Samuel B. McKee

The term "quantity and quality relatively considered" was chosen by McKee to clarify that, as the quality of the land diminished, the quantity should be increased by a factor calculated as fair by the referees. For example, Carmel Fallon had a 1/9 claim to the Augmentation—approximately 3,634 acres—but the quality of that land was so poor that the referees eventually granted her approximately 6,845 acres, nearly twice her claimed portion. In contrast, Guadalupe Averon also had a 1/9 claim to the Augmentation, but was only granted 1,308 acres because it was of a substantially higher quality and more accessible.

The next day, McKee released two partitioning decrees, outlining the manner in which Rancho Soquel and the Augmentation would be partitioned among their various owners and claimants, some of whom claimed joint or common title. Their wordings were nearly identical to the interlocutory decrees except in both decrees, some of the referees were replaced: in the Rancho Soquel decree, Wright and Drennan were replaced by Daniel Tuttle and Joseph Rufner (Younger remained the third referee); in the Augmentation decree, Dunnan, Haslam, and Younger were replaced by Wright, John W. Towne, and Godfrey M. Bockius.

In addition, three specific items were changed between the two decrees, all dealing with claims within the Augmentation:

And it is further considered, adjudged, and decreed that the defendants Roger Gibson Hinckley and John Lafayette Shelby have a good and valid lien upon the right and title and interest of the defendant Richard Savage in the lands and tenements described in the complaint by the mortgage executed

December 10, 1859 to secure the payment of $1,800 by said defendant Richard Savage to the said defendants Hinckley and Shelby, the whole of which amount together with the interest thereon from September 1, 1860, at 10% per annum is now due and payable....

And it is further considered, adjudged, and decreed that the defendants Francis R. Brady and Benjamin Cahoon Nichols, Richard Savage, James Taylor, Lyman Burrell, Luther Farnham as administrator of the estate of Joel Bates, deceased, Craven P. Hester, and Benjamin Farley have each upon said lands and tenements useful permanent and valuable improvements made at their own proper cost and expense of each of them and by his grantors....

And it is further considered, adjudged, and decreed that the defendants Roger Gibson Hinckley John Lafayette Shelby, and all parties claiming by, through, or under them the commencement of the suit, take and have their liens, mortgages, and claims as found by this decree upon the share which shall be allotted and set apart to the defendant Richard Savage, and that they shall have no lien mortgage or claims upon any other portion of the premises described in this decree.[429]

Land transfer by George Evans to John Daubenbiss

On April 22, 1863, George Evans sold the 1/18 claim to Shoquel Augmentation that he had purchased from Jones Hoy in December 1860 to John Daubenbiss. This was the same claim that Frederick Hihn was contesting due to his deed with Charles Willson signed in April 1861. In the Younger Report, it was declared that Hihn had only purchased land in Rancho Soquel, not the Augmentation.[430]

Land transfers by Benjamin Nichols and Francis Brady to Benjamin Cahoon

On April 29, 1863, Benjamin Nichols sold his half of the 1/54 portion of Shoquel Augmentation that he shared with Francis Brady, as well as the approximately 600 acres that he personally owned on adjacent land, all within the vicinity of Laurel Glen Road and the Soquel Turnpike (today's Soquel San Jose Road) to his uncle, Benjamin Cahoon. Included in this deed was his half-ownership to land in downtown Santa Cruz and a sawmill on Soquel Creek, with its accompanying structures and machinery. Exactly a month later, on May 29, Brady also sold his interest to Cahoon.[431]

John Vandenberg replaces his attorney while preparing for his appeal to the California Supreme Court

Immediately after Judge McKee issued his decrees regarding the Rancho Soquel Partitioning Suit in April 1863, John Vandenberg began preparing his appeal. He fiercely contested the findings in the Younger Report that the deed sold to him by Nicanor and Francisco Lajeunesse was void because Frederick Hihn had purchased the same claim. On August 7, Vandenberg replaced his attorney, L. Archer, with Messrs. Sloan and Provines, and the Third District Court approved this change on August 18.[432]

Partitioning Commission decree issued by Judge McKee

A Partitioning Commission decree issued by Judge McKee on August 17, 1863, was nearly identical to the previous two decrees issued in April regarding Rancho Soquel. The only significant difference was the conclusion, which reads:

> *By which it was among other things adjudged that a partition of the premises described in the complaint in this cause should be made between the plaintiffs and defendants in equal portions, quality and quantity relatively considered, and whereas it was in the same decree further ordered that a commission issue out of and under the seal of said court to you to be divided authorizing and directing you to act in the premises for the purpose of carrying the said decree into effect.*
>
> *Now therefore know ye that, confiding in your prudence and discretion, we have assigned and appointed said Daniel Tuttle, Joseph Rufner, and Charles B. Younger referees for*

> *the purpose mentioned in the said decree, and do give you full power and authority to make partition of the premises in said decree, set forth and described between said plaintiffs and the said defendants, according to their respective rights and interests therein, as the same has been ascertained, declared, determined, and adjudged in and by the decree aforesaid, a copy of which decree for your information is hereunto annexed to and made a part hereof and the decree to enable you to make the partition and perform the duties in the said decree directed, you are hereby authorized and empowered to enter into and upon the premises and view the said premises and every or any part thereof together with such surveyors and assistants as you may deem necessary and to survey the same or cause the same to be surveyed for the purpose aforesaid, and that you make a report under your hands and seals to our said court of your proceedings by virtue hereto without unnecessary delay.*
>
> Witness: Honorable Samuel B. McKee,
> Judge of Santa Cruz
>
> and the seal of said Court hereto affixed
> this 17th day of August, 1863
> signed by David J. Haslam
> Clerk of the Court

The same day, a Partitioning Commission decree was also issued for Shoquel Augmentation, with the conclusion once again being the primary difference from the previous decrees. It reads:

> *By which it was among other things adjudged that a partition of the premises described in the complaint in this cause should be made between the plaintiff and defendants in equal portions, quality and quantity relatively considered, and whereas it was in the same decree further ordered that a commission issue out of and under the seal of the said court to you to be divided authorizing and directing you to act in the*

premises for the purpose of carrying the said decree into effect.

Now therefore know ye that, confiding in your prudence and discretion, we have assigned and appointed said Thomas W. Wright, John W. Towne, and Godfrey M. Bockius referees for the purpose mentioned in the said decree and do give you full power and authority to make partition of the premises in said decree set forth and described between said plaintiff and the said defendants, according to their respective rights and interests therein, as the same has been ascertained, declared, determined, and adjudged in and by the decree aforesaid, a copy of which decree for your information is hereunto annexed to and made a part hereof and the decree to enable you to make the partition and perform the duties in the said decree directed, you are hereby authorized and empowered to enter into and upon the premises and view the said premises and every or any part thereof together with such surveyors and assistants as you may deem necessary and to survey the same or cause the same to be surveyed for the purpose aforesaid, and that you make a report under your hands and seals to our said court of your proceedings by virtue hereto without unnecessary delay.

Witness: Honorable Samuel B. McKee,
Judge of Santa Cruz

and the seal of said Court affixed
this 17th day of August, 1863
signed by David J. Haslam,
Clerk of the Court[433]

John Daubenbiss files his deed with the Third District Court

On August 20, 1863, John Daubenbiss filed with the Third District Court his deed of ownership for 1/18 of Shoquel Augmentation that he had purchased from George Evans on April 22, 1863. This is the same land to which Frederick Hihn asserted a claim.[434]

Robert Peckham's term as judge ends

With the majority of his cases in Santa Cruz County nearly completed and his one-year term as county judge at an end, Robert Peckham reopened his law office in San José in November 1863. He joined in partnership with Judge Payne two years later, and they remained partners until 1870. During this time, their firm was considered one of the best legal teams in Santa Clara County.[435]

Land transfer by John Daubenbiss to the Chase Brothers

On December 1, 1863, John Daubenbiss sold all of his 1/18 claim to Shoquel Augmentation, except for 300 acres, to Stephen and Joseph Chase.[436]

Partitioning report for Rancho Soquel submitted by Charles Younger, Daniel Tuttle, and Joseph Rufner

On December 22, 1863, Charles Younger, Daniel Tuttle, and Joseph Rufner submitted the following partitioning report for Rancho Soquel:

> *Now the Referees Charles B. Younger, David Tuttle, and Joseph Rufner, appointed under and by the several decrees by this Court, made and entered in this cause, on April 22 and 23 of 1863 A.D. and on the 31st day of August, 1863 A.D., to make partition of the lands and tenements described in the complaint as follows:*
>
> *A certain tract of land situated in the County of Santa Cruz, and State of California, known there as the Rancho Soquel, bounded on the southwest by the Bay of Monterey, on the northwest by the Soquel River, on the southeast by the Borregas Gulch, and on the northeast by the upper Soquel Ranch, so called, containing about 2,800 acres, more or less, being the same as surveyed under instructions from the United States Surveyor General for California, as the land called Soquel, confirmed to Martina Castro, having made and filed with the Clerk of this Court, on the 22nd day of*

December A.D. 1863, a full, true and correct report of the proceedings under said decree, wherein they reported to this Court:

That, having been first duly sworn, they carefully examined the rancho in said commission mentioned, to wit.

That certain tract of land lying and being situated in the Township of Soquel, in the County of Santa Cruz, in the State of California, and known as the Rancho Soquel, and bounded on the south by the Bay of Monterey, on the west by the Soquel River, on the east by the Sanjon de la Borregas, and on the north by the Soquel Augmentation Rancho, being the same patented by the United States, to Martina Castro, and have caused the said Rancho Soquel to be surveyed by Thomas W. Wright, and divided into several parcels as hereafter mentioned, and have made partition thereof, between plaintiffs Henry W. Peck and Antonia Peck, his wife, and the defendants Frederick A. Hihn, Joshua Parrish, Guadalupe Averon, Helena Littlejohn, Luisa Juan, Benjamin F. Porter, William Macondray and James Otis, as executors of the last will and testament of Frederick W. Macondray, deceased, and the heirs and devisees of said Frederick W. Macondray, whose names are unknown, and Augustus Noble, according to their several respective rights, interests, and estates therein, as the same, have been by this Court ascertained, declared, determined, and adjudged, have been designated the parcels set apart in severalty, to the respective parties by proper descriptions and monuments, as we were by said commission commanded in manner following, to wit:

We have divided said Rancho Soquel into twenty parcels, which are respectively designated by the letters Ⓐ, Ⓑ, Ⓒ, Ⓓ, Ⓔ, Ⓕ, Ⓖ, Ⓗ, Ⓘ, Ⓚ, Ⓛ, Ⓜ, Ⓝ, Ⓞ, Ⓟ, Ⓡ, Ⓢ, Ⓣ, Ⓥ, and Ⓦ on the map of the Rancho Soquel hereto attached and annexed, and herein referred to, and made a part, and marked Exhibit "B," that being in our judgment, the most equal partition, quantity and quality relatively considered, that could be made of said Rancho Soquel.

And they do further report, that for the accommodation

of the several parties herein, we have marked out and set apart, and have not assigned or set off to any one, the following mentioned roads, which are to be kept open for travel and use, to wit:

A road called the County Road [Soquel Drive]

A 33-foot wide road called Ricardo Lane [the northern portion of Cabrillo College Drive]

A 33-foot wide road called Nobles Lane [Capitola Avenue between Bay Avenue and Soquel Drive]

A 40-foot wide road called Hihn's Lane [Bay Avenue and Porter Street]

And they do further report, that for the better understanding and education of the shape and location of said Rancho Soquel, and the several parcels into which we have partitioned the same, and of the several roads herein before referred to, and of the manner in which we have partitioned said Rancho Soquel, we have caused to be made by Thomas W. Wright, by whom the same was surveyed, a map of said Rancho Soquel, designating and delineating what parcels thereof have been by us set off in severalty to the respective parties herein, as we were commanded by the said commission and by the decree of this Court therein referred to and made a part thereof, and is hereunto attached and annexed and marked as Exhibit "B."

And they do further report, that any of the parties to whom portions of said Rancho Soquel have been set apart as aforesaid, who have fences on any part of said Rancho Soquel that have been set off to another, are to be allowed to remove such fences.

Exhibit A

Present and previous owners living in Santa Cruz County: Frederick A. Hihn, Joseph Averon, Guadalupe Averon, Joseph David Littlejohn, Helena Littlejohn, Ricardo Fourcade Juan, George H. Kirby, Luisa Juan, Joshua Parrish, Dr. John P. P. Vandenberg, Miguel Antonio Lodge, Benjamin F. Porter, George K. Porter, Francisco Lajeunesse, Nicanor Lajeunesse, Pruitt Sinclair, [and] Augustus Noble.

Present and previous owners living in Santa Clara

Road to Partition 1863

County: Thomas Fallon [and] Carmel Fallon.
Present and previous owners living in Marin County: Charles H. Willson.
Present and previous owners living in San Francisco

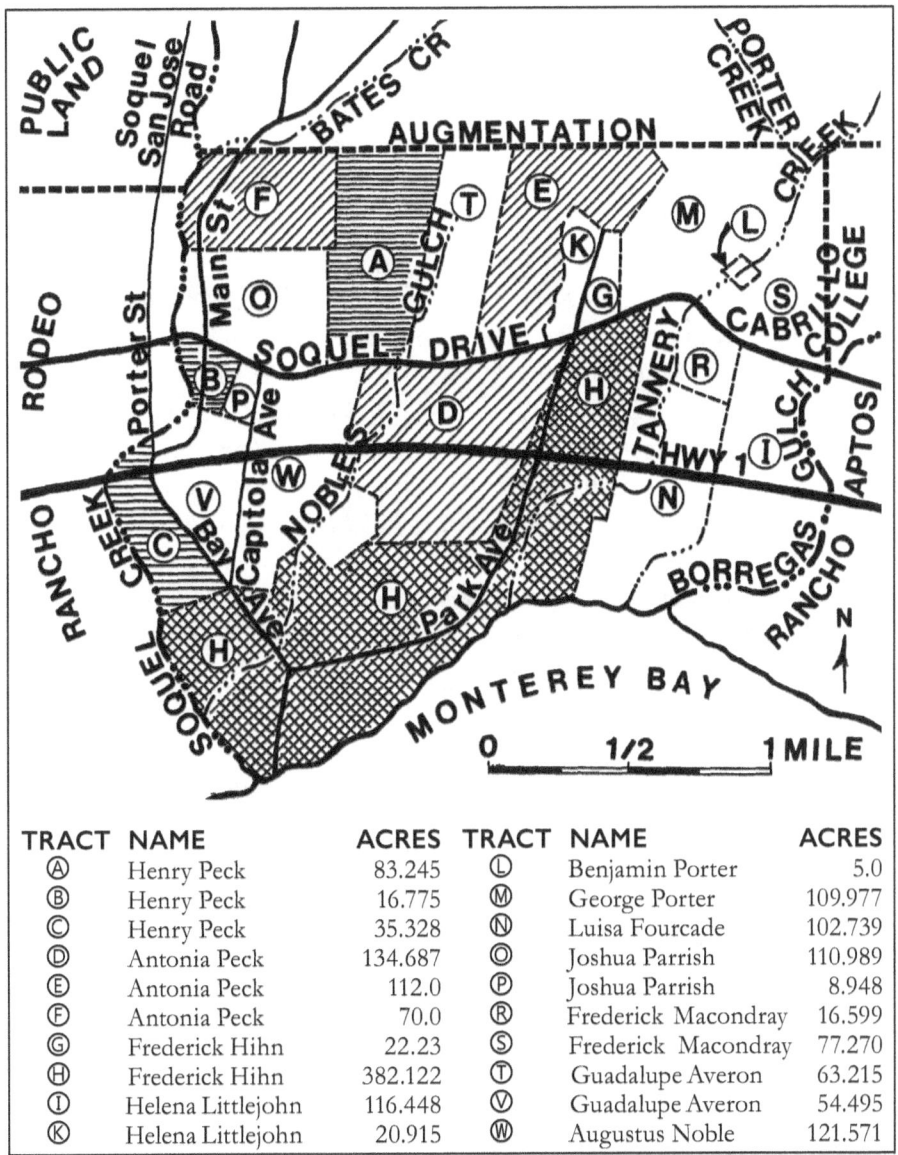

TRACT	NAME	ACRES	TRACT	NAME	ACRES
Ⓐ	Henry Peck	83.245	Ⓛ	Benjamin Porter	5.0
Ⓑ	Henry Peck	16.775	Ⓜ	George Porter	109.977
Ⓒ	Henry Peck	35.328	Ⓝ	Luisa Fourcade	102.739
Ⓓ	Antonia Peck	134.687	Ⓞ	Joshua Parrish	110.989
Ⓔ	Antonia Peck	112.0	Ⓟ	Joshua Parrish	8.948
Ⓕ	Antonia Peck	70.0	Ⓡ	Frederick Macondray	16.599
Ⓖ	Frederick Hihn	22.23	Ⓢ	Frederick Macondray	77.270
Ⓗ	Frederick Hihn	382.122	Ⓣ	Guadalupe Averon	63.215
Ⓘ	Helena Littlejohn	116.448	Ⓥ	Guadalupe Averon	54.495
Ⓚ	Helena Littlejohn	20.915	Ⓦ	Augustus Noble	121.571

FIGURE 6.7 RANCHO SOQUEL PARTITIONED TRACTS

County: William Ireland, William Macondray and James Otis as Executors of the last will and testament of Frederick W. Macondray, Henry Lawrence, William Otis Andrews, Charles W. Plum, Thomas Courtis as Administrator of John Ingoldsby, J. S. Reed, Thomas Courtis as Administrator of Benjamin P. Green, Thomas Courtis on his own behalf, [and] Mary E. J. Slade.

Submitted, as part of this Exhibit "A," is the following bill of surveyor and referees: Thomas W. Wright (for surveying, calculating, and mapping), $757; Daniel Tuttle (Referee), $247; Charles Bruce Younger (Referee), $240; Joseph Ruffner (Referee): $161, Charles Bruce Younger (for writing the report): $130—total: $1,535.

Submitted, as part of this Exhibit "A," are the following individual bills for each portion of the above bill: Joshua Parrish, $170.55; Guadalupe Averon, $170.55; Antonia Peck, $170.55; Henry W. Peck, $170.55; Helena Littlejohn, $113.70; Luisa Juan, $109.09; Benjamin F. Porter, $4.63; Frederick A. Hihn, $403.65; George K. Porter, $49.80; Frederick W. Macondray's Estate, $54.01; Augustus Noble, $127.92.

Each individual's final ownership awarded to him or her shall not be registered until the money they owe to the referees and surveyor is paid in full.

Exhibit B

Henry W. Peck, the plaintiff, is awarded the following three lots:

- Ⓐ *totalling 83.245 acres*
- Ⓑ *totalling 16.775 acres*
- Ⓒ *totalling 35.328 acres*

Antonia Peck, the plaintiff, is awarded the following three lots:

- Ⓓ *totalling 134.687 acres*
- Ⓔ *totalling 112 acres*
- Ⓕ *totalling 80 acres*

[Note: The acreage of the Pecks was at the time of this report under the ownership of Hihn due to the deed they signed with him in April 1862.]

Frederick A. Hihn, a defendant, is awarded the following two lots:
 Ⓖ *totalling 22.23 acres*
 Ⓗ *totalling 382.122 acres*

[Note: When combined with the Pecks' land, Hihn owned a total of 856.387 acres, or 52.34 percent of Rancho Soquel.]

Helena Littlejohn, a defendant, is awarded the following two lots:
 Ⓘ *totalling 116.448 acres*
 Ⓚ *totalling 20.915 acres*

Benjamin F. Porter, a defendant, is awarded a total of 5 acres, designated as follows:
 Ⓛ *totalling 5 acres*

George K. Porter, a defendant, is awarded the following lot:
 Ⓜ *totalling 109.977 acres*

Luisa Juan, a defendant, is awarded the following lot:
 Ⓝ *totalling 102.739 acres*

Joshua Parrish, a defendant, is awarded the following two lots:
 Ⓞ *totalling 110.989 acres*
 Ⓟ *totalling 8.948 acres*

William Macondray, a defendant and administrator for the deceased Frederick W. Macondray, is awarded the following two lots:
 Ⓡ *totalling 16.599 acres*
 Ⓢ *totalling 77.270 acres*

Guadalupe Averon, a defendant, is awarded the following two lots:
- Ⓣ *totalling 63.215 acres*
- Ⓥ *totalling 54.495 acres*

Augustus Noble, a defendant, is awarded the following lot:
- Ⓦ *totalling 121.571 acres*[437]

Partitioning report for Shoquel Augmentation submitted by Thomas Wright, John Towne, and Godfrey Bockius

Following in the footsteps of the Rancho Soquel partitioning report, the report for Shoquel Augmentation was delivered by Thomas Wright, John Towne, and Godfrey Bockius on December 23, 1863:

> *In pursuance of, and in obedience to the Commission dated August 17, 1863, which is here attached and annexed and made a part hereof in the Soquel Augmentation partitioning suit, better known as the Hihn vs. Peck, et al., suit, issued out of and under the seal of this Court and delivered and directed to Thomas W. Wright, John W. Towne, and Godfrey M. Bockius as Referees therein named the day of August 17, 1863, we Thomas W. Wright, John W. Towne, and Godfrey M. Bockius do report to the Court as follows, to wit:*
>
> *That having been first duly sworn, we carefully examined the Rancho in said commission mentioned to wit: that certain tract of land lying and being situated in the State of California and in the counties of Santa Cruz and Santa Clara, known thereas the Augmentation to the Soquel Ranch, bounded by a line commencing at the northwest corner of the Soquel Ranch so called, and running up the Soquel River to a place known as the Palo de la Yesca; thence to the Laguna del Sargento; thence to and including the Loma Prieta; thence to the Chuchitas; thence to the Cuatro Legues; thence to the northwest corner of the Aptos Rancho; thence to the northeast corner of the Soquel Rancho; and from thence to the place of beginning, containing 32,702 acres more or less.*

And we have caused the said Rancho to be surveyed by Thomas W. Wright and divided into several parcels as herein after mentioned and have made partition thereof between the Plaintiff, Frederick A. Hihn, and the Defendants, Carmel Fallon, Guadalupe Averon, Antonia Peck, Helena Littlejohn, Luisa Juan, Henry W. Peck, George W. Evans, Casimero Amayo, Dario Amayo, Lyman John Burrell, Luther Farnham as Administrator of the estate of Joel Bates, deceased, and the heirs of the said Joel Bates whose names are unknown, Francis R. Brady, Benjamin Cahoon Nichols, Richard Savage, Roger Gibson Hinckley, John Lafayette Shelby, Craven P. Hester, Benjamin Farley, James Taylor, George K. Porter, William Macondray and James Otis as Executors of the last will and testament of Frederick W. Macondray, deceased and the heirs or devisees of Frederick W. Macondray, deceased, whose names are unknown, and Augustus Noble, according to their several respective rights, interests, and estates therein as the same have been by this Court ascertained, declared, determined, and adjudged. And have designated the parcels so set apart in severalty to the respective parties by proper descriptions and monuments as we were by said Commission commanded in manner following, to wit:

We have divided the said Augmentation to the Soquel Ranch into 27 tracts which are respectively designated by the numbers from one to twenty-seven inclusive. On the map of said Rancho hereto attached and annexed and herein to be referred to and made a part hereof and marked Exhibit "A."

That being in our judgment the most equal partition, quantity and quality considered, that could be made of said Rancho.

And we do further report that for the better understanding and elucidation of the shape and location of said Rancho and of the several tracts into which we have partitioned the same, and of the manner in which we have partitioned said Rancho, we have caused to be made by Thomas W. Wright, by whom the same was surveyed, a map of said Rancho des-

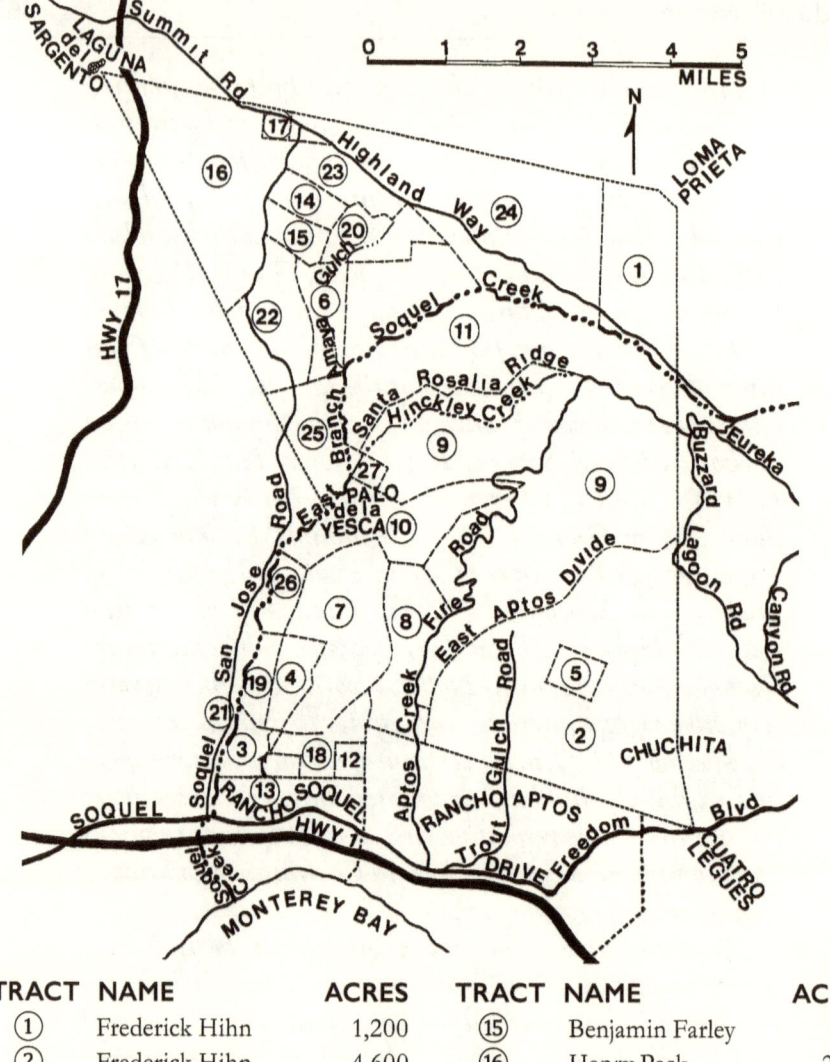

TRACT	NAME	ACRES	TRACT	NAME	ACRES
1	Frederick Hihn	1,200	15	Benjamin Farley	332
2	Frederick Hihn	4,600	16	Henry Peck	2,313
3	Frederick Hihn	480	17	James Taylor	280
4	Joel Bates	330	18	Helena Littlejohn	333
5	Luisa Fourcade	567	19	Helena Littlejohn	333
6	Luisa Fourcade	442	20	Casimero & Dario Amayo	713
7	Guadalupe Averon	1,308	21	George Evans	2
8	Frederick Macondray	1,167	22	George Evans	1,000
9	Carmel Fallon	6,845	23	George Evans	600
10	Antonia Peck	1,063	24	Lyman Burrell	3,500
11	Antonia Peck	3,513	25	Hinckley & Shelby	853
12	George Porter	180	26	Brady & Nichols	363
13	Augustus Noble	40	27	Richard Savage	140
14	Craven Hester	332			

FIGURE 6.8 SHOQUEL AUGMENTATION PARTITIONED TRACTS

ignating and delineating what parcels thereof have been by us set off in severalty to the respective parties herein as we were commanded by said Commission and by the decree of this Court therein referred to, which map is herein referred to and made a part hereof and is hereunto attached and annexed and marked Exhibit "A."

And we do further report that we have assigned to the plaintiff and defendants the following tracts:

Frederick A. Hihn, the plaintiff, has been assigned and set off in severalty the following three tracts after considering both quantity and quality:
    ① *totaling 1,200 acres*
    ② *totaling 4,600 acres*
    ③ *totaling 480 acres*

Joel Bates, a defendant, deceased, has been assigned and set off in severalty the following tract, quantity and quality <u>not</u> considered:
    ④ *totaling 330 acres*

Luisa Juan, a defendant, has been assigned and set off in severalty the following two tracts, quantity and quality considered for both....:
    ⑤ *totaling 567 acres*
    ⑥ *totaling 442 acres*

Guadalupe Averon, a defendant, has been assigned and set off in severalty the following tract, quantity and quality considered:
    ⑦ *totaling 1,308 acres*

Frederick W. Macondray, a defendant, deceased, has been assigned and set off in severalty the following tract, quantity and quality considered:
    ⑧ *totaling 1,167 acres*

Carmel Fallon, a defendant, has been assigned and set off in severalty the following tract, quantity and quality considered:
⑨ *totaling 6,845 acres*

Antonia Peck, a defendant, has been assigned and set off in severalty the following two tracts, quantity and quality considered for both:
⑩ *totaling 1,063 acres*
⑪ *totaling 3,513 acres*

[Note: The acreage of Peck was at the time of this report under the ownership of Hihn due to the deed she signed with him in April 1862.]

George K. Porter, a defendant, has been assigned and set off in severalty the following tract, quantity and quality considered:
⑫ *totaling 180 acres*

Augustus Noble, a defendant, has been assigned and set off in severalty the following tract, quantity and quality considered:
⑬ *totaling 40 acres*

Craven P. Hester, a defendant, has been assigned and set off in severalty the following tract, quantity and quality considered:
⑭ *totaling 332 acres*

Benjamin Farley, a defendant, has been assigned and set off in severalty the following tract, quantity and quality considered:
⑮ *totaling 332 acres*

Henry W. Peck, a defendant, has been assigned and set off in severalty the following tract, quantity and quality considered:
⑯ *totaling 2,313 acres*

[Note: The acreage of Peck was at the time of this report under the ownership of Hihn due to the deed he signed with him in April 1862.]

James Taylor, a defendant, has been assigned and set off in severalty the following tract, quantity and quality considered:
  ⑰ *totaling 280 acres*

Helena Littlejohn, a defendant, has been assigned and set off in severalty the following two tracts, quantity and quality not considered:
  ⑱ *totaling 333 acres*
  ⑲ *totaling 333 acres*

Casimero and Daria Amayo, both defendants and brothers, have been assigned and set off in severalty the following tract, quantity and quality considered:
  ⑳ *totaling 713 acres*

George W. Evans, a defendant, has been assigned and set off in severalty the following three tracts, quantity and quality considered:
  ㉑ *totaling 2 acres*
  ㉒ *totaling 1,000 acres*
  ㉓ *totaling 600 acres*

[Note: The acreage of Evans was at the time of this report under the ownership of Stephen and Joseph Chase due to the deed he signed with John Daubenbiss in April 1863, and the subsequent sale of the land to the Chases.]

Lyman John Burrell, a defendant, has been assigned and set off in severalty the following tract, quantity and quality considered:
  ㉔ *totaling 3,500 acres*

Roger Gibson Hinckley and his son-in-law John Lafayette Shelby, both defendants, have been assigned and set off in severalty the following tract, quantity and quality not considered:
㉕ totaling 853 acres

Francis Brady and Benjamin Cahoon Nichols, defendants and partners, have been assigned and set off in severalty the following tract, quantity and quality considered:
㉖ totaling 363 acres

[Note: The acreage of Brady and Nichols was at the time of this report under the ownership of Benjamin Cahoon due to the deeds they signed with him in April and May.]

Richard Savage, a defendant, has been assigned and set off in severalty the following tract, quantity and quality considered:
㉗ totaling 140 acres

[Note: The acreage of Savage was at the time of this report under the ownership of Benjamin Cahoon due to the deed he signed with him in August 1861.]

Referees Thomas W. Wright, John W. Towne, and Godfrey M. Bockius submit their expense report to the court...and now this day come the parties herein and also come the three referees heretofore appointed to partition the Augmentation Ranch, and move the court for an order for the payment of their fees as referees herein and of the other expenses attending and incidental to the partition of said ranch, and it appearing to the court that said referees have made partition of said ranch in pursuance of the decree in the premises and have filed their report and that the same has been by the court confirmed, and it further appearing that their [time and effort] amounts to the sum of $1,600, and that said $1,600 is payable in coin and ought to be paid immediately in coin and the parties consenting thereto.

It is therefore now here ordered, adjudged, and decreed

by the court that the parties herein in proportion to their respective interests in said ranch, as the same have been ascertained and set off to the respective parties herein, do forthwith pay David J. Haslam, as Clerk of this Court, in coin, their respective portions of the expenses of said partition as follows, to wit: Carmel Fallon, $177.89; Guadalupe Averon, $177.89; Helena Littlejohn, $112.55; Luisa Juan, $59.29; John Daubenbiss, $88.94; Dario Amayo, $29.64; Casimero Amayo, $29.64; Lyman John Burrell, $59.29; Luther Farnham as Administrator of the estate of Joel Bates, $59.29; Francis R. Brady and Benjamin Cahoon Nichols, $29.64; Richard Savage, $16.67; Roger Hinckley and John Shelby, $44.37; Craven P. Hester, $33.33; Benjamin Farley, $33.33; James Taylor, $29.64; George Keating Porter, $41.51; Augustus Noble, $8.73; William Macondray and James Otis as Executors of the last will and testament of Frederick W. Macondray, $53.36; Frederick A. Hihn, $509.98 [which included the Pecks' bills].[438]

CHAPTER 7

~

Divided and Conquered

Craven Hester and Benjamin Farley file objections to the Rancho Soquel partitioning report

Reaction to the two Partitioning Reports was swift. On the same day that Shoquel Augmentation's report was released—December 23, 1863—Craven Hester, acting on his own behalf and for Benjamin Farley, entered his objections with the Third District Court. He based these first on the descriptions of their two tracts—Nos. 14 and 15—which he stated were absurd, that the boundaries did not enclose the land that was assigned to them, and that the description was insufficient. In addition, the quantity of land that was assigned to each of them did not match the amount determined by Charles Younger, who calculated that each should receive 1/48 (681 acres). The three referees, in contrast, only granted to Hester and Farley 332 acres each, which also did not encompass all of the land where the two men had made improvements. Indeed, Hester claimed that the assigned land was nearly worthless and uninhabitable.

Another objection came due to the ruling by Judge McKee that each and every party of the partition was required to allow a right-of-way over the nearest convenient route from the lands set off and assigned to them across the lands of the others in order to reach the nearest public highway. Hester stated that, since both of their tracts were located on a high mountain with little rolling land on top to cultivate, and since they would be disturbed by travelers crossing their land, the land awarded to them would be rendered much less valuable. He concluded his list of objections by praying to the court to set aside this report and hire new commissioners to divide the Augmentation according to their proper shares as determined by the Younger Report.

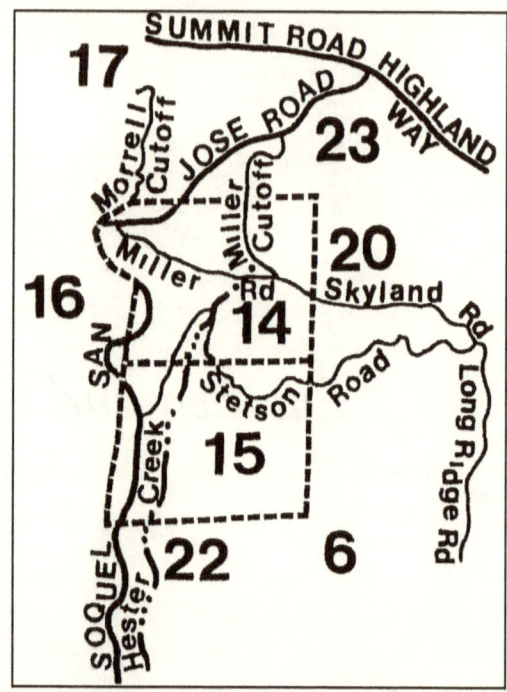

FIGURE 7.1 LOCATIONS OF TRACTS 14 & 15

After McKee filed the objection made by Hester and Farley, he adjourned the proceedings for the suit until August 1864.[439]

Benjamin Nichols and Francis Brady file objections to the Shoquel Augmentation partitioning report

On January 12, 1864, Francis Brady and Benjamin Nichols, on behalf of Benjamin Cahoon, entered into the record the following objections to Shoquel Augmentation's partitioning report:

> *First, the amount of land assigned as described in the report is insufficient and is not equivalent to the 1/54th part heretofore directed to be set off in fee simple by decree of this court. Second,*

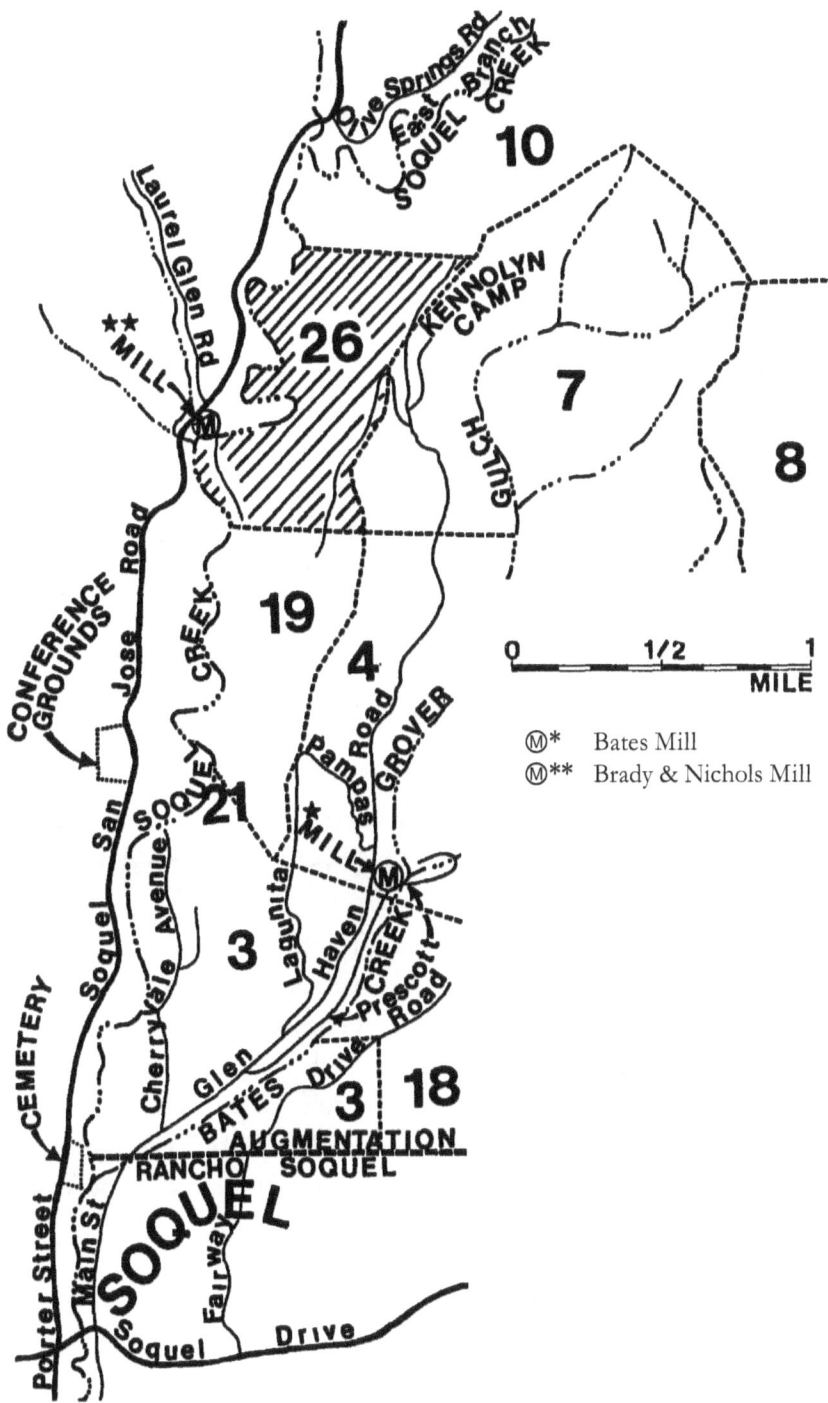

FIGURE 7.2 LOCATION OF TRACT 26 AND BENJAMIN CAHOON'S SAWMILL

> the tract of land set off does not include the land upon which we have previously erected and now have standing permanent and valuable improvements. And third, the portion of the land set off is so located as to be inaccessible from the point at which our buildings are presently located.
>
> Wherefore we, Francis R. Brady and Benjamin Cahoon Nichols, pray that the court set aside the report and that commissioners be appointed to divide the Augmentation amongst the owners thereof assigning to each his proper share of the ranch.

Of all the objections, Brady and Nichols' was probably one of the most justified. Younger had confirmed that they had a right to 1/54 of the Augmentation (606 acres). The three referees, however, only granted the partners 363 acres. But their firm was interested in logging the Augmentation and the loss of 243 acres was a substantial setback, depriving them of access to nearly nine million board feet of timber that they had planned to harvest.[440]

Land transfer by Dario Amayo to Frederick Hihn and agreement between Hihn and Casimero Amayo

Either Frederick Hihn wanted to purchase Tract 20 in Shoquel Augmentation for its water and timber or Dario Amayo wanted to sell his half of the tract and move with his family. In any case, on February 13, 1864, Dario's brother Casimero entered into an agreement with Hihn that allowed him to remain on Tract 20 and develop it for agricultural purposes as the timber was removed. Hihn, meanwhile, purchased all of Dario's claim to the tract on February 22, granting him full ownership of the timber and water on the property.[441]

California passes a law allowing an interlocutory decree to be appealed

A landmark piece of legislation was signed into law by Governor Frederick

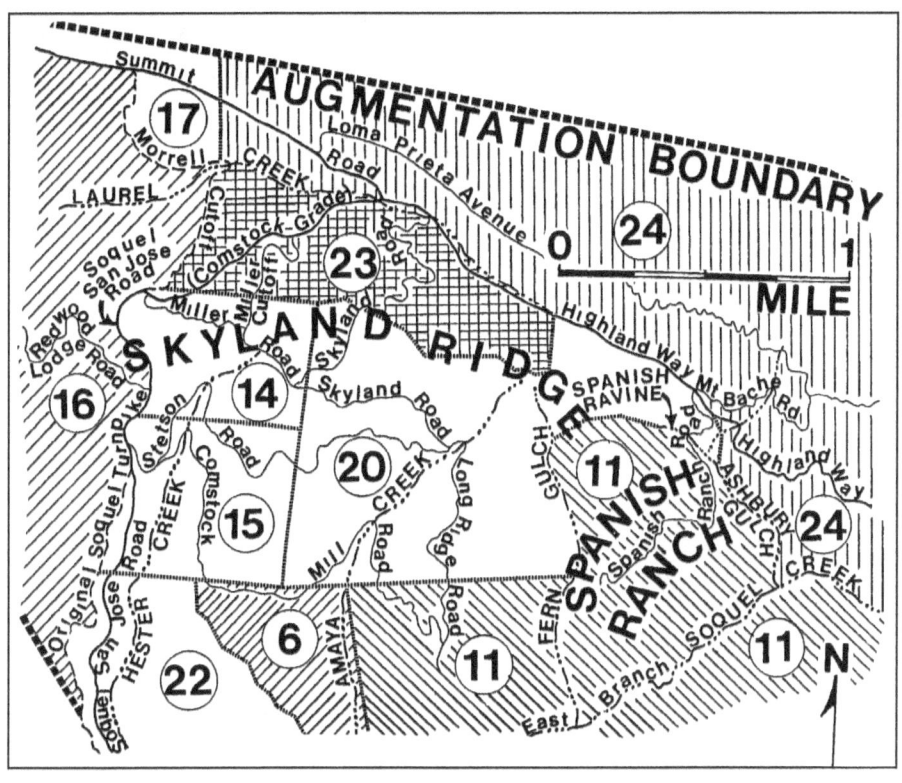

FIGURE 7.3 LOCATION OF THE AMAYO BROTHERS' TRACT 20

Low on March 23, 1864. This law had the potential to overturn the recent rulings regarding both Rancho Soquel and Shoquel Augmentation and force a new settlement. It reads:

> *This Act passed by the legislature authorizes an appeal may be made to the Supreme Court in an action for partition from the Interlocutory judgment which determines the rights of the parties and directs a partition be made* (Laws of 1862, 223).

Fortunately for those who profited from the partition and Judge McKee, the law could not be retrospectively applied and, as such, did not impact the two partitioning suits.[442]

Roger Hinckley and John Shelby file objections to the Shoquel Augmentation partitioning report

On July 19, 1864, Roger Hinckley and John Shelby filed their objections to the Shoquel Augmentation partitioning report regarding Tract 25. Their objections were as follows:

> *Gross inequality and injustice in the assignment of the joint interest of the defendants in the land partitioned by the referees, and that the same is against equity, in this that the principal part of the share set off to the defendants consists of land which can be made use of for no other purpose than for grazing.*
>
> *And that the land set off to them has very [little] quantity of which is arable land that on the whole of said land there are but two small springs of water, and the situation of the springs is such and the quantity of water afforded by them so small that they are entirely insufficient for the purpose of watering the number of cattle that the tract of land is capable of sustaining.*
>
> *That while the Soquel River, a year-round running stream, runs along the east side of our tract for about two and a half miles, and the stream would be a very great benefit and advantage in the use of the land from grazing and for other purposes, we, the defendants can reach the stream at one point only which greatly diminishes the value of the tract because the use thereof the running stream is as previously stated, greatly diminished by the denial to them of the use of the waters. And that in no other assignment of the various portions of the lands partitioned has any party holding an interest therein be barred from the free use of the waters of a boundary stream.*

In reality, Tract 25 was, for the most part, useless for the intended purposes of Hinckley and Shelby, which was mainly homesteading and raising cattle and sheep. Their tract extended from a point on the East Branch

Divided and Conquered 1864

of Soquel Creek just below Hinckley Creek along a straight line heading northwest up towards the Laguna del Sargento, while its east boundary

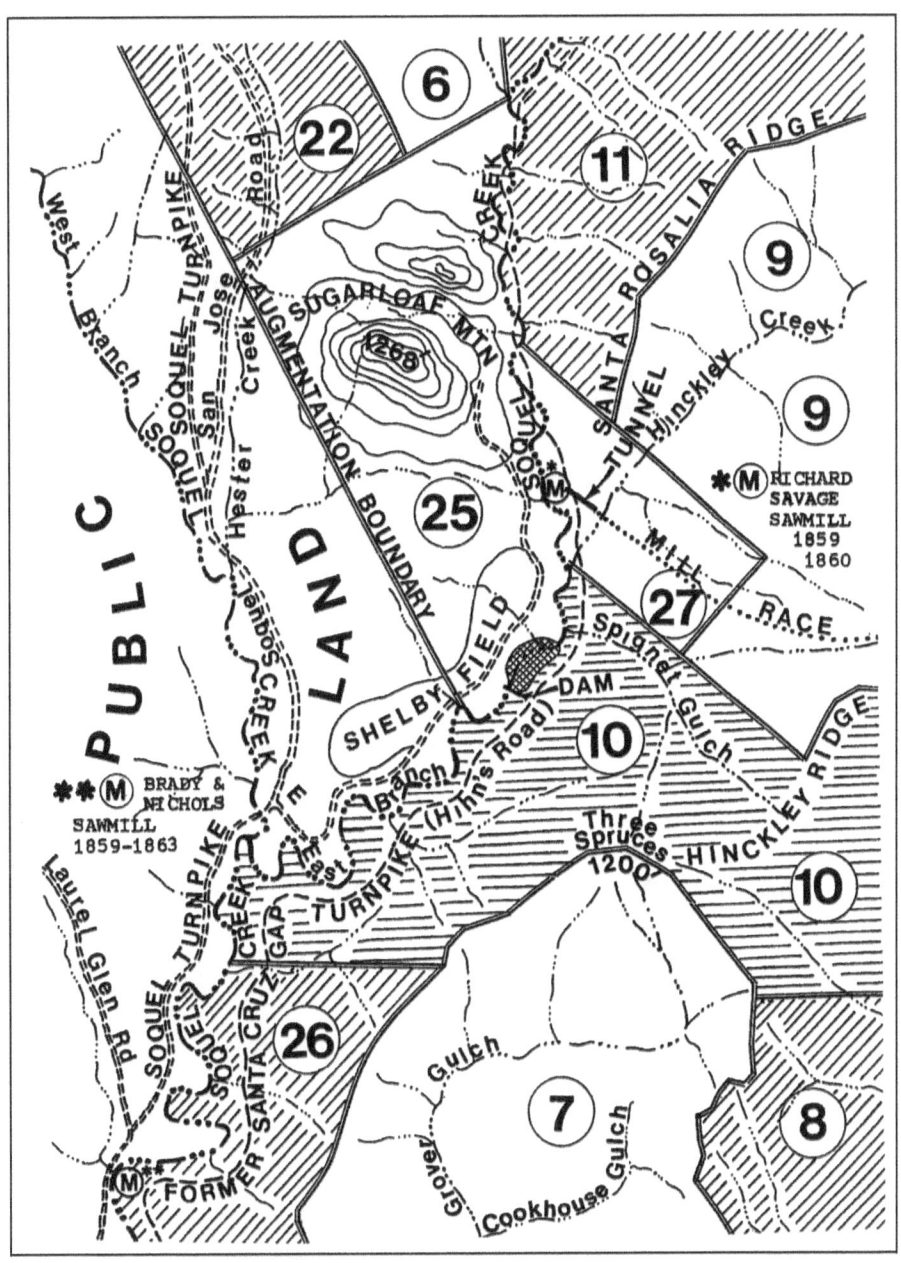

FIGURE 7.4 LOCATION OF HINCKLEY AND SHELBY'S TRACT 25

was the twisting and turning narrow channel of the East Branch of Soquel Creek for nearly two and a half miles. Access to the creek for their animals was at a narrow spot opposite the opening into Hinckley Gulch. Just to the north of the latter gulch was Sugarloaf Mountain. While the mountain made most of their land useless for grazing and cultivation purposes, a century later, the tract was taken over by the Olive Springs Quarry Company to be used as a quarry and has provided high grade rocks and asphalt products for over fifty years.[443]

Judge McKee accepts the Rancho Soquel partitioning report

On July 25, 1864, Judge McKee entered into the record his confirmation of the Younger Report for Rancho Soquel. He stated:

> *It is ordered, adjudged, and decreed by this court, and on behalf of the plaintiffs Henry Winegar and wife, Antonia, through their attorney Robert Francis Peckham that the report of the referees be confirmed, and that judgment be entered to the said report, and that the partition be effectual forever.*
>
> *And that the defendant Frederick A. Hihn be allowed the sum of $370.60 for his costs herein laid out and expended.*
>
> *And that the defendant George K. Porter be allowed the sum of $20 for his costs and disbursements laid out and expended.*
>
> *And that the sum of $370.60 to Frederick A. Hihn and the sum of $20 to George K. Porter, the plaintiffs Henry W. Peck and Antonia Peck do pay the sum of $87.67.*
>
> *And that defendant Joshua Parrish do pay the sum of $43.83.*
>
> *And that defendant Guadalupe Averon do pay the sum of $43.83.*
>
> *And that defendant Helena Littlejohn do pay the sum of $32.46.*
>
> *And that defendant Luisa Juan do pay the sum of $32.46.*
>
> *And that defendants William Macondray and James Otis do pay the sum of $13.75.*

And that defendant Augustus Noble do pay the sum of $32.55.

And that execution do issue therefore, and the same is collecting, that the sum of $10 be paid to the defendant George K. Porter, and the remainder thereof to the defendant Frederick A. Hihn.

Judgment entered July 25, 1864
by the Honorable Samuel B. McKee, District Judge

Attested to by David J. Haslam,
Clerk of the Court[444]

Judge McKee accepts the Shoquel Augmentation partitioning report

On August 8, 1864, Judge McKee entered into the record his Action for Partition decree regarding Shoquel Augmentation:

This cause coming on to be heard upon this report of the referees heretofore appointed by the court to make partition of the lands and tenements in the complaint. According to the decree of this court, swear and ordered in this court at the April term, 1863. And upon the several objections to said referees' report by the defendants Craven P. Hester, Benjamin Farley, Francis R. Brady, Benjamin Cahoon Nichols, Roger Gibson Hinckley, and John Lafayette Shelby, and the said objections of these defendants now withdrawn and the court having heard the entries in support of the objections of said defendants Francis R. Brady and Benjamin Cahoon Nichols, and having upon consideration of such evidence and denied the objections.

It is now on motion of Robert F. Peckham, as attorney for defendant Luisa Juan, considered adjudged and decreed by the court that the partition made by the referees and reported to this court, as this same now appears and remains on file in this cause, be and the same is hereby approved, ratified, con-

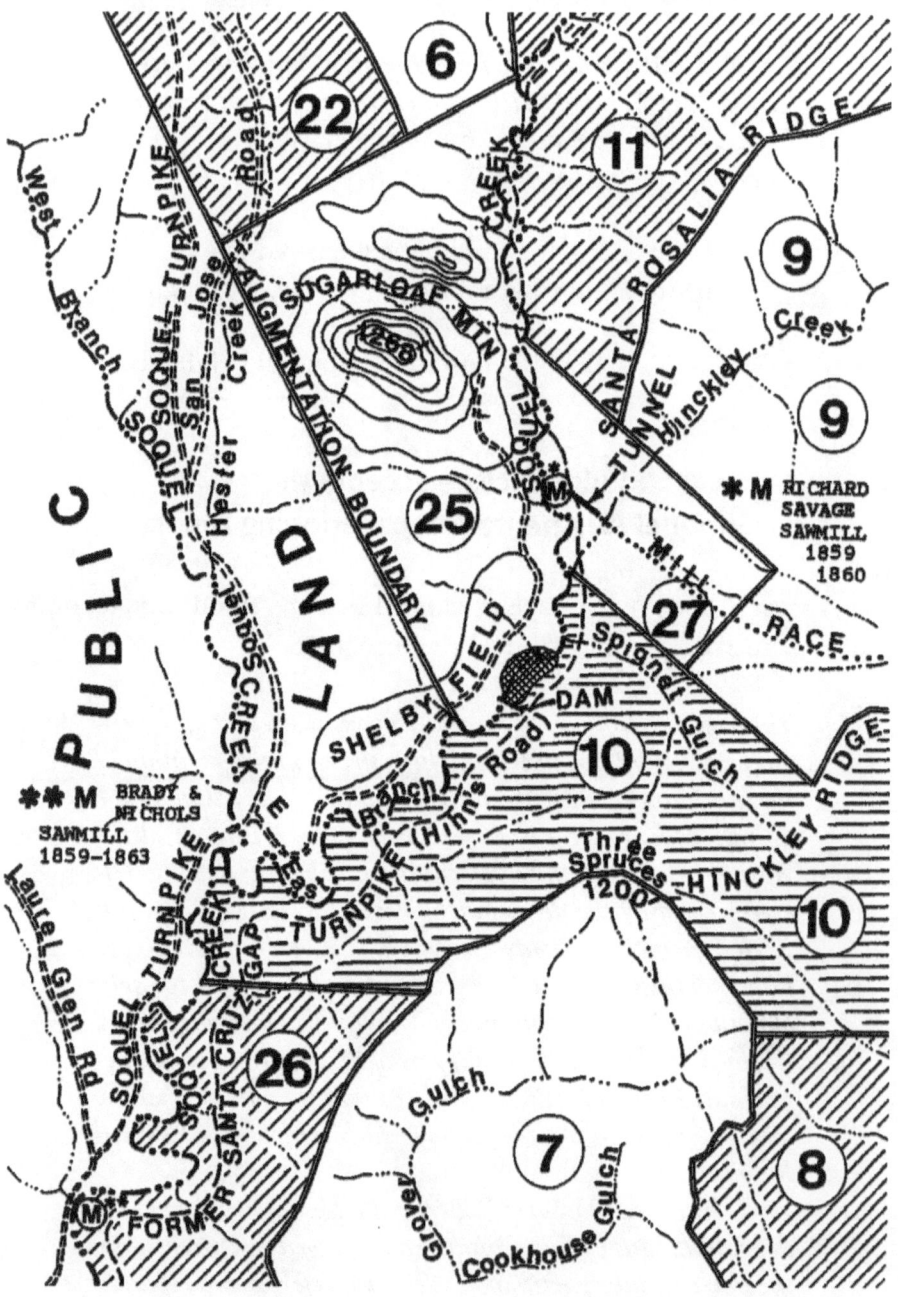

Figure 7.5 Location of dam and pond on Tracts 10 and 25

firmed, established, and made binding, firm, and effectual forever....

And that there be and is hereby reserved to each and every party to such partition a right of way over the nearest convenient route from the lands set off and assigned to him or her by this decree across the lands of the others to a public highway, and that a judgment be entered by the Clerk of the Court accordingly, and that a writ of assistance be issued from this court to put the parties in possession of the tracts of land set off and assigned to them respectively.

And that the parties to this suit have until the next term of this court to file their several bills of cost in this action and have them appertained among the parties hereto respectively.

This decree was filed on September 14.[445]

Land transfer by Frederick Hihn to Roger Hinckley and John Shelby

On August 8, 1864, Frederick Hihn uncharacteristically sold land in Tract 10 within Shoquel Augmentation to Roger Hinckley and John Shelby. However, the reason becomes clear once it is remembered that Hinckley and Shelby objected to the partitioning report because their tract lacked easy access to a source of water. Through this deed, Hihn granted the partners the right to build a dam on the East Branch of Soquel Creek opposite Spignet Gulch in Tract 25, so long as the reservoir did not interfere with the wagon road that crossed the creek further upstream. This road was vital to accessing Hihn's backcountry property, as well as reaching Benjamin Cahoon's mill.[446]

Jones Hoy land claims resolved

Although the partitioning suits had resolved the major issues regarding Rancho Soquel and Shoquel Augmentation, a serious problem still remained regarding a specific portion of land within the Augmentation. Frederick

Hihn hoped to resolve this through a series of land sales in August 1864.

Mistakes made in the Jones Hoy purchase and subsequent sale of Josefa Clements' 1/9 claim to Rancho Soquel had grown more complicated over the years, leading to rival claims and unclear ownership. As discussed before, on March 30, 1852, in the first sale based on Martina Castro's deed of August 29, 1850, Josefa and Lambert Clements sold her 1/9 claim to both Rancho Soquel and the Augmentation to Pruett Sinclair and Jones Hoy. On July 25, 1853, Hoy sold his half of that claim in Rancho Soquel to Joseph Majors. Majors immediately mortgaged the land back to Hoy with a promise to pay the balance within a short time. The next year, on October 4, 1854, Majors took out a chattel mortgage to repay a debt owed to Charles Watson, with all of Majors' livestock passing to Hoy as security. Watson sold this mortgage on April 15, 1856 to Charles Willson, who falsely believed that the mortgage included Majors' claim to 1/18 Rancho Soquel, as well as Hoy's claim to the Augmentation. A month later, on May 26, 1858, Majors was forced to sell his land at auction since he had been unable to repay the mortgage that he owed to Willson. The court included in the sale all of Majors' land, including the mistaken claim to the Augmentation. In the end, Willson made the winning bid and came into full possession of the claims.

Things became only more complicated from this point, as mistakes and false assumptions compounded. On July 3, 1858, Majors was still in debt and the court ordered that Majors sell all of his land for a second time, despite the fact that Willson had already relieved Majors of all of his land three months earlier. This time, Frederick Hihn made the winning bid and received a deed from the court on August 6 for a 1/18 claim to Rancho Soquel and the Augmentation. Willson for some reason had never received his deeds for the land he had won in April, so petitioned the court and was granted his deeds on November 1. Meanwhile, Hoy, unaware that his Augmentation property had been sold twice without his knowledge, signed the land over to George Evans on December 16, 1860.

This confusing situation came to a head during the partitioning suits. It was established that the original chattel mortgage between Majors and Watson never included a claim to any land, only to livestock. Therefore, Willson, who had bought the mortgage, had no claim to the land. However, Charles Younger ruled that Willson still had a claim to Rancho Soquel since

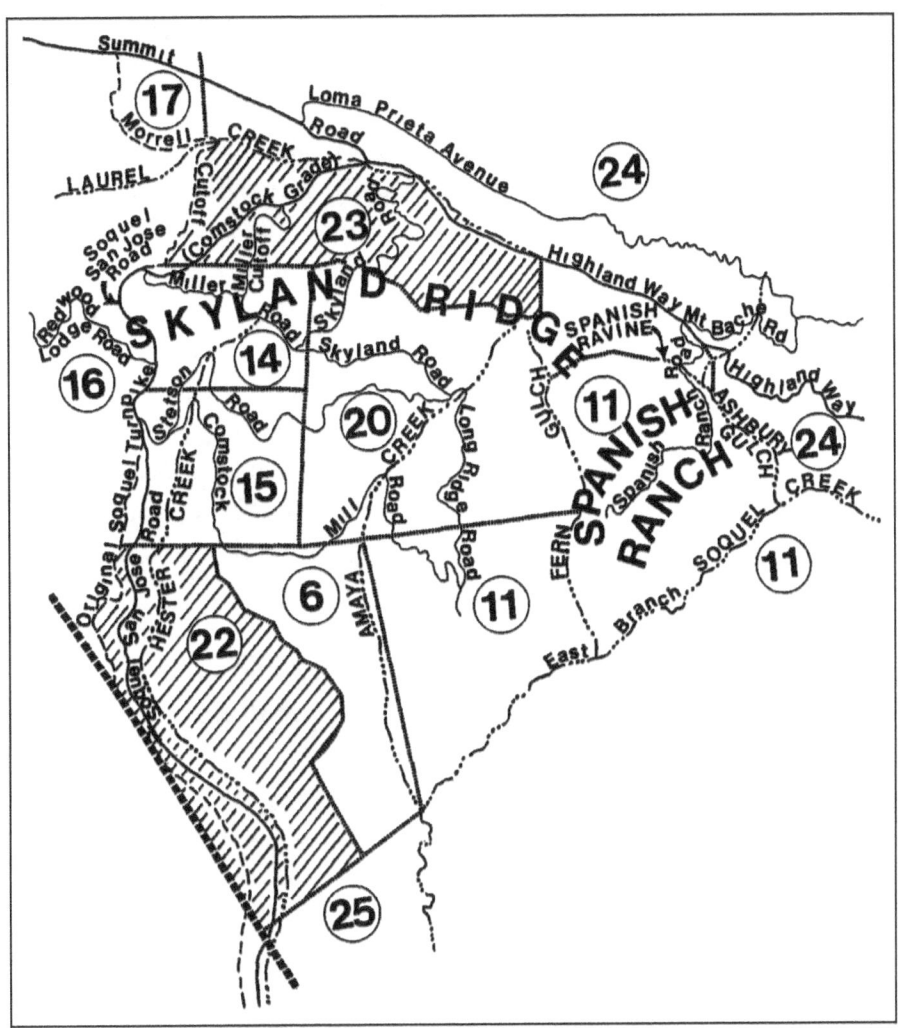

FIGURE 7.6 LOCATION OF TRACTS 21, 22, AND 23

he had purchased that land from Majors at auction in April 1858. Hihn had agreed with this ruling and promptly bought the land in Rancho Soquel from Willson on April 25, 1861. At the same time, Younger ruled that Hoy had retained possession of his land in the Augmentation, and therefore his sale of that land to Evans was legitimate.

Through the partitioning suit, Evans was granted Tracts 21, 22, and 23, totalling 1,602 acres. But on April 22, 1863, before the partitioning was finalized, he sold his land to John Daubenbiss. The latter, in turn, sold the land to Stephen and Joseph Chase on December 1, but retained about 300 acres for himself.

Hoping to resolve the lingering issue of non-adjacent lands and the 300 acres still retained by Daubenbiss, Hihn worked with the various parties to shift around ownership of the land. On August 9, two deeds were signed. The Chase cousins sold to Hihn a 1/27 claim to the Augmentation that they had acquired from Daubenbiss. Hihn then turned around and sold a different 1/27 claim that he had won from Majors to the Chases. The next day, the Chases sold Tracts 21 and 22 to Daubenbiss and, in turn, Daubenbiss sold to them the 300 acres that he had retained the previous year, which was located in Tract 23. This gave the Chases 600 acres of redwood-rich land in the north of the Augmentation, and Daubenbiss 1,000 acres of land along the western edge along the Soquel Turnpike, as well as a two-acre tract further to the south upon which sat the most significant dam and pond on Soquel Creek.[447]

John Vandenberg and Frederick Hihn file appeals concerning the Younger Report

On August 12, 1864, John Vandenberg filed an appeal to the California Supreme Court on the grounds that the Younger Report rejected his deed with Nicanor Lajeunesse, dated January 21, 1854, and instead accepted Frederick Hihn's deed of July 23 and 24, 1860 for the same 1/9 part of Rancho Soquel.

The same day, Hihn filed an appeal to the Supreme Court regarding his own objections to the Younger Report, claiming that his portion of the property should be 8/27, not the 71/270 recommended by Younger and confirmed by Judge McKee. He further argued that Augustus Noble's award should be 1/27, not 1/12; that George Porter's award should be 13/1,018, not 7/270; and that the Macondray Estate's award should be 8/243, not the 19/540.[448]

Judge McKee files two court orders

On August 13, 1864, Judge McKee signed two court orders regarding the

Rancho Soquel Partitioning Suit. The first states:

> *Let all defendants in the cause titled the Peck v. Hihn, et al., suit who are or have been represented by Selden S. Wright, or John Wilson, or both of them, have thirty days from this date in which to prepare and file a statement on appeal therein.*

The defendants represented by the two attorneys were Thomas Courtis, Mary Slade, Cyrus Coe, Charles Plum, and Henry Lawrence, while John Wilson also represented himself during certain phases of the suit.

The second court order states:

> *Upon a good cause to me by George Keating Porter, one of the defendants in the cause titled the Peck v. Hihn, et al., suit, is allowed twenty days from the 12th day of August, 1864, within which to file amendments to the statement, on appeal served herein by Frederick A. Hihn on the 12th day of August, 1864, and to serve a copy of said amendments on said appellant, Frederick A. Hihn, and it is so ordered by me this 13th day of August, 1864 at Santa Cruz.*[449]

Thomas Courtis, John Wilson, Mary Slade, Cyrus Coe, Charles Plum, and Henry Lawrence file appeals to the Younger Report

On August 15, 1864, Thomas Courtis, on his own behalf and as administrator for the estates of Father Ingoldsby and Benjamin Green, John Wilson, Mary Slade, Cyrus Coe, Charles Plum, and Henry Lawrence filed an appeal to the California Supreme Court, claiming that the findings in the Younger Report ignored their valid claims in both Rancho Soquel and Shoquel Augmentation. They argued that they had claims to the entire acreage of both properties, not only the 1/9 claim sold by Martina Castro to the Catholic Church in January 1855.

A key component of their appeal was again an attempt to prove that the deed signed by Castro in August 1850 was incorrectly filed and a product of coercion. The Supreme Court had already heard this case in the Ingoldsby v. Ricardo Juan trial in 1859, eventually overturning the decision of the lower court and deciding that the original deed of 1850 was valid, despite several errors in the paperwork. However, this second case provided Courtis and Wilson an opportunity to present evidence that had not been considered six years earlier, such as depositions given by Louis Depeaux and Peter Tracy.

Several witnesses were called in the appeal, such as José Bolcoff, Thomas Fallon, and Lambert Clements. Fallon explained:

> *In the month of August 1850, Martina Castro told me she would like to have her children around her, and I said to her that it was nothing but right, since the father was dead, that they should have their portion of the property. She said that she wanted them to have it, and to come on and settle immediately. I told her before they would go on and settle, they wanted a deed, so that they would feel independent and be secure in their improvements.*
>
> *She said get the papers written out, I am perfectly willing to give each of my children an equal ninth, and amongst them I want to include the wives of Lajeunesse and Ricardo Juan, my children by my first husband Simon Cota, and make no distinction between them and the children of Michael Lodge. Lambert Blair Clements then wrote the document, and I told him to embody therein the wish of the old lady, to give each of her children an equal ninth absolutely.*
>
> *It was the understanding between Martina Castro and her children that the title to an equal ninth of the ranch in suit should pass absolutely and forever to each of the children. Louis Depeaux and Martina Castro, during the conversation, were present at my house, and although the conversation was conducted between Martina Castro and myself, yet Louis Depeaux assented to everything that she said, and expressed himself as decided in favor of her wishes in reference thereto being carried into effect. There were several other conversations in reference thereto. The instrument of which I have been speaking was signed at Martina Castro's house and was drawn up and executed in pursuance of the aforesaid understanding and agreement.*

Clements then gave his testimony:

> *I never heard of any lease that was prepared for Martina Castro to sign whereby it was proposed to lease the ranch to her children. Previous to the 29th of August, 1850, there was a writing prepared by me whereby Martina Castro obligated herself to give to each of her children an equal right in the ranches with herself and we obligated ourselves to pay the taxes equally and keep off squatters. The paper is in the possession of Thomas Fallon, at least it was some time ago. Martina Castro and Louis Depeaux had proposed to divide off the ranches among us. There was a consultation at her house at which all the family were present. After taking into consideration the various things, pro and con, Martina Castro thought it best to let it remain until such time as the ranches were confirmed before division was made. Martina Castro then proposed that we should occupy and cultivate any portion of the ranch excepting a certain piece where the house stood. This piece was to commence at the old crossing of the Soquel River, and thence following on the line of the road to the gulch back of the house [Nobles Gulch], thence down the gulch to the Bay of Monterey, thence to the mouth of the Soquel River, and thence up the river to the place of beginning, which she desired to reserve for herself, for Louis Depeaux, her son Miguel Antonio Lodge, and her daughters Antonia, Helena and Guadalupe. With that understanding, there was drawn up and signed by Martina Castro, Ricardo Juan, Francisco Young, Thomas Fallon, and myself the document thereof—a copy is attached as Exhibit A to the deposition of Louis Depeaux herein evidence. A copy of the document was made at the time, which Louis Depeaux took. Thomas Fallon took the original.*

When Clements was asked how it was proposed to divide the ranch among the children and Martina, he answered: "It was proposed to make the division into strips, by commencing at the Bay of Monterey, and running up through the ranch in suit [Soquel], and the Soquel Augmentation Ranch." He was then asked when and where was the paper signed: "It was signed at the residence of Martina Castro and at the time the parties had consultation about it, all the parties thereto signed it at the same time, Peter Tracy, the County Recorder, was not present when it was signed."

Meanwhile, Bolcoff testified that he witnessed the transfer of the property from Castro to Fathers Llebaria and Ingoldsby in 1855, stating: "I was slightly acquainted with Louis Depeaux. I knew Martina Castro, his wife. I was with both in January of 1855 in San Francisco." When asked if he was present when Depeaux and Castro executed the deed to Llebaria and Ingoldsby, he answered, "I was present." When asked if he knew what consideration was paid, he answered, "$2,000" and confirmed that the amount was transferred. Under cross examination, Bolcoff stated: "I saw Louis Depeaux and Martina Castro sign two deeds at the time. I saw $2,000 paid to the priests Llebaria and Ingoldsby—there were several persons present when the deed was signed."[450]

Augustus Noble and the Macondray Estate propose amendments to Frederick Hihn's appeal

On August 16, 1864, Augustus Noble and the Macondray Estate proposed two amendments to Frederick Hihn's appeal of the Rancho Soquel Partitioning Suit. The first requested that some wording be changed in the appeal. Namely, that the words "plaintiff then read in evidence a conveyance from Martina Castro," be changed to "plaintiff then offered to read into evidence what purported to be a conveyance from Martina Castro." Second, they wished to record their objection to Hihn's assertion that Castro legally conveyed 1/9 of Rancho Soquel and Shoquel Augmentation to each of her eight children in 1850.

Three days later, on August 19, Hihn responded to the proposed amendments, stating "you will take notice that your proposed amendments to the statement to be used on appeal, proposed by Frederick A. Hihn, is disagreed to…and…that the proposed statement with the proposed amendments will be presented to the clerk of the court in Santa Clara County for settlement on the 13th day of September, 1864, at 10 O'clock A.M. And when and where you may appear and insist on your proposed amendments."

Hihn was given twenty days to finalize his appeal before giving it to the county clerk, at which point it was to be presented to the court for settlement.[451]

Frederick Hihn and George and Benjamin Porter agree to proposed amendments to appeal

On September 1, 1864, Frederick Hihn and George and Benjamin Porter came to an agreement regarding their proposed amendments to the appeal of the Rancho Soquel Partitioning Suit:

> *In the first stipulation, Frederick A. Hihn states that George K. Porter and Benjamin F. Porter have until and including the 10th day of September, 1864, to file and serve amendments to the statement on appeal, filed by me [Hihn] on the 12th day of August, 1864.*
>
> *In the second stipulation, the attorney for Frederick A. Hihn, Robert F. Peckham, and Selden W. Wright, representing the cousins George K. and Benjamin F. Porter, agree that the amendments being prepared by the latter two defendants, that the time they have to file their amendment is extended until and including the 20th day of September, 1864 [and] Frederick A. Hihn is allowed ten days' time additional to that allowed by law in which to bring said statement and amendments before the judge for settlement.*[452]

Agreement between Frederick Hihn and Augustus Noble, George Porter, and the Macondray Estate

On September 12, 1864, Frederick Hihn came to an agreement with Augustus Noble, George Porter, and the Macondray Estate regarding their proposed amendments to the Rancho Soquel Partitioning Suit:

> *It is hereby stipulated and agreed to by the preceding that all errors in the above named cause are hereby expressly waived, so far as the same affect the defendants in relation to each other and not otherwise.*

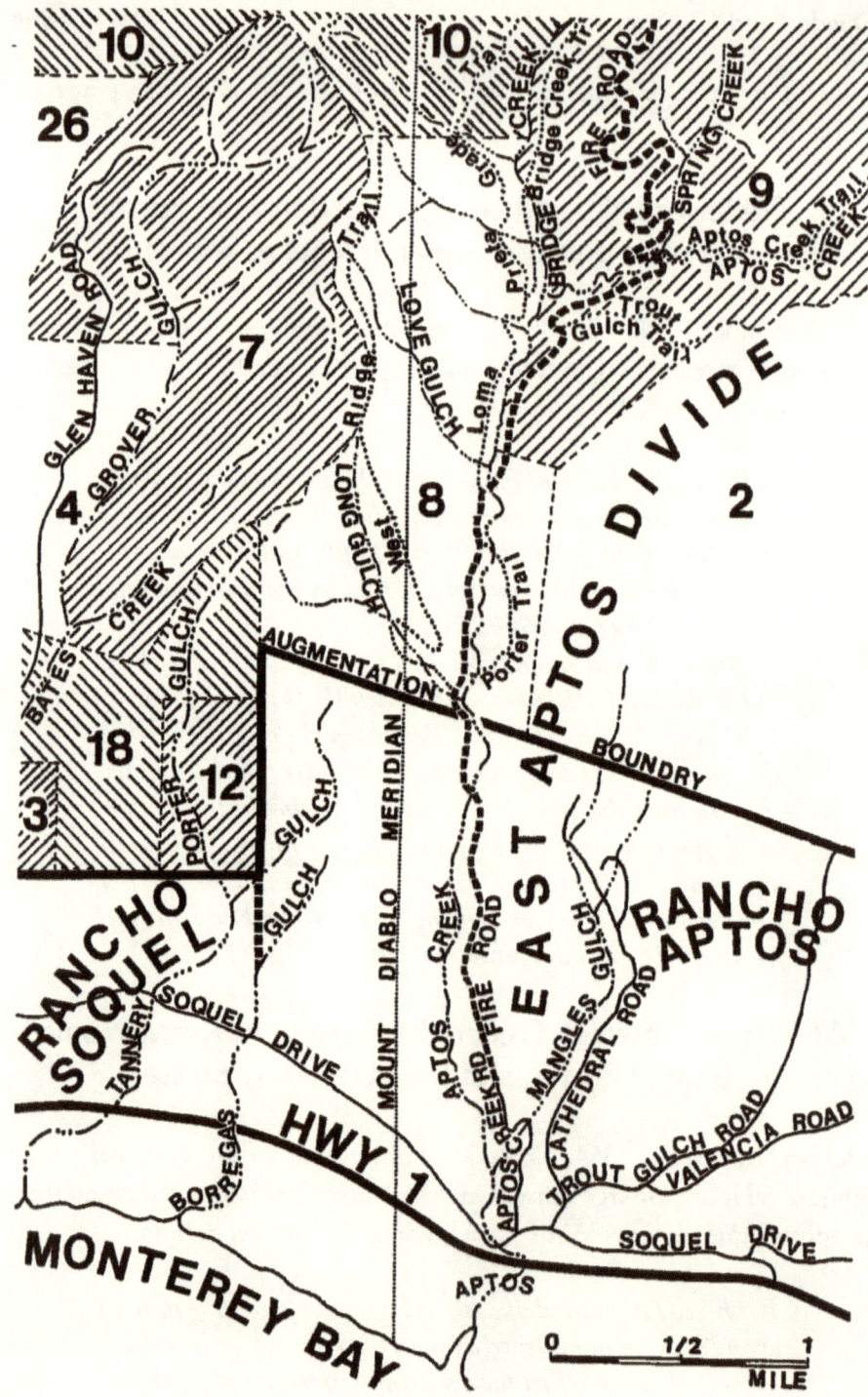

FIGURE 7.7 LOCATION OF TRACT 8

And it is further stipulated that none of the defendants shall, or will appeal from the judgment in the said cause, so far as the same affects the said defendants in relation to each other.

And Defendant Frederick A. Hihn stipulates to withdraw and hereby withdraws his statement on appeal heretofore filed in said cause, from so much the judgment of the court as affects Augustus Noble, George K. Porter, and the heirs of Frederick W. Macondray; the errors being waived and the appeal not to be taken in regard to the heirs of Frederick W. Macondray; and this stipulation and agreement, being made upon payment of $500 by Augustus Noble, George K. Porter, and the heirs of Frederick W. Macondray to Frederick A. Hihn as the consideration of his entering into the same, and waiving his rights and being it the intention of the partners hereto to make the judgment entered in the cause, final as between the defendants Frederick A. Hihn, Augustus Noble, George K. Porter, and the heir of Frederick W. Macondray, so that the same shall not be in any manner appealed from, or objected to as regards the defendants.

signed by
Frederick A. Hihn
Augustus Noble
Selden S. Wright,
attorney for George K. Porter[453]

Land transfer by the Macondray Estate to Thomas Fallon

On September 13, 1864, the Macondray Estate, acting on behalf of Frederick Macondray's widow, Lavina Capen Smith, agreed to sell 1,167 acres in Tract 8 in Shoquel Augmentation for $800 to Thomas Fallon. Carmel Fallon signed on behalf of her husband and, following the sale, the Fallons' combined holdings in the Augmentation totaled nearly twenty-five percent of the original grant or 8,012 acres.[454]

Judge McKee finalizes partition of Shoquel Augmentation

After having filed his Action for Partition decree on August 8, 1864, Judge McKee made the order final on September 14, thereby officially recognizing the partition lines within Shoquel Augmentation determined by the three referees.[455]

Craven Hester and Benjamin Farley request a new trial

Former judge Craven Hester and his friend Benjamin Farley did not simply accept their fate, but rather fought on despite appeals being filed by Frederick Hihn and the partitioning report being finalized by Judge McKee. On September 29, 1864, the two men filed an extensive rebuttal of the Shoquel Augmentation Partitioning Suit's decisions and demanded, once again, that the Younger Report be set aside and that a new survey be done that took into account claims to School Land Warrants and other factors not considered by Charles Younger, McKee, and the other referees in the case. Hester argued that:

> *The referees were duly appointed by the court to make partition of the land in the complaint so as to give to each party the quality of land equal in value to the interest decreed to him by Charles B. Younger in his report.*
>
> *That the referees reported to the court at the December term thereof 1863 their doings in that matter and that they had set off to each party land of equal value to the interest in land decreed by the court.*
>
> *And in the report made by the referees in setting off lands to the parties respectively, they made no reservation in favor of any one of the right-of-way over the lands of other parties or party in said suit, all of which will more fully appear by reference to the report and proceedings in said suit.*
>
> *That the court gave time to the parties to object to the report and some of the parties made objections which came on to be heard by the court on the first Saturday of the August term of 1864.*

The court next ordered the objections to be continued until the next succeeding Tuesday after the said Saturday, for proof by affidavits, of the matter of the objections.

When I was in court, I asked Robert F. Peckham, who was opposing the objections, whether the matter of costs in the suit be continued until the following term for decision by the court, to which he replied "Yes!"

I next asked Peckham whether other proceedings would be had at the August term in the court than the disposing of the objections and the final confirmation of the report, to which he replied, as I understood him, "no."

I next asked the plaintiff Frederick A. Hihn substantially the same questions and he replied, as I understood him, the same as his attorney, Robert F. Peckham.

After I received the preceding answers to my questions, which indicated that both the plaintiff and his attorney were not interested in the objections to the referees' report, and as nothing further was to be done in the court pertaining to the suit, I went home.

At the time the preceding occurred, Robert F. Peckham was the attorney of record in the present suit for the plaintiff Frederick A. Hihn and also for Luisa Juan and also for some other defendants in the suit. That on Monday next after the said Saturday, the objections were delivered or overruled and a decree rendered by the court of confirmation of the referees' report, as the affiant has been informed.

And also, at the same time, Robert F. Peckham, as attorney for Luisa Juan, moved the court to enter among the proceedings the following order: "And that there be and is hereby reserved to each and every party to such partition a right-of-way over the nearest convenient route from the lands set off and assigned to him or her by the decree across the land of others to a public highway."

The preceding motion was then granted and said order made by the court, as well fully appear by reference to the proceedings of this suit.

Neither I nor Benjamin Farley authorized the preced-

ing motion, nor were either of us consulted or even present when the motion was presented. Also, neither of us knew about the order until sometime after adjournment of the term of the court and that we received verbal information that some such a proceeding had been had but not of its true character.

And although the order was made as stated, yet I and Benjamin Farley have not had any notice of the motion in either writing, verbally, or otherwise, nor have either of us had since the making of the order any notice in writing within ten days after the making of the order or at any time served upon us of the order, or of a reservation of the right-of-way as let out in the order, or any reservation of the right-of-way or of the final decree in the cause.

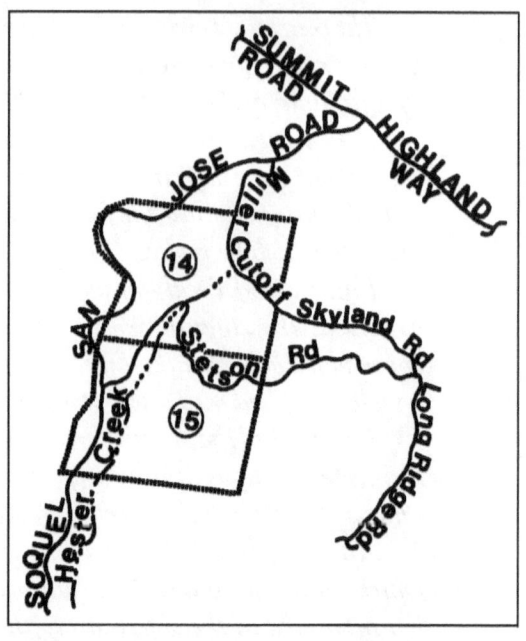

FIGURE 7.8 LOCATION OF TRACTS 14 AND 15

Neither the plaintiff, Frederick A. Hihn, nor any of the defendants or their answers therein or in any proceedings in said cause, to have reserved, in any way or form whatever, the right-of-way embraced in the order, or any right-of-way, that the recent information was not only a surprise to me, but an astonishment.

Also, the order was made by the court upon Robert F. Peckham, a motion without having any testimony in regard to the matter of it or hearing any testimony whatever, and its decision in regard to the order was not justified by any evidence or matter before the court, that no time has been given by the *court to object to the order, that no objections could be made to it under the leave given to object to the report of the referees that, if the court has power to make said order, it should have heard testimony that the land set off as aforesaid to the parties were not a just partition and their interest was not apportioned in conformity to the decree fixing their interest respectively, to said land, and that the correct way to equalize the interest was by a reservation of the way as aforesaid made.*

I, Craven P. Hester, and my client, Benjamin Farley, each had a lot of land set off to us by the referees' report, the order affects the interest of me, Craven Hester, injuriously, to the two lots that were set off to me and Benjamin Farley, and that the injury is a peculiar one to me owning to the locality of the land set off to me and Benjamin Farley, both being located on a high mountain with little following land on top that is cultivable that will now be subject to disturbance by travelers and thus rendering the land much less valuable.

The order by the court operates as a great grievance to me that I was prevented from having a fair hearing of the matter of the court order, and if set aside, I believe that I can show the court that it has no right to supply the doings of the three referees by such an order, and that I can show by testimony that the injustice and impropriety of such an order, and that because of its injurious operation upon the rights of me, Craven P. Hester.[456]

Frederick Hihn files an appeal concerning objections to the Younger Report

Throughout the Shoquel Augmentation Partitioning Suit, Frederick Hihn entered several objections into the record. In particular, after the Younger Report was produced, he objected to the loss of a 1/9 claim to the Augmentation. He had purchased a joint claim to both Rancho Soquel and the Augmentation through a court-ordered sale from Pruett Sinclair and John Hames in September 1859. However, the sheriff, when issuing the deeds, made a mistake that invalidated the deeds. Younger had accepted the

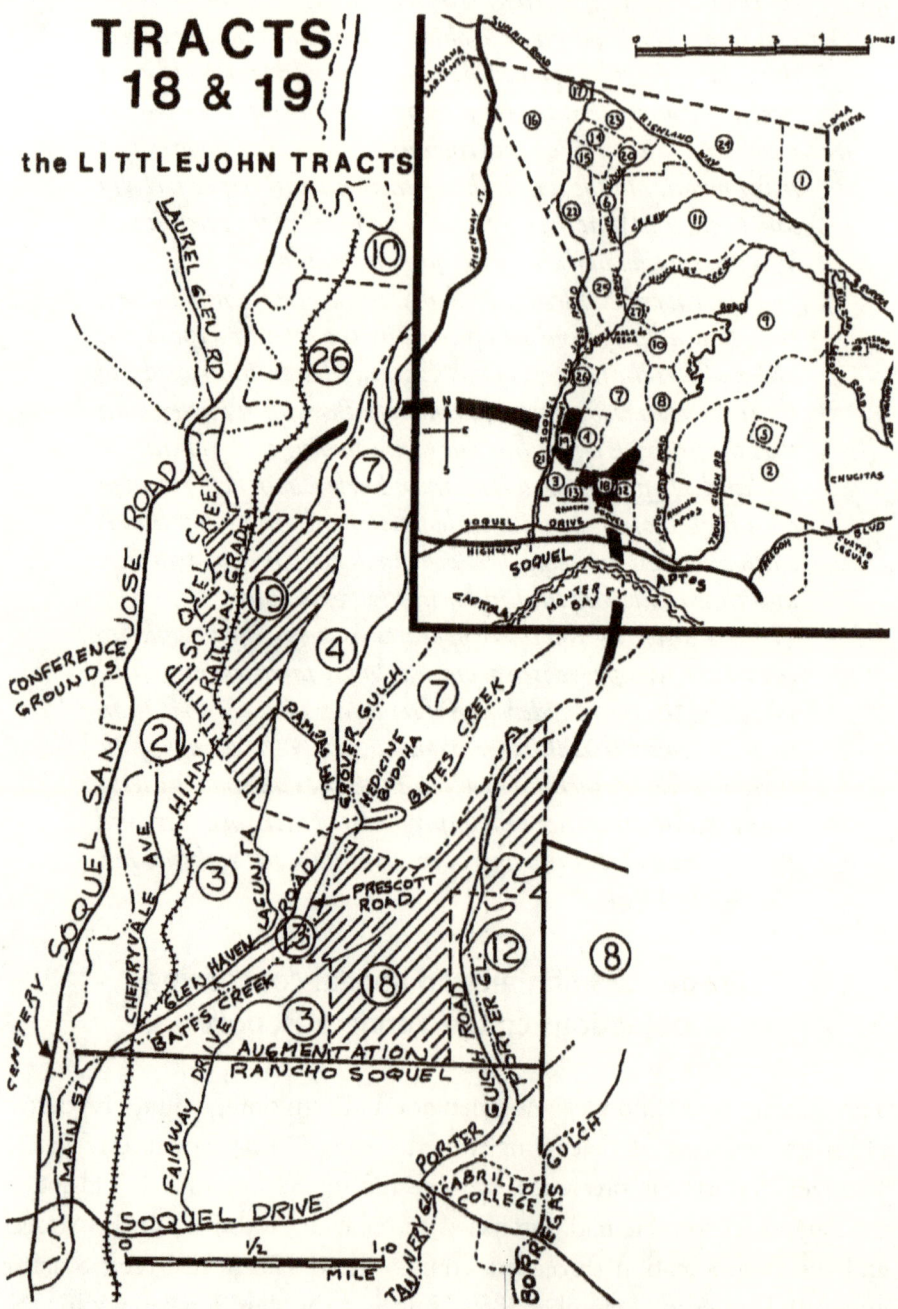

FIGURE 7.9 LOCATION OF TRACTS 18 AND 19

Rancho Soquel deed, but did not accept the Augmentation grant, depriving Hihn of 3,597 acres of land. On October 4, 1864, Hihn once more filed an appeal against the Younger Report, citing the legitimacy of his deed of 1859.[457]

Thomas Courtis, John Wilson, Mary Slade, Cyrus Coe, Charles Plum, and Henry Lawrence file an appeal concerning objections to the Younger Report

On October 25, 1864, Thomas Courtis, on his own behalf and as administrator for the estates of Father Ingoldsby and Benjamin Green, John Wilson, Mary Slade, Cyrus Coe, Charles Plum, and Henry Lawrence filed an appeal to the California Supreme Court regarding the decision in the Shoquel Augmentation Partitioning Suit. This was a parallel appeal to that lodged by the group in August regarding the decision in the Rancho Soquel partitioning suit, and they held to the same argument, that Martina Castro's agreement of 1850 was invalid and that Castro had sold all of both land grants to the Catholic Church in 1855.[458]

Land transfer by Helena Lodge to Frederick Hihn

On October 28, 1864, Helena and Joseph Littlejohn finally transferred the land that was confirmed to them within Shoquel Augmentation to Frederick Hihn, thereby fulfilling the agreement they had made with Hihn in July 1860. It will be remembered that the Littlejohns had exchanged their claims in the Augmentation to Hihn for $10,000, pending the final resolution of the partitioning case. Hihn had also agreed to pay for all court and legal fees owed by the Littlejohns. In the end, Helena had received a 5/27 claim to the Augmentation, encompassing Tracts 18 and 19, which were transferred to Hihn.[459]

Agreement between Frederick Hihn and George Kirby

Because there was a chance that George Kirby could win the appeal concerning his claim to 1/27 of Shoquel Augmentation, which he had purchased in January 1855 from Montgomery Shackleford, Frederick Hihn agreed on November 3, 1864 to sell Kirby twenty acres of land located in the southwestern corner of the Augmentation, extending along the east bank of Soquel Creek. However, Hihn required certain agreements and conditions before he would allow the sale to go through.

Shackleford's land was originally purchased in September 1852 from Nicanor Lajeunesse and totaled approximately 1,000 acres. For several years, he lived on the land and planted crops, and he enclosed the property with a fence. Along Bates Creek, he built a dam to irrigate his crops. When Kirby took over the property in 1855, he improved it further by adding an orchard and commercial tree nursery and expanding the agricultural plots. He also added new structures and expanded the fencing. However, the original deed of sale was declared invalid in the Younger Report because Lajeunesse had not properly acknowledged her mark on the document.

Wishing to move beyond the partitioning suit, Hihn stated in his agreement with Kirby that "the twenty acres should not include the little orchard next to the small house built by Kirby, that the land shall be located further north so as to include the whole of an orchard notwithstanding that by such change of location the quantity of the land hereby to be conveyed shall be increased." Hihn added a second statement that Kirby had the right to cut down only sufficient redwoods to build a fence to enclose the twenty acres, with this option expiring after six months. Furthermore, Kirby would allow a survey team to pass through his property so that a new road could be built during the winter along the northeast boundary of his property to access the Bates mill.

In exchange for all of this, Hihn would acquire all of Kirby's other claims to and physical property in Rancho Soquel and the Augmentation, and he would agree not to appeal the final partitioning decree. Kirby consented and the land was sold to Kirby on December 30 for $1.00. Through this agreement, Hihn became the undisputed owner of Lajeunesse's 1/9 claim to the Augmentation.[460]

Frederick Hihn again nominated to Board of Supervisors

In a *Santa Cruz Weekly Sentinel* article published on November 5, 1864, it was revealed that Frederick Hihn had been unanimously chosen to run

Divided and Conquered 1864

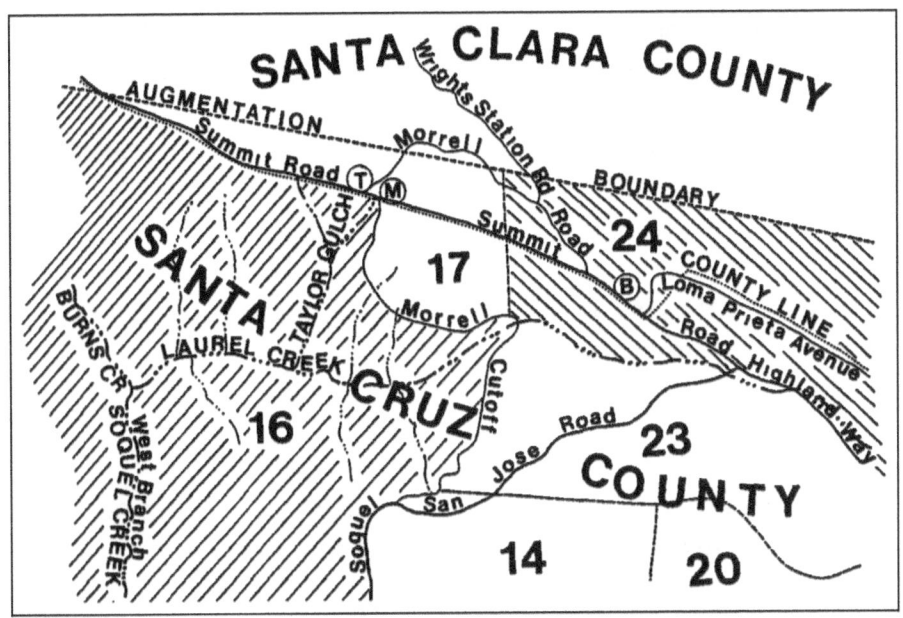

FIGURE 7.10 LOCATION OF TRACT 17

for a second term on the Santa Cruz County Board of Supervisors by the Unionist Party at a general caucus held at the County Court House on October 29.[461]

Land transfer by Frederick Hihn to James Taylor

On December 6, 1864, Frederick Hihn signed a deed that sold back to James Taylor forty-one acres of the original 180 acres that Taylor was awarded in the Younger Report as Tract 17. When precisely Hihn purchased this acreage is unclear and no deed seems to exist in the county deed books regarding the transaction. The forty-one acres returned to Taylor included the family's home as well as a small orchard and garden. Today, this property is located at the flat area where Summit Road, Morrell Road, and Morrell Cut-off converge. The remainder of Tract 17 stayed with Hihn and is one of the few places within Shoquel Augmentation where large old-growth redwoods still grow.[462]

1864 – 1865

Judgment decree served to Luisa Fourcade, Richard Savage, Francis Brady, and Benjamin Nichols for past due referee bill

On December 6, 1864, Judge McKee called to account Luisa Fourcade, Richard Savage, Francis Brady, and Benjamin Nichols for failure to pay the amounts they owed to the referees for their services in the Shoquel Augmentation partitioning suit. Only Fourcade's failure to pay, however, impacted future events. In addition to the $59.29 she owed to the court, which had a recurring fine of $2.50 added to the total, she also owed money to Frederick Hihn, who filed this delinquency of $34.56 with the court on December 8.[463]

Brad Morrell arrives in San Francisco from Maine before heading for the Gold Country

Preferring to be called Brad, Ephraim Bradbury Morrell was born in Waterville, Maine in 1831. When gold was discovered in California, both he and his younger brother, Hiram, got gold fever and headed west, but Brad, being the older, left first. Hiram joined him in 1854. While in the Sierra Nevada, Brad helped pioneer hydraulic mining techniques alongside other like-minded gold miners. By 1859, though, Hiram had grown tired of hunting for the elusive mineral and relocated to the Santa Clara Valley where he eventually settled on the Summit and farmed. Brad, meanwhile, arrived on the Summit in late December 1864 and immediately entered the Santa Cruz Mountain lumber industry. Despite his brother operating his own farm and having just married, Brad frequently asked him to help in setting up and running his mills. Brad's first known lumber mill was a small facility on Hester Creek at the mouth of Caldwell Gulch within Tract 22 of Shoquel Augmentation.[464]

Francis Brady, Benjamin Nichols, Benjamin Porter, George Kirby, and the Bates Estate file notice of appeal

On January 13, 1865, Francis Brady, Benjamin Nichols, Benjamin Porter, George Kirby, and the Bates Estate filed notice of their intent to appeal the final decision in the Shoquel Augmentation Partitioning Suit and petition for a new report to be drafted. They sent the notice to Robert Peckham, Carmel and Thomas Fallon, Antonia and Henry Peck, Helena and Joseph Littlejohn, Luisa and Jean Fourcade, and Guadalupe and Joseph Averon, all of whom benefited from the ruling.[465]

Lien placed on Luisa Fourcade's Tracts 5 and 6

As per the ruling issued to Luisa Fourcade on December 6, 1864 regarding her failure to repay the debts she owed to the referees in the two partitioning suits and to Frederick Hihn, a lien was placed on Tracts 5 and 6 within Shoquel Augmentation on February 16, 1865. Because of the complex nature of Fourcade's property, though, this lien impacted everyone who owned or occupied land within her two tracts.[466]

Francis Brady, Benjamin Nichols, and Richard Savage file notice of appeal

Having sold Tracts 26 and 27 to Benjamin Cahoon, Francis Brady, Benjamin Nichols, and Richard Savage were nonetheless responsible for defending their former land and they felt that Judge McKee had failed to award them what they were owed. Thus, on March 15, 1865, they notified Robert Peckham of their intention to appeal the partitioning decree to the California Supreme Court. The three referees for the Shoquel Augmentation partition—Thomas Wright, John Towne, and Godfrey Bockius—as well as the court clerk, David Haslam, received copies of the notice of intent. The notice was lodged on March 18 and reads:

> *On behalf of Richard Savage, we, John P. Stearns, a resident of the town of Santa Cruz, by occupation a carpenter, and William Anthony, a resident of the town of Santa Cruz, by occupation a tinsmith.*
> *Note: on behalf of Francis R. Brady and Benjamin Cahoon Nichols, John B. Arcan, a resident of Santa Cruz, also a carpenter by occupation, replaced Stearns, do undertake on the part of Richard Savage, that we are bound to the*

> *tune of $400 in coin, that if said judgment, or any part thereof, be affirmed that Savage shall pay the amount directed by the said judgment, or the part of such amount as to which the judgment shall be affirmed, if affirmed only in part, and all damages and costs which shall be awarded against Richard Savage upon the appeal, in coin not exceeding $400.*

The money was to cover the $16.07 that Richard Savage was charged by the three referees, and the $29.64 charged to Brady and Nichols.[467]

Francis Brady, Benjamin Nichols, Benjamin Porter, and the Bates Estate file an appeal

On March 16, 1865, Francis Brady, Benjamin Nichols, Benjamin Porter, and the Bates Estate filed their appeal to the Shoquel Augmentation Partitioning Suit ruling with the state Supreme Court. The four defendants' appeal stated that they objected to the Younger Report, that it did not state the facts, and that Judge McKee refused to allow a new report to be drafted.

Porter and the Bates Estate's approach was to argue that the document signed by Helena and Joseph Littlejohn in January 1858 was simply a mortgage with Frederick Hihn, not a transfer of 1/27 of the Augmentation. Similarly, they argued that Luisa and Jean Fourcade had only signed a mortgage with Hihn, too, in April 1859. Meanwhile, all four defendants disputed the legitimacy of Nicanor and Francisco Lajeunesse's deed of July 1860, claiming that it was illegal since Francisco had not signed the deed the same day and that the land was no longer available for sale since they had sold all of it to Thomas Wright, Peter Tracy, and Montgomery Shackleford in 1852.[468]

Frederick Hihn, George Porter, and Augustus Noble sign a stipulation

On April 5, 1865, Frederick Hihn, George Porter, and Augustus Noble agreed to a stipulation concerning several deeds signed between 1859 and 1860 regarding land in both Rancho Soquel and Shoquel Augmentation. It stated that after Augustus Noble and George Porter had paid the sum of

$242.50 in coin and Carmel Fallon had paid in kind, that Porter, Noble, and Fallon, as well as the heirs of Frederick Macondray, would be free from any liability in Hihn's appeal of the partitioning suits regarding the 1/30 claim to the Augmentation that he had lost to Frederick Macondray through a technical error in 1860.[469]

Craven Hester and Benjamin Farley file notice to appeal

Craven Hester and Benjamin Farley filed a notice on April 18, 1865 that they intended to appeal the decision in the Shoquel Augmentation Partitioning Suit to the state Supreme Court. The focus of their appeal was the addendum by Judge McKee that rights-of-way could be established on owners' lands in order to reach the nearest county road. More specifically, they appealed McKee's ruling against their motion for a new report to be conducted. For reasons never stated, Hester and Farley did not pursue this appeal after lodging their statement of intent.[470]

Land transfer by John Daubenbiss, Edward Porter, Jacob Parsons, A. J. Reily, and Guadalupe Lodge to Frederick Hihn for Soquel Creek water rights

Frederick Hihn had acquired much of Shoquel Augmentation before and after the end of the partitioning suit, but he did not control water rights to Soquel Creek. Indeed, the dam that John Daubenbiss and John Hames had erected in 1847 was owned by George Evans when the suit began, and was purchased by Daubenbiss while it was ongoing, eventually becoming the tiny, two-acre Tract 21. However, Hihn needed potable water for some of his projects in Soquel, so on May 5, 1865 he purchased the water rights from Daubenbiss and his wife, Margareta, as well as from several of his neighbors, including Edward Porter, Jacob Parsons, A. J. Reily, and Guadalupe and Joseph Averon.[471]

Land transfer by Benjamin Cahoon to Lucy Ann Cahoon

As Benjamin Cahoon approached his sixty-seventh year, he decided to transfer ownership of some, but not all, of his lands to his daughter Lucy Ann. On June 16, 1865, he signed a gift deed in which he passed title to the lands to his daughter, including Tracts 26 and 27 in Shoquel Augmentation. By this time, Tract 26 was almost entirely clear-cut of all valuable timber, possibly the first tract within the Augmentation to be so cleared.

Cahoon lived out his retirement from his home near the junction of Laurel Glen Road and the Soquel Turnpike (Soquel San Jose Road) until his death on June 30, 1874. His son Edwin later converted the home to a small summer resort which was popular with travelers taking the road. In later years, the home was acquired by the Casalegno family, who operated a country store and service station out of the home.[472]

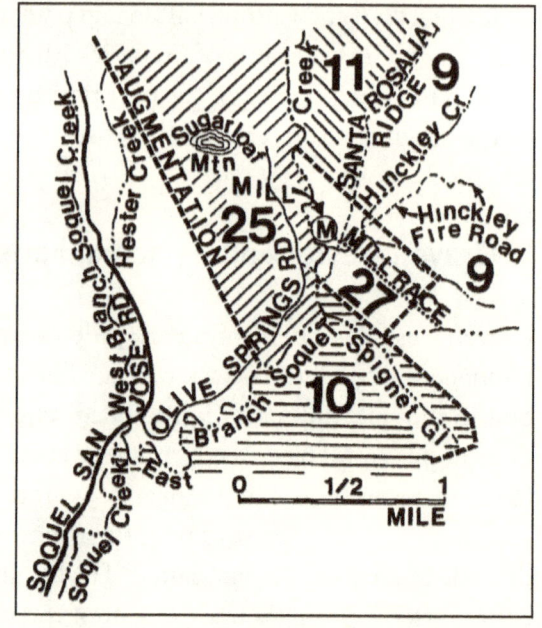

FIGURE 7.11 LOCATION OF TRACT 27

Charles McKiernan opens a hotel on the Summit

With new improvements to his property, additional sources of income, and his land cleared of redwoods, Charles McKiernan finally entered into the hospitality business in 1865. At precisely the point where the Santa Cruz Gap Turnpike became the Santa Cruz Turnpike (about a mile from the modern-day intersection of Summit and Mountain Charley Roads), McKiernan built a large, two-story hotel. It was known by several names over the years, including the Summit Hotel, the Mountain House (to differentiate it from Lyman Burrell's Mountain Home), and the Halfway House, since it was located midway between Forbes Mill (Los Gatos) and Hiram Scott's house.

A caption that sat beneath a painting of this hotel at the Los Gatos

Museum once read: "The Summit Hotel was a rest stop where people could eat, drink and rest prior to completing the trip over the mountain. It was also where the stagecoach had its six-horse exchange." Horses were added or removed as a coach climbed the mountain to overcome the steep terrain. McKiernan began accepting stagecoach passengers at his home beginning in the early 1860s after he expanded his home to make room for the new guests. Around 1870, he added a wine house and liquor store to his property, which provided alcohol to passing visitors and all the families on the Summit. The approximate location of this store today is 22196 Summit Road.

Owing to the lack of secondary schools on the Summit, McKiernan and his family moved to San José around 1874 so that his son could enroll in high school there. McKiernan built a large home at 225 West Saint Augustine Street but retained his interests on the Summit. Over the years, he leased his timber stands and sold stumpage rights to various firms. He also had a sawmill built in downtown San José to process some of his timber. On Alviso Road, he started a berry farm and erected a hay and grain warehouse. He quickly rose through the ranks of the Pacific Coast Wine Company to become its president and was a shareholder in the San Jose Light & Power Company and the San Jose Water Company. Charles McKiernan fell ill in November 1891 and died on January 16, 1892.[473]

Thomas Courtis, John Wilson, Mary Slade, Cyrus Coe, Charles Plum, and Henry Lawrence file notice to appeal

Between July 8 and 20, 1865, Thomas Courtis filed his appeal of the Rancho Soquel Partitioning Suit with the California Supreme Court. The following are the series of documents he lodged with the court:

> *Thomas Courtis, et al., file notice of intention to appeal to the California Supreme Court based on the following adverse decisions:*
> *From the order of the District Court overruling the defendants Thomas Courtis in his own right, Thomas Courtis as administrator for the John Ingoldsby and Benjamin P. Green estates, Mary E. J. Slade, Charles W. Plum, Henry H. Lawrence, Cyrus Coe, and John Wilson exceptions to the*

referees' report on April 22, 1863, and from the order therein made and entered by the court on April 22, 1863 overruling the above defendants' motion for a new trial, and from the Interlocutory Decree therein entered on April 22, 1863, and from the final Judgment therein made and entered in the District Court on July 25, 1864 in favor of the plaintiffs, Henry W. Peck and Maria Antonia Peck, his wife, and the following defendants, to wit:

> *Frederick A. Hihn*
> *Joseph and Guadalupe Averon*
> *Ricardo and Luisa Juan*
> *Benjamin F. Porter*
> *George K. Porter*
> *Joseph David and Helena Littlejohn*
> *Joshua Parrish*

and against the defendants listed in the Courtis appeal, and this appeal is taken from the whole thereof.

signed by the attorneys,
John Wilson and Selden S. Wright,
for the above defendants appealing
to the California Supreme Court

This notice was sent to the clerk of the Third District Court, to Robert Peckham as representative of the above plaintiffs, to Frederick Hihn, to Martina Castro's heirs, and to Joseph H. Skerin, representing defendants Benjamin and George Porter.

On July 8, the following was submitted:

> *Affidavit of Service Notice of Thomas Courtis, et al., Appeal, by James O. Wanzer, that after being duly sworn, disposes and says that he is a citizen of the United States, of the age of more than 21 years, that on the following days he did deliver a copy of the within notice: on July 8, 1865, he handed upon Joseph H. Skerin personally a true and correct copy at his res-*

idence in the town of Santa Cruz, and on July 20, 1865, he served a copy of the notice of appeal on Frederick A. Hihn, by handing him a copy, personally, at the town of Santa Cruz.

This was followed on July 10 by:

Affidavit by Selden S. Wright that he mailed a copy of the Thomas Court's appeal to the California Supreme Court on July 10, 1865 in the post office, in the city and county of San Francisco that was correct and true of the notice of the above defendants' appeal to the California Supreme Court.

And on July 15 with:

Affidavit by Selden S. Wright for mailing copy of Notice of Appeal by Thomas Courtis, et al. After being duly sworn, Wright states that he is a white male citizen of the United States of America, of the age of 21 years and upwards, and is one of the attorneys for the defendants in the Thomas Courtis, et al., suit.... That on the 10th day of July, 1865, he deposited in the post office, in the city and county of San Francisco, a full, true, and correct copy of the notice of the Courtis, et al., appeal to the California Supreme Court from the order of the District Court overruling their exceptions to the referee's report, and from the order of the court overruling their motion for a new trial therein, and from the Interlocutory Decree, made and entered therein April 22, 1863, and from the final decree, made and entered therein against them. The said notice was duly filed in the clerk's office of the District Court, in the County of Santa Cruz, July 8, 1865.

The copy of the notice deposited in the post office by this affiant was enclosed in an envelope and addressed to Robert F. Peckham, the attorney for the plaintiffs, and divers defendants in said action, at his place of residence, to wit: the city of San Jose, Santa Clara County, in the words following, viz: Robert F. Peckham, Esq., Attorney at Law, San Jose, Santa Clara County, California.

That this affiant prepaid the postage thereon amounting to six cents. That there is a regular communication between the said city and county of San Francisco and said city of San Jose.

Undertaking on appeal:

Whereas, Thomas Courtis, in his individual right, Thomas Courtis, the administrator of the John Ingoldsby estate, deceased, Mary E. J. Slade, Charles Plum, Henry H. Lawrence, Cyrus Coe, and John Wilson, a portion of the defendants in this action above named, have appealed to the California Supreme Court, from a judgment or decree Interlocutory, made and entered against them in said action, in the District Court in favor of the above named plaintiffs, and some of the defendants therein mentioned, on April 23, 1863, for the partition of certain lands and premises therein described, and from the order of the District Court and there entered, overruling the exceptions of said defendants, Courtis and others, to the report of the referee in said cause, and from the order of said District Court, then and there entered, overruling said appellants' motion for a new trial therein, and also from the final decree therein entered in said court, on July 25, 1864.

Now, therefore, in consideration of the premises and of such appeal, we, the undersigned, George Amerige and Moses Ellis, both residents of the city and county of San Francisco, State of California, do hereby jointly and severally undertake and promise on the part of the appellants, that said appellants will pay all damages and costs which may be awarded against them or either of them on the appeal, not exceeding $300, to which amount we acknowledge ourselves jointly and severally indebted.

George Amerige and Moses Ellis
in San Francisco July 10, 1865

George Amerige and Moses Ellis, the persons named in and who subscribe the foregoing undertaking, as the sureties thereto, being severally duly sworn, say, and each for himself deposes

> *and says, that he is worth double the amount specified in said undertaking, as the penalty thereof, over and above all debts and liabilities, exclusive of property exempt from execution.*
>
> George Amerige and Moses Ellis
> July 10, 1865 in San Francisco
> W. Willson, Notary Public
>
> Bond on appeal, filed July 12, 1865
> David J. Haslam, Court Clerk
> by James O. Wanzer, Deputy Court Clerk

On July 20, Wanzer, after being duly sworn, stated that he served a copy of the notice of Courtis's appeal to Hihn by delivering the copy directly to his hand.

Two months later, on September 22, the documents submitted for the appeal were certified by the county clerk:

> *David J. Haslam, County Clerk of the County of Santa Cruz and Ex Officio clerk of the District Court, of the 3rd Judicial District, in and for said county, do hereby certify the papers and orders contained in the annexed and foregoing 399 folios to be true, full, and correct copies of the original papers on file, and orders entered of record in said District Court, in the suit of Henry W. Peck and Antonia Peck, plaintiffs, versus Frederick A. Hihn, et al., and that the same constitute the transcript on appeal to the California Supreme Court in said cause.*
>
> *In witness whereof, I have hereunto set my hand and the seal of said court, this 22nd day of September, 1865.*
>
> David J. Haslam, clerk[474]

Thomas Courtis, John Wilson, Mary Slade, Cyrus Coe, Charles Plum, and Henry Lawrence file notice to appeal

Following on the footsteps of his appeal of the Rancho Soquel Partitioning

Suit, Thomas Courtis filed on July 21, 1865 his appeal of the Shoquel Augmentation decision as follows:

> *You will please take notice, that defendants Thomas Courtis on his own behalf, as administrator for the John Ingoldsby and Benjamin P. Green estates, Mary E. J. Slade, Charles W. Plum, Henry H. Lawrence, Cyrus Coe, and attorney John Wilson, in the above entitled action, hereby appeal to the Supreme Court of this State from the order of the 3rd District Court overruling the above defendants' exceptions to the Referee's Report entered into the record December 23, 1863, and from the order therein made and entered in the said cause by the said court, on the 23rd day of April, 1863, overruling the above named defendants' motion for a new trial, and from the Interlocutory Decree therein entered April 23, 1863, and from the final judgment therein made and entered in the said District Court on September 14, 1864 against the aforesaid defendants and in favor of the plaintiff Frederick A. Hihn, and defendants Henry W. Peck and his wife, Antonia Peck, George W. Evans, and others, and this appeal is taken from the whole thereof.*
>
> Attorney John Wilson[475]

Luisa Fourcade given sixty days to repay debts

On September 13, 1865, Luisa Fourcade (alias Juan) was given notice that her property would be sold by court order within sixty days if she did not pay her delinquent court fees plus interest and fines. The notice reads:

> *Whereas on December 8, 1864, Frederick A. Hihn recovered his judgment in the District Court against Luisa Juan for the sum of $34.56, to be paid in gold and silver coin. And whereas by an Interlocutory Decree entered in said case April 23, 1863 it was adjudged and decreed by the District Court that Luisa Juan was the owner of 1/27th undivided part of the Augmentation described in the complaint in said*

cause. Said premises being the Augmentation Ranch. And whereas by decree of partition and judgment in said cause entered September 14, 1864 there was set off to Luisa Juan in severalty in lieu of the said one undivided 27th part of the Augmentation.... And whereas the said sum of $34.56 in gold and silver coin with interest at the rate of ten per cent per annum from December 8, 1864, and also the sum of $3.00 accruing costs is a lien upon the estate rights, title, and interest of Luisa Juan, which she had on the 14th day of August, 1860, or at any time afterwards or now has of in and to the herein before described premises.

Now you, the said Sheriff, are hereby commanded to make the said sums as aforesaid due on said judgment and accruing costs to satisfy judgment out of the foregoing mentioned real estate or any other property belonging to the said Luisa Juan. And of this writ make return within 60 days with what you have done endorsed hereon.[476]

Land transfer by Helena Lodge to Benjamin Porter

On October 5, 1865, Helena and Joseph Littlejohn sold Tracts I and K, totalling 137.363 acres, to Benjamin Porter. A century later, Carrie Lodge reported in an interview the reason why the land was sold:

Uncle Littlejohn knew quite a lot about outside work. He knew horses like his hands. He knew how to drive, knew outside work, but that's about all. And the burden fell upon Aunt Helena.... The Littlejohns were married in 1852 with Joseph fathering a total of fourteen children.... And I heard how they lost their ranch. How true it is, I don't know. Uncle Littlejohn wanted a wagon, and he got it from one of the Porter cousins. And he mortgaged the ranch to buy it. Well, I guess he didn't know about mortgages, how quickly the interest mounts up, see, and they had a tremendous big family...that takes an awful lot to raise. So, they lost their ranch.[477]

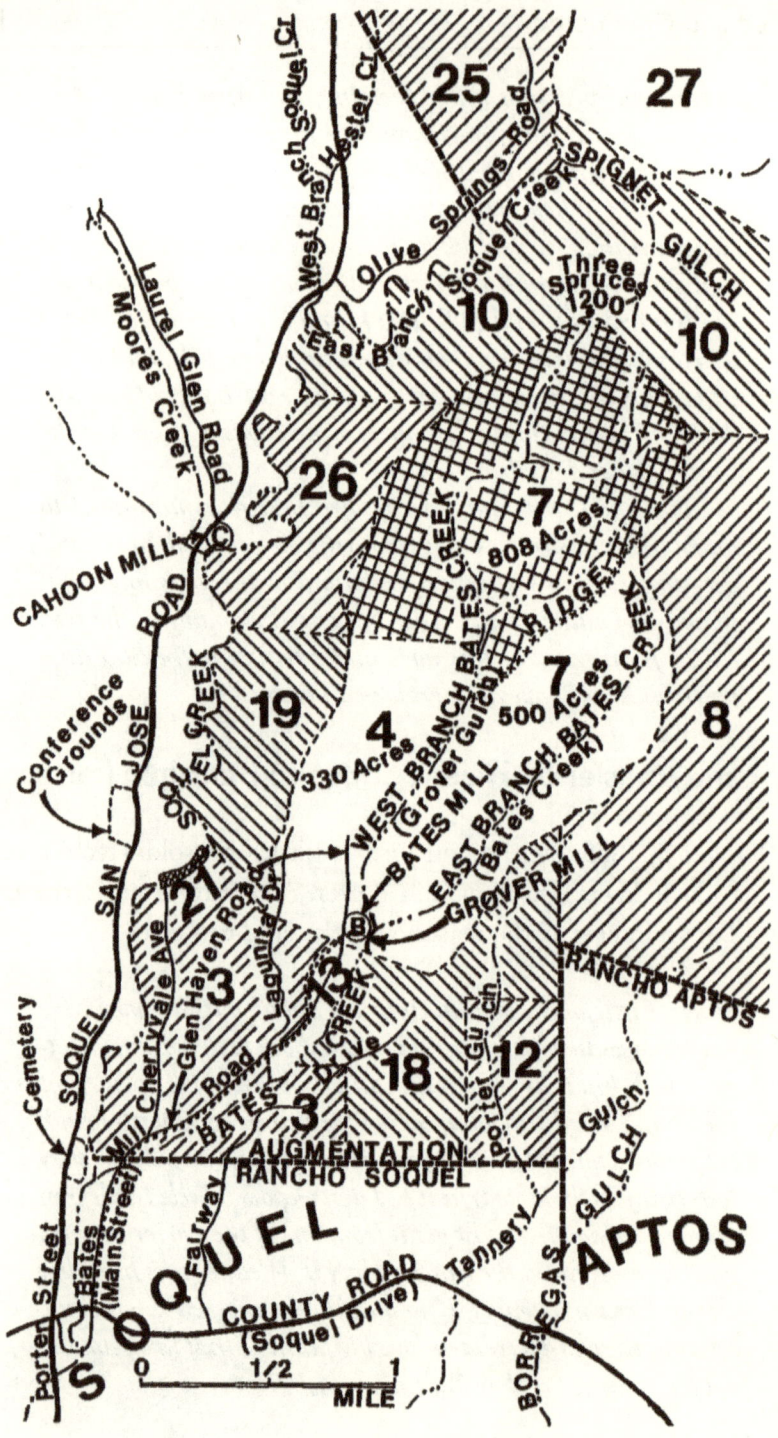

FIGURE 7.12 LOCATION OF TRACTS 4 AND 7

Public sale announced for Luisa Lodge's Tracts 5 and 6

As a procedural step prior to the sale of Luisa Lodge's land, the sheriff, as directed by the Third District Court, lodged a copy of the notice with the county clerk and advertised the sale in the *Santa Cruz Weekly Sentinel* on October 7, 1865. On December 16, it was announced that the auction for Tracts 5 and 6 in Shoquel Augmentation would occur on May 19, 1866.[478]

Rafael Castro leases land in Rancho Aptos to Benjamin, Uriah, and Merritt Nichols for logging

On February 17, 1866, the three Nichols brothers, Benjamin, Uriah, and Merritt, signed a lease agreement with Rafael Castro to refurbish John Watson's abandoned shingle mill on Aptos Creek and begin logging the surrounding redwoods. Shortly after the mill was restored and upgraded to a lumber mill, products began piling up in the storage yard. Part of the refurbishment included making the necessary repairs to the road that Watson had built in order to reach the mill.[479]

Appeals by John Vandenberg and Frederick Hihn rejected

On April 1, 1866, John Vandenberg's appeal of the decision in the Rancho Soquel Partitioning Suit was rejected by the California Supreme Court. He had attempted to prove to the court that his deed with Nicanor Lajeunesse was certified earlier than Frederick Hihn's deed for the same land. However, the case revealed that Vandenberg had certified the deed before the County Clerk, while Hihn had done so before a notary public. The law concerning conveyance of property owned by a woman mandated that only an authorized officer could certify a deed. Unfortunately for Vandenberg, a clerk was not authorized by a notary public. Therefore, the court upheld the decision by Judge McKee and confirmed that the land belonged to Hihn.

That same day, Hihn's own appeal against McKee's ruling, asserting that he should have been awarded a larger portion of Rancho Soquel and that Augustus Noble, George Porter, and the Macondray Estate should have received less, was likewise rejected.[480]

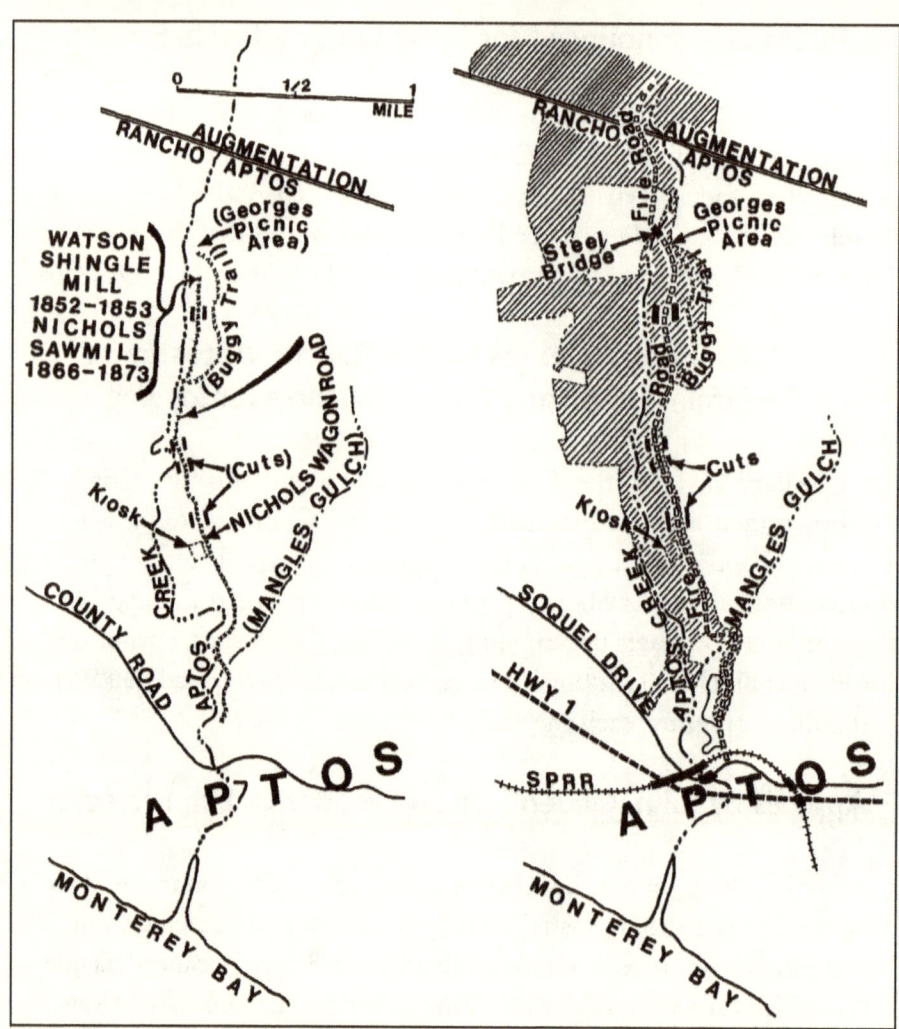

FIGURE 7.13 WATSON AND NICHOLS' MILL ACCESS ROAD IN RANCHO APTOS

FIGURE 7.14 CURRENT FOREST OF NISENE MARKS ENTRY ROAD

Land transfer by Richard Hyde to Thomas Fallon

As Thomas Fallon prepared to begin logging Tracts 8 and 9 in Shoquel Augmentation, he entered into a deed with Richard E. Hyde on April 20, 1866. In this agreement, Hyde sold Fallon 124 acres of land within Rancho Soquel along the Monterey Bay between Borregas Gulch and Porter (Tannery) Gulch.[481]

Land transfer by Luisa Lodge to Frederick Hihn

On May 19, 1866, the auction was held for Luisa Fourcade's Tracts 5 and 6 in Shoquel Augmentation, totaling 1,009 acres. The winner with a bid of $70.76 was Frederick Hihn.[482]

Appeals by Francis Brady, Benjamin Nichols, Benjamin Porter, and Frederick Hihn rejected

On July 1, 1866, the state Supreme Court once again upheld the findings of Charles Younger, ruling that he followed the law and stated the facts as he found them, and that Judge McKee was correct in declining a new report be produced regarding the partitioning of Shoquel Augmentation. The court also accepted that the two deeds between the Fourcades and Littlejohn were not mortgages. Concerning the deed signed by Nicanor Lajeunesse on July 23, 1860 and by Francisco Lajeunesse the following day, the court ruled that it was executed properly and therefore was valid evidence. The court concluded that Francis Brady, Benjamin Nichols, and Benjamin Porter had waited too long to correct any mistakes in the transactions and, as a result, had forfeited any claims that they had to the properties in dispute.

The same day, Frederick Hihn's appeal to have the court accept his deed of September 29, 1859, in which he purchased a 1/18 claim to the Augmentation from Pruett Sinclair and John Hames, was also rejected by the court.[483]

Agreements between George and Benjamin Porter and Thomas Fallon concerning a road to Tracts 8 and 9

Thomas Fallon probably began planning the logging of Tract 9 in Shoquel Augmentation shortly after the referees submitted their partitioning report on December 23, 1863. After he came into possession of Tract 8, he purchased an additional 124 acres from Richard Hyde on April 20, 1866, upon which he planned to build a lumberyard and sawmill.

At first, Fallon wanted to reach Tracts 8 and 9 with a railroad. Therefore, he hired Thomas Wright to survey a four-mile-long right-of-way up Aptos

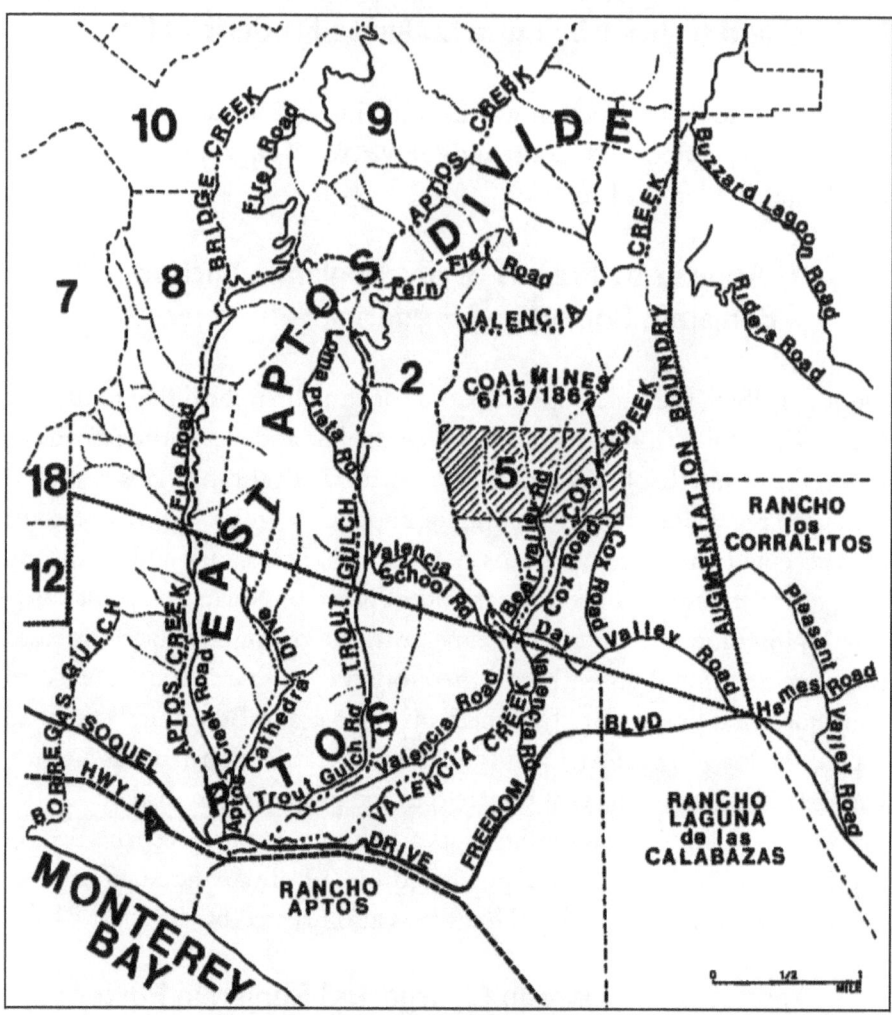

FIGURE 7.15 LOCATION OF TRACT 5 AND THE COAL MINES ON VALENCIA CREEK

Creek until Tract 9 was reached. But actual construction of this railroad required the building of a separate railroad along the coast, which did not yet exist. Because it would still be years before such a route was completed, Fallon decided to build a wagon road to his tracts. The route that this road took was through the land of George and Benjamin Porter, and so on August 22, 1866, Fallon made an agreement with the cousins to build a road through the land of their tannery in Rancho Soquel. This was followed by a second agreement with Benjamin to access the west side of Borregas Gulch in order to reach the Monterey Bay. The first agreement was as follows:

This Indenture made and entered into between Benjamin F. Porter and George K. Porter, parties of the first part, and Thomas Fallon, party of the second part, witness that, whereas the party of the second part is desirous of laying out and grading a good and substantial wagon road for the transportation of wood, lumber, and whatever else may be necessary from that part of the Augmentation, owned by Carmel Fallon, and by her purchased from Mrs. L. Macondray. Said road to commence at some point on said portions of the Augmentation and to run from thence across the lands of Rafael Castro to the easterly line on the Borregas Gulch of the Rancho Soquel, and from thence across said Rancho Soquel to the public road leading from Santa Cruz to Watsonville.

The road above described is to be used by Thomas Fallon, Carmel Fallon, his wife, and each of their heirs and assigns, tenants, servants, visitors, and all other persons who shall have occasion to pass and repass on foot, with all kinds of animals, or vehicles between the public road and that portion of the Augmentation aforesaid.

And the said parties of the first part desiring to have the use of such road as soon as the same is laid out for the purpose of transporting wood, lumber, and other materials over the same.

Now, therefore, in consideration that the party of the second part shall cause the road to be laid out and shall allow the parties of the first part the free and uninterrupted use of the road for the purpose aforesaid and for the further consideration of the sum of $25 to the parties of the first part by Thomas Fallon, at or before the delivery of these presents, duly paid. The receipt whereof is hereby acknowledged. The parties of the first part have given and granted and by these present, give, and grant unto the party of the second part, his heirs and assigns forever, the right to enter upon, locate, open, and grade a road not exceeding sixty feet in width across the lands of the parties of the first part.

Concerning the road from the westerly side of the Borregas Gulch on such grade as the party of the second part shall se-

lect...and from the lands of Rafael Castro to the county road, and also the rights within the limits of such road so located, to make all such excavations, embankments, and bridges, and to cut all such hills and undergrowth as shall be necessary to make the same a good passable road for loaded vehicles and to maintain and keep the same in repair.

And also the right for himself, Thomas Fallon, and his wife, Carmel Fallon, and each of their heirs and assigns, tenants, agents, servants, visitors, and all other persons having occasions to use the same, free rights of way to pass and repass over and along said road either on foot, with all kinds of animals, and vehicles, at all times whatsoever.

And the party of the second part, in consideration thereof, hereby covenants and agrees that as soon as the road shall be open from the Rafael Castro land to the public road, the parties of the first part, their heirs and assigns, tenants, and servants shall forever have the free use of the road for the purpose of transporting wood, lumber, and other materials over the road; but nothing herein contained shall be construed to bind either party to keep the road in repair for the use of the other or for any other person whatsoever.

And the parties of the first part have further given and granted and by these present do give and grant unto Thomas Fallon, his heirs and assigns forever, the right at any time after laying out and opening the wagon road, as aforesaid, to lay down and maintain a railroad track over and along said road and to place cars thereon with locomotives or horse power for the transportation of wood, lumber, or other materials, or for the transportation of passengers, that said track and cars shall be for his and their own use and benefit forever.

Signed and sealed by
Benjamin F. Porter,
George K. Porter,
Thomas Fallon
and acknowledged by
E. G. Joice and E. L. Williams, Notary publics

The second agreement with Benjamin Porter alone was largely the same but had several important differences. First, the purpose of the agreement was to connect Fallon's land in the north to the small acreage he had purchased from Hyde on the Monterey Bay. To accomplish this, he paid Porter $275. The right-of-way is described as follows:

> *Concerning the road from the county road between Santa Cruz and Watsonville...commencing at the latter road about four hundred and fifty feet northwesterly of where the public road crosses the Borregas Gulch, thence down the southerly side of a ravine running towards the bay of Monterey until it reaches the land purchased by Thomas Fallon from Richard E. Hyde, and also the rights within the limits of such road so located to make all such excavations, embankments, and bridges, and to cut all such hills and undergrowth as shall be necessary to make the road a good passable road for loaded vehicles and to maintain and keep the same in repair.*

The second deed was acknowledged by Williams alone and signed the same day.

At this point, it is appropriate to describe the route that Fallon eventually graded between the Monterey Bay and Tract 8 as this was one of the first thoroughfares into the Augmentation. The route probably closely followed New Brighton Beach Road from New Brighton State Beach to Highway 1, at which point it continued across the highway via Cabrillo College Drive until reaching Soquel Drive at 450 feet above sea level. This location marked the entrance to the Porters' tannery. From here, Fallon either used the county road until reaching the vicinity of the Aptos Public Library or built a skid road parallel to the county road, following it along the north side. The total length of this segment was approximately 1.4 miles.

Because the elevation of the library is close to 200 feet and the elevation north of the steel bridge that carries today's Aptos Fire Road across Aptos Creek is close to this level, it can be assumed that Fallon's road maintained this elevation between these two points and did not cross Aptos Creek prior to reaching the southern boundary of the Augmentation. Few remains of the road can be found between the library and the steel bridge along the

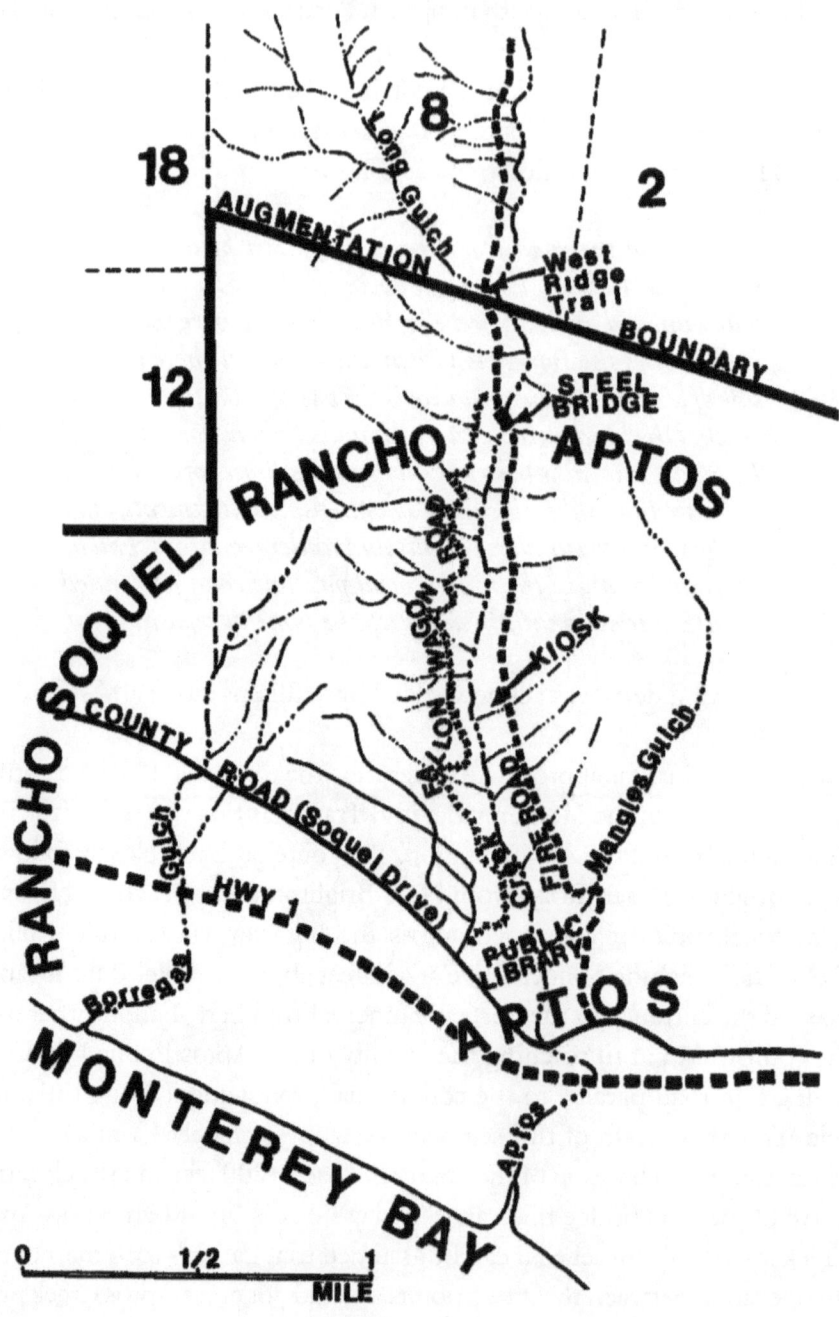

FIGURE 7.16 THE FALLON WAGON ROAD TO SHOQUEL AUGMENTATION

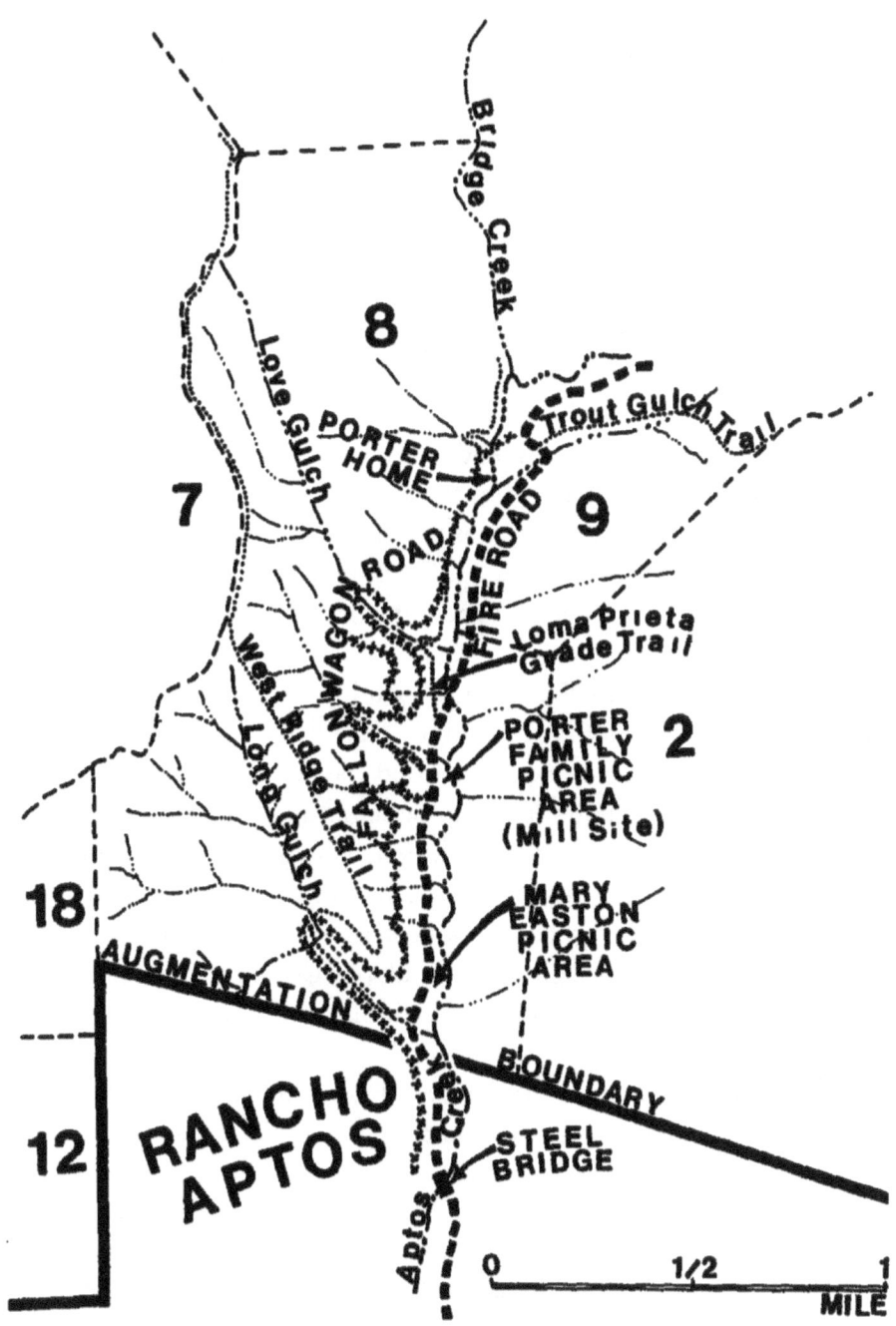

FIGURE 7.17 THE FALLON WAGON ROAD TO BRIDGE CREEK

west side of Aptos Creek due partially to the private ownership of this land. Besides, after a century of logging activity in this area, there are now homes here that make determining the original road's right-of-way nearly impossible. Today, the main access road south of the steel bridge runs along the east side of Aptos Creek along and adjacent to the old railroad alignment.

In any case, some remnants of the road can be found and one particular phenomenon is easier to track. Whenever the road approached a gulch that was too deep, the road turned sharply uphill until a point was reached where the road could safely cross. The first such section that may be identified and explored lies along the west side of Aptos Creek directly across the creek from the Forest of Nisene Marks' entry kiosk. From this area, there are trails, pathways, and several roads that parallel the creek on either side, all heading north to the steel bridge. It is at the north end of the steel bridge that the first positive indication may be found of the road's existence and location. The route from the library to the bridge was between 2.5 and 3.0 miles long, depending on how many times the route had to divert up gulches.

The steel bridge is located just south of the boundary of the Augmentation and, therefore, the start of Tract 8, which ran along the east bank of Aptos Creek to a line just beyond the top of Love Gulch. After crossing the bridge, Fallon's road can be noticed to the west of the main road after passing through a short cut. Following this former right-of-way requires permission from several private homeowners, unfortunately, but this short section can be bypassed until entering the Augmentation. By following the Fire Road through the first cut, one can see to the west several slight remains of the road. Follow these indications along the base of the ridge northward until the south side of Long Gulch is approached. The boundary of the Augmentation is halfway through the second and longer of the two cuts. How Fallon originally entered the property has been lost due to the deforestation of the area and the realignments caused by the railroad.

Donald Clark noted in his book that Long Gulch was "a not particularly long gulch running off Aptos Creek to the northwest just a few feet north of the boundary between Rancho Aptos and Rancho Soquel Augmentation, now within the bounds of The Forest of Nisene Marks State Park. Probably named after Long Ridge." Clark was unable to identify whom Long Ridge was named after, but an article in the *Loma Prieta Loglets* printed on November 20, 1889, noted that a Charles Long lived in Loma Prieta and had been quite ill but was recovering. Thus, it seems likely that this Long was the namesake of the ridge and gulch. Fallon's road did not cross the gulch over a bridge, so was probably diverted high along its flanks, creating the longest detour along the road. The point where the West Ridge Trail crosses the gulch is likely the same place where Fallon's road crossed, roughly a half mile northwest of the Fire Road.

From the crossing, Fallon's road descended the next ridge toward Aptos Creek, although it remained at a higher elevation than the current Fire Road. Almost all evidence of this section has now eroded away. It closely followed the West Ridge Trail for a short distance and then headed down an old trail that goes towards the Fire Road. About halfway down the trail, partially hidden off to the right, there are faint impressions where the wagon road reached the top, while to the left hidden in the bushes is the continuation of the road.

From the point where Fallon's road reached the next ridge, the route continued in a general northerly direction. Today it is more of a pathway than a road and it follows more or less the 400-foot contour line. While some sections of the road are easily found, other sections, due to erosion and vegetation growth, must be searched out. As previously discussed, when Fallon approached a gulch, rather than build a bridge to cross it, he would head far enough up its side until it was more easily crossed. Sometimes the journey for the wagon was far up the side of the gulch, sometimes only a short journey was needed in order to return to and remain on the 400-foot contour line. The wagon road eventually dropped down to the area that is today occupied by the Porter Family Picnic Area, the final point where cars can currently travel along the Fire Road within The Forest of Nisene Marks.

Fallon built his road for wagons that would enter the Augmentation empty and leave full of cut lumber and split stuff. But finding the site of the mill has proven problematic. Why did the wagon road suddenly drop 120 feet to reach the Porter Family Picnic Area? An obvious conclusion is that the location must have been where the sawmill was located, but there is no indication of such a facility at the site. An article in a local newspaper dated March 2, 1867 reveals much about the route:

> Mr. Thomas W. Wright has just completed a splendid map of the Soquel Augmentation Rancho, especially that portion of the princely domain, which falls to the lot of Thomas Fallon, Esq. The entire rancho contains over 32,000 acres of heavily timbered land, and is owned by different claimants, mostly heirs of the original grantee. The tract marked out to Mr. Fallon contains 8,000 acres, and is an irregular section running from one dividing ridge to another from within two or three miles of the Bay to the highest peaks of the Santa Cruz range, near Loma Prieta. It is estimated that over 200-million feet of redwood lumber can be cut off the land, besides shingles, shakes, staves, fence pickets, posts, railroad ties, etc. Large quantities of tan oak bark grows in great luxuriance, and no hoop poles, etc...., to be found on the thousand hills embraced within the tract.
>
> To give an outlet to this immense wealth, a wharf will be erected near the mouth of Tannery Gulch, from which a railroad will be built, at an easy grade, four miles long, to the point where the sawmill will be erected on the Aptos Creek. The road will eventually be extended still further, into the heart of the forest, as the timber may be cleared off along the proposed route. The Averon tract, of 2,000 acres, and the Bates tract..., now owned by Messrs. Grover & Gardner, who are running a steam sawmill, will also be benefitted by these improvements. Some of this timber is located within two miles of the flourishing village of Soquel.

The distance between Fallon's land on the Monterey Bay and the Porter Family Picnic Area is approximately four miles.

However, another clue comes from Vincent T. Leonard in an article published in the November 27, 1970 issue of the *Times & Green Sheet*. Although Leonard was the president of the Mid-County Historical Association, many of his statements have a dubious historical quality, including several that were made in this article. That being said, a statement by Leonard about the Loma Prieta Lumber Company's logging operations in the mid 1880s to late 1890s rings true. Concerning the Porters, he said: "The mill had been founded by the Porter brothers of Santa Cruz about 1870. At first it was served by a road from Soquel, but when the railroad came, it was important enough to demand and get a spur track from Aptos." With this evidence, it can be concluded that a mill was built prior to the arrival of the railroad, likely in the vicinity of the Porter Family Picnic Area.

From the picnic area, Fallon's wagon road went up a small gulch to the west, crossing at its upper end without a bridge before heading back toward Aptos Creek. The route disappears for a while but certainly climbed up Love Gulch, named after John Love, a Loma Prieta Lumber Company trimmer who worked in the mill in the late 1880s. The gulch itself is easily identified—it is the first gulch encountered on the Loma Prieta Grade Trail after leaving the Fire Road at Molino Junction, and it is crossed by a small foot bridge. One can notice as the bridge is crossed railroad ties extending from the north side of the gulch. These ties are the remains of a spur line that was extended up into the gulch in the late 1890s when the upper portion of Tract 8 was logged. Prior to this, the line was Fallon's wagon road.

From the top of Love Gulch, the road eventually returned to the current Loma Prieta Grade Trail, but not before first crossing a gulch that was too steep to bypass and too deep to ford. Given no option, Fallon built the first substantial bridge on his route.

From the bridge, the road headed north until reaching the site of the Porter House, indicated today with a sign. Because of the extensive activities that have occurred in this area, it is impossible to differentiate the wagon road from the railroad lines, pathways, and other roads. While the road's location at this point is partially based on speculation, logic dictates that, in order to reach Tract 9 located across Aptos Creek, a route in the vicinity of the Porter House was most practical. No evidence exists of a bridge across Aptos Creek in this area at this time, but such a bridge could have been erected using easy-to-obtain, simple materials such as the local redwoods. And this area was appropriate for such a crossing, as the Southern Pacific Railroad realized when it erected its own railroad bridge at the same location. It is also possible that the creek was simply forded below this site, as the water levels were relatively low during the summer and autumn months.

As a final comment concerning the existence of Fallon's wagon road, on a map prepared by the Southern Pacific Railroad Company in 1916 entitled "Loma Prieta Branch—Aptos to Loma Prieta: A Map of Real Estate and Right-of-Way Properties through Santa Cruz County, California," there is the following note: "Agreement entered into between Thomas Fallon & Loma Prieta Railroad Company dated October 2, 1882, Fallon agrees to deed right-of-way 60 feet in width across his property in the Aptos Creek above Claus Spreckels' land. This right-of-way evidently located on some abandoned location line. Auditors No. 1646." The only portion of Fallon's location line that the railroad could have occupied was from Love Gulch to the Porter House and on to Tract 9 across Aptos Creek, where the town of Loma Prieta was located.[484]

Letter asks "What is the use of being a Supervisor?"

On September 1, 1866, a letter to the editor that appeared in the *Pajaro Times* entitled "What Is The Use Of Being A Supervisor?" that reveals some details of Hihn's lands in Soquel:

> *Frederick A. Hihn owns in Soquel nearly 11,000 acres of the best and finest timber land in the state. His land was assessed at 0.47 1/2 cents per acre, and was afterwards reduced by the Board of Supervisors to 0.27 1/2 cents per acre.*[485]

Appeals by Thomas Courtis, John Wilson, Mary Slade, Cyrus Coe, Charles Plum, and Henry Lawrence rejected

On October 1, 1866, the California Supreme Court rejected another appeal of the decisions by Judge McKee regarding both the Rancho Soquel and the Shoquel Augmentation partitioning suits. These appeals were overseen by Thomas Courtis, who directly represented himself and the Ingoldsby and Green Estates, as well as John Wilson, Mary Slade, Cyrus Coe, Charles Plum, and Henry Lawrence.

Justice J. Sawyer rejected the Rancho Soquel appeal on technical grounds, ruling that, "It follows that the appeal was not in time, and this court has no jurisdiction to entertain it." Similarly, the appeal of the

Augmentation suit decision was rejected due to a technical error on the part of McKee, who had not properly dismissed the appeal in the Third District Court and, therefore, it was ruled inappropriate for the Supreme Court to hear the appeal.

The justices did give some clarity to their decision-making process, however, confirming that the earlier deed of Martina Castro in 1850 was valid due in large part to the Supreme Court decision in Ingoldsby v. Juan, which legitimized the deed. Therefore, it was inappropriate for the court to overrule an earlier court's decision on the matter, regardless of their personal feelings or new evidence. In addition, so many people had since purchased land within both properties that overturning the earlier decision would be inappropriate. The decision summarized that "to overturn the former adjudication under such circumstances, because a majority of the present court might arrive at a different conclusion from that attained by their predecessors—men equally well qualified to discern and equally conscientious in the pursuit of the right—would be to trifle with the rights of litigants and bring merited obloquy upon the administration of the justices."

In the end, the Supreme Court upheld the decision of the Third District Court, reaffirming the rights of those who received land via Castro's deed of 1850. The decisions were filed on April 1, 1867 by W. D. Harriman, the Supreme Court's clerk, thereby permanently putting to rest the rival claims by the Catholic Church to the entirety of Castro's two Mexican land grants.[486]

Letter from a Soquel resident concerning the two turnpikes

A letter by Vox Populi of Soquel to the editor of the *Santa Cruz Weekly Sentinel*, printed on November 3, 1866, reveals the ongoing consternation among locals over the rival turnpikes to the Santa Clara Valley in the mid-1860s:

> *It being a cardinal feature in all republican governments that exclusive privileges are granted to none, while equal rights are guaranteed to all, who, therefore, can not see the justice or propriety of this deeply populated and flourishing locality, both*

as to agriculture and manufacture, (the two most desirable of all pursuits for the advancement of the wealth and permanent prosperity of the County) being from all direct communication by mail with San Francisco, the great metropolis of the whole Pacific Coast, especially when it is notorious fact that all of our most important business naturally centres in that city, as the magnetic needle turns to the polar star;—furthermore, the Government, ever mindful of the interests of its citizens, has always advertised and let the contract for carrying the mail to and from Santa Cruz, to San Francisco, to come by and supply the Soquel P. O. with mail facilities; yet we have no direct mail with San Francisco, nor with San Jose Valley, which is almost in our neighborhood, or at any rate in four or five hours stage ride, if the stage came by this place, as per contract with the Government and for which the stage company is now receiving pay and we are receiving no services therefrom, but on the contrary, our letters are carried to Santa Cruz, where they should never go, and we are subjected to the inconvenient and often expensive delay of waiting for the tardy conveyance of our mail matter from Santa Cruz to Soquel, by the cross mail from Santa Cruz to Monterey via Watsonville, or by express, which is too expensive, or by private conveyance which is never reliable; either way causes a delay equal to the time that would be requisite for news to be transmitted from the remotest nook or corner of the globe that is in telegraphic communication with America, to San Francisco, and then printed in the daily papers and sent to us by rail road and stage, (if the stage ran on the route it should) while our S. F. papers are detained in the Santa Cruz P. O. Such grievous delays are not in unison with the intentions of the Government, nor in accordance with the age. As the mail is now carried, we are behind every P. O. in the County from 24 to 36 hours, whereas, if the mail were brought direct from San Jose, as per contract, we would be in advance of all other places in getting telegraphic dispatches in the daily city papers as much as the time occupied by the stage in going from Soquel to Santa Cruz, without any detriment to the last named place, as it is conceded by all that better time can be made on the Soquel route than on the turnpike or Mountain Charlie road as it is called; furthermore, there is no P. O. on the turnpike from Lexington to Santa Cruz. There is one quite respectable little settlement at Scott's Valley, the remaining portion of the intermediate country being sparsely populated, while on the Soquel route, it is one continuous succession of mills above, and cultivated farms below Soquel to the town of Santa Cruz; we think capitalists in traveling the Soquel route would form a more favorable opinion of the resources of the County, than in traveling over the comparatively uninhabited route now used, over which the timid pleasure seekers now ride, in many places with eyes dilated, fingers distended and hair erect, on account of the giddy heights of some of the precipices necessarily incurred, thereby lessening the summer resort to Santa Cruz, while no such dangers will be encountered by the proposed change. The country on the headwaters of the Soquel Creek is of easy grade,—and a safe and expeditious trip—making it incomparably the better route of the two, as well as the quickest from S. F. to Santa Cruz, until the iron horse comes thundering down the San Lorenzo Valley, laden with the almost inexhaustible timber, making the city of "The Holy Cross" the Bangor or Chicago of California for her lumber exports.[487]

Stephen and Joseph Chase move their sawmill from Burrell Creek to Los Gatos Creek

Prior to the 1867 cutting season, Stephen and Joseph Chase decided to relocate their mill from Burrell Creek on the south side of the Summit to Los Gatos Creek on the north side. The land that they had purchased stumpage rights for in Tract 23 of Shoquel Augmentation had nearly run out of viable timber and would not sustain another year of harvesting. At the same time as their relocation, another brother, Foster Chase, joined the family business. He quickly became the manager of the mill and married a local, Nancy Howard, in 1870 at Lexington.[488]

Antonia Peck and Benjamin Bayley sue Frederick Hihn over claims to land in Rancho Soquel and Shoquel Augmentation

Although the partitioning suits were settled, Antonia Peck still wanted to reclaim the land that she and her husband, Henry, had lost to Frederick Hihn through deeds signed in April 1862. Antonia continued to assert that the paper she signed was for a mortgage, not a deed, and that Tracts D, E, and F in Rancho Soquel and Tracts 10 and 11 in Shoquel Augmentation should rightly belong to them. However, for reasons not entirely known, Henry did not wish to challenge the ruling or sue Hihn for the land—he may well have been ill during this time since he died five years later on September 14, 1873 at a relatively young age. In any case, it was left to Antonia to hire Benjamin Franklin Bayley to represent her against Hihn.

On April 10, 1867, two deeds were signed. In the first, Henry sold Tracts A, B, and C in Rancho Soquel, totaling 135.368 acres, as well as Tract 16 in the Augmentation, totaling 2,313 acres, to Bayley for $7,500. In the second, Henry and Antonia sold Tracts D, E, and F in Soquel, totaling 316.687 acres, and Tracts 10 and 11 in the Augmentation, totaling 4,576

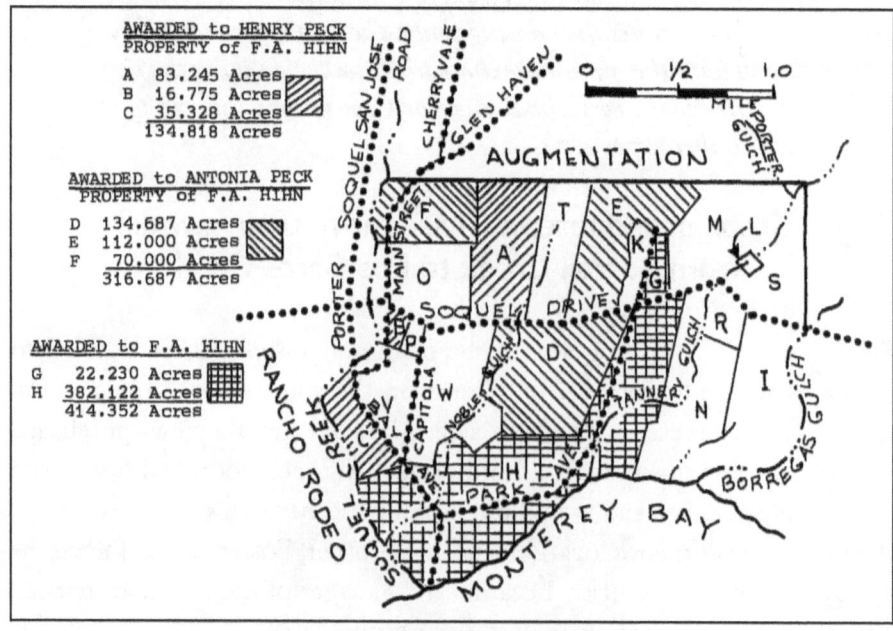

FIGURE 7.18 HIHN AND PECK TRACTS IN RANCHO SOQUEL

acres, to Bayley for $5,000. In addition—and now as the owner of all the Pecks' land in the two grants—Bayley was responsible for reviewing the legality of the deeds and challenging Hihn on any inconsistencies.

Three days later, Robert Peckham, representing Hihn, served eviction notices to Bayley and several unnamed parties concerning the contested land that Bayley had just acquired. Meanwhile, Bayley concluded that the two documents signed by the Pecks in 1862 were indeed deeds rather than mortgages, and therefore only a lawsuit would resolve the ownership dispute. As a result, on April 18, Bayley sold back to Antonia Peck all the land that she originally owned—Tracts D, E, and F in Soquel, and Tracts 10 and 11 in the Augmentation—and agreed to represent himself and her in the ensuing lawsuit. That same day, another round of eviction notices was issued by Peckham, this time to Peck and several tenants on her property.

Summons and complaints were served by Peck and Bayley to Hihn on April 20, prompting the start of Third District Court Case Nos. 608 (for Soquel) and 609 (for the Augmentation). The entire purpose of these suits was to prove that the Pecks had intended to sign mortgages, not deeds, on April 21, 1862.

The trial began shortly afterwards, presided over by Judge McKee. Tactically, Hihn once more hired Peckham to represent him in the case, which intentionally caused a conflict of interest since it was Peckham who had drafted the disputed documents in 1862. When she was called to testify, Peck recounted via a court-appointed translator that she was staying at the home of Mr. Winterham in Santa Cruz on the night that Peckham brought the documents for her to sign. Since she could not read or entirely understand English, she had the documents read to her. However, she also did not know technical subjects regarding land sales, so she trusted Peckham, even though she did not understand him, and her husband, who had already signed the documents. According to her testimony, she believed at the time that she was signing a mortgage for her lands in Soquel and the Augmentation. Peckham declined to cross-examine her.

Testifying on behalf of Antonia Peck and Bayley were James Brennan, Benjamin Cahoon, Augustus Noble, George Porter, John Hames, and Henry Peck. Testifying for Hihn were himself, Peckham, Charles Younger, County Assessor Nelson Taylor, Titus Hale, Benjamin Cahoon,

Joshua Parrish, Augustus Noble, Dickamon Rider, William Moore, John Daubenbiss, Elihu Anthony, James B. Phillips, James O. Menizer, and Henry Peck. Most of these witnesses were questioned about Henry Peck's gold prospecting in Humboldt County and his activities in Santa Cruz County related to that. When Henry himself testified, he appeared to forget many important moments in his long relationship with Hihn, such as when Hihn deeded him a 1/18 claim to the Augmentation in July 1860 for $250. Incidentally, he did remember clearly conversations with Hihn that benefited his wife's suit.

The outcome of this trial was of vital importance to Hihn, who was on the brink of starting great projects upon his lands in the Soquel area. Some of the disputed land included the future site of Camp Capitola, as well as sawmill projects on Aptos, Valencia, and Laurel Creeks. Also at stake were his water company, plans to lay out housing subdivisions, and his ultimate goal of completing a railroad along the coast. His victory against Antonia Peck and Bayley was of the utmost importance to Hihn.[489]

Hiram and Clara Morrell acquire additional sixty acres

After spending several years planting and expanding his operations on the Summit, Hiram Morrell found himself in need of more land near the end of 1867. Therefore, he purchased from James Taylor sixty acres to the west of his land that sat within Tract 17 of Shoquel Augmentation. To tend this new land, Hiram invited his brother Brad and Brad's wife to settle on the land and help develop it. Across the old and new acreage, the Morrells expanded their grape and fruit crops, planting fifty acres of vineyards, seventy-five acres of fruit trees, and thirty-five acres of prune trees. For the next seven years, Brad mostly remained out of the lumber business while helping his brother.[490]

Land transfer by Benjamin and Lucy Cahoon to James Phillips

On August 3, 1868, Benjamin and Lucy Cahoon sold Tract 27 within Shoquel Augmentation to James B. Phillips for $2,000. Included in the transaction was the water-powered sawmill originally built by Roger Hinckley and

John Shelby, then sold to Richard Savage, who lost it due to unpaid debts to Cahoon. The mill facilities occupied 126 acres and included a millpond and dam, a long flume and mill race, bunkhouses, a cookhouse, a blacksmith shop, and several other outbuildings. The mill had sat idle since the beginning of the partitioning suit in August 1860. Cahoon died six years later at his home on June 30, 1874 at the age of seventy-six.[491]

Ruling in Third District Court Case Nos. 608 and 609

Both suits between Antonia Peck and Frederick Hihn regarding Antonia and Henry Peck's alleged sale of their claims in Rancho Soquel and Shoquel Augmentation to Hihn in 1862 were conducted without a jury. Judge McKee, after hearing testimony and evidence from both sides, issued his decisions for both suits on September 26, 1868, ruling in favor of Hihn. He agreed with all parties that the actual documents signed by Antonia Peck on April 21, 1862 were indeed deeds, and that Antonia had been sufficiently informed of this fact at the time they were signed. With the conclusion of this trial, Hihn was able to begin construction of his planned resort at the mouth of Soquel Creek.[492]

Soquel Turnpike improved

Based on clues found in several local papers and discussed by historians, sometime in 1869, it is evident that portions of the Soquel Turnpike from a point just north of Olive Springs Road and south of Stetson Road (at Smith Valley Road) were improved. These included moving the road from the top of the ridge between the West Branch of Soquel Creek (to the west) and Hester Creek (to the east) down to its present-day route just to the west, and slightly above the latter creek.

While the above improvements were underway, the beginning of the turnpike was moved from Main Street to the west side of Soquel Creek on Porter Street. Instead of using Main Street and Cherryvale Avenue, it began on Soquel Drive and then headed north on Porter Street following today's Soquel San Jose Road.

Land transfer by Guadalupe Lodge to Benjamin Porter

On April 13, 1869, Guadalupe and Joseph Averon sold 598 acres of Tract 7 in Shoquel Augmentation to Benjamin Porter for $10,000. This left the Averons with 710 acres of their land, of which 500 were leased to the Grovers for logging purposes. Several years later, the couple sold 150 of the remaining acreage to John W. Wessell, while the final sixty acres were eventually sold to Max Caldwell, whose family would own and operate Kennolyn Camp.[493]

Land transfer by Lyman Burrell to Reverend James Wright

On August 25, 1869, Lyman Burrell sold to Reverend James Richard Wright 100 acres in Tract 24 in Shoquel Augmentation, located near the modern junction of Summit Road and Loma Prieta Avenue. The two men had long been aware of each other since Burrell's wife, Clarissa Vincent, was the sister of Wright's wife,

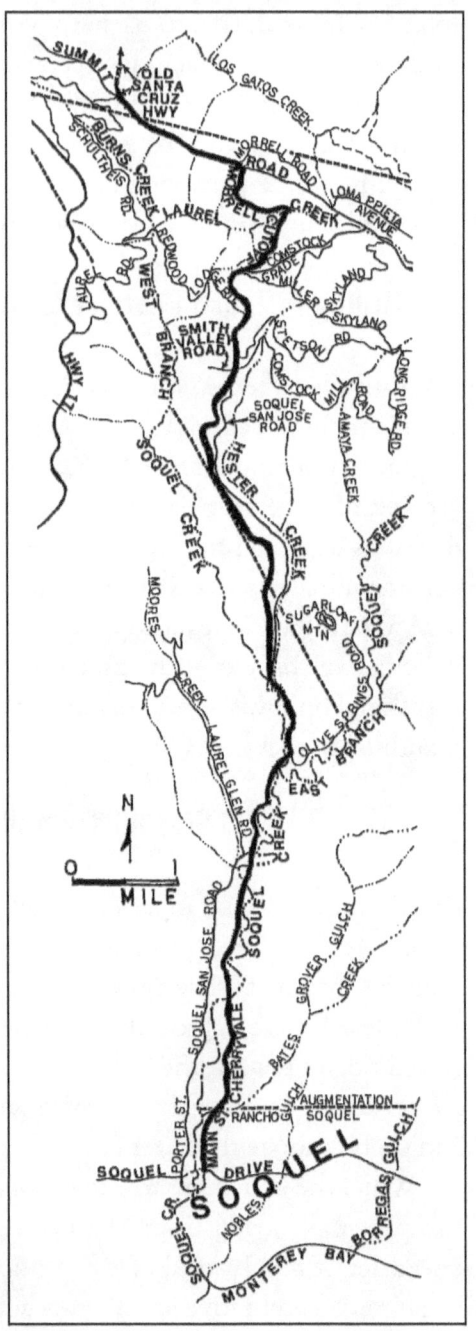

FIGURE 7.19 FINAL ALIGNMENT OF THE SOQUEL TURNPIKE

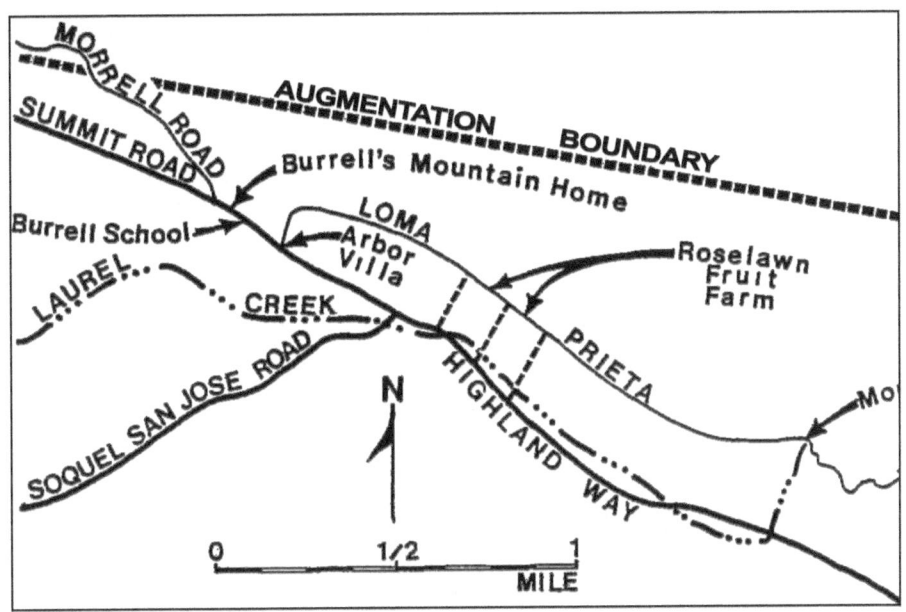

FIGURE 7.20 LOCATION OF ARBOR VILLA ON THE SUMMIT

Sarah Holmes Vincent. Wright was born on April 14, 1814 in Tallmage, Ohio. Three years after his marriage in 1844, Wright was ordained a Congregational minister. The couple soon moved to Sheffield, Ohio where he became the minister of the local Congregational church. While there, he and Sarah had ten children, eight of whom survived to adulthood.

Wanting a warmer climate, the Wrights decided to head to California where they hoped the atmosphere would better suit their health. The family arrived in San Francisco by ship and then headed straight for the Santa Cruz Mountains to visit the Burrells. After only a few weeks, the family decided to settle there and build a home. Burrell happily sold them some of his land and the Wrights began constructing a home on Whitewash Alley, just to the east of Burrell's Mountain Home.

After their home was built, the Wrights realized that they had more land than they needed, so they planted vineyards and fruit trees. Eventually, by the late 1870s, they also operated a hotel of their own called Arbor Villa. On November 15, 1886, an article in the *Santa Cruz Surf* described Arbor Villa in detail:

> *The popularity of Arbor Villa as a summer resort has long been recognized, and the crowds of visitors that 'steal away' from the fog, harsh winds, and dust of the Bay City take new lease of life, as it were, while enjoying their vacation at the pleasant and elegant mountain retreat. Surrounding Arbor Villa are fifty acres under a high state of cultivation. The improvements on the place have been made without regard to expense, and have been designed not only for utility but to please the eye as well. The Villa, a commodious and handsomely constructed building, sets back from the road on an eminence and is approached by a broad stairway, covered by an arbor or trailing vines. The well-kept grounds, fine view, and the comfortable rooms within, together with the warm welcome of the proprietors, make the visitors to this charming spot feel that life was worth the living. Though as busy as bees getting ready their first shipment of grapes for the Chicago market, they found time to show the Surf representatives over their grounds. The vineyard of twenty acres is all in bearing. These are of the different varieties of table grapes, and choice ones too. No finer grapes find their way to market than are raised in the Santa Cruz Mountains, will undoubtedly be the report from this Summit shipment when Chicago is heard from. The orchard consists of twenty acres, mainly French prunes. On the Summit, the prune makes a wonderful growth, and the yield is such that a splendid profit per acre is assured. To secure a good supply of water, a tunnel has been bored into the hill. A large reservoir laid in cement and covered receives the water, which is piped to the Villa and all parts of the premises. This splendid property is the result of seven years of enterprise and judicious expenditure on the part of the proprietors, and they have, no doubt, made it one of the most popular of our resorts, as well as a profitable piece of vineyard property.*

Arbor Villa was destroyed during a large forest fire that swept through the area in 1899. It was soon rebuilt but was severely damaged in the 1906 earthquake. By this point, James Wright was dead—he had passed away in

Divided and Conquered 1869

1896—and Sarah died shortly after the quake in 1908. It was their children who restored the hotel for a third time, but the golden age of resorts in the mountains was nearing its end and the hotel shut down in the 1910s.

Until recently, there were two buildings constructed by the Wright family still standing in the area. The third iteration of Arbor Villa survived until the Loma Prieta Earthquake on October 17, 1989, after which it was demolished. The other structure, located 300 yards to the east of the hotel, was a fruit-packing shed that was also demolished after the earthquake, although it was replaced with a modern structure. Over the years, the spacious shed hosted a grocery store, beauty shop, real estate office, and doctor's office. The site of the hotel is now the Summit Center, which includes a modern grocery store.

It is appropriate at this point to turn to the final "Recollections of an Octogenarian by Col. Lyman John Burrell," which were recorded by Mary Smith of the Summit Literary Society in 1882:

> *As the court had made a decree that all of the land of the Soquel Augmentation should be divided, he [Judge McKee] appointed three commissioners to make this partition. When this had been done and a map which designated each owner's position had been made by them, the owners were called together at Santa Cruz. They examined the map and agreed to accept the partition as shown thereon. Thereupon, they instructed the commissioners to present it to the court, which was then in session, and they departed for their homes. One commissioner [probably Thomas Wright] departed also.*
>
> *The other two commissioners then altered the map, taking off portions of one man's share and adding it to that of another. One thousand acres were thus taken from my share and given to another. The court accepted the partition map as revised by the two commissioners and it was thus recorded. As this suit lasted a month, and our farms were suffering for want of cultivation, we had no courage to engage in another lawsuit to get back our rights.*
>
> *No sooner had I reached home than the man from whom I had purchased my share, for which I had paid him $1,000*

down and given my note for $500 more, sued me for the payment of that note. He put an attachment on all of my land and my stock, being under the influence of some of those sharpers, he refused me permission to sell even a flock of sheep which I had fatted for market, and which would have brought nearly enough money to pay the bill. He placed a keeper over them to watch them. I began to feel as if people were always trying to defraud me of my farm and of everything else that I had. It had taken all that I had earned and saved for several years to defend it. But I felt determined to persevere and to surmount every obstacle. My son went to San Francisco, borrowed money of our friends, and paid the debt. We then sold our sheep and returned the money to our friends. When at last everything was settled, I turned my whole attention to fruit growing. I set out a large number of grape vines, and fruit trees in choice varieties. My friends began to caution me, urging that there would never be a market for so much fruit. But I have never seen that time yet.

Indications of petroleum were found here in those days. It created quite an excitement. With several others, I leased my land to a company. A well was commenced, but never finished. I believe there will yet be found plenty of oil in this vicinity.

Among so many misfortunes, one blessing came to us. We now had a turnpike road to Los Gatos. We could carry pickets and shakes to market as well as fruit. This was so great an improvement on the old way of packing everything on horseback that we never felt like grumbling at the toll. It soon became generally understood that the Santa Cruz Mountains were especially adapted to fruit growing. Families came flocking in and settling in every direction.

In a short time, other orchards and vineyards were set out. Sawmills commenced running here and there, and houses and barns were built. When my orchards and vineyards had reached maturity, I began to feel less interest in them and gave them into the care of others that I might go farther into the wilderness to clear up new land and to try new experiments. I brought a flock of goats, which I kept for several years.

They were of some use in clearing the brush land, but on the whole proved a failure. The lions killed a great many of them. While taking care of my goats, I prospected some for minerals. I found surface indications of silver and gold in different locations, sometimes very rich but generally of low-grade ore. I think I have reason to believe that there is a rich ledge here and I hope it will yet be found.

I prophesy a noble future for these mountains, of which the present prosperity is only a small beginning. It is pleasant for me now in my advanced age to look abroad and see the many and substantial improvements that have been made within the past few years. I see with joy and pride the orchards and vineyards so beautiful and thrifty, and the railroad which has taken the place of the long and tedious turnpike. I can hardly realize that this beautiful neighborhood was thirty years ago so wild and lonely. But I have really enjoyed the excitement of a pioneer life. It has been a satisfaction to me to make paths where no man has ever before trod, to subdue the forest and to scatter the wild animals.

I now think my work is done. I am becoming more willing to rest and to lay aside all care. I have never been a very good financier, but I have made a comfortable living. Though I have had troubles and perplexities, my blessings have far outweighed them, and my life has been a happy one. I believe I can truly say I have never knowingly wronged anyone. If the world is no better, I sincerely hope that it is no worse for my having lived in it.

Burrell died on June 3, 1884 in Santa Cruz.[494]

Epilogue

~

In the Matter of the Estate of Martina Castro, Deceased

For a woman once referred to as the "Baroness of Soquel," María Martina Castro Cota Lodge Depeaux's end came slowly and quietly. Following the confirmation of the sale of her land to the Catholic Church at the end of 1856, Castro returned to Soquel and moved into the Averon home. She came to rely increasingly on her daughters by Michael Lodge, namely Josefa Clements, Helena Littlejohn, and Guadalupe Averon.[495]

In an interview in 1965, Castro's granddaughter Carrie Lodge reflected:

> *The Averons had her in a little four-room cabin that they used to live in. Grandma likes pears, and there were five or six trees there, so she likes it there. Actually, the house that Grandma lived in was what the Averons left standing when they moved up the hill.*[496] *It had a good-sized kitchen, front room, a porch in front, and a bedroom.*
>
> *Grandma's daughter Josefa lived close by and took care of her personal needs and saw that she was comfortable. Aunt Josefa did the work and Aunt Mary* [Guadalupe] *paid for the groceries and what she had to for sickness and everything.*

> *Toward the end of her life, Grandma got erysipelas. Grandma didn't get up again after Aunt Mary brought her up to the big house, and there she just lingered, never recovering full, so it was a blessing that Grandma died. She had too much trouble—more in her life than happens to two or three people.*

The small house that Castro lived in for the final decades of her life is now gone, but its location can be found by going to the back of the former Averon home and looking down the hill onto Highway 1.

Martina Castro died at the Averon home at the age of eighty-three on December 14, 1890. While her passing was not ignored by the local newspapers, neither was it emphasized nor considered especially notable except for the fact that Castro was one of the last surviving children of José Joaquín Castro and, therefore, a relic of a time when California was still a part of Spain.

Almost exactly five years after Castro's death, on December 1, 1895, a summons was served to every person and company living on or owning property within Rancho Soquel, Shoquel Augmentation, and the one-thirteenth portion of Rancho San Andrés inherited by Castro from her father. The purpose of the summons was stated in the accompanying complaint, which announced that Mary Elizabeth Peck, the youngest daughter of Henry and Antonia Peck, sought Special Letters of Administration over Castro's estate. These letters would grant Peck the role of administrator of the estate. It was her first action in a war she hoped to win against Frederick Hihn over rival claims to Castro's land.

Carrie Lodge stated that Peck harbored resentment and deep hatred towards Hihn. For years, she had expressed her desire to reclaim the lands she felt Hihn had cheated her mother and father out of in 1862. The lands lost in the Augmentation were Tracts 10 and 11 by her mother and Tract 16 by her father. While Antonia was willing to forget the past and not reopen old wounds, forty-year-old Mary had other ideas, "for the benefit of her mother, for the memory of her dead father, and for her living aunts and uncle."

To realize her plans, Peck hired attorneys J. F. Utter, J. J. Scrivner, and A. H. Cohen to represent her. However, time was short since she had to apply for the role of Administrator before five years had elapsed since Castro's death. She established that her grandmother's estate consisted of 1,669 acres of Rancho Soquel, 32,702 acres of Shoquel Augmentation, and approximately 1,000 acres of Rancho San Andrés. On December 11, three days before any outstanding claims to the estate would lapse, her lawyers made a formal petition to the Superior Court of Santa Cruz County:

> *Your Petitioner, Mary Elizabeth Peck, respectively shows that said Martina Castro Depeaux was a resident of said County of Santa Cruz at the time of her death; that she died, interstate leaving estate in said County; that no Letters of Administration have ever been granted upon the estate of said Martina Castro Depeaux, deceased; that no application has ever been made for Letters of Administration upon said estate; that five years will soon elapse since the death of said decedent; that it is important for those interested in said estate, and essential for the preservation of their rights therein, and to avoid the bar of the statute of limitations, that before the expiration of five years from the death of said decedent, an action or actions should be commenced for the benefit of said estate, and of those interested, for the recovery of real property situated in the State of California, which was owned by said decedent, and in which she had an interest, at the time of her death, as your petitioner is informed and believes, and that an action or actions should be commenced within said five years to recover possession of said real property and to quit the title thereto for the benefit of said estate and of those interested therein; that your petitioner is about to apply for Letters of Administration upon said estate, but the delay that must necessarily attend the granting of the same, in order to give the requisite notice, would prevent the granting of such letters until after the expiration of five years from the time of the death of said Martina Castro Depeaux.*
>
> *Your petitioner states, that there is no personal property belonging to said estate, and that all of the real estate that belongs thereto which is producing any revenue is in the possession of persons claiming to hold the same adversely to said*

estate. That your petitioner is a resident of said County, and a single woman and over the age of twenty-one years, and is a granddaughter of said decedent; that your petitioner's mother, Antonia Peck, is a daughter of said decedent, and one of the heirs at law of said decedent, and entitled to succeed to a portion of any estate of the said decedent, whether real or personal, and that the said Antonia Peck has in writing signed by her, and which is herewith filed, requested that your petitioner be appointed special administratrix of the estate of said Martina Castro Depeaux, deceased.

Wherefore, your petitioner prays that she may be appointed Special Administrator of the estate of said Martina Castro Depeaux, deceased; and that your petitioner, as such Special Administratrix, be authorized and empowered to institute and prosecute any and all actions for the recovery of any real property in the State of California which the said Martina Castro Depeaux owned, or in which she had an interest, at and before the time of her death, and damages for the withholding thereof, and for the recovery of the possession of said real property, and to institute and prosecute any and all actions necessary and proper for the purpose of quitting the title of the said estate, and of those interested therein, in and to any real property which was owned by said Martina Castro Depeaux, or in which she had any interest, at and before the time of her death, and to recover and obtain the possession thereof; and that your petitioner, as such Special Administratrix, be also invested with all the power specified in section 1415 of the Code of Civil Procedure of the State of California, and with all other powers conferred upon a Special Administrator by the laws of the State of California.

Mary Elizabeth Peck
December 11, 1895

On December 12, Peck was awarded the requested Special Letters of Administration for Castro's estate and was assigned its administrator. Her court grant stated:

That Mary Elizabeth Peck be and is appointed special administratrix of the estate of the said Martina Castro Depeaux, deceased, to collect and take charge of the estate of said decedent in whatever County or Counties the same may be found, and the said special administratrix is hereby authorized and empowered to institute and prosecute any and all actions necessary and proper for the recovery of any real property in the State of California which the said Martina Castro Depeaux owned, or in which she had an interest, at and before the time of her death, and damages for the withholding thereof, and for the recovery of the possession of said real property, and to institute and prosecute any and all actions necessary and proper for the purpose of quitting the title of the said estate, and of those interested therein, in and to any real property which was owned by said Martina Castro Depeaux, or in which she had any interest, at and before the time of her death, and to recover and obtain the possession thereof; and said special administratrix is also invested with all the powers specified in section 1415 of the Code of Civil Procedure of the State of California, and with all other powers conferred upon a special administrator or administratrix by the laws of California; and that letters of such special administratrix shall issue to the said Mary Elizabeth Peck on giving bond in the sum of $100 with sureties to the satisfaction of the Judge of said Court, condition for the faithful performance of her duties and upon her taking the usual oath.

> Done in Open Court this
> 12th day of December 1895,
> J. H. Logan, Judge of the said court

Almost immediately after Peck's application was accepted by the court, she began sending out notices to all persons and companies that had acquired titles within Castro's former lands. On December 22, several people who had been issued summons filed an objection with the court on the grounds that they were not served and, therefore, were given no opportunity to voice their objection to Peck's petition.

Meanwhile, Peck set out to prove that the deed signed on August 29, 1850 that partitioned the Soquel properties between Castro and her eight children had been the product of fraud. While a court in 1858 had come to this same conclusion, the California Supreme Court overturned the ruling in 1859 and confirmed that the deed was legal. Thus, Peck restarted an argument that had been concluded thirty-six years earlier.

Peck and her attorneys depended on the Article of Agreement that Castro, her four sons-in-law, and her third husband, Louis Depeaux, signed on August 28, 1850, a day before the deed above. At the time of her petition, Peck was in possession of the original agreement, which is the only copy that has survived to the present. If Castro's deed of August 29 was declared fraudulent, then the terms of conveyance would revert to the agreement signed the day earlier, which clearly states that she wanted to give to each of her children *only* enough land upon which to build a home. If confirmed, this would leave all of her former properties intact except for eight small parcels granted to her children.

Next, to void the two deeds signed January 22, 1855 in which Castro sold all of Rancho Soquel and the Augmentation to the Catholic Church, Peck recruited several of her aunts and Miguel Lodge to testify that Castro was unsound of mind at the time that she signed the deeds. If proven to be true, this action would void the sale and the properties would hypothetically revert to the estate.

Ongoing resistance from the current occupants of the various lands formerly held by Castro, however, forced Peck to re-petition the court for her title of Administrator on May 18, 1896 so that a fresh round of summons could be sent to all concerned parties. Peck was granted new Special Letters of Administration and the title of administrator the next day.

Testimonies were given and depositions taken from the beginning of June and lasted throughout the month. The testimonies focused primarily on proving or disproving that Castro was mentally unfit to sign the deeds of January 22, 1855. Testifying on behalf of Peck was Miguel Lodge, Helena Littlejohn, Antonia Peck, and Luisa Fourcade, while testifying for the contestants were Frederick Hihn, Benjamin Porter, and Isaac Fleisig. Hihn hired Charles Younger to represent him and, in effect, all of the con-

Epilogue 1896

testants, although many of the contestants had their own attorneys as well. It must be emphasized that both sides had much to gain from arguing for or against Castro's sanity in 1855, and no testimony was above scrutiny.

Lodge was the first to give his testimony over two interviews. These have been heavily abridged. He recounted that his mother

> started to go to Mexico about 1854 or 1855. I went with her and we went to the Sandwich Islands. Depeaux beat her in the Islands and I jumped on him and from the effects of this he sent us back by the Yankee Barker to San Francisco. She stayed in San Francisco two weeks and Ingoldsby came to her and made her sign a paper. She got a little better after.

Younger then cross-examined him, asking for clarifications:

> I am 58 years old. I had seen crazy people before, Mr. _____ for one. My mother went to San Francisco two weeks before I did. We were there about two weeks before sailing for the Islands. Fare at that time was $50. I don't know what time it was that we sailed, only I know that the grass was just beginning to come up green.
>
> She was so short. She didn't come when called. She weighed about 200. We were twenty-one days going over. We sailed by D. Levertt. We stayed on the Hillman Ranch in the Islands. Captain Warren commanded the ship we sailed to the Islands on. We stayed in L_____ Islands two months and at the Ranch about three months. The natives would visit her, and they all liked her. She took seven _____ with her.
>
> I saw Father Ingoldsby ask my mother to sign a paper. I don't know what it was about. Sold furniture in the Islands, best we left there.

During a second interview, Lodge provided a little more context surrounding the journey to Hawaii:

> I reside in Santa Cruz County. I remember that my mother wanted in 1854 or 1855 to go to Mexico and then changed

to [the] Sandwich Islands. They went two weeks before I left here, determining to go to Mexico. She made [the] change to go to the Islands. I went to her room. She said the captain was a pirate and a murderer. She said they were going to kill her. When we got to the Islands, she began to feel unsteady and she began to hit at things. She used language that I did not understand.

Then we moved to the Hillman Ranch. She saw witches, then she would be calm for a while. I struck Depeaux and I _____ then he shipped us back to San Francisco. I had to watch her on the trip. The watch sang out a woman overboard. We stopped the ship and she was picked up and brought aboard.

After we got to San Francisco, Father Ingoldsby came by and gave her a paper and made her sign it. She was out of her mind completely. I stopped at Redwood City and my mother came on home. She got a little better but not much. She saw witches all the time when I saw her. She had a club to whip the devil or spirits.

Mrs. Fallon was not with us in San Francisco before I went to the Islands. After Mrs. Averon's marriage, this is when I went to the Islands. I was here at her marriage.

The furniture was sold to the bishop [probably Llebaria]. Depeaux got the money. I did not see Father Ingoldsby after I left my mother at Redwood City.

The next witness to testify was Helena Littlejohn, one of Castro's daughters. As before, her testimony has been abridged:

I was married in 1852. Mrs. Averon was married in 1854. My mother left for the Islands as soon as Guadalupe was married. I said [goodbye] to my mother after the marriage. She would say one thing and then say another thing. They told my husband to be at one place and then told him to be at another.

I was here in Santa Cruz when my mother went to the Islands. She went to the Islands in 1854. Before they went to

> *the Islands, they sent me to build a _____ and then sent us to another place and then to another.*
>
> *After my mother came from the Islands, I saw her first at my house. She was out of her mind. She pounded the roof. She said she was pounding [out] the devils. I could not see anything but the roof and the boards.*
>
> *Then she came to Mrs. Ricardo Juan's, then to Mrs. Antonia Peck in the_____ orchard here; then to Mrs. Majors; then she went to San Francisco. I next saw her in the asylum at Stockton. I had to tell a lie to find her. She was off her mind entirely.*
>
> *When I found my mother, she was off her mind, she was sick in the head. My mother said there was a man who had hit her over the head with a cane.*
>
> *I asked my mother to come away with me and my husband and I went [to] them and brought her to my house. Her condition was just the same until her death.*

Following Littlejohn was another daughter of Castro and Elizabeth Peck's mother, Antonia Peck. She provided little of use to the trial, only stating:

> *I am 60 years old; I never saw my sister [Carmel Fallon] after her marriage. She went to San Jose to live. My mother... we left Stockton on the same day which we arrived there. She knew us, asking us to take her along with us. She did not speak English.*

Another daughter, Luisa Fourcade, gave an equally brief testimony:

> *When I saw my mother at Stockton, she had on a skirt, no shoes, no stockings, and a shawl over her head and face. Her skirt came to her ankles. I went to...get my mother. I did not _____ at the _____ place because Dr. _____ would not allow it. I saw her in 1856 after she came back.*

Three short testimonies were provided on behalf of the contestants.

Benjamin Porter testified, stating:

> *I knew Martina Depeaux since 1854 until she left. I saw her frequently, I met her and communicated with her. I lived near her. I met her once or twice a month in 1854. She rented me some of her lands. Her manner was same as anybody else. She appeared to be a little above average in intelligence. She was engaged in ordinary household duties. She was then married.*

Frederick Hihn followed:

> *I met the deceased first in the early part of 1852 or 1851. My acquaintance continued with her until she left about 1855. I had a store on the lower part of the grant and she came to me to trade [often]. I called at her residence in Soquel. I passed her frequently. There was a proposition from her and her husband for me to move my store to Soquel. Sometimes I saw her twice a week, sometimes once in two months. I have an opinion as to her mental sanity, she was the same, she attended to her business as intelligently as anyone. She made her purchases, spoke about [local things], conveyed land to her children. She pointed where she wanted me to put the store.*

The final witness was a relatively unknown man, Isaac Fleisig, who had entered Castro's life in her final years. He testified:

> *I knew the deceased for sixteen years before her death. I did not _____ to her. I talked with her frequently, selling her then some goods for her. She would say _____ and take her goods to her kitchen.*

The final witness for Peck was Castro's brother, José Joaquín Castro, who provided a deposition recorded on June 6 in the office of Notary Public W. R. Pyle in the presence of J. F. Utter, for Peck, and Charles Younger, for the contestants. Joaquín did not provide a clean testimony—he often appears to either dispute or misunderstand questions from both attorneys. In many cases, he refused to answer, claiming either that he was tired or feeling ill. More generally, his lack of education, poor ability to remember when things occurred, and inability to speak English meant that his deposition requires the utmost scrutiny.

He began by stating for the record that he was seventy-eight years old and was born in California, where he has lived for his entire life. When asked if Martina Castro was ever injured in any way, he explained that his sister had fallen from a fence and landed on some redwood sticks, hurting her head, ribs, and hip. The severity of her injuries from this incident are unclear, and Joaquín muddied the waters further by stating

> *before the fall, she was frequently out of her mind when talking, and afterwards, she was sick of her head. Her head was sore, she was out of her head. She would talk about anything that came along out of her mouth. She would talk about spirits, about the sun, moon, and witches. She was always speaking of things that were not natural.*

He further explained that "the first and second husband, it was the same thing. [With the third husband] she was in the same state of mind.... She was always out of her mind from the first husband down to the third.... She was crazy from the head."

With the depositions recorded, Younger presented his case to the court on behalf of the contestants. After outlining the long and complex history of the sales and partitions of Rancho Soquel, Shoquel Augmentation, and Rancho San Andrés, as well as Castro's level of involvement in the same, Younger arrived at his primary points:

> *that at the time of the said several conveyances, the grantees and their grantees ever since have been and yet are in open, notorious, continuous, and adverse possession of the land so conveyed, and have made useful, permanent, and valuable improvements thereon of the value of more than $1,000,000. Said several ranches have been duly partitioned among the respective owners, by the judgment of the District Court, of said County, the Rancho Soquel and Augmentation in 1864, and the San Andres Rancho in 1873. The land so conveyed has*

been annually assessed by the County Assessor to the grantees in said several deeds and to their successors in interest, for State and County, School and other taxes thereon paid.

No property has been assessed to Martina Castro Depeaux since 1855, nor has she been in possession of any part of said ranches since 1855. The land described in several deeds is in the possession of more than 600 persons, who claim to own the same.

Younger then addressed the matter of Castro's mental competency and ability to convey property:

Martina Castro Depeaux, at the time of her several deeds read in evidence, was competent to execute the same. It is claimed by petitioner that Martina was of unsound mind at the time of the execution of these several conveyances by her, but it is not claimed that she was entirely without understanding.

A conveyance or other contract of a person of unsound mind, but not entirely without understanding, made before his incapacity has been judicially determined, is valid.

The grantors could not have received the property conveyed, or have quitted their title thereto, without a rescission of the conveyances, and to have rescinded they must have acted promptly.

And they must have restored or offered to restore everything of value which they had received under the conveyances.

The conveyances, even if voluntary, were good between the parties thereto and against the heirs of Martina Castro.

A consent which is not free is nevertheless not absolutely void but may be rescinded by the parties in the manner prescribed by the chapter on rescission.

The court must take into consideration the conduct of Martina Castro during her lifetime subsequent to these conveyances, and that she never set up any claim to the property or made any demand upon the parties occupying the same to deliver the possession thereof to her, or paid the taxes thereon, nor did any other act asserting ownership over the property.

Epilogue 1896

The conveyances of Mrs. Depeaux recite a consideration and are presumptive evidence of the payment of such consideration.

From and including the date of the conveyance of Martina Castro Depeaux to her children on August 29, 1850, to and including the date of her conveyances to John Ingoldsby, et al., there was nothing in her conduct indicating that she was unsound of mind. During all that time until she went to San Francisco in January 1855, she lived at her residence on the Soquel Ranch and tended to business. Her conduct in relation to the purchase of a bedroom set [in 1883], about twelve years before the hearing herein mentioned by the petitioner, proves that she was competent to transact business. At the time, she was visiting at the home of her daughter, Antonia Peck, in Santa Cruz. The mother of the petitioner, Mrs. Depeaux, gave her daughter Mrs. Averon $20 to make this purchase. Mrs. Guadalupe Averon bought an ash set from Staffler's for $35 and had it sent to Mrs. Antonia Peck's house. On arrival there, [Martina] examined it and said it was too common.

Martina attended to her household duties and continued to live on the Soquel Ranch until she left with the intention to go to Mexico. Her son Miguel lived with her during that time and worked part of the time for other people. He brought the money he earned to his mother, who provided for him. She married off her daughter, Maria Antonia, to Henry W. Peck; her other daughter, Maria Helena, to Jose David Littlejohn in 1851; and her youngest daughter, Maria Guadalupe, to Joseph Averon in 1854. She bought the necessary supplies for her household and negotiated with Frederick A. Hihn to induce him to move his store to the Soquel Rancho, and for that purpose offered to furnish him with a part of the land which she then occupied on said rancho. She invited Hihn to visit at her residence and entertained him there.

Benjamin F. Porter knew Mrs. Martina Castro Depeaux in 1854 and 1855. He met her at her residence several times, and at other places, and he testified that she was in the habit of attending to business. Frederick A. Hihn became acquainted with Martina in the latter part of 1851 or the early part of 1852. He then kept a store in Santa Cruz. He frequently met and conversed with her, and she was in the habit of trading with him at his store from the time he first knew her until she left the Soquel Rancho and went to San Francisco. And during all this time, she was perfectly sane, and his reason for thinking so was that she transacted her business in an intelligent manner and acted as sane people ordinarily do.

She left the ranch with the intention of going to the city of Mexico on business, and while in the city [San Francisco] she changed her mind and took passage with her husband and son for the Islands. All her actions up to this time indicate that she was the leader of her family and competent to transact business. She went to the Islands in the early part of 1855, after she made the conveyances in evidence of January 22, 1855. Her son, Miguel, testified that she left for the Islands while the grass was green and returned to San Francisco at the time of the next wheat harvest. This could not have been in 1854, because in that year she had a lawsuit with John Hames. On September 9, 1853, John Hames commenced an action wherein he was plaintiff and Martina Castro Depeaux was the defendant, in the District Court of Santa Cruz County, to recover from her a large sum of money. On October 1, 1853, defendant appeared in person and filed her demurrer to his complaint; on November 3, 1853, she verified and filed her answer to the complaint; on April 5, 1854, a decision was rendered in her favor, and on the same day she filed her bill of costs, duly verified and signed by her. This shows not only that Martina Depeaux was in Santa Cruz County at that time, but also that she was competent to conduct an important litigation in which she was interested.

There is no evidence of her incompetency. She kept house and attended to her household duties. She visited her children, married off all marriageable daughters; her children visited her, and she transacted business. She appeared from time to time before public officials, including the County Judge, for the purpose of acknowledging the execution of her *conveyances and leases, an examination separate and apart and without the hearing of her husband, and to make affidavits in an important litigation. She successfully defended a lawsuit brought against her for a large sum of money, and wound up the suit by filing her bill of costs. No guardian was ever appointed for her.*

The statement of her son, that she saw witches and was fighting spirits, amounts to nothing, as all this, if true, occurred subsequent to her conveyances.

After her return from the Islands, her son left her at Redwood City and saw but little of her thereafter for a long time.

Younger's conclusion, in effect, was that Castro was entirely competent and sane at the time that she made her conveyances to the Catholic priests. His points were lodged with the court on August 22, after which a final decision was debated behind closed doors. That same day, Younger, Lieutenant Governor William T. Jeter, and the latter's business partner, H. E. McKinney, petitioned the court to deprive Peck of her status as administrator of Castro's estate. The court approved the motion. Shortly afterwards, an unexpected precedent for the contestants' position came when on September 19 a similar case was concluded in the California Supreme Court. The *Santa Cruz Evening Sentinel* noted the decision "virtually settles all doubts of the land owners in the Soquel, Soquel Augmentation and San Andreas ranches being disturbed or their titles affected." The remainder of the article reads:

Mary A. Kingman owned a certain piece of property, and for a long time prior to 1878 she was insane, incompetent to transact business. But she had not been judicially declared insane and had no guardian. In 1878 one Garwood loaned Mary A. Kingman $400 and took from her a mortgage; this was foreclosed, the defendant defaulting; Garwood bought the premises in, and in due course of time sold it. The heirs in law of Mary A. Kingman brought suit to set aside the conveyance upon the ground that the original owner was incompetent. The Supreme Court holds that this can not be done, as the purchase was one in good faith and for a valuable consideration.

"A judgment entered without the appointment of a guardian, though irregular, is not void. The Court had jurisdiction of the subject matter and of the person of the defendant. It is a hardship upon the plaintiffs and it is possible that the mortgage and judgment were obtained by unfair means. But of these the defendant had no knowledge, and the wrong can not be righted at her expense." The judgment is affirmed.[497]

Only two weeks later, on October 2, the following news brief appeared in the *Santa Cruz Surf*: "Letters of Administration are denied. This will end the litigation over titles to the Soquel and Soquel Augmentation Ranchos. Judge Logan in the Superior Court today filed his decision in the Soquel land litigation by refusing to grant letters of administration to Mary Elizabeth Peck." The actual decision, filed on December 14, concludes:

That deceased conveyed away this property by deeds regular on their face over forty years ago is admitted.

It is also without question that such property has been divided into numerous subdivisions and conveyed to persons now numbering six hundred, without any notice of any adverse claim, who have improved the same by building farm houses, churches, places of business, etc., and such lands are now occupied by two towns. The lands involved aggregate about $2,000,000.

These changes were made while deceased was alive and living on part of the property surrounded by her children.

For forty years, the titles conveyed by her deeds of 1850 and 1855 were not questioned. Not only her silence and the silence of her children but every appearance favored their regularity.

The mental condition of the mother must have been known to the children who lived near and assisted in her care and support.

The only act of mental aberration proved occurred in 1855, and for forty years these children were taxing themselves for support of their mother while she was as they now allege the rightful possessor of 35,000 or 40,000 acres of land, and such ownership was kept a profound secret. After her

> death, they allowed five years to elapse before even making known their claim.
>
> It is claimed that the deeds made by Martina Depeaux were made while she was incompetent and are therefore void. That she ever was adjudged insane by any court is not claimed; that the proofs in this case of actual incompetence or insanity are very insubstantive, must be conceded. On the contrary, the evidence of the petitioner shows that deceased during all of her life was not by any means without understanding. Since the trial of this case, the Supreme Court has rendered a decision in the case of Kingman v. Greenwood; in line with this opinion, there being no property, no debts and no legacies, it follows that there is no necessity for administration. The application of Mary Elizabeth Peck for Letters of Administration on the estate of Martina Castro Depeaux is therefore denied.

On December 22, Peck filed notice that she would appeal the denial of her application for Special Letters of Administration and her removal as administrator to the California Supreme Court. Ten months later, on October 19, 1897, the court declined to hear the appeal in what was officially named Peck v. Agnew. This, in effect, confirmed the decision made by Judge Logan. The *Santa Cruz Surf* reported:

> The Supreme Court this week has handed down a decision which practically confirms the rights of the ranchers on Soquel and the Augmentation grants, who acquired their titles through Frederick A. Hihn or by subsequent purchase.
>
> Several hundred of these holders have been much disturbed during the past year by a suit brought by the Depeaux heirs to set aside the original conveyances, made forty years ago, on the grounds that the grantor was insane or of unsound mind.
>
> Although the suit is mainly directed against Frederick A. Hihn and the F.A. Hihn Company, yet all the present owners of the subdivided portions of the grant have been made defendants in the suit and most of them have made subscriptions towards attorney fees.
>
> The case in point to which reference is made would seem to

> *fully settle all doubts as to the disturbance of these secondary owners and is a strong precedent in favor of finally establishing the Frederick A. Hihn title.*

Despite the finality of the decision, Peck appealed again on November 19, claiming that her petition for a second Special Letter of Administration was a separate case, which thereby allowed for a separate appeal. But the Supreme Court rejected this argument, denied her appeal on December 19, 1898, and merged Peck v. Adams into the earlier Peck v. Agnew case. The following November, 1899, the Supreme Court rejected a third and final attempt by Peck to be named administrator of Castro's estate.

With this decision, all of the contestants in the suit were able to finally enjoy their properties on Castro's former lands without the fear of having their land seized or their boundaries redrawn. This action ended nearly half a century of dispute over the ownership of Martina Castro's Mexican land grants and allowed for the unfettered exploitation of the Soquel and Aptos Creek watersheds into the twentieth century.

T̄p

Ronald G. Powell's
story of Frederick A. Hihn
and the logging operations within
Shoquel Augmentation is continued in

The Reign of the Lumber Barons

Available from Zayante Publishing

Notes

1. Kenneth M. and Doris Castro, *Castro of California: Genealogy of a Colonial Spanish California Family* (Murphys, CA: Castro, 1975).
2. John Steven McGroarty, *California: Its History and Romance* (Los Angeles: Grafton Publishing, 1911).
3. McGroarty; Brian D. Dillon, A*n Archaeological and Historical Survey of the Soquel Demonstration State Forest, Santa Cruz County, California* (Sacramento: California Department of Forestry and Fire Protection, 1992).
4. *Cabrillo Times and Green Sheet*; Charles E. Chapman, *A History of California: The Spanish Period* (New York: Macmillan Company, 1921), p. 134; Dillon; *Sentinel*.
5. McGroarty.
6. Kenneth and Doris Castro.
7. *Cabrillo Times and Green Sheet*; Kenneth and Doris Castro; Dillon; *Sentinel*.
8. *Cabrillo Times and Green Sheet*; Kenneth and Doris Castro; Miguel Costanso, *The Narrative of the Portola Expedition of 1769-1770*, eds. Adolph van Hemert-Engert and Frederick J. Teggart, Publications of the Academy of Pacific Coast History 1:4 (Berkeley: University of California, 1910), p. 251; Dillon; *Sentinel*.
9. *Cabrillo Times and Green Sheet*; *Santa Cruz Sentinel*; Dillon; McGroarty.
10. William Wilcox Robinson, *Land in California: The Story of Mission Lands, Spanish and Mexican Ranchos, Squatter Rights, Mining Claims, Railroad Grants, Land Scrip, Homesteads, Tidelands, Chronicles of California* (Berkeley: University of California Press, 1948).
11. Dillon.
12. John Francis Bannon, ed., *Bolton and the Spanish Borderlands* (Norman, OK: University of Oklahoma Press, 1964), p. 283.
13. Bannon, 283; Kenneth and Doris Castro; Dillon.
14. Kenneth and Doris Castro; Rowland, *Early Years*.
15. McGroarty.
16. "Burrell Letters," *California Historical Society Quarterly* 29 (1950); Dillon; Bill Wulf, personal correspondence.
17. Dillon; McGroarty.
18. Kenneth and Doris Castro.

Notes

19. Dillon.
20. Donald Thomas Clark, *Santa Cruz County Place Names: A Geographical Dictionary*, second edition (Scotts Valley, CA: Kestrel Press, 2002); Stephen M. Payne, *Santa Clara County: Harvest of Change: An Illustrated History* (Northridge, CA: Windsor Publications, 1987); John V. Young, *Ghost Towns of the Santa Cruz Mountains* (Lafayette, CA: Great West Books, 1984), 68.
21. Dillon.
22. Dillon; Margaret Koch, *Santa Cruz County: Parade of the Past* (Fresno: Valley Publishers, 1973); Leon B. Rowland, *Santa Cruz: The Early Years: The Collected Historical Writings of Leon Rowland* (Santa Cruz, CA: Paper Vision Press, 1980).
23. Kenneth and Doris Castro; Dillon; Star Girky, personal correspondence; Koch; Rowland, *Early Years*.
24. Dillon.
25. Robinson.
26. Dillon.
27. Kenneth and Doris Castro.
28. Dillon.
29. Kenneth and Doris Castro; Rowland, *Early Years*.
30. Land Claims Commission, Case No. 184, transcript of the proceedings for the place named Soquel on behalf of Martina Castro.
31. Kenneth and Doris Castro.
32. Kenneth M. Castro, personal correspondence; Kenneth and Doris Castro; Rowland, *Early Years*.
33. Kenneth and Doris Castro.
34. Kenneth and Doris Castro.
35. Kenneth and Doris Castro.
36. Kenneth and Doris Castro.
37. Kenneth and Doris Castro.
38. Kenneth and Doris Castro.
39. Kenneth and Doris Castro.
40. Kenneth and Doris Castro; Rowland, *Early Years*.
41. Robinson.
42. Dillon; Koch; Rowland, *Early Years*.
43. Dillon; Rowland, *Early Years*; *San Jose Mercury News*.
44. Land Claims Commission, Case No. 184.
45. Rowland, *Early Years*; Santa Cruz County, Book of Deeds, Vol. 1, 71.
46. Land Claims Commission, Case No. 184.
47. Land Claims Commission, Case No. 184.

Notes

48 Koch; Carrie Lodge, interviews (Santa Cruz, CA: University of California, Santa Cruz, Special Collections, 1965); Rowland, *Early Years*.
49 Kenneth and Doris Castro; Rowland, *Early Years*.
50 Dillon.
51 Kenneth and Doris Castro.
52 Kenneth and Doris Castro; Rowland, *Early Years*.
53 Kenneth and Doris Castro; Clark; Rowland, *Early Years*.
54 *San Jose Mercury News*.
55 Clark; Rowland, *Early Years*.
56 Dillon; Koch; Rowland, *Early Years*.
57 Kenneth and Doris Castro.
58 Kenneth and Doris Castro; Donald M. Hayes, personal correspondence; Mission Carmel, Marriage Records, Roll No. 913161.
59 Land Claims Commission, Case No. 590, transcript of the proceedings for the place named Shoquel on behalf of Martina Castro.
60 Land Claims Commission, Case No. 590.
61 Land Claims Commission, Case No. 590.
62 Land Claims Commission, Case No. 590.
63 Land Claims Commission, Case No. 590.
64 Land Claims Commission, Case No. 590.
65 Kenneth and Doris Castro; Clark; Mildred B. Hoover, Hero E. Rensch, and Ethel G. Rensch, *Historic Spots in California*, third edition (Palo Alto, CA: Stanford University Press, 1966); Land Claims Commission, Case No. 590; Payne, *Santa Clara County*; Leon B. Rowland, personal files, ed. by Joan Gilbert Martin and Stanley D. Stevens (Santa Cruz, CA: University of California, Santa Cruz, Special Collections, 1977); Young.
66 Dillon; Hoover; Payne, *Santa Clara County*; Andrew F. Rolle, *California: A History*, second edition (New York: T. Y. Cromwell, 1969).
67 Dillon; Payne, *Santa Clara County*.
68 Dillon; Payne, *Santa Clara County*.
69 Dillon; Koch; Rowland, *Early Years*.
70 Clark; Rowland, *Early Years*.
71 Dillon.
72 Kenneth Castro, personal correspondence; Lodge, interviews.
73 Rowland, *Early Years*.
74 Gorton Carruth, *The Encyclopedia of American Facts and Dates*, tenth edition (New York: HarperCollins, 1997).
75 Rowland, *Early Years*.

Notes

76 Dillon; Koch; Rowland, *Early Years*.
77 Carruth.
78 Rowland, *Early Years*.
79 For a full history of the trial of Colonel Frémont, *see* Mary Lee Spence and Donald Jackson, eds., *Expeditions of John Charles Frémont*: Volume 2: *The Bear Flag Revolt and the Court-Martial* (Urbana, IL: University of Illinois Press, 1973), 375-486.
80 Kenneth and Doris Castro; Koch; Lodge, interviews; Rowland, *Early Years*.
81 Dillon.
82 Dillon; "Treaty of Guadalupe Hidalgo, February 2, 1848," in *Treaties and Conventions between the United States of America and Other Powers since July 4, 1776* (Washington: Government Printing Office, 1871).
83 Lodge, interviews.
84 Rowland, *Early Years*.
85 Land Claims Commission, Case No. 590.
86 Land Claims Commission, Case No. 590.
87 "The French Consulate in California, 1843-1856," *California History Quarterly*, 271.
88 J. P. Munro-Fraser, *History of Santa Clara County, California* (San Francisco: Alley, Bowen & Company, 1881); Rowland, *Early Years*.
89 Lodge, interviews; Munro-Fraser; Rowland, *Early Years*.
90 Robinson.
91 McGroarty.
92 Kenneth Castro, personal correspondence; Edna Kimbro, personal correspondence; Lodge, interviews.
93 McGroarty.
94 Kenneth Castro, personal correspondence; Kimbro; Lodge, interviews.
95 McGroarty.
96 Rowland, *Early Years*.
97 McGroarty.
98 James Miller Guinn, *History of the State of California and Biographic Record of Santa Cruz, San Benito, Monterey and San Luis Obispo Counties* (Chicago: Chapman Publishing, 1903); S. H. Willey, C. L. Anderson, Ed. Martin, W. H. Hobbs, *History of Santa Cruz County* (San Francisco: Wallace W. Elliott & Co., 1879).
99 Rowland, *Early Years*.
100 Robinson.
101 Selucius Garfielde and F. A. Snyder, eds., *Compiled Laws of the State of California* (Benicia: S. Garfielde, 1853).
102 Edward S. Harrison, *History of Santa Cruz County, California* (San Francisco:

Notes

Pacific Press Publishing, 1892); Rowland, *Early Years*.

103 Stephen Michael Payne, *A Howling Wilderness: A History of the Summit Road Area of the Santa Cruz Mountains 1850–1906* (Santa Cruz, CA: Loma Prieta Publishing, 1978).

104 Harrison.

105 California Third District Court, Case No. 280, Henry and Antonia Peck v. Frederick A. Hihn, at al., known as the Rancho Soquel Partitioning Suit (1860); Rowland, personal files.

106 California Third District Court, Case No. 280.

107 Clark.

108 McGroarty.

109 California Third District Court, Case No. 74, Thomas Fallon, et al., v. Martina Castro, et al. (1850).

110 California Province Archive, Jesuit Archives & Research Center; *New Catholic Encyclopedia*, vol. 1: A-Azt (Washington, DC: Catholic University of America, 1967); Harry B. Morrison, "Before the Sulpicians: Formation of Priests in Early Diocesan California, 1841–1885," *The Patrician* (1992).

111 California Third District Court, Case No. 280; *The Bay of San Francisco: The Metropolis of the Pacific Coast and its Suburban Cities: A History* (Chicago: Lewis Publishing, 1892).

112 George N. Darling, "Report on the Historical Retracement Survey of the Township Line Along the North Boundaries of Sections Three, Four and Five, Township Eleven, South, Range One West—Mount Diablo Base and Meridian for Santa Cruz County."

113 Robinson.

114 Archdiocese of San Francisco Pastoral Center, personal correspondence; Henry L. Walsh, *Hallowed Were the Gold Dust Trails: The Story of the Pioneer Priests of Northern California* (Santa Clara, CA: University of Santa Clara Press, 1946), 509.

115 California Third District Court, Case No. 280; California Third District Court, Case No. 608, Antonia Peck v. Frederick A. Hihn, et al. (1867); California Third District Court, Case No. 609, B. F. Bayley v. Frederick A. Hihn, et al. (1867); Lodge, interviews; *Sentinel*.

116 Clark; Hihn-Younger Archive, University Library, University of California, Santa Cruz, 1976-2003; Lodge, interviews; Rowland, *Early Years*.

117 California Third District Court, Case No. 74.

118 Los Gatos Museum, archival material; *San Jose Pioneer*, 03/16/1878, 1; *San Jose Telegraph*, 05/11/1854; Bill Wulf, personal correspondence.

119 Friedrich Gerstaecker, *California Gold Mines* (Oakland: Biobooks, 1946); Harrison.

120 The fire was on June 22. Gladys Hansen, *San Francisco Almanac*, updated and revised edition (San Rafael: Presidio Press, 1980), 26.

Notes

121 William H. Brown, trader, Washington, corner Pacific and Stockton. Charles P. Kimball, *The San Francisco City Directory* (San Francisco: Journal of Commerce Press, 1850), 18.

122 Mission San Antonio de Padua was founded on July 14, 1771, by Father Junipero Serra in Monterey County, near Jolon, southwest of King City. It was the third Franciscan mission established in California. Henry Hintch was perhaps the same person as Henry Hentsch, identified in the *Pacific Sentinel* (May 2, 1857, 1:5) as being a director of the Pacific Immigration Aid Society in San Francisco. (Unfortunately, I have been unable to identify Mrs. Hintch's given name.)

123 The general pattern of immigration from Germany is reflected in the 1875 data from the Great Register of Voters for Santa Cruz County: of 2,439 names, 163 were German, constituting about 7% of the total population (*Sentinel*, 07/31/1875, 3:1).

124 This location was Rancho Buri Buri, owned by José Antonio Sanchez in the area now occupied by Millbrae.

125 Probably at the Eighteen-mile House. At Madrone Station, eighteen miles south of San José on the Monterey Road, D. Mallory ran the Eighteen-mile House (1870). There was a series of way-side hotels-watering spots between San José and Monterey, Seven-mile House (John Ternant), Twelve-mile House (Daniel Rota, Coyote Station), Fifteen-mile House (Perry's Station), Eighteen-mile House (D. Mallory), Twenty-one-mile House (William Ternant). Just after the Twenty-one-mile House travelers had the option of going to Monterey via the Watsonville Road. W. J. Colahan and Julian Pomeroy, eds. *Sun José City Directory and Business guide of Santa Clara Co. for the year commencing January 1, 1870* (San Francisco: Excelsior Press, 1870); *Historical Atlas Map of Santa Clara County, California* (San Francisco: Thompson & West, 1876).

126 James McMahon was listed as a 35-year-old merchant from Ireland, coming to California from Pennsylvania. For information on his general merchandise store, see Isaac L. Mylar, *Early Days at the Mission San Juan Bautista* (Watsonville, CA: Evening Pajaronian, 1929), 63.

127 "Patrick Breen (c. 1805-1868), born in Ireland, went to Canada and Iowa before making his way west with the Donner Party (1846), whose dreadful experiences he recorded in a diary he kept at Donner Lake. In 1848, he became the first non-Spanish-speaking resident of San Juan Bautista." James D. Hart, *A Companion to California* (New York: Oxford University Press, 1978). The census of August 1852 indicates that Breen was 62 years old, a farmer, born in Ireland, formerly a resident of Iowa. If that age was recorded accurately, his birth year was c. 1790. There were twelve members of the Breen family recorded in the census: Patrica (62); Samuel (58); Margaret (45); John (19); Edward (18); Margaret (17); Patrick (15); Simon (12); James (10); Peter (8); Margaret (5); and William (3). The Frenchman in San Juan Bautista was probably Adolphe Vache (see Mylar, 54).

128 The Mariposa Store was owned by the Auzerais brothers, who were also partners with Johann Edvard Knoche. *The San Jose City Directory* lists "Grocers: Auzerais Bros. (A La Mariposa); John Auzerais (Auzerais Bros.), groceries,

Notes

etc., 363 Market, San Jose." Rancho Las Pulgas was near Redwood City.

129 Thomas Fisher's 750-acre ranch was located in the Burnett Township, about thirteen miles south of San José on the old Monterey Road, about one-and-a-half miles south of Coyote. *Historical Atlas Map of Santa Clara County, California*, 61.

130 Alberto Trescony arrived in Monterey in 1844. See *History of Santa Cruz County*, pages 30 and 52, for an illustration of Trescony's residence. Trescony died in 1892 at age 80. For more on the Washington Hotel, see *History of Monterey County, California* (San Francisco: Elliott & Moore, 1881), 121. Joseph Boston (d. 1874) was associated with Edward Lawrence Williams and later had a store on the Mission Plaza in Santa Cruz. Boston was also associated with the tannery owned by Richard Kirby, Jones & Co. in Santa Cruz.

131 Andrew Trust, a 27-year-old grocer from Germany was listed as a baker in 1875. L. L. Paulson's *Handbook and Directory of Santa Clara, San Benito, Santa Cruz, Monterey and San Mateo Counties* (San Francisco: L. L. Paulson, 1875). James Levy Prewitt was a 27-year-old blacksmith from Alabama, although by 1866 he was listed as a gentleman. His surname has been variously rendered as Prewitt (Hihn's diary), Prewett (1850 Poll List for Santa Cruz), Pruitt (1852 Census), and Pruett (1854 Poll of Voters).

132 Benjamin Allen Case arrived in Santa Cruz from Connecticut in January 1848. His wife, Mary Amney from Vermont, started the first school in Santa Cruz in the early 1850s. William H. Fairchild arrived in Santa Cruz sometime between 1847 and 1850 and worked as a teamster.

133 Captain Whiting was probably Colonel B. C. Whiting, who lived in Santa Cruz at this time. Perhaps Hühn misunderstood Whiting's role or the title was honorific.

134 Harrison; Rowland, personal files; David W. Heron, "The Man Who Invented Capitola: The Life and Times of Frederick Augustus Hihn," *Sun*, June 1, 1989; Frederick A. Hihn, "How I Came to Santa Cruz," *Santa Cruz County History Journal* 1 (1994); Stanley D. Stevens, "Biographical Sketch of F.A. Hihn," Hihn-Younger Archive University Library (University of California, Santa Cruz).

135 Clark; Rowland, *Early Years*.

136 Archdiocese of San Francisco Pastoral Center, personal correspondence.

137 Robinson.

138 Agreement between Martina Castro Depeaux, Durrell S. Gregory, and John Wilson, October 28, 1852.

139 Clark; Rowland, *Early Years*; Santa Cruz County, Book of Deeds 1:307.

140 Land Claims Commission, Case No. 184.

141 Payne, *Howling Wilderness* and *Santa Clara County*.

142 Darling.

143 Santa Cruz County, School Land Warrants of Santa Cruz County, as Recorded by County Surveyor Thomas W. Wright (Santa Cruz, CA: Office of the County Recorder).

Notes

144 Clark; Betty Lewis, "Watsonville Remembered—A Selection of KOMY-Radio Broadcasts," *Santa Cruz County History Journal* 1 (1994), 127-128; Rowland, *Early Years.*

145 Santa Cruz County, School Land Warrants.

146 Clark; Rowland, *Early Years.*

147 *The Bay of San Francisco.*

148 Clark; Payne, *Howling Wilderness* and *Santa Clara County*; Young.

149 California Third District Court, Case No. 74.

150 Santa Cruz County, School Land Warrants.

151 Santa Cruz County, Book of Deeds 1: 410-412.

152 Santa Cruz County, Book of Deeds 1:423-424.

153 Santa Cruz County, Book of Agreements, Volume 1.

154 Santa Cruz County, School Land Warrants.

155 Santa Cruz County, School Land Warrants.

156 Harrison.

157 *San Jose Pioneer*; Willey, et al., *History of Santa Cruz County*; Young.

158 Lyman J. Burrell, "Recollections of an Octogenarian," *Mountain Echoes*, December 12, 1881; California Third District Court, Case No. 308; Payne, *Howling Wilderness*; Rowland, *Early Years.*

159 California Third District Court, Case No. 308; Payne, *Howling Wilderness*; Rowland, *Early Years*; Young.

160 California Third District Court, Case No. 280.

161 Santa Cruz County, Book of Deeds 2:8.

162 California Third District Court, Case Nos. 280 and 308; Santa Cruz County, Book of Deeds 2:15.

163 Payne, *Howling Wilderness.*

164 Santa Cruz County, School Land Warrants.

165 California Third District Court, Case No. 308; Clark.

166 John Wilson Papers (BANC MSS C-B 420), Bancroft Library (University of California, Berkeley, 1840-1897).

167 Santa Cruz County, Book of Deeds 2:180-182.

168 Thomas A. Marshall, personal correspondence; Morrison; *New Catholic Encyclopedia* I; John J. Treanor, personal correspondence.

169 Clark; Santa Cruz County, Book of Deeds 2:187.

170 Clark; Vincent Leonard, personal correspondence; Rowland, *Early Years*; Santa Cruz County, Book of Deeds 2:184.

171 California Third District Court, Case No. 74.

172 Land Claims Commission, Case No. 593.

Notes

173 Ernest de Massey, "A Frenchman in the Gold Rush," *California Historical Society Quarterly* 5:4 (1926): 342-377.
174 California Third District Court, Case No. 78.
175 California Third District Court, Case No. 74.
176 Santa Cruz County, Book of Deeds 2:274.
177 Harrison; Stanley D. Stevens, personal correspondence.
178 Santa Cruz County, Book of Deeds 2:337.
179 John Wilson Papers; Land Claims Commission, Case No. 593.
180 California Third District Court, Case Nos. 280 and 308; Santa Cruz County, Book of Deeds 2:347 and 5:87.
181 California Third District Court, Case No. 74.
182 California Third District Court, Case No. 593.
183 Santa Cruz County, Book of Deeds 4:728.
184 California Third District Court, Case No. 78.
185 Los Gatos Museum; *San Jose Pioneer*; *San Jose Telegraph*; Wulf.
186 California Third District Court, San Francisco (Department 1), Case No. 825, In the Matter of the Estate of Martina Castro Depeaux, Deceased, 1896; Lodge, interviews.
187 Dillon; Koch, *Santa Cruz County*; Rowland, *Early Years*.
188 California Third District Court, Case No. 308.
189 California Third District Court, Case No. 308.
190 Land Claims Commission, Case No. 184.
191 Santa Cruz County, Book of Deeds 2:540.
192 Land Claims Commission, Case No. 184; Rowland, *Early Years*.
193 Santa Cruz County, Book of Deeds 4:146.
194 California Third District Court, San Francisco Department, Case No. 825; John Wilson Papers; Lodge, interviews.
195 California Third District Court, Case No. 280; Treanor.
196 California Third District Court, San Francisco Department, Case No. 825.
197 Land Claims Commission, Case No. 184.
198 California Third District Court, Case No. 308; Santa Cruz County, Book of Deeds 5:69.
199 California Third District Court, Case No. 280 and, San Francisco Department, Case No. 825; Carolyn Swift, "Stones to the Four Winds: The Sorrow of Martina Castro Lodge," *Santa Cruz County History Journal* 3 (1997): 130.
200 Santa Cruz County, Book of Deeds 3:11.
201 California Third District Court, San Francisco Department, Case No. 825; *Hawaiian Shipping News*, 03/01/1855.

Notes

202 Land Claims Commission, Case No. 593.

203 Land Claims Commission, Case No. 593.

204 Santa Cruz County, Book of Agreements 1.

205 California Third District Court, San Francisco Department, Case No. 825; *Evening Sentinel.*

206 Land Claims Commission, Case No. 593.

207 Rowland, personal files.

208 California Third District Court, Case Nos. 280 and 308; Santa Cruz County, Book of Deeds 3:121.

209 California Third District Court, Case No. 308.

210 Santa Cruz County, Book of Deeds 3:115.

211 Santa Cruz County, Book of Agreements 1:28-29 and Book of Deeds 3:110-111.

212 California Third District Court, Case No. 78.

213 Clark; Santa Cruz County, Book of Deeds 3:158.

214 Land Claims Commission, Case No. 593.

215 California Third District Court, San Francisco Department, Case No. 825; Hihn-Younger Archive; Charles V. Kieffer, Letter to Jerry Johnson, Stockton Development Center, June 12, 1992; Land Claims Commission, Case No. 593; Lodge, interviews; Penny O'Lague, Letter to Charles V. Kieffer, August 25, 1992.

216 Clark; John Wilson Papers.

217 Land Claims Commission, Case Nos. 184 and 593; United States District Court, Northern District of California, Case Nos. 295 and 343.

218 Land Claims Commission, Case Nos. 184 and 593; United States District Court, Northern District of California, Case Nos. 295 and 343.

219 Land Claims Commission, Case No. 593; United States District Court, Northern District of California, Case No. 343.

220 Land Claims Commission, Case No. 593; United States District Court, Northern District of California, Case No. 343.

221 Harrison, 343-344.

222 Land Claims Commission, Case No. 593; United States District Court, Northern District of California, Case No. 343.

223 California Third District Court, Case No. 308.

224 California Third District Court, Case Nos. 280 and 308; Santa Cruz County, Book of Deeds 3:507-509, 3:513-516, 3:559-560, 3:563, 5:39-41, 5:136-137.

225 California Third District Court, Case Nos. 280 and 308; Santa Cruz County, Book of Deeds 3:279.

226 Hubert Howe Bancroft, *The Works of Hubert Howe Bancroft*, Vol. 19 (Charleston, SC: Nabu Press, 2010); California Supreme Court, Case No. 12 Cal. 564, Ingoldsby v. Juan, et al. (1859); California Supreme Court, Case No. 31 Cal.

207, Henry W. Peck, et al., v. Thomas Courtis, et als., (1866); California Third District Court, Case Nos. 280 and 308.

227 John Wilson Papers.

228 Robert King was born in London and was known to have been a resident f Santa Cruz since 1834. He was either elected or appointed the town's first constable in 1850. He married the former Estefana Juarez, fathering four children. King died sometime before 1860.

229 California Supreme Court, Case No. 31 Cal. 207.

230 Santa Cruz County, Book of Deeds 4:549.

231 Fallon was elected the city's mayor March 29, 1859, three years after these events.

232 Lodge, interviews.

233 Santa Cruz County, Book of Deeds 3:505-506.

234 California Third District Court, Case No. 280.

235 Richard A. Beal, *Highway 17: The Road to Santa Cruz* (Santa Fe, NM: The Pacific Group, 1991); Billie J. and Reece C. Jensen, *A Trip Through Time and the Santa Cruz Mountains* (Gardnerville, NV: Ghastly Gallimaufry, 1994); Payne, *Howling Wilderness* and *Santa Clara County*; Wulf; Young.

236 California Third District Court, San Francisco Department, Case No. 825; Hihn-Younger Archive; Lodge, interviews; O'Lague.

237 Actually, the number of acres that Tracy owned in Shoquel Augmentation is somewhat confusing since it included both deeds and School Land Warrants. The number he gave here seems to only relate to the former. Regarding the latter, he owned Warrant Nos. 228 (160 acres), 90 (53 1/3 acres), 327 (160 acres), 329 (160 acres), and half of 108 (80 acres—the other half was sold to Henry Parsons). He also had briefly owned Nos. 353 and 354, although those eventually were transferred to Peck. This was the reason that Peck insisted upon the indemnification bond: he feared for the survival of his two warrants that he had purchased from Tracy.

238 California Supreme Court, Case No. 31 Cal. 207.

239 Land Claims Commission, Case No. 184.

240 California Third District Court, San Francisco Department, Case No. 825; Hihn-Younger Archive.

241 Land Claims Commission, Case No. 184; United State District Court, Northern District of California, Case No. 295.

242 William Gleeson, *History of the Catholic Church in California* (San Francisco: A. L. Bancroft & Co., 1872); Treanor; Walsh.

243 Land Claims Commission, Case No. 593; United States District Court, Northern District of California, Case No. 343.

244 John Wilson Papers.

245 John Wilson Papers.

Notes

246 Land Claims Commission, Case No. 593; United States District Court, Northern District of California, Case No. 343.

247 Payne, *Howling Wilderness*.

248 According to Francisco Alviso's crudely drawn map, Aloma Alta would be in the vicinity of today's Mount Thayer or Mount Umunhum, while Chuchita is Loma Prieta.

249 John Wilson Papers.

250 Archdiocese of San Francisco Pastoral Center.

251 John Wilson Papers.

252 Rowland, *Early Years*.

253 California Third District Court, Case Nos. 280 and 308; Gleeson; Santa Cruz County, Book of Deeds 3:587; Walsh.

254 Santa Cruz County, School Land Warrants.

255 John Wilson Papers.

256 California Supreme Court, Case No. 12 Cal. 564; California Third District Court, Case Nos. 280 and 308; John Wilson Papers.

257 California Third District Court, Case Nos. 608 and 609; *Sentinel*, 12/26/1857, 3:2.

258 Clark; Santa Cruz County, Book of Deeds 4:378.

259 John Wilson Papers.

260 California Supreme Court, Case No. 12 Cal. 564.

261 Santa Cruz County, Book of Deeds 3:671.

262 John Wilson Papers.

263 *Sentinel*, 02/06/1858, 2:1.

264 Rowland, personal files; Santa Cruz County, Book of Deeds 4:728.

265 John Wilson Papers.

266 Santa Cruz County, Book of Deeds 4:241; *The Sonoma Democrat*, February 4, 1858; *The Alexandria Gazette*, March 3, 1858.

267 California Third District Court, Case No. 308; Santa Cruz County, Book of Deeds 4:547.

268 *Pacific Sentinel*, February 13, 1858, 2:1.

269 Clark; Rowland, *Early Years*.

270 *Pacific Sentinel*, February 13, 1858, 2:1.

271 John Wilson Papers.

272 *Pacific Sentinel*, March 27, 1858, 2:3.

273 *Pacific Sentinel*, April 24, 1858, 3:1.

274 John Wilson Papers.

Notes

275 *Pacific Sentinel*, May 1, 1858, 2:2.

276 *Alta California*, December 22, 1860; Phil Francis, *Santa Cruz County* (San Francisco: H. S. Crocker, 1896); Jensen; *Sentinel*, May 8, 1858, 2:2, 8; Payne, *Howling Wilderness*; Young.

277 John Wilson Papers.

278 *Sentinel*, May 15, 1858, 2:1.

279 John Wilson Papers.

280 Santa Cruz County, Book of Deeds 3:781.

281 John Wilson Papers.

282 Santa Cruz County, Book of Deeds 3:784.

283 Santa Cruz County, Book of Deeds 4:305.

284 Santa Cruz County, Book of Deeds 3:788.

285 California Third District Court, Case No. 308; Clark; Rowland, *Early Years*; Santa Cruz County, Book of Deeds 4:13.

286 California Third District Court, Case Nos. 280 and 308; Santa Cruz County, Book of Deeds 4:39.

287 California Third District Court, Case Nos. 280 and 308.

288 John Wilson Papers.

289 Santa Cruz County, Book of Deeds 4:38.

290 California Third District Court, Case Nos. 280 and 308.

291 *Sentinel*, August 21, 1858, 2:3.

292 John Wilson Papers.

293 William Halley, *The Centennial Year Book of Alameda County, California* (Oakland: William Halley, 1876).

294 John Wilson Papers.

295 Santa Cruz County, Book of Deeds 4:129.

296 *Sentinel*, October 2, 1858 and October 16, 1858; Wulf.

297 Beal; *Sentinel* October 16, 1858; Payne, *Howling Wilderness*; Wulf.

298 Darling.

299 California Supreme Court. Case No. 12 Cal. 564.

300 John Wilson Papers.

301 California Third District Court, Case No. 608; Harrison; Heron.

302 California Supreme Court. Case No. 12 Cal. 564.

303 Santa Cruz County, School Land Warrants.

304 Burrell, "Recollections"; California Third District Court, Case No. 308; Payne, *Howling Wilderness*; Rowland, *Early Years*; Santa Cruz County, Book of Deeds 4:340; Young.

Notes

305 John Wilson Papers.
306 Santa Cruz County, Book of Deeds 4:394.
307 Santa Cruz County, Book of Deeds 4:380.
308 John Wilson Papers.
309 Marshall.
310 Santa Cruz County, Book of Deeds 4:429.
311 California Third District Court, Case Nos. 280, 308, 608, and 609.
312 Santa Cruz County, Book of Deeds 4:467.
313 California Third District Court, Case No. 308.
314 California Third District Court, Case Nos. 280 and 308; Santa Cruz County, Book of Deeds 4:556.
315 Santa Cruz County, Book of Deeds 4:524.
316 Santa Cruz County, Book of Deeds 4:513.
317 Lodge, interviews; Santa Cruz County, Book of Deeds 5:500; *Sentinel*, June 18, 1895.
318 Santa Cruz County, Book of Deeds 4:525.
319 California Third District Court, Case No. 308; Santa Cruz County, Book of Deeds 4:502.
320 John Wilson Papers.
321 Santa Cruz County, Book of Deeds 4:547.
322 Santa Cruz County, Book of Deeds 4:380.
323 Santa Cruz County, Book of Agreements 1:14 and Book of Deeds 4:582.
324 Santa Cruz County, Book of Deeds 4:565 and Book of Mortgages 1:21.
325 Santa Cruz County, Book of Deeds 4:572.
326 Santa Cruz County, Book of Deeds 4:604.
327 California Third District Court, Case No. 280.
328 Santa Cruz County, Book of Deeds 4:604.
329 California Supreme Court, Case No, 31 Cal. 207.
330 California Third District Court, Case No. 280.
331 California Third District Court, Case No. 308.
332 Burrell, "Recollections"; Clark; Payne, *Howling Wilderness*.
333 California Third District Court, Case Nos. 280 and 308; Santa Cruz County, Book of Deeds 5:3.
334 *Sentinel*, June 8, 1860; Wulf.
335 California Third District Court, Case No. 308; Santa Cruz County, Book of Deeds 5:24.
336 California Third District Court, Case No. 280.

Notes

337 California Third District Court, Case No. 303, Nicanor Cota Lajeunesse v. Francisco Lajeunesse (1860); California Third District Court, Case No. 308.
338 California Third District Court, Case No. 280.
339 California Third District Court, Case No. 280.
340 California Third District Court, Case No. 280.
341 California Third District Court, Case No. 280.
342 California Third District Court, Case No. 280.
343 California Third District Court, Case No. 280.
344 Frederick A. Hihn adopted this name in order to allow him to sit as both the plaintiff and a defendant in the lawsuit.
345 California Third District Court, Case No. 308.
346 Clark; Young.
347 California Third District Court, Case No. 280.
348 California Third District Court, Case No. 308.
349 California Third District Court, Case No. 308.
350 California Third District Court, Case No. 308.
351 Santa Cruz County, Book of Deeds No. 5:138-139.
352 California Third District Court, Case No. 308.
353 California Third District Court, Case No. 308.
354 California Third District Court, Case No. 308.
355 California Third District Court, Case No. 308.
356 California Third District Court, Case No. 308.
357 California Third District Court, Case Nos. 303 and 308.
358 California Third District Court, Case No. 308.
359 Santa Cruz County, Book of Deeds 5:96 and 270.
360 California Third District Court, Case No. 280.
361 California Third District Court, Case No. 280.
362 California Third District Court, Case No. 308.
363 California Third District Court, Case No. 280.
364 Santa Cruz County, Book of Deeds 5:100-101.
365 California Third District Court, Case No. 280.
366 California Third District Court, Case No. 308; Santa Cruz County, Book of Deeds 5:24.
367 Santa Cruz County, Book of Agreements 1:28-29.
368 California Third District Court, Case Nos. 280 and 308.
369 California Third District Court, Case No. 308.

Notes

370 California Third District Court, Case No. 308.
371 Santa Cruz County, Book of Deeds 5:136-137.
372 California Third District Court, Case No. 303; Rowland, *Early Years*.
373 California Third District Court, Case No. 308.
374 California Third District Court, Case No. 308.
375 California Third District Court, Case No. 280.
376 California Third District Court, Case No. 308.
377 California Third District Court, Case No. 280.
378 California Third District Court, Case No. 308; California Third District Court, Case No. 333, Benjamin Cahoon v. Richard Savage (1861).
379 California Third District Court, Case No. 280.
380 California Third District Court, Case No. 308.
381 California Third District Court, Case No. 308; Santa Cruz County, Book of Deeds 5:204 and 209.
382 Santa Cruz County, Book of Deeds 5:293.
383 California Third District Court, Case No. 308.
384 California Third District Court, Case No. 308.
385 California Third District Court, Case No. 308.
386 California Third District Court, Case Nos. 280 and 308.
387 California Third District Court, Case Nos. 280 and 308.
388 California Third District Court, Case Nos. 280 and 308.
389 California Third District Court, Case No. 308.
390 Santa Cruz County, Book of Deeds 5:265.
391 California Third District Court, Case Nos. 280 and 308.
392 California Third District Court, Case No. 308.
393 California Third District Court, Case Nos. 280 and 308.
394 Santa Cruz County, Book of Agreements 1.
395 California Third District Court, Case No. 308.
396 California Third District Court, Case No. 308; Santa Cruz County, Book of Deeds 5:289.
397 California Third District Court, Case No. 308.
398 California Third District Court, Case No. 308.
399 California Third District Court, Case No. 280.
400 California Third District Court, Case No. 308.
401 California Third District Court, Case No. 333; Santa Cruz County, Book of Deeds 5:343.

402 Stevens, personal correspondence.
403 California Third District Court, Case No. 308.
404 Betty Lewis, personal files; Rowland, personal files.
405 California Third District Court, Case No. 280.
406 California Third District Court, Case No. 308.
407 California Third District Court, Case Nos. 280 and 308.
408 Burrell, "Recollections"; California Third District Court, Case No. 308; Payne, *Howling Wilderness.*"
409 Clark; Santa Cruz County, School Land Warrants.
410 California Third District Court, Case No. 280.
411 Burrell, "Recollections"; California Third District Court, Case No. 308; Payne, *Howling Wilderness.*
412 California Third District Court, Case No. 308; Clark.
413 California Third District Court, Case No. 280.
414 California Third District Court, Case No. 308.
415 California Third District Court, Case Nos. 280 and 308.
416 Santa Cruz County, Book of Deeds 5:507.
417 California Third District Court, Case No. 308.
418 California Third District Court, Case Nos. 280, 308, 608, and 609; Santa Cruz County, Book of Deeds 5:561.
419 Stevens, personal correspondence.
420 Clark; *Sentinel,* June 13, 1862.
421 California Third District Court, Case Nos. 608 and 609.
422 *San Jose Pioneer,* March 16, 1878, 1; *San Jose Telegraph,* May 11, 1854; Wulf.
423 California Third District Court, Case Nos. 280 and 303.
424 Hubert Howe Bancroft, ed., *Judge R. F. Peckham: An Eventful Life* (Berkeley: Bancroft Library, 1877); Munro-Fraser.
425 California Third District Court, Case Nos. 608 and 609.
426 California Third District Court, Case No. 308.
427 California Third District Court, Case Nos. 608 and 609.
428 Clark; Payne, *Howling Wilderness*; Santa Cruz County, Book of Deeds 6:194; Young.
429 California Third District Court, Case Nos. 280 and 308.
430 Santa Cruz County, Book of Deeds 6:100.
431 Santa Cruz County, Book of Deeds 6:108 and 203.
432 California Third District Court, Case No. 280.
433 California Third District Court, Case Nos. 280 and 308.

Notes

434 California Third District Court, Case No. 308.
435 Bancroft, *Judge R. F. Peckham*; Munro-Fraser.
436 Santa Cruz County, Book of Deeds 6:404.
437 California Third District Court, Case No. 280.
438 California Third District Court, Case No. 308.
439 California Third District Court, Case No. 308.
440 California Third District Court, Case No. 308.
441 Santa Cruz County, Book of Deeds 6:500 and 7:245.
442 California Third District Court, Case No. 280.
443 California Third District Court, Case No. 308.
444 California Third District Court, Case No. 280.
445 California Third District Court, Case No. 308.
446 Santa Cruz County, Book of Deeds 6:749.
447 Santa Cruz County, Book of Deeds 4:745, 780, 782, 5:283, and 6:751-756.
448 California Third District Court, Case No. 280.
449 California Third District Court, Case No. 280.
450 California Third District Court, Case No. 280.
451 California Third District Court, Case No. 280.
452 California Third District Court, Case No. 280.
453 California Third District Court, Case No. 280.
454 Santa Cruz County, Book of Deeds 6:787.
455 California Third District Court, Case No. 308.
456 California Third District Court, Case No. 308.
457 California Third District Court, Case No. 308.
458 California Third District Court, Case No. 308.
459 Santa Cruz County, Book of Deeds 7:63.
460 California Third District Court, Case No. 308.
461 *Sentinel*, November 5, 1864.
462 Santa Cruz County, Book of Deeds 7:136.
463 California Third District Court, Case No. 308.
464 Burrell, "Recollections"; Clark; Payne, *Howling Wilderness*.
465 California Third District Court, Case No. 308.
466 California Third District Court, Case No. 308.
467 California Third District Court, Case No. 308.
468 California Third District Court, Case No. 308.

469 California Third District Court, Case Nos. 280 and 308.
470 California Third District Court, Case No. 308.
471 Santa Cruz County, Book of Deeds 7:479.
472 Koch; Santa Cruz County, Book of Deeds 7:662; *Sentinel*, July 4, 1874.
473 Clark; *San Jose Pioneer*, March 16, 878; *San Jose Telegraph*, May 11, 1854; Wulf.
474 California Third District Court, Case No. 280.
475 California Third District Court, Case No. 308.
476 California Third District Court, Case No. 308.
477 Lodge, interviews; Santa Cruz County, Book of Deeds 7:681.
478 California Third District Court, Case No. 308; *Sentinel*, October 7, 1865.
479 Santa Cruz County, Book of Leases No. 1:182.
480 California Third District Court, Case No. 280.
481 Santa Cruz County, Book of Deeds 8:245.
482 Santa Cruz County, Book of Deeds 8:302.
483 California Third District Court, Case No. 308.
484 Santa Cruz County, Book of Agreements 1:181-183.
485 *Pajaro Times*, September 1, 1866.
486 California Third District Court, Case Nos. 280 and 308.
487 *Sentinel*, November 3, 1866.
488 Clark; Payne, *Howling Wilderness*; Young.
489 California Third District Court, Case Nos. 608 and 609; Clark; Santa Cruz County, Book of Agreements 1:209, and Book of Deeds 9:339-341 and 352.
490 Clark; Payne, *Howling Wilderness*; Young.
491 Santa Cruz County, Book of Deeds No. 11:77.
492 California Third District Court, Case Nos. 608 and 609.
493 Santa Cruz County, Book of Deeds 12:137.
494 Burrell, "Recollections"; Clark; Payne, *Howling Wilderness*; Santa Cruz County, Book of Deeds 6:194; Young. For a thorough history of life on the Summit, see Stephen Payne's excellent book *A Howling Wilderness*.
495 Most of the information in this section is derived from California Third District Court, San Francisco Department, Case No. 825, and Lodge, interviews.
496 The house that the Averons moved into is located within the confines of the Capitola Mansion Apartments at 919 Capitola Avenue. The home serves as the offices for the facility.
497 *Evening Sentinel*, September 19, 1896, 2:4.

Bibliography

Newspaper articles are cited in full within the endnotes and not included in the list below. The following newspapers have had their titles simplified: *Santa Cruz Evening Sentinel (Evening Sentinel), Pacific Sentinel, Santa Cruz Weekly Sentinel*, and *The Santa Cruz Sentinel (Sentinel)*, and *Santa Cruz Surf (Surf)*.

Archdiocese of San Francisco Pastoral Center. Personal correspondence. 1993.
Bancroft, Hubert Howe, ed. *Judge R. F. Peckham: An Eventful Life*. Berkeley: Bancroft Library, 1877.
---. *The Works of Hubert Howe Bancroft*. Volume 19. Charleston, SC: Nabu Press, 2010.
Bannon, John Francis, ed. *Bolton and the Spanish Borderlands*. Norman, OK: University of Oklahoma Press, 1964.
The Bay of San Francisco: The Metropolis of the Pacific Coast and its Suburban Cities: A History. Chicago: Lewis Publishing, 1892.
Beal, Richard A. *Highway 17: The Road to Santa Cruz*. Aptos, CA: The Pacific Group, 1991.
Burrell, Lyman J. "Burrell Letters" *California Historical Society Quarterly* 29 (1950).
---. "Recollections of an Octogenarian," *Mountain Echoes* 1:1-4 (1881-1882).
California Province Archive, Jesuit Archives & Research Center.
California Supreme Court. Case No. 12 Cal. 564, Ingoldsby v. Juan, et al. 1859.
---. Case No. 31 Cal. 207, Henry W. Peck, et al., v. Thomas Courtis, et als. 1866.
California Third District Court. Case No. 74. Thomas Fallon, et al., v. Martina Castro, et al. 1850.

Bibliography

---. Case No. 78. John Hames v. Martina Castro. 1853.

---. Case No. 280. Henry and Antonia Peck v. Frederick A. Hihn, at al., known as the Rancho Soquel Partitioning Suit. 1860.

---. Case No. 303. Nicanor Cota Lajeunesse v. Francisco Lajeunesse.

---. Case No. 308. Frederick A. Hihn v. Antonia Peck, et al., known as the Shoquel Augmentation Partitioning Suit. 1860.

---. Case No. 333. Benjamin Cahoon v. Richard Savage. 1861.

---. Case No. 608. Antonia Peck v. Frederick A. Hihn, et als. 1867.

---. Case No. 609. B. F. Bayley v. Frederick A. Hihn, et als. 1867.

---. San Francisco Department. Case No. 825, In the Matter of the Estate of Martina Castro Depeaux, Deceased. 1896.

Carruth, Gorton. *The Encyclopedia of American Facts and Dates*. Tenth edition. New York: HarperCollins, 1997.

Castro, Kenneth M. Personal correspondence.

Castro, Kenneth M. and Doris. *Castro of California: Genealogy of a Colonial Spanish California Family*. Murphys, CA: Castro, 1975.

Chapman, Charles E. *A History of California: The Spanish Period*. New York: Macmillan Company, 1921.

Clark, Donald Thomas. *Santa Cruz County Place Names: A Geographical Dictionary*. Second edition. Scotts Valley, CA: Kestrel Press, 2002.

Colahan, W. J., and Julian Pomeroy, eds. *San Jose City Directory and Business Guide of Santa Clara Co. for the year commencing January 1, 1870*. San Francisco: Excelsior Press, 1870.

Costanso, Miguel. "The Narrative of the Portola Expedition of 1769-1770." Edited by Adolph van Hemert-Engert and Frederick J. Teggart. *Publications of the Academy of Pacific Coast History* 1:4 (Berkeley: University of California, 1910): 91-159.

Darling, George N. "Report on the Historical Retracement Survey of the Township Line Along the North Boundaries of Sections Three, Four and Five, Township Eleven, South, Range One West—Mount Diablo Base and Meridian for Santa Cruz County."

Dillon, Brian Dervin. *Archaeological and Historical Survey of the Soquel Demonstration State Forest, Santa Cruz County, California*. Sacramento, CA: Department of Forestry and Fire Protection, 1992.

Farquhar, Francis P. *History of the Sierra Nevada*. Berkeley, CA: University of California Press, 2007.

Francis, Phil. *Beautiful Santa Cruz County: A Faithful Reproduction in Print and Photography of its Climate, Capabilities, and Beauties.* San Francisco: H. S. Crocker Company, 1896.

Garfielde, Selucius, and F. A. Snyder, eds. *Compiled Laws of the State of California, containing all the Acts of the Legislature of a public and general nature, now in force, passed at the sessions of 1850-51-52-53.* Benicia: S. Garfielde, 1853.

Gerstaecker, Friedrich. *California Gold Mines.* Oakland: Biobooks, 1946.

Girky, Star. Personal correspondence.

Gleeson, William. *History of the Catholic Church in California.* San Francisco: A. L. Bancroft and Company, 1872.

Guinn, James Miller. *History of the State of California and Biographic Record of Santa Cruz, San Benito, Monterey and San Luis Obispo Counties: An Historical Story of the State's Marvelous Growth from its Earliest Settlement to the Present Time.* Chicago: Chapman Publishing, 1903.

Halley, William. *The Centennial Year Book of Alameda County, California, containing A Summary of the Discovery and Settlement of California.* Oakland: William Halley, 1876.

Hansen, Gladys. *San Francisco Almanac.* Updated and revised edition. San Rafael: Presidio Press, 1980.

Harrison, Edward S. *History of Santa Cruz County, California.* San Francisco: Pacific Press Publishing, 1892.

Hart, James D. *A Companion to California.* New York: Oxford University Press, 1978.

Hayes, Donald M. Personal correspondence.

Heron, David W. "The Man Who Invented Capitola: The Life and Times of Frederick Augustus Hihn." *Sun.* June 1, 1989.

Hihn, Frederick A. "How I came to Santa Cruz," *Santa Cruz County History Journal* 1 (1994): 73-81.

Hihn-Younger Archive. University Library. University of California, Santa Cruz, 1976-2003.

Historical Atlas Map of Santa Clara County, California. San Francisco: Thompson & West, 1876.

Bibliography

History of Monterey County, California, with Illustrations Descriptive of its Scenery, Farms, Residences, Public Buildings, Factories, Hotels Business Houses, Schools, Churches, and Mines. San Francisco: Elliott & Moore, 1881.

Hoover, Mildred B., Hero E. Rensch, and Ethel G. Rensch. *Historic Spots in California.* Third edition. Palo Alto, CA: Stanford University Press, 1966.

Jensen, Billie J. and Reece C. *A Trip Through Time and the Santa Cruz Mountains.* Gardnerville, NV: Ghastly Gallimaufry, 1994.

John Wilson Papers (BANC MSS C-B 420). Bancroft Library. University of California, Berkeley, 1840-1897.

Kieffer, Charles V. Letter to Jerry Johnson, Stockton Development Center. June 12, 1992.

Kimball, Charles P. *The San Francisco City Directory.* San Francisco: Journal of Commerce Press, 1850.

Kimbro, Edna. Personal correspondence.

Koch, Margaret. *Santa Cruz County: Parade of the Past.* Fresno: Valley Publishers, 1973.

Land Claims Commission. Case No. 184. Transcript of the proceedings for the place named Soquel on behalf of Martina Castro.

---. Case No. 593. Transcript of the proceedings for the place named Shoquel on behalf of Martina Castro.

Leonard, Vincent. Personal correspondence. 1961.

Lewis, Betty. Personal files. Watsonville, CA: Pajaro Valley Historical Association.

---. "Watsonville Remembered—A Selection of KOMY-Radio Broadcasts," *Santa Cruz History Journal* 1 (1994): 127-128.

Lodge, Carrie. Interviews. Santa Cruz, CA: University of California, Santa Cruz, Special Collections, 1965.

Los Gatos Museum. Archival material.

Marshall, Thomas A. Personal correspondence.

de Massey, Ernest. "A Frenchman in the Gold Rush," *California Historical Society Quarterly* 5:4 (1926): 342-377.

McGroarty, John Steven. *California: Its History and Romance.* Los Angeles: Grafton Publishing, 1911.

Mission Carmel. Marriage records.

Morrison, Harry B. "Before the Sulpicians: Formation of Priests in Early Diocesan California, 1841–1885," *The Patrician* (1992).

Munro-Fraser, J. P. *History of Santa Clara County, California, including its Geography, Geology, Topography, Climatography and Description.* San Francisco: Alley, Bowen & Company, 1881.

Mylar, Isaac L. *Early Days at the Mission San Juan Bautista.* Watsonville, CA: Evening Pajaronian, 1929.

New Catholic Encyclopedia. Volume I: A-Azt. Washington, DC: Catholic University of America, 1967.

O'Lague, Penny. Letter to Charles V. Kieffer. August 25, 1992.

Passenger list for *Yankee.* May 5, 1855.

Patten, Phyllis B. *Oh! That Reminds Me.* Felton, CA: Big Trees Press, 1969.

Paulson, L. L. *Handbook and Directory of Santa Clara, San Benito, Santa Cruz, Monterey and San Mateo Counties.* San Francisco: L. L. Paulson, 1875.

Payne, Stephen Michael. *A Howling Wilderness: A History of the Summit Road Area of the Santa Cruz Mountains 1850–1906.* Santa Cruz, CA: Loma Prieta Publishing, 1978.

---. *Santa Clara County: Harvest of Change: An Illustrated History.* Northridge, CA: Windsor Publications, 1987.

Robinson, William Wilcox. *Land in California: The Story of Mission Lands, Spanish and Mexican Ranchos, Squatter Rights, Mining Claims, Railroad Grants, Land Scrip, Homesteads, Tidelands.* Chronicles of California. Berkeley: University of California Press, 1948.

Rolle, Andrew F. *California: A History.* Second edition. New York: T. Y. Cromwell, 1969.

Rowland, Leon B. Personal files. Edited by Joan Gilbert Martin and Stanley D. Stevens. Santa Cruz, CA: University of California, Santa Cruz, Special Collections, 1977.

---. *Santa Cruz: The Early Years: The Collected Historical Writings of Leon Rowland.* Santa Cruz, CA: Paper Vision Press, 1980.

Santa Cruz County. Book of Agreements. Volume 1. Santa Cruz, CA: Office of the County Recorder.

---. Book of Deeds. Volumes 1-13. Santa Cruz, CA: Office of the County Recorder.

Bibliography

---. Book of Leases. Volume 1. Santa Cruz, CA: Office of the County Recorder.

---. School Land Warrants of Santa Cruz County, as Recorded by County Surveyor Thomas W. Wright. Santa Cruz, CA: Office of the County Recorder.

Spence, Mary Lee, and Donald Jackson, eds. *Expeditions of John Charles Frémont*: Volume 2: *The Bear Flag Revolt and the Court-Martial*. Urbana, IL: University of Illinois Press, 1973.

Stevens, Stanley D. "Biographical Sketch of F.A. Hihn," Hihn-Younger Archive, University Library. University of California, Santa Cruz. https://library.ucsc.edu/speccoll/hihn/hihn-biographies/biographical-sketch-of-fa-hihn-compiled-by-stanley-d-stevens. Accessed April 1, 2020.

---. Personal correspondence.

Swift, Carolyn. "Stones to the Four Winds: The Sorrow of Martina Castro Lodge," *Santa Cruz County History Journal* 3 (1997): 123-134.

Treanor, John J. Personal correspondence. Archdiocese of Chicago, 1992.

Treaties and Conventions between the United States of America and Other Powers since July 4, 1776. Washington: Government Printing Office, 1871.

United States District Court. Northern District of California, Case No. 295. 1856.

---. Northern District of California, Case No. 343. 1856.

Walsh Henry L. *Hallowed Were the Gold Dust Trails: The Story of the Pioneer Priests of Northern California*. Santa Clara, CA: University of Santa Clara Press, 1946.

Willey, S. H., C. L. Anderson, Ed. Martin, W. H. Hobbs. *History of Santa Cruz County*. San Francisco: Wallace W. Elliott and Company, 1879.

Wulf, Bill. Personal correspondence.

Young, John V. *Ghost Towns of the Santa Cruz Mountains*. Lafayette, CA: Great West Books, 1984.

INDEX

Alemany, Joseph S., 126-127, 129, 145, 185, 210-217, 234-238, 275, 280, 281-284, 293, 342, 376, 381, 391-392
Alviso, Francisco, 59-60, 63, 80, 85-86, 188-189, 251-253
Amador, Pedro, 18-19, 64
Amador y Noriega, María Antonia, 18-19, 23
Amayo (family), 121, 380, 392, 468-469
Andrews, William O., 254-255, 264, 315, 317, 338
Anthony, Elihu, 88, 114, 295, 302, 305-306, 327
Anza, Juan Bautista de, 11-14
Augmentation, *see* Shoquel Augmentation
Averon, Guadalupe, see Lodge, María Guadalupe
Averon, Joseph, 23, 203, 233-234, 273-274, 497, 528
Bache, Alexander D., 67, 326
Bates, Joel, 181-184, 349, 373, 374-375, 376, 378-379, 398, 406, 409

Bear Flag Revolt, 74-76, 95
bears, 6, 20, 49, 169, 171, 174, 175-176, 189, 199-203, 333-335
Blackburn, William F., 75, 80, 85-86, 98, 398
Bolcoff, José Antonio (née Osip Volkov), 23, 29, 46-48, 204-206, 311, 316
Borregas Gulch, 35, 39-42, 46, 51, 65, 68-69, 154, 178, 218, 303, 306, 339, 510-511
Botiller, María Martina, 14-16, 23
Brady, Francis R., 161, 300, 313, 349, 358, 373, 375, 376-377, 398, 407, 446-447, 466-468, 494-496, 509
Branciforte (pueblo), 16, 17, 20-24, 28, 29, 37, 55, 75, 80, 197
Branciforte County, 98
Branda, Adolphe, 255, 264, 296-298, 343, 344, 391
Briones, Rosalia, 23, 27
Burrell, Lyman J., 165-176, 332-337, 358, 372, 377, 378-379, 400, 406, 426, 428, 528-533

Index

Cabrillo, Juan Rodríguez, 4, 10
Cahoon, Benjamin, 386, 398, 404, 421, 446-447, 466-468, 475, 495-496, 497-498, 526-527
Cambustan, Henry, 62-63, 196-198, 229, 295, 345
Castro (family), 14-16, 23, 24-27
Castro, Candida, 23, 26, 29, 212, 231
Castro, Guadalupe, 23, 26-27, 43, 78, 220, 225-229, 287
Castro, Joaquín Isidro, 12, 14-16
Castro, José de Guadalupe, 23, 26, 27, 225-226, 280
Castro, José Joaquín, 16, 18-19, 23-27, 43, 544-545
Castro, Juan José, 23, 25, 225-226, 228-229, 319-320
Castro, María de los Ángeles, 23, 26-27, 53, 315, 543
Castro, María Martina, 16, 23, 25-26, 30, 31-33, 37-43, 44-46, 48-51, 56-70, 89-93, 96-97, 114-121, 123-126, 130, 145-146, 147-148, 153-154, 156-158, 162, 177-179, 193-194, 198-199, 209-217, 219-221, 223-229, 230-231, 238-239, 240-242, 263-264, 266-267, 273-275, 277-278, 357, 535-552
Castro, María Rafaela Inocencia, 25
Castro, Rafael, 23, 25, 30, 35-37, 51, 186, 240, 342, 507
Chase (family), 428, 450, 523
Chuchita, *see* Loma Prieta

Clements, Josefa, *see* Lodge, María Josefa
Clements, Lambert Blair, 23, 113, 114-121, 144, 146-147, 233-234
Coe, Cyrus, 310, 479-482, 491, 499-504, 520-521
Cota, Carmel, *see* Fallon, Carmel
Cota, María Luisa, 23, 31, 33, 56, 114-121, 153-154, 155, 189-193, 233-234, 264, 338-339, 348, 380, 392, 494, 495, 504, 543
Cota, Nicanora, 23, 31, 33, 53, 114-121, 152, 153-154, 155, 196, 363-364, 365-366, 378, 382, 492
Cota y Romero, Simón, 23, 30, 32-33
Courtis, Thomas, 243, 284, 310, 376, 380, 381, 384-386, 388, 391, 399-400, 406-407, 479-482, 491, 499-504, 520-521
Cuatro Leguas, 65, 69, 339, 369
Daubenbiss, John, 75-76, 84, 446, 450, 478, 497,
Depeaux, Louis, 23, 96-97, 114-121, 123-126, 130, 145-147, 162, 184, 186-188, 193-195, 196, 198, 203, 208-217, 219-220, 221, 230, 257-263, 264, 274, 295, 540-542
Evans, George, 264-266, 382, 383, 446, 477-478
Fallon, Carmel, 23, 32-33, 81, 146, 153, 39, 81-82, 88, 114-121, 185-186, 194, 210, 233, 485, 497, 542, 543

Index

Fallon, Thomas, 23, 75, 81-82, 88-89, 93, 114-121, 123-126, 130, 146, 153-154, 159-161, 177, 185, 186-188, 196, 207, 210, 233, 234, 246-251, 263-264, 480, 485, 508, 509-520

Farley, Benjamin, 320, 381-382, 399, 414, 426, 465, 486-489, 497

Figueroa, José, 34, 37-46

Fourcade, Jean Richard, 23, 56, 57-59, 85, 86-88, 89, 93, 97, 114-121, 153-154, 155, 163, 176-177, 189-193, 233-234, 264, 291, 312, 338-339, 348, 380, 392

Franciscan Trail, 17, 19-21, 64, 131, 173, 180-181, 265

Frémont, John Charles, 73-75, 77, 80-81, 97-98, 180

Gold Rush (California), 82, 84, 86-93, 95, 130-133, 151, 163, 190, 193, 211, 242, 284, 358, 386, 415, 423, 494, 526

Green, Benjamin P., 254-255, 312, 367, 388

Gregory, Durrell S., 117, 145, 147-148, 150-151, 156-158, 177-179, 186-188, 199, 209-210, 233-234, 238, 345

Hames, John, 75-76, 83-84, 146, 156-158, 193, 198-199, 238-239, 245-246, 347, 548

Hammond, Gervais, 145-146, 154-155, 161

Hecox, Adna A., 77-80, 84, 399

Hester, Craven P., 150, 154-155, 161, 181, 233, 285, 292, 316-317, 318-319, 320, 347-348, 359, 381-382, 399, 414, 426, 465-466, 486-489, 497

Hihn, Frederick A., 131-144, 162, 194, 232, 234, 255, 263, 288, 294-295, 302-306, 307-308, 315, 327, 337-339, 343-348, 356-357, 359, 363-365, 373-374, 380, 382, 390, 391, 398, 415-422, 425-427, 468, 475-479, 491-493, 497, 509, 520, 524-526

Hill, Henry, 78, 89, 91, 401

Hinckley, Roger B., 312-315, 348, 374, 377, 404, 445-446, 470-472, 475

Hoy, Jones, 146-147, 153-154, 185, 204, 210, 382, 475-478

Ingoldsby, John, 211-217, 234-238, 242, 254-257, 275, 278-280, 281-284, 293-294, 315, 317, 381, 388, 541-542

Ireland, William, 312, 359

Juan, Luisa, *see* Cota, María Luisa

Juan, Ricardo, *see* Fourcade, Jean Richard

Kirby, George H., 219, 363, 377-378, 404, 491-492

Laguna del Sargento, 62, 64-66, 113, 118, 124, 131, 154, 179, 180, 265, 292, 323, 326

Lajeunesse, Francisco, 23, 53, 54-55, 97, 114-121, 152, 153-154, 155, 196, 363-364, 365-366, 378, 382

Index

Littlejohn, Helena, *see* Lodge, María Helena
Littlejohn, Joseph David, 23, 129-130, 153-154, 264, 293, 364-365, 491, 505-506
Llebaria, Juan Francisco, 129, 145, 210-217, 219-220, 224-225, 234-238, 279-280, 287, 293, 342, 356, 381, 388, 391, 400, 542
Lodge, Carmel, *see* Fallon, Carmel
Lodge, Dolores, 77, 89, 92
Lodge, Efejenia, 77, 89, 92
Lodge, Ennis, 96
Lodge, Joaquín, 77, 89, 92
Lodge, Luisa, *see* Cota, María Luisa
Lodge, María Antonia, 23, 51, 89, 97, 114-121 129, 146, 153-154, 180, 211-212, 264, 332, 344, 347, 349, 351-356, 378-379, 400, 406, 425-426, 524-526, 536
Lodge, María Guadalupe, 23, 55, 89, 92, 97, 114-121, 146, 153-154, 203, 233-234, 273-274, 387, 497, 528, 535, 542, 547
Lodge, María Helena, 23, 52, 89, 97, 114-121, 129-130, 153-154, 264, 266, 293, 364-365, 387, 491, 505-506, 542-543
Lodge, María Josefa, 23, 33, 89, 97, 113, 114-121, 146-147, 233-234, 535-536
Lodge, Michael, 23, 31-33, 37-43, 48-51, 75-76, 78-80, 83-84, 89-93, 146, 156, 163

Lodge, Miguel Antonio, 23, 52, 89, 114-121, 146, 153-154, 211, 219-220, 221, 230-231, 276, 345, 346, 540, 548
Loma Prieta, 62, 65-69, 85, 118, 154, 179, 326, 369
Los Angeles (pueblo), 16-17
Luz, García, 31
Luz, Josefa, 31, 32
Macondray, Frederick W., 344, 345-346, 356-357, 382, 391, 425, 482-485
Majors, Joseph L., 23, 26-27, 53, 54-55, 185, 204, 233-234, 254, 311-312, 315, 475-478
McKee, Samuel B., 318-319, 366, 373, 374-376, 389, 407, 414-415, 428-446, 447-449, 472-475, 478-479, 494, 525, 527
McKiernan, Charles "Mountain Charlie," 64, 130-131, 180-181, 199-203, 211, 265, 278-279, 280-281, 285-286, 291-292, 293-294, 296, 302-303, 309-310, 311, 323, 423-425, 498-499
Micheltorena, Manuel, 34, 56-63, 117-118
Mission Santa Cruz, 11, 17, 18, 19-20, 24, 27-28, 37, 54, 80, 145
Monterey, 4-6, 7, 8-10, 11-13, 14, 19, 27-28, 30, 31, 49, 51, 54, 73-75, 77, 86-87, 93-95, 96, 126-127, 141, 284
Morrell, Brad, 494, 526

Index

Morrell, Hiram C., 358, 494, 526
Mountain Home, 121, 168, 171, 173, 174, 498, 529
Mountain House, *see* Summit Hotel
Nichols, Benjamin C., 152, 300, 348, 349, 358, 373-375, 376-377, 386, 407-409, 421, 446-447, 466-468, 494-496, 507-508
Noble, Augustus, 161, 242-243, 254-255, 276, 296, 301, 306-307, 309-310, 311, 312-318, 319-320, 343, 358, 359, 372, 389, 390, 482-485, 496-497
Palo de la Yesca, *see* Shoquel Augmentation
Parrish, Joshua, 54, 185-186, 233, 303, 343, 366
Parsons, Henry F., 151, 161, 211, 220, 233, 301, 392, 407
Peck, Antonia, *see* Lodge, María Antonia
Peck, Henry W., 23, 54, 129, 146, 153-154, 180, 234, 318, 331, 332, 344, 346-347, 349, 351-356, 364, 378-379, 400, 406, 415-422, 423, 425-427, 524-526
Peck, Mary Elizabeth, 536-552
Peckham, Robert F., 75, 88-89, 100, 162-165, 193-194, 196, 233, 264, 276-277, 287-288, 293, 296, 324-326, 343-344, 351-353, 367, 400, 404, 405-406, 412, 415-422, 425, 450, 525

Perez, Cornelio, 207-208
Phillips, James B., 526
Plank and Turnpike Act, 148, 181
Porter, Benjamin F., 177, 195, 291, 312, 345, 349, 366, 367, 379, 383, 386, 406-407, 483-485, 494, 496, 505, 509-513, 519, 528, 547
Porter, George K., 338, 366, 367, 379, 383-385, 406-407, 479, 483-485, 496-497, 509-513, 519
Porter, John T., 284-285, 381, 386, 399, 417-418
Post, Daniel, 113
Rancho Aptos, 35-37, 51, 56, 59, 151, 186, 195, 342, 507
Rancho Refugio, 26-27, 29
Rancho San Agustin, 29, 55, 339
Rancho San Andrés, 26-27, 35, 43, 94, 194, 536-537, 545
Rancho San Miguel, *see* Shoquel Augmentation
Rancho Soquel Augmentation, *see* Shoquel Augmentation
Rancho Soquel, 37-43, 44-51, 54, 57-63, 75-76, 78-80, 83-84, 114-121, 123-126, 130, 145-146, 147-148, 156-158, 176-177, 184, 188-193, 204-206, 210-219, 233, 239-240, 243-244, 254, 273-275, 291, 326, 340-342, 357
Rancho Soquel Partitioning Suits, 153-154, 186-188, 209-217, 255-263, 267-273, 286-288, 324-326, 328-331, 343-344,

587

Index

351-356, 365-367, 372, 379-380, 383, 385-387, 389-392, 393-395, 428-437, 447-448, 450-456, 465-466, 472-473, 478-479, 482-483, 499-504, 507, 520-521

Rancho Zayante, 54-55

San José (pueblo), 13-14, 22

Santa Cruz Gap Turnpike, 180-181, 264-266, 278, 293-294, 301-302, 303-306, 317-318, 372, 424,

Santa Cruz Turnpike, 294-295, 300-301, 302, 305-306, 307-309, 317-318, 320-323, 359, 424, 521-523,

Savage, Richard, 348, 373-375, 378, 383, 386, 398, 494, 495-496

Scarborough, James W., 236, 238, 243, 254-255, 310

School Land Warrants, 149-150, 151, 154-155, 159-161, 181-184, 207, 208, 234, 285, 331, 387, 404

Schultheis (family), 152-153

Scott, Hiram D., 302, 308, 317, 323

Serra, Junípero, 7-10, 14, 17

Shackleford, Montgomery B., 154-155, 180, 194-195, 208, 219, 378, 403, 491-492, 496

Shelby, John L., 312-315, 348, 374, 377, 404, 445-446, 470-472, 475

Shoquel Augmentation, 49-51, 57-59, 60-70, 114-121, 123-126, 130, 145-146, 177-179, 184, 188-189, 204-206, 208-210, 231-232, 233, 240-241, 243-251, 251-253, 254, 275-276, 277-278, 286-288, 326, 340-342, 357, 373-374, 400-405

Shoquel Augmentation Partitioning Suits, 223-229, 255-263, 267-273, 324-326, 328-331, 343-344, 367-372, 374-378, 379, 380, 381-384, 387-393, 395-397, 428-431, 437-446, 448-449, 456-463, 466-468, 470-471, 473-475, 483-485, 486-489, 494-495-496, 497, 509, 520-521

Sierra Azul, 65-67, 228

Sinclair, Pruett, 75, 146-147, 153-154, 204, 210, 233-234, 255, 347

Soquel Turnpike, 359-363, 424, 521-523, 527-528

Stearns, John P., 161, 363-364, 378, 387-388, 404-405

Stockton Insane Asylum, 240-242, 258, 263-264, 266-267, 342, 543

Summit Hotel, 498-499

Taylor, James, 176, 201, 349, 379, 426, 493, 526

Tracy, Peter, 81, 99, 114, 123-124, 151, 155, 159, 161, 177, 181-184, 186-187, 207, 208, 220, 256, 260-262, 264, 267-272, 276-277, 281, 331, 357-358, 387-388, 405

Valencia, Nicholas, 240

Vandenberg, John, 127, 152, 196, 263, 293-294, 357, 379-380, 399, 447, 507
Watson, Charles, 204, 254, 476
Watson, John, 150-151, 507, 508
Wesley Burnett & Company, 298, 347, 348, 349, 384, 405
Whitewash Alley, *see* Santa Cruz Gap Turnpike
Willson, Charles H., 254, 311-312, 315, 365, 366-367, 381-382, 389-390, 476-477
Wilson, John D., 31, 156-158, 177-179, 184, 208-210, 212, 219, 224, 230, 231-232, 238, 240, 244-245, 254, 255-258, 264, 287, 340-342, 381, 384-386, 391-392, 397, 399-400, 479-482, 491, 499-504, 520-521
Wright, James, 528, 530-531
Wright, Thomas W., 113-114, 154-155, 161, 177, 181-184, 207, 295, 311, 404-405, 456-463, 509-510, 518
Young, Francisco, *see* Lajeunesse, Francisco
Young, Nicanor, *see* Cota, Nicanora
Younger, Charles B., 389, 390, 393, 395, 401, 540-541
Younger Report, 389-390, 393-397, 399-400, 406-415, 426, 478, 479-482, 489-491

Ronald Gabriel Powell was an electrical engineer and local researcher from Los Altos, California. He received his engineering degree from Cogswell Polytechnic Institute in San Francisco in 1953. For most of his career, he worked at Lockheed's Missile Systems division, Rytheon, and GTE Sylvania. He retired in the late 1970s and started exploring and photographing The Forest of Nisene Marks. Around 1990, he began writing his long history of Rancho Soquel Augmentation and later donated his research to the McHenry Library at the University of California, Santa Cruz. Powell died on September 11, 2010 at the age of 79.

Derek R. Whaley is a historian, librarian, and former resident of Felton, California. He earned a doctorate in history from the University of Canterbury in 2018. He began researching Santa Cruz County history in 2011 and continues to do so from overseas. He has worked at the Santa Cruz Beach Boardwalk and The Tech Museum of Innovation, volunteered at the San Lorenzo Valley Museum and Santa Cruz Museum of Art & History, and is well-known for his Santa Cruz Trains book series and website. He currently lives in Aotearoa New Zealand.

Stanley D. Stevens is a librarian emeritus of the University of California, Santa Cruz, and the founder of the Hihn-Younger Archive of the McHenry Library. He first met Ron Powell in the mid-1990s and helped guide him in his research. In exchange, Powell provided Stevens with uncovered information related to Frederick A. Hihn and other important figures in Santa Cruz County history. It was because of this relationship that Powell donated his research collection to the library in 2005.

www.ingramcontent.com/pod-product-compliance
Lightning Source LLC
Chambersburg PA
CBHW032340170426
43194CB00035B/606